The Copyright/Design Interface

Protecting designs is complex and diverse; it involves deciding whether to protect them by design law, copyright law, or by both laws. A single protection may be under- or overprotective but two or more can be overprotective if there are no rules regulating the overlap. Legal systems in Europe and abroad have struggled to find the most adequate solution to this problem. This book traces the history of the design/copyright interface of 15 countries, selected for their diversity in the way they dealt with the interface. It examines how these countries have coped with the problems engendered by the interface, the rules they applied to it over time and the reasons for legislative changes. This analysis reveals the most appropriate rules to regulate the interface at EU and global level and will appeal to academics, practising lawyers, judges, students and policymakers all over the world.

Estelle Derclaye is Professor of Intellectual Property Law at the University of Nottingham. She is an internationally renowned author of over 100 publications and this is her sixth book. Her expert work includes working with the UK Intellectual Property Office, the European Commission, UK and foreign law firms. She is a member of the European Copyright Society, a group of European academics aiming to influence policy-making. She was a visiting scholar at the University of California, Berkeley and Melbourne Law School and a Visiting Professor at the National University of Singapore and is regularly invited to teach and present her research around the world.

Cambridge Intellectual Property and Information Law

As its economic potential has rapidly expanded, intellectual property has become a subject of front-rank legal importance. *Cambridge Intellectual Property and Information Law* is a series of monograph studies of major current issues in intellectual property. Each volume contains a mix of international, European, comparative and national law, making this a highly significant series for practitioners, judges and academic researchers in many countries.

A list of books in the series can be found at the end of this volume.

The Copyright/Design Interface

Past, Present and Future

Edited by
Estelle Derclaye
University of Nottingham

CAMBRIDGE
UNIVERSITY PRESS

CAMBRIDGE
UNIVERSITY PRESS

University Printing House, Cambridge CB2 8BS, United Kingdom

One Liberty Plaza, 20th Floor, New York, NY 10006, USA

477 Williamstown Road, Port Melbourne, VIC 3207, Australia

314-321, 3rd Floor, Plot 3, Splendor Forum, Jasola District Centre, New Delhi - 110025, India

79 Anson Road, #06-04/06, Singapore 079906

Cambridge University Press is part of the University of Cambridge.

It furthers the University's mission by disseminating knowledge in the pursuit of education, learning and research at the highest international levels of excellence.

www.cambridge.org
Information on this title: www.cambridge.org/9781107198678
DOI: 10.1017/9781108182676

First published 2018

A catalogue record for this publication is available from the British Library

Library of Congress Cataloging in Publication data
Names: Derclaye, Estelle, 1974- editor.
Title: The copyright/design interface : past, present and future / edited by Estelle Derclaye.
Description: Cambridge [UK] ; New York : Cambridge University Press, 2017. |
Series: Cambridge intellectual property and information law
Identifiers: LCCN 2017037847 | ISBN 9781107198678 (hardback)
Subjects: LCSH: Design protection (International law) | Copyright, International. | Design protection – European Union countries.
Classification: LCC K1490 .C67 2017 | DDC 346.04/84–dc23
LC record available at https://lccn.loc.gov/2017037847

ISBN 978-1-107-19867-8 Hardback

To Christopher, Astrid and Constance

Contents

Figures

Contributors

ISABELLA ALEXANDER, Associate Professor, University of Technology Sydney

LIONEL BENTLY, Herchel Smith Professor of Intellectual Property Law, University of Cambridge

ESTELLE DERCLAYE, Professor of Intellectual Property Law, University of Nottingham

JASON J. DU MONT, Lecturer in Law & Teaching Fellow for the Law, Science & Technologh Program, Stanford Law School

JANE C. GINSBURG, Morton L. Janklow Professor of Literary and Artistic Property Law at Columbia Law School, and faculty director of its Kernochan Center for Law, Media and the Arts, Columbia University, New York

MARK D. JANIS, Robert A. Lucas Chair of Law, Maurer School of Law, Indiana University, Bloomington

ANNE-EMMANUELLE KAHN, Professor, University of Lyon 2

MASAHIRO MOTOYAMA, Professor, Graduate School of Intellectual Property Law, Kokushikan University, Tokyo

ANSGAR OHLY, Professor of Private Law, Intellectual Property Law and Competition Law, Ludwig Maximilian University, Munich

MARIA-DAPHNE PAPADOPOULOU, Counsellor at law, Hellenic Copyright Organization

ANTOON QUAEDVLIEG, Professor of Private, Commercial & Economic Law, Radboud University Nijmegen

MORTEN ROSENMEIER, Professor, University of Copenhagen, Centre for Information and Innovation Law

JENS SCHOVSBO, Professor, University of Copenhagen, Centre for Information and Innovation Law

IRINI STAMATOUDI, General Director, Hellenic Copyright Organization

Preface

I have benefited from the generous help of a lot of people and organisations to make this book happen. Thanks to a grant from the German Academic Exchange Service (Deutsche Akademische Austauschdienst, DAAD), I was able to collect documents at the Max Planck Institute for Intellectual Property and Competition Law in Munich to write my chapters. Funding from the RCUK-funded Centre for Copyright and New Business Models in the Creative Economy (CREATe) enabled me to bring the contributors to Nottingham so that we could discuss our respective chapters and improve them. Lynne Chave created the graphs for the last chapter. Sabine Jacques, Giorgio Spedicato and Veronica Villa provided excellent research assistance. Jean-Michel Bruguière, Yves Gaubiac and Pascale Tréfigny sent me documents that were difficult to obtain. Alessandro Cogo, Alberto Musso, Marco Ricolfi and Elisa Vittone generously gave their time to answer my questions on some thorny aspects of the Italian legal system. The contributors to the book kept to time and patiently answered my questions on their legal systems and followed instructions. Benedikt Niedermayer translated some German documents and Peter Ganea answered questions about Japanese design law. To all of them, my most grateful thanks.

My penultimate thanks go to Kim Hughes at Cambridge University Press for her enthusiasm for the project and her continuous support, and to her assistant Rebecca Roberts and all the Cambridge University Press team for a fantastic job.

Last but not least, this book would not have seen the light of day without my husband's unfailing support and the joyful disturbance of my daughters who thankfully prevented me from working too much. I dedicate this book to them.

Estelle Derclaye,
Nottingham, September 2017

Introduction

Estelle Derclaye

The world (hi)story of the protection of designs[1] has been extremely diverse. It is so because of the special, hybrid, nature of such works: they often combine utility and beauty so that it involves deciding whether to protect the work only by design law or only by copyright law, or by both. For over a century, legal systems, not only at national but also at regional and international level, have struggled to find the most adequate solution: a single protection may be under- or overprotective and two or more can be overprotective. The relationship or interface between copyright and design law at regional and international level crystallised over the years because of the entrenched and opposite positions (from minimal protection to maximal protection) the different countries have carried on taking on the issue. Indeed, countries and periods when protection for designs changed can be grouped in five different categories according to the type of interface chosen: single protection by copyright law (i.e. no design law exists), demarcation (i.e. no cumulation between copyright and design law), partial cumulation, full cumulation and total cumulation.[2] Furthermore, the countries and periods with some cumulation can be subdivided between those with rules and those without rules regulating the interface. In addition, the criteria to regulate the interface (in the main protection requirements, term of protection, authorship and ownership, infringement) vary considerably among the cumulation countries along with the type of right (anti-copying right or monopoly right). What's more, the UK is even more special as it is the only country in the world to have a national unregistered design right along with very detailed rules regulating the registered and unregistered design/copyright interface.

Since the Design Directive was adopted in 1998, design applications from all over the world have soared especially in Europe, the United States,

[1] I use the 'neutral' term designs on purpose to include both works of applied art and industrial designs. These terms are often used to demarcate the boundary between art (the domain of copyright law) and industry (the domain of design law).

[2] For a definition of these terms, see below.

Australia and Asia.[3] EU and national case law on designs has increased as well. Therefore, design law is no longer the 'Cinderella' of intellectual property law it once was.[4] Nevertheless, the interface between copyright and design is still in disarray. Looking at the EU alone, the Design Directive legislated very minimally on the interface as the EU legislature only required the Member States to cumulate copyright and design laws without specifying rules to regulate the overlap (art. 17 Design Directive, art. 96 Design Regulation and art. 9 Infosoc Directive). Subsequently, Member States have in the main kept to their traditions, which means that some have full cumulation and others partial cumulation between the two bodies of law, with very different rules organising the interface or no rules at all. The recent CJEU *Flos* judgment,[5] which seemingly imposes the author's own intellectual creation level of originality for unregistered designs but leaves the level of originality for registered designs to Member States, has created even more uncertainty. Post *Flos*, some national courts still apply a higher level of originality for unregistered designs (e.g. Germany, the UK and Italy). The *Flos* decision also triggered the repeal of section 52 of the UK Copyright Act, which organised the overlap between registered designs and copyright.[6] The CJEU *Donner* decision also illustrates well the problems caused by the lack of harmonisation relating to designs (furniture whose protection expired in Italy parallel-imported in Germany where protection was still in force).[7] Therefore, the current state of affairs is paradoxical – design protection is gaining momentum but it is far from harmonious. Rules to regulate the overlap between copyright and design law are badly needed, at the very least at EU level. To find the most appropriate rules, it is essential to review how Member States' and other relevant countries' laws have organised the interface in the past and how successfully (or not) they have dealt with it. It is only by comparing national experience through history that an adequate solution can be found.

The book has the triple aim of:

1 tracing the history of the design/copyright interface or in other words of the protection of designs, of several countries, selected for their rules regulating the interface, for their absence of rules or for their choice to protect designs only by one body of law,

[3] See WIPO statistics at http://ipstats.wipo.int/ipstatv2/.

[4] C.-H. Massa and A. Strowel, 'Community Design: Cinderella Revamped' (2003) *European Intellectual Property Review* 68–78.

[5] Case C-168/09, *Flos SpA* v. *Semeraro Casa & Famiglia SpA* [2011] ECDR 161.

[6] For sharp criticism of *Flos* and the decision to repeal s. 52, see L. Bently, 'The Return of Industrial Copyright?' (2012) EIPR 654.

[7] Case C-5/11, *Re: Donner* [2012] ECDR 349.

2 examining how these countries have coped with the problems engendered by the rules they applied over the years and the reasons for legislative changes,
3 in order to find the most appropriate rules that can be used to regulate the interface at EU level, and even at global level.

I recognise that it is ambitious to aim to find such rules as it may not be possible. But if these rules cannot be found, at least, the book will have summarised the advantages and disadvantages of each system, allowing for a better understanding of the interface. That said, in the final chapter, I propose what I think are achievable and workable rules to regulate the copyright/design interface. I chose only fifteen countries, namely, the USA, the UK, France, Germany, Italy, Greece, the three countries that form the Benelux, Sweden, Norway, Finland, Denmark, Australia and Japan, because they are among the most striking in terms of the copyright/design interface. It is not necessary for the number of countries to be bigger let alone exhaustive to achieve the desired result. In addition, there must be sufficient differences between countries and ample case law to make the comparison worthwhile and interesting. Thus, for instance, Malaysia and Singapore have followed the UK law closely (with only very small differences) and have relatively little relevant case law. Thus taking only the UK is sufficient as it has a wealth of case law and is the prime example as former colonies modelled their law on UK law. On the other hand, Australia has departed from the UK relatively early and more drastically and has an abundant case law. There is no EU chapter. This is deliberate. Legislatively speaking, there is nothing to say as the interface was left unharmonised. On the judicial front, we only have the *Flos* decision but the judgment is obscure and by definition partial as constrained by the questions posed to the CJEU. Some commentators address it in their chapters and, otherwise, much commentary has already been written on the issue.[8]

The chapters only review substantive law, leaving procedural law (in the main, design registration and remedies) aside. This is not to say that no differences exist there but I had to work with a set word limit and the line had to be drawn somewhere. Protection of designs by unfair competition laws is also not discussed. It could have been reviewed but it is not

[8] E. Ventose, 'ECJ Rules on Legislative Limitations on Copyright Protection for Designs in Europe' (2011) JIPLP 367; L. Bently, 'The Return of Industrial Copyright?'; A. Tischner, 'Focus on the Polish Regulation of Copyright and Design Overlap after the Judgment of the Court of Justice in Case 168/09 (Flos v Semeraro)' (2012) IIC 202; B. Lauriat, 'Copyright for Art's Sake?' (2014) EIPR 275; P. Masiyakurima, 'Copyright in Works of Artistic Craftsmanship: An Analysis' (2016) OJLS 505–4; and literature cited at https://curia.europa.eu/jcms/jcms/Jo2_7083/en/.

necessary in order to find the best rules to organise the interface. As I have already explained in previous writings,[9] it is sufficient to say in this respect that the overlap between slavish imitation and any intellectual property right cannot be sustained when a specific right has been introduced simply because the intellectual property right replaces the unfair competition action for slavish imitation in this case and that there is no problem to cumulate the unfair competition action involving a risk of confusion with an infringement of copyright or design rights as the two causes for the actions (copying as opposed to causing confusion) are different.

That said, some chapters do discuss unfair competition law. This is inevitable as contributors map the history of the interface and some countries used unfair competition law instead of or in addition to copyright law before design protection existed (e.g. the Netherlands and Greece). While it would be interesting and totally comprehensive to examine the interface with trademark law, like with unfair competition law, there was no space. Furthermore, in contrast with the copyright/design interface, it is regulated at EU level, even if not fully, and is also addressed in detail elsewhere.[10]

The chapters follow the same structure, except the final chapter, which analyses all the chapters and compares countries' experiences in an attempt to find the most adequate rules to regulate the interface at international level. There is one chapter for all three Benelux countries, focusing on Dutch law and the Uniform Benelux Law on Designs and Models, one on all four chosen Nordic countries and two on US law, one focusing on copyright, the other on design patents. The chapters start with a table detailing the periods that the country has had in relation to the way it has dealt with the interface. A country could have started with full cumulation, then amended its law to adopt a partial cumulation system, etc. The table lists the different acts the country has enacted in the field of protection of designs during these periods. The table also adds if courts have followed or deviated from the legislature's mandate (e.g. an Act could have mandated demarcation but the courts applied cumulation). For each period, the tables list the total and average numbers of designs filed and registered. This data is analysed in the last chapter and shows that, in some cases, there is a link between the legal system chosen to

[9] E. Derclaye and M. Leistner, *Intellectual Property Overlaps: A European Perspective* (Oxford: Hart, 2011); E. Derclaye, *The Legal Protection of Databases: A Comparative Analysis* (Cheltenham: Edward Elgar, 2008).

[10] See E. Derclaye and M. Leistner, *Intellectual Property Overlaps: A European Perspective*; N. Wilkof and S. Basheer (eds.), *Overlapping Intellectual Property Rights* (Oxford: Oxford University Press, 2012); R. Tomkovicz, *Intellectual Property Overlaps, Theory, Strategies and Solutions* (Abingdon: Routledge, 2012); M. Senftleben, *The Copyright/Trademark Interface* (Alphen aan den Rijn: Kluwer Law International, forthcoming, 2017).

regulate the copyright/design interface and the high or low number of applications. Graphs drawn from WIPO and national IP offices data can be found in the last chapter's annex.

Each chapter then maps the history of the interface for the country or countries in question, in short the evolution of the statutory and case law on the protection of designs and the problems encountered over the years. Many chapters dealing with EU Member States stop with the implementation of the Design Directive as even if their design law was amended to comply with it, their law on the interface did not change. The chapters analyse the success or failure, advantages and disadvantages of the various mechanisms used in their countries to organise the interface over the several periods and explain why the legislatures and/or courts changed the rules over the years. Some then venture to conclude by giving their opinion as to what the best rules regulating the interface could be.

All chapters follow the same terminology regarding the different systems elaborated to deal with the interface. The terms used are: demarcation, partial cumulation, full cumulation and total cumulation. While such terminology is very rarely used by legislatures[11] or courts, many commentators used similar terminology over the years and in different countries, albeit not always consistently.[12] Accordingly, we define the several terms as follows:

Total cumulation: if the requirements of one law are fulfilled, there is automatic protection under the other law and this is whether or not the requirements of that other law are fulfilled. In other words, there is assimilation of the protection requirements of one law with that of the other. Among the countries reviewed in this book, this was the case only in France between 1902 and the implementation of the Design Directive.

[11] The European Commission's Green Paper on the legal protection of industrial design uses some of this terminology when it explains the different Member States' systems dealing with the interface.

[12] Some commentators use the term 'cumulation' to describe total cumulation, e.g. S. Ricketson and J. Ginsburg, *International Copyright and Neighbouring Rights: The Berne Convention and Beyond*, 2nd edn (Oxford: Oxford University Press, 2006), 468; W. Duchemin, 'La protection des arts appliqués dans la perspective d'un dépôt communautaire en matière de dessins et modèles industriels' (1978) 97 RIDA 4, 65. Some have used 'non-cumulation' or 'no cumulation' to describe the situation we call demarcation, among them S. Ricketson and U. Suthersanen, 'The Design/Copyright Overlap: Is There a Resolution?' in N. Wilkof and S. Basheer (eds.), *Overlapping Intellectual Property Rights* (Oxford: Oxford University Press, 2012) 159; J. Reichman, 'Design Protection After the Copyright Act of 1976: A Comparative View of the Emerging Interim Models' (1983) 31 *J. Copyright Soc'y* 267 and 'Design Protection in Domestic and Foreign Copyright Law: From the Berne Revision of 1948 to the Copyright Act of 1976' (1983) *Duke Law Journal* 1143 at 1169; Reichman (1983) *Duke Law Journal* 1143 at 1158 also uses the term 'absolute' to talk about what we call total cumulation.

Full cumulation: both copyright and design right can subsist if the protection requirements are fulfilled and the two laws apply in tandem whether it raises regime clashes and/or overprotection, or not. In other words, there are no mechanisms in the legislation to deal with these problems.

Partial cumulation: both copyright and design right can subsist if the protection requirements are fulfilled but either or both laws (i.e. the Copyright Act or Design Act) has or have one or more mechanisms to regulate the interface. For instance, if copyright and unregistered design right both subsist and are infringed, the UK Copyright Act states that only copyright infringement subsists (s. 236). Another example is alignment of rules to avoid regime clashes, e.g. same authors and owners in both copyright and design laws.

Demarcation: if something is protected or protectable by design law then it cannot be protected by copyright or by unregistered design right or vice versa.

Finally, the chapters in the book are ordered by type of system, starting with total cumulation systems and finishing with demarcation systems. Note, however, that most countries have changed systems over the years and thus the countries' place in the book reflects the longest period in which they have retained the respective system.

1 The Copyright/Design Interface in France

*Anne-Emmanuelle Kahn**

Table 1.1 *Chronological table of legislation and statistics*

Period	Legislation	Amendments	Interpretation (i.e. by courts)	Design applications	Design registrations
1. 1806–1902	19–24 July 1793 Act on literary and artistic property 18 March 1806 Act for industrial design	A Royal Order in 1825 extended protection of the law of 1806 to the whole territory (initially limited to designs on fabric in the Lyon silk industry)	Demarcation: Protection of industrial works by the 1806 Act and copyright for other works	** 1,340,765 (51,567)	* 1,250,814 (52,117)
2. 1902–1957	1902 Copyright Act	Establishes the Theory of Unity of Art	Total cumulation in case law	1,121,519 (23,364)	*** 922,777 (20,060)
	14 July 1909 Act for designs and models 12 March 1952 Act for fashion and seasonal creations	Establishes the principle of cumulation			
3. 1957–2001	11 March 1957 Copyright Act		Total cumulation in case law	369,881 (8,601)	**** 139,446 (4,980)

* The author wishes to thank Alison Davies for her help in the English translation of this contribution written in French. Thanks to Aurélie Garaudet and Francoise Gauthier for their review of this chapter.

Table 1.1 *(cont.)*

Period	Legislation	Amendments	Interpretation (i.e. by courts)	Design applications	Design registrations
4. 2001–present	Ordinance n° 2001–670 of 25 July 2001 (Act implementing Design Directive)		Partial cumulation: case law distinguishes conditions of protection	92,660 (7,127)	29,856 (2,296)

Source: Created by the author based on statistical data published by WIPO
(Figures in parentheses: average annual numbers)
* data incomplete (from 1806 to 1885 included)
** data incomplete (from 1806 to 1883 included)
*** data incomplete (1956 and 1957 included)
**** data incomplete (from 1980 to 1995 included)

1.1 Introduction

The scope of cumulation has always been unclear in France. However, historical analysis reveals that case law has appeared fairly constant since the end of the nineteenth century and that it changed only recently. In the first period (1806–1902), there was no form of cumulative protection in French law. Yet following changes in case law and under the influence of the doctrine, the French legislation established the *Unity of art* theory (forbidding discrimination between works in matter of copyright) and the cumulation principle granting a double protection to one single industrial creation: that of copyright and of specific law on industrial designs and models.

Following this legal change and for a long time, France has been the only country whose legislation enabled total cumulation. However, care should be taken in defining what a total cumulation is. Indeed, the principle of partial cumulation has been recognised in French law since 1909. The two aforementioned protection regimes can be granted to all creations of applied art (without taking into account their practicality or artistic character) provided that they fulfil the distinct and independent conditions of each regime. Therefore cumulative protection is not applied automatically. In fact cumulation was interpreted as automatic and total by case law under the influence of part of the doctrine. Thus, the criteria of protection for copyright (originality) and that of designs and models law (novelty and individual character since the Ordinance of 2001) have been considered as assimilable, which provokes not an overlay but a confusion between the two regimes. This interpretation, together with a very wide understanding of the originality criteria, has led to the protection of a large number of industrial creations by copyright. In any case, since case law assimilates the different aforementioned criteria, cumulative protection did not raise issues regarding protection of the works.

The analysis of cumulative protection for applied art from the early post-Revolutionary legislation until today will show that this situation remained unchanged in French case law until recently.[1] Indeed, despite major changes in the legal protection of designs or models law due to the transposition of the 1998 Directive, it is only in the last few years that a real evolution can be noticed in case law, changing the French system of a total cumulation to a partial or measured cumulative protection.

Furthermore, because of the total cumulative protection and the co-existence of two very different systems, serious problems have arisen which the judges, due to lack of a clear legislation, have endeavoured to solve in practice.

1.2 A History of the Protection of Industrial Design

1.2.1 First Period: 1793–1902: Uncertain Cumulation

Even though it is generally recognised that the first protection of designs and models was awarded in the aftermath of the French Revolution, the former regime had already set the wheels in motion. The Letters Patent (*lettres patentes*) enacted in 1737 and the 1744 King's Council decision had enshrined a legal protection for creations of the silk industries of Lyon (called '*Manufactures de Lyon*'), just in the same way as playwrights had managed to secure the beginnings of protection for their work just before the French Revolution. This was extended to other industrial factories throughout the kingdom by the 1787 decision of the King's Council.[2]

As the demands made by the playwrights coincided perfectly with the ideals of the Revolution, the first laws coming into effect were logically those which only applied to authors of dramatic works (Act of 19 January 1791, also known as *Loi Le Chapelier*), and to literary and artistic property (Act of 19 and 24 July 1793). The 1793 Act was indeed limited, containing only seven articles. Pursuant to article 1, authors of writings of all kinds, composers, painters and artists who engraved paintings and drawings had the exclusive right to sell and cause to be sold and distribute their works. This right to publish and distribute was granted to the author throughout his

[1] P. Kamina, 'Arts appliqués', *Juris-Classeur. Propriété littéraire et artistique*, Lexis-Nexis, Fasc. 1155, 26.

[2] This text was however criticised by the silk workers of Lyon because of certain restrictions that applied to the protection: protection was conditioned by the registration formalities of the office of their district and the length of protection was limited.

lifetime and for ten years following his death.[3] The law provided for the seizure of counterfeit objects and compensation for damages suffered by the author. Prior registration of the work was not required to secure the protection, except for literary works and engravings. Indeed, for these works, the author had to file two copies at the National Library; failing that, the copyright infringement action was not admissible (article 6). Property rights remained with the author who might transfer them in whole or in part.

On the contrary, the Revolution deprived merchants and manufacturers of the ability to protect their products. As both the privileges granted to factories and the courts settling disputes between manufacturers and workers had disappeared, fraudsters went unpunished. Finally, the Act of 18 March 1806 firmly established the operating monopoly over factory designs. This came about due to the impetus of the silk industry in Lyon[4] to remedy the imperfections of the Act of 19 and 24 July 1793 on literary and artistic property. For both doctrine[5] and the courts,[6] it was not clear if this law applied to art creation. The 1806 Act introduced for the first time a mandatory application for a registered design which has to be made to the *Conseil de Prud'hommes* newly created in Lyon (article 15) – failing that, no legal action was admissible – and charged with conservative measures for designs property ('les mesures conservatrices de la propriété des dessins').[7] The council's clerk was entrusted with the reception of the manufacturer's design and its recordal at the official register after which he would deliver a receipt. In the event of a conflict between two manufacturers, the Council would examine the specimens in detail before deciding which manufacturer would have priority (article 17). The duration of legal protection depended on the declaration of the applicant who, in exchange for payment, had the choice between a short protection (one, three or five years) or a perpetual protection (article 18). Thus those who registered their work were guaranteed national property and protection against copying of their designs.

[3] This was extended to twenty years by the Decree Law of 5 February 1810, then to thirty years by the law of 8 April 1854 in favour of the children of authors and artists.

[4] Called '*les soyeux Lyonnais*'. While on a visit to the industrial town of Lyon, Napoleon listened to the grievances of the manufacturers of the privately run silk factories who deplored the fact that there were no means available to protect their models from forgery: V. '*Manuscrit n. 1005*', Fonds Coste, Bibliothèque de la Ville de Lyon.

[5] A. Vaunois, *Des dessins et modèles de fabrique* (Paris: Marescq, 1898), p. 13, for which industrial designs and models would fall outside the intentions of the French legislator of 1793 who wished to protect only and in the strictest sense the artists of the school of fine arts. *Contra*: E. Pouillet, *Traité théorique et pratique des dessins et modèles*, 5th edn (Paris: Librairie générale de jurisprudence, 1911), p. 14.

[6] Cass. 5 brumaire an XIII: which avoided making a stand on this point in relation to models of wallpaper: V. F. Greffe, 'La protection des dessins et modèles' *Juris-Classeur. Marques et Dessins et modèles*, LexisNexis, Fasc. 3100, 9.

[7] Article 34 of the law of 1806 prescribed the creation of this institution in all other 'towns of mills and manufacturers' who so requested.

The laconic 1806 Act (indeed only six articles were devoted to design protection) had limited scope, especially as it was applied only to the designs of Lyon's silk industry. Case law decided then to extend protection first to all designs,[8] then to three-dimensional models (a protection that has never been questioned since then), by assimilating them with embossed design.[9] Finally, the 1825 Royal Order expanded the geographical scope of the Act to the whole territory, establishing the first general regime of protection of designs, which was different from that afforded to copyright and whose purpose was to protect manufacturers. This law ensured the protection of designs and models throughout the whole of the nineteenth century.[10]

Under the 1806 Act, the greatest difficulty was doubtlessly that the French legislator had not established cumulative protection and remained silent on the respective fields of application of the 1793 and 1806 Acts. For many authors, it was not the case of protecting industrial works by copyright, for which a specific law had been passed in 1806. However, in the course of action for infringement, judges were unclear as to which law should be applied to these specific creations and legal decisions fluctuated greatly. If, at first, the judges, under pressure from the operators, accepted affording protection to designs that were unequivocally industrial,[11] they very quickly tried to distinguish industrial art – which fell under the scope of specific legislation – from works that were purely artistic, which would be protected by copyright.[12] Several distinguishing criteria were put forward: the mechanical method with which the design or model in question was reproduced,[13] the ancillary nature of the factory design,[14] the demarcation according to the qualities of the author,[15] or indeed the criterion of its future industrial or artistic use according to which a design, even those of great value, would no longer fall under copyright if it were to be reproduced on an industrial and

[8] CE, avis of 30 May 1823.

[9] Cass. crim., 25 Nov. 1881, (1882) *Ann. Propr. Indust.* 133.

[10] The history of designs and models: E. Philippon, *Traité théorique et pratique des dessins et modèles industriels* (Paris: Marescq, 1880), p. 226; Vaunois, *Des dessins et modèles de fabrique*, p. 13.

[11] Cass. civ., 2 Aug. 1854, (1854) 1 *D.P.* 395: the law of 1793 'is designed to protect from counterfeiting all kinds of creation, whether it is a work of art in the strictest sense or of applied art', an informed user ('observateur averti' in French).

[12] C. Bougeard, 'Les origines équivoques de la loi de 1909: des dessins et modèles au dessin ou modèle', in *Les dessins et modèles en question* (Paris: Litec, 1986), p. 9.

[13] CE, avis of 30 May 1823. Cass. crim., 30 Dec. 1865, (1867) *Ann. Propr. Indust.* 46. But this criterion would exclude mechanically reproduced works such as printed engravings and conversely consider hand-produced models by artisans as artistic.

[14] Criteria offered by Philippon, *Traité théorique et pratique des dessins et modèles industriels.*

[15] Vaunois, *Des dessins et modèles de fabrique*, p. 39 s.: if the author of the work is an artisan or maker, the law of 1806 will apply. Whereas if he is an artist working independently, then the law of 1793 applies.

commercial scale.[16] But this 'theory of destination' led to some artistic creations being denied copyright.[17] Finally case law sided with the theory of the artistic nature of the creation.[18] This criterion, under which the protection of the 1793 Act benefited to any work of artistic character, without distinguishing the status of the author or whether the creation was destined for industry or not, left to lower courts a freedom of evaluation.[19] Only works devoid of artistic character were totally excluded from artistic property. Nevertheless, it was often tenuous to decipher whether a character was artistic or not, which meant that the judge was accorded almost full discretion and this resulted in considerable uncertainty.[20]

1.2.2 Second Period: 1902–1957: Partial Cumulation in the Texts, Total or Automatic Cumulative Protection in Case Law

This period marks a major change in the French concept of the protection of works of applied art. Indeed, towards the end of the nineteenth century, the number of attempts to have one's work included within copyright increased significantly, despite stiff opposition from the courts determined not to protect works of insufficient merit. The attempt to differentiate work that was designed for industrial use from work that was purely artistic was indeed quite artificial. Having given rise to contradictory decisions, it would quickly appear to become absurd and vain.[21] Thus, after work of doctrine and following Pouillet's belief that the law does not judge the works,[22] under the influence of

[16] Cass. civ., 17 Jan. 1882, (1883) 1 *D.P.* 119. CA Paris, 21 Jan. 1892, (1894) *Ann. Propr. Indust.* 48. Cass. civ., 8 June 1860, (1860) *Ann. Propr. Indust.* 94, braided shovels and bronze tongs.

[17] Cass. civ., 18 Aug. 1868, (1869) *Ann. Propr. Indust.* 191: for jewellery. For posters signed by the great painters and artists: T. civ. Seine, 20 June 1891, (1894) *Ann. Propr. Indust.* 51; CA Paris, 21 Jan. 1892, (1894) *Ann. Propr. Indust.* 48.

[18] P. Fressonnet, 'La protection juridique des dessins et modèles industriels', in *Dessins et modèles déposés* (Paris: CCI, 1981), pp. 13–14.

[19] Cass. req., 27 July 1903, (1903) 1 *D.P.*, 488. CA Paris, 17 Nov. 1900, (1901) 2 *D.P.* 326.

[20] Cass. crim., 15 March 1845, (1845) 1 *D.P.* 283. Cass. crim., 25 Dec. 1884, (1885) *Ann. Propr. Indust.* 319. Cass. crim., 14 June 1891, (1891) *Ann. Propr. Indust.* 388; (1891) 1 *S.* 493: 'drawings do not constitute an actual work of art'. Cass. crim., 3 March 1898, (1899) *Ann. Propr. Indust.* 72.

[21] This provoked the famous intervention of Victor Hugo at the *Chambre des Pairs* claiming that Michelangelo's chandelier, which was reproduced on a production line, should be denied copyright protection.

[22] E. Pouillet, *Traité théorique et pratique des dessins et des modèles*, 2nd edn (Librairie générale de jurisprudence, 1884), p. 28 and *Traité théorique et pratique de la propriété littéraire et artistique*, 1st edn (Marchal et Billard, 1879), p. 38: which advocated the application of the 1793 Act for all designs and forms without taking into account the designated purpose of the object, its aesthethic 'judgment of value' or the quality of its author. The doctrine quickly came to side with this idea: V. Greffe, 'La protection des dessins et modèles', pp. 18ff.

professionals,[23] the French legislator would abandon the idea of tracing a line between pure art and applied art.

This was settled with the Act of 11 March 1902, concerning copyright which established the principle of the Unity of Art, according to which protection should be extended to architects, sculptors and ornamental designers 'whatever the artistic merit and the destination of the work'.[24] Regardless of the intention of the artist or whether the work is in two or three dimensions, utilitarian or purely artistic, all creations could claim copyright protection. The law has the advantage of ending the earlier case law based on the merit or purpose of the work. Yet no cumulative protection is put forward.[25] The principle of the Unity of Art simply implies that all kinds of work, pure art as well as applied art, can benefit from the protection afforded by copyright. It is the Act of 14 July 1909 on the industrial designs and models that clearly established the principle of cumulative protection, which had already been accepted by the court. The first article provides that the law will protect those who have created designs and models 'without prejudice to the rights they obtained by other legal requirements and particularly by the Act of 19 and 24 July 1793, amended by the Act of 11 March 1902'.[26] A company that has failed to file its designs or models, a condition which was indispensable and required by the Act of 1909, would be able to exercise copyright to prohibit reproduction of its work.

In substance, the copyright law of 1902 served essentially to establish the principle of the Unity of Art. Very few reforms were made until 1957,[27] making room for case law construction of copyright, whether it concerned that of economic rights or the creation of moral rights, which is an intangible link between the author and his/her work. The right of authorship and the right of respect for the work's integrity were established

[23] Following the Congress on artistic property (Paris 1878), associations in France (Paris 1887) and the International congress of artistic property (Paris 1889), a motion was addressed to the Minister of Fine Arts in 1898 following an initiative by E. Soleau and signed by renowned artists including Rodin, Boucheron, Lalique and Christofle.

[24] See Intellectual Property Code (IPC) Art. L. 112–1. Y. Gaubiac, *La théorie de l'unité de l'art*, thesis, Paris (1980) II; 1 (1982) *RIDA* 3.

[25] N. Binctin, *Droit de la propriété intellectuelle*, 3rd edn (Paris: LGDJ, 2014), p. 902. P. Kamina, 'Droit d'auteur et droit des dessins et modèles', in J. M. Bruguière, *Articulation des droits de propriété intellectuelle* (Dalloz, 2011), pp. 85ff: 'the unity of art, which is a theory of copyright, is not a theory of cumulation (it existed previously and is applied independently to specific law). Neither does it induce an assimilation of regimes.'

[26] See IPC, Art. L. 513–2l.

[27] The Acts of 3 Aug. 1844, 8 April 1854 and 14 July 1866 allowed for protection to be extended following the author's death; the law of 9 April 1910 made a distinction between property of the hardware support of the work and intangible property of the work; the law of 20 May 1920 created the right of resale ('*droit de suite*') to authors of graphic and plastic works; the Act of 29 May 1925 annulled registration as being the condition necessary to claim infringement, signalling the end of formalities in copyright.

first,[28] followed by the author's right of disclosure.[29] This moral right, which is personal, unseizable, non-transferable, imprescriptible and perpetual, establishes, through the work, the singularity of the author which can not be appropriated.[30] Furthermore, with no mention of this matter in the law of 1793, it was also during this period that originality would appear in case law as the unique condition for the protection of works. This occurrence, favoured by the doctrine and notably by Desbois,[31] was however a little late in coming[32] and it took time for a legal link to be forged between the author and his work and for it to be defined as the imprint of the author's personality.[33] Even though the expressions were varied in case law,[34] all of them defined the subjective dimension of the notion.

At the same time, the system established by the Act of 1806 was considered insufficient, even though it was construed and finalised by the courts throughout the nineteenth century. It was replaced by the Act of 14 July 1909, which reinforced the regime of industrial property that covered designs and models. It afforded legal security to the right holder by legally dating registration, thus conferring simple presumption of ownership to the filer (article 3), without the publicity given to the design or model before filing entailing forfeiture of property right or of legal protection. The form and the duration of the filing were set in a legal framework (articles 5 to 9), but this filing had just declarative character. It was not enough thus to be the first to register a design or model in order to claim property as presumption could fall before the evidence to the contrary. The scope of protection was thus quite far-reaching; the law applied to 'any new design, any new plastic form, any industrial object that can be distinguished from similar objects by distinct and recognizable configuration affording it novelty, or by one or more exterior effects which provide its own unique physiognomy' (article 2.1). As novelty was assumed, it was incumbent on the person who attacked a design for lack of novelty to produce the proof of the existence of prior art. The law of 1909

[28] Trib. Civ. Seine, 17 Aug. 1814: quoted by A. C. Renouard, *Traité des droits d'auteur dans la littérature, les sciences et les beaux-arts* (Paris: Jules Renouard, 1838–9), t. 2, p. 332.

[29] CA Paris, 11 Jan. 1828, *Vergne*, (1828–30) 2 *S.* 5. Cass. civ., 14 March 1900, *Whistler* (1900) 1 *D.P.* 497.

[30] See on the beginnings of originality: S. Haas, *L'originalité au sens du droit d'auteur. Contribution à l'étude de la notion*, thesis, Paris 1 (1991).

[31] H. Desbois, *Le droit d'auteur: droit français, convention de Berne révisée* (Paris: Dalloz, 1950), p. 794.

[32] A. Lucas and P. Sirinelli, 'L'originalité en droit d'auteur' (1993) *JCP*, I, 3681.

[33] In French: *'l'empreinte de la personnalité de l'auteur'*: CA Paris, 1st ch., 1 April 1957, (1957) *D.* 436, 2nd decision: mentioning the imprint of the author's personality, whereas the first decision mentions a personal imprint.

[34] Regarding the notion: see A. and H. J. Lucas and A. Lucas-Schloetter, *Traité de la propriété littéraire et artistique*, 4th edn (Paris: Litec, 2012), pp. 104ff.

had also introduced the publicising of filing, the seizure of counterfeit goods (article 12) and set up sanctions against counterfeiters (articles 10 and 11). The 1909 Act was later amended by the Act of 26 November 1990, whether the formalities of registration, duration of protection (25 years, renewable once, leading to a grand total of 50 years!), and the mandatory registration on the national register for contracts concerning the designs or models.[35]

The 1909 Act was furthermore added to by the more specific Act of 12 March 1952 concerning the protection of creations from the seasonal industries of clothing and adornment. This law aimed to protect fashion creations (with specific counterfeit seizure procedures and heavy sanctions) while still affording the general protection associated with industrial design law and copyright. This creative work could thus benefit from the cumulative protection of three laws. However, having enjoyed very little success, the 1952 Act was revoked during the codification of the 1992 Intellectual Property Law, which introduced in the list of protected works those of the seasonal industries of clothing and adornment.[36]

Up until recent years, French law was still under the authority of the 1909 Act, a relatively limited law which offered few original solutions compared to copyright. This was updated very slightly by the Act of 26 November 1990. All the provisions were adopted in book V during the 1992 codification of the Code of Intellectual Property.

However, despite legislative intervention establishing the principle of cumulation, right from the outset questions were asked concerning the scope of the cumulative protection. Indeed, the definition of the object protected by the 1909 Act could quite cover works also protected by the 1793 Act; however, the 1902 Act specifying 'design and ornamental sculptures' was more restrictive and led one to believe that if the creations did not correspond to this definition, they would thus be excluded from protection by the 1793 Act. In the doctrine, two theories went head-to-head, one in favour of a restrictive interpretation of the 1902 Act, the other in favour of a more extensive interpretation. From this perspective, the domains of these two laws were identical and the conditions of originality and novelty had to be considered synonymous, thus providing the mandatory and indispensable condition for protection.

Once again, if the courts had initially refused copyright to creations that did not adhere to purely artistic considerations,[37] notably those regarding

[35] A. Françon, 'Les modifications apportées par la loi du 26 novembre 1990 au régime des dessins et modèles', in '*Vers un droit communautaire des dessins et modèles?*', (1992) Colloque IRPI, Paris, (1992), *Gaz. Pal.* Oct. 16–17, 4.

[36] See IPC, Art. L. 112–2.

[37] T. civ. Paris, 26 Jan. 1906, (1907) *Ann. Propr. Indust.* 119: protection for stills is refused. T. com. Seine, 23 May 1907, (1908) *Ann. Propr. Indust.* 28: for a watch case. CA Paris,

fashion,[38] it was a more extensive interpretation that finally prevailed. Thus, after 1930, a trend towards total or automatic cumulation gained momentum, making access to artistic creations property of the more utilitarian forms. The French Supreme Court (*La Cour de Cassation*) considered that artistic protection should be afforded to all ornamental designs, 'even industrial and without any artistic character'.[39] Cumulative protection was quickly recognised as the means to allow the creator to benefit simultaneously from two protections for the same creation and not require a choice to be made between two options, provided that the necessary conditions are met for both. A strict interpretation of this principle should have led to a distributive application of criteria of novelty and originality and that the same creation, which only responds to one criterion, can only be protected by one of legal basis (copyright or right of designs and models).[40] However, these two conditions were assimilated by the judges, thus indicating their difficulty in differentiating between the two very intertwined concepts. Moreover, French law, unlike many other laws, does not impose a minimum artistic threshold in order for a work to be recognised as original. And thus the judges swiftly opted to widen the scope of the copyright protection to industrial designs to cover even those with little artistic value, so as not to appear to judge the merit of the work.[41]

1.2.3 Third Period: The Law of 1957 to the Ordinance of 2001: Always Absolute or Quasi-automatic Cumulation

This period witnessed no major change for the assessment of cumulation. On the contrary, the liberal orientation of case law was further reinforced as the Act of 11 March 1957 relative to literary and artistic property had not put an end to the difficulties caused by cumulative protection.[42]

This time it was the authors of artistic works who called for a more precise legislation concerning their rights. The same, for the major part, were only covered by case law. The Act of 1957 thus came into effect to ensure the protection of works and authors, and the principle of the Unity

22 Jan. 1924, (1924) 1 *Gaz. Pal.* 438: for models of artificial flowers, protected by the law of 1909 but considered not to bear the necessary characteristics of a design or sculpture as defined by the law of 1793.

38 CA Paris, 25 Oct. 1905, (1906) *Ann. Prop. Indust.* 71. CA Paris, 11 March 1909, (1909) *Ann. Propr. Indust.* 234.

39 Cass. crim., 9 July 1931, (1932) *D.S.* 324. Cass. crim., 8 Dec. 1934, (1935) *D.H.* 85. Cass. crim., 30 March 1938, (1938) *D.H.* 324.

40 As proclaimed by H. Desbois, *Le droit d'auteur en France*, 3rd edn (Dalloz, 1978), p. 100.

41 For ex.: Cass. crim., 2 May 1961, (1961) *JCP*, II, 12242, note P. Aymond: for a salad basket.

42 Law codified by the law of 1 July 1992 and integrated into Books I and III of IPC (codification of established law).

of Art was held by the strategic and political choice of not discriminating between various works. The law also applies clearly to industrial creations, regardless of its destination or merit (article 2, later becoming article IPC, Article L. 112–1). In essence, the 'major law' of 1957 was clearly aimed at codifying the case law of copyright law (instituted some 150 years previously) and establishing the overriding doctrine, while taking into account technical and economic developments.[43] The law established an unlimited list of protected works which included, without the least ambiguity, works of applied art as well as seasonal creations (article 3, later to become IPC, Article L. 112–2). The French legislator, however, did not consider it relevant to introduce the only positive condition of protection of the work – that of originality. Originality remains a judicial requirement that the French legislator doubtlessly did not want to have crystallised by a legal definition, preferring to trust in the wide scope of interpretation of the judges. Furthermore, the term originality, when applied to 'the imprint of the personality of the author', has evolved, notably in the field of applied art. Today we refer to 'the creative effort',[44] the 'intellectual effort' or indeed the 'aesthetical bias' ('*parti-pris esthétique*'), thus giving the imprint of the author's personality.[45]

As far as the content of protection, the 1957 Act establishes the rights recognised to authors by the case law since the law of 1793: economic rights of reproduction and representation viewed in a broad context (article 26, later to become IPC, Article L. 121–1)[46] and moral rights (the right to authorship, right of disclosure and of respect of work, and right to repent and withdrawal: article 6, later to become IPC, Article L. 121–1). Moreover, due to the very personalistic nature of French copyright, the French legislator introduced provisions governing contracts for the exploitation of works and in particular those concerning the transfer of the creator's rights. Designed to protect the author, they are in practice very restrictive for operators of industrial works.[47]

However, by confirming the principle of the Unity of Art, and without clearly stating the subjective originality as a condition necessary to

[43] See the grounds of the Law.

[44] CA Paris, P. 5, 1st ch., 6 Nov. 2013, *Sté Christian Dior c/ Sté Brandalley et a.*, www.lamyline.fr.

[45] CA Paris, P. 5, 2nd ch., 30 Jan. 2015, n°**13/24509**, *JurisData* n°2015–002596. V. P. de Candé, 'Nouveauté – Caractère propre – Originalité', *Juris-Classeur Marques – Dessins et modèles*, LexisNexis, Fasc. 3230, 68. C. Bernault, 'La notion d'œuvre protégée', *Juris-Classeur Propriété littéraire et artistique*, LexisNexis, Fasc. 1135, 57. See below.

[46] To which the right of resale (*droit de suite*) was added to graphic and plastic works: article 42, later becoming IPC Article L. 121–8.

[47] See below.

protect the work (except for the titles of the works), the Act of 1957 did not shed light on how far-reaching the cumulation was to be. This explains why the case law that analysed this cumulative protection as an almost automatic combination of legal regimes was upheld and even reinforced.[48] One of the most salient effects of this total cumulation was the confusion of the criteria of validity of each property regime. The judges took into consideration the novelty of the designs and models (which would appear to exclude subjectivity) in a very relative way, which looked so like the originality of copyright that they were often confused. Indeed, the line between the idea of originality and novelty is difficult to draw. Furthermore, the traditional opposition between originality and novelty, as Desbois advocated, does not stand up to analysis, as originality is deeply intertwined with novelty.[49] As has already been pointed out, 'the two concepts of originality and novelty were so close that they degenerated'.[50]

Indeed, in practice, the courts subordinated the legal protection of designs and models to the proof of novelty *and* originality of the work. Thus, one was able to judge that 'it is not contested in virtue of the provisions of the law of 1909, that for a work to be protected it must not only be new and distinguishable from similar works . . . but also, since its provisions are extended to all "creators" . . . to qualify as a "creation", clearly implies that it must bear the "imprint" of the author's personality'.[51] It was often the case that the protection from specific law was refused as the work in question was not new *and* original or, on the contrary, protection was granted because it was new *and* original.[52]

Furthermore, even the Commercial Chamber of the French Supreme Court stirred up trouble by confirming this case law. In numerous decisions made on the legal authority of the 1909 Act, the Court clearly defined that the single observation of novelty was insufficient and that the design or model, in order to be considered new, should also 'be marked with the imprint of the personality of the author' and be the result

[48] Cass. crim., 11 Apr. 1975, (1975) *D.* 759, Desbois.

[49] C. Caron, *Droit d'auteur et droits voisins*, 2nd edn (Litec, 2009), 86. M. Vivant and J. M. Bruguière, *Droit d'auteur et droits voisins*, 2nd edn (Dalloz, 2012), 255: 'originality is only the other way in which something new is viewed'. Binctin, *Droit de la propriété intellectuelle*, p. 30.

[50] Lucas and Lucas-Schloetter, *Traité de la propriété littéraire et artistique*, p. 115.

[51] CA Paris, 4th ch., 25 Sept. 1996, (1997) 624 *PIBD*, III, 52: relating to car rims. CA Paris, 22 Sept. 1986, (1988) *JCP E*, II, 15155, 60, obs. J. J. Burst and J. M. Mousseron. CA Paris, 4th ch. B, 21 Jan. 2005, *Thi Dong Thai Le c/ Mme B. Cintius*, (2005) 17 *Propr. Intell.* 448, obs. P. de Candé.

[52] CA Paris, 23 Nov. 1963, (1964) *D.* 291, Greffe: for a hairbrush due to its slender and tapered shape.

of a creative effort – in essence, be original[53] – which is criticised in the doctrine.[54] At the same time, originality, the unique condition for copyright, was the feature relevant to differentiating the creation from previous work or from an overall impression (at a time when the individual character, '*caractère propre*' in French, did not exist as a condition of protection in Book V). Thus it was regularly judged that 'if all parts of the design do not invoke prior works, it must thus be considered as an original creation and thus merits protection'.[55] During this period, this extremely liberal interpretation of originality in case law was allowed to continue to protect numerous works of industrial art by copyright,[56] especially when formalities were deleted in 1925, leading companies to register fewer designs and models, preferring to claim copyright as the single legal means of defending their creations.

1.2.4 Fourth Period: Following the Ordinance of 25 July 2001: From Total Cumulation to Partial Cumulation (Reasoned Cumulative Protection in Case Law)

By transposition of the Directive 98/71 of 13 October 1998, this Ordinance n° 2001–670 of 25 July 2001[57] modified essential elements

[53] See e.g.: Cass. com., 13 Feb. 1996, (1996) *JCP E*, I, 562, obs. F. Greffe: concerning a cigarette lighter. Cass. com., 17 July 2001, (2002) 3 *Propr. Intell.* 65, obs. P. de Candé: for a model of a packet designed to hold seeds. Cass. com., 28 Jan. 2003 and 6 May 2003, (2003) *Propr. Intell.*, comm. 64, obs. P. Kamina. Cass. com., 20 Feb. 2007, (2007) 851 *PIBD*, III, 315; (2007) *Propr. Intell.*, comm. 43, obs. J. P. Gasnier: which requires a demonstration of originality as well as novelty, while considering that it was possible to infer 'the originality of a registered model by its aspect of novelty without examining if it bears the imprint of the author's personality'. Cass. com., 26 Feb. 2008, (2008) 873 *PIBD*, III, 291: concerning a wintering float for swimming pools.

[54] See e.g.: J. Schmidt-Szalewski and J. L. Pierre, *Droit de la propriété industrielle*, 4th edn (Litec, 2007), p. 148. P. Kamina, 'Le nouveau droit des dessins et modèles' (2001), 40 *D. affaires* 3258.

[55] In French, we say that there is no 'antériorité de toutes pièces': CA Paris, 22 Nov. 1988, (1989) *PIBD*, III, 243. Cass. com., 23 March 1965, (1965) *Bull. civ.* III 229. Cass. crim., 22 June 1967, (1968) *D.* 241, note Costa: 'the sketch of the silhouette by "Citroën"' is a protectable work 'because it embodies something new and original'. Cass. crim., 9 Oct. 1974, (1976) *JCP*, II, 18311, note A.C.: for a model of bottle opener. CA Paris, 4th ch., 13 July 1976, (1977) *Ann. Propr. Indust.* 59. Cass. com., 10 Sept. 2013, *Sté BPI c/ Sté Coscentra et a*, (2013) 993 *PIBD*, III, 1536.

[56] E.g. Cass. 16 Jan. 1957, (1957) *Ann. Propr. Indust.* 304: for lamp sockets. Cass. Crim., 30 Oct. 1963, (1964) *D.* 678, note A. Françon: protection for a salad basket which used plastic in a way that was 'new, original and pleasing to the eye' and was easily distinguishable from other models. Cass. crim., 9 Oct. 1974, (1976) *JCP G*, II, 18311: for a model of bottle opener. Cass. com., 15 Apr. 1982, *Casadamont*, (1982) 4 *RIDA* 110. Cass. com. 16 June 1992, *JurisData* n° 1992–001471: for twisted cable necklace chains. Cass. 1st civ., 11 Feb. 1997, (1997) *JCP G*, II, 22973, note X. Daverat: for a bolt.

[57] See F. Greffe, 'Ordonnance du 25 juillet 2001: transposition de la directive communautaire du 13 octobre 1998 sur la protection juridique des dessins et modèles. Une

of the Law on designs and models, such as the definition of the object of legal protection which became more objective and far-reaching, focusing on the appearance of the product (a condition which is not required in copyright).[58] The substantive conditions of protection evolved with the introduction of individual character,[59] as well as novelty becoming a relative novelty (IPC, Article L. 511–2 s).[60] Moreover, designs and models which are contrary to public policy or morality were denied protection (IPC, Article L. 511–7). This exclusion does not exist in copyright, as well as creations dictated solely by a technical function (IPC, Article L. 511–8). But the judge transfers this exclusion to copyright when certain technical or functional elements do not affect the originality of the work as a whole.[61] The Ordinance also amends the content of exclusivity, its limits and the duration of protection (IPC, Article L. 513–1). The filing of the design now has a constitutive effect and not a declarative one. It has to be filed within one year from the disclosure of creation. The applicant (whether he or she is the creator or not) gets a property right that he or she is free to assign or to grant a licence (IPC, Article L. 513–2).[62]

Concerning the principle of cumulation, the Ordinance of 25 July 2001 contains a similar wording as the previous text, since the right given by registration is granted 'without restricting the rights resulting from other legal provisions, chiefly Books I and III of the present code', i.e. copyright. This principle is to be found in the new Article L. 513–2 of the IPC (in chapter III relative to rights assigned by registration) and, even if its former pride of place has been lost, it is still a point of reference.[63]

This reform once again raised the question of whether the scope of cumulative protection should be revised, especially with the new change in the law on designs and models. If indeed some authors still believe in total cumulation and that the required conditions should still remain

harmonisation limitée et inutile', (2001) *JCP E*, 1900. P. Kamina, 'Le nouveau droit des dessins et modèles' (2001) 40 *D. affaires* 3258. F. Pollaud-Dulian, 'L'Ordonnance du 25 juillet 2001 et la réforme du droit des dessins et modèles', (2001) *JCP E*, act. 1737. J. Raynard, 'Du nouveau droit français des dessins et modèles: de l'influence de l'ordonnance du 25 juillet 2001 sur le principe de l'unité de l'art', (2002) *Propr. Industr.*, chron. 2.

[58] IPC, Art. L. 511–1. [59] IPC, Art. L. 511–3: '*caractère propre*' in French law.

[60] The Directive mentions the 'individual character' and 'the overall impression produced on an informed user'.

[61] CA Paris, P.5, 2nd ch., 6 Nov. 2009, *Sotuals Sarl c. Delsey SA et a*, (2010) 913 *PIBD*, III, 158, for a suitcase model.

[62] Cass. Com., 23 Sept. 2008, n°07–16970, (2008) 884 *PIBD*, III, 642.

[63] M. A. Perot-Morel, 'A propos du maintien de l'unité de l'art dans le nouveau droit des dessins et modèles', (2005) *Propr. Indust.*, étude 8.

assimilated,[64] the overriding doctrine quickly opted for change, deciding that the new provision of the IP code had a strong bearing on the Theory of the Unity of Art and cumulation. In the specific law of designs and models the French legislator introduced the notion of individual character (*caractère propre*) based on the objective opinion of an informed user (*observateur averti* in French) – whereas copyright still depends on a subjective evaluation of originality based on the personality of the author. Thus, due to specific law taking on a more objective slant or 'objectification', cumulation can no longer be automatic and must be understood as a juxtaposition of protection and not a confusion. Double protection is thus only possible if distributive application of the conditions stipulated in each text is applied and the latter must be clearly distinguished and analysed separately.[65] A same creation may benefit from the protection of copyright and designs and models law, but, depending on the case, the protection should be either alternative or cumulative. Thus if the novelty is ruined because of a previous disclosure of a request to register a design or model, it does not get in the way of the originality of the creation and copyright protection. On the contrary, a functional creation could benefit from the specific law of designs and models as it would not be considered 'exclusively' functional (IPC, Article L. 511–8), even if this creation does not fulfil the condition of orginality.

1.2.5 The Status Quo Period

Despite the position taken by the doctrine, it must be acknowledged that change was not as radical as some had hoped. Indeed, case law initially sided with those who claimed that the Ordinance of 2001 had very little impact. The judge continued to enforce total cumulation and in doing so maintained the confusion between novelty and originality but also between individual character and originality. In substance, the individual character of the work struggled to be seen as a stand-alone

[64] F. and P. Greffe, *Traité des dessins et modèles*, 9th edn (LexisNexis, 2014): who believe that the individual character was only introduced to facilitate the assimilation of regimes and must be considered original. D. Cohen, *Le droit des dessins et modèles*, 4th edn (Economica, 2014), p. 287.

[65] See J. Passa, *Traité de la propriété industrielle*, 2nd edn (LGDJ, 2009), pp. 688–98. C. Bernault, 'Droit d'auteur et droit des dessins et modèles: l'émancipation?', (2015) *Propr. Indust.*, étude 23. V. L. Bénabou, 'Les nouveaux critères de protection des dessins et modèles: une protection "sur mesure"', in *La protection des créations de mode*, (2002) 100 *Dr. et patrimoine*, p. 43. P. de Candé, 'Nouveauté – Caractère propre – Originalité', pp. 1 ff. M. A. Perot-Morel, 'A propos du maintien de l'unité de l'art dans le nouveau droit des dessins et modèles'. M. C. Piatti, 'Autonomisation du droit français des dessins et modèles?', (2004) *Propr. Indust.*, étude 20. F. Pollaud-Dulian, '*La propriété industrielle*' (Economica, 2010), p. 1027. P. Kamina, 'Arts appliqués', 30.

condition. As for demonstrating its originality, the *creative effort* reflecting *an aesthetic bias hallmarked with the author's personality* (*'parti-pris esthétique empreint de la personnalité de son auteur'* in French) often brought with it the notion of individual character.[66] It is still possible to see today legal decisions perpetuating this confusion.[67] It may even be perceived that the change in appreciation of the conditions necessary for protection relate more to a purely formal and disciplined way of thinking (as the judges distinguish very clearly the nuance between the conditions) than to a real change in the characterisation of the latter.

Finally, far from clarifying the link between the laws, the Ordinance of 2001 seems to complicate further the judges' task. The decisions taken confirm the difficulty which they still experience, despite legislative changes, to clearly distinguish originality, novelty and the individual character of industrial creations. Can we consider another way at looking at this? Indeed, when appreciating the individual character of a work, we must take into account the degree of liberty given to the creator to carry out his or her design or model. In turn this makes it tricky not to fall into the trap of confusing this with originality (which is already difficult to distinguish from novelty).[68] The two notions influence each other. Also, not only does the judge sometimes refer to an 'overall impression' (*'impression d'ensemble'* in French) or 'overall visual impression' to characterise the originality of the work,[69] but in the field of applied art, he or she also takes into account the degree of liberty given to the creator.[70] As French law does not impose a minimum creative threshold, the judge is thus allowed to determine how the author is able to express his or her personality through his or her work and thus find the means of defining originality. However, the risk of over-protection is blatant

[66] CA Paris, 4th ch. A, 28 Jan. 2004, *Sté Dispaly Factory c/ Péjoine, inédit*. CA Paris, 4th ch., 17 Jan. 2003, n°02/00158, (2003) 765 *PIBD*, III, 299.

[67] E.g. CA Paris, P.5, 1st ch., 13 Jan. 2015, *Cipa Distribution c/ Opel*, n°13/09274: originality is a necessary condition in design right. CA Paris, P.5, 1st ch., 15 Jan. 2014, *Sarl Pinkiss c/ Sarl Brin de Fille, JurisData* n°2014–001706. Cass. com., 31 Jan. 2012, n°11/14024. Cass. com., 21 Oct. 2008, (2009) *Propr. Indust.* 16, note F. Greffe: originality 'is a condition of protection right of a model however the legal basis claimed'.

[68] A. Tricoire, 'Le droit d'auteur au service de l'industrie ou la mort de l'autonomie de l'art', in *Mutations des industries de la culture, de l'information et de la communication* (Colloque, Sept. 2006): www.observatoire-omic.org/colloque-icic/pdf/TricoirereTR2.pdf.8.

[69] E.g. CA Paris, P.5, 1st ch., 8 June 2011, *Chrystal Denim c/ BA&Sh*, (2011) *Com. com. électr.*, chron. 8, obs. A. E. Kahn. CA Paris, P.5, 1st ch., 1 Feb. 2012, *JurisData* n°2012–002239. Cass. com., 20 Feb. 2007, *JurisData* n°2007–037741. Comp. CA Paris, 4th ch. A, 7 June 2006, (2006) 2 *Propr. Intell.* 455, obs. P. de Candé: referring to the experienced user as being the best placed to judge the originality of the work.

[70] TGI Paris, 3rd ch., 2nd sect., 18 Sept. 2015, n°14/02358, (2016) *Propr. Intell.* 241, obs. P. de Candé.

as originality could be expressed in very limited aspects of the design.[71]

All these difficulties go a long way to explain why for so many years, and in line with previous case law, whenever these two legal bases were raised, no decision accepted the protection of one while cancelling the other. Still today, the majority of decisions tend either to keep[72] or refuse[73] the protection of a creation based on the two legal bases with the same method of analysis.

Moreover, the judge continues to use copyright rather liberally for applied art creations,[74] whereas filing of a design or model has not been claimed, and is therefore out of any cumulation. For many years now the courts have agreed to exclude the style of a creation and its artistic elements[75] from protection. This is also the case for designs that fall into the public domain and for those that have purely technical and functional features.[76] However, the combination of these elements can be protected if it produces something original.[77] Thus, numerous designs with similar and non-protected features (often displaying a fashion statement or a functional necessity), if combined in an original way, can benefit from copyright without infringing upon the liberty of each creator. The courts highlight that the described elements when put together confer 'an own physiognomy which distinguishes them from other designs of the same kind and this in turns expresses an esthetic bias

[71] See P. de Candé: commentaire in (2016) *Propr. Intell.*

[72] CA Paris, P.5, 2nd ch., 28 March 2014, *SA Desmazières c/ Sarl Menport* (2014), *Com. com. électr.*, chron. 8, obs. A. E. Kahn, 4: model of ankle boot. CA Paris, P.5, 2nd ch., 7 Feb. 2014, *Mode Ecran* v. *Babou et Valta*, *JurisData* n°2014–001722: model of a tunic. CA Paris, P.5, 1st ch., 15 Jan. 2014, *JurisData* n°2014–001706: a style of dress. CA Paris, P.5, 2nd ch., 27 Nov. 2015, (2016) 1043 *PIBD*, III, 54: model of a sandal.

[73] TGI Paris, 3rd ch., 24 Oct. 2014, (2014) *Com. com. électr.*, chron. 8, obs. A. E. Kahn: a model of shoe.

[74] CA Paris, P.5, 2nd ch., 30 Jan. 2015, *JurisData* n°2015–002596: for a perfume bottle in the shape of a male torso. CA Paris, P.5, 1st ch., 12 May 2015, *Sté CFI c/ Sarl Highnesse*, n°14/11880: model of trousers. CA Paris, P.5, 1st ch., 21 Oct. 2014, *JurisData* n°2014–028509: model of a watch.

[75] CA Paris, 4th ch. B, 6 Feb. 2004, (2004) 791 *PIBD*, III, 461: 'l'appréciation de l'originalité doit tenir compte de ce qui appartient au domaine public' ('The appreciation of originality must take account of what is in the public domain'). Restyling fashionable items (elastic band attached to the inside of a pair of trousers) is not enough to give the model the imprint of the author's personality.

[76] CA Pau, 2nd ch., 4 Sept. 2006, *Jaspe Vert c/ Société Axara*, *JurisData* n°2006–313400.

[77] CA Paris, P.5, 2nd ch., 6 Nov. 2009, (2010) 913 *PIBD*, III, 158: for a type of suitcase. Cass. com., 17 March 2009, (2009) 895 *PIBD*, III, 1036: for model of a shoe. Cass. 1st civ., 10 Dec. 2014, n°13–23.076, *Groupement européen d'achats SAS et a. c/ Les produits de santé sélectionnés Sarl et a*, (2015) 1021 *PIBD*, III, 137. Cass. 1st civ., 9 Apr. 2015, n°13–28.768, (2015) 1029 *PIBD*, III, 424.

and the imprint of the author's personality'.[78] This phrase has since become standard wording. The appreciation of originality is done case by case in relation to the specific layout of diverse elements stemming from a creative effort.[79] And this is so whenever the originality can be found in the fine details due to a small degree of liberty of the creator that the judge decides to take into account. French copyright is thus proven to embrace industrial creations with open arms and there are many examples that illustrate this.

1.2.6 Recent Developments

However, change, timid though it may be, is underway and it appears that recent case law tends to have a more disciplined approach and is turning away from absolute cumulation towards one that is partial or reasoned. This was confirmed many times by the French Supreme Court considering that the texts issued by the Directive of 1998 'do not impose total cumulation or full rights to various protection, but authorize only such a cumulation when all the respective possibilities of different forms of protection are met'.[80] This understanding is clearly in the mind of the French legislator, and thus in line with the texts, and deserves to be highlighted and should be approved.

It is often brought to attention that the notion of prior art[81] and the individual character are unknown in copyright.[82] Copyright does allow

[78] In French: 'physionomie propre qui les distingue des autres modèles du même genre et qui traduit un parti-pris esthétique empreint de la personnalité de l'auteur': CA Paris, P.5, 1st ch., 6 Oct. 2010, *Sté LS Sarl c/ Sté Eve et Lou, JurisData* n°2010–021871. CA Paris, P.5, 2nd ch., 25 Oct. 2013, (2014) 999 *PIBD*, III, 132. CA Paris, P.5, 2nd ch., 30 Jan. 2015, *BPI c/ Attractive Fragrances & Cosmetics, JurisData* n°2015–002596.

[79] E.g. CA Paris, P.5, 2nd ch., 27 Nov. 2015, (2016) 1043 *PIBD*, III, 54: 'l'originalité des sandales revendiquées réside dans la combinaison des éléments qui les caractérisent – position des nœuds, choix de leur emplacement, taille des empiècements de cuir couvrant partiellement le dessus du pied, dessin des espaces vides laissés entre ces empiècements, selon un agencement particulier' ('the originality of the claimed sandals lies in the combination of elements that characterise – position of the nodes, choice of location, size leather inserts partially covering the top of the foot, drawing empty spaces between the panels, in a particular arrangement').

[80] Cass. crim., 13 Dec. 2011, (2012) 957 *PIBD*, III, 180. Cass. crim., 26 Nov. 2013, *JurisData* n°2013–027182. Cass. crim., 5 Oct. 2010, *Peugeot PSA Citroën Autosud*, n°09–85695.

[81] CA Paris, P.5, 1st ch., 21 May 2014, *JurisData* n°2014–012530. CA Paris, P.5, 2nd ch., 5 Sept. 2014, *Tod's Spa et al. c/ Basicitalia*, n°13/08513. CA Paris, P.5, 2nd ch., 6 Dec. 2013, (2014) *Com. com. électr.*, chron. 8, obs. A. E. Kahn. Cass. crim., 5 Oct. 2010, (2011) *RTD com.* 100, obs. F. Pollaud-Dulian. Cass. com. 20 Feb. 2007, (2007) *Propr. Intell.*, comm. 43, obs. J. P. Gasnier.

[82] CA Paris, P.5, 1st ch., 12 May 2015, *Sarl Ash Distribution C/ SA Eden*, n° 14/00989. CA Paris, P.5, 2nd ch., 21 Feb. 2014, (2014) *Propr. Intell.* 53. CA Paris, P.5, 2nd ch., 19 Apr. 2013, *Sté Leyla Style c/ Sarl The One, JurisData* n°2013–010405. CA Paris, P.5, 1st ch., 28 Nov. 2012, *Sas The Kooples et al. c/ Sté Gysele, JurisData* n°2012–030273.

for the existence of prior art to be made known (especially concerning those belonging to the public domain), as this can help prove the absence of originality. However, the judge does not rely on this criteria (which is specific to designs and models) to determine the originality of a design.[83] The existence of prior art thus is not sufficient to exclude the originality of a work.

In the same way, based on specific law, the judges are able to differentiate more clearly between the originality and the individual character of a design which is no longer assimilated[84] and rightly consider that the originality and artistic value are unknown qualities in design and model law.[85]

This leads to the logical conclusion, though not freely admitted enough, that the protection of a creation is accepted based on specific law while protection from copyright is denied,[86] or inversely when a cancelled registration of design remains under the protection of copyright.[87] All these decisions indicate that the criteria for protection are today more clearly distinguished.

The following crucial remark can be made – judges, for some time, do not hesitate to deny copyright protection to industrial designs even when the designs and models law has not been claimed.[88] The French Supreme Court exercises its control only over the characterisation of originality or the lack thereof in the light of the judges' appreciation.[89]

[83] P. de Candé, 'Nouveauté – Caractère propre – Originalité', 31.

[84] E.g. CA Paris, P.5, 2nd ch., 28 March 2014, *JurisData* n°2014–006788. CA Paris, P.5, 2nd ch., 31 May 2013, n°11/19345, (2013) 989 *PIBD*, III, 1381. CA Paris, P.5, 2nd ch., 8 Feb. 2013, (2013) 982 *PIBD*, III, 1144: judging that the law of designs and models does not require any specific creative effort. CA Paris, P.5, 2nd ch., 24 June 2011, *Cyrillus c/ Tod's Spa et Tod's France*, (2011) 41 *Propr. Intell.* 426, obs. P. de Candé.

[85] E.g. CA Paris, P.5, 2nd ch., 18 Nov. 2011, (2012) *Propr. Indust.* 27, obs. J. P. Gasnier. CA Paris, P.5, 1st ch., 7 Apr. 2015, *JurisData* n°2015–008797.

[86] Cass. 1st civ., 5 Apr. 2012, n°10/27373, (2012) *Com. com. électr.*, chron. 8, obs. A. E. Kahn. Cass. com., 10 Feb. 2015, (2015) *Propr. Indust.* 30, obs. J. P. Gasnier: a model of a fishing reel. TGI Paris, 3rd ch., 1st sect., 22 May 2014, (2014) *Propr. Intell.* 53: models of furniture. CA Paris, P.5, 2nd ch., 16 March 2012, (2012) *RLDI* 82, L.C.: designs that will be displayed on umbrellas. CA Paris, P.5, 1st ch., 8 June 2011, (2011) 948 *PIBD*, III, 625: a model of label that will be displayed on clothes.

[87] Cass. 1st civ., 11 Dec. 2013, n°12/14030, *JurisData* n°2013–028869.

[88] CA Paris, P.5, 2nd ch., 6 Dec. 2013, *SA Van Cleef & Arpels et al. c/ Sarl Actuelle*, (2014) *Com. com. électr.*, chron. 8, obs. A. E. Kahn. TGI Paris, 3rd ch., 1st sect., 6 Oct. 2009, (2010) 909 *PIBD*, III, 41. TGI Paris, 3rd ch., 2nd sect., 24 Oct. 2014, (2015) *Com. com. électr*, chron. 8, obs. A. E. Kahn: style of shoe.

[89] Cass. 1st civ., 15 May 2015, *Sté Cassegrain, Sté Longchamp c/ Sté Vivadia*, *JurisData* n°2015–011326: style of bag. Cass. 1st civ., 10 Sept. 2014, n°13/21996, www.legifrance.gouv.fr: style of cups. Cass. 1st civ., 2 Oct. 2013, *Sté ZV France*, (2014) *Com. com. électr.*, chron. 8, obs. A. E. Kahn: for a tee-shirt. Cass. com., 29 Jan. 2013, n°11/27351, www.legifrance.gouv.fr: models of furniture. Cass. 1st civ., 20 March 2007, (2008) *Propr. Intell.* 467, obs. P. de Candé: a bottle top in the shape of a warhead.

Figures 1.1 and 1.2. 'Tracksuits of French design can be considered eligible of protection under the provision of Book V of IPC (but there had not been filing in this case) but not that of Books I and III of the same IP code as the company making the request does not point out in what way the outfit is the result of a personal effort of creation and reflects originality which is not limited to the individual character of the design' (TGI Paris, 3rd Chapter, 1st section, 11 January 2011).

And so copyright protection was refused for a style of shoes[90] and also a style of tracksuit (see Figures 1.1 and 1.2).[91]

The trial judges appear much more exacting concerning the description of the features that characterise the imprint of the author's personality, especially when the design incorporates elements that belong to the public domain in a layout claiming to be original. The author has to clearly characterise how his work is original. It is not enough to claim the existence

[90] CA Paris, P.5, 2nd ch., 5 Sept. 2014, *Tod's Spa c/ Basicitalia Spa et a.*, *RG* n°13/08513. Cass. 1st civ., 20 March 2014, *Sté Tod's et al. c/ SAS Santiago Pons Quintana et al.*, *JurisData* n°2014–006515. CA Paris, P.5, 1st ch., 12 May 2015, n°14/00989, (2015) *Comm. com. électr.*, chron. 8, obs. A. E. Kahn: simple colour difference between two models is not enough to justify '*a special and distinct contribution reflecting the creative effort of the author and the imprint of his personality*'.

[91] TGI Paris, 3rd ch., 1st sect., 11 Jan. 2011, *Sarl Jacob H c/ Sarl G-Sport*, (2011) *Comm. com. électr.*, chron. 8, obs. A. E. Kahn.

Figures 1.1 and 1.2. *(cont.)*

of an original combination. The author must go on to describe and explain the aesthetic choices which were made in order for his work to achieve its 'own physiognomy' and thus expresses an '*aesthetic bias and the imprint of the author's personality*'.[92] Whoever is defending must then bring proof of prior art or evidence that the work is devoid of originality. The rights-holder to the creation does not benefit whatsoever from the presumption of originality.[93]

The doctrine sees this as a clear evolution, though timid move forward in case law, towards partial cumulation which is no longer

[92] E.g. CA Paris, P.5, 1st ch., 11 May 2011, *La Redoute c/ Caroll International*, *JurisData* n° 2011–008582. CA Paris, P.5, 2nd ch., 6 Dec. 2013, *SA Van Cleef & Arpels et al. c/ Sarl Actuelle.*

[93] CA Paris, P.5, 1st ch., 19 Jan. 2016, (2016) *Propr. Intell.* 240, obs. P. de Candé: 'the plaintiff in a copyright infringement action must characterise the elements that make the originality of the work'. Comp. CA Paris, P.5, 2nd ch., 12 June 2015, *Sarl Christy c/ Sas Paris Première* (2015) *Propr. Intell.* 454.

automatic, thus reinforcing the objective line ('objectification') of specific law.[94]

1.3 The Practical Implementation of Cumulation

In France numerous designs of applied art are being protected by copyright due to the Theory of the Unity of Art combining with cumulative protection, which gives access to rights. The implementation of these rights in turn causes awkward practical consequences to appear. Indeed, right from the outset, it was widely understood that both types of protection were 'juxtaposable'. However, it is necessary to have agreement on what that means and how the two situations can be clearly defined. When only specific law is concerned, or is the only law that can be enforced because the design in question lacks originality, and thus cumulative protection is not applicable, the Theory of the Unity of Art cannot be used to transfer the provision of copyright to a registered design. Cumulation means the overlapping (or superposition) of regimes[95] and not a confusion of both, and copyright should not irretrievably come to the rescue when the specific law falls short.

On the contrary, when both legal regimes can be applied, thus allowing the rights-holder the most favourable provision of each regime, copyright is applied in the same way as specific law, especially when the latter is devoid of any particular clause. This is of interest to us here. By allowing the cumulative protection of the two differently inspired laws and including their very separate clauses, the French legislator, throughout the years, has failed to address the issue of the overlapping of sometimes contradictory texts, at the very least restrictive, for the operators.

Some differences between the two regimes do not raise issues of a practical nature and have not called for legislation whether it concerns the aim of the protection (with the exclusion of technical designs and models or those which are contrary to public policy or morality in the designs and models law) or the exceptions to rights of which some may be in contradiction (the exception of a short quote in copyright is more restrictive than the exception given to illustrations in the designs and models law; the exception for parodies does not exist in Book V).

On the other hand, other legal provisions, because of the personalistic viewpoint of French copyright which is very protective of the creator, lead to a difficult cumulation in practice for those who market industrial works. The

[94] C. Bernault, 'Droit d'auteur et droit des dessins et modèles: l'émancipation?' P. de Candé, 'Nouveauté – Caractère propre – Originalité'. A. E. Kahn, 'Un an de droit de la mode', (2013–14) *Com. com. électr.*, chron. 8.

[95] See Lucas and Lucas-Schloetter, *Traité de la propriété littéraire et artistique*, p. 170. Contra: Passa, *Traité de la propriété industrielle*, p. 742.

root of the problem is working out who has property of rights. Book V indicates that this right belongs to the creator or to his or her successor and the right to protection is, until proven otherwise, granted to the author of application for registration of a design, and this could be done by a legal person or corporation (IPC, Article L. 511–9). On the contrary, the principle in copyright according to which an individual can be entitled to this right *ab initio*[96] – except for a collective work – means that corporations cannot hold rights to a creation until this is specifically granted by the author.[97] Corporations can of course register a design or model in their name, but this only amounts to mere presumption of property which can always be cancelled out if the author claims property of his work (IPC, Article L. 511–10).

The solution is awkward for companies when it concerns the work of a paid employee. If common ground cannot be found within the European Union, copyright expressly indicates that all rights belong to the employee.[98] Thus if copyright is applicable (in a single or cumulative measure) and without instruction from Book V which remains silent on this matter, it is not possible to infer from looking only at the work contract (or order contract) that the author is willing to yield his rights on his forthcoming work.[99] A specific transfer in favour of the employer is necessary and cannot take the form of a general clause within the work contract (or order contract) as *global cession on future works* from the author is prohibited (IPC, Article L. 131–1).

In contrast and where the designs and models law is silent on the point,[100] the rights belong to the employee who created the work. However, nothing forbids a clause in a work contract from attributing the rights to the employer.[101] In this case, as two sets of rules are in force,

[96] A principle that has not always been respected in applied art, but these decisions date back a while: Cass. crim., 21 Nov. 1979, (1980) *PIBD*, III, 78. CA Paris, 4th ch., 10 June 1977, (1978) *JCP G*, 18830, obs. F. Greffe – CA Paris, 4th ch., 10 Dec. 1980, (1981) *D.* 517, obs. F. Greffe.

[97] Cass. 1st civ., 15 Jan. 2015, *JurisData* n°2015–000315: a legal person cannot be qualified as an author.

[98] IPC, Art. L. 111–1: '*L'existence ou la conclusion d'un contrat de louage d'ouvrage ou de service par l'auteur d'une œuvre de l'esprit, n'emporte aucune dérogation à la jouissance du droit reconnu par l'alinéa premier.*'

[99] Cass. 1st civ., 16 Dec. 1992, (1993) 156 *RIDA* 193, obs. P. Sirinelli: refusing implied assignment to the employer.

[100] The only text that allows provision is article 14.4 of the ruling (CE) n°6/2002 according to which the employer retains the rights, 'unless contrary clause in national legislation is applicable'. When only Book V is applicable, Article L. 111–1 of IPC cannot be considered as 'a national contrary clause'. See TGI Paris, 3rd ch., 27 Jan. 2011, (2011) *Propr. Indust.* 59, obs. J. P. Gasnier. See also Lucas and Lucas-Schloetter, *Traité de la propriété littéraire et artistique*, p. 170.

[101] The economic dimension in Industrial Property law explains why the link between the creator and the creation does not have the same power as in copyright.

the employee would retain copyright even though the employer is in his legal rights to register the design under the Book V ruling. We can clearly see the difficulties this poses in practical terms as even if the employer attempts registering the design following the Book V ruling, if he or she infringes on the worker's rights the latter can assert his or her rights or have the registration annulled (IPC, Article L. 512–4).

Until progress is made on this matter, the qualification of collective work seems to offer the best alternative to offset the shortcomings of common law regarding designs made by employees. Courts readily recognise the legal qualification (IPC, Article L. 113–2) which provides a range of rights,[102] including moral rights,[103] to the individual or legal person that produced, published and promoted the work under his name when a designer claims property rights for a design (IPC, Article L. 113–2).[104] Admittedly, in practice, works of applied art are often made in design studios by teams of creators who follow the company's guidelines, and in doing so the conditions for a collective work of art are met. However, ligation regarding works made by employees is marginal, as the majority of employees never claim property for their creative work.

Secondly, if Book V has few rules concerning operating agreements (which need a written act and publication), copyright has been on the other hand a lot more restrictive since the 1957 Act. A written document is required *ad probationem* for some contracts such as editing contracts (IPC, Article L. 131–2), and even when the former is not legally required, each assigned right must be clearly identified in its scope (destination, place and duration: IPC, Article L. 131–3). The author's remuneration is 'proportional to the revenue from the sale or exploitation', with the option to substitute in some cases a lump sum (IPC, Article L. 131–4). Finally, transfer of copyright only concerns property rights, as moral rights are unassailable. The author's rights are thus well protected within a strong legal framework.

The courts, by pragmatism, have tried to set up a 'safety valve' to free applied art from the binding rules of copyright. Attempts have been made to bind the two as well, sometimes by setting aside rules, sometimes adjusting them. In an attempt to combat conterfeiting, the French Supreme Court, since 1993, guarantees 'presumption of ownership of the legal person in whose name the design is released, without taking

[102] IPC, Art. L. 113–5. Cass. 1st civ., 22 Oct. 1991, (1992) *Ann. Propr. Indust.* 320. Cass. crim., 10 June 1991, (1991) *RJDA*, 771: relating to models of car bodywork.

[103] Cass. 1st civ., 22 March 2012, *JurisData* n°2012–005215.

[104] Cass. soc., 26 March 2014, *Van Cleef & Arpels c/ Berthelot*, *JurisData* n°2014–006028; (2014) *Com. com. électr.*, chron. 8, obs. A. E. Kahn. Cass. soc., 22 Sept. 2015, *Mme X. c/ Sté Lalique*, (2016) *Propr. Intell.* 58, obs. J. M. Bruguière. CA Paris, P.5, 2nd ch., 11 Sept. 2015, *Triangle Expositions c/ Sté Volvo Trucks France*, (2015) 1036 *PIBD*, III, 681.

into account any qualification of the creation and in the absence of a claim made by the original creator'.[105] This is done with or without the presence of the author in question.[106] However, the company must prove unequivocal exploitation under its name,[107] or the disclosure under its name.[108] Some decisions go as far as demanding that the marketing of the work is done 'in an unambiguous manner'.[109] This presumption, which sides most favourably with the company, would pose a problem if the creator reclaims property rights or if he or she joins the action taken by the company that benefits from presumed property as he or she would have to prove that he or she is indeed the author of his or her work.[110]

In the same way, the rules governing the transfer of copyright have all been tailored to suit those who sell industrial creations in order to take into account technical, commercial and economic constraints. Indeed, judges have sometimes admitted 'implicit' or 'tacit cession of rights' on industrial works.[111] The French Supreme Court made an important ruling in limiting the demands of Article L. 131–3 of the IPC to transfers that need a written document according to Article L. 131–2, which is not normally the case in applied art as assignment often only applies to reproduction rights (without being a publishing contract). The assignment of rights and its scope can be proven by a multitude of means.[112] With regard to remuneration, Article L. 131–4 of IPC allows in some cases for the author to receive a lump sum rather than a proportional payout. This is especially true when the author's contribution does not play a fundamental intellectual role in the creation of the work or when

[105] Cass. 1st civ., 24 March 1993, two decisions: *Sté Bezault c/ Michallon et Prat* et *Sté Aréo c/ Syndicat d'initiative de l'Office de tourisme de Villeneuve Loubet*, (1993) *JCP G*, II, 22085. Cass. 1st civ., 9 Jan. 1996, *Sté C. Dior c/ C.L. Design*, *JurisData* n°1996–000052: concerning a model of tray. Here, case law is plentiful and constant.

[106] Cass. com., 20 June 2006, *JurisData* n°2006–034149.

[107] Cass. 1st civ., 19 Oct. 2004, (2005) 1 *RIDA*, 271. Cass. 1st civ., 6 Oct. 2011, n°10/17018, *JurisData* n°2011–021600. Cass. 1st civ., 4 May 2012, *JurisData* n°2012–009214.

[108] Cass. 1st civ., 16 March 2004, (2004) *Propr. Intell.* 636, obs. P. Sirinelli.

[109] CA Paris, 4th ch. B, 16 Jan. 2009, (2009) *Propr. Intell.* 272, obs. A. Lucas.

[110] Cass. 1st civ., 15 Nov. 2010, *JurisData* n°2010–021417. CA Paris, P.5, 1st ch., 31 March 2010, *JurisData* n°2010–013011.

[111] Cass. com., 20 Feb. 1980, (1981) *JCP*, II, 10619, obs. Burst and Kovar: the creator allowed his work to be released under the name of the company. Cass. 1st civ., 27 May 1986, (1987) 2 *RIDA* 61: transfer deducted from the invoice. CA Paris, 4th ch. B, 13 Dec. 1990, (May 1991) *Cah. Dr. Auteur* 22: according to which the formal rules 'are very rarely imposed in matters of applied art'. Cass. com., 27 Oct. 1992, (1993) 2 *RIDA* 190: transfer deducted from an order contract relative to designs reproduced on clothes. CA Paris, 1st ch., 29 Oct. 2001, (2002) 2 *RIDA* 441: transfer deducted from usages.

[112] Cass. 1st civ., 21 Nov. 2006, (2007) *Com. com. électr.*, chron. 8, obs. A. E. Kahn. CA Paris, P.5, 1st ch., 29 June 2011, (2011) *Propr. Ind.* 84.

the way in which the work is used plays a secondary role to the object itself. The latter holds true especially in the case of industrial works.[113] These adjustments, which may seem punctual, become more frequent in applied art, leading to a regime derogating from the copyright.

Moreover, industrial creations due to their nature or destination are not easily assessed in terms of moral rights.[114] This is why the courts consider that, due to constraints linked to the industrial use of these creations, authors should sometimes accept certain limitations of their moral rights, whether it be authorship[115] or the right of respect for the work's integrity.[116] Limitation clauses of moral right have also been allowed, either to pre-validate some forms of use or to accept knowingly the modifications concerning the works.[117]

Finally, the stringency with which the conditions of protection of copyright and of the designs and models law were appreciated has obviously affected the way in which counterfeiting is assessed. Judges who had sometimes appeared flexible today show a clearer appreciation between Books I and V. In copyright law the judge must check whether the essential features of the work which denote its originality have been replicated in the forged copy. In the law on designs and models, he or she must judge the overall visual impression that this would have on an informed user. These criteria have become somewhat confused because of cumulation. Thus, the judge, on the basis of copyright, has sometimes required an inspection to determine whether the two designs create an effect of resemblance.[118] The French Supreme Court has recently

113 TGI Paris, 16 Dec. 1980, (1981) 109 *RIDA* 223: for freely distributed advertising brochures. TGI Paris, 3rd ch., 11 March 2010, *F. Sofia et al. c/ Erard et al.*, (2010) 921 *PIBD*, III, 471. CA Paris, P.5, 1st ch., 31 Oct. 2012, n°10/21777, *JurisData* n°2012–026025: for a model of perfume bottle which is considered accessory to the perfume itself.

114 Unseizable, non-transferable, imprescriptible and perpetual: IPC, Article L. 121–1.

115 Cass. 1st civ., 13 Feb. 2007, *M. X. c/ Manufacture de Beauvillé*, (2007) *Propr. Indust.* 52, obs. F. Greffe. See also: CA Paris, 29 March 1978, (1979) *PIBD*, III, 34, concerning an emblem. CA Paris, P.5, 1st ch., 31 Oct. 2012, *JurisData* n°2012–026025: for a bottle of perfume.

116 Cass. 1st civ., 11 June 2009, *Brit Air c/ Aedifis*, (Oct. 2009) *Propr. Intell.* 397, obs. P. de Candé: but modifications to the work must not exceed 'what is strictly necessary' or 'disproportionate to the original aim'. See, however: CA Paris, 4th ch. B, 5 Dec. 2008, (2009) 893 *PIBD*, III, 936, confirmed by Cass. com., 16 Feb. 2010, *Ph. Reddon c/ L'Oréal*, (2010) *Com. com. électr.*, chron. 8, obs. A. E. Kahn: which allows, in a more restrictive manner, only modifications that are necessary from a technical point of view and not those that are purely economic.

117 Cass. com., 6 Feb. 2013, (2013) 980 *PIBD*, III, 1083. TGI Paris, 3rd ch., 14 May 2010, *Idéal Sarl et al. c/ Chanel*, (2010) 925 *PIBD*, III, 646.

118 CA Paris, 4th ch. A, 19 Sept. 2007, (2008) 26 *Propr. Intell.* 114, obs. A. Lucas. CA Paris, P.5, 1st ch., 9 Dec. 2011, (2012) 45 *Propr. Intell.* 458, obs. P. de Candé. Cass. com., 17 June 2003, *Novasque et Fibleuil c/ SA Nicole Olivier*, (2004) *Propr. Intell.* 9, obs. J. Schmidt-Szalewski.

silenced this confusion by clarifying that trial judges are not bound to 'make a decision from an overall impression' in line with copyright law.[119] Similarly, it has also put paid to errors made by trial judges who highlighted the likelihood of confusion when analysing counterfeiting.[120]

Acts of counterfeiting are determined differently depending on whether copyright or the law of designs and models is applied and this is notably the case in unregistered community design. What is deemed counterfeit or infringing in one is not necessarily replicated in the other, and judges are more careful in characterisation of what constitutes infringement. It is either based on rulings in Book I and/or Book V that companies win their case.[121] Cumulative protection is thus clearly applied in this field also. However, one practical and key question still remains unanswered: can the law on designs and models be claimed under appeal for the first time while only copyright was claimed before the first court and vice versa? Insofar as 'the object and function of each law are clearly separate and they serve different purposes',[122] 'new considerations' under appeal should not be submitted (Code of Civil Procedure, Articles 564 and 565). Nevertheless, the question remains, as contradictory decisions have been made by the Paris Court of Appeal.[123]

Finally, by using a more flexible approach to copyright and allowing texts to juxtapose, judges have made cumulation possible for applied art. However, if the Ordinance for 2001 gives rise to a specific pro-industry regime for designs and models and in doing so distances itself from copyright,[124] it appears that in practice the gap is widening in the

[119] Cass. com., 8 Apr. 2014, (2014) 52 *Propr. Intell.* 271, obs. A. Lucas.

[120] Cass. com., 26 March 2008, (2008) 875 *PIBD*, III, 349. Cass. com., 23 Sept. 2008, (2008) 883 *PIBD*, III, 608. Cass. 1st civ., 15 May 2015, (2015) 56 *Propr. Intell.* 298, obs. J. M. Bruguière.

[121] TGI Paris, 3rd ch., 2nd sect., 5 Dec. 2014, n°13/12390, *INPI, basis of jurisprudence*, réf. D20140252: for models bearing differences, the litigious model cannot be considered a slavish imitation and infringement cannot be claimed by UCD as copyright is in force. TGI Paris, 3rd ch., 3rd sect., 5 Dec. 2014, n°12/16235, *INPI, basis of jurisprudence*, réf. D20140247: infringement under UCD for slavish imitation for a jacket is recognised, but infringement under copyright is refused due to the reproduction of elements which characterise the work.

[122] J. P. Gasnier, 'Un an de droit des dessins et modèles', (2014) *Propr. Indust.* chron. 4, 15. See also: C. Bernault, 'Droit d'auteur et droit des dessins et modèles: l'émancipation?'

[123] Refusal of the possibility of invoking on appeal the benefit of UCD: CA Paris, P.5, 2nd ch., 19 Apr. 2013, *Sté Leyla Style c/ Sarl The One*, *JurisData* n°2013–010405. CA Paris, P.5, 2nd ch., 26 Apr. 2013, *Sarl Giovanni c/ Sas SAM*, n°11/18809, inédit. CA Paris, P.5, 1st ch., 5 June 2013, *Sas Sandro c/ sarl Timely*, n°12/09557, inédit. On the contrary, acceptance of Book I or Book V being invoked for the first time under appeal: CA Paris, P.5, 2nd ch., 1 March 2013, *SARL Sarahdavid c/ SA Jus d'orange*, (2013) *Propr. Indust.* 62, obs. P. Greffe.

[124] M. A. Perot-Morel, 'A propos du maintien de l'unité de l'art dans le nouveau droit des dessins et modèles'.

copyright between industrial creations and the other, more artistic creations. We thus reach a paradox with harmful consequences where the creator of a design or model has greater protection from general law (copyright) than from the law that was specifically designed for him or her. The principle of cumulation in France has seen the empowerment ('*autonomisation*' in French) of the creations of applied art within copyright. This is largely due to the establishment of a widely derogatory regime in order to avoid rules protecting authors, which can act as barriers for those who market industrial creations.

1.4 Conclusion

Full and even total and automatic cumulation has been applied in French law for centuries. Today this is evolving towards a partial or reasoned cumulative protection. Having applied the new law for designs and models for sixteen years, judges are aware that the conditions of protection afforded by copyright and the law for designs and models need to be determined in a clear and independent manner. This will doubtlessly cause industry to rethink their strategy in terms of design protection. For French companies copyright has always been their standby – an easy and inexpensive way to protect their works of applied art. As case law becomes more stringent we have noticed that companies that did not register their creations are claiming in increasing numbers the benefit of unregistered community design, and this can only be commended. Before the Ordinance of 2001, specific law was considered only as a complement to copyright which protects all original works. Today, this dynamic is beginning to change.

Developing partial cumulation is the best way forward so that every industrial creation does not fall automatically under the protection of copyright. The latter has immense adaptability and flexibility but cannot keep accepting all demands and 'risk losing its soul or at the very least its coherency'.[125] Partial cumulation will bring balance to the system as a whole. Copyright will thus preserve its coherence and companies will benefit from a stronger legal framework.

A closer look needs to be taken concerning the originality of the creation, which bears the imprint of its author. French courts are not helped by not being able to appreciate the merit of the work or have a minimum creative threshold. But this would not, however, prevent a certain subjectivity when appreciating the work, and decisions made by the judges

[125] J. P. Gasnier, 'Cumul, vous avez dit cumul?', in '*Les dessins et modèles, dix ans après. Bilan & perspectives*', (2011) 63 *RLDA*, 87ff.

would, even here, lack objectivity. A more exacting examination of the originality, on which the European Court of Justice will intervene, will perhaps encourage companies to look towards specific law which was designed for their industrial creations.

As cumulative protection often leads to industrial creations being protected twice over, clear planning must be key, right from the outset in French law, to provide safer solutions for industrial works. Rather than adopting a specific regime in copyright for creations in applied art (which would only weigh down copyright further and add to undermine its coherence), it is now time for copyright to be updated, especially regarding creations made by employees of a company. This could be done by either a legal transfer of rights to the employer (in exchange for financial compensation, as is done with patents) or by simplifying laws relating to assignments. However, this is still met with a lot of reticence, and the solution to the issue may indeed come from the European Union.

2 The Copyright/Design Interface in the Netherlands

Antoon Quaedvlieg

Table 2.1 *Chronological table of legislation and statistics*

Period	Legislation	Amendments	Interpretation (i.e. by courts)	Further information
1912–1953	Copyright Act of 1912		Varying degrees between simple originality and a (modest) degree of artisticity are required by the courts.	Intense debate in the doctrine about the absence of a full protection for models.
1953–1975			As before.	1953, Protection against confusion allowed under the law of unfair competition. 1966, Benelux Treaty on Models and Designs is concluded but the law will not enter into force until 1975.
1975–2003	1975, Uniform Benelux Law on Designs and Models		Partial cumulation. 1987, the Benelux Court of Justice rules that no 'higher' degree of originality is required.	Article 14(5) UBLDM categorically excludes protection by the law of unfair competition. Article 21 makes cumulation with copyright dependent on the

Table 2.1 *(cont.)*

Period	Legislation	Amendments	Interpretation (i.e. by courts)	Further information
				design showing a 'clearly artistic character'.
2003–present	2003, implementation of the European Design Directive.	2006, the UBLDM is inserted as Title III into the new Benelux Convention on Intellectual Property.		2003, the 'ban' on protection by unfair competition law is lifted.

2.1 General Overview of Design Law in the Netherlands

2.1.1 History of Dutch Design Protection

Dutch design law is not Dutch; Belgium, Luxembourg and the Netherlands share a Uniform Benelux Law on Designs and Models, which was integrated in 2006 into the Benelux Convention on Intellectual Property.

However, the Dutch Copyright Act is of national origin. Until 1975, when – relatively late – the Uniform Benelux Law on Designs entered into force, the way copyright dealt with models and designs developed independently from Belgium and Luxembourg; so did the national law of unfair competition, the interference of which may have been of considerable influence on the relation between design law and copyright in the Netherlands. For these reasons, the interface between design law and copyright law will here be dealt with from the Dutch perspective only. Its history can be divided into four stages.

2.1.2 First Period: 1912–1953: Only Copyright Protection

Until 1975, the Netherlands had no design law at all. As from 1912, however, models and designs could be protected on the basis of copyright. Under the earlier Copyright Act of 1881,[1] neither works of the visual arts, nor designs and models, figured in the list of works eligible

[1] Law of 28 June 1881, *Staatsblad* 1881, 124, for the regulation of Copyright.

for copyright protection. In answer to questions in Parliament, the Minister had asserted that separate laws should be preferred for these categories.[2] Article 10 (10°) (presently: 11°) of the Copyright Act 1912[3] provided that *works of art applied to industry* were to be considered as works of literature, science or art. The Explanatory Memorandum declared that the Act thus met a *longstanding wish* of interested circles.[4] The Dutch were well aware that this meant that foreign design would have to be protected in the Netherlands, whereas the opposite would not necessarily be the case;[5] the 1908 Berlin version of the Berne Convention did not yet include this category of works. Moral rights protection for works of applied art was only granted in 1972.[6]

2.1.3 Second Period: 1953–1975: Slavish Imitation Added

In 1953, the Dutch Supreme Court framed a protection against slavish imitation under the general clause of unlawful behaviour in the Dutch civil code.[7] The pressure to create some kind of protection for design had been high. Although the Netherlands had agreed, in 1928,[8] to the Hague Agreement, they had failed to create protection for designs themselves.[9] In the 1930s, this led to debates in the Dutch legal press which would not stop until the introduction of the Benelux Design Law in 1975.[10]

[2] Memorandum of reply of 22 September 1880, session 1880–1, Annexes Lower House (Tweede Kamer), 15, nr 1; taken from Marijke Reinsma, *Auteurswet 1881. Parlementaire geschiedenis wet 1881 – ontwerp 1884* (Zutphen: Walburg Pers, 2006), p. 51.

[3] Law of 23 September 1912, *Staatsblad* 1912, 308, holding a new regulation of copyright, entry into force 1 November 1912.

[4] Explanatory Memorandum, TK 1911, at Article 9, under 10°.

[5] L. G. van Praag, *De Auteurswet 1912 en haar verband tot de herziene Berner Conventie* (Rotterdam: Nijgh & Van Ditmar's Uitgevers-Maatschappij, 1912), pp. 40–1.

[6] Following the Brussels revision of the BC. Lower House session 1964–5, no. 7877, Explanatory memorandum (nr 3), p. 10.

[7] Supreme Court of the Netherlands, 26 June 1953, *Machinefabriek Thole* v. *Hyster Company* ('Hyster Karry Krane'), NJ 1954, 90, note PhANH; BIE 1953, 113; *Ars Aequi* III, 10, note Hijmans van den Bergh.

[8] Act of 15 March 1928, *Staatsblad* 196.

[9] Article 1 of the Agreement read:

'Les ressortissants de chacun des pays contractants ainsi que les personnes ayant satisfait sur Ie territoire de l'Union restreinte aux conditions établies par l'article 3 de la Convention générale, pourront s'assurer dans tous les autres pays contractants la protection de leurs dessins ou modèles industriels, au moyen d'un dépôt international effectué au Bureau international de la propriété industrielle a Berne.'

[10] Supreme Court of the Netherlands, 31 May 1991, *Borsumij* v. *Stenman* ('window stay'), NJ 1992, 391, note Verkade; BIE 1992, 50, note Steinhauser; IER 1991, 116, note Vriesendorp; *Ars Aequi* 1993, 680, note H. Cohen Jehoram.

2.1.4 *Third Period: 1975–2003: Benelux Design Protection*

A special design law was finally introduced in the form of the Uniform Benelux Law on Designs and Models (UBLDM),[11] entered into force on 1 January 1975.[12] Chapter II of the UBLDM contained a regulation for cumulative protection by copyright and design law. It provided that in order to be eligible for copyright protection, designs had to show 'a clearly artistic character'.[13] It further regulated the consequences of the deposit of the design and the assignment of either the design or the copyright, and designs made on commission. It also contained a provision, revoked in 2003, that before the expiry of the design right, right holders had to deposit a declaration for maintenance of copyright in order to keep their copyright.

2.1.4.1 Revocation of the Protection under the Doctrine of Slavish Imitation

The UBLDM strived at a register as complete as possible. Consequently, Article 14(5) UBLDM categorically excluded designs from after 1 January 1975 from the protection under the doctrine of slavish imitation. Protection of this kind was thought to undermine the willingness of right holders to have their designs registered. However, designs from *before* that date would, as Article 25 explicitly provided, continue to enjoy the same protection as had previously been granted to them under national law.[14]

2.1.4.2 The Disappointment of the UBLDM

The UBLDM turned out to be a disappointment.[15] Timely registration was often omitted, either for reasons of ignorance or negligence, or because it was felt that the costs were high or the registration cumbersome. The

[11] Part of the Benelux Treaty on Designs and Models of 25 October 1966, *Tractatenblad* 1966, 292 and 1974, 66. Also see the Act of ratification of 18 April 1973, *Staatsblad* 1973, 203, Articles 1 and 2; which already entered into force on 19 April 1973 (Article 5).

[12] According to Article 13 of the Benelux Treaty on Designs and Models.

[13] 'Een duidelijk artistiek karakter' or 'un caractère artistique marqué'; other authors translated 'duidelijk' as: 'marked' or 'distinctly'. However, as will be explained further, this criterion of a clearly artistic character would eventually be interpreted as meaning no more than that the design had to be original.

[14] Article 25 UBLDM 1975: 'Subject to Article 26, designs which prior to the entry into force of this Law enjoyed protection, in any form, under the national law in any one of the Benelux countries shall continue to enjoy the same protection in that country.'

[15] Jaap H. Spoor, 'The Impact of Copyright on Benelux Design Protection Law', and Charles Gielen, 'Design Protection and Unfair Competition', both in Jan J. C. Kabel and Gerard J. H. M. Mom (eds.), *Intellectual Property and Information Law. Essays in Honour of Herman Cohen Jehoram* (The Hague/London/Boston: Kluwer Law International, 1998), pp. 59–68; Anselm Kamperman Sanders, '100 Years of Copyright – The Interface with Design Law Coming Full Circle?', in Bernt Hugenholtz, Antoon Quaedvlieg, Dirk Visser, *A Century of Dutch Copyright Law. Auteurswet 1912–2012* (Amsterdam: deLex, 2012), pp. 99–114, at 109–10.

situation was aggravated by the strictness of the novelty requirement, which (until 1999[16]) was not mitigated by any grace period. In that constellation, the suppression of the supplementary protection has probably contributed to the sharp increase of cases in which copyright protection for designs was invoked and granted.

2.1.5 Fourth Period: 2003–Present: Design Directive and Other New Rules

2.1.5.1 Copyright

As from 1 December 2003, the law of 1975 was amended[17] in order to implement European Design Directive 98/71. This operation significantly changed the design law, including the Chapter on cumulative protection with copyright law. The requirement of a declaration for maintenance of copyright mentioned above was abolished and the ban on supplementary protection of designs by the law of slavish imitation was lifted.[18] However, slavish imitation would henceforth play a secondary role. Copyright had become the primary ground for invoking protection.

2.1.5.2 2006: Benelux Convention on Intellectual Property

On 1 September 2006, the UBLDM was 'merged' with the Uniform Benelux Law on Trade Marks into the consolidated Benelux Convention on Intellectual Property (BenCIP) of 25 February 2005.[19] Consequently, the numbering of the articles was changed. Article 5.3 BenCIP provided that the rights existing under the UBLDM would be maintained. According to the Explanatory Memorandum, this included the rights flowing from transitional provisions. That meant that 'old' designs from before 1 January 1975 continued to enjoy the

[16] The grace period, created in the Protocol of 28 March 1995, *Tractatenblad* 1995, 133, entered into force on 1 May 1999.

[17] On the basis of the Protocol of 20 June 2002, *Tractatenblad* 2002, 129; entry into force on 1 December 2003, on the first day of the third month after ratification by the third Benelux state (Luxembourg, on 30 September 2003). See Article VIII as well as *Tractatenblad* 2003, 181.

[18] The original Article 14(5) was deleted. It had been renumbered 14(7) in 1997 and 14(8) in 2000. See for 1997: Benelux Protocol of 28 March 1995, *Tractatenblad* 1995, 133; approved for the Netherlands on 27 June 1997 (*Staatsblad* 1997, 253); entry into force 1 May 1999 (BIE 1999, 39). For 2000: Benelux Protocol of 7 August 1996, *Tractatenblad* 1996, 226, entry into force 1 January 2000 (*Tractatenblad* 2000, 381).

[19] Benelux verdrag inzake de intellectuele eigendom, *Tractatenblad* 2005, 96. Entry into force on the first day of the third month after the third ratification instrument has been deposited (Article 6.2): on 1 September 2006, after the deposit of the ratification instrument by the Netherlands on 29 June 2006 (for the Dutch Act of ratification of 10 May 2006 see *Staatsblad* 2006, 262). The old UBLDM was repealed in the Netherlands on the same date of 1 September 2006; see *Tractatenblad* 2006, 182.

protection under the doctrine of slavish imitation flowing from Article 25 UBLDM.[20]

2.2 The Object of Protection

2.2.1 Design Law: Novelty and Specialty

2.2.1.1 Novelty

Until the implementation of the European Design Directive in 2003, mere novelty was sufficient to be eligible for protection as a design or model under the UBLDM.[21] According to Article 4(1) a design was not new when: (a) at any time during the 50 years preceding the date of deposit or the date of priority under the Paris Convention, a product identical in appearance with the deposited design or differing only in minor respects had enjoyed a de facto notoriety in the relevant industrial or commercial circles in Benelux territory; (b) a design identical with the deposited design or differing only in minor respects had been the subject of an earlier deposit followed by the publication provided for in Article 9.3 of this Law or in Article 6(3) of the Hague Agreement.

2.2.1.2 Specialty

Article 1 UBLDM protected as a design the new appearance of a *product having a utility function*. This was the statutory basis of the doctrine of specialty: the object of protection was only the registered design as applied to a specific useful product. Consequently, the scope of protection of the design was restricted to a certain category of goods or branch of industry. The Explanatory Memorandum of the UBLDM stated that independent registrations would have to be made with regard to the same Scottish tartan applied to wallpaper, ties or blankets.[22]

In 1995 the Dutch Supreme Court embraced a draconian interpretation of the doctrine of specialty in the case of *Van der Lans* v. *Floral*.[23] A third party, which was not involved in the procedure, sold Ferrari pedal cars on the market. Van der Lans bought such pedal cars, removed the pedal mechanism and mounted the car model on the support of a hairdresser's

[20] Of the same opinion, Gielen, *Kort begrip van het intellectuele eigendomsrecht*, 11th edn (Deventer: Kluwer, 2014), no. 191, p. 155; Hendrik Vanhees, *Het Beneluxmodel* (Brussels: Larcier, 2006), no. 442.

[21] Article 1: 'The new appearance of a product having a utility function may be protected as a design.'

[22] Verkade signalled several potential problems flowing from this system: see D. W. F. Verkade, *Bescherming van het uiterlijk van produkten. Commentaar op de Benelux-Modellenwet en andere relevante regelingen* (Deventer: Kluwer, 1985), pp. 22–3 and 41.

[23] Supreme Court of the Netherlands, 10 March 1995, *Van der Lans* v. *Floral*, NJ 1995, 670; BIE 1998, no. 63, p. 312; GRUR Int 1997, 756, note Ruijsenaars at 687.

chair, thus creating a product that turned small boys, not always an easy public for hairdressers, into happy, amenable customers; both they and the hairdresser could now have the illusion to race. Van der Lans registered his pedal car-hairdresser's chair as a model. Floral started to produce the same product, albeit mounted on a different support. Accused by Van der Lans of infringement on his model, the President of the District Court as well as the Court of Appeal turned down that action with the argument that it lacked novelty, as the Ferrari pedal car which characterised it most had been on the market before the hairdresser's chair had been registered by Van der Lans. However, the Hoge Raad found that Van der Lans' product had a new function and that, therefore, the pedal car-chair did constitute a new model.

When the Design Directive, and after the implementation thereof the statute itself, made no specific reference any more to *a product having a utility function*, this caused uncertainty in the Benelux,[24] and especially in the Netherlands.[25] Eventually, the conclusion crystallised that the 'informed user' and the 'relevant sector' in the Directive formed references which could restrict a universal protection resulting from the Directive.[26]

2.2.1.3 Article 3.1 Benelux Convention on Intellectual Property: Novelty and Individual Character

As from 2003, Article 1 UBLDM (Article 3.1 BenCIP as from 2006), consisting of a mixture of Articles 1 and 3(2) of the Directive, defined the object of design rights as follows:

1. A design shall be protected to the extent that it is new and has individual character.
2. The appearance of the whole or a part of a product shall be regarded as a design.

[24] H. M. H. Speyart, 'Het gewijzigde voorstel van de Europese Commissie voor de modellen-richtlijn', BIE 1996, 222–31, at 230; Heijo Ruijsenaars, 'Die Zukunft des Designschutzes in Europa aus der Sicht des französischen und des Benelux-Rechts', GRUR Int 1998, 378–85, at 379; L. A. G. Meijer, 'Moet de BTMW in de steigers?', IER 1998, 1–11, at 2; Freya van Schaik, 'De toekomstige Benelux-regeling inzake de modelrechtelijke bescherming van reserveonderdelen. Is de tijd wel rijp om de huidige regeling overboord te zetten?', IER 2002, 282–90, at 285; Charles-Henry Massa and Alain Strowel, 'Community Design: Cinderella Revamped' [2003] EIPR 68–78.

[25] C. J. J. C. van Nispen, J. L. R. A. Huydecoper, Y. Cohen Jehoram, *Industriële Eigendom. Deel 3: Vormen, namen en reclame* (Deventer: Wolters Kluwer, 2012), nos. 1.4.1–1.4.1.1 (pp. 45–7); nos. 1.4.2.4.11–1.4.2.4.12 (pp. 81–4).

[26] Gregor Vos, 'De weggeharmoniseerde gebruiksfunctie en de ingewijden in de betrokken sector', *BMM Bulletin* 2004, 191–3, at 193; A. A. Quaedvlieg, 'Eigen karakter, technische functie en specialiteit in het nieuwe modellenrecht', BIE 2004, 529–34, at 530–1; Gielen, note with President of the District Court, The Hague, 12 April 2005, *Ferrari* v. *Asian Gear*, IER 2005, no. 48 at 216–18; A. A. Quaedvlieg, 'De redelijk speciale universaliteit van de modellenrichtlijn. Geïnformeerde gebruiker kijkt verder dan gebruiksfunctie', BIE 2006, 406–11.

3. The appearance of a product shall be imparted, in particular, through the features of the lines, contours, colours, shape, texture and/or materials of the product itself and/or its ornamentation.
4. A product shall mean any industrial or handicraft item, including inter alia parts intended to be assembled into a complex product, packaging, get-up, graphic symbols and typographic typefaces. Computer programs shall not be regarded as a product.

2.2.2 Copyright: Originality

Works of applied art, designs and models are mentioned in Article 10, under 11° (before 1 August 1985[27] under 10°) of the law of 1912. The eligibility for copyright of designs has therefore never been an issue, but the level of originality required for protection stayed uncertain until the end of the twentieth century.

2.2.2.1 1912–1964: Originality is Vague

The Dutch Copyright Act contains no formal requirement of originality. The legislative history of the Act of 1912 is silent as to the required level of originality, with the exception, however, of works of *architecture* – a category of works fairly close to models and designs. The Minister remarked that 'the bill would contain a grave mistake' when the expression 'works of architectural art' would solely apply 'to works of a certain clearly perceptible artistic value', and that this restriction was nowhere contained in the legislative proposal.[28] Still, some level of originality definitely was required. In a judgment of 1926, the District Court of Groningen found that, in order to be eligible for copyright protection, a product of architectural art had to show 'something own, new and original'.[29] In 1929, the District Court of Amsterdam used the criterion of 'an own, original character' in relation to the design of mattress cloth.[30]

[27] Act of 30 May 1985, *Staatsblad* 370, entered into force 1 August 1985 (Royal decree of 11 July 1985, *Staatsblad* 412).

[28] Memorandum of Reply, in L. De Vries (ed.), *Parlementaire geschiedenis van de Auteurswet 1912, loose leaf edition* (Den Haag: SDU), at p. 10.14.

[29] In Dutch: 'iets eigen nieuw origineels moet bevatten'; District Court of Groningen, 19 November 1926, *Smit* v. *Meersma*, NJ 1927, 162–6, at 163. Endorsed by the Advocate-General Van Lier in Supreme Court of the Netherlands (Hoge Raad), 27 May 1929, 'Objects of delftware', NJ 1929, 1315–16.

[30] District Court of Amsterdam, 14 October 1929, *Baekers en Raymakers' Textielfabrieken* v. *Leeuwin*.

The Act of 1912 did, however, speak of 'works of literature and *art*', and this convinced many judges that it was required that a work showed some degree of *artistic* level in order to be eligible for protection. Terms such as 'beauty', 'aesthetic' or 'artistic sense' appear in numerous decisions,[31] but the actual threshold might still be low. The Dutch Supreme Court[32] endorsed a decision of the Court of Appeal of Arnhem[33] that found originality on the basis of two expert statements considering decisively whether 'the designer has meant to evoke, ... an impression of beauty with the observer'. The subjective *intention* of the maker therefore sufficed.[34]

After the war, the courts kept recycling the same variety of formulas.[35]

2.2.2.2 1964–1967: Pressure on Copyright as Compensation for the Lack of Industrial Property Protection

In 1964, a bill was proposed in the Netherlands to make the country adhere, with great delay, to the Brussels text of 1948 of the Berne Convention.[36] As to industrial design, it was proposed to replace the wording of 'works of art applied to industry' in the existing Dutch Act in line with the new wording of 'works of applied art' in the Berne Convention.[37]

The Minister distinguished between 'works of applied art' on the one hand and 'designs and models of industry' on the other.[38] The delimitation between these two categories was a matter left to the national legislator. For designs and models of industry no special legislation was in force as yet in the Netherlands,[39] but the Benelux Bill that had been offered on 10 June 1963 to the Advisory Interparliamentary Benelux Council[40] was to provide for that.[41] The Permanent Commission for

31 Court of Appeal of Amsterdam, 14 March 1935, *De Zwaan* v. *Fabriek en handelbureau 'Nederland'* (bollards), NJ 1936, 37 is one example out of many.

32 Supreme Court of the Netherlands (Hoge Raad), 27 May 1929, 'Objects of delftware', NJ 1929, 1315–16. It concerns, like most lawsuits of that period, a criminal case.

33 Court of Appeal of Arnhem, 30 October 1928, *Weekblad van het Recht*, no. 11921.

34 Approving H. L. de Beaufort, *Auteursrecht* (Zwolle: W. E. J. Tjeenk Willink, 1932), at 78.

35 Th. Limperg, *Bescherming van vormgeving tegen plagiaat. Een handleiding voor de praktijk* (Amsterdam/Brussels: Agon Elsevier, 1971), p. 19.

36 Bill of 5 November 1964, TK (Lower House) 1964–5, 7877, nos. 1 and 2.

37 At p. 1, Article 10.

38 In the Explanatory Memorandum of 10 November 1964 accompanying Bill 7889 for the ratification of the Berne Convention, which was introduced days after Bill 7877 for the revision of the Copyright Act.

39 Notwithstanding the fact that the country had adhered to the Lisbon Agreement of 31 October 1958, Article 5 quinquies, which obliged the signatory countries to protect designs and models of industry.

40 'Raadgevende Interparlementaire Beneluxraad'.

41 Explanatory Memorandum with the Bill of ratification of the revised Berne Convention concluded on 26 June 1948 in Brussels, TK (Lower House) 1964–5, 7889 (R 446), no. 3, p. 2; Provisional Report of 17 November 1965, TK (Lower House) 1964–5, 7877, 7889 (R 446), no. 5, p. 2.

Justice of parliament, however, protested that (all) 'productions of industrial design' were to be eligible for protection under the *Copyright* Act. The Minister objected that the proposed solution would be at variance with the impending Benelux unification.[42]

2.2.3 *Copyright in the UBLDM: A 'Clearly Artistic Character'*

The text of the UBLDM, drafted in 1963[43] and signed by the three Benelux countries on 25 October 1966,[44] entailed an important restriction of the number of designs eligible for the – longer – copyright protection. Chapter II of the UBLDM bore the title 'Designs or models with a clearly artistic character' and the Explanatory Memorandum[45] made clear that the UBLDM would reserve copyright protection for the situation where an 'artistic work' of an 'artist' had been incorporated into the model.

Indeed, the spirit that had inspired the UBLDM seems to have been one of distrust with regard to the long duration of copyright and the absence of registration.[46] Both were considered to hamper economic progress. The UBLDM limited the term of protection to a maximum of merely fifteen years.

The drafting of the UBLDM may furthermore have been inspired by the restrictive approach of the merger doctrine developed shortly before by the US Supreme Court in *Mazer* v. *Stein*.[47] It strikes that the Explanatory Memorandum with Article 21 consistently refers to the case that an *independent*, pre-existing[48] work of art is incorporated into the model;[49] *Mazer* v. *Stein* dealt precisely with such a case.

2.2.3.1 1972: The Dutch Openly Ignore the Artistic Character Required by the UBLDM

In 1972, parliament accepted an amendment[50] providing that on the same day that the UBLDM would enter into force, the wording of 'works of applied art' in the Dutch Copyright Act would be completed with the

[42] Additional Memorandum of Reply of 24 February 1971, TK (Lower House) 1970–1, 7877, 7889 (R 446), no. 11, pp. 2–3.
[43] *Publicatieblad van de Benelux Economische Unie* 1963–3.
[44] *Tractatenblad* 1966, 292 and 1974, 66.
[45] Published in *Tractatenblad* 1966, 292 at 35 ff.
[46] Th. Limperg, *Bescherming van vormgeving tegen plagiaat*, p. 212.
[47] *Mazer* v. *Stein*, 347 US 201, 203 (1954).
[48] Cf. para. 9 of the Explanatory Memorandum with Article 21: 'It may happen that, without the permission of the designer, a work of art is incorporated in a useful article by a third, who subsequently registered it.'
[49] A detail often overlooked: A. A. Quaedvlieg, *Auteursrecht op techniek* (Zwolle: W. E. J. Tjeenk Willink, 1987), pp. 15–17.
[50] Amendment no. 22 of 9 May 1972.

phrase: 'and designs and models of industry'.[51] Thus, Dutch national copyright legislation would openly contradict the Benelux Treaty as from the day it entered into force on 1 January 1975.[52] Indeed, after 1975, Dutch jurisprudence[53] showed 'no trace that higher requirements were applied with regard to the copyright protection of models'.[54] However, it was understood that the protection would only extend to such designs and models as complied with the general Dutch originality criterion.[55]

2.2.3.2 1987: *Screenoprints*

In 1987, the problem was finally solved when the Benelux Court of Justice confirmed, in *Screenoprints*, that in order to be eligible for copyright protection under Article 21 UBLDM, it was required 'that a design or a model could be considered as a work – that is to say, as a production with an own, original character, which bears the personal stamp of the maker – in the domain of the (applied) art'.[56] The 'normal', low originality criterion therefore also applied to designs and models. The Benelux Court considered that the requirement of a 'clearly' artistic character had to be explained against the background of the former Belgian system, which had been one of full cumulative protection of copyright law and design law.[57] The requirement only meant that where in doubt whether a design or model actually was a work in the sense of the copyright law, protection would have to be withheld. The rule of the UBLDM also applied to models and designs that had not been registered.[58]

It still is questionable whether, from a historical viewpoint, the interpretation given by the Benelux Court was right;[59] but in 1987, the rejection

[51] Article Ia of the Act of 27 October 1972, *Staatsblad* 579.

[52] According to the system provided for in Article 13 of the Uniform Benelux Treaty, reading: 'This Convention shall enter into force on the first day of the month following the deposit of the third instrument of ratification. The Uniform Law shall enter into force one year after the entry into force of this Convention.'

[53] Court of appeal Den Bosch, 24 September 1980 (and partial decision of 6 February 1980), *Olly* v. *Optima*, AMR 1984, 34; BIE 1982, 313, was the only one to explicitly address the question. It held that there was no reason to conclude that the UBLDM was meant to put aside the system of the Copyright Act.

[54] Cf. H. Cohen Jehoram in his note with BenCJ Screenoprints, *Ars Aequi* 1987, at 724.

[55] In the decision of the Supreme Court of the Netherlands of 29 November 1985, *Screenoprints* v. *Citroën* ('Car shades'), NJ 1985, 880; BIE 1986, no. 15 at 55, this was regarded as 'generally acknowledged': cf. no. 3(4).

[56] Paragraph 23, in Benelux Court of Justice, 22 May 1987, *Screenoprints* v. *Citroën* ('Car shades'), NJ 1987, 881, note L. Wichers Hoeth; BIE 1987, no. 49 at 196, note Steinhauser; *Ars Aequi* 1987, 717–25, note H. Cohen Jehoram; AMI 1987, 78–83, note J. H. Spoor.

[57] BenCJ Screenoprints, nos. 15–18. [58] BenCJ Screenoprints, no. 31.

[59] Cf. in their respective notes with BenCJ Screenoprints H. Cohen Jehoram, *Ars Aequi* 1987, at p. 723; J. H. Spoor, 'The Impact of Copyright on Benelux Design Protection Law', in Jan J. C. Kabel and Gerard J. H. M. Mom (eds.), *Intellectual Property and*

of a criterion of artistic value had become even more massive than in 1972,[60] whereas it had become clear that the UBLDM in practice often failed to meet its purpose.[61] Without copyright protection, many designers in the Netherlands – and the Benelux – would have been in serious trouble. As it was practically impossible to change the Benelux Treaty, judicial interpretation was the only way left open to correct the rule, and this was done in a fairly elegant way by the Benelux Court.

In 1989, Spoor stated in his inaugural lecture that the copyright threshold for designs and models continued to drop.[62] Case law yielded examples of thresholds so low that they tended towards a protection of *all* designs and models.[63]

2.2.4 *Recent Developments in Copyright*

2.2.4.1 ***Van Dale* v. *Romme* (1991) and *Heirs of Endstra* v. *Nieuw Amsterdam* (2008)**

In the *Van Dale* v. *Romme* case of 1991,[64] the Dutch Supreme Court copied the Benelux *Screenoprints* formula to make it the general criterion of Dutch copyright law: 'In order to be considered as a work of literature, science or art it is required that a product has an own, original character and bears the personal stamp of the maker.'[65]

In 2008 the Supreme Court elucidated, in *Endstra*,[66] that the requirement that the work must bear the personal stamp of the maker meant 'that there

Information Law. Essays in Honour of Herman Cohen Jehoram (The Hague/London/Boston: Kluwer Law International, 1998), pp. 59–68, at 63; idem, in AMI 1987, at 82.

[60] Cf. the long list of authors quoted by Verkade, *Bescherming van het uiterlijk van produkten* (Deventer: Kluwer, 1986), pp. 148–9.

[61] Steinhauser, in his note with BenCJ Screenoprints, BIE 1987, at 201.

[62] J. H. Spoor, *De gestage groei van merk, werk en uitvinding* (Zwolle: W. E. J. Tjeenk Willink, 1989), pp. 22–3.

[63] Court of Appeal of Arnhem, 16 March 1999, *Vredestein* v. *Ring 65* ('Z-profile of a bicycle tyre'), IER 1999, no. 34 at 182; also see the note of Spoor in NJ 2002, 55; Court of Appeal of The Hague, 3 February 2000, *Slagboom Electric* v. *Koz Products* ('cable clamps'), AMI 2001, no. 1 at 48–50, note Quaedvlieg; President of the District Court of The Hague, 12 December 1996, *Bodegraven* v. *GEBU* ('element for isolation material'), AMI 1997, at 128–30, note D. W. F. Verkade, IER 1997, no. 20 at 75–7; President of the District Court of The Hague, 4 June 1993, *Ozonex* v. *Exozon* ('ozon filters'), BIE 1995, no. 92 at 356–7; President of the District Court, Utrecht, 29 November 1994, *Boels* v. *Quadri* ('key rings'), IER 1995, no. 11 at 59–61.

[64] Supreme Court of the Netherlands, 4 January 1991, *Van Dale* v. *Romme*, NJ 1991, 608, note D. W. F. Verkade; AMI 1991, 177, note Spoor; IER 1991, no. 38, pp. 96–9, note F. W. Grosheide; *Ars Aequi* 1992, 31, note H. Cohen Jehoram; *Computerrecht* 1991, 68, note P. B. Hugenholtz; GRUR Int 1994, 259.

[65] Often abbreviated in Holland as 'EOKPS', for 'Eigen en Oorspronkelijk Karakter en Persoonlijk Stempel'.

[66] Supreme Court of the Netherlands, 30 May 2008, *Endstra* v. *Uitgeverij Nieuw Amsterdam* ('Endstra papers'), IIC 2013, 103; GRUR Int 2008, 955–960, Anm. F.

must be a form which is the result of creative human labour and therefore of creative choices, and therefore is a production of the human mind. Outside this falls in any case[67] a form which is so trivial or banal, that no creative labour of whatever kind can be shown behind this.'[68] Consequently, one sole element of creativity can establish originality. That is no theoretical possibility: in the *Tripp Trapp* case reported below, the originality was essentially derived from *one* element which was held creative: the slanting ***L***-shape of the side supports. However, a threshold of originality only excluding products which contain no creative labour of whatever kind seems too low.[69]

2.2.4.2 When Creativity is Subordinate to Random Practical or Functional Choices

Should functional shapes be encompassed by the low originality criterion even if no discernible creative effort has been devoted to their design? This can be illustrated at the hand of the water treatment machine, which was denied protection by the District Court of Amsterdam in 2006.[70]

Such models consist of a number of functional elements – a tank, meters, handles, tubes, etc. – that must be assembled. There often is a broad variety of ways to do this. Their appearance consequently may show an own character as a result from *arbitrary* choices. Under present Dutch law, the position of such artefacts is unclear. It would be difficult to sustain that 'no creative labour of whatever kind can be shown behind it' in whatever of its elements. Still, some judges maintain that copyright simply is not meant for such artefacts. One reason that might justify that position is that it would be wrong to sacrifice serious interests in the free (functional) domain for virtually absent interests in creative expression.

Henning-Bodewig; NJ 2008, 556, note Dommering; AMI 2008, no. 12 at 136–42, note M. R. F. Senftleben; IER 2008, no. 58 at 227–31, note J. M. B. Seignette; *Ars Aequi* 2008, 819–22, note P. B. Hugenholtz.

67 In my view, the Hoge Raad has probably meant to maintain the criteria already used in *Van Dale* v. *Romme*, adding no more than that decisions of the judges of the facts will only be *quashed* if they cross the 'absolute' line by granting protection to productions without any creative element. The rest belongs to the facts.

68 Cf. *Endstra*, para. 4.5.1:

'4.5.1 . . . The requirement that the work must bear the personal imprint of the maker means that there must be a form which is the result of creative human labour and therefore of creative choices, and therefore is a production of the human mind. Outside this falls in any case a form which is so trivial or banal, that no creative labour of whatever kind can be shown behind this.'

69 A. A. Quaedvlieg, 'The Tripod of Originality and the Concept of Work in Dutch and European Copyright', GRUR Int 2014, 1105–12.

70 District Court of Amsterdam, 9 February 2005, *Holland Marine Services Amsterdam* v. *DVZ Services*, BIE 2006, no. 17, at 100.

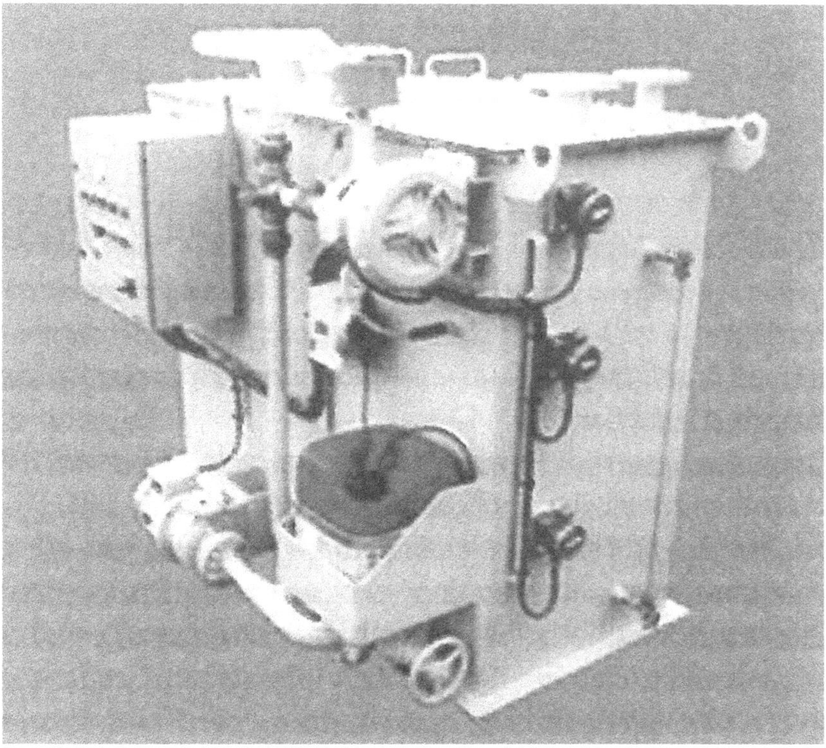

Figure 2.1 Water treatment machine by Holland Marine Services Amsterdam
Source: Bijblad bij de Industriële Eigendom, 2006, p. 101

2.2.4.3 Compliance with the European Originality Requirement

The conviction is widely shared in the Netherlands that present Dutch law complies with the harmonised concept of originality developed in the jurisprudence of the Court of Justice of the European Union (further: CJEU).[71] This it is not in every respect certain. First, whereas in the Netherlands protection must only be refused in case 'no creative

[71] As already explained above, we do not entirely share this optimism. The extremely low Dutch originality requirement seems more lenient than the European one, and the technical exclusion in Dutch law might be less strict than the European one. Apart from that, however, conditions for copyright protection of designs and models probably are fairly close.

labour of whatever kind can be shown', the European approach seems to require that the design *as a whole* reflects the author's personality, which constitutes a less indulgent threshold. Further differences will be discussed in the paragraph concerning the technical exclusion.

Another thing is that the Supreme Court held in the *Fire stoves* decision of 2013[72] that the 'harmonisation by stealth'[73] of the originality criterion also extended to *designs*. Seeking support in the CJEU *Flos* judgment of 2011,[74] it held that the freedom as to the standard of originality that the Design Directive and Regulation had left to the Member States had been limited by the case law developed by the Court of Justice as from 2009.

Article 17 of the Design Directive provides that *registered* designs shall also be eligible for protection under the law of copyright, but that the *extent* to which, and the *conditions* under which, copyright protection is conferred, including the level of originality required, shall be determined by each Member State.[75] The Court of Justice decided in *Flos* that this obligation to create cumulative protection was *limited* to registered designs (nr 32).[76] However, it added that it was 'conceivable that copyright protection for works which may be unregistered designs could arise under other directives concerning copyright, in particular Directive 2001/29, if the conditions for that directive's application are met' (nr 34).

However, as several commentators observed, granting copyright protection for unregistered designs under Directive 2001/29 would create

[72] Supreme Court of the Netherlands, 25 October 2013, *S&S Import en Export* v. *Esschert Design* ('Fire stoves'), IER 2014, no. 6, pp. 48–55, note P. G. F. A. Geerts; AMI 2014, no. 6, pp. 65–7; ECLI:NL:HR:2013:1036. In the same sense, Supreme Court of the Netherlands, 22 February 2013, *Stokke* v. *H3*; LJN BY1529; AMI 2013, 158, note K. J. Koelman; also see M. van Eechoud, *Along the Road to Uniformity – Diverse Readings of the Court of Justice Judgments on Copyright Work*, 2012 *JIPITEC*, 60–80, at 69, no. 70.

[73] Term introduced by Lionel Bently, *inter alia* at 'InfoSoc@Ten', CRIDS – IViR conference 2012 in Brussels.

[74] Case C-168/09, *Flos* v. *Semeraro*, ECR 2011 I-00181.

[75] Article 17 of Directive 98/71, entitled 'Relationship to copyright': 'A design protected by a design right registered in or in respect of a Member State in accordance with this Directive shall also be eligible for protection under the law of copyright of that State as from the date on which the design was created or fixed in any form. The extent to which, and the conditions under which, such a protection is conferred, including the level of originality required, shall be determined by each Member State.'

[76] CJEU *Flos*, nr 32: 'As regards the first case (that of designs which have never been registered as such), Article 17 of Directive 98/71 provides that only a design protected by a design right registered in or in respect of a Member State in accordance with that directive may be eligible, by virtue of the directive, for protection under the law of copyright of that State.'

the massive contradiction of non-harmonised copyright applying to harmonised registered designs, and harmonised copyright applying to non-harmonised unregistered designs. Moreover, as Bently has very convincingly demonstrated,[77] such an interpretation would be at odds with Article 9 of the Copyright Directive itself, which provides that the Directive is without prejudice to design rights.

The *Flos* decision should therefore be read with caution. The Court said no more than that it is 'conceivable' that copyright for unregistered designs could arise. Visser[78] and Klos[79] rightly argued that the Supreme Court should have put questions to the European Court of Justice.[80]

2.3 Exclusions from the Protected Domain

Technical subject-matter, style and trend, ideas and concepts cannot be the object of protection of copyright or design law. These exclusions are of great importance for contemporary design, both because of its often *functional* nature, as for the fact that many an 'iconic' design merges functional and aesthetic features within one binding *concept*. Contemporary Dutch case law deeply inquires into the accurate determination of the scope of these exclusions.

2.3.1 The Exclusion of Technical and Functional Forms

2.3.1.1 The Technical Exclusion in the UBLDM

What is 'necessary for the achievement of a technical effect'?

Article 2(1) UBLDM (old) read: 'From the protection of this Act is excluded that what is necessary for the achievement of a technical effect.'

For years, a debate raged on how far this technical exclusion reached. The main opposition was between those who followed the theory of *multiplicity of forms*, or, as we prefer to call it, a narrow, 'effect-oriented' exclusion of

77 Lionel Bently, 'The Return of Industrial Copyright?' [2012] EIPR, 654–72, at 661–2.

78 D. J. G. Visser, 'Hoge Raad had in de Tripp-Trapp zaken prejudiciële vragen moeten stellen aan over het auteursrecht', B9 12245; IEF 12542; NJB 2013, 979–88.

79 Sven Klos, 'Het toepassen van de kunst & de kunst van het toepassen', in A. M. E. Verschuur, P. G. F. A. Geerts, R. C. K. van Oerle (eds.), *gIElen, een bekend begrip.* Liber amicorum prof. Ch. Gielen (Deventer: Wolters Kluwer, 2015), pp. 183–205.

80 Advocate-General Hammerstein, however, argued, in another case, that the Supreme Court should as far as it could maintain that there was no difference between the two criteria, so that the Dutch jurisprudence about the concept of work could keep its meaning, at the same time respecting as much as possible the formal place of the CJEU in the European legal order: Conclusion with Supreme Court of the Netherlands, 19 September 2014, *Erno Rubik* v. *Beckx* ('Rubik cube'), NJ 2015, 179, endorsed by D. W. F. Verkade in his note (no. 8).

functional aspects,[81] and others who preferred a broader, 'aspect-oriented' exclusion.[82]

An *effect*-oriented exclusion[83] solely excludes shapes *indispensable* in order to obtain the technical result. As soon as, however, reasonable alternatives to attain that result are available, the shape is not 'indispensable' and can be protected, despite its technical nature. Even for purely functional shapes, protection could in principle be conceivable, on the condition that technical alternatives exist capable of achieving the same result. As alternative solutions are almost always available, the technical exclusion will only rarely apply.

The effect-oriented exclusion therefore only strives at avoiding genuine product monopolies. That may make the outcome of the test less predictable: whether a particular shape represents or not an indispensable solution may depend on individual qualities of the customer, the circumstances under which the product is used and the aim it is used for.[84]

The 'aspect-oriented exclusion'[85] by contrast excludes from protection *every* technically determined feature of a design, whether or not alternatives are available.[86] It uses the systemic argument of the reflex of patent law: the protection of technically determined features should be reserved for patent law alone. No back-door protection should be granted via design law.

Both exclusions only regard the purely technical aspects of the shape. To the extent that the design also shows arbitrary features, it can of course always be eligible for design protection.

The classic example to show the difference between the aspect- and the effect-oriented approach is the spiral-shaped part of a corkscrew. Of course, this spiral element is (almost) purely technically determined. However, a number of reasonably available technical alternatives exist, such as the *tire bouchon bilame* with two thin metal blades instead of a

81 In Dutch: 'resultaatgerichte leer'.

82 More elaborately: A. Quaedvlieg, 'Overlap/relationships between Copyright and Other Intellectual Property Rights', in Estelle Derclaye (ed.), *Research Handbook on the Future of EU Copyright* (Cheltenham: Edward Elgar, 2009), pp. 480–516.

83 Supported *inter alia* by Braun and Evrard, *Droit des dessins et modèles au Benelux* (Brussels: Larcier, 1975), pp. 49–60; H. Cohen Jehoram, *R. M. Themis*, 1976, 187.

84 As can also be illustrated in the example of the corkscrews given below: although on average the spiral corkscrew and the *tire bouchon bilame* could be regarded as more or less equivalent solutions, the latter has unsurpassed qualities for removing old and crumbling natural corks, whereas it is unfit to remove certain types of modern synthetic corks.

85 In Dutch: 'apparaatgerichte leer'.

86 A. A. Quaedvlieg, *Auteursrecht op techniek* (Zwolle: Tjeenk Willink, 1987), pp. 31ff, 40–4.

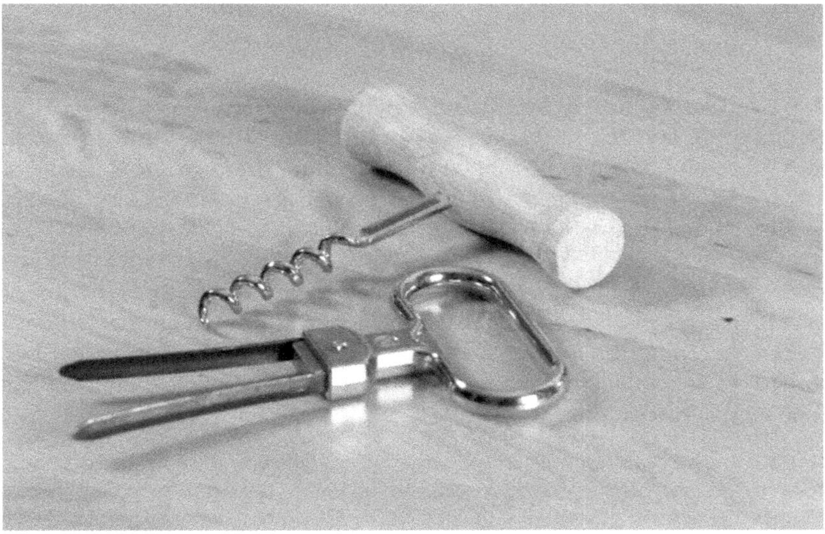

Figure 2.2 Corkscrew with two thin metal blades instead of a spiral and cork screw based on a vacuum technique

In the aspect-oriented approach both the spiral and the metal blades are excluded from protection for being of a technical nature.

In the effect-oriented approach only one of them is excluded. The one which has last become available is not indispensable any more to reach the solution because there exists a reasonable alternative.

spiral, or cork screws based on a vacuum technique. In the effect-oriented exclusion, the spiral shape – supposed it were developed after the alternative solutions – would be eligible for protection. Under the aspect-oriented exclusion, however, the alternatives play no role as the technical nature of the spiral shape as such suffices to apply the technical exclusion.[87]

The *Screenoprints* decision[88] did not resolve the ambiguity of the law, and although Article 7(1) of the Design Directive appears

[87] The literature distinguished not always clearly between either the effect- or the aspect-oriented doctrine: A. A. Quaedvlieg, *Auteursrecht op techniek*, pp. 33–8.

[88] Benelux Court of Justice, 22 May 1987, *Screenoprints* v. *Citroën* ('Car shades'), discussed by H. Cohen Jehoram in 'Cumulation of Design Protection: A System for the EC' [1989] EIPR 83; and 'Cumulation of Protection in the EC Design Proposals' [1994] EIPR 514. NJ 1987, 881, note L. Wichers Hoeth; BIE 1987, no. 49, p. 196, note Steinhauser; *Ars Aequi* 1987, 717–25, note H. Cohen Jehoram; AMI 1987, 78–83, note J. H. Spoor.

to favour the aspect-oriented exclusion,[89] many in the Benelux still hesitate.[90]

2.3.1.2 The Technical Exclusion in Copyright Law

In copyright law, the problems in essence are no different than in design law. Here also, the main problem is the conflict between the doctrine of *multiplicity of forms* on the one hand and a broad, comprehensive exclusion of all technical shapes on the other hand.

In 2013, the design of Stokke's *Tripp Trapp* high chair unleashed in a firework of no less than three decisions in cassation within three months.[91] All three were preceded by an identical 'charter', in which the standard rules concerning the object and scope of copyright protection were laid down. As to the exclusion of technical subject-matter, it contained the following consideration:

> (c) This concept of work finds its limitation where the own, original character only concerns that which is indispensable in order to obtain a technical result. Elements that merely serve a technical effect or are too much the result of a choice limited by technical constraints are excluded from protection ... It must be remarked that this exclusion of technical protection does not extend to all elements having a technical function: thereby, industrial design would wrongly be placed beyond the reach of copyright.

The criterion formulated here is complicated. A first phrase only excludes shapes that are *indispensable* in order to obtain a technical result; the next one however extends the exclusion to *all* 'elements that merely serve a technical effect or are too much the result of a choice limited by technical constraints'.

In practice, this seems to lead to the following system. Shapes that are *indispensable* in order to obtain a technical result will be excluded at all times. Elements that are not indispensable for the result – other shapes or means to the same result are available – but still merely serve a technical effect, or that are too much the result of a choice limited by technical constraints, will also be excluded, *unless* they show particular aesthetic qualities. Perhaps this follows from the word 'merely': a shape with

[89] Article 7(1): 'A design right shall not subsist in features of appearance of a product which are solely dictated by its technical function.'

[90] A. A. Quaedvlieg, 'De techniek, het Hof en de duivel – De technische uitsluiting bij merken, modellen en de slaafse nabootsingsleer', BIE 2013, 231–44.

[91] Supreme Court of the Netherlands, 22 February 2013, *Stokke* v. *H3*; LJN BY1529; AMI 2013, 158, note K. J. Koelman; Supreme Court of the Netherlands, 12 April 2013, *Stokke* v. *Fikszo*, NJ 2013, 502 (note Hugenholtz under 503); AMI 2013, 158, note K. J. Koelman; IER 2013, no. 50, pp. 412–22, note P. G. F. A. Geerts; ECLI:NL:HR:2013: BY 1532; IEF 12554; Supreme Court of the Netherlands, 12 April 2013, *Hauck* v. *Stokke*, NJ 2013, 503, note P. B. Hugenholtz; ECLI:NL:HR:2013:BY 1533.

aesthetic qualities does not *merely* serve a technical effect. This will now be illustrated at the hand of leading case law.

Functionality and 'Vision': Technip

In 1993, the Court of Appeal of The Hague[92] found the *thesaurus*[93] of the Dutch standard dictionary '*Van Dale*' to be the expression of a personal *vision.*[94] This was the start of a doctrine which allowed copyright protection for products of scholarly 'vision'. The doctrine reached its peak in the 2006 decision in *Technip*,[95] where it was held that selections of a scientific or technical nature were eligible for copyright, but seems to have been abandoned since then.

Originality as 'Effect': Tripp Trapp

In the *Tripp Trapp* decision of 2013, originality was based on the 'effect' or 'appearance' of the design, regardless of the technical function performed by the shape.

The Tripp Trapp is a highly ergonomic high chair. It is continuously adjustable to the size of the child as it grows, by means of a system of horizontal slits at the inside of the two side supports of the chair. The author applied an austere, Scandinavian design style, which meant that minimal use was made of the margins left for free creativity.

The Court of Appeal of The Hague[96] considered that originality resulted from two elements: the slanting side supports into which all elements of the high chair had been integrated, resulting in a 'taut, "geometrical" appearance'; and the L-shape resulting from the combination of the slanting side supports and the horizontal bottom legs, which created a 'suspended effect'. Thus, in essence it was the aesthetic *appearance* or *effect* produced by the design that made it eligible for protection, despite the fact that the Court of

[92] Court of Appeal of The Hague, 1 April 1993, *Van Dale* v. *Romme* II, NJ 1994, 58; Informatierecht AMI 1993, 134, note H. Cohen Jehoram; Computerrecht 1993, 165, note Hugenholtz; IER 1993, 82; GRUR Int 1994, 259.

[93] It concerned the sheer selection of the entries only; not other elements such as the descriptions.

[94] The expression of 'personal vision' as a criterion for originality was first used in Supreme Court of the Netherlands, 4 January 1991, *Van Dale* v. *Romme* (footnote 78).

[95] See para. 3.5, Supreme Court of the Netherlands, 24 February 2006, *Technip Benelux* v. *Goossens*, IIC 2007, 615–23, note Quaedvlieg; NJ 2007, 37; BIE 2007, no. 23, p. 144; IER 2006, no. 39, pp. 140–7; AMI 2006, no. 13, p. 153, note Quaedvlieg.

[96] It concerned two cases: Court of Appeal of The Hague, 31 May 2011, *Hauck* v. *Stokke*, IER 2012, no. 3, p. 10, note J. M. B. Seignette; LJN BQ6773; Court of Appeal of The Hague, 30 May 2009, *Stokke* v. *Fikszo*, IER 2009, no. 77, pp. 312–18, note F. W. Grosheide; BIE 2010, no. 25, p. 152, note A. A. Quaedvlieg; AMI 2009, 211–12; LJN BK8037. This last one was an interlocutory decision; the final decision was given on 10 October 2010, AMI 2011, 37.

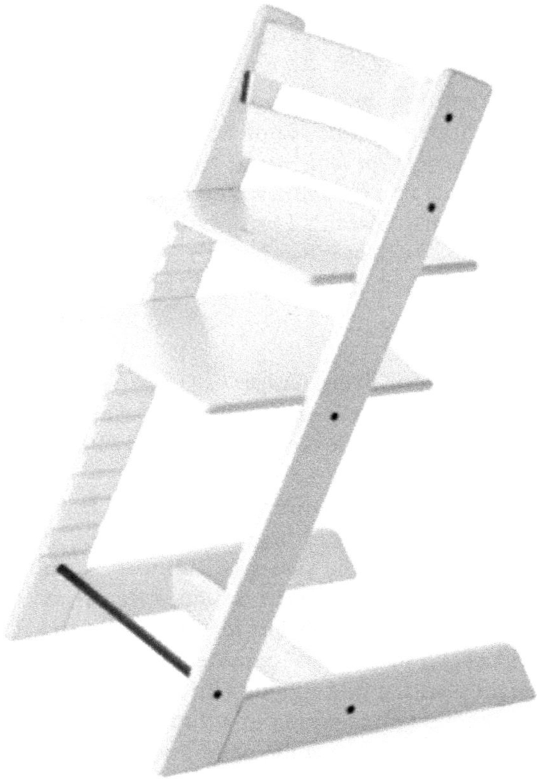

Figure 2.3 Stokke Tripp Trapp chair, created by Peter Opsvik
Source: Stokke/Jamak decisions of the Court of Appeal of Amsterdam published on the internet (rechtspraak.nl), ECLI:NL:GHAMS:2012:BV3404

Appeal acknowledged the functional nature of the slanting side supports and the L-shape:

(c) This judgment is not altered by the fact that the angle between the supports and the horizontal bottom legs of the Tripp Trapp is partly determined by the anatomy of man (the child) and furthermore by practical and functional conditions, such as the length of the horizontal bottom legs and the supports and the stability of the chair.

The Court of Appeal moreover considered that the Tripp Trapp chair was a revolutionary design with a high degree of originality and therefore deserved a 'broad scope of protection'. It inferred from this that even the copying of only one of the two protected features of this creation – the L-shape – could lead to an infringement. Strong copyright protection was thus granted to weak (functional) copyright elements. The Hoge Raad, however, approved of this finding.[97]

The Tripp Trapp chair was found not to be *indispensable* in order to obtain a technical result, as the Court of Appeal had established that the alternative of a high chair with (almost) 90 degree vertical supports was also available on the market.[98]

Court of Appeal of Amsterdam: An Opposite Approach

The Court of Appeal of Amsterdam,[99] however, emphasised, in another Tripp Trapp conflict, that elements that are *too much the result of a choice limited by technical constraints* are excluded from protection. Given that, in principle, other parties had to be free to copy functional aspects, the Court denied the Stokke design a broad scope of protection. Although the result was diametrically opposed to the one reached by the Court of Appeal of The Hague, the Supreme Court[100] endorsed that judgment, *too.*[101] Such conflicting results obviously create great legal uncertainty.

The European Court of Justice

The application of the technical exclusion by the European Court of Justice seems to support the approach of the Amsterdam judges. In *Football Dataco*,[102] it was ruled that technical constraints preclude a *personal touch*, which according to *Eva-Maria Painer*[103] results from

[97] Court of Appeal of The Hague, 30 May 2009, *Stokke* v. *Fikszo*, para. 6.3.2.

[98] It is a rather juicy detail that, in first instance, the District Court had found that another chair with an almost vertical version of the side supports constituted an infringement: District Court of The Hague, 7 February 2007, *Stokke* v. *Fikszo*, AMI 2007, no. 13, pp. 99–103, note Dirk Visser; BIE 2008, no. 62, pp. 449–56; IER 2007, no. 74, p. 265, note F. W. Grosheide. It concerned the so-called Tamara-chair, one of four types that were accused of being an infringement.

[99] Court of Appeal of Amsterdam, 17 January 2012, *Stokke* v. *Jamak* ('Leander chair'), AMI 2012, 81, LJN BV3404; Court of Appeal of Amsterdam, 15 March 2011, *Stokke* v. *H3*, LJN BQ3808.

[100] Supreme Court of the Netherlands, 22 February 2013, *Stokke* v. *H3*, LJN BY1529; AMI 2013, 158, note K. J. Koelman.

[101] Note that there appears to be growing irritation within the Supreme Court about 'complaints that in fact ask for a new factual assessment in cassation'; but this problem definitely concerns a legal question.

[102] Case C-604/10, *Football Dataco* v. *Yahoo!*, ECLI:EU:C:2012:115 (paras. 38 and 39). Also see case C-393/09, *Bezpečnostní softwarová asociace*, ECR 2010 I-13971: components which are differentiated only by their technical function cannot meet the criterion that the work must be the author's own intellectual creation (para. 48). AMI 2011, no. 6, p. 95, note A. van Rooijen; BIE 2011, no. 21, p. 59, note Quaedvlieg.

[103] Case C-145/10, *Eva-Maria Painer* (paras. 88–9), ECR 2011 I-12533; GRUR 2012, 166; IIC 2012, 612; AMI 2012, 66–75, note M. M. M. van Eechoud; IER 2012, no. 16,

free creativity, whose concept is the central element of originality.[104] It would have been wise if the Supreme Court had put questions to the CJEU.[105]

2.3.2 The Exclusion of Style and Trend

2.3.2.1 The Exclusion of style and Trend in out Copyright Law

The basis for the exclusion of style was laid out in a Supreme Court decision of 1946[106] where it was held that 'using the same material, treating that material with the same method yielding a specific artistic effect, following the style do not mean that there is an adaptation of the work'. The style exclusion proved strong enough to produce a reflex effect on the doctrine of slavish imitation: in 2015, the Supreme Court held that no supplementary protection under this doctrine could be available for an artistic painter, the style of whom had been closely and systematically imitated by a colleague.[107]

Although elements of style, trend and fashion are not eligible for protection, the *combination* of unprotected elements may be original. This will be elaborated on when we deal with the scope of protection.

The Style Exclusion as a Warrant against Monopolistic Effects of the Exclusive Right

In Dutch copyright, the exclusion of style is increasingly seen as an important warrant against monopolistic effects of copyright protection. That means that the exclusion may go far beyond the abstract artistic vocabulary of long-established, general styles like Bauhaus, Art Nouveau or Cubism. It may also cover 'young' and more concrete design, especially where this represents a concept which, as a 'potential style',[108] is deemed fit also to be used, in different ways, by other designers.

pp. 143–62, note P. G. F. A. Geerts; Mediaforum 2012, no. 8, pp. 100–7, note Vivien Rörsch.

[104] Joined cases C-403/08 and C-429/08, *Football Association Premier League* and *Murphy*, ECR 2011, I-9083; GRUR 2012, 166; commented on in the Netherlands in NJ 2012, 164, note P. B. Hugenholtz; AMI 2012, no. 1, pp. 13–24, note F. W. Grosheide; IER 2012, no. 26, pp. 227–46, note M. de Cock Buning and H. M. H. Speyart; Computerrecht 2012, 73–5, note Sophie van Loon; *Markt en Mededinging* 2011, 243, note P. J. Kreijger.

[105] D. J. G. Visser, 'De kopstaande cursieve T', IE-Forum 11842.

[106] Supreme Court of the Netherlands, 28 June 1946, *Van Gelder* v. *Van Rijn*, NJ 1946, 712. It concerned a method according to which wood was first burnt and then brushed out with a steel brush, with the effect that the grains came out dark, whereas the wood in between contrasted in a lighter colour.

[107] Supreme Court of the Netherlands, 29 March 2013, *Duijsens* v. *Broeren*, NJ 2013, 504, note P. B. Hugenholtz; AMI 2013, no. 5, pp. 108–17, note J. C. S. Pinckaers; IER 2013, no. 40, pp. 338–50, note F. W. E. Eijsvogels; LJN BY8661.

[108] A. A. Quaedvlieg, '"Style is Free": Designs Beware' [2001] EIPR, 445–53.

This is accompanied by a shift in justification. In case of general styles, the fact alone that they have found expression in thousands of works and that their boundaries are vague suffices to state that they do not constitute a concrete work eligible for copyright. 'Potential styles', however, may very well be retraced to one or a few works of one artist. The justification is not that the style is too general, but rather that exclusive rights in such design achievements might stifle the cultural development.

In the proceedings leading to the Hoge Raad decision in *Decaux* v. *Mediamax*,[109] Decaux had created a line of 'street furniture' and more specifically an innovative billboard, called the 'Mupi Senior'. Its design meant a significant breach with the ugly, morbidly dull billboards which previously existed in the Netherlands, randomly knocked together with the sound aversion to aesthetic distractions typical of the people that conquered its territory on the sea. The billboard was held between a tubular steel U-frame (the 'U' upside down). The upper part of the U-frame showed a characteristic buckle forward which made the horizontal tube on top stand out. In this horizontal tube, lights were hidden which could illuminate the surface of the billboard.

The parties had agreed that both billboards were the expression of a current fashion or style for street furniture. The Court of Appeal considered that elements determined by fashion, style or functional requirements were not eligible for copyright. It therefore adopted the criterion, endorsed by the Supreme Court, whether *keeping account of the fashion, trend or style in the field at issue*, the defendant had maintained enough distance from the plaintiff's design.[110] It found that precisely the *main* features of Decaux's billboard were an expression of the prevailing trend or fashion.[111] Consequently, copying those features did not amount to an infringement of design rights or copyrights. The case illustrates how the concept of 'style' may also touch the main features of a concrete and relatively fresh, individual design.

109 Supreme Court of the Netherlands (Hoge Raad), 29 December 1995, *Decaux* v. *Mediamax* ('Billboards'), NJ 1996, 546, note Verkade; Informatierecht AMI 1996, 199–207, comment Quaedvlieg 195–8; BIE 1997, no. 66, p. 343; LJN ZC1942.

110 Nr 4(6).

111 In the light of the facts as established by the President of the District Court of Utrecht, these main features probably concern the characteristic buckle forward, the tubular frame and the fact that the billboard is attached to the frame with a number of rings. President of the District Court of Utrecht, 15 July 1993, *Decaux* v. *Mediamax*, AMI 1994, 77–8; IER 1993, no. 37, pp. 180–2; ECLI:NL:RBUTR:1993:AK2149.

Figure 2.4 Billboards from Mediamax and from Decaux
Source: AMI 1996, p. 195. The illustration below shows the original from Decaux, the photo on top the billboard from Mediamax

2.3.2.2 The Exclusion of Style and Trend in Design Law

Does the style exclusion also apply in design law? Advocate-General Asser argued in his Opinion with *Decaux* v. *Mediamax*[112] that it did not: as design protection could – on the ground of the then applying rule of specialty – not extend beyond the concrete object which had been registered, there was no need to create safeguards against the appropriation of a style. The Supreme Court dismissed the argument,[113] but in our view the Advocate-General was right. Benelux design law protected against confusion. The style that is chosen for a design can be highly distinctive; consequently, copying that style may be highly confusing. Even now, under the regime of Directive 98/71, it remains true that the application of a certain style to a model may embody an element of a distinct novelty and individuality, which deserves protection. Finally, distinguishing style aspects from individual design elements can be extremely difficult, and that may be especially the case with innovative design concepts, as will be dealt with below.

2.3.3 The Exclusion of Ideas

Ideas as such are not eligible for copyright protection. In the case of abstract ideas without a concrete form, the exclusion is obvious. Less obvious is whether the exclusion of ideas extends to designs embodying a concept (and consequently, an 'idea'). This category of shapes provides a platform for a bitter struggle between conflicting tenets of copyright protection and freedom of competition.

2.3.3.1 The Exclusion of Ideas in Copyright Law

In 1934, the District Court of Rotterdam ruled in a special case. It opposed the well-known Dutch designer Mart Stam and the furniture producer Gispen.[114] Mart Stam was the spiritual father of the first design of a chair with a steel-tubing cantilever frame which created a 'freely suspended effect'. His creation inspired both Mies van der Rohe and Marcel Breuer, who shortly after him created their own cantilevered tubular-steel chairs. The chair thus established a trend.

Gispen imitated this idea on an industrial scale. Mart Stam rightly put all emphasis on the fact that Gispen's cantilevered tubular-steel

[112] Conclusies RvdW no. C21, no. 2.56.
[113] Supreme Court of the Netherlands (Hoge Raad), 29 December 1995, *Decaux* v. *Mediamax* ('Billboards'), para. 3.3.
[114] District Court of Rotterdam, 16 March 1934, NJ 1934, pp. 826–7.

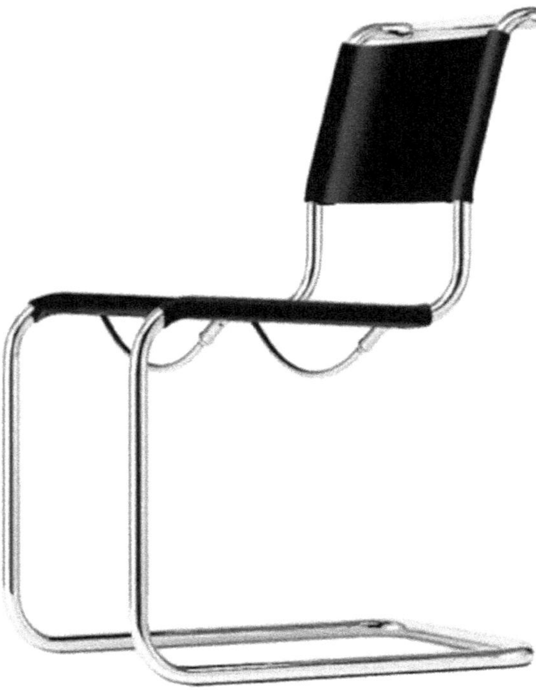

Figure 2.5 Mart Stam chair S33 from 1926
Source: en.shop.thonet.de

chairs copied the 'freely suspended effect' of his own design – that is, the concept which makes the chair highly unique. The District Court, however, was of the opinion that this effect resulted from the application of a technical invention in the field of industry, and therefore did not belong to the domain of copyright – and that is *also* correct. The case illustrates a major dilemma haunting the modern law of the protection of designs. Stam came up with a revolutionary new product concept deserving protection. But the concept also sparked artistic as well as commercial innovations with others. They were imitations that unmistakably bore the mark of Stam's initial design; but should copyright have prevented Mies van der Rohe and Marcel Breuer from making a design inspired by Stam? And should copyright forbid the imitation of the technical aspect of the cantilevered tubular-steel solution, which to a great extent determined the shape?

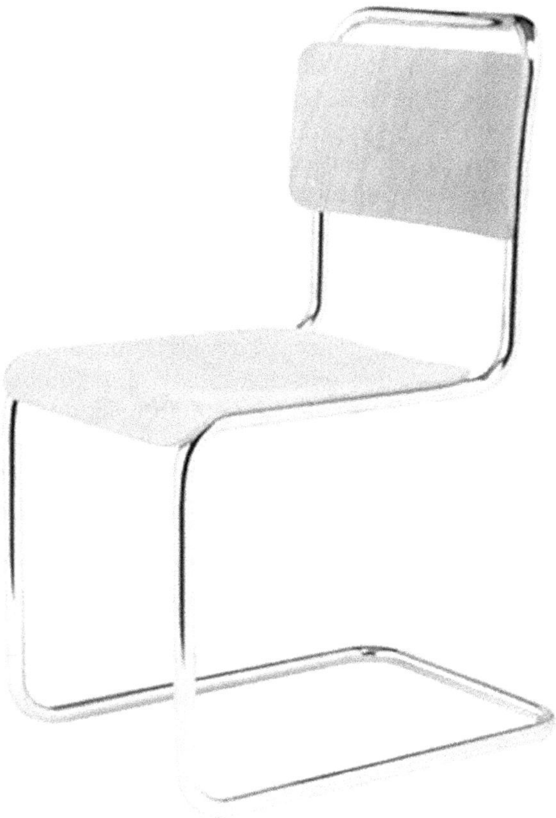

Figure 2.6 Gispen imitation from 1931: chair 101
Source: NederlandsDesign.com

Aesthetic Inventions

The case of the tubular steel chair is not unique. It is an example of a larger category of product concepts. Product concepts of this kind have in common that it is extremely difficult to make a distinction between the style, the functional features and the concrete expression of the design. They all merge into one integral product idea; that is why we will speak here of 'aesthetic inventions'. Illustrative for aesthetic inventions is a remark of the Court of Appeal in *Decaux* v. *Mediamax*.[115] The Court observed that the characteristic buckle forward of the Mupi Senior

[115] *Decaux* v. *Mediamax*, Court of Appeal, as quoted in NJ 1996, 546, para. 4.11.

billboard followed, if not from trend or fashion, from functional requirements, namely an adequate illumination of the billboard. In other words: if not from free aesthetical requirements (trend and fashion), from free functional requirements. The same circumstance can be observed in the *Stokke* case. In the slanting, L-shaped side supports, beauty and function coincide. The tubular chair, the billboard-with-buckle and the L-shaped high chair are all examples of 'aesthetic inventions'.

The Competitive Footprint of 'Aesthetic Inventions'

Aesthetic inventions are characterised by a binding concept. That concept makes the shape highly individual and lends it a particularly strong, expressive profile. The central concept strongly dominates the shape. Whatever variation or adaptation one could think of, it will be stamped with that original concept. The 'iconic' design of the Tripp Trapp chair has inspired countless other products; in all these versions one immediately recognises the basic idea of the Tripp Trapp.

As, due to the natural dominance of its concept, it often is impossible to follow an aesthetic invention without the result keeping a strong reference to the original, the protection of aesthetic inventions may have a large 'competitive footprint': an exclusive right in such designs restricts competition more than usual. That may be even more problematic when, as often is the case, such concepts respond particularly well to a modern sense and taste of living of the consumer, thus creating a considerable lead for them on the market. In that case, competitors are in fact forced to find a new *concept* equally evocative and inventive, and that means that the restriction on competition reaches much further than in a situation where cosmetic changes would suffice to create a design able and allowed to compete.

The Interests of the Author

Despite all this, aesthetic inventions often constitute marvellous design achievements. Denying protection to those designs, or curtailing it, will mean that copyright fails to fulfil its mission to protect designers – and, more in particular, the best among them. This constitutes an enormous dilemma which may be hard to solve within the existing system.

2.3.3.2 The Exclusion of Ideas in Design Law

As design law only protects the concrete design of a concrete useful object, it is clear that the protection cannot extend to 'general' ideas. As to integral design or 'aesthetic inventions', the fact that the term of protection is restricted to a maximum of twenty-five years makes a very considerable difference with the potential restriction on competition formed by the long term of copyright protection. If that might be an argument to plead for design protection as the preferred regime for 'aesthetic inventions', the novelty requirement in design law makes that choice less attractive. Moreover, if a protection of seventy years p.m.a. is long, a term of twenty-five years for top design achievements is too poor.

2.3.4 Conclusion

The present system offers no satisfactory solutions yet to meet the challenge of the 'aesthetic inventions', the integral designs.[116] New solutions will have to be developed for this most valuable category of design achievements.

2.4 Rights and Infringement

2.4.1 Rights

2.4.1.1 The UBLDM

Article 14(1) UBLDM granted the right holder the exclusive right to prevent the manufacture, importation, sale, offering for sale, hire, offering for hire, exposition, delivery or use, or the holding for any of these objects, of the design for industrial or commercial purposes. The scope of the exclusive right was considered so broad that any need for supplementary protection could hardly be imagined.[117] Nevertheless, it is not quite clear whether *depicting* the design is encompassed by the exclusive right. The authoritative handbook of Van Nispen, Huydecoper and Cohen Jehoram is of the opinion that the design right does not cover the depicting of the design in a context in which there is no relation with the putting into circulation or the commercialisation of concrete embodiments of the model.[118]

2.4.1.2 The Copyright Act

Article 1 of the Dutch Copyright Act defines the exploitation right by only two very broad concepts:[119] first, a 'right of copying' ('recht om te

[116] A. A. Quaedvlieg, 'The Tripod of Originality and the Concept of Work in Dutch and European Copyright', GRUR Int 2014, 1105–12, at 1108.
[117] D. W. F. Verkade, *Bescherming van het uiterlijk van produkten. Commentaar op de Benelux-Modellenwet en andere relevante regelingen* (Deventer: Kluwer, 1985), no. 60, pp. 90–1.
[118] C. J. J. C. Van Nispen, J. L. R. A. Huydecoper, T. Cohen Jehoram, *Industriële Eigendom Deel 3. Vormen, namen en reclame* (Deventer: Kluwer, 2012), no. 1.10.3, at p. 158.
[119] The broad concepts of article 1 are further defined – and broadened – in articles 12–14.

verveelvoudigen'), comprising the reproduction right as well as the adaptation right;[120] secondly, a 'right of making public' ('recht om openbaar te maken'), encompassing all the ways to put the work at the disposal of the public, including the right of first publication, the distribution right, the rights of communication to the public and the representation right.[121] Apart from that, the author disposes of his moral rights.

The Dutch system of exploitation rights has proved remarkably flexible and resistant against the strain of the numerous technical developments. It could absorb them all without too much difficulty. The proven quality of the system made the Dutch hesitant to abandon it too quickly by harmonising it according to emerging European copyright law. The Copyright Committee, asked by the government to advise whether the Dutch system should be subjected to a fundamental review, advised in 2001 to wait until a clear European system would have emerged.[122] The Dutch subsequently maintained the existing system until the present moment.[123]

2.4.2 *Infringement: Legal Criteria in the UBLDM and the Copyright Act*

To an important degree, the scope of protection is determined by the definition of what is eligible for protection. This has already been dealt with. What remain to be discussed here are the formal criteria for establishing an infringement.

2.4.2.1 The UBLDM: Difference in Minor Aspects and the Concept of Confusion

Article 14(1) of the Benelux Design Law provided that the right holder could oppose the exploitation of products showing the same outer appearance as the deposited design or model, or only *minor differences*.[124] The Common Governmental Comment explained that products showing 'minor differences' meant products showing so little

120 'Adaptation' ('bewerking') also covering the transformative rights in general such as translation, arrangement and alteration.

121 See the contributions of J. H. Spoor, D. J. G. Visser and M. de Cock Buning in Bernt Hugenholtz, Antoon Quaedvlieg, Dirk Visser, *A Century of Dutch Copyright Law. Auteurswet 1912–2012* (Amsterdam: deLex, 2012), pp. 197ff, 225ff, 261ff.

122 Advice of July 2001, pp. 4–5.

123 Explanatory Memorandum, pp. 12ff.

124 Article 14 UBLDM:

'1. By virtue of his exclusive right to a design, the proprietor may prevent any of the following acts, performed for industrial or commercial purposes: the manufacture, importation, sale, offering for sale, hire, offering for hire, display, delivery or use, or the holding for any of these objects, of a product identical in appearance with the design as deposited or differing only in minor respects.'

difference with the model, 'that the public could easily confuse them with each other'.[125] Therefore, as later confirmed in *Decaux* v. *Mediamax*,[126] the scope of protection was framed on the basis of the concept of 'confusion'.[127]

As a product, in order to be infringing, had to show the same outer appearance as the deposited design or model, it seems that the mere copying of parts of a model would, in general, not have entailed an infringement.

2.4.2.2 The Copyright Act

The Dutch Copyright Act grants a broad right of 'copying' ('*verveelvoudigen*'), encompassing the reproduction right as well as the adaptation right. The adaptation right is laid down in Article 13 of the Copyright Act. According to this provision, 'any partial or full adaptation or imitation in a modified form, which cannot be regarded as a new, original work', will be considered as an infringement. Highly original design is allowed a broad scope of protection.[128]

The Dutch Copyright Act explicitly includes *partial* adaptations. The same obviously applies to reproductions. It likewise is obvious that in order to constitute an infringement, the copied parts must independently comply with the requirement of originality.

[125] The comment refers at this place to the remarks made with regard to the same concept in Article 4, whose provision dealt with the condition of novelty of the design. Also see D. W. F. Verkade, *Bescherming van het uiterlijk van produkten*, nos. 39 and 40, pp. 58–60.

[126] Dutch Supreme Court, 29 December 1995, *Decaux* v. *Mediamax*, para. 3.3; in that case it more specifically concerned the organisations and institutions involved in buying and placing billboards.

[127] Antoine Braun and Jean-J. Evrard, *Droit des dessins et modèles au Benelux* (Brussels: Larcier, 1975), no. 187, pp. 145–7, limited the application of the criterion of confusion to models that clearly distinguished themselves from earlier creations. Other designs were only to be protected against identical or almost identical imitation. The handbook of Van Nieuwenhoven Helbach contains, as from 1983, a clear reference to the concept of confusion mentioned in the Common Governmental Comment: E. A. Van Nieuwenhoven Helbach, *Nederlands handels- en faillissementsrecht. II Industriële eigendom en mededingingsrecht*, 7th edn (Arnhem: Gouda Quint, 1983), nos. 473–4 at p. 219 and no. 404 at pp. 188–9. The handbook of Drucker et al. only repeated, in its 1976 edition, the text of the law; Drucker, Bodenhausen, Wichers and Hoeth, *Kort begrip van het recht betreffende de industriële eigendom*, 5th edn (Zwolle: W. E. J. Tjeenk Willink, 1976), p. 77. As from the 7th edition of *Kort begrip*, however, issued in 1993, with a chapter on designs authored by R. Ebbink, it is acknowledged that the criterion of minor differences was 'an application of the doctrine of confusion' (p. 103).

[128] In the *Stokke* decision, the Supreme Court upheld the decision of the Court of Appeal of The Hague where it was held that a broad scope of protection could be allowed to 'a revolutionary design with a high degree of originality'; this despite strong opposition of Advocate-General Verkade, Supreme Court of the Netherlands, 12 April 2013, *Stokke/Fikszo*, para. 6.3.1: NJ 2013, 503, note P. B. Hugenholtz; AMI 2013, no. 8, pp. 158–63, note K. J. Koelman; ECLI:NL:HR:BY1532.

2.4.3 The Criterion of the 'Overall Impression'

2.4.3.1 Basis of the Assessment in Copyright and Design Law: Aims

In both copyright and design law, the criterion of the overall impression produced by the two products decides whether there is an infringement.[129] First, it aims at preventing the 'atomisation' by splitting up the assessment in lists of similar and/or different elements of the respective designs. Secondly, it extends the scope of protection to adaptations that are not identical to the original. If, despite the differences, these produce the same 'overall impression', they are considered to be an infringement.

As will be elucidated below, the 'overall impression' under design law is not necessarily the same as under copyright law. The uniformity of criterion does therefore not always produce the practical advantage of uniformity as to the result.[130]

2.4.3.2 The Constructive Nature of the Concept of 'Overall Impression'

The 'overall impression' cannot be based on the concrete appearance of the product. Such an assessment would be biased, as this concrete appearance contains many elements which (either under both laws or under one of them) are not eligible for protection, such as elements which are not new, individual or creative, elements which are determined by free style, or by functional and technical requirements, or elements which embody a free concept. Such elements must be disregarded,[131] for the finding of an infringement cannot be based on similarities in the free domain.

The 'overall impression' therefore only concerns those aspects of the design that do matter for protection. The rest of the products must be 'thought away'. The 'overall impression' therefore is a constructive concept, which only partly matches with the concrete appearance of the product.

This constructive nature of the criterion of the 'overall impression' explains why it will not necessarily produce the same result for copyright and design law. In copyright, the overall impression is determined by the original elements; in design law, by those elements which are new and individual. Of course, the overall impressions resulting from these tests may be close or identical, but that is not guaranteed. If, for example, one thinks that elements of style and idea are eligible for design protection but

[129] Dutch Supreme Court, 29 December 1995, *Decaux* v. *Mediamax*, para. 3.3: 'de totaalindrukken van de produkten'.

[130] As did Advocate-General Asser in *Decaux* v. *Mediamax*, paras. 2.20–2.25.

[131] Dutch Supreme Court, 29 December 1995, *Decaux* v. *Mediamax*, para. 3.4.

not for copyright, the overall impression for the assessment under either law could be quite different.

2.4.3.3 Criticisms of the Criterion of 'Overall Impression'

The criterion of the 'overall impression' has been criticised consistently and severely.[132] It is argued that it creates confusion, for it easily invites one to compare the appearance of the concrete products instead of the constructive appearance of the protected substrate. Moreover, if correctly applied, the criterion is complex. The construction of a correct image of the 'overall impression' requires painstaking efforts to sort out exactly what is protected and what is not, and demands counterintuitive conclusions where those features which are the most characteristic for the concrete form must be 'thought away'.

2.4.3.4 The Overall Impression and the 'Combination Rule'

However, it is the 'combination rule' that complicates most the construction of the 'overall impression'. The combination rule means that *combinations* of free elements can be eligible for protection, provided that the way they have been combined is original, or new and individual.[133] If a design consists of an already complicated mixture of protected and unprotected elements, one must first neatly distinguish these, and then assess whether the unprotected elements may still contribute to the overall impression by their combination with protected, or other unprotected, elements. Clearly, however, that should not result in the protection of the unprotected as such, which remains free domain. An infringement will only occur if the original *combination* is copied. The application of this combination rule to design poses problems for specialists, let alone for judges not specialised in intellectual property.[134]

[132] Can be mentioned, in a non-exhaustive enumeration, D. J. G. Visser, note with Dutch Supreme Court, 29 November 2002, *Accordo* v. *Tros* ('Una voce particolare'), AMI 2003, no. 1, p. 21; Ch. Gielen, 'De totaalindruk in het auteursrecht', IER 2004, no. 55, pp. 255–8; Grosheide, 'Totalitair Auteursrecht(?)', in *Album Amicorum Feer Verkade*, BIE 2008, pp. 158–64; Spoor, 'Hoezo, totaalindrukken?', in N. A. N. M. van Eijk and P. B. Hugenholtz (eds.), *Dommering bundel Opstellen over informatierecht* (Amsterdam: Cramwinckel, 2008), pp. 321–32; Lieke Quanjel-Schreurs, 'Harry Potter en de strijd tegen het Lexicon', IER 2009, no. 37, pp. 163–72, at pp. 169ff; Hugenholtz in his note with Dutch Supreme Court, 22 February 2013 (*Stokke* v. *H3*), NJ 2013, 503.

[133] Supreme Court of the Netherlands, 22 February 2013 (*Stokke* v. *H3*), para. 3.4(e), NJ 2013, 503, note P. B. Hugenholtz; AMI 2013, no. 8, pp. 158–63, note K. J. Koelman; ECLI:NL:HR:BY1529.

[134] D. J. G. Visser, *Het ABC van iedere IE inbreuk*, inaugural lecture, Leiden (Den Haag: Boom, 2004), p. 14.

2.4.3.5 Arguments in Favour of the Criterion of the 'Overall Impression'

Heavy as these criticisms may be, they do not justify the conclusion that the criterion of the overall impression must be abandoned. The problems encountered under the overall impression criterion cannot be avoided.[135] The adaptation right will have to cover non-identical imitations: the only way to deal with that is to compare the 'overall impressions' of the two designs. In the frame of that comparison, neither is it possible to escape the distinction of protected and unprotected elements. What the criterion of the overall impression reveals is not some defect inherent in the rule, but the huge complexity of the infringement question.

2.4.3.6 Design Directive 98/71: The Overall Impression Produced on the Informed User

Under the regime of Design Directive 98/71, the scope of the protection includes 'any design which does not produce on the informed user a different overall impression'.[136] Most authors agree that this means that the criterion of confusion has been abandoned.[137]

2.5 Ownership, Transfer and Presumptions of Ownership

2.5.1 Initial Ownership, Transfer and Presumption of Ownership

2.5.1.1 Article 3 UBLDM: The Exclusive Right Is Acquired by Him Who Deposits

According to Article 3(1) UBLDM, the exclusive right to a design was acquired by the first deposit made within Benelux territory and registered with the Benelux Designs Office. This meant that anyone could in

[135] A. A. Quaedvlieg, 'De totaalindruk, kern van het bewerkingsrecht', in A. M. E. Verschuur, P. G. F. A. Geerts, R. C. K. van Oerle (eds.), *gIElen, een bekend begrip. Liber amicorum voor prof. Mr. Ch. Gielen* (Deventer: Wolters Kluwer, 2015), pp. 229–41.

[136] Article 9:

'Scope of protection

1. The scope of the protection conferred by a design right shall include any design which does not produce on the informed user a different overall impression.
2. In assessing the scope of protection, the degree of freedom of the designer in developing his design shall be taken into consideration.'

[137] Gielen (ed.), *Kort begrip van het intellectuele eigendomsrecht*, 11th edn, 2014, no. 208, p. 181. The Belgian author Vanhees is of the opinion that the criterion of confusion was abandoned: Hendrik Vanhees, *Het Beneluxmodel* (Brussels: Larcier, 2006), no. 259, p. 113. The handbook on industrial property of Van Nispen et al. does not once mention the criterion of confusion in relation to models and designs (however, it neither says that it cannot be used any more): Van Nispen, Huydecoper, Cohen Jehoram, *Vormen, namen en reclame*, no. 1.9ff, pp. 144ff.

principle acquire the design right by making the first legal deposit, whether he was the designer or not.

2.5.1.2 Article 5 UBLDM: The Creator May Claim the Benelux Deposit

Article 5(1) UBLDM partly corrected the rule following from Article 3 by allowing the creator of the design – or the person deemed under Article 6 to be the creator – to claim, during the five years following publication of a deposit, the Benelux deposit of that design if the deposit had been effected by a third party without the creator's consent; or at any time invoke the nullity of the deposit.

2.5.1.3 Copyright

According to the Dutch Copyright Act, the initial copyright belongs to the maker, except where provisions of constructive ownership apply. According to Article 2 of the Copyright Act, the assignment of the copyright as well as exclusive licences must be in writing.

2.5.2 'Works Made for Hire'

2.5.2.1 Copyright: Rules of Constructive Ownership

Article 7 Copyright Act

The general regime for the attribution of copyright in employment relationships has as from 1912 been laid down in Article 7 of the Dutch Copyright Act.[138] It provides that where the labour consists in the making of a work, the employer is taken to be the maker. The provision is strongly in favour of employers insofar as it creates a fictitious *initial* ownership: there is no presumption of *transfer* of the copyright, but the employer is considered to be the maker of the work. On the other hand, that presumption is a rebuttable one: the parties may contract otherwise.

As to works made on commission, Article 7 is interpreted *a contrario*: outside a genuine labour agreement, the general rule has always applied that the copyright belongs to the author.[139]

[138] Article 7 Copyright Act reads: 'Where labour which is carried out in the service of another consists in the making of certain literary, scientific or artistic works, the person in whose service the works were created is taken to be the maker, unless parties have agreed otherwise.' (Translation: M. Van Eechoud, in *A Century of Dutch Copyright Law* (Amsterdam: deLex, 2012).)

[139] See Verkade, note with Supreme Court of the Netherlands, 25 October 2013, *S&S* v. *Esschert* ('fire stoves'), NJ 2015, 178, paras. 3–4; Quaedvlieg, 'Aspecten van Intellectuele Eigendom', in C. J. Loonstra and W. A. Zondag (eds.), *SDU Commentaar Arbeidsrecht* 2005/6 (Den Haag: SDU, 2005), pp. 1337–90, at C.5.1, pp. 1357–8; Proceedings of the

Article 8 Copyright Act vests in public institutions, legal persons or companies the copyright in works that these have published as stemming from them without mentioning any natural person as the maker, unless the publication under these circumstances must be deemed to be unlawful.

2.5.2.2 Design Right

Article 6 UBLDM: 'Designs Made for Hire'

Article 6 UBLDM,[140] presently Article 3.8 BenCIP, contained a special regime for designs made in the course of employment relationships or in the execution of commissioning contracts. It created a fictitious initial ownership of the design right not only for employers, but also for commissioners. It has the form of a rebuttable presumption: the parties can contract otherwise, and then the initial ownership of the design right stays with the designer.

As to *employment* relationships, it is required that the design or model was designed 'in the execution of the function' of the employee. As under Dutch national copyright law, the same rule applies (see hereafter); the interface between copyright and design right would not pose great problems here.

As regards designs *made on commission*, the two laws differed. Whereas the copyright in a work made on commission is vested in the author, the UBLDM contained a statutory attribution of the design right to the commissioning party. A rule was therefore needed in order to avoid contradictions in case of cumulative protection by copyright and design right. It was laid down in Article 23 UBLDM, which will be dealt with below.

Article 6.2 added the important condition that the commission had been done 'with the aim of the use in commerce or industry of the product in which the design or model is incorporated'. In *Electrolux*,[141] the BenCJ interpreted this[142] as a commission for a standard model designed with

Lower House of Parliament, 4 July 1912, pp. 3059–63; L. de Vries, *Parlementaire Geschiedenis van de Auteurswet 1912* (Den Haag: SDU), 7.5–7.11, at 7.6.

140 Text of Article 6 UBLDM (old):

Article 6

1. Where a design has been created by a worker or employee in the execution of his function, the employer shall be deemed to be the designer, unless otherwise agreed.
2. Where a design has been made pursuant to a commission, the person commissioning the design shall be deemed to be the designer, unless otherwise agreed, provided that the commission was made with a view to the commercial or industrial use of the product embodying the design.

141 BenCJ, 22 June 2007, *Electrolux* v. *Sofam*, NJ 2007, 500; BIE 2007, no. 129, p. 601; IER 2007, no. 82, pp. 309–10, note Gielen.

142 With a reference to the Explanatory Memorandum (Benelux-Publicatieblad 1966–6, p. 40).

the view on production on an industrial scale in the enterprise of the commissioner. Only in that case the law attributed the rights to the commissioner.[143]

2.5.3 Rules for Cumulation

2.5.3.1 Article 22 UBLDM: Presumptions of Assignment and of Copyright Ownership

Article 22 UBLDM, presently Article 3.28 BenCIP,[144] provides that the authorisation given by the creator of a work protected by copyright to a third party to effect a design deposit entails the assignment of the copyright in that work to the extent of its embodiment in the design (Article 22(1)). The applicant in the case of a design eligible for copyright is presumed also to be the owner of the copyright therein; this presumption does not, however, apply to the true creator or to persons acting under his authority (Article 22(2)). The assignment of the copyright in a design eligible for copyright entailed the assignment of the design right, and vice versa (Article 22(3)).

2.5.3.2 Article 23 UBLDM: Design Regime for Copyright Ownership Extended to Unregistered Designs

Article 23 UBLDM[145] extended the fictitious initial ownership of the design right of Article 6 UBLDM to the *copyright* in the design. In 2007, the Benelux Court[146] decided, despite a differing Opinion of Advocate-General Dubrulle, that Article 23 even applied when the work had never been registered under design law. The Benelux Court considered that if the commissioning party did not, as from before the deposit of the design under the law of models and designs, also possess the quality of right holder of the copyright, he would not, vis-à-vis the real designer, be entitled to deposit the design.

[143] BenCJ, *Electrolux*, nos. 14, 15.

[144] Article 3.28 BenCIP was one of only two provisions on cumulative protection to survive the implementation of the Design Directive in 2003.

[145] Article 23 UBLDM read: 'Where a design having a marked artistic character is created in the conditions referred to in Article 6, the copyright in that design shall belong to the person deemed to be the creator in accordance with that Article.'

Presently in the slightly modified Article 3.29 BenCIP: 'Where a design is created in the circumstances referred to in Article 3.8, the copyright relating to the design shall belong to the party deemed to be the designer, in accordance with the provisions of that Article.'

[146] BenCJ, 22 June 2007, *Electrolux* v. *Sofam* (footnote 141 above).

It is not certain that the court's reasoning was correct. Under Article 3 of the UBLDM, *everyone* – thus including the commissioning party – was free to deposit a design, whether or not he was entitled to it; in case one was not, Article 5 allowed the party with the better right to claim the registration. The commissioning party could therefore deposit and register the right, or revindicate the registration in case someone else would deposit or register it. The fact that the commissioning party's entitlement to the copyright would only arise with the registration could in no way prevent the commissioner from registering the design.

Apart from that, the decision of the BenCJ created a conflict with the system of European design right. According to Article 14(3) Community Design Regulation, as interpreted by the CJEU in its decision in *FEIA* v. *Cul de sac*,[147] the initial registered and unregistered design rights in a commissioning relationship are vested in the creator, not in the commissioning party. For these and other reasons, *Electrolux* has been criticised.[148]

In the *Fire Stoves* decision[149] the Hoge Raad decided that Article 3.29 BenCIP – the successor of Article 23 UBLDM – applied whether or not a model complied with the requirements of novelty and of individual character, in other words regardless of whether cumulative protection can in reality occur.[150]

2.6 Duration, Expiry and Formalities

2.6.1 Comparison of Terms

The term of protection of the UBLDM was fifteen years. Article 12 provided that the registration was for a term of five years as from the date of deposit and that it could be renewed for two successive terms of five years. That was short in comparison to copyright, which protected

[147] Case C-32/08, *FEIA* v. *Cul de sac* [2009] ECR I-05611.

[148] Verkade, note with Supreme Court of the Netherlands, 25 October 2013, *S&S* v. *Esschert* ('fire stoves'), NJ 2015, 178, paras. 3–4; Vanhees, 'Opdrachtgeversauteursrecht: een (Belgische) reactie', AMI 2009, 179–81; Quaedvlieg, 'Het opdrachtgeversmodel als Fremdkörper', BIE 2009, 393–6.

[149] Supreme Court of the Netherlands, 25 October 2013, *S&S Import en Export* v. *Esschert* ('fire stoves'), NJ 2015, 178; IER 2014, no. 6, pp. 48–55, note P. G. F. A. Geerts; AMI 2014, no. 6, pp. 65–7; ECLI:NL:HR:2013:1036.

[150] The decision was sharply criticised by Senftleben: M. R. F. Senftleben, 'Spelen met vuur. Over de nodeloze uitbreiding van fictief makerschap in het *Vuurkorven*-arrest van de hoge Raad en de onvermijdelijke afschaffing van het opdrachtgeversauteursrecht in de toekomst', AMI 2014, 41–6.

until fifty years *post mortem auctoris*, and as from 29 December 1995,[151] until seventy years p.m.a.

In 2003, the maximum duration was extended to twenty-five years, on the basis of Directive 98/71:[152] the registration could now be renewed for four successive periods of five years.[153]

2.6.2 *Articles 21(3) and 24 UBLDM Declaration for the Maintenance of Copyright*

A peculiarity of the UBLDM was that once the registration of a design would lapse, the copyright in that design would lapse with it, unless the right holder would make a 'special declaration'. This system was laid down in Articles 21(3) and 24 UBLDM.

Article 21(3) of the UBLDM read, until it was abolished in 2003:

> Where the deposit of a design having a marked artistic character is declared null and void or the exclusive right resulting from the deposit of such a design has lapsed, the copyright in that design shall lapse at the same time insofar as both rights belong to the same proprietor; such right shall not lapse, however, if the proprietor of the design makes a special declaration in accordance with Article 24 for the maintenance of his copyright.

Article 24 UBLDM read, until 2003:

> Article 24
>
> 1. The declaration under Article 21.3 must be made, in the manner to be prescribed by the Rules and on payment of the fee to be fixed therein, during the year preceding the lapse of the exclusive right to the design. In the case of the annulment of the right, the declaration must be made within the three months following the date on which the court's declaration of nullity takes on force of law.
> 2. The declaration under Article 21.3 shall be recorded and the corresponding entry shall be published.

2.7 Exceptions

The UBLDM contained only very few exceptions. Article 14(3) formulated a rule of exhaustion, geographically limited to products that had been put on the market in the Benelux territory by the right holder or with

[151] Act of 21 December 1995, *Staatsblad* 651, entered into force on 29 December 1995 (cf. Article III of the Act).

[152] Article I, K of the Protocol of 20 June 2002, *Tractatenblad* 2002, 129; entry into force on 1 December 2003, Article VIII as well as *Tractatenblad* 2003, 181.

[153] See the present Article 3.14 BenCIP.

his permission. Article 14(4) excluded the enforcement of the design right against products which had been put on the market in the Benelux territory before the deposit of the design, and Article 14(5) formulated the rule described above, that excluded models from after 1 January 1975 from the protection of the doctrine of slavish imitation.

Article 17 provided rules for a right of 'prior use' or 'personal possession' in favour of any third party who, prior to the date of the deposit, had manufactured identical products in the Benelux territory, or had started to carry out his intention to manufacture, unless the design had been copied. The owner was allowed to continue the manufacture and to perform all the other acts falling under the exclusive right.

2.7.1 The Interface with Copyright

No or minimal attention was paid by the literature as to the interface with the exceptions formulated in the Copyright Act. Of course, the design right did not encompass a general right of reproduction – but only the rights to manufacture and to sell, and only the right to do this, in view of the doctrine of specialty, with regard to the product concerned. This meant an important limitation of the exclusive right in comparison to copyright, leaving free many uses which would require special limitations in the Copyright Act.

In the UBLDM, exhaustion of the right will also cover the right to *use* the design. That might have been an interesting element in the debate, in copyright, about the exhaustion of the right to use computer software – for those who were inclined to support such a broad scope of the exhaustion principle.

2.8 Conclusion

2.8.1 General: Object of Protection

In the Netherlands, copyright remains the primary regime for the protection of models and designs. Copyright protection has been available as from 1912, whereas design protection was only introduced more than sixty years later, in 1975. Paradoxically, the introduction of the Uniform Benelux Law on Models and Designs may in the end have reinforced the role of copyright. First, practice reacted sluggishly on the new protection regime: registration was very often neglected. Designers therefore sought refuge under the shelter of copyright, and as courts may, despite the absence of registration, have felt reluctant to justify shameless imitations, it was natural that they were inclined to allow such shelter. Secondly, although the concurring protection of slavish imitation had been abolished for models introduced *after* 1975, it was maintained for the 'old' ones of before that date. The provision was meant as a legal tomb for a design heritage supposed to quickly fade away. Instead, it developed into a festival tent where eternal old models lushfully partied to the rhythm of an ever-expanding, benevolent jurisprudence. Rather than concluding from this that 'old models' were spoilt with far too much protection, many felt that unregistered designs from after 1975 also deserved some protection; and again it was copyright which offered a solution.

When finally, in 1987, the Benelux Court of Justice assured that to Benelux models and designs the quite moderate, general threshold of originality applied, copyright protection for design in the Netherlands exploded.

As to the originality criterion, even if its threshold is 'low', it still remains a question *how* low exactly it is, and models and designs could well serve to make certain nuances visible at this level. For example, even devices which are plainly functional and were meant to be nothing more – no attempt aiming at any conscious 'design' is visible – may contain arbitrary choices which contribute to that device showing an 'own' character, as was the case with the water treatment machine depicted above. Some jurisdictions in the Netherlands nevertheless consistently refuse to grant copyright in such creations, as, in their view, not every arbitrary choice amounts to a creative choice – even if it results in an appearance showing individuality.

2.8.2 Boundaries of Protection

As it is in this field of the boundaries of protection that Dutch law shows some interesting developments, it was dealt with in some detail. Dutch case law shows itself aware of the monopolising effects that may be inherent in the protection of certain models and designs. That applies especially in the case of copyright, because of its long duration and its 'universal' scope of protection. The universal scope of protection means that the exclusive right is not limited to a specific useful object or category of useful objects, but applies to all forms with the same appearance.

Although the exclusion of *technical subject-matter* is, in principle, strict, its application in practice may not always be. The Supreme Court allows a very large measure of freedom to the appreciation of the facts by the lower judges. Moreover, the original 'appearance' and its aesthetic 'effect' may justify eligibility for copyright despite the technical nature of the model. Whether that complies with the rules of European copyright remains uncertain. By contrast, the Supreme Court recently (in 2013) took an adamant position as to the exclusion of *style*.

The doctrine of the exclusion of *ideas* is less developed. It was sustained above that it is precisely at this point, however, that the greatest risk might lurk of monopolising effects. In fact 'iconic' and 'revolutionary' design often resides in a concept, an idea, frequently encompassing technical aspects as much as aesthetic qualities. It is in such cases that restrictions on competition might have the most important consequences. On the other hand, it is precisely in such cases that a generous reward for the designer seems most justified. This constitutes a dilemma that may be hard to solve.

Although many consider it self-evident that the same restrictions apply in design law, it is very questionable whether the apparently prevailing opinion is right. The inclusion of elements of style and ideas in the design protection would at the same time be more justified and less harmful as in copyright, and its anti-competitive effects would be fairly innocuous.

2.8.3 Rights and Infringement

Copyright and design right both offer a broad exclusive right, although it is assumed that the design right does not encompass the right to *depict* a model or design. Infringement remains a question that is, to a great extent, inevitably ruled by factual appreciations. In 1995, the Dutch Supreme Court ruled that, in copyright as well as in design right, the scope of protection was governed by the criterion whether there was similarity in the *overall impression* of the respective designs. Although certainly motivated by a laudable pursuit of simplicity, such a 'unification' of the infringement criterion only has sense where it is certain that, as to their object of protection as well as to their excluded subject-matter, copyright and design law exactly concur. As it is almost certain that – at least at the time of the UBLDM – this was not the case, the identity of the infringement criterion stayed, at least from a doctrinal point of view, a rather nominal affair.

2.8.4 Ownership, Transfer and Presumptions of Ownership

Contrary to the basic copyright rule, the Benelux law on designs and models provides that, under certain circumstances, commissioners are regarded as initial copyright holders. In 2007, the Benelux Court ruled that this rule also applied to designs that had never been deposited. It would have been better, however, to limit the application of the rules for concurrence of design law and copyright law to cases where this concurrence actually occurs.

2.8.5 *Final Remarks*

As a final note, we should perhaps consider why copyright law developed into the primary IP-regime for designs and models in the Netherlands, and not design law which nevertheless constitutes the *specialis* rule, and therefore might be expected to respond best to the needs of the right holders. Of course, copyright had built up a head start of more than fifty years before the design law was introduced. But because of the perpetual legal uncertainty as to the question what level of originality exactly was required, the conditions for a successful start of the new design law were given.

If, in the end, copyright nevertheless prevailed, it is difficult to find reasons for this other than the condition of registration. Perhaps this is a lesson in modesty. The popular sense of justice condemns imitation. The existing protection under copyright as well as the law of unfair competition had made the Dutch confident that the law supported this moral judgment. From there, it proves to be extremely hard to bend and subject this sense of justice to administrative requirements.

As a consequence, design law remained a tree that grew up in the shadow of other regimes, bereaving it of the sunshine of confidence and the rain of case law a young regime needs to fully deploy all its potential. Sometimes one has the impression that case law, in a vain pursuit of efficiency, enforces analogies on the two regimes where it would also have been conceivable to see differences. To be concrete: in view of the limitations already inherent in the object, the right as well as the duration of the design right, there is no necessity to subject it to certain restrictions applying to copyright. A registered design right is restricted to a specific category of goods; it – probably – does not cover the right to depict the model; it will last no more than twenty-five years. That raises the question whether there is any need to be as strict in design right as in copyright where it concerns the freedom of style and even the freedom of ideas; and likewise whether certain statutory copyright limitations have only been 'forgotten' when they were not copied in the design law, or were with good reason omitted. In that light, all the weight which in the Netherlands has been levelled on the copyright approach may, despite obvious advantages, also have entailed disadvantages for the right holders.

3 The Copyright/Design Interface in Greece

Irini Stamatoudi and Maria-Daphne Papadopoulou

3.1 Introduction

Greece was late in adopting legislation on industrial designs and models and it may well be amongst those countries that were the last ones to do so. Protection of industrial designs and models can be divided into two phases: (a) from 1920 to 1996 where copyright protection was the only protection possible together with unfair competition law[1] and (b) from 1996 to date when special legislation was enacted in Greece for the protection of industrial designs.[2] Since 1996 industrial designs and models can be protected both as industrial designs (under this special legislation) and as works of applied art (by copyright) if the conditions for such protection are met.

During the first phase (copyright) protection was not uniform. There were variations depending on the laws enacted and on how these laws were each time interpreted by the courts. There was also protection under unfair competition law but this falls outside the scope of this chapter and therefore it is not examined. This phase is divided into three periods, which are examined separately. The law in the second phase, i.e. from 1996 to date (partial cumulation), is more or less settled. This phase is also examined separately. At the end an assessment is made with regard to the protection of industrial designs and models during all those years, whilst at the same time conclusions are drawn as to where we stand today.

NOTE: For the purposes of this chapter the term 'partial cumulation' shall mean that both copyright and industrial design protection co-exist in the same subject-matter to the extent that the requirements for each type of protection are met. The term 'full cumulation' shall mean that to the extent that the requirements for one type of protection (only) are met, this protection is automatically extended to cover the other type, too, irrespective of whether the requirements for this other type of protection are met. The terms 'full cumulation' and 'partial cumulation', as used in this chapter, correspond to the definitions of 'total cumulation' and 'full cumulation', respectively, as the two latter terms are defined in the introduction of this book.

[1] These two forms of protection did not necessarily co-exist. A design or a model could be protected either by copyright or by unfair competition law or by both.

[2] Presidential Decree 259/1997, which was enacted on the basis of the statutory authorisation provided in Article 4 Law 2417/1996; see section 3.3.

Table 3.1 *Chronological table of legislation and statistics*

Period	Acts	Amendments	Interpretation (i.e. by courts)	Further information	Design applications	Design registrations
1920–1975	Copyright Law 2387/1920	Law Decree (L.D.) 12/15.6.1926 Law 4301/1929 Law 4489/1930 L.D. 619/1941 L.D. 2179/1943 Law 763/1943 Law 988/1943	Protection by copyright	Protection of designs and models under unfair competition law		
1975–1993	Copyright Law 2387/1920 Copyright Law 100/1975 Law 213/1975		Protection by copyright irrespective of originality	Protection of designs and models under unfair competition law		
1993–1996	Copyright Law 2121/1993 Copyright Law 100/1975		Express protection of designs and models as works of applied art by copyright	Protection of designs and models under unfair competition law		
1996–date	Law 2417/1996	Presidential Decree No. 161/2002 (adaptation to Directive 98/71/EC)	Partial	Protection of designs and models under unfair competition Law	4,124 * (229)	3,785 ** (222)

Table 3.1 *(cont.)*

Period	Acts	Amendments	Interpretation (i.e. by courts)	Further information	Design applications	Design registrations
	Presidential Decree 259/1997 on industrial designs and models Copyright Law 2121/193	Law 3966/2011 (adaptation to Directive 2004/48/EC)	Cumulation	Law 2417/1996 is a law frame, i.e. protection for designs and models in Greece actually starts with Presidential Decree 259/1997		

Source: Created by the authors based on statistical data published by WIPO

Figures in parentheses: average annual numbers

* 2015 is included

** 2015 is not included

3.2 First Phase: 1920–1996: Protection by Copyright Law

3.2.1 *First Period: 1920–1975*

The first law on copyright was adopted in Greece in 1909 (Law 3483) with the aim to protect dramatic works. Designs were neither mentioned nor protected. In 1920, Law 2387[3] was enacted and extended protection to 'original works or works based on adaptation or duplication or translations'.[4] Although originality was not an express requirement in the Law, it was one established by literature and case law.[5] According to them, originality was the outcome of the author's creative intellectual labour and contribution, due to which the work presents a special individuality, which distinguishes it from commonplace (everyday) intellectual productions.[6]

The term of protection was fifty years *post mortem auctoris*.[7] If the work was a collaborative work (created by two or more authors), the term was calculated from the death of the last surviving author.[8] Authors, i.e. writers, music composers, painters, draughtsmen, sculptors and engravers, as expressly provided in the Law,[9] had the exclusive right to publish or reproduce their works in any manner or form. They could also transfer their rights to third parties.[10] The buyer of a work of visual arts did not have the right to reproduce it in any way.[11] Some few exceptions were

[3] Act 2387/1920 'On Copyright Law' (*Official Gazette* A' 148/3.7.1920).

[4] This law repealed Articles 2 to 6 Law 3483/1909 and constituted the basic Copyright Law till 1993, which has been revised and supplemented on several occasions since then. It contained only seventeen articles.

[5] G. Koumantos, *Copyright Law* (Athens: Ant. N. Sakkoulas, 1967), p. 3 (in Greek); I. Likiardopoulos, 'Copyright Law on Copies' (1938) *Greek Jurists' Review*, 574; K. Papaioannou-Silts, *The Scope of Author's Right in Musical Sector* (Thessaloniki: 1990), pp. 69ff (in Greek). Judgment No. 1989/1937, Board of Appeals, Athens, 1938 *Greek Jurists' Review* 216; Judgment No. 2032/1938, Board of Appeals, Athens, 1939 *Themis* 425; Judgment No. 3402/1968, Court of First Instance (Multimember Panel), Athens, 1969 *Legal Tribune* 572; Judgment No. 567/1974, Supreme Court, 1975 *Legal Tribune* 151; Prosecution of Court of First Instance, Athens 3/1959, 1960 *Jurists Archive* 305–6 = 1960 *New Law* 219–21, comment I. Sakellaropoulos.

[6] Prosecution of Court of First Instance, Athens 3/1959, 1960 *Jurists Archive* 305 = 1960 *New Law* 219, comment Sakellaropoulos. Yet, there are instances where the courts confuse originality with novelty, such as Judgment No. 3402/1968, Court of First Instance (Multimember Panel), Athens, 1969 *Legal Tribune* 572, comment K. Asprogerakas-Grivas and Indictment No. 1989/1937, Court of Appeal, Athens, 1938 *Greek Jurists' Review* 216, proposal of I. Papanikolaou, which found that for a work (in this case city plans included in a book) to be original, it has to be completely different from the pre-existing ones regarding its composition and formulation.

[7] Article 2. [8] Article 3.

[9] There was no list of protected subject-matter. There was only a reference to a list of authors, and from this list we derive what the protected subject-matter was.

[10] Article 1. [11] Article 8.

provided to authors' rights, which however were of limited significance to designs and models.[12]

During this period no special legislation existed for industrial designs and models, although in 1963 an attempt was made to this end.[13]

Concerning the protection of industrial designs and models, the literature was divided. Some commentators[14] argued that the external form of industrial products could be protected by both copyright (i.e. Law 2387/1920) and unfair competition law, whilst others[15] argued that protection could only take place on the basis of unfair competition law (and in particular under Articles 1, 13(3) and 17 Law 146/1914).

Case law seems to be more uniform. In most reported cases[16] industrial designs and models were found to be protected on the basis of unfair

[12] Articles 7, 9, 10 and 13.

[13] In 1963 the then Minister of Commerce by Decision 23479 established a Committee to draft a relevant law. Yet, no law was produced at the end.

[14] M. Minoudis, 'The Draft Law on Industrial Designs' (1980) *Commercial Law Review* 382; M. Minoudis, 'The Protection of Industrial Designs and Models', in Argiriadis, Beier, Georgakopoulos et al., *The Evolution of Industrial Property Law*, Studies in Commercial and Maritime Law, A. Argiriadis (Athens/Komotini: Ant. N. Sakkoulas, 1988), p. 89 (in Greek); P. Papadrosou-Arhaniotaki, 'Models and Designs of Utility–Industrial Designs and Models or Models and Aesthetic Form Designs in the Paris Convention' (1986) *Armenopoulos* 310; D. S. Oekonomidis, 'Signification du terme nouveauté en tant que condition premiere pour la protection des dessins et modeles en droit allemande et en droit francais avec une reference au droit grec' (1966) *Revue Hellenique de Droit International* 71, 117; A. Mikroulea, *Utility Models* (Athens: Nomiki Vivliothiki, 1999), p. 84 (in Greek); N. Rokas, *Unfair Competition* (Athens: Nomiki Vivliothiki, 1996), p. 147 (in Greek); Th. Liakopoulos, *Industrial Property* (Athens: P. N. Sakkoulas, 2000), p. 276 (in Greek); S. Vrellis, 'Concerning the Distinction between Designs and Models and Their Mode of Protection', 1971 *New Law* 409; G. Koumantos, 'Contemporary Issues of Copyright Law' (1953) *Legal Tribune* 216; G. Koumantos, 'La protection des artes applicques a l'industrie en Grece' (1962) *Revue Hellenique de Droit International* 284, who initially argued that designs and models may be protected only under the provisions of unfair competition, but later argued that after the ratification of the Berne Convention by Greece every industrial design or model is presumed to satisfy the requirements of protection as a work of art and it is consequently protected under copyright law and, more specifically, under Law 2387/1920; G. Koumantos, 'The Greek Legislation on Copyright after the Stockholm Revision of the Berne International Convention' (1969) *Commercial Law Review* 152; G. Koumantos, *Copyright Law*, 8th edn (Athens/Komotini: Ant. N. Sakkoulas, 2002), p. 124. It was also argued that Article 60 Civil Code applied granting a general action for the protection of the products of one's intellect, Papadrosou-Arhaniotaki, 'Models and Designs', 311, n. 72. In the absence, however, of a specific law for the protection of industrial designs and models, such a protection was infeasible, N. Tsotsos, 'The Recent Reform of Patent Law and Industrial Models Law' (1980) *Armenopoulos* 943; Minoudis, 'The Protection of Industrial Designs and Models', p. 90.

[15] P. Selekos, *The Right in Industrial Design and Model* (Athens: Ant. N. Sakkoulas, 1999), p. 51 (in Greek); L. Kotsiris, *Copyright Law*, 4th edn (Athens/Thessaloniki: Sakkoulas, 2005), p. 69 (in Greek); K. Karavas, *Commercial Law*, vol. 1 (Athens, 1962), p. 649 (in Greek); N. Rokas, *Industrial Property*, 2nd edn (Athens: Nomiki Vivliothiki, 2011), p. 69 (in Greek), who only mentions the view of protecting industrial designs and models under copyright law.

[16] Judgment No. 3599/1974, Court of First Instance, Athens, 1974 *Legal Tribune* 1085 and Judgment No. 5498/1974, Court of First Instance, Athens, 1974 *Commercial Law Review* 270.

competition law only. The reason for that was, on the one hand, that only authors expressly mentioned in Article 1 Law 2387/1920 enjoyed protection and, on the other, that designs and models were not expressly provided as protected subject-matter. There was a single case though (Case 3651/1962 of the Three-Member Misdemeanours Court of Athens)[17] where the Court found that the plastic reproductions of known pictures were protected as works because – as stated – works are protected by copyright irrespective of their purpose, i.e. whether they are produced for aesthetic reasons or for practical use and in particular for industrial application.

3.2.2 Second Period: 1975–1993

In 1971 the Berne Convention for the Protection of Literary and Artistic Works was revised in Paris. Article 2(7) second and third subparagraphs provide that 'Works protected in the country of origin solely as designs and models shall be entitled in another country of the Union only to such special protection as is granted in that country to designs and models; however, if no such special protection is granted in that country, such works shall be protected as artistic works.' This provision was incorporated into Greek law by Law 100/1975.[18] Since Greece did not have special laws on industrial designs and models, these had to be protected by copyright even if the requirements for such protection (and especially the criterion of originality) were not met.[19] Yet, there were also voices in the literature that argued that originality was a necessary requirement for copyright protection (despite what was provided in the Berne Convention (Paris Act)) and had to be met in order for industrial designs and models to be protected.[20]

[17] Judgment No. 3651/1962, Criminal Court (Three-Member Panel), Athens, 1962 *Copyright and Industrial Property Review* 39, comment T.I.

[18] Law 100/1975 'On the Validation of a) the Convention on the Formation of the World Organization of Protection of Property of Intellectual Works, signed in Stockholm on July 14th, 1967 and b) the Diplomatic Conference of Paris, carried out in July 1971 for the Revision of the Berne Convention of 1886' (*Official Gazette* A' 162/01.08.1975).

[19] Koumantos, 'The Greek Legislation on Copyright', 152, 160; Koumantos, *Copyright Law*, 8th edn, pp. 124ff, n. 305; K. Pampoukis, *The Law of Distinctive Marks* (Thessaloniki/Athens: P. Sakkoulas, 1965), pp. 42ff (in Greek); K. Pampoukis, *Industrial Property Law and Copyright Law in Practice* (Thessaloniki: Sakkoulas, 1996), p. 53 (in Greek); V. Antonopoulos, *Industrial Property Law*, 2nd edn (Athens/Thessaloniki: Sakkoulas, 2005), pp. 157ff, 292ff (in Greek); M. Marinos, *Copyright Law*, 2nd edn (Athens/Komotini: Ant. N. Sakkoulas, 2004), p. 35; Selekos, *The Right in Industrial Design and Model*, p. 53, n. 64; P. Selekos, 'The Substantial Conditions of Industrial Design and Models Protection according to Presidential Decree 259/1997' (1998) *Commercial Law Reports* 643, n. 2; Th. Liakopoulos, *Industrial Property*, Law and Economy, 5th edn (Athens: P. N. Sakkoulas, 2000), p. 276, n. 1 (in Greek); Papadrosou-Archaniotaki, 'Models and Designs of Utility', 311.

[20] Kotsiris, *Copyright Law*, p. 70, argues that the provision at issue should not be interpreted in a way that each design or model is considered as such in order to satisfy the conditions

During this period courts granted protection to industrial designs and models on the basis of the Berne Convention (Paris Act), which was ratified in Greece by Law 100/1975.[21] According to case law[22] copyright protection is granted to all products of the human intellect to the extent that they present a 'height of creativity' (or a certain level of creativity) so as to qualify as works. Without creativity a work could not be considered a

for its protection as a 'work of art'. It is not that by definition a design is assimilated to a work of art but rather that designs are considered to come within the subject-matter of copyright protection to the extent that they satisfy the relevant requirements for such a protection, as is the case with works of applied art. See also Mikroulea, *Utility Models*, p. 84, n. 194.

[21] Some rulings (Judgment No. 447/1981, Court of Appeal, Athens, 1982 *Armenopoulos* 33 = 1982 *Commercial Law Review*, p. 313; Judgment No. 7829/1979, Court of First Instance, Athens, 1979 *Commercial Law Review* 488ff; Judgment No. 10070/1984, Court of First Instance (Multimember Panel), Thessaloniki, 1985 *Commercial Law Review* 354; Judgment No. 8773/1983, Court of First Instance, Athens, 1983 *Commercial Law Review* 686; Judgment No. 16073/1979, Court of First Instance (Multimember Panel), Athens, 1980 *Commercial Law Review* 692ff; Judgment No. 17299/1982, Court of First Instance, Athens, 1985 *Commercial Law Review* 356, comment I. Georgakis) did not refer to Law 100/1975, which ratified the Berne Convention (Paris Act, 1971) but inaccurately to Law Decree 3356/1956, which ratified an earlier version of the Berne Convention (i.e. Brussels Act, 1948). In this earlier version (i.e. Brussels Act, 1948) it was provided in Article 2(5) that: 'Works protected in the country of origin solely as designs and models shall be entitled in another country of the Union only to such special protection as is granted in that country to designs and models.' Yet, the Berne Convention was amended in Paris, so as the favourable provision (Article 2(7) third subpara.) was included, which provides that if no special protection for industrial designs and models is granted in one country, such works are protected as artistic works. In all these cases the courts applied the earlier version of the Berne Convention, failing to recognise to the designs at issue copyright protection, as they had to do on the basis of the Paris amendment (i.e. Paris Act, 1971). The most interesting among these rulings is Judgment No. 447/1981, Court of Appeal, Athens, 1982 *Armenopoulos* 33 = 1982 *Commercial Law Review* 313. In this case in relation to painted depictions on canvas for embroidery, the court held that they constituted the product of an artistic and intellectual creation in which the creator's personal and original contribution could be identified. In fact, she was inspired to create the work at issue and attributed to it individuality and originality in comparison to the pre-existing ones.

[22] Judgment No. 8773/1983, Court of First Instance, Athens, 1983 *Commercial Law Review* 686, and Judgment No. 10070/1984, Court of First Instance (Multimember Panel), Thessaloniki, 1985 *Commercial Law Review* 354, held that painted depictions printed on special synthetic fabrics (canvases) were protected under copyright law, in conjunction with Article 60 Civil Code and the provisions of unfair competition law. Also relevant is Judgment No. 525/1985, Supreme Court, 1986 *Legal Tribune* 195, which expressly took into account Law 100/1975. See also Judgment No. 7829/1979, Court of First Instance, Athens, 1979 *Commercial Law Review* 488; Judgment No. 400/ΑΦ/1990, Court of First Instance, Veroia, 1991 *Commercial Law Review* 151; Judgment No. 1064/1982, Court of First Instance (Multimember Panel), Thessaloniki, 1982 *Commercial Law Review* 320; and Judgment No. 237/1991, Court of First Instance (Multimember Panel), Veroia, 1991 *Commercial Law Review* 724. A similar reasoning is found in the ruling of Judgment No. 2/1992, Court of First Instance, Veroia, 1992 *Armenopoulos* 29, in which the dispute concerned knitwear designs. The court held that even though the subject designs did not present originality or did not have the necessary 'level of creativity', they were protected as artistic works, since in Greece no special legislation on industrial designs and models had been enacted.

literary or artistic work. Designs and models though, according to Article 2(7) third subparagraph Berne Convention (Paris Act), were protected as artistic works (irrespective of any creativity) given that the specific country in which their protection was sought (in the case at issue Greece) did not provide for any special laws for them.

There were also cases involving, for example, plastic components of assembled toys (i.e. Lego),[23] where it was judged that they constituted works of applied art because they presented originality and individuality by reason of their specific dimensions and special distinctive features, which distinguished them from existing similar designs. The court also referred to the fact that even if that were not the case (i.e. qualifying as works of applied art), they would still be protected by copyright on the basis of the Berne Convention (Paris Act) given that no special laws were provided for them in Greece. In all these cases the designs and models at issue were also found to be protected by unfair competition law.

Courts' stance was not always uniform though. There were rulings[24] which provided that designs and models were only protected under unfair competition law and did not qualify for copyright protection. These rulings did not consider designs and models to form independent intangible products in the same sense as works of applied art, which were considered to possess a higher level of creativity.

[23] Judgment No. 400/ΑΦ/1990, Court of First Instance, Veroia, 1991 *Commercial Law Review* 151 and Judgment No. 1064/1982, Court of First Instance (Multimember Panel), Thessaloniki, 1982 *Commercial Law Review* 320, which ruled at second instance that the plastic components of children's constructions (i.e. assembled Lego blocks) were works of applied art protected under Article 2(7) Berne Convention (Paris Act) as artistic works. The same objects, that is, plastic components of children's constructions in the form of assembled table games, were also dealt with in Judgment No. 237/1991, Court of First Instance (Multimember Panel), Veroia, 1991 *Commercial Law Review* 724, which ruled in the same way, also recognising that according to the Berne Convention, as ratified by Law 100/1975, the relevant designs and models are protected as artistic works. In the given case though, the court held that the said plastic components of children's constructions (blocks) present individuality and originality anyhow and are protected as artistic works. Judgment No. 3000/1979, Court of First Instance (Multimember Panel), Athens, 1981 *Commercial Law Review* 595 held that the external distinctive elements of toys (automobiles in miniature form) are considered as works of applied art according to the Berne Convention (Paris Act) and Law 100/1975 and are protected according to Law 2387/1920 in combination with Article 60 Civil Code. The same reasoning was applied in the ruling of Judgment No. 1200/1996, Court of First Instance, Athens, 1996 *Commercial Law Review* 414, according to which plastic components of children's constructions (assembled Lego blocks) present originality and individuality and therefore are protected by copyright law.

[24] Judgment No. 16073/1979, Court of First Instance (Multimember Panel), Athens, 1980 *Commercial Law Review* 692ff (overruled by Judgment No. 447/1981, Court of Appeal, Athens, 1982 *Armenopoulos* 33 = 1982 *Commercial Law Review* 313); Judgment No. 17299/1982, Court of First Instance, Athens, 1985 *Commercial Law Review* 356, comment I. Georgakis; Judgment No. 8773/1983, Court of First Instance, Athens, 1984 *Commercial Law Review* 685.

A common feature in all the aforementioned cases was the fact that the applicants (right holders) who sought to protect their works by reason of the external configuration of their industrial products either as industrial designs or models, or as works of applied art, invoking the Berne Convention, were foreigners. Greek citizens had also the right to invoke the provisions of the Berne Convention (as revised in Brussels in 1948), according to Article 1 Law Decree 4264/1962, if those provisions were more favourable compared to the ones of the Greek law.[25] Given that this was the case, designs and models created by Greek citizens at the time enjoyed in Greece copyright protection, since no special legislation for industrial designs was in place.[26]

During this period two more attempts were made (one in 1977[27] and one in 1991[28]) to draft laws on the protection of industrial designs and models. Yet, both of them failed.

In 1975 Greece ratified by Law 213 the 1883 Paris International Convention on the Protection of Industrial Property (as revised in Stockholm in 1967).[29] Although this Convention (and the ratifying Law) provided in Article 5quinquies that all Union countries had to protect industrial designs, that was a blank cheque. Industrial designs were listed in Article 1(2) Law 213/1975 as protected subject-matter but no further rules were provided. Therefore, such a protection was not applied in practice.[30]

3.2.3 *Third Period: 1993–1996*

In 1993 Law 2121 was enacted.[31] This is the Copyright Law, which currently applies in Greece (after several revisions). Article 2(1)

[25] Law Decree 4264/1962 (*Official Gazette* A' 187/12.11.1962).

[26] Koumantos, 'The Greek Legislation on Copyright', 152; Rokas, *Industrial Property*, p. 69; Georgakis, comment on Judgment No. 17299/1982, Court of First Instance, Athens, 1985 *Commercial Law Review* 356.

[27] The then Minister of Commerce established by Decision 7947/1355/15.2.1977 a Legislative Committee in order – among other things – to draft a law for industrial designs and models. In August 1978 the draft law had been deposited but it never became a law. M. Minoudis, 'The Draft Law on Industrial Models' (1980) *Commercial Law Review* 381ff; Minoudis, 'The Protection of Industrial Designs and Models', p. 91; M. Minoudis, 'Der Entwurf eines griechischen Geschmacksmustergesetzes' (1980) *Gewerblicher Rechtsschutz und Urheberrecht, Internationaler Teil* 145ff; and Tsotsos, 'The Recent Reform of Patent Law', 939.

[28] Georgakopoulos, *Commercial Code Draft and Introductory Report (Report to the Ministry of Justice)* (Athens, 1991), pp. 40ff.

[29] Law 213/1975 on the 'Ratification of the Paris International Convention of 1883 on Protection of Industrial Property, as revised in Stockholm on 14th July 1967' (*Official Gazette* A' 258/20.11.1975).

[30] Liakopoulos, *Industrial Property*, p. 8.

[31] Law 2121/1993 on the 'Copyright, Related Rights and Cultural Matters' (*Official Gazette* A' 4.3.1993), available in English at www.opi.gr/index.php/en/library/law-2121-1993.

Copyright Law provides for an indicative list of copyrightable subject-matter within which works of applied art are also included.

The main characteristic of works of applied art against any other type of work is their utility and, on most occasions, their industrial or handicraft production as well as their marketability. These works were essentially considered to be products rather than works in the narrow sense of the word, such as classic/conventional copyright works.[32] They are used to improve the looks of industrial products or their utility.[33] That, of course, does not seem to create any problem for their copyrightability given the fact that copyright protection is independent of the value, aim, purpose or any moral judgment with regard to the work.[34] This is also the reason why there is an express reference to these works (as protectable subject-matter) in the Greek Copyright Law.[35]

Copyright Law 2121/1993 protects original creations of the mind.[36] Therefore originality is a precondition for copyright protection.[37] The notion of originality has been shaped on the basis of literature and case law but no significant changes had been introduced compared to what applied until then. A work is considered to be original if it is statistically unique, i.e. no other person with the same aim in mind and under the same or similar circumstances would reasonably have reached the same creative outcome. The work needs to present individuality or a modicum of creativity such that the work can be distinguished from everyday productions or from other similar and known works.[38] This also applies to works of applied art, including industrial designs.[39]

[32] I. Stamatoudi, Comment on Article 2/74, in L. Kotsiris and I. Stamatoudi (eds.), *Commentary on the Greek Copyright Law* (Athens/Thessaloniki: P. N. Sakkoulas, 2009); Kotsiris, *Copyright Law*, p. 68; Marinos, *Copyright Law*, p. 93; P. Koriatopoulou and Ch. Tsigou, *Copyright Law – Entries Interpretation* (Athens: Nomiki Vivliothiki, 2008), p. 207.

[33] D. Kallinikou, *Copyright Law and Related Rights*, Law and Economy, 3rd edn (Athens: P. N. Sakkoulas, 2008), p. 49.

[34] Koumantos, *Copyright Law*, pp. 122ff; I. Stamatoudi and G. Koumantos, *Greece* 2[1][b], in P. E. Geller (ed.), *International Copyright Law and Practice* (New York: LexisNexis, 2013), vol. 2.

[35] Koumantos, *Copyright Law*, p. 123.

[36] Article 2(1).

[37] Except from originality regarding computer software programs, which is defined in Article 2(3) Law 2121/1993.

[38] Judgment No. 2028/2003, Court of First Instance (Multimember Panel), Athens (legal information database Nomos). For commentary, see Stamatoudi, Comment on Article 2/27, in *Commentary on the Greek Copyright Law*. This criterion of originality has also been applied to maps of Thessaloniki's urban complex as well as its building coefficients, Judgment No. 1710/2011, Court of Appeal, Thessaloniki, 2012 *Mass Media, Information and Communications Law* 74.

[39] See also Judgment No. 4091/2010, Court of Appeal, Athens, 2011 *Private Law Annals* 455, comment D. Kallinikou (finding that designs of ceramic lamps, vases and other works of utilitarian nature were not original because they did not present statistically

The unique elements of a work can be found in one of the work's attributes (the subject, how the idea was conceived and turned into a work, its formulation, particular expression, combinations used, etc. in relation to the whole or parts of the work) depending on the type and nature of the work. The mere fact that the work is not a copy/duplication of another work (even with some variations) is not enough to render it original. Also originality is not found in the effort, skill or labour invested in the creation of a work and is not assessed with regard to its usefulness.[40] Originality depends on the author's creative choices and the margin she or he has to make such choices.

General copyright provisions also apply to works of applied art. Copyright protection is automatic, is not subject to formalities and is vested *ab initio* to persons who qualify as authors.[41] It is only persons who qualify as authors and it is to them that rights are first vested.[42] Presumptions (which can be rebutted) are provided in certain cases, e.g. the person whose name appears on embodiments of a work in any way usually employed to indicate the author of the work is presumed to be its author.[43] In a case of a 'collaborative' work created by a number of authors working together to create it, the authors are the initial joint owners in equal parts of the entire copyright in the resulting work, to the extent that their respective contribution cannot be separately exploited.[44] In the case of a 'composite' work, consisting of different parts created separately and later brought together in a work, all authors own copyright in the entire composite work jointly and each of them owns copyright in the separate part she or he created to the extent that this part can be separately exploited.[45]

With regard to ownership and transfer of rights, special provisions apply. The economic rights of authors-employees in the private sector are transferred *ipso jure* to the employer to the extent necessary in order for the purpose of the employment contract to be fulfilled.[46] The economic rights of authors-employees in the public sector in works created in the context of their duties are automatically transferred to their employer.[47] Copyright law does not deal with works that authors create as independent contractors (freelancers) on the orders and under the commission of other persons. According to the general copyright rules though, rights

unique elements so as to distinguish them from usual and commonly known forms on the market).

[40] Judgment No. 4087/1995, Court of First Instance, Athens, 1998 *Greek Justice* 221.

[41] Article 6(2). [42] Article 6(1). [43] Article 10(1). [44] Article 7(1). [45] Article 7(3).

[46] Article 8 first subpara. [47] Article 8 second subpara.

remain with the author unless it is otherwise provided in the contract. Economic rights can be transferred either between living persons or by inheritance.[48] Copyright in a work may be transferred as a whole or in parts. Rights may be transferred by assignment or be licensed, exclusively or non-exclusively.[49] Yet, a licensee cannot transfer a contractually acquired licence to a third party without the licensor's consent.[50] Moral rights are only partially subject to contractual waiver and for particular acts (or omissions) only and devolve on heirs.[51] Any agreement concerning the transfer or licensing of copyright should be in writing. Yet, it is only the author who may invoke the invalidity of a contract due to the fact that it is not in writing.[52] In Article 1(1) Law 2121/1993 it is explicitly stated that copyright is made up of both economic rights[53] and moral rights.[54] An exhaustive list of limitations and exceptions are provided to the economic rights.[55] Amongst them is Article 26, which provides for an exception with regard to the use of images of works sited in public spaces. According to it the occasional reproduction and communication by the mass media of images of – amongst others – works of applied art, which are sited permanently in a public place, are permissible, without the author's consent and without paying her or him a fee. Finally, Article 3(1) fifth subpara. Law 2121/1993 provides that the rights of rental and public lending do not apply to works of applied art.

Although Law 2121/1993 was enacted to afford a comprehensive legal regime of protection to creative expressions of the mind (i.e. works), Judgment No. 1200/1996 of the Court of First Instance of Athens[56] erroneously considered at the time that Greece fulfilled (by this Law) its international obligation to afford special protection to industrial designs and models, due to the fact that works of applied art were expressly provided in its scope of protection. Generally, though, courts were reluctant to protect industrial designs by copyright. In the only other judgment during this period the Court of Appeal in Thessaloniki[57] found that a design for a chair, which enjoyed international protection as an industrial design but for which Greece was not declared as a third interested party, was only protected by unfair competition law. It did not qualify for copyright protection.

[48] Article 12(1). [49] Article 13(1), (2). [50] Article 13(6). [51] Articles 16 and 12(2).
[52] Article 14. [53] Articles 3 and 5. [54] Article 4. [55] Articles 18–28C.
[56] Judgment No. 1200/1996, Court of First Instance, Athens, 1996 *Commercial Law Review* 414.
[57] Judgment No. 4098/1995, Court of Appeal, Thessaloniki, 1996 *Commercial Law Reports* 657ff, comment I. Soufleros.

During this period no other case law regarding the protection of designs and models, neither as works of applied art nor as industrial designs or models, has been reported.

Finally, Article 72 Law 2121/1993 repealed Law Decree 4264/1962. Thus Greek citizens from 1993 to 1996 (when special legislation was enacted for industrial designs and models) could no longer invoke the provisions of the Berne Convention (Paris Act), which provided that industrial designs and models should be afforded copyright protection if the country where protection is sought has no special laws for their protection. This differentiation in treatment concerned designs that were published for the first time in Greece or were unpublished.[58] That meant that it was only foreigners that could take advantage of this provision and have their industrial designs and models protected by copyright irrespective of whether these were original. Greek nationals had to prove originality as a precondition in order for designs to be protected by copyright.

3.3 Second Phase: 1996 to Date: Protection by Industrial Design and Copyright Law (Partial Cumulation)

During this phase Greek Copyright Law remains the same. Yet, in 1996 Greece enacted special legislation on the protection of industrial designs and models. In fact, Law 2417,[59] which ratified the Hague Agreement on the international deposit of industrial models and designs, defines the notion of an 'industrial design or model'[60] and provides that these are

[58] See Judgment No. 1200/1996, Court of First Instance, Athens, 1996 *Commercial Law Review* 414 and Judgment No. 7518/2000, Court of First Instance (Multimember Panel), Athens, 2001 *Greek Justice* 1422 = 2001 *Business and Company Law* 708 = 2001 *Commercial Law Review* 364 = 2001 *Private Law Annals* 461, according to which the said protection of the Berne Convention did not extend to all designs and models, but only to those of international character, and the Convention did not apply to designs and models created by Greek citizens and published for the first time in Greece or were unpublished. Same in F. Karagiannopoulos, comment on Judgment No. 6489/1999, Court of First Instance, Athens, 1999 *Business and Company Law* 408.

[59] Law 2417/1996 'Validation of the Hague Settlement on the International Submission of Industrial Plans and Models of November 6th, 1925, as revised in the Hague on November 28, 1960, and of the Supplementary Act of Stockholm of July 14th, 1967, as amended in Stockholm on September 28, 1979' (*Official Gazette* A' 139/3.7.1996), available in English at www.obi.gr/obi/?tabid=247.

[60] Article 3: 'For the implementation of the national legislation "a design or model" is considered to be the outward visible image of the whole or part of a product, which derives from its specific features and mainly the line, contours, colors, shape, form and/or materials of the product itself and/or its ornamentation . . .'

governed by special rules analogous to patents. It also provides in Article 4 for the issuance of presidential decrees that would regulate further modalities of the Law.

In 1997 Presidential Decree 259 was issued.[61] This Decree constitutes the main legislative instrument for the protection of industrial designs and models in Greece. It was enacted before the 98/71 Directive for the legal protection of designs and models came into force,[62] but took into account drafts of the Directive and the Regulation on the Community Design.[63] Decree 259/1997 introduced provisions on the requirements for the protection of national designs and models, on disclosure, exceptions to protection, invalidity, ownership, rights, term of protection and procedures.

With regard to ownership, Presidential Decree 259/1997 provides that the right to register a design or model is vested in the designer or his successor in title (Article 17(1)). In fact, a rebuttable presumption is introduced to the favour of the person who files the application for the registration of the design or model.

If one holds the rights in a design or model and a third party has filed an application for the registration of this design or model or one containing substantial elements of it, without his consent, the holder may demand by action against that third party either the recognition on his behalf of the rights conferred by the application or, in case a certificate for registration has been issued, its transfer. The co-owner of a registered design or model may also demand the recognition of his right (Article 18(1)). The time limitation for such an action is two years from the publication date of the registration of the design or the model in the Industrial Property Bulletin (Article 18(2)).[64]

If two or more persons have created a design or model under a common creative effort, provided that no different agreement has been concluded, the right to the design or the model is vested in them jointly and in equal parts. Each co-owner is entitled to transfer freely his share and supervise the protection of the common

[61] Presidential Decree 259/1997 'Provisions on the Application of the Hague Settlement on the International Submission of Industrial Plans and Models, which was validated by Law 2417/1996 and Provisions on the National Protection Title' (*Official Gazette* A' 185/ 19.9.1997), available in English at www.obi.gr/obi/?tabid=248.

[62] 98/71/EC Directive of the European Parliament and of the Council of 13 October 1998 on the legal protection of designs, OJ 1998 No. L 289/28.

[63] Proposal for a European Parliament and Council Directive on the legal protection of designs, COM (1993) 344, COD 464, OJ 1993 No. C 345/14 and also Proposal for a European Parliament and Council Regulation on the Community Design, COM (1993) 342, COD 463, OJ 1994 No. C 29/20.

[64] See for example Judgment No. 2542/2009, Court of Appeal, Athens, 2009 *Business and Company Law* 928.

registered design or model (Article 17(2)). Yet, if two or more persons have created substantially similar designs or models independently the one from the other, the right is vested in the person who first filed the application for registration of a design or model or to the one who has a priority right with regard to an international application (Article 17(4)). If the design or the model has been created by an employee, the relevant provisions of patent law apply (Article 6(6)–(7) Law 1733/1987). According to them the right holder is deemed to be the employer.[65] The right to the registration of a design or model and the registered design or model may be transferred upon written agreement or inherited. The transfer is deemed to take place upon registration of the agreement or of the certificate of inheritance in the Design and Model Register and is published in the Industrial Property Bulletin. The holder of a registered design or model may license his design or model to third parties upon written agreement. This licence is registered in the Design and Model Register and is published in the Industrial Property Bulletin (Article 19(1)–(2)).

Directive 98/71 was implemented into Greek law by Presidential Decree 161/2002,[66] which amended Presidential Decree 259/1997. In 2011, Article 53 Law 3966/2011[67] amended Presidential Decree 259/1997, in order to bring it in line with Directive 2004/48 on the enforcement of intellectual property rights.[68]

After the enactment of special legislation in 1996, the favourable treatment of industrial designs and models under the Berne Convention (i.e. their protection by copyright irrespective of whether they were original) could no longer apply. Industrial designs and models can only be protected by copyright if they are original – as is the case with any other work[69] – and as is provided under Article 30 Presidential Decree

[65] Judgment No. 46/2011, Court of First Instance (Multimember Panel), Theba, 2014 *Armenopoulos* 481, comment D. Chatzimichail, and Judgment No. 19827/2010, Court of First Instance (Multimember Panel), Thessaloniki, 2010 *Business and Company Law* 1041.

[66] Presidential Decree No. 161/2002 'Adaptation of the 259/1997 Presidential Decree towards the Provisions of the 98/71/EC Directive of the European Parliament and of the Council of 13 October 1998 on the Legal Protection of Designs and Models' (*Official Gazette* A' 149/26.06.2002).

[67] Law 3966/2011 'Harmonization of National Law with the 2004/48/EC Directive of the European Parliament and of the Council of 29 April 2004 on the Enforcement of Intellectual Property Rights' (*Official Gazette* A' 118/24.05.2011).

[68] 2004/48/EC Directive of the European Parliament and of the Council of 29 April 2004 on the enforcement of intellectual property rights, OJ 2004 No. L 195/16.

[69] Judgment No. 7518/2000, Court of First Instance (Multimember Panel), Athens, 2001 *Greek Justice* 1422 = 2001 *Business and Company Law* 708 = 2001 *Commercial Law Review* 364 = 2001 *Private Law Annals* 461.

259/1997. In fact, Article 30[70] provides for the system of 'partial cumulation'.[71] According to it, a registered industrial design or model can also be protected by copyright, provided that it meets the requirements for such a protection, i.e. the conditions rendering it an original work.[72] Thus if a design or model has been regarded as an industrial design or model it is protected as such, plus by copyright if it is original. Copyright protection exists independently irrespective of any registration.[73]

The notion of originality in Greek Copyright Law has been explained in section 3.2.3 above and no changes have been introduced so far.[74] Yet,

70 'The design or model that has been registered under the provisions of the present presidential decree is also eligible to protection under the current copyright legislation in Greece from the moment it was created or fixed in any form.' See also Recital 8 of the Preamble of the 98/71 Directive.

71 Koumantos, *Copyright Law*, p. 126. See, relatively, Judgment No. 220/2004, Court of Appeal, Piraeus, 2004 *Business and Company Law* 748 = 2006 *Justice* 1456; Judgment No. 7518/2000, Court of First Instance (Multimember Panel), Athens, 2001 *Business and Company Law* 708 = 2001 *Greek Justice* 1442 = 2001 *Commercial Law Review* 364; Judgment No. 484/2008, Court of Appeal, Piraeus, 2009 *Business and Company Law* 322, comment Ch. Tsene; Judgment No. 2015/2010, Court of Appeal, Thessaloniki, 2011 *Commercial Law Reports* 731, comment K. Pampoukis; Judgment No. 5863/2008, Court of Appeal, Athens, 2009 *Greek Justice* 585; Judgment No. 6152/2012, Court of First Instance (Multimember Panel), Piraeus, 2013 *Greek Justice* 801; Judgment No. 2398/2008, Court of Appeal, Athens, 2009 *Business and Company Law* 572, comment Apostolopoulos; Judgment No. 1486/2007, Court of First Instance, Athens, 2007 *Mass Media, Information and Communications Law* 257, comment M. D. Papadopoulou; Judgment No. 220/2004, Court of Appeal, Piraeus, 2004 *Business and Company Law* 748 = 2006 *Greek Justice* 1456; Judgment No. 7518/2000, Court of First Instance (Multimember Panel), Athens, 2001 *Greek Justice* 1422 = 2001 *Business and Company Law* 708 = 2001 *Commercial Law Review* 364 = 2001 *Private Law Annals* 461; Judgment No. 2398/2008, Court of Appeal, Athens, 2009 *Business and Company Law* 572, comment Ch. Apostolopoulos; Judgment No. 5863/2008, Court of Appeal, Athens, 2009 *Greek Justice* 585, which found that the specific jewellery was protected under an industrial design right, but due to the fact that there was an international registration to which Greece was not included in the determining countries, the industrial design protection could not be implemented and, thus, the jewellery was protected under copyright law as a work of applied art, given that it satisfied all the prerequisites for protection, including originality. See, relatively, Judgment No. 220/2004, Court of Appeal, Piraeus, 2004 *Business and Company Law* 748 = 2006 *Justice* 1456 and Judgment No. 7518/2000, Court of First Instance, 2001 *Business and Company Law* 708 = 2001 *Justice* 1442 = 2001 *Commercial Law Review* 364 but also comment Karagiannopoulos in Judgment No. 6489/1999, Court of First Instance, 1999 *Business and Company Law* 409.

72 Rokas, *Industrial Property*, p. 62; Liakopoulos, *Industrial Property*, p. 275; Koumantos, *Copyright Law*, p. 126. Judgment No. 220/2004, Court of Appeal, Piraeus, 2004 *Business and Company Law* 748 = 2006 *Greek Justice* 1456.

73 Judgment No. 2398/2008, Court of Appeal, 2009 *Business and Company Law* 572, comment Apostolopoulos.

74 Judgment No. 537/2010, Supreme Court; Judgment No. 936/2006, Supreme Court; Judgment No. 152/2005, Supreme Court (all published in legal information database *Nomos*); Judgment No. 1248/2003, Supreme Court, 2005 *Greek Justice* 452; Judgment No. 885/2009, Court of Appeal, Athens, 2009 *Business and Company Law* 707; Judgment

the Court of Justice's recent case law[75] seems to throw new light on the concept of originality.[76] The EU originality criterion, which was expressly provided in EU law for three types of works only (i.e. photographs,[77] software[78] and databases[79]), now extends to all types of works irrespective of their type or nature and constitutes the sole requirement for their protection. According to it, in order for a work to be copyright protected, it should be an intellectual creation and in particular its author's own intellectual creation. Substantial skill and labour do not suffice. The author should be able to make free and creative choices and should stamp his work with his personal touch.[80] No Greek case law

No. 4172/2008, Court of Appeal, Athens, 2009 *Business and Company Law* 190; Judgment No. 80/2008, Court of Appeal, Athens, 2008 *Armenopoulos* 1852; Judgment No. 281/2005, Court of Appeal, Piraeus, 2005 *Piraeus Case Law* 174; Judgment No. 2768/2003, Court of Appeal, Athens, 2004 *Legal Tribune* 51; Judgment No. 3252/2002, 2003 *Business and Company Law* 293; Judgment No. 4091/2010, Court of Appeals, Athens, 2011 *Private Law Annals* 455, comment D. Kallinikou; Judgment No. 4519/ 2010, Court of Appeal, Athens, 2011 *Business and Company Law* 443, comment N. Kiprouli; Judgment No. 4627/2012, Court of First Instance (Multimember Panel), Piraeus, 2013 *Mass Media, Information and Communications Law* 218, comment P. Koriatopoulou-Aggeli; Judgment No. 6193/2006, Court of Appeal, Athens, 2007 *Greek Justice* 1461; Judgment No. 2330/2007, Supreme Court (Penal), 2008 *Penal Annals* 2; Judgment No. 8153/1999, Court of Appeal, Athens, 2000 *Commercial Law Review* 171, comment N. Kiprouli. Koumantos, *Copyright Law*, pp. 105ff, where there is extensive case law; Stamatoudi, Comment on Article 2/27ff, in *Commentary on the Greek Copyright Law*; Kotsiris, *Copyright Law*, pp. 58ff; Kallinikou, *Copyright Law and Related Rights*, pp. 34ff; Marinos, *Copyright Law*, pp. 76ff; M. Marinos, 'The Infringement of Copyright Law and Related Rights', 35 *Greek Justice*, 1441ff.

75 Case C-5/08, *Infopaq International A/S* v. *Danske Dagblades Forening* (Judgment of 16 July) [2009] ECR I-656; Cases C-403/08 and C-429/08, *Football Association Premier League Ltd and Karen Murphy* (Judgment of 4 October 2011) [2011] ECR I-9083; Case C-145/10, *Eva-Maria Painer* v. *Standard VerlagsGmbH and Others* (Judgment of 1 December 2011) [2011] ECDR 297; Case C-604/10, *Football Dataco Ltd and Others* v. *Yahoo! UK Ltd and Others* (Judgment of 1 March 2012) [2012] 2 CMLR 24; Case C-393/ 09, *Bezpečnostní softwarová asociace – Svaz softwarové ochrany* v. *Ministerstvo kultury* [2010] ECR I-13971 (Judgment of 22 December 2010); Case C-406/10, *SAS Institute Inc.* v. *World Programming Ltd* (Judgment of 2 May 2012) [2012] 3 CMLR 4; Case C-355/12 *Nintendo Co Ltd* v. *PC Box Srl* (Judgment of 23 January 2014) [2014] ECDR 6.

76 See I. Stamatoudi, 'Originality in the EU Copyright Law' (2016) *Mass Media, Information and Communications Law* 49 and I. Stamatoudi, 'Originality under EU Copyright Law ' in P. Torremans (ed.), *Research Handbook on Copyright Law*, 2nd edn (Cheltenham: Edward Elgar, 2017), p. 57.

77 2006/116/EC Directive of the European Parliament and of the Council of 12 December 2006 on the term of protection of copyright and certain related rights, OJ 2006 L 372/12, Article 6.

78 91/250/EEC Council Directive of 14 May 1991 on the legal protection of computer programs, OJ 1991 L 122/42, Article 1(3).

79 96/9/EC Directive of the European Parliament and of the Council of 11 March 1996 on the legal protection of databases, OJ 1996 L 77/20, Article 3(1).

80 Case C-145/10, *Eva-Maria Painer* v. *Standard VerlagsGmbH and Others* (Judgment of 1 December 2011) [2011] ECDR 297; C-604/10, *Football Dataco Ltd and Others* v. *Yahoo! UK Ltd and Others* (Judgment of 1 March 2012) [2012] 2 CMLR 24, [2012] ECDR 10;

has been reported so far applying the jurisprudence of the Court of Justice of the EU.

Existing case law, though, seems to have difficulty, in certain cases, distinguishing between the notions of 'novelty' and 'individual character' on the one hand, and the notion of 'originality' on the other.[81] Many cases seem to treat those concepts in the same manner, thus rendering difficult the distinction between industrial designs and works of applied art and confusing the implementation of the two types of laws. There have also been cases that have had general difficulties in applying these notions. There have been, for example, cases where the courts took into account the labour and long effort needed for the creation of a design in order to assess whether it could be protected both by copyright[82] and as a design or model,[83] when in both instances labour should not have been a requirement. Another example is a judgment by the Court of Appeal of Athens[84] where a brooch bearing the shape of a dragonfly was examined in terms of 'novelty', 'individual character' and 'originality' in exactly the same manner. More specifically, the judgment was based on the fact that the brooch required for its production several hours of delicate work and substantial effort. This was the reason for which the design was considered finally to be new, possess an individual character and qualify as original at the same time. According to the court the design was cumulatively protected both as an industrial design and as a work of applied art for the same reasons.

In another case concerning designs of cubes, drawers, hives and boxes, the Court of First Instance of Athens[85] found that they were not 'new' and did not possess an 'individual character' since identical objects already existed in the past on the market. Therefore, they could also not be protected as intellectual creations. In another case[86] concerning designs

C-403/08, and C-429/08 *Football Association Premier League Ltd and Karen Murphy* (Judgment of 4 October 2011) [2011] ECR I-9083.

81 Judgment No. 484/2008, Court of Appeal, Piraeus, 2009 *Business and Company Law* 324, comment Tsene; Judgment No. 1486/2007, Court of First Instance, 2007 *Mass Media, Information and Communications Law* 257, comment Papadopoulou; Judgment No. 2398/2008, Court of Appeal, 2009 *Business and Company Law* 572, comment Apostolopoulos; Judgment No. 6489/1999, Court of First Instance, Athens, 1999 *Business and Company Law* 405, comment Karagiannopoulos; Judgment No. 4091/2010, Court of Appeal, Athens, 2011 *Private Law Annals* 455, comment Kallinikou = 2011 *Business and Company Law* 40.

82 Judgment No. 1289/1999, Supreme Court, 2001 *Greek Jurists' Review* 151, which accepted that the specific toy's components (Lego blocks) are protected as works of applied art due to the strenuous and multiannual scientific effort.

83 Judgment No. 5863/2008, Court of Appeal, Athens, 2009 *Greek Justice* 585 and Judgment No. 5863/2008, Court of Appeal, Athens, 2009 *Greek Justice* 585.

84 Judgment No. 5863/2008, Court of Appeal, Athens, 2009 *Greek Justice* 585.

85 Judgment No. 6489/1999, Court of First Instance, Athens, 1999 *Business and Company Law* 405, comment Karagiannopoulos.

86 Judgment No. 4091/2010, Court of Appeal, Athens, 2011 *Private Law Annals* 455, comment Kallinikou = 2011 *Business and Company Law* 40.

of ceramic lamps, vases and other works of utilitarian nature, the Athens Court of Appeal found that they were not original because they did not present any statistically unique elements. Similar designs were known on the market and their forms were so common – both presently and in ancient times – that they could not be distinguished from other usual and existing forms on the market. In this case the court seems to confuse 'novelty' with 'originality'.[87] Novelty is not a prerequisite for originality. Originality is a subjective notion, whilst novelty is based on objective criteria.[88]

There have also been cases, though, that make an accurate distinction between 'new' and 'original'. The Athens Court of Appeal[89] in a case concerning a brooch in the shape of a dragonfly found that the design was both 'new' and 'original'. The design possessed an 'individual character' due to its aesthetic/visual configuration (shape or outer image) attributed to it by its creator's intellectual effort. Moreover, the overall impression it made on the informed user distinguished it from existing creations with the same subject and indicated it originated from a specific jewellery house. In fact, no other same design as that of the applicant had been circulated either in the Greek market or abroad. Also the designer contributed creatively to its production and therefore the design constituted her own intellectual creation.

We should also note that, apart from having difficulties distinguishing between new and original, the courts are also generally reluctant to acknowledge that a design or model is original and thus protected by copyright as a work of applied art.[90] In 2014, the Athens Court of

[87] See also on the same subject, the opposite Judgment No. 9259/2010, Court of Appeal (Penal), Athens, 2011 *Penal Annals* 538.

[88] Comment Kallinikou on Judgment No. 4091/2010, Court of Appeal, Athens, 2011 *Private Law Annals* 455; Kallinikou, *Copyright Law and Related Rights*, p. 36.

[89] Judgment No. 2398/2008, Court of Appeal, Athens, 2009 *Business and Company Law* 572, comment Apostolopoulos.

[90] See also Judgment No. 4091/2010, Court of Appeal, Athens, 2011 *Private Law Annals* 455, comment Kallinikou (see above text accompanying n. 88); Judgment No. 1445/2006, Court of Appeal, Athens, 2007 *Business and Company Law* 49, comment N. Kiprouli, which did not accept that a ring (ornamented with spirals) is protected as a copyright work, because it does not present originality and uniqueness; Judgment No. 446/1999, Supreme Court, 1999 *Business and Company Law* 1010 = 1999 *Legal Tribune* 1184 = 2000 *Piraeus Case Law* 98 = 1999 *Penal Justice* 681 = 2000 *Penal Annals* 56 = 1999 *Defense* 1171, which repeals a Court of Appeal Judgment that had by inadequate reasoning characterised as intellectual creations sewing designs or clothing manufacturing designs (jeans); Judgment No. 2015/2010, Court of Appeal, Thessaloniki, 2011 *Commercial Law Review* 731, comment K. Pampoukis, which does not confer protection under copyright law as works of applied art to clothing designs (jeans); Judgment No. 7118/2001, Court of First Instance, Athens, 2002 *Commercial Law Review* 280, comment K. Pampoukis, that refers to designs and clothing patterns; Judgment No. 4627/2012, Court of First Instance (Multimember Panel), Piraeus, 2013 *Mass Media, Information*

Appeal[91] found that stamps on clothing are not copyright protected since 'by definition' they cannot be statistically unique or present any level of creativity. In another case, again the Athens Court of Appeal[92] found that clothing designs are not protected because they are not original since similar ornamentations are used widely by fashion designers in a similar manner and therefore this mode of decoration at issue did not present any individuality.

On the contrary, there are some cases[93] where designs or models were found to be original and thus protected by copyright as works of applied art. An example is a ruling[94] by the Court of First Instance of Athens with regard to ceramic table lamps in the shape of a church

and Communications Law 218, comment P. Koriatopoulou-Aggeli, that found that stools cannot be protected as works of applied art; Judgment No. 9799/2000, Court of First Instance, Athens, 2004 *Private Law Annals* 67, comment E. Nikolopoulou, that found that jewellery design is not original (the judgment mentions the 'new' and 'original' element with 'individual character' as a prerequisite of copyright protection); Judgment No. 6489/1999, Court of First Instance, Athens, 1999 *Business and Company Law* 405, comment Karagiannopoulos, that found that specific designs of cubes, drawers, hives and boxes are not protected as works of applied art since the preconditions of their protection as industrial designs do not apply – that is to say, they are not 'new' and 'original' with 'individual character'; Judgment No. 266/1999, Court of First Instance, Kilkis, 1999 *Business and Company Law* 1280, comment N. Karamitsanis, that does not accept the protection of special designs of battery construction as works of applied art, since their originality was not adequately determined.

91 Judgment No. 3269/2014, Court of Appeal, Athens, 2014 *Mass Media, Information and Communications Law* 546, comment E. Velissaropoulou.

92 Judgment No. 4519/2010, Court of Appeals, Athens, 2011 *Business and Company Law* 43.

93 Copyright protection was recognised to a jewellery design, Judgment No. 7475/2008, Court of First Instance, 2009 *Private Law Annals* 162, comment D. Kallinikou; to a jewellery design, brooch in the shape of a dragonfly, Judgment No. 2398/2008, Court of Appeal, Athens, 2009 *Business and Company Law* 572, comment Apostolopoulos; to plastic toy's components (Lego blocks), with Judgment No. 17390/1999, Court of First Instance, Athens, 1999 *Commercial Law Review* 593, but also with Judgment No. 1289/1999, Supreme Court, 2001 *Greek Jurists' Review* 151; to kiosk construction design with Judgment No. 6152/2012, Court of First Instance (Multimember Panel), Athens, 2013 *Greek Justice* 801; to humoristic designs as decorative elements of clothing, gifts and memorabilia with Judgment No. 6193/2006, Court of Appeal, Athens, 2007 *Greek Justice* 1461, because they derive from the author's personality and they present originality which consists in and is determined and evidenced by the choice of the elements they use, such as the shape and size of the designs, the colouring, movements or expressions and the conceptual content, which is mainly humorous. Protection as work of applied art was also granted to mannequins (figures for model clothing) with Judgment No. 1720/2004, Supreme Court (Penal), 2005 *Legal Tribune* 753 = 2005 *Penal Justice* 160 = 2004 *Penal Word* 2206. Also a design for a suitcase was found to be protected under copyright law because it was original due to its specific dimensions, individuality, configuration and its own new form, Judgment No. 2519/1997, Court of First Instance, Athens, 1999 *Greek Justice* 453, comment M. Marinos = 1997 *Commercial Law Review* 358, comment M. Minoudis.

94 Judgment No. 281/2005, Court of Appeal, Piraeus, 2005 *Piraeus Case Law* 174.

and a mill (souvenirs). In this case the court found that the lamps were not mere copies of traditional buildings but also reflected their author's personality by way of including elements that were attributed to their author and his own creative inspiration, mainly in the manner and details of their production, and as such were protected as works of applied art.

The common feature between works of applied art and industrial designs or models is that both involve objects of practical utility whose purpose is to serve everyday needs, and which also have an aesthetical aspect.[95] The difference – at least according to the prevalent view in the literature[96] and case law[97] – is found in the qualities of the aesthetic aspect, which in copyright law are interpreted as 'level of creativity' and in industrial property law as 'individual character'. Copyright law puts at the centre the author and her or his personality that is imprinted/stamped or reflected on her or his work. This is also the reason why a work is considered to be an intellectual creation. In industrial designs or models law, the focus is rather placed on the product, since a product is rendered aesthetically attractive with the aim to increase its marketability (besides, it is not a coincidence that copyright law refers to intellectual creations and industrial property to products).[98]

The focus of the distinction between works of applied art and industrial designs or models is creativity.[99] In order for a work of applied art to be copyright protected it needs to be original, i.e. statistically unique, and

95 Antonopoulos, *Industrial Property Law*, p. 834.

96 Marinos, *Copyright Law*, p. 94; Koumantos, *Copyright Law*, p. 126; Antonopoulos, *Industrial Property Law*, p. 835; Rokas, *Industrial Property*, p. 62; Selekos, *The Right in Industrial Design and Model*, pp. 60ff; Karagiannopoulos, comment on Judgment No. 6489/1999, Court of First Instance, Athens, 1999 *Business and Company Law* 408.

97 Judgment No. 1064/1982, Court of First Instance (Multimember Panel), Thessaloniki, 1982 *Commercial Law Review* 320; Judgment No. 220/2004, Court of Appeal, Piraeus, 2004 *Business and Company Law* 748 = 2006 *Greek Justice* 1456; Judgment No. 7518/2000, Court of First Instance (Multimember Panel), Athens, 2001 *Business and Company Law* 708 = 2001 *Greek Justice* 1442 = 2001 *Commercial Law Review* 364; and Judgment No. 2015/2010, Court of Appeal, Thessaloniki, 2011 *Commercial Law Reports* 737, comment K. Pampoukis.

98 Marinos, *Copyright Law*, p. 94; Koumantos, *Copyright Law*, p. 123; Antonopoulos, *Industrial Property Law*, p. 835; Rokas, *Industrial Property*, p. 62.

99 Rokas, *Industrial Property*, p. 62; Antonopoulos, *Industrial Property Law*, p. 834; Nikolopoulou, comment on Judgment No. 9799/2000, Court of First Instance, Athens, 2004 *Private Law Annals* 71. Judgment No. 3269/2014, Court of Appeal, Athens, 2014 *Mass Media, Information and Communications Law* 548, comment Velissaropoulou, according to which the exclusive artistic and creative level is the decisive criterion that differentiates the work of art protected under Law 2121/1993 from industrial designs, the latter being protected under Law 2417/1996 and Presidential Decree 259/1997, in the sense that it obviously cannot be considered that under the same circumstances and with the same aim no other designer-author under reasonable probability could have achieved a similar design.

present individuality or a modicum of creativity.[100] Industrial designs or models do not necessarily present creativity. The fact that the external configuration or (outer) image of industrial designs or models is aesthetically attractive does not render them an intellectual creation.

The notion of 'originality' should be distinguished from the notions of 'novelty' and 'individual character' in the same sense that works of applied art should be distinguished from industrial designs and models.[101] The notions of 'novelty' and 'individual character' are notions which are alien to copyright law in the sense that whether a particular work pre-exists or not carries no weight for copyright purposes.[102] The requirement of 'individual character' (according to Presidential Decree 259/1997) refers to whether a design differs from an existing one (identical or almost identical, i.e. different only in immaterial details). This should be irrelevant from a copyright point of view. A design may be different from an existing one but it may not reflect the author's personality and may not present a modicum of creativity. In other words, someone else under the same or similar circumstances with the same aim in mind could reach the same creative outcome (statistically unique).[103]

3.4 Conclusions

Although legislation on the protection of industrial designs and models was only introduced in Greece in 1996, industrial designs were – by and large – protected during all those years by copyright and/or unfair competition law. Yet, the absence of a tailor-made regime of protection led at the beginning (from 1920 to 1975) to a limited or inconsistent protection and from 1975 to 1996 to their overprotection.[104] In this latter period industrial designs and models were unjustifiably placed in a particularly favourable position compared to other types

[100] Under similar conditions and with the same aim no other author could in reasonable probability have created a similar work: see above, n. 74.

[101] See Karagiannopoulos, comment on Judgment No. 6489/1999, Court of First Instance, 1999 *Business and Company Law* 409.

[102] Apostolopoulos, comment on Judgment No. 2398/2008, Court of Appeal, Athens, 2009 *Business and Company Law* 572.

[103] Koriatopoulou-Aggeli, comment on Judgment No. 4627/2012, Court of First Instance (Multimember Panel), 2013 *Mass Media, Information and Communications Law* 229.

[104] Koumantos, 'The Greek Legislation on Copyright', 160; P. Selekos, 'Die Zukunft des Designschutzes in Europa der Sicht des griechischen Rechts' (1998) *Gewerblicher Rechtsschutz und Urheberrecht, Internationaler Teil* 371; Selekos, *The Right in Industrial Design and Model*, p. 52; Papadrosou-Arhaniotaki, 'Models and Designs of Utility', 311; Minoudis, 'The Protection of Industrial Designs and Models', p. 90; I. Kakavouli, *The Conditions of Protection of Industrial Designs in the EEC Members* (Athens, 1981), p. 51. See a similar approach in Judgment No. 3599/1974, Court of First Instance, Athens, 1974 *Legal Tribune* 1086.

of works or subject-matter.[105] In fact their protection was on many occasions considerably higher compared to the one they would be entitled to if special legislation on industrial designs and models were in place. This was – from a systematic point of view – wrong.[106] Yet, even during this period, the case law was not uniform as to how designs and models were protected.

In addition, the protection of industrial designs and models (without any formalities) by copyright law did not provide for speed and security in the transactions as would have been the case with tailor-made legislation. It has been argued[107] that, on top of it, the duration of protection (afforded to them by copyright) was excessive and did not sit well with the rights' economic purpose since industrial designs and models relate to products with short market life.[108] Besides, the pressure exercised through the provision of the Berne Convention (Paris Act) (Article 2(7) third subpara.) aimed at exactly that: to oblige States to introduce special legislation on industrial designs and models that would meet their needs and those of the market; not afford them (copyright) protection on more favourable terms and conditions compared to other types of works or subject-matter.

Special legislation was finally enacted in 1996[109] and 1997.[110] This legislation affords protection to industrial designs and models and regulates the relationship between this protection and copyright law by establishing a system of 'partial cumulation'. According to it, designs and models may be protected both as industrial designs and models and by copyright if the conditions for each type of protection are met. This is assessed on a case-by-case basis. Yet, the courts seem to have difficulty distinguishing between the conditions of protection for each type of rights. In fact (by reason of the fact that designs – either as industrial designs or as works of applied art – place the emphasis on the looks and

[105] Liakopoulos, *Industrial Property*, p. 277.

[106] It has been argued that the extension of copyright protection to industrial designs and models downgrades the notion of art and intellectual creativity given the fact that industrial designs and models should only be protected by copyright in exceptional cases and not by definition. See Papadrosou-Arhaniotaki, 'Models and Designs of Utility', 311.

[107] Kakavouli, *The Conditions of Protection of Industrial Designs*, p. 51.

[108] According to Greek unfair competition law in force at that time, claims for omission or damages were barred after a period of six months from the time when the person entitled to such a claim gained knowledge of the act and of the identity of the party liable and, in any case, three years from the time when the act was committed. Regarding claims for damages, time did not start to run before the damage incurred (Article 19 Law 146/1914).

[109] Law 2417/1996; see above under n. 59.

[110] Presidential Decree 259/1997; see above under n. 61.

appearance of a work/product), they seem to confuse the notion of 'originality' with the notions of 'novelty' and 'individual character'. Courts seem in most cases to examine these notions in such a manner and form that they either reject both types of protection altogether or accept them both.

The difference between industrial property law and copyright law on this aspect is a qualitative one. It is not that in any of the two types of protection additional criteria are at stake but rather that the subject-matter is assessed on different grounds. From that point of view there is a difference in the value judgements made and in the nature/content of the criteria applied.

The point of friction or confusion seems to be that according to industrial property law a design needs to possess an 'individual character'.[111] In fact, in Article 12(4) and (5) Presidential Decree 259/1997 it is provided that '4. [a] design or model shall be considered to have an individual character if the overall impression it produces on the informed user differs from the overall impression produced on such a user by any design or model which has been made available to the public before the date of filing of the application for registration, or, if priority is claimed, the date of priority. 5. In assessing the individual character the degree of freedom of the designer in developing the design or the model in relation to the technical requirements shall be taken into consideration.' On the basis of this provision, courts focused on whether a design or model is different from existing ones. That means that the overall impression that it creates to an informed user should differ from those created by any other designs or models in the area[112] (which, of course, have become available to the public before the date of

[111] Directive 98/71 on industrial designs requires that industrial designs registered in a country in accordance with the Directive also be eligible for protection under the copyright law of that country. However, the conditions under which this protection is conferred, 'including the level of originality required', are to be determined by each State (Article 17 – Relationship to copyright: 'A design protected by a design right registered in or in respect of a Member State in accordance with this Directive shall also be eligible for protection under the law of copyright of that State as from the date on which the design was created or fixed in any form. The extent to which, and the conditions under which, such a protection is conferred, including the level of originality required, shall be determined by each Member State').

[112] 'In order for a design to be considered to have individual character, the overall impression which that design produces on the informed user must be different from that produced on such a user not by a combination of features taken in isolation and drawn from a number of earlier designs, but by one or more earlier designs, taken individually': Case C-345/13, *Karen Millen Fashions Ltd* v. *Dunnes Stores and Dunnes Stores (Limerick) Ltd* (Judgment of 19 June 2014), [2014] Bus LR 756, available at eur-lex.europa.eu/legal-content/EN/TXT/?qid=1462906626743&uri=CELEX:62013CJ0345.

applying for registration). It has been argued that the criterion of 'individual character' complements and further specifies that of novelty.[113]

The differences between existing designs and the one at issue are assessed on an *ad hoc* basis taking into account the characteristics of each case. The comparison is not one of quantity but rather one of quality. It is not how many differences exist between the designs (in terms of quantity) but rather a general assessment of the overall image and features of the design at issue.[114] It is this overall impression that is produced, which in fact is nothing more than a value/subjective judgement, that is conclusive as to whether a design possesses an individual character or not.[115] In other words, it is not the number of differences that counts but rather the overall impression that is created on the basis of those differences. This can also be derived from Article 27 Presidential Decree 259/1997, which concerns the scope of protection and provides that '[t]he protection conferred by a design or model right shall include any design or model which produces on the informed user a *similar* impression'.[116] In that sense the design at issue should not be similar to existing designs. It should be different. And, although this is not expressly provided in the law, the difference should subsist in the outer image, the looks and aesthetics of the product,[117] and should be such that it makes the product appealing to the consumers.[118]

In assessing the 'individual character' of a design or model the degree of freedom of the designer in developing the design or the model in relation to the technical requirements is taken into consideration. In other words, if a design or model could be developed in one way only that is dictated by the needs of the utility, function or technical specifications of the particular product or statutory requirements, it is not considered to possess an individual character. Those constraints result in a standardisation of certain features, which will

[113] Judgment No. 1044/2011, Court of Appeal, Thessaloniki, 2012 *Commercial Law Reports* 412.

[114] Case C-345/13, *Karen Millen Fashions Ltd* v. *Dunnes Stores and Dunnes Stores (Limerick) Ltd* (Judgment of 19 June 2014), [2014] Bus LR 756.

[115] Judgment No. 42143/2007, Court of First Instance (Multimember Panel), Thessaloniki, 2008 *Business and Company Law* 320 = 2008 *Greek Justice* 308.

[116] Emphasis added. [117] Rokas, *Industrial Property*, p. 75.

[118] Selekos, 'The Substantial Conditions of Industrial Design and Models Protection', 642ff; Judgment No. 1044/2011, Court of Appeal, Thessaloniki, 2012 *Commercial Law Reports* 412; Judgment No. 19827/2010, Court of First Instance (Multimember Panel), Thessaloniki, 2010 *Business and Company Law* 1041; Judgment No. 42143/2007, Court of First Instance (Multimember Panel), Thessaloniki, 2008 *Business and Company Law* 320 = 2008 *Greek Justice* 308.

thus be common to the designs applied to the product concerned.[119] According to the General Court (Case T-337/12):

> the greater the designer's freedom in developing a design, the less likely it is that minor differences between the designs at issue will be sufficient to produce a different overall impression on the informed user. Conversely, the more restricted the designer's freedom in developing a design, the more likely minor differences between the designs at issue will be sufficient to produce a different overall impression on the informed user. Accordingly, if the designer enjoys a high degree of freedom in developing a design, this reinforces the conclusion that the designs which do not have significant differences produce the same overall impression on the informed user.[120]

Although the criterion of 'individual character' seems akin to that of 'originality', this is not always so. In fact, in industrial property law the designer needs to exercise a degree of freedom in relation to the product's technical requirements. This degree of freedom may translate (at least) in small variations with regard to existing designs. It, however, may not present any creativity in the sense that although the designer may have some free choices these choices were not necessarily creative ones (as the notion of originality requires: 'free and creative choices') and he or she may not have stamped the design with his or her 'personal touch'. Still, in this case, though, the design may produce a different overall impression from existing designs. From this point of view, a design may have an 'individual character' but may not qualify as 'original'. Yet, if the design is 'original', it will certainly also have an 'individual character'. That does not necessarily mean that it will also be 'new'. In our view in most cases it will also qualify as 'new' as it will qualitatively differ from existing designs in the area. From this aspect, on most occasions an original design will

[119] Case T-337/12, *El Hogar Perfecto del Siglo XXI, SL* v. *Office for Harmonisation in the Internal Market (Trade Marks and Designs) (OHIM)* (Judgment of 21 November 2013), para. 32, [2014] ECDR 1; Case T-11/08, *Kwang Yang Motor* v. *OHIM – Honda Giken Kogyo (Internal combustion engine)* (Judgment of 9 September 2011) (EU: T: 2011: 447), para. 32 and the case law cited; Cases T-83/11 and T-84/11, *Antrax It Srl* v. *Office for Harmonisation in the Internal Market (Trade Marks and Designs) (OHIM)* (Judgment of 13 November 2012) (EU: T: 2012: 592). Rokas, *Industrial Property*, p. 76.

[120] Case T-337/12, *El Hogar Perfecto del Siglo XXI, SL* v. *Office for Harmonisation in the Internal Market (Trade Marks and Designs) (OHIM)* (Judgment of 21 November 2013), para. 33, [2014] ECDR 1; Case T-11/08, *Kwang Yang Motor* v. *OHIM – Honda Giken Kogyo (Internal combustion engine)* (Judgment of 9 September 2011) (EU: T: 2011: 447), para. 32; Cases T-83/11 and T-84/11, *Antrax It Srl* v. *Office for Harmonisation in the Internal Market (Trade Marks and Designs) (OHIM)* (Judgment of 13 November 2012) (EU: T: 2012: 592). Liakopoulos, *Industrial Property*, pp. 30ff.

also qualify as an industrial design, whilst the opposite may not always be the case.

Given that the notion of 'individual character' has been harmonised in the EU (defined in the EU Directive on industrial designs and elaborated upon by the Court of Justice of the European Union), and given also that in the light of the Court of Justice's recent case law this is the case for the notion of originality in copyright, too, we can argue that Article 17 Directive 98/71 on industrial designs is no longer applicable with regard to its second subparagraph and in particular with regard to the conditions and level of originality (i.e. 'The extent to which, and the conditions under which, such a protection is conferred, including the level of originality required, shall be determined by each Member State').[121] Member States can no longer determine any level of originality since there is only one level which applies throughout the EU, that of a work being its 'author's own intellectual creation'.[122] Since, according to the CJEU's case law, originality forms the sole requirement for the protection of a work, designs are only copyright protected if they are considered original as originality is defined in EU law (i.e. the author should have free and creative choices and should have stamped the work with his 'personal touch'). That notion of 'originality', as explained above, cannot and should not automatically coincide with those of 'novelty' and 'individual character'. From that point of view, Member States are only obliged to protect industrial designs and models by copyright insofar as they are original. If they are not, they cannot (according to the EU) be protected by copyright.[123]

From the above, it can be argued that EU law imposes a system of partial cumulation rather than full cumulation; and that is the case because there are differences between the requirements of protection for each type of right, as explained. Full cumulation would lead to the unjustified protection for a number of designs by extending the

[121] See also Recital 8, 98/71 Directive. This is also applicable for the term of protection. See in this respect Case C-168/09, *Flos SpA* v. *Semeraro Case Famiglia SpA* (Judgment of 27 January 2011) [2011] ECR I-181.

[122] 2006/116/EC Directive of the European Parliament and of the Council of 12 December 2006 on the term of protection of copyright and certain related rights, OJ 2006 L 372/12, Article 6; Council 91/250/EEC Directive of 14 May 1991 on the legal protection of computer programs, OJ 1991 L 122/42, Article 1(3); 96/9/EC Directive of the European Parliament and of the Council of 11 March 1996 on the legal protection of databases, OJ 1996 L 77/20, Article 3(1).

[123] The same approach with regard this time to the term of copyright protection for designs is taken in *Flos* (Case C-168/09, *Flos SpA* v. *Semeraro Case Famiglia SpA* (Judgment of 27 January 2011) [2011] ECR I-181). According to it, no variations on the basis of Member States' national laws are valid insofar as they contradict notions that have been harmonised under EU law (see para. 39 *Flos*).

scope of copyright protection to non-original subject-matter and would necessarily lead to overprotection. Extending copyright protection to non-original matter is something that is not allowed under EU law.[124] In addition, it would also unjustifiably give rise to competition law issues.

[124] C-30/14, *Ryanair Ltd* v. *PR Aviation BV* (Judgment of 15 January 2015) [2015] ECDR 13.

4 The Copyright/Design Interface in Scandinavia

*Jens Schovsbo and Morten Rosenmeier**

Table 4.1 *Chronological table of legislation and statistics*

Period	System	Interface	Supplementary information	Country	Design applica-tions	Average annual numbers of appli-cations	Design registra-tions	Average annual numbers of appli-cations
1741–1904/1907	Copyright didn't accept works of applied art No Design Act	Not relevant	Sweden and Norway: Similar for copyright. Swedish Design Act 1899 (ornaments in the metal industry)	NO DK SE FI	No Data No Data No Data No Data		No Data No Data No Data No Data	
1905/1908–1960	Design Act 1905 Copyright Act 1908	Partial cumulation	Similar in Sweden. For Norway: Demarcation. (Data from 1911 onwards. No app data for NO in 1945)	NO DK SE FI	43,134 85,085 6,388 –	880 1,702 128 –	59,827 80,689 3,385 –	1,197 1,614 68 –
1961–2009	Copyright Act 1961 Design Act 1970 Copyright Act 1995 Design Act of 2000	Full cumulation	Sweden coming closer to full cumulation. Norway retains partial cumulation.	NO DK SE FI	43,738 48,295 91,708 30,087	893 986 2,038 813	30,501 45,908 63,658 23,606	743 937 1,415 638
2009–2015	CJEU Judgments in Infopaq (combined with *Flos* in 2012)	Full cumulation (?)	Full cumulation (?)	NO DK SE FI	5,600 818 2,564 1,014	1,120 164 513 203	3,776 818 2,051 952	756 164 410 190

* Professor, Dr Jur., PhD Jens Schovsbo and Professor PhD Morten Rosenmeier both at the Centre for Information and Innovation Law (CIIR) at the University of Copenhagen, Denmark.

4.1 Introduction

The base-line for describing the relationship between copyright and design law in the Nordic countries was established with the passing of common Design Acts in 1970 (Denmark, Norway and Sweden) and 1971 (Finland).[1] The legislative process that led to these Nordic Design Acts was initiated in the 1960s when a joint inter-Nordic committee was founded.[2] A decade prior to the initiative in design law a reform of the Nordic copyright legislation was initiated.[3] Also this eventually led to closely coordinated Nordic Copyright Acts. For these reasons the legal landscape in the field of copyright and design law is quite similar in the Nordic countries. As will be seen, however, important differences also exist (or have existed) regarding the policing of the relationship between design law and copyright law.

The chapter uses the Nordic design law reform as its *pièce de résistance* and will thus focus on the development after 1970. It opens, however, by briefly describing the situation prior to the pan-Nordic Design Acts, which was characterised by national and uncoordinated solutions. After this follows an account for the development after 1970 and leading to the present, including the latest period of EU harmonisation. We will use Danish law as our starting point but will also include accounts for

1 Denmark (Lov om mønstre No. 218 of 27 May 1970), Finland (Mönsterrättslag No. 221/1971 of 12 March 1971), Norway (Lov om mønster No. 33 of 29 May 1970) and Sweden (Mönsterskyddslag 1970:485).

2 See for Denmark the *Parliamentary Report leading to the Danish Design Act* No. 417/1966, 34 (Betænkning 417/1966 vedrørende en ny dansk lov om mønstre udarbejdet af den af handelsministeriet den 5.2.1960 nedsatte kommission i samarbejde med tilsvarende finske, norske og svenske kommissioner ('mønsterlovsbetænkningen')). The Report is available (in Danish) at www.foxylex.dk/media/betaenkninger/Betaenkning_vedroerende_en_ny_dansk_lov_om_moenstre.pdf. The Nordic countries set up a joint committee and on this basis national reports were drafted. See for an account of the discussions from a Swedish perspective (and in English), S. Ljungman, 'The Scandinavian Approach in Design Protection – Aims and Outcome – in Comparison with the New Benelux Legislation 117–128', in H. C. Jehoram (ed.), *Design Protection* (Leyden: Sijthoff, 1976), p. 117 and S. Ljungman, 'The New Nordic Design Legislation Under Comparative Aspects' (1973) *International Review of Intellectual Property and Competition Law* 336–51 at 350–1. A recent account for the Scandinavian experience based on the Nordic Design Acts is given by J. Schovsbo and S. Teilmann-Lock, 'We Wanted More Arne Jacobsen Chairs but All We Got Was Boxes – Experiences from the Protection of Designs in Scandinavia from 1970 till the Directive' (2016) 47(4) *International Review of Industrial Property and Competition Law* 418–37.

3 See for Denmark the Parliamentary Report *Lov om Ophavsretten til Litterære og Kunstneriske Værker*, 1951, available at www.statensnet.dk/betaenkninger/0601-0800/0621-1951/0621-1951_pdf/printversion_0621-1951-u.pdf.

developments in the other Scandinavian countries (i.e. Norway and Sweden).[4]

4.1.1 A Note on Terminology

In the following we will apply the specific terminology developed for the present project, i.e.:

- ***demarcation:*** If something is protected by design law then it cannot be protected by copyright or vice versa;
- ***partial cumulation:*** The middle between demarcation and (full) cumulation (below). Thus both copyright and design right can subsist if the protection requirements are fulfilled but either or both laws (i.e. the Copyright Act or Design Act, or else the case law) has or have one or more mechanisms to regulate the interface;
- ***full cumulation:*** Both copyright and design right can subsist if the protection requirements are fulfilled and the two laws apply in tandem whether it raises regime clashes and/or overprotection, or not.

4.2 History of the Copyright/Design Interface in Denmark (Scandinavia)

4.2.1 First Period: Before 1970: Partial Cumulation (Denmark and Sweden) and Demarcation (Norway)

The acceptance in copyright of works of 'design'/'applied art' came gradually to the Scandinavian countries where copyright at first was limited to printed matters.[5] In Denmark a first movement towards a broadening of copyright's reach could be detected in the 1864 Act on

[4] The Nordic countries of Finland and Iceland are excluded because of the languages. Denmark and Sweden are both members of the EU whereas Norway is a member of the EEA. For all practical purposes the EU legislation and the case law from the CJEU in design law and copyright are binding also for Norway.

[5] In Denmark copyright protection for printers and publishers in their prints goes back to an Ordinance from 7 January 1741. The protection for prints was extended by Lov om Eftertryk of 29 December 1857. See generally on Nordic law in these regards M. Levin, *Formskydd* (Stockholm: LiberFörlag, 1984) and M. Rosenmeier, *Værkslæren i ophavsretten* (Copenhagen: Jurist- og Økonomforbundets Forlag, 2001). For a recent and detailed study in English of the historical developments in Danish law, see S. Teilmann-Lock, *The Object of Copyright: A Conceptual History of Originals and Copies in Literature, Art and Design* (Abingdon: Routledge, 2016), e.g. pp. 18ff.

the copying of artworks[6] which granted exclusivity to manufacturers and craftsmen against the use of their protected works of 'pure art' (paintings or drawings, etc.) as decoration on articles (e.g. as a print on a handkerchief). In 1908 the Act on Authorial and Artistic Rights was amended to acknowledge works of applied art as being copyright protected, even in cases where the works were mass-produced.[7] Despite the legislative mandate, Danish courts continued to regard works of applied art with some scepticism and evidently found it hard to get used to the fact that objects which were both mass-produced and serving a practical purpose could be considered artistic.[8] Thus it was not until 1961 that the category of 'works of applied art' was recognised in the Danish Copyright Act alongside the types of works traditionally protected.[9] A reluctant attitude towards giving copyright protection to applied art was also seen in the other Scandinavian countries. Most notably, in *Sweden* works of applied art were not accepted in copyright until 1926 and then only granted a

[6] Lov of 31 March 1864 om Eftergørelse af Kunstarbejder (which amended and extended the protection granted to 'artists' (apart from writers and producers of prints) by Ordinance of 13 December 1837).

[7] Lov 39 of 28 February 1908 om ændret Affattelse af § 24 i Lov om Forfatterret og Kunstnerret, 29 March 1904. According to the amendment 'original artistic works intended to be prototypes for industrial art and handicrafts, as well as the *objects* created on the basis of such works, are to be considered works of art whether or not these are produced individually or in a larger quantity ...' (italics added). See Teilmann-Lock, above note 5, 129ff (who has also translated the provision, ibid. 129). This system was upheld by amendments of the Act in 1912 and 1933, Teilmann-Lock, ibid., pp. 132ff.

[8] The introduction of the protection of applied art into the Copyright Act in 1908 was the reaction to a Supreme Court decision in (1907) *Ugeskrift for Retsvæsen* 619 which had denied protection of a blue fluted porcelain coffee pot since this was – according to the Court – 'a common industrial item whose main function is to serve a practical purpose': see T. Lund, *Loven om Forfatterret of Kunstnerret af 26. April 1933* (Copenhagen: G. E. C. Gads Forlag, 1933), p. 19. Even after 1908, Danish courts were somewhat reluctant to grant copyright protection to works of applied art, most markedly in three notorious decisions in (1935) *Ugeskrift for Retsvæsen* 692, 695 and 699, which denied protection to Mart Stam and Marcel Breuer's Freischwinger chairs and tables. A sceptical attitude towards copyright protection of applied art was also reflected in the decisions reported in (1946) *Ugeskrift for Retsvæsen* 35 (shop dummies), (1956) *Ugeskrift for Retsvæsen* 237 (bread slicer which the Supreme Court characterised as being 'a mere tool by which the artistic shaping of a part of the tool was of totally minor importance in relation to the practical purpose'), (1958) *Ugeskrift for Retsvæsen* 1211 (blouses denied protection, i.a. since one of them was mass-produced) and (1960) *Ugeskrift for Retsvæsen* 762 (lamp serving a 'merely practical' purpose denied protection). Protection was granted in (1931) *Ugeskrift for Retsvæsen* 376 (Poul Henningsen's 'PH-'lamps), (1944) *Ugeskrift for Retsvæsen* 1185 (jewellery), (1948) *Ugeskrift for Retsvæsen* 883 (rattan cane tea table) and (1960) *Ugeskrift for Retsvæsen* 483 Ø (Wegner chair). For further reading see Rosenmeier (above, note 5), p. 244.

[9] Lov 158 of 31 May 1961, and on the development in practice against this basis, see below, 4.2.2.

ten-year term of protection.[10] In *Norway* applied art did not get copyright protection until 1930.[11]

In *Denmark* a *sui generis* Design Act was enacted in 1905.[12] The scope of the Act was very broad and allowed for the protection of 'designs' ('mønstre') relating to the outer appearance of industrially produced items ('Forbilleder for Industrifrembringelserns ydre Udstyr og ydre Skikkelse') (para. 1) which were novel (in the patent law sense, i.e. 'global and objective') or 'characteristic' ('Ejendommelige') (para. 4). Protection could be extended to fifteen years and was dependent upon registration. The examination of the Office was limited to formalities and *ordre public* and morality. Despite its neutral starting point, the development in case

10 See Levin (above, note 5), p. 288 with references and specifying that for works which had been made public the term was calculated on the date of the publication. Otherwise it was calculated according to the year of the death of the author. The Swedish jurisprudence is modest compared to the Danish one. A restrictive attitude was reflected in (1935) *Nytt Juridiskt Arkiv* 712 (Freischwinger chairs) and (1943) *Nytt Juridiskt Arkiv* 547 (shop dummy heads which were found to be 'mere industrial products' rather than artistic). On the other hand, protection was granted in (1931) *Nytt Juridiskt Arkiv* 506 (engraved drinking glasses). From the late 1950s the Swedish jurisdiction began to reflect a more relaxed and liberal administration of the requirements for protection of applied art. See the decisions of the Swedish Supreme Court in (1958) *Nytt Juridiskt Arkiv* 68 (arm chair), (1962) *Nytt Juridiskt Arkiv* 750 (wooden shelves in a simple steel rack) and (1964) *Nytt Juridiskt Arkiv* 532 (simple, round mirror). Also the so-called *Svensk Forms Opinionsnämnd* – i.e. a private tribunal under the association *Svensk Form* (previously *Svenska Slöjdföreningen*) which gives expert opinions on the protectability of applied art for use in pending cases – applied the requirements for protection in a liberal manner. See the opinions of the tribunal in *Upphovsrättsligt skydd för brukskonst 1954–63* (Stockholm, 1965), p. 62 (plastic milk pail), p. 78 (plastic salad cutlery), p. 170 (glass piggy bank). For further reading see Rosenmeier (above, note 5), p. 237.

11 B. Stuevold Lassen and A. Stenvik, *Designrett – En innføring*, Cappelen (Oslo, 2006), p. 16 and Levin (above, note 5), pp. 290ff (pointing out that the Norwegian Copyright Act from 1893 would seem not to have covered works which were used industrially). See also B. Wyller, 'Om Forholdet mellem Kunstnerret og Mønsterret i Norge' (1936) *Nordiskt immateriellt rättsskydd* 2. The Norwegian jurisprudence of the time is, however, sparse and consists to a great extent of decisions from municipal courts. The cases reflect a restrictive administration of the requirements for protection and only very few Norwegian court decisions gave copyright protection to works of applied art. The Norwegian Supreme Court granted protection in a decision printed in (1963) *Nordiskt immateriellt rättsskydd* 204 concerning a combined sofa and worktable made by the famous Danish architect Wegner. Also, protection was granted by the Municipal Court of Oslo in (1968) *Nordiskt immateriellt rättsskydd* 227 (wrought iron keyhole furnishings) and (1968) *Nordiskt immateriellt rättsskydd* 323 (toy troll). On the other hand, protection was denied by Jæren Herredsret in (1957) *Nordiskt immateriellt rättsskydd* 225 (two knitting patterns, a knitted sweater and a diagram) and by the municipal court of Oslo in (1958) *Nordiskt immateriellt rättsskydd* 125 (architect-designed table), (1961) *Nordiskt immateriellt rättsskydd* 196 (upholstery fabric design) and (1967) *Nordiskt immateriellt rättsskydd* 440 (carpets).

12 Lov 107 of 1 April 1905. The literature on the Act is very limited. See for an overview J. Schovsbo and N. H. Svendsen, *Designret*, 2nd edn (Jurist- og Økonomforbundets Forlag, 2013), pp. 30ff.

law led to a limitation of the applicability of the Act to designs with an aesthetic effect or that were designed according to aesthetic intentions (so-called 'smagsmønstre' ('Geschmackmuster')).[13] Purely functional designs, in other words, could not be protected under the Design Act despite the neutral and broad wording of paragraph 1 of that Act. At the time of the Nordic design reform, *Sweden* had a Design Act from 1899. This, however, was rudimentary and limited to ornaments within the metal industry. *Norway* had a Design Act from 1910. The Norwegian Act provided for a protection of up to fifteen years after the first registration. The Act applied a neutral definition of protectable design and even products whose shape depended on functional concerns could be protected provided that they were novel (patent style). The examination was limited to the formal requirements and *ordre public* and morality (and did not include novelty).[14]

As far as the relationship between copyright and design law is concerned *Denmark* has traditionally not restricted access to copyright protection for products which were also protected as designs, i.e. a principle of cumulation applied. A specific rule to that effect was found in the Design Act 1905 (see para. 31) and in 1961 it was clarified by the enactment of a corresponding rule in the Copyright Act.[15] The position in *Sweden* (and in Finland) was similar.[16] In *Norway*, however, the Design Act from 1910 contained a rule which limited the protection for works of applied art which had also been registered as designs.[17] For such works copyright could not be invoked against 'industrial use' after the lapse of the fifteen-year protection term. For other uses the right holder could invoke copyright in the full term (at the time fifty years p.m.a.).

Summing up: In *Denmark* and *Sweden* double protection was allowed but for works of applied art the threshold in copyright was higher than for other types of works: partial cumulation. In *Norway* a rule based on demarcation applied.

[13] See Olsen J, 'Nogle spørgsmål om mønsterbeskyttelse og illoyal konkurrence' (1960) *Nordiskt immateriellt rättsskydd* 227 and Schovsbo and Svendsen, *Designret*.

[14] The *Parliamentary Report leading to the Danish Design Act*, pp. 25ff.

[15] See para. 10 in Lov 158 of 31 May 1961. According to the preparatory work, this rule merely clarified the existing position. Similarly, the *Report of the Nordic Design Law Committee*, 91.

[16] See the *Parliamentary Report leading to the Danish Design Act*, 92ff (remarking *inter alia* that because of the very limited coverage of the Swedish 1899 Design Act the issue of double protection had had no practical importance).

[17] See the *Parliamentary Report leading to the Danish Design Act*, pp. 91ff. The Norwegian position was abandoned with the adoption of the Design Act in 1970.

4.2.2 Second Period: 1970–2001: Full Cumulation (Denmark) and Partial Cumulation (Norway and Sweden)

The common Design Acts marked a new beginning for the protection of designs in the Nordic countries. They aimed to protect what was perceived as being the 'modern design', i.e. the so-called 'functional design' where – as it is often said – 'form follows function'. As described above, design which was shaped to perform a function would normally not qualify for protection: *neither* under the Danish Design Act of 1905 *nor* under copyright. For this reason it was to fill what was perceived as a 'legal void' in the IPR-protection system that the Design Acts were put in place.

For the copyright/design law interface Denmark and Sweden retained the principle of cumulation and this principle was also adopted in Norway.

4.2.2.1 The Design Acts

The Nordic Design Acts were based on a full 'patent approach': to obtain protection it was thus necessary to submit an application to a Registration Authority (i.e. the national Patent and Trademark Offices (PTO) of the individual countries) and the Office carried out a full investigation, i.e. both of the formal and of the substantive requirements. Protection could be extended up to fifteen years. The Acts defined the object of protection as 'a model for a commodity's appearance or for an ornament'. The definition is neutral as it was the intention to allow protection of the appearance of purely functional designs. Design was not protected in 'the abstract' but only against the use of similar design in regard to goods which incorporate the design or goods of a similar kind. Specific limitations were contained for prior use (para. 6) and repair of aircrafts (para. 7). A narrowly defined (and never relied upon) rule on compulsory licensing was provided for in cases where a third party had 'very particular reasons' and had no knowledge of the application and, moreover, had not reasonably been able to acquire such knowledge (para. 28).

In the examination of an application for registration of a design, the PTO should examine whether the conditions for registration of the design were fulfilled, including the requirements of novelty and 'essential difference'. In principle, the search was to include all information available to the PTO. However, in practice it was limited to design registrations in force, applications and previous registrations which had been cancelled within the past five years. These limitations obviously affected the validity of the registrations negatively.

Interestingly, despite their (almost) identical starting points, registration practices in the different countries did not develop in the same way. The most stringent requirements are usually said to have developed in Sweden and the mildest in Denmark.[18] National differences were fuelled by the lack of clarity in the Acts as well as uncertainties as to the extact role of the Patent and Trademark Offices and of the examination procedure as such. This point may be illustrated by the discussions regarding so-called 'trivial designs': whether such designs were to be rejected when the offices were unable to point to specific known designs. While discussions were related to differences in the wordings of the Nordic reports,[19] they also had a principal dimension, viz. the role and function of the offices as either 'gate keepers' or as 'registrars'.[20] The Swedish[21] (and the Finnish[22]) position was that the Offices were to reject trivial design even though no specific older design could be pointed out. At first this stance was rejected in Denmark: it was not considered to be appropriate for the Patent and Trademark Office to deny protection to designs against which no protests had been raised. More generally, as was maintained, it had not been the intention of the registration system to keep invalid designs out of the register.[23] Eventually, however, the position in Denmark changed in the Swedish (Finnish) direction.[24] Overall, however, the Nordic Design Acts

[18] M. Levin, 'Die Zukunft des Designschutzes in Europa aus der Sicht des Rechts der nordischen Staaten' (1988) *GRUR-Int.* 371–7 at pp. 372ff and G. O. Hæreid, 'Skildnadskravet i mønsterretten' (1995) *Nordiskt immateriellt rättsskydd* 550–94 at 586ff. See from Danish practice notably the decision from the Maritime and Commercial Court reported in (1990) *Ugeskrift for Retsvæsen* 334 upholding the registration of the design for a T-shape diaper. Even though the court acknowledged that the shape was largely limited by technical and economic considerations resulting from production, the design was found to be sufficiently different. In Norway the similar design had been rejected: Hæreid, ibid., 587.

[19] According to the Danish and Swedish reports the requirement of 'essential difference' implied that designs which were 'ordinary' (Danish: 'helt almindelige'; Swedish: 'banale') did not live up to the requirements. The Norwegian Report was silent on this.

[20] Generally Levin (above, note 5), pp. 339ff.

[21] Ljungman (above, note 2) (1973), p. 343, and S. Ljungman, 'Mönsterlagen i praxis' (1977) *Nordiskt immateriellt rättsskydd* 42, 47ff, G. Moore, 'Första året med mönsterskyddslagen' (1972) *Nordiskt immateriellt rättsskydd* 125 at 132ff, G. Moore, 'Mönsterskyddslagens skillnadskrav' (1973) *Nordiskt immateriellt rättsskydd* 40ff.

[22] Hæreid (above, note 18), p. 587.

[23] R. Carlsen, 'Skal der indføres et banalitetsbegreb i nordisk mønsterret?' (1974) *Nordiskt immateriellt rättsskydd* 158–63 at 160ff (also pointing out that determining what is 'banal' is very complicated and far from clear). See also Levin (above, note 5), 340 (in support of the Danish and Norwegian positions and pointing out that in practice no major differences existed).

[24] See the decision from the Board of Appeal of 25 September 1989 in case M 2/86 and Schovsbo and Svendsen (above, note 12), p. 89. For Norway the position in practice came close to that in the other countries: see Hæreid (above, note 18), pp. 557ff. Whereas the design protection was generally seen as being inadequate and to lead to underprotection, the competition law concerns in relation to spare parts were identified almost from

have left remarkably little trace in case law.[25] In Denmark merely two examples of successful infringement cases were reported in the entire thirty-year history of the Act.[26]

4.2.2.2 Copyright

As explained above, it was a starting point for the common Design Act initiative that the overlap between copyright and design law was slim because works which were shaped to perform a technical function would often not pass the threshold for copyright. A similar position had been expressed in the 1950s when a reform of the Nordic copyright legislation was initiated.[27]

For *Denmark*, the sceptical attitude towards copyright protection of applied art was softened, however, by the time the proposal for a Copyright Act had made its way through the legislative process. In the Danish Parliamentary Report from 1960, which formed the basis of the Copyright Act of 1961, it was thus specified that works of applied art (which were at the same time recognised as a class of works alongside copyright's traditional work categories) were to be protected as first amongst equals viz. according to the 'normal standards', i.e. those which applied to all other types of works.[28] It was clearly the intention of the legislator to emphasise that the mere fact that functional considerations had shaped the product – even to a substantial degree – should not

the outset. The committees did not pay much attention to the issue. No specific limitation for forms 'dictated by function' were instituted since the monopoly situation was considered as being too unlikely to occur for specific regulation to be adopted. See on spare parts, Schovsbo J, *Grænsefladespørgsmål mellem immaterialretten og konkurrenceretten* (Copenhagen: Jurist- og Økonomforbundets Forlag, 1996), pp. 178ff (pointing out that spare parts were being protected and that requirements were very low).

[25] Schovsbo and Teilmann-Lock, above, note 2.

[26] I.e. the decision from the Maritime and Commercial Court reported in (1990) *Nordiskt immateriellt rättskydd* 269ff and the decision from the Western Court of Appeal reported in (1996) *Nordiskt immateriellt rättskydd* 335ff. See Schovsbo and Svendsen (above, note 12), p. 38. For the other Nordic countries the experiences were equally limited.

[27] See for Denmark the Parliamentary Report *Lov om Ophavsretten til Litterære og Kunstneriske Værker*, 1951, available at www.statensnet.dk/betaenkninger/0601-0800/0621-1951/0621-1951_pdf/printversion_0621-1951-u.pdf. Among other things the report explained that according to court practice the distinction between works worthy of copyright protection and works which would have to settle for design protection depended on the works' aesthetic value.

[28] The Parliamentary Report, *Folketingstidende* 1960–1961, Till. B 628–9 ('Emphasis ought to be on whether the article is an artistic creation which fulfils the usual requirements for a work as defined by the law. In that case it ought to be protected without taking into account its practical purpose even when the consideration of the functionally appropriate has had a decisive role in the shaping of the article').

exclude copyright protection.[29] The reception by legal theory and courts of these (far from crystal clear) remarks left a somewhat murky picture. Following the Act the basic test for copyright protection was that the work should both be 'artistic' and 'original'. It was implied that the works should be 'new to the author' (i.e. not copied) and have a certain element of 'novelty and independence'. There was agreement, however, that this did not imply a certain 'artistic quality' and that creative effort should not be judged against a quantitative basis. Some level of 'personal effort' was required and the mere 'sweat on the brow' or technical assistance was not enough. The precise content of the abovementioned principles is not just difficult to describe on paper. They were also difficult for the courts to apply, and this resulted in a jurisprudence in which the results would often be difficult to predict. Basically, however, under the Copyright Act of 1961 and till the onset of the EU harmonisation (below), the Danish courts applied fairly moderate originality requirements in cases concerning works of applied art.[30] Danish courts have also consistently decided the copyright cases on the merits of the Copyright Act and have in no instance stated that the originality requirement had been affected because of the Design Act of 1970. In practice the decisive element in many copyright cases became whether or not a claim for copyright could be supported by statements from experts (e.g. architects) on the artistic qualities of the product in question.[31] At the same time as Danish courts were beginning to relax entry-level criteria, it was suggested in legal theory that courts should combine a 'low protection' with a 'narrow' one, i.e. limit the scope of protection in order to avoid overprotection notably in the area of functional design.[32] It was not, however, till the next period

[29] Rosenmeier (above, note 5), pp. 245ff (pointing out that the remarks were meant to reject the very strict criteria which the Supreme Court had used in its decision reported in (1956) *Ugeskrift for Retsvæsen* 273 to reject a bread-cutter from copyright).

[30] In (1961) *Ugeskrift for Retsvæsen* 1027 a very simple ribbed handle design on cutlery was found to be protectable under Danish copyright law. Protection was also granted in (1965) *Nordiskt immateriellt rättsskydd* 103 (rubber troll) as well as in (1967) *Ugeskrift for Retsvæsen* 482 (folding dish drainer), (1969) *Ugeskrift for Retsvæsen* 851 (coffee mill), (1998) *Ugeskrift for Retsvæsen* 941 (metal rack holding a dishcloth and a washing-up brush), (2000) *Ugeskrift for Retsvæsen* 212 ('Mag-Lite' torches) and (2012) *Ugeskrift for Retsvæsen* 3189 (the design of electrical switches). Protection was denied in (1968) *Ugeskrift for Retsvæsen* 189 (lamella lamp), (1979) *Ugeskrift for Retsvæsen* 588 (sailboat) and (1991) *Ugeskrift for Retsvæsen* 335 (lamp). For further reading see J. Schovsbo, M. Rosenmeier and C. Salung Petersen, *Immaterialret*, 4th edn (Copenhagen: Jurist- og Økonomforbundets Forlag, 2015), pp. 104ff.

[31] See Rosenmeier (above, note 5), pp. 251ff and M. Rosenmeier, 'Nogle bemærkninger om sagkyndiges medvirken i ophavsretssager' (2001) (B) *Ugeskrift for Retsvæsen* 102 at 104ff.

[32] See Trolle (1962) *Tidsskrift for retsvidenskab* 149ff and M. Koktvedgaard, *Immaterialretspositioner – Bidrag til læren om de lovbestemte enerettigheder og deres forhold til*

that this suggestion clearly crystallised in case law (see below on the two Supreme Court decisions from 2001 and 2002).

In *Norway*, unlike in Denmark, the original common Scandinavian position – viz. that 'relatively strict requirements' would apply for works of applied art to qualify for copyright protection[33] – was not softened in the passing of the copyright reform. Instead it came to constitute the basis for the development in case law. Case law from Norway remains, however, that scarce. It is, therefore, difficult to assess precisely whether the originality requirement applied did in fact correspond to the starting point indicated in legislation. In the legal literature it was maintained, however, that the originality requirement towards applied art was being administered in accordance with the indications in the legislation and in a more strict and conservative manner in Norway than in the other Nordic countries.[34] However, since these assumptions were to a great extent based on Norwegian municipal court decisions from the mid-nineteenth century, their general applicability is hard to test.[35] For this reason, it is arguably difficult to describe precisely the extent of the overlap between copyright and design law in Norwegian law at the time. See, on the *Tripp Trapp* decision from the Norwegian Supreme Court in 2012, below.

In *Sweden* the originality requirement towards works of applied art was being administered in a rather mild, relaxed manner during the 1950s and 1960s. This was especially clear from the Supreme Court decisions referred to above concerning an arm chair, a shelf system and a mirror.[36] Mildness also characterised the opinions of Svensk Forms Opinionsnämnd.[37] This position was reversed, however, in 1965 when

den almindelige konkurrenceret (Jurist- og Økonomforbundets Forlag, 1965), e.g. at pp. 258ff.

[33] Above, note 11 and the Norwegian Report, Innstilling til lov om mønster of 9 June 1967, 40.

[34] See Levin (above, note 5), p. 302 and pp. 299ff and Stray Vyrje, *Opphavsrettens ABC* (Oslo, 1987), p. 118. See also Rosenmeier, above, note 5.

[35] The few relevant court cases seem to be the following: Decision of the municipal court of Oslo, 10 March 1972, briefly referred to in Sijthoff Stray, *Opphavsrett* (Oslo, 1989), p. 48 (pleasure boats and naval vessels, protection denied), and the decision of the Supreme Court in (2014) *Nordiskt immateriellt rättsskydd* 161 which granted copyright protection to a Tripp Trapp chair. In the case the infringer claimed that the originality requirement towards works of applied art is strict. The court agreed upon this, referring to the views in O.-A. Rognstad, *Opphavsrett* (Oslo: Universitetsforlaget, 2009), pp. 94ff. The court also noted that it is doubtful whether this means that works of applied art must meet a strict originality requirement or simply that such works have difficulties meeting the basic originality requirement which all works must meet: see para. 67.

[36] See above, note 10. [37] Above, note 10.

the Nordic Design reform made its way through the Swedish legislative system. The proposal's suggestion to introduce a registered design protection for 'all' designs thus was combined with a suggestion to extend the term of protection for works of applied art (then just ten years) to the (then) standard term of protection, i.e. fifty years p.m.a. In so doing it was made clear that in order to avoid overcompensation of authors the prolongation should be accompanied by a strict application of the originality requirement, and that this would imply that the threshold for works with a functional character would be very high.[38] In the *travaux préparatoires* it was stated that the tightening of the originality requirement should take place through application of the so-called 'principle of unicity', i.e. a principle according to which a work can only be considered original if it is unlikely that two authors could have created it independently.[39] Further, it was stated that the above-mentioned Supreme Court decisions were incompatible with the new restrictive interpretation of the originality requirement. This led to a significant toughening in Opinions from Svensk Forms Opinionsnämnd, which from 1970 to 1984 found the originality requirement to be met in only 10 per cent of the cases compared to 75 per cent in earlier years.[40] From the mid-1980s, however, the practice of Svensk Forms Opinionsnämnd was gradually relieved. Following this, the pendulum began to swing again, and beginning in the 1990s Swedish case law administered the originality requirement in a way which cannot be described as especially strict.[41] This period culminated with a Supreme Court decision in 1995 which granted copyright protection to a knitted tunic.[42] In the case, the Supreme Court expressly stated that the Design Act of 1970, and the sharpening of the originality requirement following the passing of this Act, had not resulted in a satisfactory protection of works of applied art.

[38] SOU 1965:61 Mönsterskydd, pp. 206ff (available at http://weburn.kb.se/metadata/342/SOU_626342.htm). See e.g. Rosenmeier (above, note 5), 236ff.

[39] Read more of the principle of unicity in Rosenmeier (above, note 5), 132ff. The principle was originally invented in Kummer, *Das Urheberrechtlich Schützbare Werk* (Bern, 1968) and later imported to Nordic copyright law by the Swedish professor Seve Ljungman. See Rosenmeier, ibid. The principle has also enjoyed some success in Norway and Denmark. However, it is first and foremost a Swedish phenomenon.

[40] See M. Levin in *Festskrift till Sveriges Advokatsamfund 1887–1987* (Stockholm, 1987), p. 328. See also Rosenmeier (above, note 5), p. 237.

[41] See, among other things, the decisions of the Swedish Supreme Court in (1990) *Nordiskt immateriellt rättsskydd* 671 (plastic bag with Gotland drawings, protection granted) and (1994) *Nordiskt immateriellt rättsskydd* 143 (upholstery fabric with strawberry motif, protection granted).

[42] (1995) *Nordiskt immateriellt rättsskydd* 411.

4.2.2.3 Evaluation of the Interface in this Period

For *Denmark* it was expressly stated in the legislation's preparatory works that works of applied art were to be protected according to the 'normal criteria'. This starting point was not taken by the courts to imply that *all* 'works of applied art' were protected. It just meant that no special concessions were to be made for the category of work of applied art. In this way *full cumulation* would seem to describe the Danish position.

For *Norway* and *Sweden* it would seem to be more accurate to describe their position as being based on *partial cumulation*. This is the clearest for Norway, where courts were instructed to apply a high threshold and would seem to have done so (despite the meagre practice).

4.2.3 Third Period: 2001–2009: Same but More So

The EU Design Directive was implemented in Denmark and Sweden in 2001 and in Norway in 2003.[43] This ended the reign of the pan-Nordic Design Acts. Few people (if any) had any regrets: The Nordic Design Acts had failed to deliver the intended protection for the 'modern' designs and designers.[44] The patent approach proved to be too cumbersome, and since the Offices were in practice unable to guarantee the validity of the design registrations, the legal certainty which constituted the *raison d'être* of the registration process evaporated and only the costs remained. Apart from its inner weaknesses and flaws, the demise of the design system was fuelled by a tendency by courts to extend the scope of copyright by a lowering of the threshold.[45]

The present Design Acts are based closely on the Design Directive and mirror the registration system for the EU-design. For this reason, no account will be given.[46] Also no changes occurred regarding the availability of copyright protection or for the relationship between copyright and design law; cumulation still applies.

[43] See for Denmark Designloven, currently Consolidated Act (lovbekendtgørelse) No. 89 of 28 January 2009 as later amended (available in English at www.dkpto.org/media/23033727/the%20consolidate%20designs%20act%202017%20tospaltet%20-%20ikke%20markeret.pdf), for Norway Lov om beskyttelse av design (designloven) 2003–03-14 nr 15 and for Sweden Mönsterskyddslag 1970:485 (as amended following the EU rules).

[44] Notably the critique by Levin (above, note 5 and note 18), p. 373.

[45] Schovsbo and Teilmann-Lock (above, note 2) and J. Schovsbo and T. Riis, 'Design Law: Caught between Chairs?', in G. Ghidini et al., *Kritika* Vol. 2 (Cheltenham: Edward Elgar, 2017), p. 88.

[46] See on the Danish Design Act, Schovsbo and Svendsen (above, note 12) and Schovsbo, Rosenmeier and Salung Petersen (above, note 30).

Even though no formal changes took place, some of the developments which had been set in motion in the previous period matured in this one. For *Danish* law the most important development was the explicit adoption by the Supreme Court in 2001 and 2002 of the 'protect low *but* narrow' position which had been advocated in legal theory in the 1960s. This happened in two cases: The first one[47] concerned whether the Tripp Trapp high chair for children was infringed by another high chair. The second one[48] concerned whether Arne Jacobsen's iconic design chair 'The Ant' was infringed by a cheap copy. Since then the 'protect low *but* narrow' position has been repeated in a number of Supreme Court decisions on works of applied art.[49] The Danish position is remarkable because it does not reflect the classic copyright principle according to which a work's scope of protection depends upon the degree of originality. Rather, the view is that the scope of protection for the *category* of works of applied art is *a priori* narrower than for other works according to Danish law, no matter the level of originality. Unlike for work of pure art, authors of works of applied art are thus only protected against 'close copying'. Apart from this, the period confirmed the tendency towards the rather low threshold required for copyright and even rather mundane creations were found worthy of protection, including a dish drainer, a coffee grinder, a holder for a dishwashing brush and a pocket-torch.[50] In this way Danish courts even in this period continued to treat works of applied art in a distinctly different way when compared to other types of works. Only the discrimination was not directed at the entry-level criteria ('originality') but rather took place *ex post* in determining the scope of protection.

In this period *Swedish* law probably moved in the direction of Danish law in terms of the threshold for originality.[51] The Swedish originality

[47] Judgment from the Supreme Court reported in (2001) *Ugeskrift for Retsvæsen* 747.

[48] Judgment from the Supreme Court reported in (2002) *Ugeskrift for Retsvæsen* 1715/2.

[49] See the references in Schovsbo, Rosenmeier and Salung Petersen (above, note 30), 226ff.

[50] See respectively: Judgment from the Supreme Court reported in (1967) *Ugeskrift for Retsvæsen* 482, Judgment from the Supreme Court reported in (1969) *Ugeskrift for Retsvæsen* 851, Judgment from the Maritime and Commercial Court reported in (1998) *Ugeskrift for Retsvæsen* 941 and Judgment from the Maritime and Commercial Court reported in (2000) *Ugeskrift for Retsvæsen* 212. According to Rosenmeier (above, note 31), 252, works of applied art are usually granted copyright protection as long as an expert opinion statement declares that the product in question is 'original' or 'new'. The case law is comprehensive: for an overview see Schovsbo, Rosenmeier and Salung Petersen (above, note 30), pp. 100ff.

[51] See M. Rosenmeier (2009) *Nordiskt immateriellt rättsskyd* 498ff in a comment to the decision from the Swedish Supreme Court reported in (2009) *Nytt Juridiskt Arkiv* 159 to grant copyright protection to the 'Maglite' torch. The Danish Maritime and Commercial Court had arrived at the same conclusion already in its judgment of 29 October 1999 reported in (2000) *Ugeskrift for Retsvæsen* 212. For Sweden, the lowering of the requirements was noted already by M. Levin (above, note 5), p. 375.

requirement in connection with works of applied art was discussed again in a Supreme Court decision from 2009 concerning a Maglite torch.[52] Here the court stated that the originality requirement which must be met by works of applied art does not differ significantly from the originality requirement which other works must meet. However, the court noted, the originality requirement of works of applied art is still a stricter one than the one which applied before 1970.[53]

For *Norway*, however, the Supreme Court in a decision from 2012 regarding the Tripp Trapp would seem to have upheld the traditional Norwegian strict position.[54] In the most recent textbook on copyright law in Norway, Professor Ole-Andreas Rognstad explains that this is based on a general 'friholdelsesbehov' ('requirement of availability/ 'Freihaltebedürfnis') according to which copyright protection should not be extended so as to foreclose access to purely functional elements.[55] Taking this position as its starting point, the Norwegian Supreme Court was clearly in doubt as to whether or not to accept the chair as a work. Eventually, the Norwegian court found that the chair did in fact constitute a work which was protected according to the stringent criteria which applied. It is not entirely clear whether the court applied the 'raised bar' criterion because the chair was considered as being a work of 'applied art'[56] or because its functional character made it more difficult for the author to exercise his personal choices.[57]

As in Denmark, Norwegian and Swedish courts often relativise the scope of protection. In cases involving functional works courts thus normally apply a narrow test which implies that only products which are 'very similar' to the protected one are considered as infringing the copyright. Unlike in Denmark, however, these countries relate the breadth of the scope of protection to the degree of originality of the work in question:

[52] Reported in (2009) *Nordiskt immateriellt rättsskydd* 509.

[53] For further reading, see M. Rosenmeier (2009) *Nordiskt immateriellt rättsskydd* 498ff.

[54] For Norway, see A. Lund, 'Høyesteretts dom om Tripp Trapp-stolen – et gjennomslag for Tharp? Vern for verket eller også for den kunstneriske idé som det uttrykker' (2014) *Nordiskt immateriellt rättsskydd* 178–203 (pointing out that the decision by the Norwegian Supreme Court in its judgment of 27 June 2012, HR-2012–1325-A, reported in (2014) *Nordiskt immateriellt rättsskydd* 161–77 to accept copyright protection for the Tripp Trapp chair was based on the traditional stringent criteria). The Tripp Trapp chair has also been accepted under copyright by the Danish Supreme Court, below, and by the Swedish Hovrätten for Western Sweden in a judgment of 7 December 1998, T 548–97; see M. Levin, *Lärobok i immaterialrätt*, 10th edn (Stockholm: Norstedts Juridik, 2011), p. 102. Lund, ibid., pp. 179ff. See below on the position in EU law.

[55] Rognstad (above, note 35), pp. 94ff.

[56] As Lund (above, note 54), p. 181 would seem to suggest.

[57] As would seem to be preferred by Rognstad (above, note 35).

the more original the work, the broader the protection.[58] In this manner the positions in Sweden and Norway differ from the one in Denmark where protection for the category of 'works of applied art' is *a priori* narrower than for other types of works.

4.2.3.1 Evaluation

Denmark and Norway: as before (i.e. full and partial cumulation respectively). Sweden: in the Danish direction.

For Denmark the full cumulation position did not imply that works of applied art were being treated like all other types of work. However, unlike in earlier periods (i.e. pre-1961), the discrimination was factored into the assessment of the scope of protection (i.e. *ex post*) where works of applied art could only be relied upon to prevent 'close copies'.

4.2.4 Fourth Period: 2009–present: EU harmonisation

For the current period, no formal legislative changes have taken place – neither of the Copyright[59] nor of the Design Acts.[60] Instead, the CJEU has handed down a number of important decisions. The full ramifications of these decisions remain to be seen and more need to follow for the full picture to emerge. It is, however, obvious that the freedom for national courts to decide on issues such as originality and scope of protection now must be viewed within the developments in EU law. As will be demonstrated in the following, these developments have made the relevance of the national positions identified above doubtful.

On 16 July 2009, the CJEU handed down its Judgment in *Infopaq*.[61] The case involved a Danish newspaper and a news agency and it was

[58] See the decision of the Norwegian Supreme Court in (2014) *Nordiskt immateriellt rättsskydd* 71, para. 86. See also the decision of the municipal court of Oslo in (1968) *Nordiskt immateriellt rättsskydd* 323 where broad protection was given to a troll doll since it reflected a new type of troll. On Sweden see the Supreme Court decisions in (1966) *Nordiskt immateriellt rättsskydd* 74 (mirror) and (1994) *Nordiskt immateriellt rättsskydd* 143 (upholstery fabric with strawberry motif). For further reading, see Rosenmeier (above, note 5), p. 240.

[59] See, for Denmark, Consolidated Act on Copyright No. 1144 of 23 October 2014 (available in English at http://kum.dk/fileadmin/KUM/Documents/English%20website/Copyright/Act_on_Copyright_2014_Lovbekendtgoerelse_nr._1144__ophavsretslove n__2014__engelsk.pdf).

[60] Above, note 43.

[61] Judgment of 16 July 2009, Case C-5/08, *Infopaq International A/S* v. *Danske Dagblades Forening*, ECLI:EU:C:2009:465.

considered as an important judgment on the effects of the Infosoc-Directive[62] for the use of digital material in the form of texts (and perhaps even pictures) used. Certainly, nobody at the time thought that this judgment would come to redefine the concept of a 'work'. The importance of the decision grew in the coming years, however, and it gradually became clear that a horizontal and harmonised test for deciding whether something constitutes a 'work' was emerging.[63] It is arguably not as yet clear whether this also involves works of applied art. One could thus (well!)[64] argue that because of Article 17 of the Design Directive which leaves it to the Member States to determine *inter alia* 'the level of originality' Member States would in fact be left to do so. On the other hand, the CJEU's Judgment in *Flos* in 2012 could be understood to imply that the Infopaq-criteria do in fact extend even to works of applied art.[65] Presently, it is thus arguably unclear to what extent EU countries are free to rely on the principles developed in national law for regulating the border-area between design and copyright law.

Nowadays, the basic requirement in contemporary *Danish* copyright law is that the work should represent the 'personal and creative effort of the author'. The work thus has to reflect a certain amount of creativity

[62] Directive 2001/29/EC of the European Parliament and of the Council of 22 May 2001 on the harmonization of certain aspects of copyright and related rights in the information society, OJ 2001 L 167/10–19 (22 June 2001).

[63] Judgment of 22 December 2010, Case C-393/09, *Bezpečnostní softwarová asociace – Svaz softwarové ochrany* v. *Ministerstvo kultury*, ECLI:EU:C:2010:816; Judgment of 4 October 2011, Joined Cases C-403/08, C-429/08, *Football Association Premier League Ltd and Others* v. *QC Leisure and Others*, ECLI:EU:C:2011:631; Judgment of 1 December 2011, Case C-145/10, *Eva-Maria Painer* v. *Standard Verlags GmbH and Others*, ECLI:EU:C:2011:798; and Judgment of 2 May 2012, Case C-406/10, *SAS Institute Inc.* v. *World Programming Ltd*, ECLI:EU:C:2012:259.

[64] L. A. F. Bently, 'The Return of Industrial Copyright?' (2012) 34(10) *EIPR* 654–72.

[65] Judgment of the CJEU of 27 January 2012 in Case 168/09, *Flos* v. *Semeraro Casa*, ECLI:EU:C:2011:29, para. 34. In its decision on the Tripp Trapp chair (above, note 54), the Norwegian Supreme Court implicitly rejected this view, stating that the notion of what constitutes a work has not been harmonised. In the same direction, the German Supreme Court in its Birthday Train case on the protectability of a toy train under German copyright law found that EU law did not bind national courts with regards to defining which works to protect: Judgment from the Bundesgerichtshof of 13 November 2013 – I ZR 143/12 'Birthday Train (Geburtstagzug)' 2014 *International Review of Intellectual Property and Competition Law* 831 (*GRUR* 2014 175). Yet, the German Supreme Court added that for the sake of consistency in the field of copyright law it would use the EU criterion as the benchmark also for works of applied art. Even if no formal obligation extends from *Infopaq* etc., the indirect effect of the case may thus still be harmonisation of the test for copyrightability. See for a comment on the German case and for an insightful discussion, A. Ohly, 'Where is the Birthday Train Heading? The Copyright-Design Interface in German Law', in G. Karnell et al. (eds.), *Liber Amicorum Jan Rosén* (Visby: eddy.se ab, 2016), pp. 589–605.

and aesthetic choice.[66] This would seem to be in conformity with the originality definition of modern EU law according to the decisions from the CJEU. However, as mentioned above, Danish courts have traditionally combined a 'low' (i.e. a non-discriminatory) threshold with a 'narrow' scope of protection for the *category* of works of applied art. The latter part of this approach would seem to conflict with the 'Gertrude Stein' approach of the CJEU – i.e. that 'a work is a work is a work' – which was established in *Painer* and where, furthermore, the CJEU remarked that the protection conferred to works must be given 'a broad interpretation' (para. 96). Also in this decision, the court explicitly rejected that the extent of protection should depend on 'possible differences in the degree of creative freedom in the production of various categories of works' (para. 97). The CJEU concluded that: 'Therefore, as regards a portrait photograph, the protection conferred by [the Infosoc. Directive] cannot be inferior to that enjoyed by other works, including other photographic works' (para. 98). If one accepts that these remarks apply to *all* types of works (as we believe that the CJEU indeed does) then Danish courts cannot continue to provide for a narrow scope of protection for works of applied art as such. Instead they will have to decide each case on its merit.

Because of this uncertainty it is difficult to predict exactly how Danish and Scandinavian courts (and all other courts in EU countries) are going to be developing case law in the border area between copyright and design law.

4.3 Analysis

In dealing with works of applied art in copyright, Scandinavian courts have historically employed several strategies to limit copyright protection of works of applied art. These have included: (1) 'raising the bar' to keep works with 'clear functional intentions' out of copyright (as seen in Norway and until recently also in Sweden) and (2) narrowing the scope of protection (seen in all three nations).

Both of these models involve an element of legal discrimination of works of applied art and in this way bear evidence of the difficulties Scandinavian courts have had – and indeed continue to have – in applying the normal copyright regime to products which perform a function apart from having an appealing shape. Even though such works have long been accepted as part of copyright's family they have been treated like stepchildren.

[66] See Schovsbo, Rosenmeier and Salung Petersen (above, note 30), pp. 76ff.

All the Scandinavian countries originally applied a 'raised bar' approach for works of applied art and sought to reject functional products from copyright *ex ante*. As seen over time, however, the raised bar approach has proven to be most difficult to uphold. The lowering of the requirements has taken place at different times in the three countries. In Denmark, it began already in the 1960s, in Sweden it took place in the 1990s and in Norway it would seem that the original position has not (yet) been abandoned. These differences are most likely due to both cultural and legal factors (all of which are closely interrelated). Despite the cultural similarities it is thus probably fair to say that amongst the three Scandinavian countries it is mainly in Denmark where 'design' has for the most part of the twentieth century been hailed as an important part of the cultural identity. The names of the Danish Modern designers such as Arne Jacobsen, Hans Wegner, Poul Henningsen and Finn Juhl and indeed their furniture, lamps, etc. are household names and items to many Danes. For this reason, case law involving the copying of the products of these designers has been much more plentiful in Denmark than in, for example, Norway. The cultural status of the designers may also explain the readiness of the Danish legislator – and (perhaps even more importantly) the courts – to accept the modern functional design as part of the realm of copyright. This development in turn made the designers orient themselves towards the copyright system and its free, long-term and comprehensive protection scheme. In this way a system based on feed-back loops between designers, courts and legislators gradually expanded the area occupied by copyright and eroded the basis for the kind of registered and 'industrial-style' design protection offered by the common Design Acts of the 1970s.[67]

Presently, it is doubtful, however, to what extent the development in EU law will allow the models developed in national law to deal with these concerns. If one continues the trajectories of the suite of cases following *Infopaq* and *Painer* the result will most likely be a position where no discrimination is allowed, neither in terms of the threshold nor the scope of protection.

Moving forward on the basis of a harmonised (and most likely 'low') originality criterion, the need to control the overlap between design law and copyright will in our minds increase and mechanisms should be found to limit copyright's reach. Based on the experiences in Scandinavia it would be very difficult to rein in the scope of copyright's protection. We submit, however, that attempts should be made to seek to demarcate the boundaries of copyright to avoid protection to products which are to a large extent shaped to perform a specific function. Such

[67] Schovsbo and Teilmann-Lock (above, note 2).

products, we suggest, should be channelled out of copyright and towards either design law or unfair market law. In this way, we suggest that any attempts to police the boundary between copyright and design should involve a holistic approach whereby both copyright and design law interests are included. The European design system is under review now and we suggest that the relationship to copyright is included in these considerations.[68]

[68] See Legal review on industrial design protection in Europe, published on 6 June 2016, available at file:///C:/Users/js/Downloads/ET-04-16-452-EN-N%20(2).pdf. The Report addresses the relationship between design and copyright in several places and recommends that Member States implement the cumulation prescribed by the *Flos* decisions, ibid. 96 and 161. Furthermore, this principle is said to imply the 'total cumulation' known in the French approach, ibid. 149ff, i.e. a situation where products which pass the threshold for design protection are also protected by copyright. For this reason, spare parts etc. are expected to be protected by copyright and limitations suggested to ensure that the special design law exceptions and limitations for spare parts are not circumvented by copyright protection, ibid. The authors of the report thus foresee a further expansion of copyright's reach, at least as seen from a Scandinavian perspective. No attempts are made, however, to counter such a development on a more general level.

5 The Case for Partial Cumulation in Germany

*Ansgar Ohly**

Table 5.1 *Chronological table of legislation*

Period	Legislation	Interface/interpretation
1876–1907	Act on Copyright in Works of Art 1876 Act on Copyright in Designs and Models [Design Act] 1876	Demarcation
1907–1964	Act on Copyright in Works of Art 1907 Design Act 1876	Partial cumulation
1965–2003	Copyright Act 1965 Design Act 1876	Partial cumulation
2004–2013	Copyright Act 1965 Design Act 2004	Partial cumulation
2014	Copyright Act 1965 Design Act 2004	Partial (or total?) cumulation

5.1 The Origins: From Unfaithful Lacemakers to the Copyright Package of 1876

Although both philosophers and legal scholars had already discussed the issue of reprinting in the eighteenth century,[1] copyright legislation in Germany started later than in other European countries. At the beginning of the nineteenth century Germany was split into many territories. Some

* Dr (Munich), LL.M. (Cantab.), Chair for Private Law, Intellectual Property and Competition Law, Ludwig Maximilian University, Munich, Visiting Professor at the University of Oxford.

[1] On the 'reprinting debate' ('Nachdruckdebatte'), to which many legal scholars but also philosophers such as Immanuel Kant and Johann Gottlieb Fichte contributed, see L. Gieseke, *Vom Privileg zum Urheberrecht* (Baden-Baden: Nomos, 1995), pp. 115–36; U. Andersch, Die Diskussion über den Büchernachdruck in Deutschland bis ca. 1815 (Tübingen Mohr Siebeck, forthcoming); M. Vogel, in U. Loewenheim, M. Leistner and A. Ohly (eds.), *Schricker/Loewenheim, Urheberrecht*, 5th edn (Munich: Beck, 2017), Einleitung, paras. 117–22.

states such as the Austrian Empire or the Kingdoms of Prussia and Bavaria were among Europe's larger countries, but some principalities and dukedoms were extremely small. When the German Confederation (Deutscher Bund) was founded at the Congress of Vienna in 1815, Article 18(d) of the Final Act called upon all member states to protect writers and publishers. Indeed, in all of these territories books and works of art or music could be protected by privileges against unauthorised reprinting.[2] But the territorial scope of these privileges remained restricted to that state.[3]

Due to the lack of mass production, design protection was not a major issue at that time. The only need for regulation seems to have arisen in textile manufacturing. Saxony, in particular, was known for its laces. They were often made by women in homework on the basis of patterns, which were provided by the person or company organising manufacture and distribution. Apparently some women were tempted to pass the patterns on to other producers or to produce more lace than agreed and to sell the extra products underhand. A Saxonian order for the 'punishment of disloyal lacemakers'[4] is an early example of a criminal provision against the unauthorised use of textile designs. Similar statutes were passed elsewhere.[5] Curiously, one of these provisions has survived until today.[6] In the framework of trade secret protection, § 18 of the German Act against Unfair Competition provides that a person who, 'acting without authorisation, uses or communicates to another person models or instructions of a technical nature, particularly drawings, prototypes, patterns, segments or formulas, entrusted to him for the purposes of competition or for personal gain', is liable under criminal law.

The first copyright legislation in Germany[7] was the Prussian Copyright Act of 1837. For the first time it afforded general protection against

[2] On the nature of privileges see B. Dölemeyer and D. Klippel, 'Der Beitrag der deutschen Rechtswissenschaft zur Theorie des gewerblichen Rechtsschutzes und Urheberrechts', in F.-K. Beier et al. (eds.), *Gewerblicher Rechtsschutz und Urheberrecht in Deutschland* (Weinheim: VCH, 1991), pp. 187, 189–94.

[3] Before 1806 Imperial Privileges granted by the Emperor for the entire German Empire had also been available.

[4] Order of Elector Friedrich August of 4 April 1721, reprinted in P. Schmid, 'Zur Geschichte des Musterschutzes', GR 1893, 143–4. The order is restated in a Circular of 6 February 1804, No. 4, published in the Codex Augusteus, the Saxonian Collection of Statutes, Vol. III, Dresden 1824, p. 204.

[5] Schmid, GR 1893, 143–5.

[6] Although it is likely that this provision will be repealed once Germany implements the EU trade secrets directive (Directive 2016/943, OJ 2016 L 157/1).

[7] Apart from areas west of the Rhine, where French law was applicable in Napoleonic times and partly still thereafter; see B. Englert, *Grundzüge des Rechtsschutzes der industriellen Formgebung* (Cologne/Berlin/Bonn/Munich: Carl Heymanns, 1978), p. 13.

copying to authors of works of literature, science, music and art. But the Act contained an explicit exception allowing the use of works of art as models for industrial production. § 25 of the Act provided:

> The use of works of art as models for the products of manufactures, factories and crafts is permitted.

In the first half of the nineteenth century, models and sketches of furniture, glassware and china which were copied from the works of architects and designers such as Karl Friedrich Schinkel were in wide use.[8] Legislation had no intention of stopping this practice. It was even hoped that the industrial copying of designs could enhance industrial production.[9] In many respects Germany in those days was what we would today refer to as a threshold country. Outside the narrow field of literature and fine arts there was no clear evidence that intellectual property protection would benefit industry. On the contrary, the copying of foreign technology was widely accepted.[10] In 1854 the Prussian government conducted an inquiry among chambers of commerce and comparable institutions about the need for design protection, and forty-six of sixty-two of the responding organisations found such legislation unnecessary.[11]

With respect to design, the general attitude towards protection changed in the second half of the century. The German performances at the World Exhibitions in London in 1862 and in Vienna in 1873 were widely regarded as a disaster.[12] While the growing economy allowed the increasingly affluent middle classes to buy decorative furniture, and table- and glassware, the popular style was backward-looking and overloaded with ornaments. This was increasingly seen as bad taste,[13] and

[8] S. Zentek, *Geschichte des Designschutzes – Industrialisierung, Beginn der Moderne, Nachkriegsjahre, bis heute* (Dortmund: Lelesken-Verlag, 2016), pp. 24–8.

[9] E. Gerstenberg, 'Die Entwicklung des Geschmacksmusterrechts', in F.-K. Beier et al. (eds.), *Gewerblicher Rechtsschutz und Urheberrecht in Deutschland* (Weinheim: VCH, 1991), p. 694.

[10] Kurt Biedenkopf, the former prime minister of Saxony, stresses that the development of the Saxonian textile industry in the nineteenth century was not least made possible by the copying of British technology: see K. Biedenkopf, 'Geistiges Eigentum – Prosperitätsgarantie nur für die Industriestaaten?', in O. Depenheuer and K.-N. Peifer (eds.), *Geistiges Eigentum: Schutzrecht oder Ausbeutungstitel?* (Berlin/Heidelberg: Springer, 2008), pp. 23, 30.

[11] M. Eck, *Neue Wege zum Schutz der Formgebung* (Köln/Berlin/Bonn/München: Carl Heymanns Verlag, 1993), p. 21.

[12] Schmid, GR 1895, 309, 311; Gerstenberg, 'Entwicklung des Geschmacksmusterrechts', p. 695; Zentek, *Geschichte des Designschutzes*, p. 43.

[13] H. Albrecht, *Das Kunstgewerbe in der deutschen Urheberrechtsgesetzgebung*, doctoral thesis (Erlangen, 1933), p. 42: 'Imitation, in particular of foreign products, monotonous classicism and horrid conglomerates of styles of all periods were the guideline and the characteristic feature of design at that time.'

there were calls for the improvement of German design. The final push towards design protection came when in 1871 Alsace-Lorraine was included in the newly founded German Empire. The flourishing textile industry of this region had benefited from French copyright and design legislation, and producers lobbied for protection against copying.[14]

This resulted in what one might call the 'Copyright Package' of 1876. Three copyright Acts were passed on three consecutive days: the Act on Copyright in Works of Visual Art of 9 January, the Act on the Protection of Photographies of 10 January and the Act on Copyright in Patterns and Models of 11 January 1876. While the latter Act used the terminology of copyright law, it was in fact the first German Design Act. It largely remained unchanged for more than 100 years. Hence from 1876 onwards design law and copyright went separate ways.

5.2 Design Law and Unfair Competition Law

5.2.1 Design Law

The Act on Copyright in Patterns and Models of 11 January 1876 remained in force until the implementation of the EC Design Directive in 2004.[15] During this period, substantive design law remained largely unchanged, whereas the registration procedure underwent a major reform in 1986. At the time of its repeal in 2004 the Act was one of the oldest German intellectual property statutes.[16] Until then, the word 'copyright' and terminological references to 'the author' were retained, although already towards the end of the nineteenth century the Act had become known as 'Geschmacksmustergesetz', which literally translates into 'Act on Aesthetic Models'. Since the Act was the legal basis of German design law, it will be referred to here as the Designs Act 1876. This chapter will not cover the modern German Designs Act of 2004, by which the EC Design Directive was implemented, since a discussion of the present design law has little to add to the analysis of the copyright/design interface.

[14] Gerstenberg, 'Entwicklung des Geschmacksmusterrechts', p. 694; Englert, *Grundzüge*, p. 14.

[15] The 1876 Act was repealed by the Design Law Reform Act of 12 March 2004, Bundesgesetzblatt I, p. 390.

[16] R. Nirk and H. Kurtze, *Geschmacksmustergesetz*, 2nd edn (Köln/Berlin/Bonn/München: Carl Heymanns Verlag, 1997), Einführung, para. 1.

Under § 1(2) Designs Act 1876, there were three substantive conditions of protection, which remained unchanged for more than 125 years: the design had to be (1) a 'pattern' ('Muster') or 'model' ('Modell'), which was (2) new and (3) individual ('eigentümlich'). Protection was granted for an initial period of three years, which could be extended to a maximum of fifteen years, and it was against reproduction only.

The distinction made by the Act between two-dimensional ('patterns') and three-dimensional designs ('models') did not have any practical relevance.[17] What mattered was that the feature had the purpose of having and the capability to have an impact on the aesthetic perception of the viewer.[18] This criterion mainly served to distinguish aesthetic from functional features. Soon after the enactment in 1876 there was general agreement that design law did not extend to exclusively functional shapes.[19] In order to fill this gap, the Utility Model Act of 1891 ('Gebrauchsmustergesetz') was enacted. For a long time, 'model law' ('Musterrecht'), consisting of 'aesthetic model law' and 'utility model law', was regarded as a distinct category of intellectual property law.[20] The development of utility model law into a right in inventions, which is, apart from examination and its shorter term, largely similar to a patent, is a more recent development.[21]

The design had to be new. For a long time it was disputed whether the concept of novelty in design law was objective (as in patent law) or subjective (as in copyright law). The courts tended to apply an objective standard,[22] whereas most scholars advocated a subjective approach.[23] This dispute was finally laid to rest by the Federal Supreme Court in 1968, when it came down in favour of an objective-relative concept of novelty.[24] The court based its decision

[17] Nirk and Kurtze, *Geschmacksmustergesetz*, § 1, para. 109.

[18] BGH GRUR 1958, 510 – *Schlafzimmermodell [Bedroom Model]*; BGH GRUR 1960, 256, 257 – *Chérie.*

[19] BGH GRUR 1966, 97, 99 – *Zündaufsatz [Igniter Top]*; BGH GRUR 1981, 269, 271 – *Haushaltsschneidemaschine II [Household Slicer II].*

[20] See J. Kohler, *Musterrecht – Geschmacks- und Gebrauchsmusterrecht* (Stuttgart: Verlag Ferdinand Enke, 1909).

[21] For a detailed account of this development see R. Übler, *Die Schutzwürdigkeit von Erfindungen: Fortschritt und Erfindungshöhe in der Geschichte des Patent- und Gebrauchsmusterrechts* (Tübingen: Mohr Siebeck, 2014), pp. 228–42, 311–30.

[22] See the references in BGH GRUR 1969, 90, 91 – *Rüschenhaube [Frilly Bonnet].*

[23] H. Furler, 'Die Neuheit im Geschmacksmusterrecht', GRUR 1956, 49–51; K. Nicolini, 'Die Neuheit im Geschmacksmusterrecht', GRUR 1963, 407–13, giving further references.

[24] BGH GRUR 1969, 90, 91–5 – *Rüschenhaube [Frilly Bonnet].*

on the *travaux préparatoires* and on the consideration that the condition of 'individuality' already implied subjective novelty and that, hence, the novelty requirement would be superfluous under a subjective approach. While the court noted that design and copyright law were related, it also pointed out that double creations were much more likely in design law than in copyright law. In this case the court considered it as appropriate to give the designer a right to prevent similar and younger designs.

The requirement of 'individuality' was seen as closely related to copyright law, which, in Germany, also requires a work to be 'individual' rather than 'original'.[25] There had to be a personal creative effort which went beyond what was usual in the respective sector and what would have been created by an average designer,[26] who was seen as closely related to the 'person skilled in the art' in patent law. Practically courts used to compare the design to all pre-existing designs, often referred to as the 'wealth of shapes' ('Formenschatz'). This test also applied when items of nature were imitated: the naturalistic reproduction in an artificial flower was seen as insufficient for design protection, whereas a flower pattern on a plate could well qualify.[27] The approach bore some resemblance to the copyright approach and was not regarded as qualitatively different. As will be explained below, the difference was seen as one of degree. Whereas designs which were different from pre-existing patterns or shapes were usually seen as individual, only extraordinary designs qualified for copyright protection.

The formal requirement for protection under the 1876 Act was registration and the deposit of a specimen or depiction. Both had to occur before the first marketing of the product.[28] They had to be made at the local court at the owner's main place of business. There was no substantive examination. A central national registration, which had for a long time been suggested by critics,[29] was only introduced in 1986. These formalities made design protection unattractive in some sectors of trade and industry. Fashion designers, in particular, found it difficult to deposit a specimen or depiction before first marketing. In particular the time between application and registration often turned out to be longer than

[25] Whether this has changed in the light of the recent CJEU judgments on the concept of work is another matter, which is not relevant here. On the influence (or the lack of it) of the CJEU case law on the concept of applied art, see below at III 9–10.

[26] BGH GRUR 1960, 395, 396 – *Dekorationsgitter [Decoration Grid]*; BGH GRUR 1966, 97, 99 – *Zündaufsatz [Ignition Top]*.

[27] RGZ 135, 385, 391 – *Künstliche Blumen [Artificial Flowers]*.

[28] § 7 Designs Act 1876.

[29] Gerstenberg, 'Entwicklung des Geschmacksmusterrechts', pp. 700–1.

a fashion season. These considerations led the Supreme Court to grant liberal protection for fashion novelties under unfair competition law,[30] as will be discussed below.

To sum up, German design law before 2004 was a hybrid between copyright and industrial property law.[31] The terminology of the 1876 Act was rooted in copyright law, as was the individuality requirement. As in copyright, designers were only protected against reproduction, not against independent creation. On the other hand, both the novelty requirement and the formal conditions of protection are reminiscent of industrial property law.

Design law has always played an important role in practice. The relatively easy and decentralised application and deposit procedure seems to have been widely used. In the years around 1900, around 180,000 applications were made per year.[32] This number decreased over time, but it still remained at a high level. In the 1960s there were around 60,000 applications per year; in the 1990s the German Patent Office received between 65,000 and 80,000 applications per year.[33] Nevertheless many reported cases show that claimants in design cases often sought copyright protection or remedies in unfair competition law. The reasons are not always made explicit, but they are probably threefold. First, as discussed above, the lack of an unregistered design right caused problems. Registration was regarded as burdensome, in particular when the design concerned a broad range of products, and in some sectors the time between application and registration prevented effective protection. Secondly, for successful designs the term of protection of fifteen years was rather short. Thirdly, design articles were often produced by small and medium-sized enterprises which just may not have been sufficiently aware of the need to obtain intellectual property protection.

5.2.2 *Unfair Competition Law*

The first German Act against Unfair Competition was passed in 1896. It contained provisions against misleading advertising, against trade libel and against the misappropriation of trade secrets, but there was no general tort of unfair competition. This restrictive approach was criticised by many authors who pointed out that a flexible, open-textured provision was needed in order

[30] Which was the reason for the Federal Supreme Court to grant liberal unfair competition protection to fashion designs; see BGH GRUR 1973, 478, 480 – *Modeneuheit* = [1973] IIC 458, 462 – *Fashion Novelty*.

[31] Nirk and Kurtze, *Geschmacksmustergesetz*, Einführung, paras. 39–40; Eck, *Neue Wege*, p. 109.

[32] Gerstenberg, 'Entwicklung des Geschmacksmusterrechts', p. 696; Englert, *Grundzüge*, p. 21.

[33] Nirk and Kurtze, *Geschmacksmustergesetz*, Einführung, para. 10; Englert, *Grundzüge*, p. 21.

to allow the courts to react to flexible markets. *Kohler* compared unfair practices to Proteus: they took on a thousand different forms in order to steal the fruits of labour from fair traders.[34] The new Act against Unfair Competition of 1909 contained what is known in German terminology as the 'general clause' ('Generalklausel') of unfair competition law:

> Injunctive relief and damages can be claimed against anyone who, in the course of trade and for purposes of competition, commits acts which conflict with honest practices ('die gegen die guten Sitten verstoßen').

At first the courts were hesitant to apply this new and broad provision. But from the 1920s onwards the general clause became the basis of new doctrines, which developed on a case-by-case basis, but which gradually turned into rules. Methodologically this process bears striking parallels with the development of the common law.[35] Some of these rules were codified by Parliament in later years. Areas which came to be governed by case law on the basis of § 1 Unfair Competition Act 1909 were, *inter alia*, comparative advertising, the obstruction of other competitors or the breach of statutory duties. The most important category in relation to design protection was unfair product imitation.

Especially a common lawyer might frown on this category of unfair competition, as this kind of protection seems to undermine the limits of intellectual property law and to unduly restrict competition.[36] The freedom of imitation is the necessary corollary of intellectual property. The Supreme Court was aware of this problem. Already in its first decisions under § 1 Unfair Competition Act 1909 it held that imitation was not unfair per se. There had to be additional elements of unfairness which went beyond the mere copying. In early years not only academic authors regarded 'reaping without sowing' as unfair,[37] the Supreme Court also tended to regard the sale of imitated products at a lower price as such an additional element.[38] But it soon recognised that this approach amounted to a ban on imitation per se.[39] From the 1930s onwards the categories of

[34] J. Kohler, *Recht des Markenschutzes* (Würzburg: Staehl, 1884), p. 60.

[35] See A. Ohly, *Richterrecht und Generalklausel im Recht des unlauteren Wettbewerbs* (Köln/Berlin/Bonn/München: Carl Heymanns, 1997), pp. 253–310, 315–26.

[36] See the criticism of doctrines of 'unfair copying' by Jacob J. in *Hodgkinson Corby* v. *Wards Mobility Services* [1995] FSR 169, 175.

[37] Two years before the U.S. Supreme Court used this expression in its famous *INS* v. *AP* judgment, 248 US 215, 239–40, Lobe referred to product imitation as 'plowing with someone else's calf': A. Lobe, 'Der Hinweis auf fremde gewerbliche Leistung als Mittel zur Reklame', MuW XVI (1916–17) 129 (which begs the obvious question of why one should use a calf rather than an ox or a horse for ploughing).

[38] RGZ 73, 294, 297 – *Schallplatten [Records]*.

[39] RG, GRUR 1929, 483 – *Spielzeugsignalscheibe [Toy Signalling Disk]*; RGZ 135, 385, 394 – *Künstliche Blumen [Artificial Flowers]*.

unfairness developed,[40] which have meanwhile been codified in § 4 No. 9 Unfair Competition Act 2004 = § 4 No. 3 Unfair Competition Act 2015.[41] Although this provision was only enacted in 2004, it reflects the approach developed by the courts in the 80 years prior to the enactment. § 4 of the Act provides:

Unfair commercial practices are committed by a person who
1., 2. . . .
3. offers goods or services which are imitations of the goods or services offered by a competitor, provided the person
   a) causes avoidable confusion as to the origin of the imitated goods or services among consumers,
   b) takes unfair advantage of or causes damage to the reputation of the imitated goods or services,
   c) has acquired the knowledge or the documents necessary for the imitation by unfair means;
4. . . .

This provision reflects the conditions of protection which first emerged in the 1930s.[42] First, a product offered by a competitor must have been imitated. Secondly, the original product must satisfy certain requirements. It must be of 'competitive individuality' ('wettbewerbliche Eigenart'), i.e. it must have features which identify the product's commercial origin or quality. Thirdly, there must be additional factors of unfairness. By far the most important category is the one now codified in § 4 No. 3(a): causing confusion as to the origin. Despite differences in detail, this category has obvious parallels with the common law tort of passing off. The second category goes beyond passing off: taking unfair advantage of another trader's reputation by means of an 'image transfer' is considered as unfair, even if there is no likelihood of consumer confusion. The conditions of imitation, competitive individuality and additional factors or unfairness are interrelated. The closer

[40] See P. Nerreter, 'Wettbewerbsrechtlicher Schutz technischer und ästhetischer Arbeitsergebnisse', GRUR 1957, 408, 409–15; A. Ohly, 'UWG und Urheberrecht', GRUR Int. 2015, 693, 694–6, both giving further references.

[41] In a major reform in 2004 much of the former case law was cast into statutory provisions. The former judge-made categories of unfairness were compiled in a statutory list (§ 4 Nos. 1–11 Unfair Competition Act 2004). In 2008 the Unfair Commercial Practices Directive (2004/29/EC) was implemented, but the Commission was not satisfied with the implementation. Hence the Act was amended again in 2015, which *inter alia* led to a change of the numbering: § 4 No. 9 of the 2004 Act became § 4 No. 3 Unfair Competition Act 2015. For an overview see A. Ohly, 'Das neue UWG im Überblick', GRUR 2016, 3, 4.

[42] On the conditions under § 4 No. 3 Unfair Competition Act 2015 see A. Ohly in A. Ohly and O. Sosnitza (eds.), *UWG*, 7th edn (Munich: Beck, 2016), § 4 paras. 3/25–3/80.

the imitation and the higher the degree of competitive individuality is, the lesser are the requirements for additional factors. In cases of identical imitation, the courts are much more easily prepared to find a likelihood of confusion or an actionable misrepresentation.[43]

The case law of the Supreme Court on unfair imitation is so extensive that it cannot be recounted in any detail here. Between 2004 and 2014 the Supreme Court decided around forty cases under what is now § 4 No. 3 Unfair Competition Act 2015, so that the total number of Supreme Court judgments in this category will amount to several hundreds. Some general observations will have to suffice.

First, the approach of the Supreme Court to the additional requirements of unfairness over the decades resembles a wave with crests and troughs. After the court had provided protection rather liberally at first, it took the additional requirements more seriously in the 1930s. After the Second World War the Supreme Court, in a period that could generally be regarded as one of judicial activism, was more prepared to use § 1 Unfair Competition Act 1909 in order to fill what it perceived as gaps in the intellectual property system, and protection again reached a high-water mark. In the last decades the extension of intellectual property law resulted in a stricter approach to the additional requirements. In particular, the category of 'taking unfair advantage' has been applied more restrictively in recent years.[44] While some authors in German literature take issue with the principle of freedom of imitation and are in favour of stronger protection,[45] others criticise the courts for not taking the additional requirements of unfairness seriously enough and for sometimes getting close to prohibiting imitation per se.[46]

Secondly, the Supreme Court has been more prepared to grant unfair competition protection to aesthetic than to functional features. While there is an extensive case law on when confusion is 'avoidable', the courts have repeatedly stressed that the imitation of a technical solution is unobjectionable, as long as consumer confusion is avoided by sufficient

[43] See BGH GRUR 2015, 909 – *Exzenterzähne [Eccentric Teeth]*, recently confirmed in BGH GRUR 2017, 734 – *Bodendübel* [*Ground Plug*], where the Supreme Court enjoined the sale of identical imitations of wall-plugs on the basis of unfair competition law although the patent on the plugs had expired. See the comments by H. Nemeczek, case note, GRUR 2015, 914–15 (for) and by Ohly, in Ohly/Sosnitza, § 4 para. 3/62 (against).

[44] See BGH GRUR 2007, 795 – *Handtaschen [Handbags]*.

[45] G. Fezer, 'Modernisierung des deutschen Rechts gegen den unlauteren Wettbewerb auf der Grundlage einer Europäisierung des Wettbewerbsrechts', WRP 2001, 989, 1004–5; A. Lubberger, in H. J. Ahrens, J. Bornkamm and H. P. Kunz-Hallstein (eds.), *Festschrift für Eike Ullmann* (Saarbrücken: Juris, 2006), p. 737.

[46] A. Peukert, *Güterzuordnung als Rechtsprinzip* (Tübingen: Mohr Siebeck, 2008), pp. 389, 812–18; A. Ohly, 'Hartplatzhelden.de oder: Wohin mit dem unmittelbaren Leistungsschutz?', GRUR 2010, 487, 494.

labelling.[47] When it comes to aesthetic features, the courts are more prepared to require the imitator to change his product.

Thirdly, while the advantage of this area of law is its flexibility, its disadvantage is its uncertainty. 'Confusion', 'avoidable' and 'unfair advantage' are open terms which allow the courts to balance interests and to consider the merits of each individual case. Over time the courts have developed many principles and sub-principles that governed the application of the former case-law doctrine and that now govern the application of § 4 No. 3 Unfair Competition Act 2015. Nevertheless a critic inspired by American Legal Realism might observe that in many cases you can identify both a principle favouring the claimant and a counter-principle favouring the defendant.

Fourthly, the courts have repeatedly used § 1 Unfair Competition Act 1909 in order to fill gaps in the intellectual property system. A prominent example is the protection of inventions between the end of the Second World War and the re-opening of the German Patent Office in 1949.[48] Since then, § 1 Unfair Competition Act 1909 has been used to protect well-known marks,[49] plant varieties,[50] neighbouring rights[51] and databases[52] before the respective intellectual property provisions were enacted. *Ulmer* referred to this phenomenon as the 'pace-maker function' of unfair competition law.[53] One example in point is the *Fashion Novelty* case decided by the Supreme Court in 1973.[54] Fabric patterns used for haute couture clothing had been imitated and sold to a clothing discounter. There was no likelihood of confusion, and it was also questionable whether the defendant had taken unfair advantage of the claimant's reputation. The Supreme Court granted protection on the basis of § 1 Unfair Competition Act 1909 and explained very openly why the law of registered designs did not provide sufficient protection. Hence the court considered it appropriate to protect fashion against identical or almost identical imitation, but also decided that protection was restricted to one season. By doing this, the Supreme Court came close to creating an unregistered design right judicially.

Whether the categories of intellectual property should be closed or whether the courts should be able to grant additional low-level and short-term protection in cases not covered by intellectual property

[47] BGH GRUR 2012, 58, para. 46 – *Seilzirkus [Spacenet]*.
[48] BGH GRUR 1952, 562 – *Schuhsohle [Shoe Sole]*; Nerreter, GRUR 1957, 408, 416–17.
[49] BGH GRUR 1985, 550 – *Dimple*.
[50] BGH GRUR 1959, 240 – *Nelkenstecklinge [Carnation Shoots]*.
[51] BGH GRUR 1962, 470 – *AKI*. [52] BGH GRUR 1999, 923 – *Tele-Info-CD*.
[53] E. Ulmer, *Urheber- und Verlagsrecht*, 3rd edn (Berlin/Heidelberg/New York: Springer, 1980), p. 40.
[54] BGH GRUR 1973, 478 – *Modeneuheit* = [1973] IIC 458 – *Fashion Novelty*.

legislation is a fundamental question, which is too broad to be discussed here.[55] A closed system protects the freedom of imitation, but it may also cause legislature to over-react by creating unnecessary or unnecessarily broad statutes, and it may cause the courts to force square pegs into round holes. Restricted intellectual property rights, combined with flexible low-level protection, could allow a 'more economic approach' to intellectual property law. But this issue goes well beyond the scope of this chapter.

5.3 Copyright Law: From Demarcation to Partial Cumulation

5.3.1 Demarcation under the 1876 Act

The Act on Copyright in Works of Visual Arts of 1876 did not define the term 'work of visual arts', although works of architecture were explicitly excluded. The drafters gave more attention to a list of acts that amounted to a reproduction and to a corresponding list of what was not a reproduction. According to the motives, the crucial criterion for distinguishing between artistic and industrial reproductions was which purpose prevailed. Hence the demarcation according to the purpose became known as the 'prevalence theory'. The main reason for this demarcation was the concept of 'art pour l'art' prevailing at that time. The distinction between high art, which served to enlighten, edify and educate the public, and industry seems to have been well entrenched. This becomes evident in the following passage taken from a judgment handed down by the Supreme Court in 1883. According to the court, copyright protection could only be granted if the work was

> not a means for an external end but a beautiful creation, drawing from an individual intellectual spirit and representing in harmony the purity of lines, the glow of colours and the sterling solidity of materials, which fill its author when creating and its beholder when viewing with the ideal joy of beauty.[56]

Hence a typeface[57] or models for carved backrests[58] were held not to be protected by artistic copyright.

[55] For some further thoughts on this point, see A. Ohly, 'The Freedom of Imitation and Its Limits – A European Perspective' [2010] IIC 506, 520–4.

[56] RGZ 14, 46, 54–5 – *Buchstabenformen [Letter Shapes]*.

[57] RGZ 14, 46, 54–5 – *Buchstabenformen [Letter Shapes]*.

[58] BGH GRUR 1976, 649, 650 – *Hans Thoma-Stühle [Hans Thoma Chairs]*. In this case the Federal Supreme Court had to decide whether artistic chair designs produced around 1900 by an artist who died in 1924 were still protected by copyright law in 1966. The Federal Supreme Court applied the prevalence theory and held that the designs had been in the public domain before 1907. Following judgments handed down by the Supreme Court after 1907 the Federal Supreme Court held that copyright protection did not resurge in 1907.

But in addition the Act provided for a further demarcation. While § 5 No. 3 listed the reproduction of the work on 'works of architecture, industry, factories, crafts or manufacture' as a relevant category of reproduction, § 14 of the Act provided:

> If the author of a work of visual arts allows it to be reproduced on a product of industry, factories, crafts or manufactures, he will not enjoy protection against further reproductions on works of industry etc. under the present Act, but only under the Act on Copyright in Patterns and Models.

Thus a work which qualified as a work of art was protected under copyright law against reproduction for artistic purposes, but protection against mass production was only granted under the Design Act. If an artist painted a picture and allowed its reproduction on plates, cups, tables, paperweights or album covers, he would still be granted copyright protection against the reproduction of the picture in a painting. But protection against counterfeit tableware was only available under design law with its formal and temporal restrictions.[59] A practical example of how the demarcation was applied is given by a case decided by the Supreme Court in 1889. The case concerned an advertising poster commissioned by Norddeutscher Lloyd, one of Germany's leading shipping companies at that time. The poster showed a passenger ship at full steam (Figure 5.1).

The Supreme Court regarded the picture as artistic and held that it did not lose its artistic quality just because the artist had created it for the purposes of advertising. But copyright protection against the reproduction on posters could not be granted because, according to § 14 of the Artistic Copyright Act 1876, the advertising posters were 'products of industry'.

Hence the law between 1876 and 1907 combined a partial subject-matter exclusion with an exception. Only artistic designs qualified for copyright protection in the first place. But even artistic works which qualified were not protected by copyright against industrial reproduction if the owner had allowed it. This part of the former German approach is reminiscent of s. 10 of the UK Copyright Act 1956 before its amendment in 1968.[60]

5.3.2 *From Demarcation to Partial (or Even Total?) Cumulation: The 1907 Act*

Around the turn of the century German design became increasingly innovative. Inspired by the British Arts and Crafts Movement, the

[59] BGH GRUR 1976, 649, 650 – *Hans Thoma-Stühle [Hans Thoma Chairs]*.
[60] See Chapter 6 on UK law.

Figure 5.1 The 'Norddeutscher Lloyd' advertising poster
Designer: Themistokles von Eckenbrecher (1842–1921), scan: Wikimedia Commons. This poster is not identical, but similar to the one assessed by the Supreme Court in 1889.

architects and designers of the Jugendstil (Art Nouveau) started creating buildings, furniture and ornaments characterised by curved lines and floral ornaments. A reform movement among designers started fighting against the excessive decorations of the nineteenth-century style and advocated clarity and simplicity. In 1907 the Werkbund was founded, an association of artists, designers, architects and producers who rejected the 'l'art pour l'art' approach and who were convinced that a new beginning in architecture and style had to start from crafts and from industrial production.[61] At the same time the restrictions of copyright law were increasingly criticised. Designers not only complained that many of their creations remained unprotected, they also pointed out that German works of applied art were not protected abroad under the Berne Convention due to the reciprocity principle. The German Association for the Protection of Industrial Property, which was later to become the German Association for the Protection of Intellectual Property (GRUR), took the lead and conducted a study among artists, experts and producers which showed that there was a widespread desire for a more extensive copyright protection.[62] Legislation, which had already passed a new Act on Copyright in Works of Literature and Musical Art in 1901, reacted by proposing a Copyright Bill in 1905.

The new Act on Copyright in Works of Visual Arts and Photography was passed on 9 January 1907. It did not define the concept of 'work' either, but it now included works of architecture and works of artistic craftsmanship ('Kunstgewerbe'). The old restriction concerning industrial reproduction was abolished. § 17 of the Act provided:

> Any reproduction without the consent of the right owner is inadmissible, independent of the process by which it is achieved; it does not make any difference whether the work is reproduced in one or several copies.

The Motives to the Act, i.e. the explanatory memorandum, point out that artists increasingly turned their attention to objects of everyday life and shaped them in aesthetic ways. Thus the distinction between pure art and applied art had become anachronistic. The memorandum also pointed out that foreign copyright Acts tended to treat both areas alike.[63]

Thus demarcation in Germany only lasted for thirty-one years. The new Act explicitly provided for an overlap between copyright and design protection. But it did not clarify the relation between both rights any further. In particular it was not clear from the provisions of the Act whether any design also qualified as a work of artistic craftsmanship or whether the copyright threshold was higher than the threshold of individuality in design law. The Motives, however, indicated that there could

[61] See Englert, *Grundzüge*, p. 17; Zentek, *Geschichte des Designschutzes*, pp. 106–18.
[62] Zentek, *Geschichte des Designschutzes*, p. 120. [63] GRUR 1906, 17ff.

be creations such as textile designs, wallpapers, clothes and simple combinations of shapes which attracted design protection but which could not be regarded as works of art.[64]

It took four years before the Supreme Court had the chance to consider this issue. In this period, the relationship between copyright and design law was moot and much disputed in legal literature.[65] The prevalence theory, which distinguished between works of art and designs according to their purpose, had some supporters.[66] Others, most notably Kohler, rejected this approach and thought that works of art on the one hand and designs on the other hand were of a different nature. According to Kohler, works of art were the embodiments of a creative idea,[67] whereas designs were aesthetic shapes. Schanze restricted the concept of 'works of art' to images of the outside world and argued that such images had to be independent, i.e. not parts of a complex product, and indivisible, i.e. unlike a pattern which could be cut or repeated.[68] But there were also influential writers who argued that all distinctions between designs and 'works of arts and craft' had been abolished by the 1907 Act and who advocated full cumulation.[69] According to Osterrieth, the new Act protected 'the whale and the bacillus alike'.[70] Copyright protection did not depend on artistic merit. In the course of the legislative process the qualification initially made in the Bill that 'products of craft are considered as works of art if they pursue artistic purposes' had been struck from the text.

5.3.3 *Setting the Tone for the Next 100 Years: The* School Typeface *Judgment (1911)*

But the uncertainty did not last for long. In 1911 the Reichsgericht handed down its *Schulfraktur* (*School Typeface*) judgment,[71] which set

64 GRUR 1906, 17ff.
65 See the overview by O. Schanze, 'Geschmacksmustergesetz und Kunstschutzgesetz', Leipziger Zeitschrift 1908, 652–60, 754–64, 822–40.
66 K. Runge, *Urheber- und Verlagsrecht* (Bonn/Hannover/Stuttgart: Ferd. Dummlers Verlag, 1953), p. 289; for a more modern variant of the prevalence theory see W. Reichel, 'Die Formgebung und die Formgestaltung von Schriftwerken und ihr rechtlicher Schutz', GRUR 1963, 124, 126; W. Nordemann, 'Zur Abgrenzung des Geschmacksmusterschutzes vom Urheberschutz', (1967) 50 *UFITA* 906, 910.
67 Kohler used the term 'Weltschöpfungsidee' ('world creation idea'); see Kohler, *Musterrecht*, p. 44.
68 Schanze, Leipziger Zeitschrift 1908, 762–3.
69 P. Allfeld, *Kommentar zu dem Gesetze betreffend das Urheberrecht an Werken der bildenden Künste und der Photographie* (Munich: Beck, 1908), p. 39; A. Osterrieth, *Lehrbuch des gewerblichen Rechtsschutzes* (Leipzig: Deichert'sche Verlagsbuchhandlung, 1908), pp. 222–3; E. Riezler, *Deutsches Urheber- und Erfinderrecht*, Vol. I (Munich/Berlin: J. Schweitzer Verlag, 1909), p. 459.
70 A. Osterrieth, *Kunst und Recht* (Berlin: Puttkammer & Mühlbrecht, 1909), p. 24.
71 RGZ 76, 339 – *Schulfraktur [School Typeface]*.

the tone until today. The principles of this case have governed the relationship between design and copyright law since then. Even the recent *Birthday Train* judgment contains language that can be traced back to the 1911 case.

The claimant had been the owner of design rights in a Gothic typeface known as the 'school typeface'. It retained the shapes of the traditional Gothic types, which prevailed in German books at that time, but simplified them in order to make them clearer and hence better suited for schoolbooks and newspapers.[72] The Supreme Court considered the typeface to be new and original in the sense of design law. But in the course of the proceedings design protection had lapsed. Hence the claimant also relied on copyright. The court reviewed the literature and adopted the theory of (only) partial cumulation. The main argument in the reasons is that full copyright protection would undermine the limits of design law:

> If every item which has so far been protected as a design, for a fee, subject to formalities and for up to 15 years only, should now enjoy copyright protection for free, without any formalities and for much longer, the retention of the Design Act would not have made sense ... Thus it remains the case that industrial products which can be protected as designs must be classified into those which do and those which do not attract copyright protection.[73]

But the court also recognised the problem inherent in this approach:

> The difficulty, however, lies in the practical application.

It felt unable to draw a clear and bright line:

> The difference is a gradual one. Not every little ornament, not every aesthetic arrangement lifts an industrial product into the sphere of art ... A work of applied art ... is only present if the aesthetic surplus which is added to the utility of the shape, independently of its artistic value, reaches a level at which it is possible, according to the views held in life, to speak of art.[74]

In the case at hand the court considered the design of the typeface to have been dictated by functionality. It compared the typeface to the examples mentioned in the explanatory memorandum – patterns for textiles and

[72] As far as can be reconstructed, the typeface in Figure 5.2 was registered as a design in 1893 and was one of the typefaces the Supreme Court considered in its judgment of 1911.
[73] RGZ 76, 339, 343 – *Schulfraktur [School Typeface]*.
[74] RGZ 76, 339, 344 – *Schulfraktur [School Typeface]*.

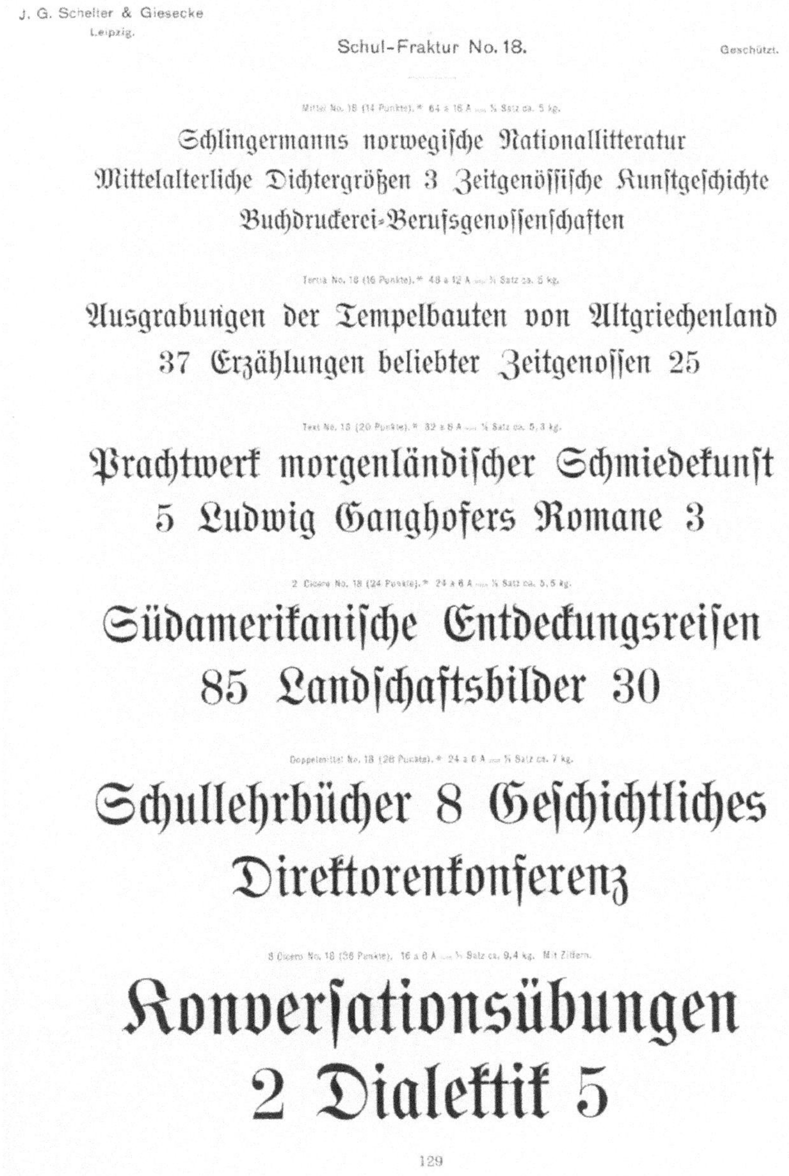

Figure 5.2 The 'School typeface': Schelter and Giesecke, Schulfraktur No. 18
Source: Specimen book J. G. Schelter and Giesecke, *Proben*, Vol. I, Leipzig, around 1899, p. 129, courtesy of Klingspor Museum, Offenbach

wallpapers and models for clothes – and decided that the typeface was even less inspired by aesthetic considerations.

The judgment clearly highlights the dilemma faced by the court. On the one hand, granting full copyright protection to all designs would have undermined the conditions and limits of design law. On the other hand, the court could not have applied a full or partial demarcation approach. Full demarcation had been given up by legislation; partial demarcation, which could have consisted in a shorter term of protection, would also have required legislative intervention. Hence the court had to draw a line between copyrightable and non-copyrightable designs.

The court introduced two criteria, both of which have obvious drawbacks. First, the court required an 'artistic surplus', an artistic addition to the mere shape. This criterion reminds of nineteenth-century design which allowed the distinction between the functional object and added ornaments. Under a modern 'form follows function' approach this separation is often not feasible, as cases concerning Bauhaus design soon showed. The second criterion, which could be called the 'informed observer test', is extremely vague. Drawing the line between art and simple objects of craft is next to impossible, and the court at first did not specify whether this question was to be determined from an expert's or from a consumer's perspective. At least in one respect the courts could rely on external expertise. According to § 46 of the Act on Copyright in Works of Visual Arts of 1907, chambers of experts were to be established, from whom courts could request opinions. In the *School Typeface* case the Supreme Court had had the benefit of such an expert opinion. The experts had advised against considering the typeface as a work of art.

5.3.4 *The Bauhaus Challenge: Stam's Cantilever Chair and the Gropius Door Handle (1932–1933)*

While the *School Typeface* criteria remained the guiding principles, the Supreme Court was prepared to grant copyright protection to designs rather liberally in the following years. Examples are a simple food label decorated with the picture of a bullfinch[75] and a lamp in the shape of a juggler.[76] The high-water mark of copyright protection was probably

[75] RGZ 117, 230, 234 – *Dompfaff-Marmelade [Bullfinch Jam]*.

[76] RG of 10 April 1929, case I 366/1928 (unpublished), but see RGZ 115, 180, 182 – *Puppenjunge [Boy Doll]*, confirming the appeal court's decision against copyright protection of a doll with certain individual characteristics.

reached in a judgment of 1929 which concerned a cutlery set. The knives, forks and spoons had ordinary shapes, but the handles were designed in a fan-like way.

Figure 5.3 The 'Fan-style' cutlery set: WMF cutlery set model 900 'Fächer'.
Photograph: Heinz Scheiffele

The Supreme Court acknowledged that this was a borderline case. But it was prepared to follow the opinion of the chamber of experts and the judgments of the courts of instance, which had all considered the cutlery set to be a work of art.[77]

Meanwhile the heavily ornamented design of the pre-war period had given way to a modernism characterised by austerity and objectivity. This movement was led by the Bauhaus designers. The Bauhaus, an academy of architecture and design, was founded in Weimar in 1919. In 1925 it moved to Dessau and in 1933 it was closed after repressions by the Nazi authorities. The name 'Bauhaus' (literally 'building house') is reminiscent of the artisans who joined up to build cathedrals in medieval times and who referred to their communities as 'Bauhütten' ('building huts'). The Bauhaus designers saw themselves in the tradition of these medieval artisans. Much like cathedral builders, they regarded themselves as craftsmen with artistic ambition.[78] They were pioneers of a modern design which preferred simple, basic and functional shapes. While there is some evidence that the Bauhaus designers took design protection more seriously than copyright,[79] cases soon reached the courts in which design protection for groundbreaking objects had lapsed. These cases presented a challenge to the idea of 'artistic surplus', which is hard to discern in Bauhaus design.

The first Bauhaus judgment handed down by the Supreme Court concerned a cantilever chair design by *Mart Stam*. The District Court and the Berlin Court of Appeal had regarded the chair as a work of applied art. The Supreme Court upheld both judgments and cited the reasons given by the lower courts with approval:

> The District Court and the Court of Appeal regard Mart Stam's steel tubular chairs as works of applied art [literally: arts and crafts] (§ 2 Artistic Copyright Act 1907) ... [According to both courts of instance] Mart Stam had produced an independent, individual creation. As a solution to the problem of constructing a chair out of tubular steel, several variants would have been possible. The main characteristic of Stam's chair was the strict, consequent layout which avoided all superfluous elements and embodied the New Objectivity in a minimal shape with simplest means. It was immaterial for individuality whether the shape was also determined by technical concerns. Especially in present times a mode of art was considered as particularly valuable which lent a good, simple expression to a purpose. For a work of artistic craftsmanship it sufficed that an object of everyday life received a certain aesthetic shape which was agreeable to the eye. These requirements had been met in the present case.

[77] RGZ 124, 68, 72.

[78] A rich account of the Bauhaus history and of all copyright and design issues concerning Bauhaus design is given by S. Neurauther, *Das Bauhaus und die Verwertungsrechte* (Tübingen: Mohr Siebeck, 2013).

[79] Neurauther, *Bauhaus*, pp. 286–90, 347–54.

Shortly after, however, the Supreme Court reached a different conclusion in the case of a door handle designed by Walter Gropius. The handle had an extremely basic shape. It consisted of a cubic part and of a handle in the shape of a cylinder.[80]

Figure 5.4 The *Gropius* door handle
Photograph: Harald Wetzel

What has by now become a usual design feature of modern buildings was revolutionary in early 1933. The chamber of experts had stressed that the handle was designed according to the modern taste in art without any artistic ornaments. In modern design the purpose of the shape could not be separated from its aesthetic value. But, following the Berlin Court of Appeal, the Supreme Court rejected this view and stressed that for a shape to attract copyright protection it had to have an 'artistic surplus'. Whether this was the case had to be determined from the perspective of an 'educated public, which is reasonably familiar with artistic views and susceptible to objects of art'.[81] This version of the 'informed observer test', first formulated in the *School Typeface* judgment, has become well entrenched since then.

The Supreme Court upheld the Court of Appeal's judgment and repeated both arguments given by the appeal court. First, the handle only consisted of basic shapes which had been combined 'in their exclusivity, one might say: in their nakedness'. Such basic shapes could not

[80] See Figure 5.4. [81] RGZ 139, 214, 218.

attract protection, as otherwise every object of modern design had to be regarded as protected.[82] Secondly, the claimant's series comprised several door handles in different dimensions. Hence the court concluded that he did not claim protection for one object, but rather for a style.[83]

5.3.5 Influences of Nazi Ideology? (1933–1945)

The *Gropius* judgment, which was handed down on 14 January 1933, two weeks before Hitler came to power, has recently been interpreted as foreshadowing the Nazi attitude towards modern art and design.[84] Indeed, unlike the court in its *Stam* judgment and unlike the chamber of experts, the *Gropius* court did not find any warm words for modern design. One senses that the author of the judgment regarded the modern design concept with scepticism. But when analysing the judgment it seems important to exclude hindsight. Whereas we now know that designs like the Gropius handle were pioneers of what is today's mass taste, they were disputed in the 1930s. Unlike the cantilever chair, which had a highly original shape, the handle did consist of extremely basic forms which could not have been protected as such. Since the court followed earlier judgments in rejecting a theory of full cumulation, it had to draw a line. Also the *Gropius* design did not satisfy the 'artistic surplus' test, objectionable as this test may have already been at that time. From this perspective, it was at least arguable to exclude the combination of basic shapes from copyright protection.[85] Thus it seems difficult to argue that the judgment was tainted by ideology.[86]

What is true, however, is that the Supreme Court adopted a more restrictive attitude to copyright protection in the following years,[87] *inter alia* by denying copyright protection to a pattern of upholstery fabrics.[88] In 1939 the court again had to decide about copyright protection for a cutlery set, which, in terms of artistic merit, is difficult to distinguish from the set which was given protection in 1929. The Court of Appeal applied

[82] RGZ 139, 214, 219. [83] RGZ 139, 214, 219–20.

[84] Zentek, *Geschichte des Designschutzes*, pp. 177–8. On design during the Nazi period see S. Zentek, *Design(er) im Dritten Reich* (Dortmund: Lelesken-Verlag, 2009).

[85] The Supreme Court's approach also found support in legal literature: see, e.g., W. Pinzger, 'Die Reform des Geschmackmusterrechts', GRUR 1934, 396, 398.

[86] This view is shared by Neurauther, *Bauhaus*, p. 26.

[87] Copyright legislation did not change between 1933 and 1945. In 1939, the Academy of German Law presented a draft Copyright Act which was based on a pre-Nazi draft prepared by the Ministry of Justice in 1932, but which never entered into force. Typically for commercial law legislation between 1933 and 1945, the draft was a mixture of politically neutral provisions with some ideology interspersed.

[88] RGZ 155, 199, 201; see also Neurauther, *Bauhaus*, pp. 26–7.

the reasoning of the *Gropius* case and denied copyright protection. The Supreme Court upheld this judgment. Whether the cutlery set amounted to a work of applied art had to be determined not according to the views of the general public, but from the perspective of an educated member of the public,[89] who is reasonably familiar with artistic views and susceptible to objects of art. The Court of Appeal had been correct in applying a rather strict standard, because the law drew a distinction between design law and copyright law. Not every aesthetic and tasteful design could be regarded as copyrightable.

5.3.6 *Continuity: The First Post-war Supreme Court Judgments*

Not long after its establishment on 1 October 1950, the Federal Supreme Court (Bundesgerichtshof, BGH) had to decide its first case concerning a work of applied art. The claimant produced 'Hummel figures', i.e. china figures of children in traditional local costumes, which many people in the 1950s enjoyed on their mantelpieces and shelves. The defendant had imitated these figures. The case was brought on the basis of copyright, trade dress and unfair competition law, whereas design law was not invoked. As regards copyright, the Supreme Court cited the *Upholstery Fabric* judgment of 1937, in which the Reichsgericht had applied its 'informed observer test', in an obiter dictum. It did not elaborate on the subsistence of copyright, since it was evident that there had not been infringement.

Judgments handed down in the following years clarified that the Supreme Court considered the principles developed by the Reichsgericht as still applicable and as well established. As the Supreme Court before 1945, the Federal Supreme Court rejected the prevalence theory and stressed that the purpose for which a work was made was irrelevant. All that mattered was whether a creation would be seen as artistic rather than as merely aesthetic by members of the public who were susceptible to art and reasonably familiar with artistic views. In several cases the Supreme Court considered expert opinions obtained by the lower courts as helpful, but not as determinative.

In the practical application, the court adopted the same strict approach that had become the rule in the wake of the *Gropius* case. Repeatedly it stressed that the threshold for copyright protection should not be set too low. *Inter alia*, the Supreme Court denied copyright protection to a newspaper logo and to a modern, asymmetric china vase produced by one of Germany's leading china companies.[90]

[89] Following Nazi terminology, the court used the term 'Volksgenosse' ('national comrade'). But there are no other references to Nazi ideology in the judgment.

[90] BGH GRUR 1959, 289 – *Rosenthal-Vase*.

Figure 5.5 The *Rosenthal* vase 'Schwangere Luise' ('Pregnant Louise')
Designer: Fritz Heidenreich, picture: Rosenthal

But when the Federal Supreme Court, like the court in 1932, had to decide a case concerning an imitation of Mart Stam's cantilever chair, it followed its pre-war case law and considered the chair as protected by copyright.[91]

5.3.7 *The Copyright Act of 1965*

As seen above, there had already been initiatives for copyright reform in the 1930s. After the war they gained momentum. The 1907 Acts had become outdated due to both the technological development and the Rome and Brussels revisions of the Berne Convention. In 1954 the Ministry of Justice prepared a draft which was followed by a government proposal in 1959. Both drafts proposed to define the term 'work' as a

[91] BGH GRUR 1961, 635 – *Stahlrohrstuhl I [Tubular Chair I]*.

'personal intellectual creation' and to include 'works of artistic craftsmanship' (1954 draft) or 'works of applied art' (1959 proposal) into a non-exhaustive list of categories of work.

Not everyone was happy with this approach. Two alternative proposals were made. Some authors recommended repealing the Designs Act, integrating design protection into copyright law but providing a shorter term of protection for designs. According to one proposal, works 'merely intended for commercial exploitation' were to be protected for ten years only, provided they were not of significant originality.[92] The Association of German Industry, on the other hand, recommended abolishing copyright protection and introducing *sui generis* protection for utilitarian works.[93] The Legal Committee of the German Parliament was attracted to this proposal, but recommended retaining copyright protection of works of applied art until the creation of a *sui generis* system.[94]

None of these alternative proposals was ultimately successful. The new Copyright Act, which entered into force on 1 January 1965, merged the 1907 Acts into one, stressed the importance of moral rights and distinguished more clearly than before between copyright and related rights and but it did not change the legal regime for designs. With respect to the copyright/design interface the Act aimed at continuity and left the exact distinction between works of applied art and non-copyrightable designs to the courts.

Thus, nothing changed. The Supreme Court reiterated the 'informed observer test' in many judgments between 1965 and 1995,[95] which do not need to be analysed in detail here. But two aspects gradually developed over time and are worth noting.

First, in many judgments the courts apply the rather vague test by comparing the alleged work with pre-existing products.[96] The mere adoption of a combination of common shapes did not amount to a personal individual creation. The same applied to naturalistic copies of objects of nature. There are also several judgments in which the courts took the freedom of the designer into account. Features determined by technical constraints or by rules of logic did not give rise to copyright protection.

92 E. Henssler, 'Der Schutz der angewandten Kunst nach geltendem Recht und nach dem Ministerialentwurf 1959 zum Urheberrechts-Gesetz', GRUR 1961, 397, 402.

93 Henssler, GRUR 1961, 397, 403; Englert, *Grundzüge*, p. 28.

94 BT-Drucks. [Bundestagsdrucksache = Parliamentary Proceedings] IV/3401, p. 2; Englert, *Grundzüge*, p. 31.

95 See, e.g., BGH GRUR 1967, 315, 316 – *Skai-cubana*; BGH GRUR 1972, 38, 39 – *Vasenleuchter [Vase Lamp]*; BGH GRUR 1979, 332, 336 – *Brombeerleuchte [Blackberry Lamp]*; BGH GRUR 1983, 377, 378 – *Brombeer-Muster [Blackberry Pattern]*.

96 Eck, *Neue Wege*, p. 57.

Secondly, the threshold of protection was rather high, at least until 2014.[97] Simple everyday designs usually failed to meet the copyright threshold. Great artistic designs, however, were held to be protected. As a rule of thumb one could apply the 'museum test': Would a design museum such as the Victoria & Albert Museum, the Architecture & Design Department of the Museum of Modern Art in New York or the Pinakothek der Moderne in Munich acquire the object for its collection? Examples are pieces of furniture created by *Le Corbusier*,[98] lamps designed by *Wilhelm Wagenfeld*[99] or the *Tripp Trapp* chair,[100] whereas simple everyday furniture such as office desks, a step stool or chairs did not normally qualify.

Clothes, fabric patterns and jewellery could attract copyright protection in exceptional cases, but practically copyright protection was denied in the majority of reported cases. The closer designs came to classical categories of works, the more likely they were to be protected. Toy figures, for example, were granted protection in most reported cases. The same applied to advertising posters, whereas simple logos were mostly seen as not protected.

5.3.8 Silver Thistle, *the 'Two-tier Theory' and Its Critics*

While the distinction between non-copyrightable designs and works of applied art had become well established by 1965, the 'informed observer test' lacked precision and theoretical coherence. One of the critics was *Ulmer*.[101] He acknowledged that not every design could be protected by copyright law, but he also rejected earlier attempts to regard art and craftsmanship as different by nature. Since both design and copyright law required an individual creation, they were of a similar nature ('wesensgleich'). Thus the difference had to be one of degree. While literary or musical works of little originality, often referred to as the 'small coin' ('kleine Münze') of copyright law, were protected by copyright law, design law could be seen as providing the base or substructure ('Unterbau') of copyright law in the area of applied arts. Hence design law was in some ways comparable to

[97] See the case analysis by S. Zech, *Der Schutz von Werken der angewandten Kunst im Urheberrecht Frankreichs und Deutschlands* (Munich: Beck, 1999), pp. 187–93.
[98] BGH GRUR 1987, 903, 905 – *Le-Corbusier-Möbel*.
[99] BGH GRUR 2007, 871, 873 – *Wagenfeld-Leuchte*.
[100] OLG Hamburg ZUM-RD 2002, 181, 187, affirmed by BGH GRUR 2009, 856 – *Tripp-Trapp-Stuhl*.
[101] Ulmer, *Urheber- und Verlagsrecht*, pp. 149–50.

neighbouring rights which protect non-original subject-matter, such as the right in non-original photographs which exists in many EU Member States or (after Ulmer's day) the *sui generis* right in databases. Thus, according to Ulmer, it made sense to exclude the 'small coin' of creativity ('kleine Münze') from copyright protection and to make it dependent on what he termed an 'artistic level of creativity' ('künstlerische Gestaltungshöhe'). This approach has become known as the 'two-tier theory' or 'two-step theory' ('Stufentheorie'): new and individual designs are protected by design law (step 1); highly creative designs qualify for copyright protection (step 2).

The Supreme Court, which had not clearly distinguished between different levels of originality before, adopted Ulmer's approach in the *Silver Thistle* judgment, but held that it was consistent with the court's established case law. The court recounted the arguments mentioned above and held that works of applied art were only protected by copyright if they reached a level of creativity which was well above the level of average design.[102] The 'silver thistle' earclips failed to meet this requirement. The Supreme Court pointed out that they were modelled on nature and that they were the result of creative craftsmanship rather than of a personal individual creation.

In the following years it became rarer for the Supreme Court to cite the 'informed observer test' and to adopt the perspective of 'members of the public susceptible to art and familiar with artistic views'. Referring to the *Silver Thistle* case, the court applied the two-tier theory and enquired whether the alleged work showed a level of individuality which was well above the average. For practical purposes the matter seemed to be settled: between 1995 and 2011 the Supreme Court decided several cases concerning works of applied art, including cases resulting from the lack of protection in Italian law at that time. But none of these cases concerned the issue of whether the work in question was copyrightable. The Federal Constitutional Court confirmed that it neither amounted to an excessive interference with property rights nor to an unjustified unequal treatment.[103]

But there was a growing debate in legal literature. Some authors agreed with the Supreme Court's approach.[104] They argued that liberal copyright protection could undermine the requirements of design law and that creativity in the area of designs required breathing space which would be unduly restricted if copyright law provided for almost

[102] BGH GRUR 1995, 581, 582.

[103] BVerfG GRUR 2005, 410 – *Laufendes Auge [Running Eye]*.

[104] H. Schack, *Urheber- und Urhebervertragsrecht*, 7th edn (Tübingen: Mohr Siebeck, 2015), para. 237; A. Ohly, 'Designschutz im Spannungsfeld von Geschmacksmuster-, Kennzeichen- und Lauterkeitsrecht', GRUR 2007, 731, 733.

eternal protection without registration. Even demarcation was advocated.[105]

But the proponents of full cumulation were in the majority.[106] They pointed out that the application of different thresholds under one single statutory definition was doctrinally inconsistent and that it was impossible to distinguish between 'artistic craftsmanship' and an 'artistic level of creativity' with any certainty. It was also pointed out that the 'small coin' of copyright was protected with respect to works of photography, although German law granted 'second-tier' *sui generis* protection to non-original photographs. Treating photography and applied art alike meant that the 'small coin' had to be copyrightable in both areas. The doctrinal foundations of the 'two-tier theory' were also weakened when the Designs Act 1876 was repealed and the European Design Directive implemented in 2004. The drafters of the Directive intended to replace the 'patent' and 'copyright' approaches, which had existed in Europe, with a novel 'design' approach.[107] Under the new law, a design right was not a similar, if lesser, form of copyright, but an independent type of intellectual property. It is remarkable that for most of the critics, in line with the general academic tendency in the 1990s, the aim was not a fair balance between protection and the public domain, but an optimal protection of designers which left as few gaps as possible.

5.3.9 The Exclusion of Technical Features in Rope Circus *(*Spacenet*)*

Gradually, the Supreme Court moved away from the 'two-tier theory'.[108] The first indications[109] of this development were given in the *Spacenet*

[105] F. Wassner, *Kunst, Geschmack und unlauterer Wettbewerb* (Berlin: Schweitzer, 1975), pp. 33–40.

[106] U. Loewenheim, 'Höhere Schutzuntergrenze des Urheberrechts bei Werken der angewandten Kunst?', GRUR Int. 2004, 765; A. Nordemann and F. N. Heise, 'Urheberrechtlicher Schutz für Designleistungen in Deutschland und auf europäischer Ebene', ZUM 2001, 128, 137–40; G. Schricker, 'Der Urheberrechtsschutz von Werbeschöpfungen, Werbeideen, Werbekonzeptionen und Werbekampagnen', GRUR 1996, 815, 818–19; U. Koschtial, 'Zur Notwendigkeit der Absenkung der Gestaltungshöhe für Werke der angewandten Kunst im deutschen Urheberrecht', GRUR 2004, 555 (558ff); Zech, *Schutz*, pp. 246–52; E.-I. v. Gamm, *Die Problematik der Gestaltungshöhe im deutschen Urheberrecht* (Baden-Baden: Nomos, 2004), pp. 91ff, 233.

[107] F.-K. Beier, 'The Future of Intellectual Property in Europe – Thoughts on the Development of Patent, Utility Model and Industrial Design Law' [1991] IIC 157, 175.

[108] An earlier version of 5.3.9 was published in G. Karnell et al. (eds.), *Liber Amicorum Jan Rosén* (Visby: eddy.de, 2016), pp. 591–607. On the development leading to the *Birthday Train* case, see also K.-N. Peifer, '"Individualität" or Originality? Core Concepts in German Copyright Law', GRUR Int. 2014, 1100.

[109] An even earlier hint is given in BGH GRUR 2011, 803, para. 31 – *Lernspiele [Learning Games]*, where the Supreme Court refrains from citing the *Silver Thistle* judgment and returns to the 'informed observer test' instead.

(*Seilzirkus*) case.[110] The claimant was the producer of climbing structures made of ropes, designed for playgrounds. The defendant had copied the structures. They had a certain aesthetic appeal, although the main purpose of the design was functional.[111]

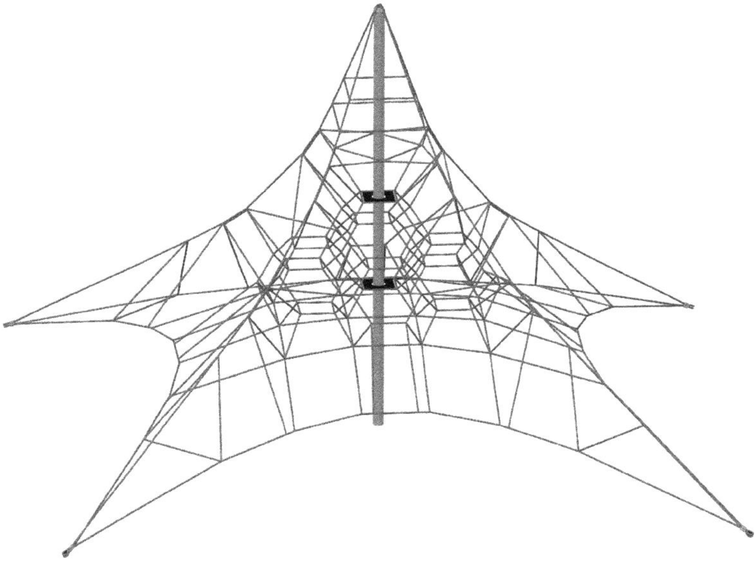

Figure 5.6 The 'Spacenet' ('Seilzirkus') climbing structure
Designer: Conrad Roland, drawing courtesy of COROCORD Raumnetz GmbH

The Supreme Court had several options. It could have denied copyright protection on the basis of the 'two-tier theory', it could have jettisoned the theory or it could have referred the case to the CJEU. The court did not choose any of these paths. It recounted the criticism advanced against the theory,[112] but left the issue open and denied copyright protection on the basis of a robust notion of functionality.[113] First, creativity required a certain freedom of choice which did not exist when features were determined by technical considerations. Secondly, the state

[110] BGH GRUR 2012, 58 – *Seilzirkus [Rope Spacenet]*. The word 'Seilzirkus' literally translates into 'rope circus', but the product is distributed in the English-speaking word under the name 'Spacenet'.
[111] See Figure 5.6. [112] BGH GRUR 2012, 58, para. 35.
[113] BGH GRUR 2012, 58, paras. 18ff.

of the art in technology had to remain free, as the functionality exceptions in both trademark and design law showed. Since nobody could be allowed to monopolise the free state of the art, copyright required an artistic creation of an aesthetic nature. That was not the case here: the *Spacenet* decision solved the technical problem of constructing a climbing structure consisting of a mast and ropes. Even if there would have been design alternatives, the features were chosen for technical reasons.

This judgment was remarkable for several reasons. First, it cast doubt on whether the 'two-tier theory' was still good law. If it had been, the Supreme Court could have disposed of the case with much less argumentative effort. Secondly, the court applied a functionality doctrine which was clearer and more robust than previous cases showed. Thirdly, the CJEU judgments on the European concept of work were not mentioned with one single word. The Supreme Court seemed to assume that national law was still free to determine the requirements of copyright protection on its own. At the same time, the reasoning of the judgment is, albeit tacitly, in line with judgments such as *BSA*[114] and *Football Association Premier League*,[115] in which the CJEU had held that copyright did not subsist in features which were dictated by rules and technical constraints.

5.3.10 The Abolition of the Two-tier Theory in Birthday Train *(*Geburtstagszug*)*

The Birthday Train is a wooden toy train which can be decorated with numbers and candles – the number six and six candles for a child's sixth birthday, for example.[116]

The Supreme Court had to decide whether the toy train was protected by copyright law. It should be noted, however, that this was not an infringement case. It arose under one of the provisions of German copyright contract law which give an author a claim to adequate remuneration when either the remuneration on which the parties have agreed has been inadequate from the beginning or if it becomes inadequate due to the commercial success of the work.[117] The designer had received the equivalent of 200 Euros for her design of the train. Then the train turned out to be a bestseller. The designer claimed additional remuneration. Since design law does not contain similar provisions, the claimant could only be successful if the train attracted copyright protection. At the same time,

[114] CJEU, Case C-393/09, *BSA* v. *Ministerstvo kultury*, ECLI:EU:C:2010:816, para. 49.
[115] CJEU, Case C-403/08, *Football Association Premier League* v. *QC Leisure*, ECLI:EU:C:2011:631, para. 98.
[116] See Figures 5.7 and 5.8. [117] §§ 32, 32a German Copyright Act.

Figure 5.7 The 'Birthday Train'
Designer and photograph: Heike Wiechmann

EU law was not relevant, since the case did not hinge on the interpretation of Articles 2–4 InfoSoc Directive.

Under the 'two-tier theory' copyright protection would have been highly unlikely. Since wooden toy trains have been around for a while and since the design is nice, but in no way extraordinary, the train is the result of 'artistic craftsmanship'. So the Supreme Court had to decide the issue, and gave up the 'two-tier theory':

> The Senate abandons its former approach under which copyright protection for works of applied art eligible for design rights required a level of creativity which is well above the average. In principle no other conditions apply to the copyright protection of works of applied art than to the copyright protection of works of non-utilitarian fine arts or literary or artistic creations. It is thus sufficient for them to reach a level of creativity which can be referred to as an 'artistic' creation, according to the perspective of persons susceptible to art and reasonably familiar with artistic views.[118]

One might have expected that the Supreme Court would justify this departure from established case law with the recent developments in EU law. But this was not the case. In a way which could almost be regarded as CJEU-sceptic, the Supreme Court argued that it was not bound by the Court of Justice's case law on the concept of work.[119] The InfoSoc Directive only provided that the copyright owner had rights with respect

118 BGH GRUR 2014, 175, para. 26 – *Geburtstagszug [Birthday Train]* (author's translation); see also the translation in [2014] IIC 831 – *Birthday Train*.
119 BGH GRUR 2014, 175, paras. 27–32 – *Geburtstagszug [Birthday Train]*.

to a work, but it did not define what a work was. The definitions given in EU law with respect to computer programs, databases and photographs did not apply to works of applied art. They explicitly stated that a work was the 'author's own intellectual creation' and ruled out other criteria. Similar restrictions did not exist with regard to other types of work. In addition, the Supreme Court referred to Article 17(2) Design Directive, which left it to the Member States to determine the level of creativity required for the copyright protection of designs. Thus the Supreme Court considered the former German approach to be fully reconcilable with EU law.

Instead, the Supreme Court based its decision on the changed nature of design law.[120] After the implementation of the Design Directive, design law could no longer be regarded as similar to and as a substructure of copyright law. Both areas of law set forth different conditions of protection. Hence they were independent of one another. At the same time the court stressed that the level of creativity required for the protection of works of applied art should not be too low. For three reasons, the freedom of competition and the creative freedom of other designers did not risk being unduly restricted under the new approach. First, the court revived the 'informed observer test': a work would only be protected if it would be referred to as an 'artistic creation' by members of the public reasonably susceptible to the arts and reasonably familiar with artistic views. Secondly, features dictated by technical constraints did not qualify for copyright protection. Thirdly, the scope of protection depended on the level of individuality: works of little creativity would receive only a narrow scope of protection.

Academic comments reflect the former disagreement about the merits of the 'two-tier theory'. Those who liked it tend to be critical of the new approach.[121] The criticism will be explored in more detail below. Others agree with the Supreme Court that there should only be one single threshold of protection in copyright law[122] and applaud the extended protection against counterfeits.[123] Many also think, unlike the Supreme Court, that this step was required by EU law.

[120] BGH GRUR 2014, 175, paras. 33–40 – *Geburtstagszug [Birthday Train]*.

[121] H. Schack, case note, JZ 2014, 207–8; T. Hoeren, case note, MMR 2014, 337–8.

[122] E. I. Obergfell, 'Abschied von der "Silberdistel": Zum urheberrechtlichen Schutz von Werken der angewandten Kunst', GRUR 2014, 621, 627; G. Schulze, case note, NJW 2014, 475.

[123] N. Rauer and D. Ettig, 'Urheberrechtsschutz für Werke angewandter Kunst – BGH gibt ständige Rechtsprechung auf', WRP 2014, 135, 140.

Both critics and supporters alike can only speculate about whether the judgment has actually lowered the threshold of copyright protection. On the one hand, the Supreme Court has given up the 'two-tier theory'. Works of applied art do not have to pass a higher threshold of individuality any more. The court also stressed that design was an independent intellectual property right, not a 'substructure' to copyright. This might make it less necessary to draw a line between both areas of law and might point towards more generous copyright protection.[124] On the other hand, the Supreme Court returned to the old 'informed observer test'. While it may be reminiscent of the 'informed user' standard in EU design law, it should be noted that precisely this test was the basis of the rather restrictive approach to copyright protection between 1911 and 1995. In its *Silver Thistle* judgment, the Supreme Court had only considered the 'two-tier theory' as a restatement of the well-established approach. The *Gropius* formula will still allow the courts to exclude everyday designs from copyright protection.[125] It can also be argued that there is still a difference between works of applied art and other types of works: with regard to literary works, for example, German courts have never enquired whether, according to members of the public reasonably familiar with novels and poems, a text can be referred to as literature.

So the *Birthday Train* judgment is inherently ambiguous. While the Supreme Court will not require a higher level of creativity for works of applied art any more, it is likely to apply a more robust functionality exclusion than in design law and to exclude utilitarian features from copyright protection on that basis.[126]

5.3.11 The Present: Where is the Birthday Train *Heading?*

The fate of the birthday train has meanwhile been decided. The Supreme Court had referred the case back to the Schleswig Court of Appeal and had ordered it to decide the case on the basis of the new criteria. The Schleswig Court denied copyright protection.[127] It compared the birthday train to pre-existing toy trains, some of them produced by the defendant, but created by other designers.

[124] Obergfell, GRUR 2014, 621, 624; Schulze, NJW 2014, 475: 'Thanks to this welcome decision, the Birthday Train should be heading towards copyright protection with full steam. But the scope of protection might be narrow.'

[125] Schack, JZ 2014, 207, 208.

[126] M. Leistner, 'Urheberrecht unter dem Einfluss der EuGH-Rechtsprechung', EuZW 2016, 166, 167.

[127] OLG Schleswig, GRUR-RR 2015, 1 – *Geburtstagszug II [Birthday Train II]*.

None of them had been a 'birthday train' with holes for numbers and candles, but some of them had looked similar. The court considered the idea of a 'birthday train', which the claimant had apparently not even developed herself, to be outside the ambit of copyright protection. If one applied this idea to the pre-existing trains, the novel features of the claimant's design were not creative. Interestingly, however, the court gave judgment for the claimant with respect to another design which had not been considered by the Federal Supreme Court: the 'Birthday Caravan', which consisted of a line of wooden animal figures on wheels rather than of a train. There had been no toys of this sort before, and the court held that the designer had exercised its artistic freedom by creating the animals in a way which children like.

Since then, some courts of instance have given judgments on works of applied art. In a recent judgment the Cologne Court of Appeal considered the bow of a cruise ship, painted with a mouth, eyes and eyebrows painted on the bow, as a work protected by copyright:

> Now that the Supreme Court has given up its requirement of a specific level of creativity for works of applied art, this design ... has the necessary degree of creative individuality.[128]

The same court considered a green urn decorated with a bellowing stag[129] as protected.[130] The court adopted with approval the rather florid description of the urn given by the court of first instance, found that all pre-existing designs were rather different and rejected the defendant's argument that the motif only depicted a landscape in a naturalistic way. Although the language used by the court seems to indicate a more generous approach, both judgments would probably not have been different under the old law, since the designs in both cases consisted of pictures and hence resembled works of 'pure' art, which have always received more generous protection than mere shapes or patterns.

The District Court of Hamburg recently considered labels of beer bottles to be protected by copyright, although the labels were designed in a rather simple, almost puristic way.[131] The court held that precisely

[128] OLG Köln GRUR 2016, 495, para. 11 – *AIDA Kussmund [AIDA Kissing Lips]*.
[129] *De gustibus non est disputandum*.
[130] OLG Köln, GRUR-RR 2015, 275, 276 – *Airbrush-Urnen [Airbrush Urns]*.
[131] LG Hamburg, ZUM-RD 2017, 227.

this simplicity distinguished the labels from other bottles. This judgment is reminiscent of some judgments the Supreme Court handed down in the 1920s, before the *Gropius* judgment.

A judgment of the Nuremberg Court of Appeal[132] shows the interplay between individuality, functionality and scope. The leading German football magazine had offered a poster which showed the tables of the first three German football leagues, superimposed on the picture of a stadium. Users could update the table by sticking cardboard riders with the logos of the top league football clubs into slits corresponding to the respective positions. The court considered most features of this poster as determined by functional considerations, but thought that the graphic display of the tables could attract copyright protection. But apparently the court was not entirely certain. 'Even if copyright subsisted', the level of creativity was so low that the scope of protection was very narrow. Since the defendant's version of the table was sufficiently different, it did not infringe.

Some of these judgments show that there is some degree of uncertainty about the new approach. But they also suggest that the threshold of copyright protection has been lowered. However, it is still too early to tell with any certainty whether this is really the case and whether there are any new, individual and non-functional designs left which do not qualify for copyright protection.

5.4 Analysis: The Merits of Partial Cumulation

5.4.1 The German Experience Evaluated

5.4.1.1 The Model of Partial Cumulation

Table 5.2 summarises the historical analysis. It shows that all potential solutions to the copyright/design interface have either been realised or at least been proposed in Germany at some stage. But the prevailing model has been one of partial cumulation, based on a distinction between a lower threshold for design protection and higher requirements under copyright law.

5.4.1.2 Advantages

The strength of the German model of partial cumulation is that it takes the formal and substantive limits of design law seriously. As early as 1911 the Supreme Court stressed that specific design legislation did not make any sense if there was full copyright protection for new and individual designs.

[132] OLG Nürnberg, GRUR 2014, 1199 – *Kicker-Stecktabelle [Kicker Football Chart]*.

This argument has even more force today. The Community Design Regulation draws a clear and reasonable distinction between unregistered designs, which are only protected against imitation for three years, and registered designs, which are granted absolute protection for up to twenty-five years. This distinction would be undermined if every design which is new and original from a design law point of view would attract copyright protection. Compared to a model of full cumulation, the German approach thus allows more creative freedom for other designers who wish to use pre-existing shapes.

Also, the German model has limited the potential for 'asymmetric convergence'[133] between copyright and design law. As far as can be seen, there are next to no cases in which the difference between the exceptions allowed by copyright and by design law would have been an issue. A recent case[134] concerned the quotation right: a research organisation which had contributed to the development of the ICE had depicted the train in its catalogue. The Supreme Court considered this to be an infringement of the German Railway Company's design right in the train. Since there had been no precedents on quotation in design law, the court interpreted § 40 No. 3 Designs Act 2004 (= Article 13(1)(c) EU Design Directive) in accordance

Table 5.2 *The German approaches to demarcation and cumulation over time*

	Copyrightable subject-matter	Rights and exceptions
demarcation	subject-matter already registered as design / qualifying for design protection not copyrightable → *sui generis* legislation excluding copyright proposed before 1965, but never realised	exclusion of copyright protection in case of industrial reproduction → **Artistic Copyright Act 1876 – 1907**
partial cumulation	higher originality standard for copyright protection → **the law since 1907, modified (?) but not abolished by 2013 *Birthday Train* judgment**	shorter term of copyright protection or restricted rights in case of industrial reproduction → proposed before 1965, but never realised
full cumulation	identical standards, term and rights → proposed by academic authors, both after 1907 and under the Copyright Act 1965	

[133] I.e. an overlap of rights while exceptions remain incongruent; see A. Kur, 'A New Framework for Intellectual Property Rights – Horizontal Issues' [2004] *IIC* 1, 20.
[134] BGH GRUR 2011, 1117, paras. 42–50 – *ICE*.

with copyright law. But this case was not one of overlap: German Railway had only invoked design protection. Disputes about ownership have apparently not reached the higher courts, although German copyright law exclusively allocates ownership to the author,[135] whereas designs made by employees are owned by the employer.[136]

Compared to models of demarcation which restrict copyright protection against industrial reproduction, German law grants more protection to exceptional designs. The demarcation approach of the Artistic Copyright Act of 1876 was criticised because it also restricted the scope of protection for highly creative works, once there was industrial reproduction. Arguably great designs are equivalent to fine arts. The furniture created by Arne Jacobsen or Mart Stam has enriched our cultural heritage. For good reasons it is not only sold, it is also displayed in design museums. There is a case for granting copyright to these 'great' designs. But the same cannot be said for birthday trains or football sticker posters.

5.4.1.3 Drawbacks

However, the German experience also shows that this model has evident disadvantages. In particular, the criteria for distinguishing between ordinary designs and works of applied art are unclear. This is particularly true for the 'informed observer test'. The criterion of 'artistic' creativity is highly uncertain and theoretically unsound. Neither modern theorists of art nor judges who have to rule on issues of 'artistic freedom' have felt able to draw the line between art and routine. According to the Supreme Court the decision is to be made from the 'perspective of persons susceptible to art and reasonably familiar with artistic views'. These persons are probably related to the 'average consumer', the 'informed user' of designs and the 'person skilled in the art'. The four siblings are not real persons but normative devices. Their perceptions cannot be determined as questions of fact, although the Supreme Court has sometimes relied on expert evidence. The normative considerations behind these devices only become apparent in the course of time. Meanwhile there is a host of sub-criteria which determine the perception of the 'average consumer' or the knowledge and skills of the 'person skilled in the art'. But the perception of the 'person susceptible to art' has very much been determined on a case-by-case basis. It was difficult to determine how this person would perceive *Gropius* door handles, and it is difficult to say how he or she feels about beer labels or urns decorated with the picture of a bellowing stag.

[135] § 7 Copyright Act 1965. [136] § 7(2) Designs Act 2004.

The 'two-tier test' is conceptually slightly clearer. It draws a distinction between everyday designs which differ from pre-existing forms and extraordinary creations. Many of the decisions handed down by the courts have a certain intuitive appeal. Whereas from a design law perspective a step stool with some individual features[137] and the *Tripp Trapp* chair[138] are treated alike, one is a rather usual shape which is to a high degree dictated by functional constraints, whereas the *Tripp Trapp* chair could be considered as a paradigm shift in the design of children's chairs. Nevertheless the reported cases show that the distinction is fraught with uncertainty.

Another problematic feature of German law is the strong role of unfair competition law, on which many claimants whose design rights had elapsed have based their cases. Designers, but also many judges, have the strong intuition that at least the identical imitation of a competitor's product is wrong. When this intuition cannot be accommodated by copyright law, it finds other channels. While German law does not prohibit the 'slavish imitation' of product shapes outside intellectual property law, the courts have often been prepared to find consumer confusion when they felt that the defendant should not have copied. Thus it is not safe for a competitor to imitate a product which has been on the market for more than three years and which is not protected by a registered design, because there is always the likelihood that the sale of the product will be regarded as unfair by the courts. The codification of the rules on unfair product imitation in § 4 No. 3 Unfair Competition Act 2015 has reduced the legal uncertainty and the courts seem to be more aware of the limits of intellectual property law, but a serious uncertainty remains.

5.4.2 *A Model for Europe?*

5.4.2.1 Would It be Consistent with EU Law?

The tension between Article 17 Design Directive and the concept of work as developed by the CJEU in *Infopaq* and subsequent judgments[139] is discussed elsewhere in this volume. The wording of Article 17(2) of

[137] Copyright protection denied in BGH GRUR 1981, 517, 518, 519 – *Rollhocker [Step Stool]*.

[138] Copyright protection accepted by OLG Hamburg ZUM-RD 2002, 181, 187, affirmed by BGH GRUR 2009, 856 – *Tripp-Trapp-Stuhl*.

[139] CJEU, Case C-5/08, *Infopaq* v. *DDF*, ECLI:EU:C:2009:465, paras. 33–7; Case C-145/10, *Painer* v. *Standard*, ECLI:EU:C:2011:798, paras. 87–99; see also the overviews given by E. Rosati, 'Towards an EU-wide Copyright? (Judicial) Pride and (Legislative) Prejudice' [2013] *IPQ* 47, 55–65; M. Leistner, 'Der europäische Werkbegriff', *ZGE/IPJ* 5 (2013) 4–45.

the Directive strongly suggests that Member States remain free to determine the conditions under which designs are protected under copyright law. Indeed, the Supreme Court made this point in its *Birthday Train* judgment and stressed that its departure from its previous case law was not mandated by EU law.[140] It is a 'home-made' rather than a European solution. At the same time, the court was eager to avoid a conflict with the CJEU case law. By adopting a single threshold of protection, the Supreme Court abolished a theory which was at least arguably irreconcilable with the *Infopac* doctrine and chose an approach which is beyond European criticism. The Supreme Court also refers to European criteria such as the 'freedom of choice'.

Leistner has argued that the Supreme Court tried to 'fly under the European radar' and to stress its independence while avoiding open conflicts.[141] He thinks that an open dialogue between the Supreme Court and the CJEU would have better served the development of EU copyright law. There is much to be said for this view. Cases like *Spacenet* or *Birthday Train* would have had the potential of becoming EU law precedents. They represent two typical situations: 'technical features with some aesthetic appeal' and 'attractive, but small, designs'. It would have been good to have a European guideline for these situations. At the same time, it is one of the methodological problems of the CJEU case law that the court ignores the rich experience of Member States in all areas of intellectual property law. The preliminary reference procedure gives a national court the possibility to feed its own arguments into the European discourse. The Supreme Court has identified two principles which can counterbalance excessive protection: the freedom of the state of the art and the freedom of common shapes. Both principles should have been presented to the CJEU. The Supreme Court has missed this opportunity. To be fair, however, the *Birthday Train* case concerned unharmonised law,[142] so the Supreme Court could not ask for the interpretation of Articles 2–4 InfoSoc Directive. This exposes a weakness of the *Infopaq* doctrine: the CJEU used Article 2 InfoSoc Directive to harmonise the concept of work, which is only addressed indirectly by this provision. The concept is obviously of much broader importance, also for areas which are as yet unharmonised and hence outside the powers of the CJEU.

At some stage the CJEU will have to clarify the relationship between copyright and design law. It is to be hoped that the court will get the

[140] BGH GRUR 2014, 175, paras. 27–32 – *Geburtstagszug [Birthday Train]*.

[141] M. Leistner, 'Urheberrecht an der Schnittstelle zwischen Unionsrecht und nationalem Recht', GRUR 2014, 1145, 1147.

[142] See above, 5.3.11.

opportunity to do so in a suitable case with appropriate questions, which force the CJEU to produce a nuanced result. In a case concerning trivial or technical features, the court might dodge the issue by holding that the result is already clear under cases such as *Painer* or *Football Dataco*.[143] In a case concerning a 'great' design, however, the court could be tempted to allow parallel protection by copyright and design law with overly broad considerations.

5.4.2.2 Demarcation, Partial Cumulation or Full Cumulation?

Ultimately every IP lawyer's views on the copyright/design interface are determined by his or her basic convictions about intellectual property. IP pessimists will favour demarcation. They will point out that the limits of design law protect the public domain and that these limits are undermined if every design is also protected by copyright. It is not surprising that this attitude prevailed, to varying degrees, in Germany in the late nineteenth and early twentieth century, because Germany had embraced intellectual property only hesitantly. IP optimists will try to protect designers in an optimal way. They will point to gaps if the formal and substantive limits of design protection are conclusive, and they will argue that the long term of copyright protection does no harm: if a design is successful, it deserves longer protection; if it is not successful, it will be forgotten anyway. This view prevailed among German academics at a time when intellectual property protection was widely seen as deficient and when the quest for strong protection had reached its high-water mark.

The appeal of the German model is that it steers a middle course: it grants full protection to designs which, due to their high level of creativity, can be compared to fine art, but it excludes everyday design from copyright protection. If the 'small coin' of design protection is protected in the same way as texts or musical works are, the fine-tuned system of design law is in danger of being undermined. At the same time, the specific benefit of a claim for additional remuneration, which German law provides, can only be justified in the case of truly individual creations. A model of graded protection – three years' protection against imitation for unregistered designs, up to twenty-five years' absolute protection with registration, full copyright term for highly creative designs – is by no means outdated. On the contrary, it takes account of the need to allow future designers the freedom they need.

[143] CJEU, Case C-145/10, *Painer* v. *Standard*, ECLI:EU:C:2011:798; Case C-604/10, *Football Dataco* v. *Yahoo*, ECLI:EU:C:2012:115.

A possible alternative, at which the Supreme Court hints in *Spacenet* and *Birthday Train*, can consist in full copyright protection, tempered by a robust functionality doctrine and by the principle of 'relativity of scope', under which 'small works receive small protection'. But it seems doubtful if both doctrines can sufficiently safeguard the public domain. As for functionality, the devil is in the details. There are few cases in which functional constraints leave no freedom at all – a telephone directory is one of the few examples. But in most cases there are several ways of implementing a functional concept. In this sense, there is no clear and bright line between the *Spacenet* and a sculpture. While the *Spacenet* serves a technical purpose, it also has aesthetic appeal. Many trivial ornaments do not even have a functional purpose at all. Here, the 'freedom of choice' criterion is entirely unhelpful. It is also unclear whether copyright should adopt the principle which is expressed in Article 5(2) of the Design Directive: 'In assessing individual character, the degree of freedom of the designer in developing the design shall be taken into consideration.' In design law, protection is not excluded when there is little freedom. On the contrary, smaller differences from previous designs can justify protection under this theory. So the criterion of 'freedom of choice' is ambiguous: it may exclude copyright protection when there is little freedom, but it may also be used to justify the contrary result. The principle of 'relativity of scope' can partly contain the risks created by extending protection. Nevertheless there are reasons for restricting protected subject-matter. First, the scope of protection is only determined by an infringement court. Before proceedings start, however, intellectual property rights can be used as threats. Competitors who try to behave lawfully and to avoid the risk of infringement can be prevented from using shapes which may or may not turn out to be outside the scope of protection. Secondly, courts may be influenced by the rhetoric of property law. The InfoSoc Directive is committed to a high degree of protection. This may convince courts, in particular inexperienced ones, to give strong protection to intellectual property and to disregard the relativity of scope.

Hence, in my view, copyright protection for all new and individual designs would go too far in many respects. Graded protection consisting of short-term protection for unregistered designs, medium-term protection for registered designs and copyright protection for highly creative designs seems systematically and economically sound. While it is certainly difficult to apply the criterion of 'high creativity' in practice, the application of thresholds is a part of every intellectual property lawyer's everyday life. At a time of growing concerns about over-protection, intellectual property should resist the tendency to cover broader and broader areas. In a time of increasing copyright scepticism, copyright lawyers should fight for strong protection of truly personal creations. But they should also be aware that restricted and short-term regimes may be more appropriate to protect lower levels of creativity.

6 The Design/Copyright Conflict in the United Kingdom: A History

*Lionel Bently**

6.1 Introduction

This chapter offers an historical account of the evolution of British design and copyright laws as falling into three broad periods. In the first period (1787–1911), design protection, initially granted automatically but from 1839 requiring registration, sat alongside the specific copyright regimes for engravings, sculptures and drawings, without much consideration of, or concern with, potential overlap. I call this the period of 'quiet co-existence'. The second period, dating from 1912 through to 1968, is the period of demarcation. During this era attempts were made at 'demarcation', that is, at ensuring that material eligible for protection under the registered design regime was excluded from copyright protection. Further clarifications sought to ensure that material that was regarded as appropriate subject-matter for copyright law was to be excluded from eligibility in the registered design regime. The third period, dating from 1968 to the present, is the era of culmulation. In this period, some form of cumulation between the copyright and registered design regime has been admitted (and regarded as desirable). The period began with only partial cumulation, that is, permitting cumulation between copyright and registered designs, but curtailing the term of copyright as applied to designs to that available through registration. As of 2016, the arrangement approximates to full cumulation.

How are we to understand this evolution? I want to suggest that the particular history of nineteenth-century Britain as an industrial nation – the self-styled 'workshop of the world' – explains the special status accorded during the second period to the registered design regime in the regime of protection of the appearance of mass-produced products. The design system was heavily used, particularly by the Lancashire cotton

* Herchel Smith Professor of Intellectual Property, University of Cambridge. I am grateful to Isabella Alexander and Jason Du Mont for their comments on an earlier draft of this chapter.

Table 6.1 *Chronological table of legislation and statistics*

Period	Legislation	Amendments	Interpretation (i.e. by courts)	Further information	Design applications	Design registrations
1787–1839	Engravers Acts, 1735, 8 Geo. II, c. 13; 1766, 7 Geo. III, c. 38; 1777, 7 Geo. III, c. 57; Calico Printers Act 1787, 27 Geo. III, c. 38	Calico Printers Acts, 1789, 29 Geo. III, c. 19 (renewing 1787 Act); 1794, 34 Geo. III, c. 23 (making perpetual and extending term to 3 months) 2 Vict., c. 13 (extending to Ireland and to other fabrics)		Protection for engravings and designs for patterns for printing on fabrics, neither requiring registration	Application not required nor possible	Application not required nor possible
1798–1839	Models and Busts Act 1798, 33 Geo. III, c. 71	1814, 54 Geo. III, c. 56		As yet, no protection for designs of three-dimensional articles	Application not required nor possible	Application not required nor possible
1839–1842	Copyright of Designs Act 1839, 2 Vict., c. 17			Registration introduced for most designs (but not for patterns for cotton fabrics)	No data available	1,035,672 (total) 14,187 (average)
1842–1850	Designs Act 1842, 5 & 6 Vict., c. 100	Utility Designs Act 1843, 6 & 7 Vict., c. 65; Designs Act 1850, 13 & 14 Vict., c. 104; Copyright of Designs Act 1858, 21 & 22 Vict., c. 70;		Registration extended to all ornamental design. Sculptures protected by copyright excluded from registration as designs (s. 3, Sch. C). Sculptures permitted to be registered under 5 & 6 Vict., c. 100	No data available	

		1861, 24 & 25 Vict., c. 73; 1865, 28 Vict., c. 3; Copyright of Designs Act 1875, 38 & 39 Vict., c. 93				
1862–1883	Fine Art Copyright Act 1862		*Dick* v. *Brooks* (1880)	Paintings and drawings protected	No data available	
1883–1907	Patents, Designs and Trade Marks Act 1883	49 & 50 Vict., c. 27, s. 3; Patents, Designs and Trade Marks Act 1888, 51 & 52 Vict., c. 50		Sculptures protected by copyright excluded from definition of registrable design	645,852 (total) 23,066 (average)	
1907–1912	Patents and Designs Act 1907	Patents and Designs Act 1919				
1912–1956	Copyright Act 1911		*King Features* v. *Kleeman*	**Demarcation** for designs capable of registration, but **partial cumulation** if work not intended to be used industrially at time of creation	794,578 (total) 14,189 (average)	717,940 (total) 12,820 (average)
1949–1989	Registered Designs Act 1949; Designs Rules 1949, esp. r. 26	Copyright, Designs and Patents Act 1988, ss. 265–272, Sch. 3, Sch. 4; Registered Designs Regulations 2001, SI 2001/3949 (implementing EC Directive)		Exclusion of works primarily of a literary or artistic character from registrability		

Table 6.1 *(cont.)*

Period	Legislation	Amendments	Interpretation (i.e. by courts)	Further information	Design applications	Design registrations
1956–1968	Copyright Act 1956		*Dorling* v. *Honnor Marine* (indirect protection through copyright for functional designs that would not be registrable)	Demarcation where design is capable of registration		
1968–1989		Copyright of Designs Act 1968	*British Leyland* v. *Armstrong*	**Partial cumulation** of copyright and design protection during term of registration (15 years)	307,521 (total) 6,543 (average)	284,949 (total) 6,063 (average)
1989–2001	Copyright, Designs and Patents Act 1988; Registered Designs Act 1949 as amended and codified in Sch. 4 to the 1988 Act			**Partial cumulation** of copyright and registered design protection during term of registration (25 years): s. 52 **Demarcation** of copyright and unregistered design right: CDPA, s. 51		

2001–2016	Registered Designs Act 1949 (as amended by Registered Designs Regulations 2001, SI 2001/3949)	Enterprise and Regulatory Reform Act 2013; Intellectual Property Act 2014	*Flos* Judgment (CJEU)	Criteria of protection of registered designs modified to implement Designs Directive, but interrelation with copyright left largely untouched [Rule 26 of Registered Designs Rules, relating to designs of articles of primarily a literary or artistic character, abolished]		
2016–				ERR 2013 in force. **Full cumulation** with no limit on copyright term (except for section 51)		

The UK table is more complex than other countries' tables owing to the different regimes often used during the same period for different types of creations (e.g. demarcation for some creations and partial cumulation for others). To enable some sort of comparison, the table uses the three broad periods determined in this chapter but inevitably oversimplifies the picture so the data analysis (totals and averages) is not as precise as for other chapters and only is a rough guide to the differences that the change of regimes may have produced.
Source of the data: National Archives (1855–75), Department of Science and Art Reports (1839–55), Parliamentary Papers (1875–83), WIPO (1883–2014) and UKIPO Annual Reports. Applications are only available from 1884 onwards and registrations from 1839 onwards.

industry, the pre-eminent symbol of British industrialisation,[1] during the century from 1840 to 1940, reaching a peak just prior to the First World War. At that time, as pressures emerged to broaden copyright law to encompass so-called 'works of applied art', British industries were familiar with, and content with, the compromises between protection and competition embodied in the registered design regime. It was recognised that affording copyright protection to designs (broadly understood) would undermine the operation of the registration system. Hence, the legislature embarked on a series of initiatives to try and demarcate the boundary between 'copyright' and 'designs'.

These attempts at demarcation proved both problematic and contentious. Over the latter half of the twentieth century, the relative significance of Britain as an industrial nation diminished, and with it the resolve to maintain the Design Registry as the primary source of legal protection. Other local industries, such as jewellery, fashion and furniture manufacture, as well as merchandising, which found the system of registration cumbersome, gained in influence. This shift was reflected in a change in the subject-matter of many contentious cases, which now included furniture,[2] children's toys,[3] clothes,[4] and merchandise generated by broadcasting and film companies and their licensees.[5] This change in *who* was interested in the design/copyright interface, as well as the nature of their commercial practices,[6] gradually informed policy-making: attempted 'demarcation' between the two systems gave way to a regime of partial overlap and systemic coordination. By the last third of the century, the landscape of legal protection seemed to have reversed: the

[1] D. A. Farnie, *The English Cotton Industry and the World Market, 1815–1896* (Oxford: Clarendon, 1979), p. 21; Roger Lloyd-Jones and M. J. Lewis, *Manchester and the Age of the Factory: The Business Structure of Cottonopolis in the Industrial Revolution* (London: Croom Helm, 1988), p. 1; C. Knick Harley, 'Cotton Textile Prices and the Industrial Revolution' (1998) 51 *EcHR* 49 ('cotton textile technology defined the British industrial revolution').

[2] *George Hensher* v. *Restawile Upholstery (Lancs)* [1976] AC 64 (three-piece suite).

[3] *Interlego AG* v. *Tyco Industries Inc.* [1989] AC 217 (PC) ('Lego').

[4] *Lewis Trusts* v. *Bambers Stores; Infabrics* v. *Jaytex* (1981, HL); CA, 18 Feb. 1983; *Merlet* v. *Mothercare* [1986] RPC 115 ('raincosy'); *Vermaat* v. *Boncrest* [2001] (5) FSR 49 (bedspread); *Guild* v. *Eskandar* [2001] (38) FSR 645 (clothes); *Lambretta Clothing Co. Ltd* v. *Teddy Smith (UK)* [2005] RPC (6) 88 (clothes).

[5] *Lucasfilm Ltd* v. *Ainsworth* [2011] UKSC 39 ('Star Wars'); *BBC Worldwide Ltd* v. *Pally Screen Printing Ltd* [1998] FSR 665 ('Teletubbies').

[6] As Bellido has perceptively written, 'the character of copyright was . . . transformed in the twentieth century from an exclusive right to particular copyright subject matter to a platform for commercial activities centred on . . . merchandising, licensing and franchising opportunities'. J. Bellido, 'Copyright in Toys', in J. Bellido (ed.), *Landmarks in IP Law* (Oxford and Portland, Oregon: Hart Publishing, 2017.

registered design system now appeared as an anomaly, copyright as the norm.

Further moves towards 'full cumulation' were a consequence of the United Kingdom's participation in the European Union. This brought the need to locate a workable compromise between Member States, some of whom had substantial experience of full cumulation. Although it initially appeared that EU harmonisation of designs law was not intended to affect a Member State's treatment of the design/copyright interface, the legislative wording was not sufficiently robust to resist the pressure of former design right holders (particularly in the furniture sector) intent on securing the huge economic gains of lengthier copyright terms. Relying on the integrationist instincts of the Court of Justice, the avaricious right holders argued that Member States were bound to confer full copyright protection on all designs that constitute 'intellectual creations'. In the face of such pressures, the United Kingdom ultimately abandoned any attempt to channel designers into the registered design regime.

6.2 The Period of Quiet Co-existence

6.2.1 The Beginnings

The regulation of the making, sale and consumption of designed goods by the grant of exclusive rights has normally been dated to the eighteenth century. Not long after the abolition of legislative restrictions on the sale and wearing of calicoes in 1774,[7] Parliament passed laws granting a right lasting two months to the 'inventor and designer' of patterns applied to calicoes, cottons, muslins and linens, thereby enabling the designer to control the copying of such patterns.[8] The Calico Printers

[7] (1720) 7 Geo. I, c. 7 (prohibiting use of printed callicoes for clothing and furniture); (1736) 9 Geo. II, c. 4 (so-called 'Manchester Act' permitting printing of fabrics as long as mixture of linen and cotton); (1774) 14 Geo. III, c. 72 (allowing printing of cottons, subject to duty). See E. Baines, *The History of the Cotton Manufacture in Great Britain* (London: Fisher, Fisher & Jackson, 1835), p. 166; G. Turnbull, *A History of Calico Printing* (Altrincham: John Sherratt & Son, 1951), pp. 25–6, 134ff; P. J. Thomas, 'The Beginnings of Calico-printing in England' (1924) 39 *Eng. Hist. Rev.* 206 (describing background to legislation and noting its relative ineffectiveness).

[8] An Act for the Encouragement of the Arts of designing and printing Linens, Cottons, Calicoes and Muslins, by vesting the properties thereof in the Designers, Printers and Proprietors, for a limited time, (1787) 27 Geo. III, c. 38. The Act was renewed by 29 Geo. III, c. 19 (1789) and made perpetual by (1794) 34 Geo. III, c. 23. These laws have, with the benefit of hindsight, been characterised as the first 'design laws': Lewis Edmunds, *The Law of Copyright in Designs* (London: Sweet & Maxwell), Ch. 1. However, at the time of their adoption it was by no means obvious that they were a category of laws that were distinct from those granting exclusive rights to engravers under 8 Geo. II, c. 13 (1735) and

Acts, as they were known, had been modelled on the Engravers Acts which protected engravers against the reprinting of their engravings, though they differed from the latter in key respects.[9] Apart from the short term of protection (two or three months, compared with twenty-eight years), the Calico Acts were enforceable by action in common law courts (whereas the Engravers Acts had provision as to penalties and costs) and conferred rights only on 'new and original' patterns. (See Table 6.2.)

The 1787–1794 laws had been passed in response to the petitions of London calico printers, most notably William Kilburn, and were targeted at copyists in Lancashire and Scotland. In fact, the only two cases under the Act which have been reported followed that geographical pattern.[10] By the 1830s, the calico printing industry had left London behind (as a site of production), but the tensions heightened between those that invested in design (such as Hargreaves & Co., Sherriff & Co.) and those (such as Coates & Co.) that were happy to copy or rework successful designs marketed by others. Indeed, Lancashire calico houses ended up in a civil war, which had begun with an attempt to enforce the exclusive right conferred under the 1794 Act by injunction in Chancery.[11] The litigation strategy was only partially successful, the Court recognising the

7 Geo. III, c. 38 (1766), that were later categorised as copyright laws. Indeed, many treatments of copyright also included registered designs, and, later in the nineteenth century, a number of colonial laws on 'copyright' would allow for registration of designs: see W. A. Copinger, *The Law of Copyright* (1870), Ch. XV; Brad Sherman and Lionel Bently, *The Making of Modern Intellectual Property Law* (Cambridge: Cambridge University Press, 1999), p. 164; Alexander, herein, Chapter 7.

[9] R. Deazley, 'Commentary on the Calico Printers' Act 1787', in L. Bently and M. Kretschmer (eds.), *Primary Sources on Copyright (1450–1900)*, www.copyrighthistory.org (2008); Ada Longfield, 'William Kilburn and the Earliest Copyright Acts for Cotton Printing Designs', (1953) 95 *The Burlington Magazine* 230–3.

[10] *Mackmurdo and Another* v. *Smith and Others* (December 1797), *Morning Chronicle*, 4 October 1798 (Lord Kenyon Chief Justice, sitting with a Special Jury of Merchants at The Guildhall) (in which London linen-draper Edward Longdon Mackmurdo and calico printer Francis Hickes were awarded £100 damages plus costs by the Court of Kings Bench against 'Smith', a house in the same line 'in the Country'); *Williams and Burford* v. *Merry, Millar & Co.*, *The Times*, 30 July 1808 (Common Pleas, James Mansfield CJ, with a Special Jury) (Ephraim Burford, selling from The Poultry, was awarded 1 shilling damages plus 40 shillings in costs against a Manchester competitor found to have counterfeited Burford's designs): *Lancaster Gazette*, 6 August 1808. Note also *Mackmurdo and Hickes* v. *Donald, Crick & Co.* (*Morning Chronicle*, 4 October 1798) (settled on basis that defendant £100 be paid in damages, and that defendant purchase claimant's remaining stock).

[11] *Hargreaves and Dugdale* v. *Thomas Coates & Co.*, Bills and Answers in TNA: C13/921/43 (Manchester firm of calico printers brought four separate claims seeking injunctive relief against Thomas Coates, a calico printer, and various London drapers who distributed textiles sourced from Coates & Co.).

Table 6.2 *Comparison of protection given to engravings and calico designs*

	Engraving	Calico designs
Acts	(1735) 8 Geo. II, c. 13; (1766) 7 Geo. III, c. 38; (1777) 7 Geo. III, c. 57	(1787) 27 Geo. III, c. 38; (1789) 29 Geo. III, c. 19; (1794) 34 Geo. III, c. 23; (1839) 2 Vict., c. 13
Subject-matter	'any historical print or prints, or any print or prints of any portrait, conversation, landscape, or architecture, map, chart, or plan, or any other print or prints whatsoever' (1766)	Patterns for printing linens, calicoes, cottons or muslins (from 1839, 2 Vict., c. 13, wool, silk, hair or mixture of these)
Standard	'invent ***and*** design' (1735) or 'invent ***or*** design, engrave, etch or work . . .' (1766)	Invent, design and print new and original patterns
Formalities	Date of publication and name of proprietor	Notice of the date of publication and name of the proprietor 'at each end of every such piece of linen, cotton etc'
Ownership	'invent ***and*** design' or 'from his own works and invention, shall cause to be . . .' (1735); 'cause or procure to be designed and engraved, etched, or worked' (1766)	'invent, design and print, or cause to be invented, designed and printed and become the proprietor of any new and original pattern'
Infringement	'any other manner copy in the whole, or in part, by varying, adding to, or diminishing from, the main design' (1777) *West* v. *Francis* 5 B&A 737	'print, work or copy such original pattern'
Term	14 years' protection from publication (1735, s. 1); 28 years (1766, s. 7)	3 months from first publication
Remedies	Penalties: 5 shillings/sheet (qui tam) damages and double costs: (1777) 7 Geo. III, c. 57, s. 1	Action on the case for damages and costs; Injunctions? *Hargreaves* v. *Coates*

possibility of injunctive relief, but sending the parties to Law in situations where the patterns were not identical.[12]

12 *Morning Chronicle*, 23 Jan. 1830; *The Standard*, 23 Jan. 1830. But five years later Thomas Gibson stated in his evidence to the Select Committee on Arts and Manufactures that injunctive relief in Chancery seemed to work to the satisfaction of the cotton trade:

The argument for protection of designs across the whole field of industrial production was made forcefully before William Ewart's *Select Committee on Arts and Manufactures*, which sat between 1835 and 1836,[13] hearing witnesses from a range of sectors, including manufacturers of iron stoves and fenders,[14] silk manufacturers,[15] lace making[16] and japanning,[17] as well as retailers, painters, sculptors and architects.[18] The task of the Ewart Committee was to determine 'the best means of extending a knowledge of the arts and of the principles of design among the people (especially the manufacturing people) of this country'. The Report found that design in British manufacturing was inferior to that of competitor nations, particularly France. The Committee attributed this inferiority to a lack of taste amongst the public, as well as the failure to invest in improved designs caused by the absence of effective legal protection. The Report proposed the establishment of galleries and museums that would display good design, design schools that would teach design, as well as protection for designs similar to that which already was recognised in France. Given the overwhelming evidence of 'piracy', and the problems of enforcement of any existing rights, the Report favoured a new system with protection. While it declined to offer a conclusion as to the appropriate term of protection, the Ewart Committee took the view that registration was 'indispensable' to a system of protection that could operate with the 'greatest promptitude'.[19] A closer look at the evidence indicates that registration was assumed to offer a host of advantages: it

Evidence (1835), Q 393; while Charles Toplis suggested that injunctions had been resorted to by the Manchester trade, but 'not very extensively': ibid., QQ 1567–72.

13 *Report from the Select Committee on Arts and Manufactures* (1835), [598]; (1836), [568] (hearafter Ewart Committee).

14 Ewart, *Evidence* (1835), QQ 99ff (John Jobson Smith of Sheffield iron founders, Stewart, Smith & Co.).

15 Ewart, *Evidence* (1835) QQ 358 ff (Thomas Field Gibson, Spitalfields); QQ 455ff (Robert Harrison of Brydges, Campbell and Harrison).

16 Ewart, *Evidence* (1836), QQ 144ff (John Millward, Olney, Bucks).

17 Ewart, *Evidence* (1835) QQ 748ff (Samuel Wiley of Jennings and Betteridge, Birmingham).

18 In 1835 the Committee heard twenty-seven witnesses; the 1836 Committee, thirty-six.

19 Ewart, *Report*, vii; Ewart, *Evidence* (1835), Smith, QQ 108ff (registry at National Gallery or Somerset House); James Morrison MP, Q 233 (proposing deposit); Gibson, QQ 401–5 (proposing registration but dubious about a central office); John Howell, Q 440; Harrison, Q 479 (registration valuable but dubious about stamping on fabric); Robert Butt, QQ 606–10 (registration at local town plus stamping on a number on copies); Rennie, Q 975 (central board with branches in 'principal manufacturing towns'); James Skene, Q 1153 (registration 'in the metropolises'); Charles Toplis, QQ 1567–72 (favouring central registration and local tribunals); cf. John Henning, Q 856 (suggesting automatic protection); Ewart, *Evidence* (1836), Millward, Q 171 (registry at Somerset House); D. R. Hay, QQ 474–5 (central and local registration might be possible).

would give design proprietors more certainty;[20] it would provide design users notice of what was protected;[21] and it would create a reservoir of formerly protected designs for the edification of the public.[22]

The idea of a registration system was taken forward by the president of the Board of Trade, Charles Poullett Thomson.[23] As initially envisaged, however, a system of protection premised on registration was not attractive to many of the Manchester calico printers. Given their experience of systematic copying of designs as soon as they were displayed in London shops, the Manchester printers feared that a central register would inevitably facilitate copying rather than protect against it. They therefore sought exclusion from the new regime, and instead achieved only extension of protection to other fabrics (silk and wool, and mixtures) as well as to Ireland.[24] The legislature did, however, adopt a registration system for all other designs,[25] both three and two dimensional,[26] protection being awarded for a limited term of one year from registration (though it further provided that for designs applied to articles of metal this was to be three years).[27] The link to the Calico Printers Acts was maintained at least in the standard for protection, namely that the designs were 'new and original'.[28]

Once the registration system was in operation,[29] the Manchester calico printers who wanted lengthier protection found that their previous fears that the Register would facilitate piracy were mistaken: the inaugural Registrar, F. B. Long, had made regulations restricting third-party access to registered designs during the period of their protection.[30] Therefore

[20] Ewart, *Evidence* (1835), Charles Toplis, QQ 1567–72.
[21] Ewart, *Evidence* (1835), Smith, QQ 153–4.
[22] Ewart, *Evidence* (1835), George Rennie, QQ 980–1.
[23] (1799–1841), MP for Manchester (1832–9) and President of the Board of Trade (from April 1835 until September 1839).
[24] 2 Vict., c. 13 (1839).
[25] An Act to secure to Proprietors of Designs for Articles of Manufacture the Copyright of such Designs for a Limited Time, (1839) 2 Vict., c. 17 establishing 'Registrar of Designs for Articles of Manufacture': s. 5.
[26] 'Pattern or print, to be either worked into or worked on, or printed on or painted on, any Article of Manufacture, being a Tissue or Textile fabric, except Lace, and also any other Article within the meaning of the Acts mentioned in the Schedule hereto annexed' – those being the four 'Calico Printers Acts'.
[27] Registration of Designs Act 1839, 2 Vict., c. 17, s. 1 (listing three categories of protected designs and specifying terms).
[28] Registration of Designs Act 1839, 2 Vict., c. 17, s. 1.
[29] Registration of Designs Act 1839, 2 Vict., c. 17, s. 12 (1 July 1839).
[30] *Report from the Select Committee on Copyright of Designs* (1840), *Evidence*, [7740]; (1842) 5 & 6 Vict., c. 100, s. 17 (on limited entitlement of access to registered designs prior to expiry of term); 1883 Act, s. 52 (registry closed during term, then five years) (a position defended by the Herschell Committee (1888), [52], in the face of arguments to the contrary by, e.g., Ernest de Pass, QQ 1402ff, and Alfred Julius Boult, QQ 1655ff); 1907 Act (closed for two years); 1949 Act, s. 22 (presumptively open, but powers conferred to make rules restricting access). On the practice, post-1949, see Board of Trade, *Report*

the calico printers petitioned Parliament for lengthier protection and inclusion in the registration regime, the Belfast MP James Emerson Tennant taking the role of lead advocate in the Commons.[31] However, Tennant's proposal was met with fierce opposition.[32] In the face of this division of opinion, the Commons appointed a Select Committee,[33] which took evidence from both sides,[34] and generated acrimonious literature putting the case for one side or the other. Caught in the cross-fire, the Select Committee divided 6–6 as to whether to report at all,[35] with Tennant casting the deciding vote. The Report declared simply that 'it is expedient to extend Copyright of Designs'.

After one failed attempt at legislation in 1841,[36] the following year, a new Registration Act was passed in 1842, allowing for registration of 'ornamental design' (including calicoes).[37] The act of registration involved the submission of two representations of the design,[38] and each application was given a number.[39] Applications were allocated to one of thirteen classes of article,[40] and the applicant was required to pay a registration fee, the amount varying depending on the classes.[41] The identities of the

of Departmental Committee Industrial Designs (1961, Cmnd 1808) (hereinafter *Johnston Report*), [10] ('Since 1932 most designs have become open to inspection from the date of registration . . .').

31 1804–1869. Turnbull, *A History*, pp. 143–8.

32 The debate is reviewed in Lara Kriegel, 'Originality and Sin. Calico, Capitalism, and the Copyright of Designs, 1839–1851', Chapter 2 of her *Grand Designs: Labor, Empire and the Museum in Victorian Culture* (Durham, NC/London: Duke University Press, 2007).

33 *Report from the Select Committee on Copyright of Designs*, 1840 (442).

34 Thirty-six witnesses appeared before the Committee.

35 Ewart, a committee member, had suggested that, rather than report, the Select Committee just submit the evidence it had collected to the House.

36 For opposition, see 'Advertisement: Bill To Extend Copyright In Designs On Woven Fabrics', *The Times*, 3 Mar. 1841, p. 6.

37 An Act to Consolidate and Amend the Laws relating to the Copyright of Designs for Ornamenting Articles of Manufacturer, 5 & 6 Vict., c. 100 (Ornamental Designs Act) (in operation from 1 September 1842).

38 The 1839 Act had required three copies: 2 Vict., c. 17, s. 6. Some flexibility was introduced by the Designs Act (1850), 13 & 14 Vict., c. 104, s. 11, to substitute a specification or description in place of a representation; and by the Copyright of Designs Act 1858 (permitting samples in some cases). See further 1883 Act, s. 48(1) (allowing photographs); Designs Rules 1883, r. 9 (requiring three copies). A statement of the nature of the design was also required under r. 9, and in the Design Rules 1908 this became a 'statement of novelty'.

39 (1839) 2 Vict., c. 17, s. 6; (1842) 5 & 6 Vict., c. 100, s. 15 (setting out duties of Registrar).

40 Ornamental Designs Act, s. 3 (specifying terms for each of thirteen classes); s. 4 (applicant to specify class for which registration was being sought). The 1883 Act increased the number of classes to fourteen: Designs Rules 1883, Sch. 3; and the 1907 Act to fifteen classes. Classes were ultimately abandoned in 1949, following the House of Lords' decision in *Stenor Ltd* v. *Whitesides (Clitheroe) Ltd* (1948) 65 RPC 1 (HL) and the recommendation of the Swan Committee, [289]–[295].

41 (1839) 2 Vict., c. 17, s. 8; (1842) 5 & 6 Vict., c. 100, s. 18 (setting statutory maxima).

proprietors were entered by hand in separate books, by class, and in chronological order, cross-referenced to the representations via the registration number. Each proprietor was given a certificate.[42] The Registry did not, at this stage, purport to search or examine (though it would come to do so later);[43] and the Register was not printed or circulated.

With the calico printers on board, the numbers of registrations multiplied from under 500, in both 1840 and 1841, to over 10,000 in 1843. The cotton industry – the number one British export industry from 1803 to 1938 – was to be the primary user of the design regime for the next century. In fact, calico designs would become such an important component in the system that a separate branch of the Designs Office would eventually be established in Manchester in 1907 to deal with textiles in 'the cotton classes'.[44] As will become clear, the cotton industry views about design registration would be critical to policy-making for well over a century.

6.2.2 *Overlap: 1839–1911*

The 1839 Act said nothing explicitly about overlap, either to acknowledge the possibility and permit cumulation or to seek demarcation. Looking back, one might have expected the question of the relationship with copyright law to arise immediately following the introduction of a design registration system. By 1839, the statutes offering 'copyright' – a term by then in common currency – covered both engravings and sculptures. Indeed, the references to modelling and engraving in the 1839 Registration Act immediately evoke the expressive techniques to which the Engravers Acts and Models and Busts Acts had already extended protection.[45] Even though the most obvious reading of the Engravers Acts might have suggested that they concerned 'artistic' engravings, not mere 'patterns' or 'designs', the 1735 Act had been interpreted as early as 1740 to extend to engraved images of plants,[46] which remained a common feature of many textile designs.

[42] (1839) 2 Vict., c. 17, s. 7; (1842) 5 & 6 Vict., c. 100, s. 16; 1883 Act, s. 49.

[43] 1883 Act, s. 47 (power to refuse); Registered Designs Act 1949 (as enacted), s. 3(2); *Johnston Report*, [12]. See L. Bently, 'Requiem for Registration? Reflections on the History of the UK Registered Design System', in A. Firth (ed.), *Perspectives in Intellectual Property: Vol. I. The Prehistory and Development of Intellectual Property* (London: Sweet & Maxwell, 1997), pp. 1, 18 (giving indication as to increased levels of refusals after 1883, going as high as 2,400 in 1938).

[44] By then, classes 13–15 of the fifteen classes established by Design Rules 1908.

[45] The 1839 Act referred to designs for '*Modelling* or the Casting, or the Embossment, or the Chasing, or the *Engraving*, or for any Kind of Impression or Ornament, on Any Article of Manufacture, not being a Tissue or Textile Fabric'.

[46] *Blackwell* v. *Bickham, Harper and Others* (8 Dec. 1740) Barn C. 209. (LC, holding that the scope of the 1735 Act was not limited to mere inventions of the mind: 'a new Print, tho' taken from Nature, will be within the Act, provided it be not copy'd from any other Print

Moreover, there were reasons a designer might have wanted to take advantage of the potential overlap. Perhaps the most obvious of these related to registration and term: registration being required under the Design Acts but not under the Engravings or Sculpture Acts; and the term of protection of registered designs being rather short compared to the twenty-eight years granted under the Engravers Acts, and two periods of fourteen years under the Sculpture Acts. On the other hand, the Design Acts offered the enticing remedy of penalties of £5–£30 per offence, twenty to one-hundred-and-twenty times the sum under the Engravers Acts, and recoverable by summary proceedings before two justices having jurisdiction where the party offending resided.[47]

However, the question of overlap hardly seems to have arisen. Possibly this was because it was clear that the two regimes had different fields of application.[48] More specifically, the Acts were targeted at very different sorts of goods: while the 'plates' protected under the Engravers Acts might be made of wood or metal, the output of the process of printing was engravings *on paper*,[49] whereas the 1787–94 Acts protected patterns to be printed on 'linens, calicoes, cottons or muslins', and the 1839 and 1842 Registration Acts were concerned with 'articles of manufacture'. Seen in this way, there was a narrow field of overlap covering patterns for printing on wallpaper. In any event, even if there had been overlap, it is not clear that it would have been of much interest to operators in the printed design field: the chief difference – the term of protection – was probably an irrelevance given that designs had a very short life-span; while the formalities required by the Engravers Acts, requiring the name of the

or Prints'. A copy of a tapestry, itself based on a drawing, would not, however, be protected.)

47 Registration of Designs Act 1839, 2 Vict., c. 17, s. 4; Ornamental Designs Act (1842) 5 & 6 Vict., c. 100, s. 8. The provisions for penalties were retained until 1949 but the enforcement before justices of the peace was removed in 1883 when instead the penalties were made recoverable as an action for debt in any court of competent jurisdiction: 1883 Act, s. 58; Patents, Designs and Trade Marks Act 1888, 51 & 52 Vict., c. 50, s. 7 (implementing *Herschell Report* (1888), [57], and inserting a cap of £100 for any design); Patents and Designs Act, s. 60(2). Writing in 1930, Russell-Clarke observed that 'Nowadays, however, damages are almost always asked for and not the penalty': A. D. Russell-Clarke, *Copyright in Industrial Designs* (London: Pitman, 1930), p. 77. With the cap of £100 there was a real possibility that the penalty might not compensate the claimant sufficiently. From 1949, the primary remedies were injunctions and damages.

48 *Dick* v. *Brooks* (1880) 15 Ch D 22, 35 (James LJ) (stating that he could not 'conceive that such a reproduction of a subject in tapestry, or Berlin wool, or upon china, or in earthenware, is within the meaning of the Act of Parliament'). Ricketson sees this as an example of 'the courts' reluctance to condone overlap of protection under the various pre-1911 copyright acts': S. Ricketson, *The Paris Convention for the Protection of Industrial Property: A Commentary* (Oxford: OUP, 2015), p. 495 n. 77.

49 The Act specifically referring to 'sheets' ('such offender or offenders shall forfeit the plate . . . and all and every sheet or sheets').

proprietor and date of publishing on 'every print', might have proved commercially problematic with wallpaper or textile designs. The Calico Acts, in contrast, only required formal notice of proprietorship 'at each end of every such piece of linen, cotton'.

The issue of overlap with the Models and Busts Acts may have proved marginally more problematic. Certainly, in promoting the Design Registration Act, it had been said that the Sculpture Acts were limited in scope, and the view seems to have prevailed for some time that the Sculpture Acts only related to models and busts of people and animals,[50] and thus would not extend to sculptures of vegetation, or indeed abstract shapes.[51] This meant that the overlap between sculpture and design protection was limited, though by no means non-existent: indeed, Henry Cole states in 1848 that he could instance 'several cases in art manufactures where the design, already protected by the Copyright Act for fourteen years, has been registered under the Ornamental Designs Act, merely to obtain the summary mode of redress which the latter Act gives'.[52] Although this narrow interpretation of protected sculpture was prevalent until virtually the end of the nineteenth century, it was rejected in 1892 in *Caproni* v. *Alberti*, when Mathew J found that the 1814 Act's reference to 'matter of invention in sculpture' protected certain plaster models of 'groups of shaddock and foliage, apples and leaves and peaches'.[53]

The question of overlap between sculpture and registrable designs was of sufficient concern to receive legislative treatment (even if such treatment generated very little comment). When the 1839 Act was repealed and replaced with effect from 1 September 1842, a specific exclusion ('demarcation', in the terms of this volume) was created so that 'sculpture' protected under the 1814 Act could not be registered. Moreover, from 1851 to 1883, that rule was reversed, and the statute explicitly allowed registration of sculptures under the procedures of the 1842 Act.[54] The aim was to make available the summary remedies – actions

[50] Robert Butt, of Regent Street retailer Messrs Howell and James, giving Evidence to Select Committee on Arts and Manufactures (1835) [598], QQ 592ff; Anon, 'Occasional Chapters on Copyright in Designs. Chapter 1 – The Inconsistency and Obscurity of the Law' (1849) 1 *Journal of Designs and Manufactures* 19, 20.

[51] All but one of the thirty-nine surviving representations of sculptures that were registered under the Designs Act, between 1850 and 1883, are for sculptures of people and animals. The exception, No. 41, was for an obelisk. See TNA: BT48/5.

[52] Letter from H. Cole to Sir Denis Le Marchant, 6 Sept. 1848, in *Report of Select Committee on the School of Design* (1849) [576], Appendix 1, p. 341.

[53] (1892) 65 LT 785; 40 WR 235. Mathew J found it to be a 'matter of invention in sculpture' and thus protected by copyright because of the 'ingenuity, artistic taste, judgement and arrangement'.

[54] 13 & 14 Vict., c. 104, ss. 6–7.

Table 6.3 *Comparison of protection given to engravings, sculptures and registered designs*

	Engraving	Sculpture	Registered designs
Acts	(1735) 8 Geo. II, c. 13; (1766) 7 Geo. III, c. 38; (1777) 7 Geo. III, c. 57; (1836) 6 & 7 Will. IV, c. 59	(1798) 33 Geo. III, c. 71; (1814) 54 Geo. III, c. 56	(1839) 2 Vict., c. 17; (1842) 5 & 6 Vict., c. 100; (1843) 6 & 7 Vict., c. 65
Subject-matter	**1766**: 'any historical print or prints, or any print or prints of any portrait, conversation, landscape, or architecture, map, chart, or plan, <u>or any other print or prints whatsoever</u>'	**1798** (s. 1): model, bust, cast of whole or part of human or animal figure **1814** (s. 1): or 'matter of invention in sculpture'	**1839–42**: three categories, but excluding designs protected under Calico Acts **1842**: all ornamental designs except sculptures (note: expanded to include calico) **1843**: added designs for purposes of utility **1850**: sculpture made registrable **1883**: eliminated distinction between ornament and utility: **1883** Act, s. 60 ('any design applicable to any article of manufacture') (excluding sculpture)
Standard	'invent ***and*** design' (1735) or 'invent ***or*** design, engrave, etch or work . . . ' (1766)	New (1798 Act); New and original (1814 Act)	New and original; 1883 Act, s. 47
Formalities	Day of publication; name of proprietor *Brooks* v. *Cock*	Name of proprietor and date 'put thereon': 1798, s. 1; 1814, s. 1	(1839) s. 1; (1842) 5 & 6 Vict., c. 100, s. 4; 1883 Act, ss. 50–51 (registration; stamping). On failure to mark, see *Pierce* v. *Worth* (1868)
Ownership; Assignment	'invent ***and*** design' or 'from his own works and invention, shall **cause to be** . . . ' (1735); 'cause or procure to be designed and engraved, etched, or worked' (1766)	'make or cause to be made' (1798, s. 1) Transfer of right by deed with two witnesses (1814, s. 4)	(1839), s. 1 (author or commissioner for valuable consideration); s. 2 (transferee) (1842) 5 & 6 Vict., c. 100, s. 5 ('author' or commissioner for good and valuable consideration); s. 6 (registration of transferee) 1883 Act, s. 61 (same)

Infringement	Copying: *West* v. *Francis* 5 B&A 737 But not selling or distribution: *R* v. *Powell*, *The Times*, 10 Nov. 1862, p. 11	Copying by adding or diminishing (1798, s. 1); Make pirated copy or cast (1814, s. 3)	**1839–42**: applying whole or any original part: (1839) 2 Vict., c. 17, s. 3 **1842**: 'fraudulent imitation': (1842) 5 & 6 Vict., c. 100, s. 7 **1883**: 'fraudulent or obvious' (1883 Act, s. 58)
Term	1735–1766: 14 years 1766–1912: 28 years 1842–1912: maps if in books, life +7 or 42 years	14 years (1798, s. 1), but 14 more if alive and still proprietor (1814, s. 6)	**1839–42** (12 mths; 3 yrs for metal) **1842–83** (9 mths; 12 mths; 3 yrs) **1850–83** (possible extension by BT of term for specified classes up to further 3 years, under 13 & 14 Vict., c. 104, s. 9) **1883–1907**: 5 years: 1883 Act, s. 50 **1907**: 5 years renewable to 15 years
Remedies	(1735) Forfeiture and penalties, 5 shillings/sheet (1766) Damages From 1862, penalties under 1862 Act, s. 8	Special action on the case: 1798, s. 2; 1814, s. 3	(1839) 2 Vict., c. 17, ss. 3, 4; (1842) 5 & 6 Vict., c. 100, s. 8: penalties £5–£30, recoverable either by action for debt, action on the case or summary proceedings before two justices having jurisdiction where the party offending resides; s. 9 (damages) Note also Copyright of Designs Act 1858, c. 70, permitting proceedings for damages to be brought in the County Court 1883 Act, ss. 58 and 59: penalty of £50 (made a simple contractual debt, only recoverable by action)
Costs	(1766) Double costs	Full costs, 1798, s. 2; Double costs, 1814, s. 3	(1842) 5 & 6 Vict., c. 100, s. 12 (costs to successful party)
Limitation	3 months for penalties (1735, s. 3); 6 months for penalties, 1767, s. 6. Six-year limit for damages: *Graves* v. *Mercer* (1868) 16 WR 790	6 months (1798, s. 4; 1814, s. 5)	(1842) 5 & 6 Vict., c. 100, s. 12: 12 months from offence

for penalties before magistrates – from which registered design proprietors benefited.[55] As far as I am aware, however, there were only fifty-nine registrations in thirty-three years, and only one case in which the penalty procedure was used.[56] More significantly for our purposes, the lack of discussion as to the removal in 1883 of sculpture from protectability by registered designs suggests that the interface between the design regime and copyright was one which was largely regarded as technical.[57] The exclusion of sculptures from design registration remained in place from 1883 until 1919.[58]

The first signs that the relationship between sculpture and the designs registration system might prove an issue came in *Britain and Others* v. *Hanks Brothers & Co.*, in 1902, where the claim was made that lead toy soldiers, depicting mounted yeomen on horseback, were sculptures. The soldiers had been modelled by William Britain junior from photographs and had his name stamped on them. Evidence was accepted by the Court that 'the anatomy is good, and that the modelling shows both technical knowledge and skill'. Wright J said that while he had 'great doubt as to the meaning of the [1814 Sculpture Copyright] Act', he was nevertheless prepared to hold that these toy soldiers were sculptures.[59] The outcome clearly raised the possibility of copyright protection for some mass-produced designs and also foreshadowed in an important way the desire of toy-manufacturers for the longer, cheaper and simpler system of protection offered by copyright rather than the shorter term of protection dependent on prior registration under designs law. However, given the statutory exclusion of 'sculpture' from the scope of

[55] This seems to have been inspired by Sir Henry Cole: Letter from H. Cole to Sir Denis Le Marchant, 6 Sept. 1848, in *Report of Select Committee on the School of Design* (1849) [576], Appendix 1, pp. 340ff (referring to the reluctance of sculptors to utilise the 'hazardous action at law' under the 1814 Act and suggesting the Act might be aligned with Registration Acts); Anon., 'Amended Act for the Copyright of Designs' (1850) 3 *Journal of Designs and Manufactures* 177, 178 (change intended to save sculptors from 'the ordeal of an action at common law').

[56] *Stark* v. *Fenzi*, Bell's Life, 15 Sept. 1866 (£10 fine for each reproduction of bust of Gladstone). Registration No. 14 (25 April 1866): TNA: BT 48/5 (Register of Sculptures); www.bonhams.com/auctions/15506/lot/102/.

[57] TNA: BT/22/26/4 (Henry Reader Lack, the Commissioner for Patents, stating that the Royal Commission on copyright thought sculpture should fall into the domain of 'copyright' rather than 'designs').

[58] Patents, Designs and Trade Marks Act 1883 (46 & 47 Vict., c. 57), s. 60; Patents and Designs Act 1907, s. 93. The effect of the repeal of the 1814 Sculpture Act in 1912 left the position unclear: S. Robertson, *The Law of Copyright* (1912), pp. 26–7. However, the definition of design was clarified by the Patents and Designs Act 1919 (amending the Patents and Designs Act 1907, s. 93, by removing the exclusion of sculpture as such). Thereafter, the demarcation turned on the definition of 'industrial process'.

[59] 86 *Law Times* 765 (2 August 1902) (Wright J).

registrability of designs, one effect of the decision should have been to make such designs unregistrable.

Little potential was seen for the overlap between the Fine Arts Copyright Act 1862, which offered copyright protection to original drawings, and the design regime.[60] Although the title of the Act referred to 'fine art', it was widely recognised that this did not preclude the protection of works as simple or functional as the drawing of a hand for use on voting cards.[61] Indeed, there was some litigation in situations where artistic works were applied as labels to mass-produced products,[62] as well as some concerning Christmas cards.[63] However, copying in three dimensions was not considered likely to be infringement of copyright in a two-dimensional drawing. Contemporary commentaries indicated that copying was limited to copying on flat surfaces, e.g. another painting or engraving. This view derived from *Hanfstaengl* v. *Empire Palace*, a case which concerned '*tableaux vivants*' or living pictures, in which people dressed up and posed in the same manner as in famous paintings. Asked whether such performances were infringing

[60] 'Copyright Bill. Differences between clauses 16–31 of the Bill and the Existing Law', CCXXIX(1) (27 June 1911), in TNA: BT 209/474 (on clause 23) ('at present the law as to copyright and the law of designs do not to any considerable extent overlap'); 'Copyright Bill: Analysis', CXL(1) (6 April 1911), in TNA: BT 209/474 (on clause 23 and differences, if any, in existing law) ('Very few registrable designs could be protected under existing copyright law').

[61] *Kenrick* v. *Lawrence* (1890) 25 QBD 99. See also Evan J. MacGillivray, *A Treatise upon the Law of Copyright: in the United Kingdom and the Dominions of the Crown, and in the United States of America* (1902), 168 (a mere label would not be an artistic work; but if it had a picture on it then there 'would undoubtedly be copyright, as the use to which a work of art is put is immaterial').

[62] *Levi* v. *Champion* (1887) 3 TLR 286 (question of ownership of copyright in artistic work which was used for labels for mustard tins); *Hildesheimer* v. *Faulkner* [1901] 2 Ch 552 (on penalties); *Hanfstaengl* v. *Holloway* [1893] 2 QB 1 (where infringement was admitted in making copies of a painting, Bernard Plockhorst's *The Guardian Angel*, for defendant's pill boxes).

[63] *Hildesheimer and Faulkner* v. *Mendelssohn*, *The Standard*, 9 November 1887, p. 2 (awarding damages for reuse in defendant's Christmas card of images taken from plaintiff's children's book); *Hildesheimer* v. *Dunn* (1891) 64 LT 452 (Kekewich J) (Christmas card comprising cardboard hand, with lines on palm and verses on back, was properly registered under both the Fine Art Copyright Act and the Literary Copyright Act, and the defendant was enjoined from copying it); *Millar and Lang, Ltd* v. *Polak*, *Times*, 21 Dec. 1907; [1908] LR 1 Ch 433 Neville J (holding that Christmas cards comprising pictures and writing could be protected under the Fine Arts Copyright Act 1862, rejecting the defendant's argument that these were 'designs'). On penalties under the Fine Arts Copyright Act 1862, see *Hildesheimer* v. *Faulkner* [1901] 2 Ch 552 (1 million copies of image as cigarette card). See also J. M. Easton, *The Law of Copyright: In Works of Literature and Art: including that of the drama, music, engraving, sculpture, painting, photography, and designs by W. A. Copinger*, 4th edn (London: Stevens & Haynes, 1904), p. 344; Russell-Clarke (above, note 47) (1930) 22 ('before 1911, it could probably have obtained protection either as an artistic work … or as a design').

reproductions, the Court of Appeal responded that the term 'copy' implied 'the reproduction of something of a character similar to that of which they were the authors'.[64] The leading commentary, Copinger, observed that 'according to these views a sculpture apparently could not be an infringement of the copyright in a picture'.[65] Lobbyists shared this view: for example, speaking to a 1908 Committee on copyright, David Croal-Thomson (art dealer, painter and editor of the *Art Journal*), from the Artistic Copyright Society, said that the 1862 Act was limited to flat copying, not copying 'in the round'.[66]

In practice, the real issue of boundary drawing in the mid- to late nineteenth century lay between the design registration system and the archaic and expensive patent system. The 1839 Registration Act allowed for the registration of designs 'for the shape or configuration of any article of manufacture', a mysterious formula that was soon recognised as offering the possibility of protection through registration to any article, including those whose functioning could be linked to its form.[67] In today's terms, the 1839 Act was thought to offer both design protection and protection of 'utility models'. As is explained in detail elsewhere,[68] faced with a spate of such registrations, the Registry sought to devise a mechanism to differentiate between different types of application. Consequently, from 1843 through to 1883, the Office operated two registers, one for designs for the purpose or ornament and the other for designs for the purpose of utility.[69] Even though the numbers of registrations of non-ornamental designs were in the hundreds, there was widespread concern over the character and usefulness of the protection offered under the 1843 Act. Even after the reform of the patent system and the merger of the two design regimes in 1883,[70] the courts and legislature continued to struggle to delineate a boundary line between the registered design regime and patent

[64] [1894] 2 Ch 1, 5 (Lindley LJ). [65] Copinger (1904), p. 393.

[66] Gorell (below, note 93), *Evidence*, [267]–[268], [282]; W. Reynolds-Stephens, [2206]; also written evidence at p. 184 on how the 1862 Fine Art Copyright Act did not apply; *Gregory Report* (1951), [230] (little overlap because of narrow construction by courts of copyright statutes); *Johnston Report* (1961) (below, note 152), [140] ('This problem did not arise before the Copyright Act 1911. Until the introduction of this Act, a two-dimensional representation did not, it was thought, give rights in a three-dimensional form').

[67] Report of the Proceedings of the Designs Office, *First Report of the Department of Science and Art* (1854) 28 PP 269, 464–5, 480–95.

[68] L. Bently and B. Sherman, 'The UK's Forgotten Utility Model: The Utility Designs Act 1843' (1997) *IPQ* 265.

[69] (1843) 6 & 7 Vict., c. 65.

[70] The system was recognised to have offered a 'cheap patent' for up to four years, and now that the 1883 Act would permit patenting at the same price, the utility designs register was regarded as unnecessary: Joseph Chamberlain, Board of Trade, (1883) 278 *Hansard (HC)* 349–50 (16 April 1883).

law. In the end, specific exclusions were inserted in the definition of design: it would not encompass (from 1919) a 'method or principle of construction' or a 'mere mechanical device',[71] or (from 1949) 'features . . . dictated by function'.[72] These exclusions reflected a clear desire to channel innovations that related to function into the patent system and away from the Designs Register. There is no need in our context for further elaboration of these developments; though, as we will come to see, they did have important indirect effects on the copyright/design interface, and in no small part informed the evolution of so-called 'industrial copyright', the great concern of the latter part of the twentieth century.

6.2.3 *The End of the Nineteenth Century*

In many ways, the design system of the nineteenth century appears to have been a roaring success. Numbers of registrations grew to a phenomenal level of 40,000 just before the First World War (the exact moment that the cotton industry reached its peak level of production, export and employment).[73]

The registered design system was copied in some of the British colonies,[74] and the 'registration' model adopted in 1839 constituted a model first (in 1852) for reform of the system of patents,[75] and later (in 1875) for inauguration of a system of registered trade marks (which also utilised a system of classification of goods in relation to which marks were registered). Coinciding with the latter initiative, the three offices were consolidated in one place, the Patent Office,[76] and the three regimes were, in 1883, brought under the same Act.[77] Designs were granted a five-year period of protection, but now with no differentiation according to class,[78] and this term was extended to fifteen years in

[71] Patents and Designs Act 1907, s. 93 (defining design), as amended by the Patents and Designs (Amendment) Act 1919, 9 & 10 Geo. V, s. 19. Russell-Clarke explained that these exclusions merely codified judicially developed limitations on what was registrable under the 1883 Act: Russell-Clarke (above, note 47), p. 14.

[72] Following the recommendation of the Swan Committee (below, note 130), [282]. The terms had been regarded as synonymous: Russell-Clarke (above, note 47), p. 15.

[73] Farnie (above, note 1), p. 8.

[74] Alexander, herein, Chapter 7 (Victoria, Western Australia and Queensland).

[75] Protection of Inventions Act (1851, 14 Vict., c. 8) (provisional registration of inventions at the Designs Registry). The real reform of the patent system was carried out the following year by the Patent Law (Amendment) Act 1852, 15 & 16 Vict., c. 83.

[76] Copyright of Designs Act 1875, c. 93, s. 4. On the background, see TNA: BT 13/8/4, TNA: BT 13/5, TNA: BT 13/4 (Tomlinson's embezzlement of registration fees).

[77] Patents, Designs and Trade Marks Act 1883 (46 & 47 Vict., c. 57), s. 50(2).

[78] Patents, Designs and Trade Marks Act 1883 (46 & 47 Vict., c. 57), s. 50(2). For extensions under section 9 of the Designs Act 1850, see BT 22/8/9 (16 Dec. 1872). For criticisms of the system, see Benjamin Armitage and Thomas Browning, 'Memorial

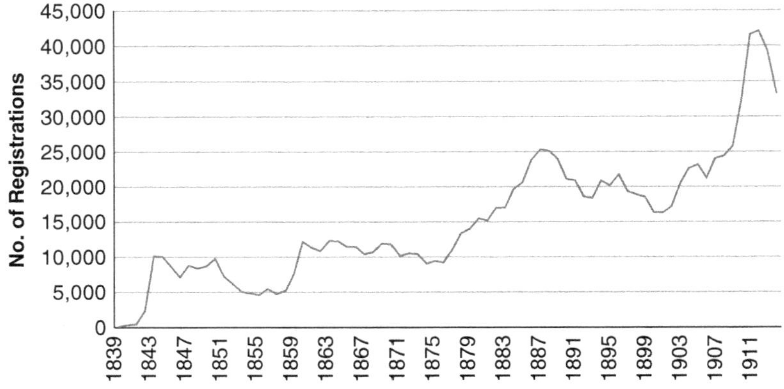

Figure 6.1 UK design registrations 1839–1914
Sources: Parliamentary Papers; Reports of Department of Science and Art; Design Registry books at TNA (1855–75); Annual Reports of Comptroller General; WIPO collated statistics

1907.[79] The 1883 Act also conferred on the Registrar the power to refuse registration,[80] and with that a system of cursory examination.[81]

It was at this point, with the registered design system at its zenith, that internal and external pressures started to emerge to expand the copyright regime in various ways that could affect the registration regime. The internal pressures came from the growing recognition that the various copyright laws, comprised in an array of distinct statutes, needed to be rationalised and, if possible, codified. By the final quarter of the century, the 'law of copyright' comprised fourteen copyright Acts, as well as common law principles. The Royal Commission, which sat between 1875 and 1878, reported as its first observation that the law was 'wholly destitute of any sort of arrangement, incomplete, often obscure' and that

to Rt Hon R A Cross MP, Sec of St for Home Dept, from Directors of Manchester Chamber of Commerce', 25 Feb. 1880, in TNA: BT 26/4.

79 Patents and Designs Act 1907, 7 Edw. VII, c. 29, s. 53. For background, see C. N. Dalton, 'Suggested Legislation for the Consolidation and Amendment of the Patents, etc., Acts', in TNA: BT 209/458 (period of protection is too short); BT 209/465 (Lloyd George amendment for 3rd five-year term).

80 1883 Act, s. 47(6).

81 *Report of the Committee Appointed by the Board of Trade to Inquire into the Duties, Organisation, and Arrangements of the Patent Office ... so far as relates to Trade Marks and Designs* (1888), C. 5350 (hereafter Herschell Committee), [51] (recommending maintenance of system of examination on the basis of novelty). For different views, see QQ 1354ff (Ernest de Pass, opposed); Alfred Julius Boult, QQ 1670ff (supportive).

some of the Acts were 'hardly intelligible'.[82] The Report's first and most important recommendation was that the law be codified, that is, reduced to a systematic and intelligible form.[83] The Committee did not, however, consider the interaction with design registration, explaining that the subject of design registration differed 'in many important particulars'.[84]

In the two decades that followed the Commission's Report, bills devoted to copyright were repeatedly presented to Parliament, culminating in three consecutive years (1898–1900) in which Bills were discussed before the Select Committee in the House of Lords. Just prior to 1898, a 'Committee of Artists', aided by the barrister and copyright expert Thomas Scrutton, drew up a bill to protect 'artistic works', not just sculptures, engravings, paintings and photographs.[85] The Bill defined 'work of fine art' as 'painting, drawing, engraving, sculpture or other artistic work', and specifically protected sculptures 'though made for or applied to the decoration of any article of manufacture'. Moreover, clause 26 defined copying to include copying 'in any other form, and in any material and in any size'. These proposals were included in Lord Monkswell's Copyright (Artistic) Bill which was discussed in the Select Committee of 1899. There Lord Thring questioned Edmund Cutler QC,[86] copyright barrister, asking him repeatedly about the breadth of the subject-matter protected, saying 'it is all important, because we must not override copyright in design'.[87] Cutler seemed caught off-guard, only responding that the problem did not appear any greater than under the 1862 Act.[88] When he had time to consider the matter further, Cutler added that the issue was largely theoretical, and that any *a priori* attempt to resolve the overlap through 'demarcation' was doomed to failure. He indicated that he thought that there might be some situations where cumulation was possible, but he foresaw little difficulty.[89] In 1900, the issue of the design/copyright boundary cropped up again when solicitor Herbert Bentwich gave evidence to the Select Committee, arguing that protection afforded to the design of a picture

82 *Royal Commission on Home, Colonial and International Copyright, Report* (1878), C. 2036, [5]–[9].
83 *Royal Commission, Report,* [13]. 84 *Royal Commission, Report,* [4].
85 *Report from the Select Committee of the House of Lords on the Copyright Bill [H.L.] and the Copyright (Amendment) Bill [H.L.]; together with the proceedings of the committee, minutes of evidence, and appendix,* 1898 Parliamentary Papers (393), 261, Appendix E. The background is described in the evidence of Edwin Bale, at 168ff, QQ 2654ff.
86 1831–1916.
87 *Select Committee of the House of Lords on the Copyright Bill [H.L.] and the Copyright (Artistic) Bill [H.L.]* (1899), 150, Q 2167; 185.
88 *1899 Select Committee,* 151, Q 2179.
89 *1899 Select Committee,* 185–6, QQ 2667–80.

should extend to its use, for example as a pattern for a cushion cover. Lord Monkswell, chairing the Committee, retorted that these moves would bring copyright 'perilously near to infringing the provinces of copyright in designs, which is a different branch of the law'.[90]

Although the desire to replace concrete, particular, subject-matter categories with ones which were abstract and open-ended (such as 'artistic work') raised the question of the copyright-design border, a more significant impetus was the external pressure associated with the growing internationalisation of copyright. As is well known, the Berne Convention was agreed in 1886, with Great Britain as a signatory. The 1908 Revision at Berlin radically extended the significance of the Treaty, requiring the abandonment of national regimes of formalities. At the behest of the French, the Berlin Revision saw the addition of a requirement that 'works of art applied to industry are protected'. However, on the basis of the objections of the British delegation, which had received instructions that inclusion of designs within the Convention was 'inadvisable', the extension of the subject-matter was qualified, so that the obligation was only to offer protection 'to the extent permitted by the internal legislation of each country'.[91] As the delegates explained, the effect was that countries were left free to choose whether to protect works of applied art as 'artistic works' or 'industrial designs'.[92]

The Gorell Committee, established to examine changes to British law necessary to implement the Berlin Revision of Berne, reported in December 1909. While acknowledging that it was unnecessary to reach a conclusion on the protection of industrial designs by copyright, the Committee nevertheless received substantial evidence on the topic, and the Report was sympathetic to allowing cumulation of protection.[93] The Committee had considered a Bill drafted for the Artistic Copyright Society, which included in the scope of subject-matter any 'design of an artistic nature applicable or applied to any articles of manufacture'.[94]

90 *Report from the Select Committee of the House of Lords on the Copyright Bill [H.L.] and the Copyright (Artistic) Bill [H.L.]; together with the proceedings of the committee, minutes of evidence, and appendix* (1900) (377), 82, Q 1097.

91 Article 2(4). For background see Actes (1908), 42, 231, 233; TNA: BT 13/44/6; Ricketson and Ginsburg, *The Berne Convention and Beyond* (2006) [3.11], p. 95, [8.61], pp. 456–7. For perceptions of UK law, see [1909] *Droit d'Auteur* 125ff.

92 *Correspondence respecting the revised convention of Berne for the protection of literary and artistic works, signed at Berlin, November 13, 1908* (1909) Cd. 4467, 6 (report of delegates), 116–17 (proceedings).

93 *Law of Copyright Committee. Report of the Committee on the Law of Copyright* (1910) Cd. 4976, pp. 10–11.

94 Gorell, *Evidence*, [263]; [2221] (Reynolds-Stephens), pp. 243ff, esp. clause 29(1) (defining 'work of art') and clause 24(2) (articulating relationship with Designs Acts). It seems

That Bill received the approval of John Scarratt Rigby,[95] from the Institute of Decorative Designers, who objected to the registration system because it required multiple applications for protection of the same design in different classes (e.g. wallpaper, chintz, tapestry). William Ernst Reynolds-Stephen, from the Society of British Sculptors, also complained about the 'difficulty and cost' of registration, advocating the 'great principle' that all art should be given the same protection on the same conditions.

On 16 July 1909, further evidence was given to the Committee by George Maillard, a barrister at the Paris bar and President of the *Association Littéraire et Artistique Internationale*, an organisation established in the late 1870s by Victor Hugo to promote the international recognition of copyright. Maillard explained the history of the French law on copyright and designs, arguing that experience demonstrated the impossibility of resolving the question of the boundary between authors' rights protection under the revolutionary legislation of 1793 and protection of designs under the 1806 Act.[96] Because of this impossibility, France embraced the idea of 'l'unité d'art' in its Law of 11 March 1902, protecting ornamental designers in the same ways as other artists, and granting copyright whatever the merit or use of the work.[97] Maillard recognised that adoption of such a broad approach to copyright subject-matter necessarily raised the question, 'What is to be done with the "Designs" Act?' He advised the Committee that they need not decide, but one option was to exclude works protected by copyright from design registration, the other to 'accept the cumulative effect in both systems'.

While the Gorell Committee was sympathetic to a broad definition of copyright-protected subject-matter and the possibility of cumulation,[98] the Board of Trade was well aware that cumulation would not be welcomed by the industrial interests. The Board appreciated that the registration system was highly valued.[99] In fact, when Scarratt Rigby had already made a proposal for cumulation back in 1907,[100] the Board of

that the proposal implicitly required an artist to elect between the two systems: Gorell, *Evidence*, [270]–[281].

[95] Gorell, *Evidence*, [337]. Edward Haviland Davis (d. 1957), a designer of wallpaper, silks and tapestries, also testified as to the inadequacy of the designs system to protect against copying in multiple materials.

[96] See also Maillard's written evidence at 194ff and the *Memorandum on Protection of Designs in France and Germany* at pp. 260–1.

[97] Gorell, *Evidence*, [3004]. On the theory, widely attributed to Eugene Pouillet, see Ricketson and Ginsburg (below, note 120), [8.60], 454–5.

[98] *Gorell Report*, 10–11.

[99] Deputation from the Manchester Chamber of Commerce, 2 Feb. 1907 ('We value very highly the advantages of the Designs Acts . . . '), in TNA: BT 209/467.

[100] John Scarratt Rigby, Letter to Board of Trade, 11 Feb. 1907 in TNA: BT 209/467.

Trade had suggested that such a view would not receive *any* support.[101] The evidence to the Gorell Committee showed that the Board was wrong, and that the idea of copyright protection as an alternative at least had *some* support, but the Department remained sceptical.[102]

6.3 The Period of Demarcation

6.3.1 The Policy of Demarcation: 1911–1940

With growing pressures to generalise the field of application of 'copyright',[103] and concern to take advantage of the Berne Convention,[104] the British Government decided on a policy of 'demarcation'. It would confer copyright protection on any work of applied art as long as it was not intended to be mass-produced, in which case the appropriate form of protection was by way of design registration.[105] To have done otherwise, it was believed, would be to undermine the functioning of the registration system for designs.[106] Copyright would be permitted to expand, but not at the cost of the design registration system. According to the Manchester Chamber of Commerce, reflecting the views of the cotton trade, automatic copyright protection would be 'disastrous to manufacturing industries, and extremely disadvantageous to designers'.[107] Because the protection afforded by copyright would be 'superior in every respect to

[101] The Comptroller-General of Patents, C. N. Dalton, observed that Rigby's proposal 'undoubtedly would be bitterly opposed. I doubt it would receive any support': 2 March 1907, TNA: BT 209/467.

[102] On 18 February 1910, the Comptroller-General of Patents, William Temple Franks (1863–1926), responded that he thought these problems were outweighed by commercial considerations.

[103] Sherman and Bently, *The Making* (above, note 8), p. 163.

[104] TNA: BT 209/835, 'Copyright Convention', predicting that, if France made a reservation in relation to works of applied art, most countries would follow suit so that works of applied art would have no protection and expressing concern that 'English artists would undoubtedly be very angry and we should get the blame'. In fact, only France and Tunisia made the predicted reservations: Ricketson, *The Paris Convention* (2015), 497, [11.38].

[105] W. Temple Franks, 4 March 1910, TNA: BT 209/835, remained vehement in his opposition to extending protection of UK copyright law to works of applied art. 'It seems clear at any rate that it would seriously affect, if it did not render largely inoperative, the Designs Act and registration of Industrial Designs.'

[106] On 31 May 1910, Temple Franks had sought views on 'the value and efficiency' of the present system: 'The Protection Afforded to Artist Designs' (20 June 1910) *Manc. Cham. Com. Monthly Record* 165.

[107] 'Manchester Chamber of Commerce. New Textiles Designs Committee' (30 Sept. 1910) 21(19) *Manc. Cham. Com. Monthly Record* 264, 265 (treating designs as 'artistic works' would be 'disastrous to manufacturing industries, and extremely disadvantageous to designers'). See also 'The Protection Afforded to Artist Designs' (30 July 1910) *Manc. Cham. Com. Monthly Record* 198 (responding to Franks, stating that the benefit of

that given by the Design Acts',[108] copyright would undermine the registration system. This would 'destroy the efficacy' of the Acts, 'which are regarded as valuable by the manufacturers which use designs (e.g. calico printers)'.[109] Not surprisingly, the Artistic Copyright Society was not impressed by this feature of the Bill, and made representations to the Board of Trade (though without success).[110]

A draft bill of 3 June 1910 defined an 'artistic work' open-endedly as including 'every work of painting, drawing, sculpture, architecture or other artistic process, and every print or photograph or other work of art produced by any process, mechanical or otherwise, by which impressions or representations of the work can be taken or multiplied'.[111] However, a week later a much simplified definition stated that 'artistic work' included 'works of painting, drawing, sculpture, architecture and *artistic craftsmanship*, and engravings and photographs' (emphasis added); with further definitions of 'work of sculpture', 'work of architecture', 'engravings' and 'photographs'.[112] George Maillard wrote to the Department on 8 August 1910, noting that 'the Bill certainly means to protect works of

the existing system was 'inestimably great' and a proposal that protection be equivalent to that being proposed for copyright would 'be absurd, unworkable and very detrimental if applied to industrial designs'); 'The Law of Copyright and Designs' (31 Jan. 1911) *Manc. Cham. Com. Monthly Record* 4 (cumulation would have 'very prejudicial results for the mercantile interests of this district'); Walter Speakman 'Copyright Act: Designs' (31 May 1912) 23(5) *Manc. Cham. Com. Monthly Record* 142 (Speakman, Secretary to the Manchester Chamber of Commerce from 1904 to 1920, explaining that 'what . . . is desired by this Chamber, viz., that designs for textiles should not come within the purview of or be controlled by the Copyright Act 1911').

108 J. M. Easton, *The law of copyright, in works of literature, art, architecture, photography, music and the drama: including chapters on mechanical contrivances and cinematographs by W.A. Copinger*, 5th edn (London: Stevens & Haynes, 1915), p. 96.

109 Board of Trade, 'Notes on Memorandum of Artistic Copyright Society', 28 Nov. 1910, TNA: BT 209/477.

110 'Memorandum of the Artistic Copyright Society on the Copyright Amendment Bill 1910', in TNA: BT 209/477. In 'Copyright Bill: Notes on Memorandum of Artistic Copyright Society', doubts were expressed as to how far the Society represented 'the ordinary working designer, e.g. for textiles. The Society certainly does not represent the views of manufacturers who use the designs.' It goes on to note that the grant of full copyright to designs 'would destroy the efficacy of the Patents and Designs Act, which is regarded as valuable by the manufacturers who use the designs'. The Board of Trade met with the ACS on 24 November 1910 and on the issue of clause 23 'the Society's representatives appeared to acquiesce'. In separate correspondence, George Maillard asked 'why the theory of cumulative protection has been excluded?' J. W. Phillips proposed a reply to the effect that 'the question has been very carefully examined, with regard to the British conditions, and the proposals in the Bill go as far as seemed possible in the circumstances'. TNA: BT 209/477.

111 Copyright Bill, Confidential Draft XXXIV(7) of 3 June 1910, in TNA: BT 209/474. The draft already included a provision to prevent cumulation in clause 24.

112 Copyright Bill, Confidential Draft XXXIV(8) of 9 June 1910, in TNA: BT 209/474. The definition of 'work of architecture' is amended by hand on Confidential Draft XXXIV(12) of 23 July 1910, a change reflected in Bill 282 of 26 July 1910.

art applied to industry, since in the definition of the words "artistic work" it includes … "works of artistic craftsmanship"'. But he recognised the uncertainties in the concept (with which lawyers continue to struggle), asking for clarification: 'what is the exact meaning of "craftsmanship"? Does it include works executed by an artisan for industrial purposes?'[113]

Given the breadth of the definition of artistic work to include sculptures and works of artistic craftsmanship,[114] as well as the broadening of the circumstances in which a work might be infringed,[115] the Act sought to 'demarcate' the two systems so as to prevent overlap. This was done by section 22, which excluded from protection by copyright any work that was capable of registration as a design and which was intended to be applied by an industrial process. The intention was that the subject-matter of designs would not be protected by copyright.[116] Rules followed defining the concept of an 'industrial process' as multiplication of more than fifty articles, or the application of the design to certain specified types of article.[117]

The French continued to promote aggressively the recognition of '*l'unité d'art*' as an international norm both at the revisions of the Paris Convention on industrial property (first at Washington in 1911,[118] and

[113] TNA: BT 209/477. See also Robertson, *The Law of Copyright*, p. 22 ('appear[s] to mean works executed artistically … and would include such things as art jewellery, art needlework, art beadwork, art basketwork, and so on'); A. Russell-Clarke, *Copyright and Industrial Designs* (London: Sweet & Maxwell, 1951), p. 54 ('What is included under this head is not so easy to define').

[114] 'Difference Between Clauses 16–31 of the Bill and the Existing Law', 27 June 1911, in BT 209/474 (explaining that 'At present the law as to copyright and the law of designs do not to any considerable extent overlap' but noting this would change because copyright was to extend to works of artistic craftsmanship 'unless some demarcation were drawn').

[115] Copyright Act 1911, s. 1(2). The extension to reproduction 'in any material form' had significant implications for the scope of protection of design drawings: *Chabot* v. *Davies* (1936) 155 LT (NS) 525; F. E. Skone James, *Copinger on the Law of Copyright* (7th edn, 1936), p. 65; Russell-Clarke, *Copyright and Industrial Designs*, p. 235; *Gregory Report* (below, note 13), [230].

[116] Russell-Clarke (1930) (above, note 47), 4 ('Section 22 … prevents artistic copyright and industrial copyright overlapping').

[117] Designs Rules 1912 (26 June 1912) (reprinted in Copinger (5th edn, 1915)), p. 744; Designs Rules 1920, SI 1920/337, r. 89; Designs Rules 1932, r. 92; Copyright (Industrial Designs) Rules 1949, SI 1949/2367, r. 2. When these were discussed internally within the Board of Trade in 1957, A. V. King noted that fifty was purely an 'arbitrary figure' but as reasonable as any other: Note by A. V. King, 21 Jan. 1957, in TNA: BT 209/598.

[118] *Actes de la Conférence réunie à Washington du 15 mai au 2 juin 1911* (Berne: Bureau International de l'Union, 1911), p. 221 (French proposal that designs and models enjoy protection of laws and treaties relating to artistic property), 289–91 (5th Report of Commission to consider proposal, chaired by Maillard with Osterrieth acting as reporter); M. Innes, A. Bateman and W. Temple Franks to Sir Edward Grey, 'Report of the British Delegates', 28 July 1911, in *Industrial property and merchandise marks. Papers and*

then at The Hague in 1925)[119] and in those of Berne (in Rome in 1928, and again in Brussels in 1948).[120] Each attempt generated a plethora of satellite initiatives and discussions, such as an International Chamber of Commerce meeting in Amsterdam in July 1929.[121] Nevertheless, well into the twentieth century, the registered designs regime continued to be regarded by British industrialists and policy-makers as valuable territory that was not to be undermined through automatic regimes,[122] and the United Kingdom led the opposition to the repeated French endeavours.

The most clear expression of resolve to resist further international pressure to abandon demarcation was the *Peto Report* of 1935.[123] The Peto Committee had been appointed to consider proposals put forward by the Belgian Government for the forthcoming Brussels conference on the revision of the Berne Copyright Convention, which it was thought would take place in 1936.[124] One proposal was for mandatory protection

correspondence relative to the recent conference at Washington, for the revision of the International Convention for the Protection of Industrial Property and the arrangement for the prevention of false indications of origin on goods, Cd. 5842 (1912), 100 (explaining the French proposal and British opposition, given content of draft Copyright Bill); S. Ricketson, *The Paris Convention* (2015), pp. 478–9, [11.07].

119 *Actes de la Conférence réunie à La Haye du 8 octobre au 6 novembre 1925* (Berne: Bureau International de l'Union, 1926), p. 332 (French proposal to add to Article 1 the sentence 'Les oeuvres artistiques restent protégées par la legislation sur les oeuvres artistiques même si elles ont un emploi ou une destination industrielle'), 412–14 (Report of First Sub-Committee, chaired by Llewelyn Smith, with British objection); Anon., 'Patents and Trade Marks', *The Times*, 9 Dec. 1925, p. 26 (reporting that the French proposal was defeated).

120 *Actes de la Conférence réunie à Rome, 7 mai au 2 juin 1928* (Berne: Bureau Internationale pour la Protection des oeuvres littéraire et artistique, 1929), pp. 64–5 (explaining proposal), p. 190 (report of sub-committee, explaining opposition from Great Britain, Japan and Norway), pp. 227–8 (Main Report), pp. 287–9 (statement of George Maillard as to French position); TNA: BT 209/734 (Report of the British Delegates to the Rt Hon. Sir Austen Chamberlain, Secretary of State for Foreign Affairs); Ricketson and Ginsburg, *The Berne Convention and Beyond* (2006), [3.30], p. 109, [8.62], pp. 457–9.

121 'Industrial Designs', *The Times*, 17 June 1929, p. 9.

122 W. W. Shepherd, Letter to the Editor, 'Industrial Design: The French Proposals', *The Manchester Guardian*, 28 Oct. 1930, p. 13 (explaining the benefits of the existing system and the risks involved in giving it up).

123 *Report of the Departmental Committee on International Copyright* (1935), TNA: BT 209/330.

124 As things turned out, the Brussels Revision was postponed until 1948, when 'works of applied art' made their way on to the list of protected works in Article 2 of the Convention, though subject to a qualification that countries were free to determine the extent of application of their laws to works of applied art and the conditions under which such works would be protected: Brussels, Art. 2(5). For background, see Plaisant, *Report*, 94; *Documents*, 122 (report of sub-committee), 141–8, 158; Ricketson and Ginsburg (above, note 120), [3.38], p. 115; [8.65], pp. 462–5.

by copyright of works of applied art, a shift that would have required the United Kingdom to repeal section 22 of the Copyright Act 1911.[125] The Report rejected the proposition, explaining that 'important interests in this country are opposed to such an alteration of the law'.[126] The 'important interests' were, of course, the textile design companies. The Manchester Chamber of Commerce submission to the Committee stated that cumulation with copyright 'would deprive the textile industry of such benefits as are inherent in the present system of registration under the Patents and Designs Act, which benefits are appreciated notwithstanding various anomalies and defects which are also inherent in the system'.[127] The basis for this resistance was similar to that expressed in 1910:

> registration with deposit of specimens is a useful means of asserting proprietorship, and that the system of official search affords *prima facie* evidence that priority has been established before registration, and to that extent brings about a sense of security which is desirable in an industry dependent on a constant and enormous replenishment of new designs.

6.3.2 *Challenges to Demarcation: 1941–1968*

The principle of demarcation was disturbed by the litigation in *King Features* v. *Kleeman*.[128] In that case, the claimant owned copyright in comic strips featuring the cartoon character Popeye, and had licensed the making of brooches and toys based on the Popeye character. The defendant, who had applied for and been refused a licence, sought to import Popeye toys into the United Kingdom from Japan. The claimant was granted an injunction on the basis that the toys and brooches were reproductions of the artistic works in which they held copyright. The defendant's argument that copyright lapsed once the claimant had permitted the artistic works to be used as a basis for the manufacture of articles by an industrial process, which had succeeded in the Court of

[125] *Peto Report*, [20] (recommending that the Government resist the proposed changes, explaining that while the copyright might seem attractive, the enormous numbers of designs which are required in the textile industry from year to year meant attractions of automatic protection would be 'largely illusory'). The Committee had discussed the issue at its 10th meeting on 22 July 1935: TNA: BT 209/367, Minutes of 10th Meeting, [29].

[126] *Peto Report*, [17].

[127] Manchester Chamber of Commerce, 18 Jan. 1935, in TNA: BT 209/346. The position was supported by others, such as the Trade Marks, Patents and Designs Federation (now the 'IP Federation').

[128] *King Features Syndicate Inc. and Betts* v. *O & M Kleeman Ltd* [1941] AC 417; 58 RPC 207 (HL). For an analysis of the background, see Jose Bellido, above, note 6.

Appeal,[129] failed in the House of Lords. Their Lordships ruled that section 22 was applicable only if the creator intended, at the time of the creation of the cartoons, that they would be reproduced on articles by an industrial process. Thus, where no such intention existed or was proved, later use in this way would not deprive the works of copyright.

The *King Features* decision, handed down in May 1941, threw the previous system of demarcation into disarray. One effect was to introduce a rather odd distinction between artistic works that were commissioned to be used as designs applied to articles (where copyright in design drawings would be lost), and designs based on existing copyright works which had not originally been intended as industrial designs (for which full copyright existed, alongside registered design rights in the later application of the artistic work to a product). This remained the position for the next fifteen years, when Parliament gave effect to two Government reports, both of which had criticised the decision of the Lords and recommended re-instatement of 'demarcation'.

The first call to reinstate demarcation came from the Swan Committee, which had been appointed to investigate the patent and registered design regimes.[130] The Swan Report objected that *King Features* opened the door to protection of the same intellectual creation both by copyright and by design registration, and that the rights conferred might even be in different hands. The Report also observed that the decision deprived potential copyists of any way of ascertaining whether, once a registration of a design had lapsed, the design was in fact in the public domain.[131] It proposed therefore that demarcation be reinstated. However, the Swan Committee was of the view that the precise point of demarcation of the line between the registered designs system and copyright required some adjustment. While section 22 of the 1911 Act sought to exclude registrable designs from copyright, the Swan Report also recommended that certain works ought properly to be regarded as copyright, and these should be excluded from design registration. For example, following views that had been expressed in Copinger,[132] the Swan Report recommended that the registered design regime should not cover postcards and

[129] Russell-Clarke (1930) (above, note 47), 24 ('if he subsequently proceeds to industrialize it he will lose all protection').

[130] *Departmental Committee on Patents and Designs* (1947, Cmd. 7206) (the Swan Committee), 62, [311]–[312].

[131] Ibid., [311]–[312].

[132] Copinger (1936) (above, note 47), 68 (discussing problem of distinguishing mass-produced artistic works, such as engravings, from registrable designs). See also Russell-Clarke (1930) (above, note 115), 21–2 (whether certain conceptions fall within Designs Acts or are protected by copyright is 'a matter of considerable importance' that 'it is sometimes extremely difficult to decide').

calendars which, if original, should be within the copyright regime.[133] In addition, the Report said sculptures should be treated like other artistic works.[134] Following the recommendation, the Registered Designs Act 1949 provided for the exclusion from registrability of articles of 'primarily literary or artistic character'.[135] Implementing rules sought to clarify more precisely what was meant, excluding from registrability works of sculpture (apart from casts and models used or intended to be used as models or patterns to be multiplied by any industrial process), wall plaques and medals, as well as printed matter of various sorts (book-jackets, dressmaking patterns, maps, postcards and stamps).[136]

A further call to reinstate demarcation came from the Gregory Committee (1951),[137] established to investigate what changes to copyright were necessary to implement the Brussels Revision of Berne (which had occurred finally in 1948 rather than 1936, as had been initially planned). Like the Swan Committee before it, the Gregory Committee was concerned that the decision in *King Features* raised the possibility that an artistic work which was the basis of a design might be protected even once the protection conferred by registration had come to an end. It was impossible for a person to know whether a lapsed registered design was in the public domain or not because of the possible existence of a copyright work that had not, at the time of its conception, been intended for mass production. While approving the goal of demarcation,[138] the Committee concluded that the words 'used or intended to be used' in section 22 of the 1911 Act were 'a matter of some difficulty'. Seeking to avoid an 'intention-based' mechanism for demarcation, the Report proposed instead utilising acts of 'registration'

133 Cf. *Gunston* v. *Winox Ltd* [1920] 1 Ch 165, 38 RPC 40 (showcards for advertising medicated wine registered in Class 5); *Con Planck Ltd* v. *Kolynos Inc.* [1925] 2 KB 804 (showcards of clown were engravings but denied copyright because of s. 22).

134 *Swan Committee*, [310]. Cf. *Pytram Ltd* v. *Models (Leicester) Ltd* [1930] 1 Ch 639 (model of wolf cub's head to be used as totem for poles was registrable as design so excluded from copyright).

135 Registered Designs Act 1949, s. 1(4).

136 Design Rules 1949, SI 1949/2368, rule 26. Later, the Johnston Committee was critical of the logic of excluding sculpture and other matter listed from registration and recommended the exclusion be limited to printed matter: *Johnston Report* (below, note 152), [139]. For a situation in which a court had difficulty applying the rules, see *Klarmann (H.) Ltd* v. *Henshaw Linen Supplies* [1960] RPC 150 (Roxburgh J).

137 Board of Trade, *Report of the Copyright Committee*, Cmd. 8662 (hereinafter *Gregory Report*), [227]–[251].

138 The Gregory Committee argued that permitting copyright protection of designs as artistic works would defeat the intention of the registered design regime, in particular the limitation of term, and add undesirable uncertainty: *Gregory Report*, 87, esp. [237], [240].

or 'industrial use' as criteria that would cause the scope of copyright to be reduced.[139]

The reinstatement of demarcation proposed by the Swan and Gregory Committees was carried into effect by section 10 of the Copyright Act 1956.[140] Whereas under section 22 of the Copyright Act 1911 the aim had been to give effect to the principle of demarcation by using a subject-matter exclusion, in the Copyright Act 1956 the legislature chose to use a defence or exception. Although section 10 would acquire some notoriety for being 'a long and complex section',[141] it sought to provide that where a work was capable of registration as a design, and the design either had been registered or used in mass production, it was not thereafter an infringement of copyright in the artistic work to do an act that fell within the scope of the rights that would be given to an owner of a corresponding registered design.[142] The defence was, for fifteen years, limited so as to excuse only uses on the *same* article (as that for which a design had been registered or to which the design had been industrially applied), but after that period the defence applied to uses on *all* articles to which the design could have been applied. It is worth noting that the limitation of the defence to matter 'capable of registration' meant that material that was incapable of registration, such as that excluded from registration on account of its 'literary or artistic character' (under section 1(4) of the 1949 Act and rule 26 of the Design Rules), benefited from copyright as normal: thus sculptures (unless intended for mass production), medals, maps, postcards and football pools coupons, for example, remained subject to full copyright.

139 *Gregory Report*, [241] (referring to a proposal from the Chartered Institute of Patent Agents). The Committee also sought to modify the rules on novelty, so that the requirement of registration prior to publication would not adversely affect the protection of products, such as Popeye brooches, based on published cartoons or comic strips.

140 In a Joint Memorandum by the President of the Board of Trade and Postmaster General the change was said to be 'to rule out double protection which may now exist for the same thing under two Acts. This is a highly technical [but comparatively non-controversial] question.' See TNA: BT 209/533, item 55A. The 1956 Act also sought to limit the impact of copyright protection of technical drawings on the ability to make products that corresponded to those drawings by enacting the so-called 'non-expert defence', in section 9(8) of the 1956 Act. In *LB (Plastics) Ltd* v. *Swish Products Ltd* [1979] RPC 551, 636, Lord Salmon described this as a 'strange sub-section'.

141 *Johnston Report*, [36] ('the precise effect of section 10 . . . is very difficult to determine'); Russell-Clarke, *Copyright in Industrial Designs*, 3rd edn (London: Sweet & Maxwell, 1960), p. 99 (noting that the section and its schedule ran to over 1,000 words); TNA: BT 209/1408 (observation by William Wallace that even leading barristers did not understand the effect of the section). A parallel provision was later adopted by Australia: J. Lahore, 'Industrial Designs and the Copyright Act 1968 – The Problem of Dual Protection' (1969) 43 *ALJ* 139; and Isabella Alexander, Chapter 7, herein.

142 On the background to the Copyright (Industrial Designs) Rules 1957, SI 1957/867, see TNA: BT 209/598.

6.3.3 *Questioning Demarcation: The Road to 1968*

Despite the resolve to maintain the policy of demarcation, the numbers of registrations continued to fall. The peak in 1913 was followed by an inter-war recovery, only to return to low levels during the Second World War, from which there was little movement in the 1950s and 1960s. In fact, the number of registrations in the post-Second World War decades was similar to those a century earlier.

Consequently, it must have been eminently clear that the importance of design registration was fading.[143] In contrast, patent numbers did pick up and soon came to surpass pre-war levels, suggesting that whatever the causes were lay with the design industries rather than the economy more generally. As I have argued elsewhere,[144] the shift primarily reflects industrial change: the contraction in British manufacturing generally, and the virtual elimination of the textile industries more specifically.[145] The effect of industrial change, and the decline of the Manchester calico industry, did not just affect the statistics, i.e. the reduction in design registrations, but it altered the politics. There remained people who advocated demarcation, but these no longer came from the industrial powerhouses. Alongside them other voices emerged who could see real benefits from protecting design investment through copyright rather than registration.[146] Key amongst these were the new 'cultural industries' of the twentieth century: furniture makers, such as Ercol, Hille (which distributed Robin Day chairs) and Conran;[147] toy manufacturers, such as Britains, who were said to be suffering with the effects of Hong Kong-based copiers;[148] jewellery designers, such as Andrew

[143] Compare the 1949 *Swan Committee*, [254] (expecting a revival) (above, note 130) with the 1961 *Johnston Committee* (below, note 152), [14] (acknowledging that use of present design system has diminished).

[144] L. Bently, 'Requiem for Registration?' (above, note 43), 9–12.

[145] The total value of textile exports in 1969 was £187 million: 'Textile Council Move' (May 1970) 257 *Design* 21. The total value of textile exports in 1913 had been around £185 million (of which cotton comprised £127 million), and the total value of all exports £525 million: *Statistical Abstract for the United Kingdom from 1900 to 1914*, Table No. 46, PP.

[146] For an early expression of the view that automatic protection by copyright was in British interests because properly protected industrial design could be an 'important export', see Louis A. De Pinna, *The Times*, 15 Jan. 1948, p. 6.

[147] The British Furniture Manufacturers Federated Associations, the Society of Industrial Artists and Designers and the British Joint Copyright Council made submissions to the Board of Trade arguing for copyright protection: J. W. Noel Jordan, 'Design Protection' (letter) (Nov. 1964) 191 *Design* 69; Noel Jordan, letter (Jan. 1964) 181 *Design* 59 (emphasising international advantages of following New Zealand's lead and protecting designs by copyright); Staff Reporter, 'Easy Chair Design Stealing', *The Times*, 26 Jan. 1967, p. 10 (reporting Leslie Julius, of Hille & Co., describing the Registered Designs Act as 'a waste of time').

[148] F. J. Erroll to R. A. Butler, First Secretary of State, 13 May 1963, in TNA: BT 209/1278.

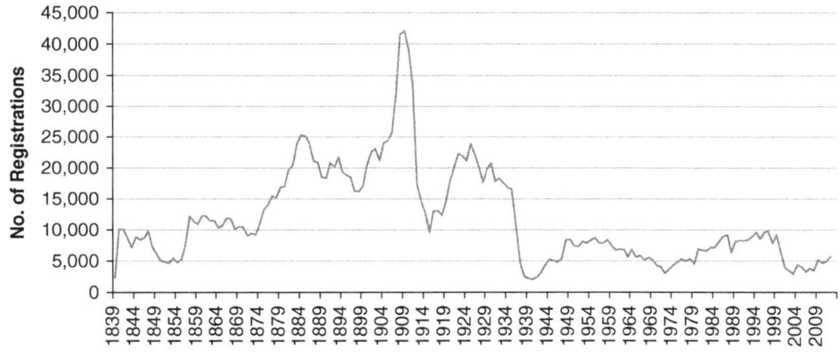

Figure 6.2 UK design registrations 1839–2015

Grima (1921–2007); film and broadcasting companies, which were starting to see the importance of merchandising;[149] and dress and fashion designers, such as Mary Quant. For these groups, the registered designs regime was 'out of date, time-consuming and ineffective'.[150]

The first signs of a change in resolve (to support demarcation) appeared in the 1961 Report of the Johnston Committee. The Committee had been established in 1959 to investigate the law of designs.[151] While it acknowledged that there remained strong support for the retention of the registered design regime,[152] for the first time, the Johnston Committee recognised that there were design sectors for whom the existing system

[149] Walt Disney had made submissions on the 1956 Act (supporting the House of Lords decision in the Popeye case), proposed further amendment after its passage, appeared before the Johnston Committee, and made submissions following the report. Indeed, on 16 April 1964 in TNA: BT 209/1287, the Comptroller-General Gordon Grant wrote that '[t]he day went against [Disney] when the 1956 Copyright Act was under discussion and they have been lobbying ever since'.

[150] John E. Blake (Feb. 1967) 218 *Design* 19.

[151] The Committee was promised to induce Alan Green MP to withdraw his Registered Designs Act (Amendment) Bill, No. 26, proposing a three-year interim copyright for all designs, which had received a second reading on 21 March 1958.

[152] Board of Trade, *Report of the Departmental Committee on Industrial Designs* (1961, Cmnd. 1808), [12], [14], [28], [49], [51]. At the 26th meeting of the Committee, on 21 December 1960, in TNA: BT 209/1443, it was observed that 'whether or not there was sufficient justification for retention of the present system, in view of the amount of evidence in its favour (particularly from the textile trade) it would, as a matter of practical politics, be necessary to maintain it'. The strongest support was from (what was left of) the textile industries, but other supporters included the pottery industry (British Pottery Manufacturers' Federation to Patent Office, 9 Nov. 1962, in TNA: BT 209/1255), the Chartered Institute of Patent Agents and the Association of British Chambers of Commerce.

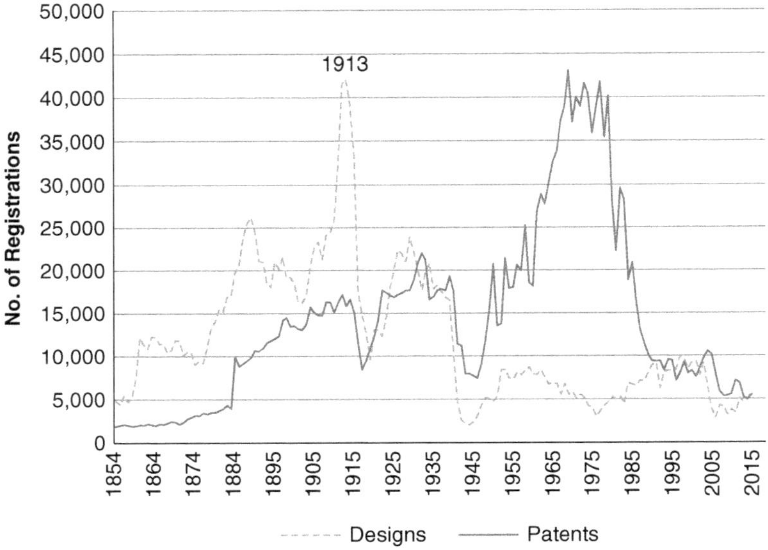

Figure 6.3 UK design and patent registrations 1854–2015
Source: Patent statistics: UKIPO

was not offering the sort of protection that was wanted.[153] As a result, the Committee was no longer prepared to prop up the registered design system on behalf of the textile industry,[154] by making it the sole form of protection in the field. Instead the Report proposed cumulation of traditional registered designs,[155] which it dubbed a 'design monopoly' regime, with a new less bureaucratic system, which it called 'design copyright'.[156] The latter was intended to respond to the needs of those who were not well served by the existing registration system, but was to be formulated so as not to undermine it. What was meant by 'design copyright' was a

[153] *Johnston Report*, [4].

[154] *Johnston Report*, [14], [28], [49], [51]. The Committee recognised that the Registry was regarded by the textile industry as a critical tool for facilitating search of prior art, and a finding that a design could be registered was understood as indicating it was not infringing, allowing production to go ahead. Registration thus served as 'a rough and ready test of infringement and this fact to a large extent accounts for the popularity of the existing design system in the textile industry'. As a result, the Committee accepted that this required some sort of provision for search and examination: [26].

[155] *Johnston Report*, [49]. [156] *Johnston Report*, [47].

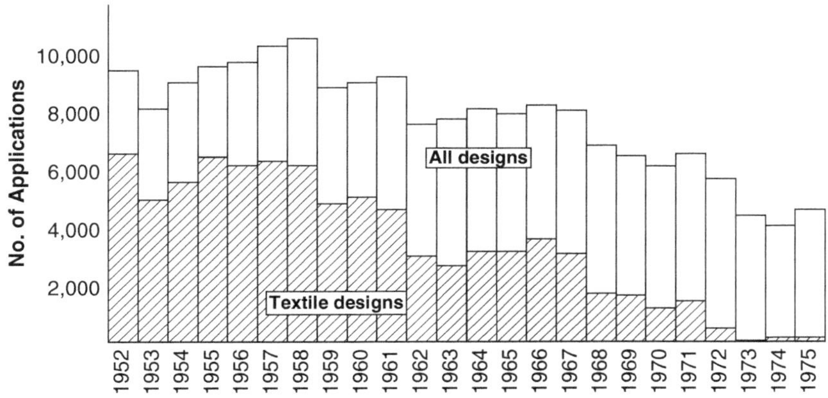

Figure 6.4 Registered designs – applications received 1952–1975
Source: Whitford Report (1977)

'copyright' regime in the sense that protection was to be grounded in originality (origination) rather than novelty, and its scope limited to preventing copying (and dealing in copies).[157] It was to apply to all industrial design, not limited, as in many other countries, to 'applied art' or designs having some mysterious 'artistic quality'.[158] However, in contrast with the regime applicable to artistic works under the 1956 Copyright Act, 'design copyright' protection was premised on deposit of a representation of the design. Such deposit was to be a mechanism to secure priority, rather than define the scope of protection.[159] Under the Johnston proposal, 'design copyright' was to last only fifteen years, the same term as the registered design regime, rather than the life plus fifty years conferred on artistic works by the 1956 Act.[160] The Committee also recommended that there should not be 'cumulation' between 'design copyright' and copyright.

[157] *Johnston Report*, [47](3). The Committee did, however, recommend that the statutory presumptions not apply so that the onus fell on a claimant to prove 'the design to be original as well as proving infringement'.

[158] *Johnston Report*, [47](5) (but conceding a power to exclude specified fields, such as footwear, clothing and hosiery).

[159] *Johnston Report*, [48](2) (stressing that deposit would offer the public a 'means of knowing which articles are protected and which are in the public domain'). Cf. the Law Society's proposal for ten-year automatic right: '"Unfair Copying" of Designs', *The Times*, 1 July 1961, p. 6.

[160] *Johnston Report*, [48](6).

The Johnston Committee's recommendations garnered industry support,[161] but never made their way on to the statute book. This was primarily because of lack of Parliamentary time,[162] though it might be said that the scheme had some obvious problems. Indeed, while one of the Parliamentary draftsmen who had been charged with drawing up a draft bill to give effect to the Johnston recommendations found he was suffering from 'mental arthritis', his superior 'professe[d] to have great philosophical doubts about the whole proposition on which he [was] asked to draft'.[163] Moreover, neither the Board of Trade nor the Patent Office was overly enamoured with the Johnston proposals, one civil servant observing that 'we should have preferred to have got rid of the existing system [of registration] instead of having both running side by side'.[164] What is important for our purposes, however, is that the Johnston Report signals the end of the commitment to strict demarcation given in the previous half century.

The abandonment of the sanctity of the Register as the sole source of design protection, and with it the principle of demarcation, reflected not only the shift in the centre of gravity of British lobbying interests (from textiles to toys, jewellery and furniture), but also three other significant influences. The first was the position of the Patent Office (and Board of Trade): from being staunch defenders of registration, the evidence suggests that it now wanted to be rid of the register altogether. This, in turn, seems both to reflect the decline in the number of registrations, and a belief that the system did not work well. This change in attitude is visible between 1959 and 1962. In 1959, responding to Alan Green's

161 British Pottery Manufacturers' Federation to Patent Office, 9 Nov. 1962 and Michael Tree, Council of Industrial Design, to Peter Thornton, Board of Trade, 26 Nov. 1962, both in TNA: BT 209/1255. See also 'Copyright and Design Law' (Dec. 1962) 168 *Design* 62; B. Weatherill, *The Times*, 2 Nov. 1966, p. 13 (proposing implementing legislation).

162 See E. Heath, Hansard (HC), 19 Mar. 1964, col. 1566 (Government accepts principal recommendations but has no plans to legislate in present Parliament). For background, see TNA: BT 209/1278; TNA: BT 209/1287; TNA: BT 209/1310.

163 G. Ryder (BT) to Bird, 16 Feb. 1967, in TNA: BT 209/1287. Parliamentary Counsel, Harold Chorley, wrote to BT (G. M. E. White) on 5 Aug. 1965 seeking a discussion of 'first principles' and observing that the difference between 'design monopoly' and 'design copyright' was 'virtually imperceptible' and stating he was 'utterly unable to see what advantage is gained by having two systems'.

164 J. Leckie, 12 June 1962, TNA: BT 209/1255. The sentiment found its way into the BT paper of April 1963 for the Home Affairs Committee: 'The Board of Trade would have preferred that the Design Copyright system should replace the present system completely since it is troublesome and the advantages it is supposed to give are largely illusory. Nevertheless, given the evidence, it seems that the existence of two systems must be accepted unless and until it is found that the Design Copyright has largely replaced the Registration system in practice.'

proposal for a three-year copyright for registrable designs, which it saw as 'radical', the Board of Trade expressed 'the general feeling of the representatives of those interested organisations with which we have discussed the Bill is that it would not be feasible to work separate systems on "copyright" and "patent" lines simultaneously and that the remedy proposed by the Bill seemed worse than any disease existing in the present system'.[165] In contrast, soon after the establishment of the Johnston Committee, Gordon Grant, the head of the Patent Office, stated bluntly that '[t]he Patent Office would like to be rid of the present system'. Indeed, the Assistant Comptroller observed that 'protection of industrial designs on copyright lines (though for a shorter period than the copyright life plus fifty) is something which I have always felt desirable'.[166]

The second factor was a changing consciousness as to what was meant by 'design', and a wider belief in the common cause of 'design'. This is most visible through organs like the Council on Industrial Design and magazines, such as *Design*, which from the late 1950s were pushing for effective protection of *all* designs, which meant, in its view, embracing a much simpler mechanism for protection.[167] The third influence was an increasing desire to be part of an effective international and regional design protection regime. A key date in this was 1960, the year of the revision of the Hague Convention on Industrial Designs. The Hague system presupposed national regimes were based on deposit of designs and models, rather than an examination-based registration system. The Johnston Committee's vision of 'Design Copyright' would have allowed access to that regime; while including designs in copyright proper (under the 1956 Act) might offer greater possibility of utilising the Berne regime of international copyright. Not coincidentally, the leading voices in the Patent Office who had abandoned the goal of

[165] TNA: BT 209/1157, 'Note on Mr Alan Green's Registered Designs (Amendment) Bill', J. L. Girling, 12 Feb. 1958 ('radical').

[166] W. Wallace, 'Committee on Designs', 28 May 1962, in TNA: BT 209/1255.

[167] For the common cause, see e.g. 'Design is Indivisible' (1950) (Dec.) 24 *Design* 1 (the 'interdependence of design from industry to industry'). Legal issues start to be a concern from 1956: 'Legal Protection for Industrial Designs' (1956) (Sept.) 93 *Design* 15 (special issue); J. Noel Jordan, 'Legal Protection' (1956) (Nov.) 95 *Design* 66; Anon., 'Better Protection for Industrial Design' (1957) (Sept.) 105 *Design* 35. These continue through the 1960s: Anon., 'Copyright and Design Law' (1962) (Dec.) 168 *Design* 63; Anon., 'The British View on Copyright' (1963) (Oct.) 178 *Design* 51; J. W. Noel Jordan, 'Copyright – Insularity or Internationalism?' (1964) (Jan.) 181 *Design* 59; 'Design Protection' (1964) (Nov.) 191 *Design*; 'Time for a Change in Design Law' (1967) (Feb.) 218 *Design* 19; 'A Chance to Get Action on Design Protection' (1967) (Mar.) 219 *Design* 21; R. Welham, 'Design Plagiarism and the Manufacturer' (1967) (Sept.) 225 *Design* 67; Hoscher and Tye, 'Design Plagiarism' (1967) (Oct.) 226 *Design* 67.

demarcation were also those who were closely interested in such international negotiations (of both the Hague Agreement of 1960 and the Berne Revision).[168]

6.4 The Era of Cumulation

6.4.1 Partial Cumulation and the Era of 'Industrial Copyright': 1968–1989

In 1968, the political economy of intellectual property had so altered that Parliament abandoned the policy of demarcation to which it had adhered at least since 1911, instead adopting a policy of 'partial cumulation'. The move was made in response to a Private Member's Bill, brought by Jill Knight, MP for Edgbaston, motivated by the goal of ensuring copyright protection for jewellery.[169] In the background, however, were the machinations of the Patent Office, and especially William Wallace,[170] who had, from the end of 1965, been advocating for a short instrument giving copyright protection to designs.[171] An internal note proposing this in April 1968, and signed by the Comptroller, Gordon Grant,[172] observed that:

> This solution, although perhaps not very elegant, would be as effective as anything in this field is ever likely to be. It would involve no formalities, no extra stuff in the Patent Office and would give a measure of protection abroad without the need to register at all. But it must be admitted that it is so revolutionary to British ideas on the subject that it is likely to lead to opposition . . . It is the view of the Patent Office that it is worth trying.

[168] William Wallace was the British representative at the Conference of International Experts on the Hague Revision, 28 Sept.–8 Oct. 1959; and later would represent the United Kingdom at the Stockholm Revision of the Berne Convention (1967).

[169] 'Renewing control on prices and incomes', *The Times*, 27 Mar. 1968, p. 8; *Copyright and Designs Law. Report of the Committee to Consider the Law of Copyright and Designs* (1977, Cmnd. 6732) (hereinafter *Whitford Report*), 30, [101].

[170] A. Hope, 'Inquiry into Working of Laws on Copyright', *The Times*, 28 Feb. 1974, p. 25. In fact, it seems clear that the idea was Wallace's: see TNA: BT 209/1288 (reporting meeting between Knight, Wallace, Russell-Clarke and Cawley).

[171] TNA: BT 209/1287. See also William Wallace, 'Legislative Committee: Mrs Jill Knight's Designs Bill. Brief for Board of Trade Ministers', 6 May 1968 ('Mrs Knight got the idea for her draft from Board of Trade officials . . .'), in TNA: BT 209/1287.

[172] Gordon Grant, 'Protection of Industrial Designs', 9 April 1968, in TNA: BT 209/1287. Grant predicted that '[t]his would produce some grumbling from those who are attached to the existing system since they would suspect us of trying to kill the existing system by attrition. We should indeed have no regrets if this happened.'

However 'revolutionary' it may have seemed to the Patent Office, Knight's Bill sailed through Parliament unopposed and received Royal Assent on 25 October 1968.[173] The 1968 [Design Copyright] Act amended section 10 of the 1956 Copyright Act so as to allow copyright to be recognised for fifteen years (a term equivalent to the period of design registration) even where the design had been industrially applied to articles, but leaving the rest of defence introduced in the 1956 Act to operate thereafter as it had before. The effect was that for fifteen years the designer had a choice between using the registration regime, or relying on copyright, or using both. The policy of demarcation was dead. Partial cumulation had become a reality.[174]

As anticipated, this opened the door to the use of copyright to protect mass-produced works, with one of the first uses being by George Hensher against Debonair Upholstery Ltd over use of the former's 'Bronx' three-piece suite.[175] Contemporaries commented favourably on the benefits that accrued to various design industries, including fashion design[176] and furniture manufacture.[177] Not surprisingly, given that copyright protection now seemed to be available for registrable designs, designers were presented with a choice, and increasingly few seemed to see advantages in the registered design regime. Design registrations, already in decline, slumped to a low of 3,019 in 1976. Of course, the decline is not attributable solely to the availability of copyright, as the British economy had fallen into a deep recession from 1973 to 1975, with a fall in GDP of between 3 and 4 per cent (and 2.4 per cent in the first quarter of 1974).

Copyright protection, however, was not without its own limitations, as Hensher soon discovered. While copyright protection might be grounded on design drawings, and action taken against three-dimensional reproductions (whether direct, or indirect), in the absence of such drawings, a claimant hoping to rely on copyright would need to establish that the designed artefact (or a prototype) itself fell within the limited list of copyright subject-matter. Hensher sought protection for its Bronx suite by arguing that a prototype constituted a work of artistic craftsmanship: in 1974, the matter went up to the House of Lords, ending in

173 25 May 1968 (HC, second reading); 25 July 1968 (HC, third reading). It was steered through the House of Lords by Lord Cawley without opposition: 29 July 1968 (HL, second reading); 22 Oct. 1968 (third reading); W. Wallace, 'Protection for Designs in the United Kingdom' (1974) 22 *Bull. Copyright Soc'y USA* 437, 440–1.

174 Anon., 'News: Design is Copyright' (Dec. 1968) 240 *Design* 25.

175 *Cabinet Maker and Retain Furnisher* 387 (21 Aug. 1970).

176 A. Hope, 'Fending off the Fashion Pirates', *The Times*, 9 Nov. 1976, p. 23.

177 K. Owen, 'Need for Protection of Designs Emphasized', *The Times*, 11 July 1978, p. 18; *Whitford Report* (above, note 169), [133] (reporting that some were pleased with the effect of the 1968 Act).

disappointment for the furniture designer, and leaving the concept of 'artistic craftsmanship' mired in confusion to this day.[178] The outcome was, however, a useful reminder that the registered design regime was not redundant. As the British economy recovered slowly from the recession, the number of design registrations gradually increased.

At this juncture, other problems with the Copyright Act 1956 started to become increasingly apparent. Section 10 had made non-cumulation dependent on *registrability* and the 1968 Act now offered the possibility of dual protection for *registrable* designs, but with a limited fifteen-year term. However, because registered design protection was *not* available for functional shapes, copyright *could* protect functional designs embodied in design drawings (as 'artistic works') precisely because those designs were so functional and unappealing that they were *unregistrable*.[179] This became clear in *Dorling* v. *Honnor*,[180] where functional parts of a dinghy were recognised as falling outside the section 10 defence, and thus were fully protected by copyright.[181] The issue became a more urgent concern following a decision of the House of Lords in October 1971 which gave a broad reading to the exclusion of functional designs from the registration system.[182] Thereafter, for example, drawings of a rivet, bolt or screw,[183] washers,[184] pulley wheels,[185] spare parts for vacuum cleaners[186] and exhaust pipes[187] all came to be regarded as

[178] *George Hensher* v. *Restawile Upholstery (Lancs)* [1976] AC 64.

[179] Such an outcome was not inevitable: it would have been possible to interpret 'capability' of registration as referring to the generic subject of registration (namely, at that stage, features of shape, configuration, pattern or ornament), rather than specifically registrable subject-matter. For various appraisals as to who was to blame see Dworkin (below, note 204), 694 ('a result of historical accident, misunderstanding and judicial construction, there is an overlap in the legal protection which is now offered'); Louis Stevenson, 'Protection for Industrial Designs under the British Copyright Act 1956' (1986) 8 AIPLAQJ 369 ('a series of mistakes and oversights on the part of the legislative draftsmen').

[180] [1963] RPC 205, [1964] RPC 160 (CA).

[181] William Wallace had noted these implications in a note, 'Designs Law Amendment: *Dorling v Honnor Marine Ltd, and another*', in TNA: BT 209/1287. Wallace's colleague J. A. E. Davies referred to the 'embarrassment implicit in this decision', and when instructions were sent to Parliamentary Counsel on 13 August 1964 they included a proposal that *Dorling* be reversed.

[182] *Amp* v. *Utilux* [1971] FSR 572, [1972] RPC 103 (HL) (effectively narrowing the breadth of design subject-matter and thus extending the availability of copyright). For the previous understanding of this exclusion, see *Johnston Committee*, [6] ('Very few design registrations have been held invalid for this reason'); Michael Hesketh-Pritchard, 'Copyright and Design Law' (Dec. 1962) 168 *Design* 62 (stating that the existing law did 'not disqualify any design from protection because it has functional merit').

[183] *British Northrop Ltd* v. *Texteam Blackburn Ltd* [1973] FSR 241, 255 (Megarry J).

[184] *Ocular Sciences Ltd* v. *Aspect Vision Care Ltd and Others* [1997] RPC 289, 421 (Laddie J).

[185] *Solar Thomson Engineering Co. Ltd* v. *Barton* [1977] RPC 537, 558 (CA).

[186] *Hoover plc* v. *George Hulme (Stockport) Ltd* [1982] FSR 565, 571–2 (Whitford J).

[187] *British Leyland Motor Corporation* v. *Armstrong Patents Co. Ltd* [1986] AC 577.

protected by copyright.[188] Widely known as 'industrial copyright',[189] the resulting situation was described as 'bizarre', 'logically odd' or simply 'daft'.[190] Apart from rendering the design/copyright interface illogical, many commentators objected that conferring copyright protection on such 'works' might have deeply anti-competitive implications.[191] Chief amongst such critics were the makers of spare parts for automobiles who quickly found themselves as defendants in litigation.[192]

The Department of Trade and Industry monitored the situation closely.[193] For much of 1972, it was considering a short Bill to limit the term of protection to fifteen years, and to exclude functional designs from copyright altogether.[194] The matter proved, however, more controversial than anticipated.[195] Some commentators defended the protection of functional designs by copyright, arguing that it made up for the absence of a 'petty patent';[196] others asserted that such was justifiable as preventing 'free-riding'.[197] Ultimately, the Department recognised that

188 Stevenson (above, note 179); Christine Fellner, *Industrial Designs Law* (London: Sweet & Maxwell, 1995), [1.023], 9.

189 J. G. Drysdale and H. G. Hands, 'Designs Copyright Act 1968 – A Review – And Some Implications and Suggestions for Amendment' [1971–2] CIPA 363; W. R. Cornish, 'Cumulative Protection for Industrial Designs' (1973) *U B Col LR* 219, 237, 243; *Whitford Report*, [154]; Bernard Budd, 'The Future of Industrial Copyright' [1978] EIPR 2; *Ocular Sciences Ltd* v. *Aspect Vision Care Ltd and Others* [1997] RPC 289, 421 (Laddie J); Hugh Laddie, 'Copyright: Over-Strength, Over-Regulated, Over-Rated?' [1996] EIPR 253.

190 *Whitford Report*, 29, [96]; Dworkin (below, note 204) ('logically odd, legally confusing and economically potentially chaotic'); Robin Jacob, 'Reform of UK Copyright Law. Do the Necessary' [1987] EIPR 123 ('daft').

191 J. M. Nugent, WCB Containers, *The Times*, 5 Feb. 1973, p. 16; Eric Taylor, *The Times*, 26 Jan. 1973, p. 18.

192 Anon., 'Automotive Products' Writ against Quinton Hazell', *The Times*, 22 Jan. 1973, p. 17 (litigation over clutch mechanism); Quinton Hazell, *The Times*, 5 Feb. 1973, p. 16. The Hazell litigation was eventually settled: Clifford Webb, 'Automotive Products Buys French Clutch Plant', *The Times*, 24 Sept. 1973, p. 18. It was not just motor vehicle spare parts that were implicated: Granville Kirkup, *The Times*, 25 Jan. 1973, p. 2 (highlighting implications for manufacture of spare parts for cameras).

193 TNA: BT 209/1362 (collecting case transcripts).

194 John Groser, 'Government May Alter Law to Reduce Copyright Period for Mass-produced Goods', *The Times*, 18 Aug. 1972, p. 13. For correspondence, see TNA: BT 209/1408.

195 For press comment and responses, see David Jones and Adrian Hope, 'The Jewellers' Charter Becomes an Engineer's Nightmare', *The Times*, 22 Jan. 1973, p. 19; Kenneth Johnston, *The Times*, 30 Jan. 1973, p. 18; Jill Knight, 'Need for Urgent Amendment to the Design Copyright Act 1968', *The Times*, 24 Jan. 1973, p. 20; C. P. Tootal, *The Times*, 24 Jan. 1973, p. 20; Stanley Coleman, *The Times*, 24 Jan. 1973, p. 20; Cawley, 'Anomalies of Design Copyright Act 1968', *The Times*, 25 Jan. 1973, p. 2.

196 O. W. Jaques, *The Times*, 25 Jan. 1973, p. 2.

197 W. R. Farwell, *The Times*, 26 Jan. 1973, p. 18; Richard Stevens, Society of Industrial and Artistic Designers, *The Times*, 5 Feb. 1973, p. 16; O. J. R. Allen, *The Times*, 25 Jan. 1973, p. 2.

the issue was trickier than it had first seemed and decided that it would best be considered as part of the broader investigation into copyright law that was about to commence under High Court judge Jack Whitford.[198]

The Whitford Committee, however, struggled with the 'very large number' of submissions it received, which were by no means unanimous.[199] In the end the Committee was hopelessly divided (4–3–2) over which designs should be protected and how. A majority of seven favoured a system of automatic protection of designs of products whose appearance influenced purchasers in some respect.[200] The protection was to last for twenty-five years, and damages were only to be available if the design carried a copyright notice. The two dissenters would have limited availability of copyright to 'aesthetic designs' and were also of the view that functional designs should not benefit from any protection whatsoever.[201] In contrast, while four of the nine were happy for functional designs to be protected automatically for twenty-five years (and would have abolished registration altogether), three thought such protection should be based on registration by way of deposit and last for fifteen to twenty-five years (in line with the 'design copyright' system proposed by the Johnston Committee, rather than the 'design monopoly' system, which they, too, would have abolished).[202] These three would have permitted non-functional designs to be deposited too, without prejudice to the automatic protection.[203]

Not surprisingly, given the divided nature of the conclusions of the Whitford Report, it received a luke-warm reception.[204] Despite continuing despair at the state of the law,[205] there was no legislative action. Indeed, two further Green Papers were published in 1981 and 1983, and each offered up different prescriptions to remedy the problem. In the 1981 consultation, the Government indicated that it preferred the

198 Christopher Sweeney, 'Committee Will Report on Copyright Laws', *The Times*, 15 Aug. 1973, p. 2; Adrian Hope, 'Inquiry into Working of Laws on Copyright', *The Times*, 28 Feb. 1974, p. 25.

199 *Whitford Report*, Ch. 3, [129].

200 *Whitford Report*, [180] (expressing conclusion), [167] (defining category A).

201 *Whitford Report*, [185]–[187]. 202 *Whitford Report*, [192].

203 *Whitford Report*, [192].

204 Gerald Dworkin, 'Report of Committees' (1977) 40 MLR 685, 693 (the majority preference for protecting functional designs by copyright 'builds illogicality upon illogicality').

205 Bernard Budd QC (above, note 189); J. Drysdale, 'The Application of UK Copyright Law to Manufactured Articles' [1980] EIPR 75, 77; S. Gratwick QC, 'UK Design Copyright – A Gilbertian Situation' [1980] EIPR 243 (calling the situation a 'scandal').

minority view of the Whitford Committee, namely that functional designs should receive no protection at all, and suggested that indirect protection could be avoided by a rule that it was not an infringement of copyright in a plan to make an article corresponding to the plan unless that article would itself be protected by copyright.[206] The Green Paper suggested that in other respects copyright protection should be available for twenty-five years to all works the appearance of which is not solely dictated by function (not just works of artistic craftsmanship). It thus rejected the requirement that the Whitford minority had proposed that only aesthetic articles benefit from protection.[207] It left open the question of abolition of the registration system (which four of the Whitford Committee had explicitly supported), noting that there had been something of a resurgence in registrations (to over 5,000 per year). It anticipated a 'lively debate' on the issue. However, only two years later a further study by Robin Nicholson, Chief Scientific Adviser to the Cabinet Office, proposed removing 'industrial copyright' (which it confusingly called 'design copyright') and instead incorporating functional designs within the registered design regime (with corresponding limitations on duration and remedies).[208] The *New Scientist* remarked that Nicholson's report contained 'something to offend everyone'.[209]

With no legislative action, the issue of 'industrial copyright' came before courts and other regulatory fora. From the early 1970s, British Leyland and other car manufacturers targeted manufacturers of spare parts, arguing that manufacture of spare parts indirectly infringed copyright in the design drawings of its automobiles.[210] The litigation was designed either to force spare parts producers to obtain licences, or to exclude competition from the spare parts market altogether. The latter practices were of concern to competition authorities, as exclusivity in one market (cars) was being used to prevent competition in another, adjacent, market (spares), apparently to the detriment of consumers (many of

[206] *Reform of the Law Relating to Copyright, Designs and Performers' Protection. A Consultative Document* (1981, Cmnd. 8302), Ch. 1 ('Industrial Design'), [11], [15].

[207] 1981 Green Paper, [14].

[208] *Intellectual Property Rights and Innovation* (December 1983, Cmnd. 9117), [4.19], [4.21].

[209] *The New Scientist*, 5 Jan. 1984, p. 5.

[210] Clifford Webb, 'Panel Makers Unite to Face Leyland's Threat of Legal Action', *The Times*, 10 Sept. 1974, p. 17; Peter J. Brown, Association of Motor Repair Panel Manufacturers, Letter to Editor, *The Times*, 24 Oct. 1974, p. 22; Clifford Webb, 'BLMC Move in Panel Repair Row', *The Times*, 19 Nov. 1974, p. 20; Clifford Webb, 'Rival Carmakers May Follow Leyland over Pirate Spares', *The Times*, 16 Sept. 1974, p. 17; *British Leyland* v. *Wyatt* [1979] FSR 583; *British Leyland* v. *TI Silencers* [1979] FSR 591, [1980] FSR 408; Stevenson (above, note 179), 386ff.

whom did not factor in the high price of spares into their initial purchasing decisions). In March 1985, the Monopolies and Mergers Commission (MMC) found Ford's refusal to license the manufacture and sale of replacement parts to be anti-competitive, but that the remedies available to the MMC to prevent such action were inadequate. Given this limitation, the MMC recommended legislative reform of the registered designs and copyright regimes so as to limit protection of designs for spare parts to a five-year period.[211]

Sensing that Parliament was not going to legislate on the topic, the House of Lords also came up with its own radical solution to the problem of copyright holders using their rights to prevent the emergence of competition in the market for replacement parts. In *British Leyland* v. *Armstrong*, Lord Templeman adapted a doctrine from land law, the so-called 'principle of non-derogation from grant', to free producers of spare parts from copyright liability.[212] The idea was that the sale of a car was akin to the disposition of a legal estate (a 'grant') of land, and implied into any such grant was an undertaking that the grantor would not use any of the rights it retained to hinder the use of the land. By analogy, the seller of a car should not use the rights it retained (the copyright) to hinder use of the car. As far as the House of Lords was concerned, for the principle to be effective, the purchaser should not merely be able to repair their car, but be able to do so by purchasing spare parts from a competitive market. It was a strained analogy, but it allowed the Lords to limit the most obvious detrimental effect of industrial copyright.

6.4.2 *The 1988 Act: Partial Cumulation and a* Sui Generis *System for Functional Designs: 1989–2012*

In April 1986, the Government published the White Paper *Intellectual Property and Innovation*, in which it sketched a new vision of the relationship between copyright, registered designs and a solution to the problem of protection of 'functional designs'.[213] The key to the new compromise was the introduction of a new right, to be called 'unregistered design right', modelled on a European proposal that Member

[211] MMC, *Report on the policy and practice of the Ford Motor Company Ltd of not granting licences to manufacture or sell in the United Kingdom certain replacement body parts for Ford vehicles* (1985, Cmnd. 9437), [6.65], [6.66].

[212] *British Leyland Motor Corporation* v. *Armstrong Patents Co. Ltd* [1986] AC 577. This was later referred to by the Supreme Court as a 'radical and controversial solution': *Lucasfilm Ltd* v. *Ainsworth* [2011] UKSC 39, [2012] 1 AC 208, 218, [12].

[213] White Paper, *Intellectual Property and Innovation* (1986, Cmnd. 9712), [3.17]–[3.39].

States protect 'semi-conductor chips'.[214] The proposed right would, like industrial copyright, arise automatically and protect features of shape and configuration of an article that were original, whether the design was functional or not.[215] The idea was to replace industrial copyright with a right that would give designers a 'market lead' over copiers, thereby satisfying those who had argued that *some* protection was justified.[216] However, to meet the criticism that industrial copyright was anti-competitive, the 'unregistered design right' would be short: influenced by the report of the Monopolies and Mergers Commission, the White Paper proposed five years of exclusivity, with a further five-year entitlement to remuneration for use of identical or substantially similar designs.[217]

The idea of an unregistered design right did not escape criticism. On the one side, the Confederation of British Industry argued this was inadequate;[218] on the other, many remained unconvinced the protection of such designs was necessary or desirable.[219] Robin Jacob suggested that the controversy might further postpone reform, so urged the introduction of a short Bill removing 'conversion damages' and the 'daft' effect of conferring lengthier copyright protection on functional designs than of those with eye appeal.[220] In the end, the Government pushed ahead, and following lengthy and intense debate ranging across a wide range of issues (going well beyond designs), the law was reformed in the Copyright, Designs and Patents Act 1988.

[214] Council Directive 87/54/EEC of 16 Dec. 1986 on the legal protection of semiconductor products, OJ 1986 L 24/36. The Commission Proposal, COM (85) 775 final, OJ C 360/14, had been published on 31 December 1985, and bears many features that would come to characterise the United Kingdom's unregistered design right: for example, as to the standard for protection ('original' and 'not commonplace'), the scope of protection and the term (fifteen years from fixation or ten years from marketing).

[215] The proposal was adopted, and this aspect is reflected in the Copyright, Designs and Patents Act 1988, s. 213. Design right does not subsist in 'surface decoration': CDPA 1988, s. 213(3)(c).

[216] White Paper, [3.26].

[217] This was given effect to in CDPA, s. 216 (fifteen years from making or ten from making available); s. 237 (licences of right available in last five years of design right).

[218] Norma Rose, 'CBI Criticizes Copyright Bill', *The Times*, 29 Feb. 1989, p. 2.

[219] A. Tettenborn, 'Copying Manufactured Articles – Proposals and Problems' (1986) *Comp Lawyer* 239 (case for unregistered design right 'not proven' and proposals 'unconscionably vague'); E. Armitage [1987] EIPR 191, 194 (calling on Government to reconsider right which 'will drive a coach and four through the principle that only inventive technical design should be protected'). See further H. Carty and K. Hodkinson, 'Copyright, Designs and Patents Act 1988' (1989) 52 MLR 369, 379 (criticising complexity of new scheme and lack of evidence of need for the new right); T. A. Blanco White, 'Intellectual Property: A Future for British Concepts' [1988] EIPR 229, 233 (proposed UK UDR 'far too complicated, and that it is anti-European').

[220] R. Jacob (above, note 190).

Under the 1988 regime, copyright, registered design and the new unregistered design right were organised into a complex relationship, albeit one with its own logic. The three regimes targeted in principle different sorts of results: copyright protected artistic works as such; registered designs (now twenty-five years in length) protected 'aesthetic' designs with eye appeal,[221] but not works of a purely artistic character;[222] whereas unregistered design right protected original shape and configuration generally,[223] even if it was non-aesthetic or even functional, but only against 'copying'.[224] As the three regimes could overlap, their relationship was coordinated to ensure that copyright did not undercut the limits built into the registered design regime (partial cumulation), and to make the unregistered design right give way to copyright where protection related to an article which was itself artistic (in effect, a sort of demarcation). In the light of the *British Leyland* v. *Armstrong* decision, which had effectively removed any protection from 'spare parts', the Registered Designs Act was amended and the new unregistered design right regime was drafted to leave unprotected 'must fit' and 'must match' features, that is, those aspects of a design that were necessarily reproduced by anyone who wanted to make replacement parts.[225]

The possible cumulation of automatic protection of copyright and registration-based design protection was not regarded as a problem in principle: copyright was to be permitted to subsist in artistic works even though those works had been, or could be, registered as designs. However, section 52 of the Act continued the policy introduced in 1956 (and modified in 1968) of providing a defence where a copyright work had been 'applied industrially'. That is, where copies of an artistic work, with due authorisation, have been industrially made and then marketed, after the end of the twenty-fifth year in which the licensed copies were first marketed, it was no infringement to copy the artistic work so as to 'make articles of any description'. Moreover, section 52 stated that 'anything may be done in relation to articles so made, without infringing copyright in the work'. An article was regarded as 'made by an industrial process'

[221] In addition to the requirement of 'eye appeal', the amended Registered Design Act 1949 henceforth required that the appearance of the article to which the design was applied be one that was 'material' to consumers: Registered Designs Act 1949 (as amended by CDPA 1988), s. 1(3). See Fellner (above, note 188), 4, 44–7, [2.068]–[2.078]. The requirement was removed when the UK implemented the Designs Directive in 2001: Registered Designs Regulations 2001, SI 2001/3949.

[222] RDA (as amended in 1988), s. 1(6); Registered Designs Rules 1989, SI 1989/1105, rule 26.

[223] CDPA 1988, s. 213(1), (4) (originality requirement).

[224] CDPA 1988, s. 226 (infringement).

[225] CDPA 1988, s. 213(3)(b); RDA 1949, s. 1(1)(b)(ii) (as amended in 1988) (must match).

where more than fifty copies have been made. However, reproduction in the form of certain articles of primarily a literary or artistic character (for example, by way of postcards, posters or book jackets or sculpture) did not trigger its operation.[226] Equally, reproduction of an artistic work by making fifty copies of a film on which the work was reproduced was disregarded.[227] The overall effect was to continue the policy of 'partial cumulation' of copyright and protection of designs through registration that had been in place since 1968.

In contrast, a policy of demarcation was established between the two automatic rights, unregistered design right and copyright. This was effected through a combination of two defences. The first, seeming to give primacy to copyright, declared that there was no infringement of unregistered design right by doing an act that infringed copyright.[228] Thus, although both rights might arise in relation to the same design, unregistered design right was to have no role where copyright applied. However, by limiting the operation of copyright, section 51 of the CDPA 1988 seeks to ensure that unregistered design right applies in relation to designs for shape and configuration of an article *other than an artistic work*. The section states:

> It is not an infringement of copyright in any design document or model recording or embodying a design for anything other than an artistic work or a typeface to make an article to that design or to copy an article made to the design.

Although section 51 has occasionally been interpreted expansively so as to deny copyright protection even in some situations where unregistered design right might not offer an alternative action,[229] on the whole it has worked effectively to exclude the operation of copyright from the field of functional industrial designs.[230] Copyright applies instead only where a design is itself for an 'artistic work' (including, for example, a work of artistic craftsmanship or a sculpture), or insofar as features fall outside the definition of design in section 51(3) because they are 'surface decoration'.[231]

226 Copyright (Industrial Process and Excluded Articles) (No. 2) Order 1989, SI 1989/1070.

227 CDPA 1988, s. 52(6) ('references to articles do not include films').

228 CDPA 1988, s. 236.

229 *Lambretta Clothing Co. Ltd* v. *Teddy Smith (UK) Ltd* [2005] RPC (6) 88 (CA) (holding, by majority, that section 51 operates in relation to the entire 'design document', so that copyright in an arrangement of colours on a tracksuit top could not be enforced against a person making an article according to the design, at least in a case where the colours could not exist conceptually or physically apart from the shapes).

230 Government spokesman Lord Beaverbrook explained that 'the function of [section 51] is to take industrial designs out of copyright': 491 *Hansard* (HL) 185 (8 Dec. 1987) (Committee Stage).

231 *Hi-Tech Autoparts Ltd* v. *Towergate Two Ltd (No. 2)* [2002] FSR 270 (design of rubber non-slip mats was not 'surface decoration').

The effect of the 1988 Act may well have been to give design registration something of a boost, though in truth registration numbers had steadily increased since the trough in the mid-1970s. Perhaps a key factor in this recovery had been the rather limited, and certainly uncertain, interpretation of the notion of 'work of artistic craftsmanship' in the House of Lords decision in *George Hensher* v. *Restawile Upholstery (Lancs)*.[232] This might well have removed some of the confidence from those, such as furniture makers, who had initially been so pleased with the fact that the 1968 Act offered them an alternative system of automatic protection. The 2011 decision of the Supreme Court, offering a narrow interpretation of 'sculpture' that would exclude 'Stormtrooper helmets', has likely reinforced the sense that registration might prove worthwhile.[233] By 1988, there were 7,140 registrations, and, with the exception of 1992 (when the number slipped back to 6,271), during the 1990s and early 2000s, the figures sat in the 8/9,000 area (see Figure 6.5).

6.4.3 Europe and the Road towards Full Cumulation

The 1988 Act's experiment – a product of twenty years of debate – did not last long. The need to complete the Internal Market of the European Community led to the adoption of a Directive harmonising designs law in Europe,[234] and, in 2001, a Regulation establishing a unitary Community designs regime.[235] The Directive was limited to harmonising the registered design system. Although full demarcation was now ruled out, in other respects the Directive expressly left the unregistered regimes (copyright and the UK's unregistered design right) unaffected.[236] The Community Regulation introduced both a Community-wide registered right, and a short-term unregistered Community Design Right. Once again, it sought only to deal with the copyright/design interface by

[232] [1976] AC 64 (HL).

[233] *Lucasfilm Ltd* v. *Ainsworth* [2011] UKSC 39, [2012] 1 AC 208, [49]. In the High Court and Court of Appeal the conclusion was also regarded as relevant to the application of CDPA 1988, s. 52.

[234] Directive 98/71/EC of the European Parliament and of the Council of 13 October 1998 on the legal protection of designs.

[235] Council Regulation (EC) No. 6/2006 of 12 December 2001 on Community Designs.

[236] Directive, Article 17; European Commission, *Green Paper on the Legal Protection of Industrial Design*, 111/F/5131/91-EN (Brussels: June 1991), [11.3.4] (a) ('no design should be denied protection under copyright law for the "sole" reason that it has been registered either at national or at Community level'); Patent Office, *Legal Protection of Designs: A Consultation Paper on the Implementation in the United Kingdom of EC Directive 98/71/EC* (2001), 17, [49] ('There does not appear to be any requirement for amendment to the Copyright, Designs and Patents Act 1988'). For the background, see L. Bently, 'The Return of Industrial Copyright?' [2012] EIPR 654.

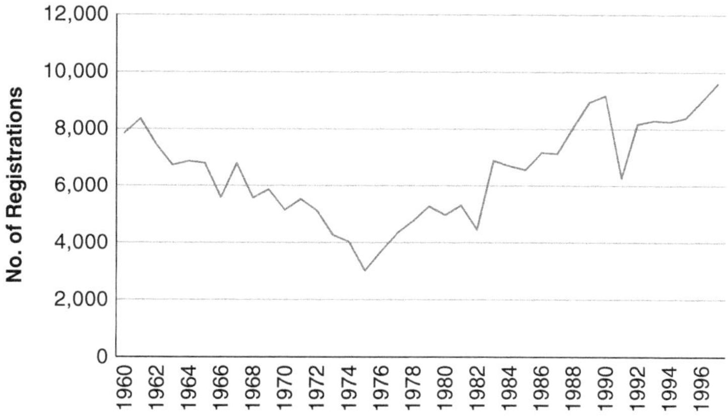

Figure 6.5 UK design registrations 1960–1997

prohibiting copyright rules that removed copyright protection from registered designs (demarcation), purporting to leave all other aspects of copyright (such as originality, scope and length of protection) untouched.[237]

There were three immediate effects on the UK regime that flowed from these EU initiatives. First, the logic of the 1988 reforms was disturbed, as the registered design regime had to be modified in various respects, most notably by removal of its focus on designs whose appearance was material to consumers. Secondly, the design protection system was suddenly much more complex. As copyright and UK unregistered design right were maintained, protection of designs in the United Kingdom thereafter depended on the interaction of five rights: Community Registered and Unregistered designs, UK registered and unregistered designs, as well as copyright. Bill Cornish dubbed it an 'absurd maze'.[238] Thirdly, the introduction of the Community register in 2003 led inevitably to a fall in domestic design registrations. By 2006 these figures were down to 3,000 or so per year (see Figure 6.6). One response to this decline was to bring examination practice in the UK into line with OHIM practice, and therefore from 1 October 2006 the grounds for refusal were greatly restricted.[239]

[237] Regulation, Art. 96(2).

[238] W. R. Cornish, D. Llewelyn and T. Aplin, *Intellectual Property*, 7th edn (London: Thomson, 2010), p. 632, [15–52].

[239] RDA, s. 1A was repealed by the Regulatory Reform (Registered Designs) Order 2006, SI 2006/1974, r. 3.

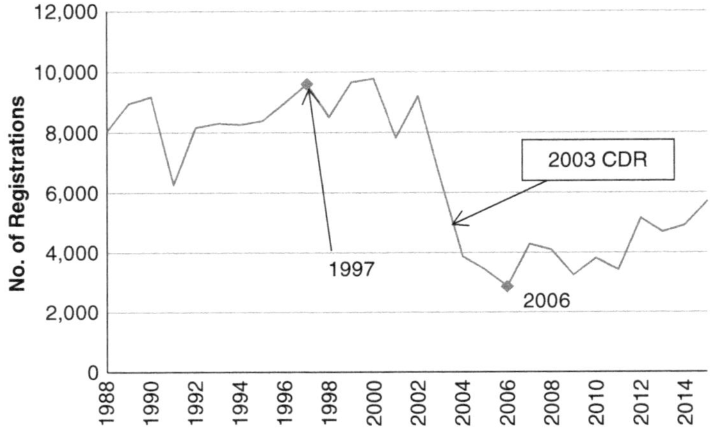

Figure 6.6 UK design registrations 1988–2015

Almost certainly, the decline in UK applications reflected a preference for the Community system, which had obvious attractiveness to foreign entities who had formerly filed in the United Kingdom: in the decades before the Community system came into being, foreign applicants often comprised more than 50 per cent of UK applications, whereas today they are as few as 2 per cent. Moreover, British design proprietors have also migrated to the EU regime, which has tended to attract between 4,000 and 6,000 applications from UK proprietors per annum since 2005.[240] While there will doubtless be some level of overlap, with super-cautious/acquisitive proprietors obtaining both UK registered design rights and Community Registered designs, the combined total number of registrations originating in the UK now seems to be running at around 8–10,000.[241] (See Figure 6.7.)

Recent years, however, have completely reconfigured the relationship between copyright and the registered designs regimes, so that as of 31 July 2016 the United Kingdom has moved to almost complete cumulation. The shift was prompted by statements of the Court of Justice in response

[240] HM Treasury, *Gowers Review of Intellectual Property* (London: HMSO, 2006), 42, [3.44] (citing OHIM statistics that 10% of applications for 2003–5 came from the UK).

[241] An independent review of the intellectual property system in 2006 reported that there were no calls to abandon UK registration: *Gowers Review*, 43, [3.46]. In fact, the only area of design protection that was seen as problematic was enforcement: 43, [3.48].

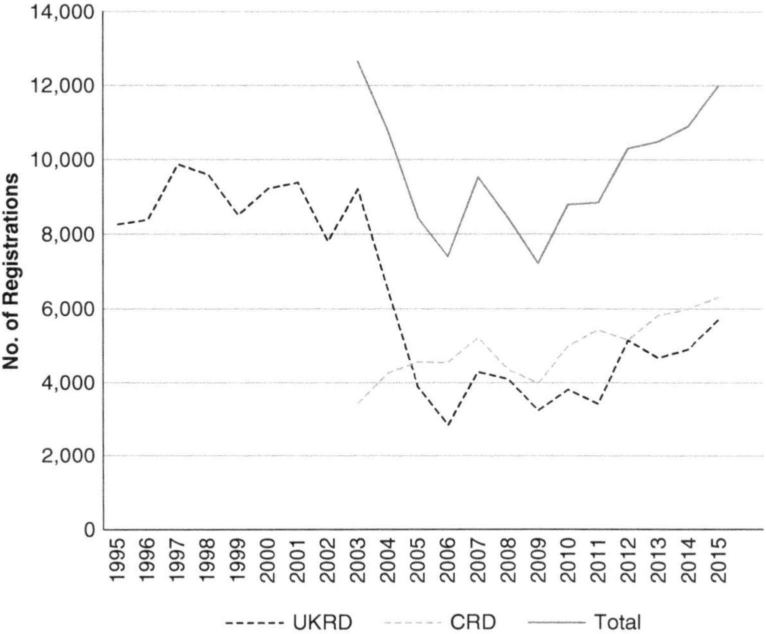

Figure 6.7 UKRDs and CRDs from UK 1995–2015
Source: OHIM (for CRD); UKIPO Annual Reports (UKRD)

to a reference from the Italian courts in the case of *Flos*.[242] The Court hinted that the progressive harmonisation of copyright through the Term and Information Society Directives had deprived Member States of the freedom to regulate the relationship between copyright and designs (that on its face had been preserved in Article 17 of the Designs Directive and Article 96(2) of the Regulation).[243] Lobbyists working for companies that held rights in classic mid-century designs jumped on the Court's dictum,[244] calling on the United Kingdom Government to remove the restriction in section 52 on the availability of copyright for mass-produced articles after twenty-five years of production. Fearing *Francovich* liability,

242 Case C-168/09, *Flos SpA* v. *Semararo Case e Famiglia SpA* (27 Jan. 2011) (CJEU, 2nd Ch.).
243 For counter-arguments, see L. Bently (above, note 236).
244 These included Artek, Cassina, Flos, Stokke, Thonet GmbH and Vitra.

and without conducting any formal consultation, the Government announced it intended to repeal section 52 of the 1988 Act. This was done by section 74 of the Enterprise and Regulatory Reform Act 2013. The Government met criticisms of its failure to consult, and concerns about the implications of what was in substance (if not form) a 'revival' of long-lapsed rights, with a promise of lengthy transitional provisions.[245] Having initially honoured this promise by adopting Regulations creating a five-year transition, the Government spinelessly responded to an application for judicial review by revoking them.[246] A further 'consultation' suggested that, in settling the judicial review, perhaps the Government had now committed itself to a very short transitional period.[247]

The repeal of section 52 took effect on 31 July 2016, so that the full copyright term (seventy years *post mortem auctoris*) applies to all artistic work created since 1 June 1957. A further instrument, which took effect on 6 April 2017, brought pre-1957 designs back within the copyright field (from which they had been excluded by section 22 of the Copyright Act 1911).[248] Even with these changes, 'full cumulation' is not absolutely complete. Section 51 of the 1988 Act remains in place, limiting protection by copyright of design drawing or models 'for something other than an artistic work', so that copyright in the drawing is not infringed by making an article to the design. As a result, Eames chairs, Arco lamps and George Nelson clocks will only be protected against replication if, and only if, the articles themselves can be regarded as 'artistic works', that is works of artistic craftsmanship, sculptures or engravings. Vested interests will be tempted to challenge the compatibility of the provision under EU law

245 IPO, *Call for Evidence: Transitional provisions for repeal of section 52 of the Copyright, Designs and Patents Act 1988* (2013). In its response of February 2015, the Government accepted that some businesses and other interests needed a phase-out period of five years, and thus proposed to delay bringing the repeal of section 52 into operation until 2020: IPO, *Transitional provisions for the repeal of section 52 of the Copyright, Designs and Patents Act 1988: Government response to the consultation and announcement of transitional provisions* (Feb. 2015). The Government implemented this decision on 10 Mar. 2015 by the Enterprise and Regulatory Reform Act 2013 (Commencement No. 8 and Saving Provisions) Order 2015, SI 2015/641, bringing section 74 of the 2013 Act into force from 6 April 2020.

246 The Enterprise and Regulatory Reform Act 2013 (Commencement No. 8 and Saving Provisions) (Revocation) Order 2015, operative from 20 July 2015.

247 IPO, *Consultation on transitional arrangements for the repeal of section 52 of the Copyright, Designs and Patents Act 1988* (Oct. 2015).

248 The Copyright (Amendment) Regulations 2016, SI 2016/1210 (disapplying CDPA 1988, Sch. 1, para. 6 for artistic works protected by copyright in another EEA state on 1 July 1995). The change followed a consultation: IPO, *Changes to Schedule 1 of the Copyright, Designs and Patents Act 1988 and the Duration of Copyright and Rights in Performances Regulations 1995* (July 2016). There are no transitional provisions.

before the United Kingdom leaves the European Union, as it seems destined to do some time in the Spring of 2019 following the result of the referendum of 23 June 2016.

6.5 Conclusion

There is a danger that any account of the historical evolution of law, such as that offered here, from 'quiet co-existence' to 'demarcation' to almost 'full cumulation', is liable to be understood as implying either the inevitability or desirability of the developments described. That is not my intention. Instead, I have tried merely to describe and, where possible, explain the changes, by highlighting how they reflected shifts in the nature and interests of the primary economic entities operating in the field, and their interactions with policy-makers. If there is one overarching reflection, it is that from the end of the nineteenth century the boundaries between legal categories of exclusive rights have been especially prone to the actions of rent-seekers who have recognised they have much to gain from dismantling barriers between these categories. Over the same period, the intuitive appeal of the legal distinction between 'art' and '[industrial] design', which was perhaps common sense in the nineteenth century, seems to have weakened, as its aesthetic grounding has been repeatedly challenged. Unfortunately, the question of what arrangements best promote consumer welfare has only rarely featured in, much less been at the forefront of, the debates. Can it really be the case that to incentivise optimal levels of design of clocks, tables, lamps, chairs, wallpaper and dresses, it is necessary to confer rights lasting for seventy years after the designer's life?

7 The Copyright/Design Interface in Australia

*Isabella Alexander**

7.1 Introduction

The law relating to designs in Australia has long been the subject of dissatisfaction. As long ago as 1936, Sir Owen Dixon referred to the Designs Act 1906 as 'rather peculiar',[1] while the interface between copyright and designs has garnered even more pointed criticism, being called 'troubled',[2] 'vexed'[3] and an area of '(perennial) confusion'.[4] At different times Australia has adopted different approaches to the overlap, moving from potential cumulation (or dual protection as it is more commonly known in Australia) to demarcation and then to partial cumulation (for two-dimensional works) combined with demarcation (for three-dimensional works). Legislative implementation of these policies, however, has been far from straightforward. At each stage, Australia looked to the United Kingdom to inform its legislative approach. While never simply slavishly copying the UK's legislative language, the tendency was at first to follow generally where the UK led. From 1968, however, the position of the two countries diverged, with Australia pursuing a stricter approach of demarcation until it adopted partial cumulation in 1989. Moreover, while the UK simplified its legislative provisions, Australia's approach was to add further detail – an approach that has not necessarily resulted in greater clarity.

The next section of this chapter examines the history of designs and the copyright/design interface in Australia from 1852 to the present, while the

* I am grateful to Eloise Chandler and Kosta Hountalas for research assistance and to Jill McKeough for reading this chapter in draft. All errors remain my own.

[1] *Macrae Knitting Mills Ltd* v. *Lowes Ltd* (1936) 55 CLR 725, 729; (1936) 10 ALJR 201; [1936] HCA 43.

[2] Jani McCutcheon, 'Too Many Stitches in Time? The Polo Lauren Case, Non-infringing Accessories and the Copyright/Design Overlap Defence' (2009) 20 *Australian Intellectual Property Journal* 39, 52.

[3] Sam Ricketson, 'Towards a Rational Basis for the Protection of Industrial Design in Australia' (1994) 5 *Australian Intellectual Property Journal* 193, 194.

[4] Advisory Council on Intellectual Property, *Review of the Designs System: Options Paper* (2014), 30.

Table 7.1 *Chronological table of legislation and statistics*

Period	Legislation	Amendments	Interpretation (i.e. by courts)	Further information	Design applications	Design registrations
1. 1852–1906	Copyright Act 1869 (Vic) Copyright Act 1878 (SA) Copyright Act 1879 (NSW) Patents, Designs and Trade Marks Act 1884 (Qld) Designs and Trade Marks Act 1884 (WA) Patents, Designs and Trade Marks Act 1893 (Tas)	Exhibitors Protection Act 1872 (Vic) Designs and Trade Marks 1884 and Patent Act Amendment Act 1886 (WA) Copyright Act 1890 (Vic)	Cumulation (Vic, NSW, SA, Qld) Partial demarcation (WA & Tas) – excluded sculptures	Some early colonial legislation dealt with designs and patents for inventions in the same Acts: Letters of Registration for Inventions Act 1852 (NSW) Patent Act 1859 (SA)	No data	No data
2. 1907–1912	Copyright Act 1905 (Cth) Design Act 1906 (Cth)		Cumulation?		WIPO 1,151 (192)	WIPO 988 (165)
3. 1913–1968	Copyright Act 1912 (Cth)		Demarcation, no copyright		WIPO 51,936 (944)*	WIPO 42,459 (772)*

Table 7.1 *(cont.)*

Period	Legislation	Amendments	Interpretation (i.e. by courts)	Further information	Design applications	Design registrations
	Design Act 1906 (Cth)		protection for acts within scope of design protection			
4. 1969–1980	Copyright Act 1968 (Cth)	Designs Act 1968 (Cth)	As above, period 3		WIPO 29,294 (2,441)	WIPO 21,239 (1,770)
	Design Act 1906	Design Regulations 1969 (Cth)			IP Australia (1972 to 1980) 6,936 (771)**	IP Australia (1972 to 1980) 3,156 (351)**
5. 1981–1989	Copyright Act 1968 (Cth)	Designs Amendment Act 1981 (Cth)	As above, period 3		WIPO 35,401 (3,933)	WIPO 24,337 (2,704)
	Designs Act 1906 (Cth)				IP Australia 28,394 (3,155)	IP Australia 21,531 (2,392)
6. 1990–2003	Copyright Act 1968 (Cth)	Copyright Amendment Act 1989 (Cth)	Partial cumulation for two-dimensional artistic works, demarcation for three-dimensional works applied industrially, demarcation for works of artistic craftsmanship,		WIPO 58,575 (4,184)	WIPO 47,804 (3,415)
	Designs Act 1906 (Cth)				IP Australia 58,645 (4,189)	IP Australia 47,801 (3,414)

			buildings and models of buildings (copyright protection unless register a design)			
7. 2004–2015	Copyright Act 1968 (Cth) Design Act 2003	Designs (Consequential Amendments) Act 2002	As above, period 6	Definition of 'building or model of building' altered so as not to include portable buildings, pre-constructed swimming pools and demountable buildings	WIPO (to 2014) 66,236 (6,021) IP Australia (to 2015) 73,496 (6,125)	WIPO (to 2014) 64,085 (5,826) IP Australia (to 2015) 70,639 (5,887)

* No data for 1941.

** The huge discrepancy between data from WIPO and data from IP Australia in the period prior to 1981 must raise serious doubts as to the accuracy of the data in this period. IP Australia suggests that the WIPO data is more likely to be accurate (personal communication with author).

following section briefly looks at some of the ongoing problems in this area. Although issues also arise as to the interrelationship between patents and designs, and to a lesser extent between trademarks and designs, this chapter does not address these in any detail.

7.2 History of the Copyright/Design Interface in Australia

7.2.1 First Period: 1852–1906: Varying Approaches in the Colonies Prior to Federation

After many years of comparative neglect, recent years have seen growing levels of academic interest in the history of intellectual property in Australia.[5] Design rights, however, have not yet seen the benefits of this emergent interest and the copyright/design interface still less so.[6] This section thus briefly sketches the early years of intellectual property laws and the legal background against which they developed.

When the tall ships of the First Fleet arrived in Botany Bay in January 1788, they carried with them all English laws applicable to the conditions of the new colony. During the colony's infant years, few if any of the new arrivals – the majority of whom had not travelled there by choice but under Her Majesty's pleasure – would have considered England's panoply of intellectual property laws applicable or relevant to the situation in which they found themselves. However, as the settlement expanded, with new arrivals bringing valuable skills both technical and entrepreneurial, opportunities for commerce, industry and cultural production began to grow. Governors, and soon the Legislative Councils of the two colonies of New South Wales and Van Diemen's Land, had power to pass local laws, as long as they were not 'repugnant' to the Laws of England, and in 1828 the imperial Parliament enacted the Australian Courts Act 1828 (UK) which stated explicitly that English statutes and judicial decisions were operative in New South Wales and Van Diemen's Land.[7] However,

[5] See the references in Catherine Bond, '"Cabined, Cribbed, Confined, Bound In": Copyright in the Australian Colonies', in Isabella Alexander and H. Tomás Gómez-Arostegui (eds.), *Research Handbook on the History of Copyright Law* (Cheltenham: Edward Elgar Publishing, 2016), pp. 374–81 and Kimberlee Weatherall, 'The Emergence and Development of Intellectual Property Laws in Australia and New Zealand', in Rochelle C. Dreyfuss and Justine Pila (eds.), *The Oxford Handbook of Intellectual Property Law* (OUP, forthcoming 2017).

[6] Weatherall, 'The Emergence and Development of Intellectual Property Laws' (1.2 'Note on Sources and the State of the Scholarship').

[7] Bruce Kercher, *Unruly Child: A History of Law in Australia* (St Leonards: Allen & Unwin, 1995), pp. 69–74.

English Acts passed after 1828 were not operative unless they applied by paramount force – in other words, stated that they applied to the colony in question.[8]

The British statutes relating to copyright, patents and designs thus passed prior to those dates formed part of the colonies' law, and some later statutes were expressed to apply by paramount force.[9] The colonial legislatures also had the power to enact local laws and this included the ability to issue patents by parliamentary act.[10] However, it was soon realised that the UK statutes did not apply to books published or inventions first made in the colony in question.[11] Moreover, the Patent Law Amendment Act 1852 (UK) provided patents would not apply automatically to the colonies,[12] and the 1868 decision of *Routledge* v. *Low*[13] confirmed in the field of copyright that books published in the colonies would have protection in a colony, and only in that colony, if it had passed a copyright statute (which none of them had).[14]

These developments spurred the colonies to a legislative response and patent law was the first area to command attention. It was the patents regime, broadly conceived, which encompassed designs. The first colony to act was New South Wales, which had the largest population and the greatest concentration of industrial activity,[15] and it enacted the Letters of Registration for Inventions Act 1852.[16] The Act empowered the NSW Governor General, acting with the advice of his Executive Council, to grant Letters of Registration 'for the exclusive enjoyment and advantage for a period of not less than seven nor more than fourteen years for all

[8] Ibid., p. 75. The 1828 Act also applied to Victoria, Queensland and the Australian Capital Territory, as they were carved out of New South Wales and thus took its law with them at the time of separation. Western Australia and South Australia were established separately and it was assumed that they took with them the laws of England in force at the time of settlement, 1829 and 1836 respectively.

[9] The 1842 Copyright Act applied by paramount force but neither the 1942 Ornamental Designs Act nor the 1843 Utility Designs Act did so.

[10] Jeremy Finn, 'Particularism versus Uniformity: Factors Shaping the Development of Australasian Intellectual Property Law in the Nineteenth Century' (2000) 6 *Australian Journal of Legal History* 113, 119.

[11] Bond, '"Cabined, Cribbed, Confined, Bound In"', pp. 381–2.

[12] An Act for Amending the Law for Granting Patents for Inventions 1852, 15 & 16 Vict., c. 83 (UK).

[13] *Routledge* v. *Low* (1868) LR 3 HL 100.

[14] Bond, '"Cabined, Cribbed, Confined, Bound In"', p. 386.

[15] In 1851, the population of NSW was 181,400: G. J. R. Linge, *Industrial Awakening: A Geography of Australian Manufacturing 1788 to 1890* (Canberra: Australian National University Press, 1979), p. 53.

[16] An Act to authorize the Governor General with the advice of the Executive Council to grant Letters of Registration for all inventions and improvements in the Arts or Manufactures to have the same effect as Letters Patent in England so far as regards this Colony 1852, 16 Vic. 24.

inventions and improvements in the Arts or Manufactures to the author or authors or designer or designers thereof'.[17]

In its focus on improvement of 'arts and manufactures', the Act demonstrates its influences lay not in the 1852 Patent Law Amendment Act recently enacted in the United Kingdom, but rather in earlier British proposals for a general law of arts and manufacture.[18] It was concerns surrounding the applicability of English patent laws, combined with proposals for the first Australasian Industrial Exhibition, driving enactment of this first statute.[19] The question of whether the colonial Legislature was competent to grant patents or pass a patent law occasioned some debate in the press,[20] but it was nonetheless passed.

The colony of Victoria was established in 1851, and three years later, with the gold rush well underway, it passed a Patent Act which allowed for the granting of letters patent to 'the originator or discoverer of any new invention or improvement in the arts or manufactures'.[21] The language of arts and manufactures remained, but the reference to designers was gone.[22] Tasmania largely copied the Victorian Act in its own statute in 1858,[23] as did Western Australia in 1872.[24] South Australia drew on the New South Wales Act in its Patent Act of

[17] Ibid., s. 1.

[18] The 1836 Select Committee on Arts and Manufactures was established to 'inquire into the best means of extending a knowledge of the Arts and of the Principles of Design among the People (especially the Manufacturing Population of the Country)'. Select Committee on Arts and Manufactures, House of Commons; Report from the Select Committee on Arts and their Connexion with Manufactures with the minutes of evidence, appendix and index (1836 9 PP 1), 568, iii. Several bills following its recommendations were subsequently presented to Parliament in the late 1830s. Brad Sherman and Lionel Bently, *The Making of Modern Intellectual Property Law* (Cambridge: Cambridge University Press, 1999), pp. 104–5.

[19] Following the Australasian colonies' disappointing showing in the Great Exhibition of 1851, more concerted efforts were made to make the most of opportunities offered by international exhibitions and to organise local ones, with the first being held in Sydney and Melbourne in 1854. See Peter H. Hoffenberg, '"Nothing Very New or Very Showy to Exhibit"? Australia at the Great Exhibition and After', in Jeffrey A. Auerbach and Peter H. Hoffenberg (eds.), *Britain, the Empire and the World at the Great Exhibition of 1851* (Hampshire: Ashgate, 2013); *The Maitland Mercury and Hunter River General Advertiser*, 9 April 1851, p. 2; *Sydney Morning Herald*, 9 April 1851, p. 3; *Sydney Morning Herald*, 11 April 1851, p. 3.

[20] *Sydney Morning Herald*, 11 April 1851, p. 3.

[21] An Act to regulate Grants of Patents for Inventions in the Colony of Victoria 1854, 17 Vic. c. 15.

[22] This Act too was repealed and replaced in 1857 with a new Act, referring now only to the need to 'promote and encourage the discovery of new manufactures'. An Act concerning Letters Patent for Inventions 1857, 20 Vic. c. 3, s. 1.

[23] An Act to regulate the granting of Letters Patent for Inventions 1858, 22 Vic. No. 22 (Tas).

[24] An Act to regulate Grants of Patents for Inventions in the Colony of Western Australia 1872, 36 Vic. No. 1 (WA).

1859[25] and thus adopted the same approach of a general law of arts and manufactures covering inventors and designers. Queensland adopted its own Patents Act in 1867, but although its title referred to inventions and improvements in the arts and manufactures, its aim was limited to giving temporary protection to inventors more cheaply than the current cost of obtaining letters of registration by government petition.[26]

At this stage, protection of designs shifted into the copyright sphere in some of the colonies. The first colonial copyright statute was passed in Victoria in 1869, at the urging of a deputation including designers,[27] and its very first operative section related to 'copyright of designs for articles or works of manufacture or art'.[28] While the provisions of this Act were clearly based on British legislation relating to designs, the Victorian legislature did not follow the British approach of splitting designs into ornamental and useful categories. The Act in fact was a blend of the 1842 Ornamental Designs Act[29] and the 1843 Utility Designs Act.[30] Section 3 of the Act protected 'the proprietor of any new and original design for any article or work of manufacture or art, and whether such article or work be for purposes of utility ornament or otherwise'.[31] The Act also differed from its UK forebears in some reordering of words and sections and, more significantly, in the periods of protection.[32] This Act was amended in 1872 and repealed and

[25] An Act to authorize the Governor-in-Chief, with the advice of the Executive Council, to grant Letters of Registration for all Inventions and Improvements in the Arts or Manufactures, to have the same effect as Letters Patent in England, so far as regards the Province of South Australia 1859, 22 & 23 Vic. No. 18 (SA).

[26] An Act to Amend the Law relating to Letters of Registration for Inventions and Improvements in the Arts or Manufactures by granting Provisional Certificates of Registration for a Limited Period 1867, 31 Vic. No. 26 (Qld); *The Queenslander*, 30 November 1867, p. 6.

[27] The Leader, 17 April 1869, p. 12; Victoria, *Parliamentary Debates*, Legislative Assembly, 31 August 1868, pp. 1837–8 (G. Paton Smith).

[28] An Act to secure to Proprietors of Designs for Articles and Works of Manufacture and Art, and to Proprietors of Works of Literature and Fine Art, the Copyright of such Designs and Works for a limited period 1869, 33 Vic. No. 350, s. 3.

[29] An Act to Consolidate and Amend the Laws Relating to the Copyright of Designs for Ornamenting Articles of Manufacture 1842, 5 & 6 Vic. c. 100.

[30] An Act to Amend the Laws Relating to the Copyright of Designs 1843, 6 & 7 Vic. c. 65.

[31] Ibid., s. 3.

[32] The 1842 British Ornamental Designs Act offered three different levels of protection: three years for goods in classes 1 to 6, 9 and 12, twelve months for articles in classes 13 and 14 and nine months for articles in classes 8, 10 and 11. Moreover, the 1843 Utility Designs Act gave three years of protection for useful designs. By contrast, the Victorian Act gave three years of protection to articles registered in classes 1 to 5 and two years of protection to the remainder. The classes were almost identical to the British classes of the 1842 Ornamental Designs Act, with an additional class covering articles made of ivory, bone, papier-mache and other solid substances not already included.

replaced in 1890 with a new copyright statute, in which the design provisions were unchanged.[33]

The next colony after Victoria to pass copyright legislation was South Australia, in 1878.[34] This Act was closely modelled on the Victorian Statute but South Australia did away with the notion of different classes in which designs should be registered, leaving it to the proprietor to determine whether they would register for one, two or three years of protection.[35] New South Wales passed its Copyright Act the following year, and the provisions on design copyright were effectively identical to those of Victoria.[36]

Western Australia, Queensland and Tasmania, however, took a different approach. Rather than including designs in their copyright Acts, they followed the more recent UK approach. The WA legislature provided protection for designs in its Designs and Trade Marks Act 1884.[37] In the same year, Queensland passed the Patents, Designs and Trade Marks Act 1884.[38] In 1893 Tasmania passed an Act which repealed its existing patents and trade marks legislation.[39] All were closely modelled on the UK Act of 1883 (although Western Australia continued to treat patents separately). They thus covered 'new *or* original' designs, to be protected for a period of five years from registration. They also excluded protection for sculptures.[40]

A final point to be made about the provisions on designs in every one of the colonies is that they contained penal provisions. Anyone who applied any designs, or fraudulent imitation of a design, for the purposes of sale,

[33] The 1872 Act provided that designs falling under s. 3 and fine art works falling under s. 36 of the Copyright Act 1869 would retain their protection under that Act even in the event they were publicly exhibited at an exhibition of works of industry and art: An Act to protect Exhibitors of New Inventions and Works of Industry and Art 1872, 36 Vic. No. 422 (Vic). See also An Act to consolidate the Law relating to Copyright 1890, 54 Vic. No. 1076 (Vic).

[34] An Act to regulate the Law of Copyright and for other purposes 1878, 41 & 42 Vic. No. 45 (SA).

[35] Ibid., s. 3.

[36] An Act to secure to Proprietors of Works of Literature and Fine Art and to Proprietors of Designs for Articles and Works of Manufacture and Art the Copyright of such Works and Designs for a limited period 1879, 42 Vic. No. 20 (NSW).

[37] An Act to regulate the Registration of Designs and of Trade Marks in the Colony of Western Australia 1884, 48 Vic. No. 7, amended by An Act to alter the law relating to the procedure under 'The Designs and Trade Marks Act 1884 (Vic)' and An Act to regulate grants of Patents for Inventions in the Colony of Western Australia 1886, 50 Vic. No. 5.

[38] An Act to amend and consolidate the law relating to Patents for Inventions, and the Registration of Designs and Trade Marks 1884 (WA), No. 13 of 1884.

[39] An Act to amend the Law relating to Patents for Inventions, and the Registration of Designs and Trade Marks 1893, 57 Vic. No. 6 (Tas).

[40] Designs and Trade Marks Act 1884 (WA), s. 17; Patents, Designs and Trade Marks Act 1884 (Qld), s. 3; Patents, Designs and Trade Marks Act 1893 (Tas), s. 4.

or who sold or exposed such designs knowing they did not have the consent of the proprietor, would be liable to a penalty of between five and fifty pounds.[41] While civil actions were also available, it was the summary conviction that was used and appealed in the only officially reported case I am aware of involving colonial design rights. In *R* v. *Radke, ex parte Dyke*, Radke appealed his conviction under the Copyright Act 1869 (Vic) for selling a safe to which a registered design had been applied, knowing that the proprietor Dyke did not consent.[42] The judges quashed the conviction, accepting Radke's argument that an 'iron frame for a safe' was not an appropriate subject-matter for copyright protection, but was more suited to a patent, commenting: 'Shape and configuration are not the same as a combination of parts.'[43]

At the end of the nineteenth century, protection of designs in what was yet to become Australia was subject to a confusing array of laws, both colonial and imperial.[44] This reflects the fact that the colonies were introducing their laws at the time when, as Sherman and Bently have argued, intellectual property was shifting from its pre-modern to its modern form.[45] While they suggest that in Britain the new logic was emerging by the 1850s, the Australian colonies were still experimenting with different structures and categories, looking to the 'mother country' for guidance but also, at least in the case of the larger colonies, striking out with a few tentative steps on their own. While there was no explicit prohibition against protecting something using both copyright and design registration (except for sculpture in WA, Tasmania and Queensland), it seems that the general assumption was that different regimes applied to different types of subject-matters and products, and that it was up to the

[41] Copyright Act 1869 (Vic), s. 10; Copyright Act 1879 (NSW), s. 41; Copyright Act 1878 (SA), s. 10; Designs and Trade Marks Act 1884 (WA), s. 15; Patents, Designs and Trade Marks Act 1884 (Qld), s. 58; Patents, Designs and Trade Marks Act 1893 (Tas), s. 66.

[42] *R* v. *Radke, ex parte Dyke* (1882) 8 VLR (L) 23.

[43] Ibid., 25. A criminal prosecution was also pursued in *McLean* v. *Wood*, The Age, 30 October 1877, p. 4, but a civil action was contemplated in *Rosenthal* v. *Kaufman*, The Argus, 6 September 1893, p. 7.

[44] For more on the interaction of imperial law with colonial legislation in this field see: Acland Giles, 'Literary and Artistic Copyright in the Commonwealth' (1905–6) 3 *Commonwealth Law Review*, 107, 113; Lionel Bently, 'The "Extraordinary Multiplicity" of Intellectual Property Laws in the British Colonies in the Nineteenth Century' (2011) 12 *Theoretical Inquiries in Law* 161; Sam Ricketson, 'The Imperial Copyright Act 1911 in Australia', in Uma Suthersanen and Ysolde Gendreau (eds.), *A Shifting Empire: 100 Years of the Copyright Act 1911* (Cheltenham: Edward Elgar Publishing Ltd, 2013), pp. 53–62; Bond, '"Cabined, Cribbed, Confined, Bound In"'; Robert Burrell, 'Copyright Reform in the Early Twentieth Century: The View from Australia' (2006) 27 *The Journal of Legal History* 239, 240–6.

[45] Sherman and Bently, *Making of Modern IP Law*.

relevant creator (whether they be author, inventor or designer) to decide which was the most appropriate path of protection.[46]

7.2.2 Second Period: 1907–1912: Cumulation?

In 1901, the six colonies joined together to form the Commonwealth of Australia. The new Constitution gave to the new Federal Parliament the power to legislate in relation to 'copyrights, patents of inventions and designs, and trade marks'.[47] Within five years, Parliament had exercised that power in relation to each of the intellectual property subject-matters, passing the Patents Act in 1903,[48] the Copyright Act[49] and the Trade Marks Act[50] in 1905, and the Designs Act[51] in 1906. The Designs Act was, in a sense, the final piece of the intellectual property puzzle. Senator Keating, who introduced the Bill into the Senate on 20 June 1906, informed the House that it was necessary to pass the Bill because 'correspondence between the Governments of the Commonwealth and of the United Kingdom has revealed that we are not entitled to the measure of international protection which Britain obtained for herself and her Colonies by the Convention of 1894[52] unless our legislation covers the whole field of patents, designs, and trade marks'.[53]

The Bill, which became the Designs Act 1906, did not echo the UK Patents, Designs and Trade Marks Act 1883 in the same way as the Western Australian and Tasmanian statutes had done. Rather, it sought to express those legislative principles alongside their judicial interpretation and development.[54] It was the places where the Australian Bill differed from the UK Act that occasioned most debate. One of the first objections related to the division of the different subject-matters into separate legislative instruments, rather than in a single Act as in the UK. However, as Keating pointed out, given that separate patents, copyright and trade marks statutes had already been enacted, 'the time for the consideration of that point has passed'.[55]

[46] A far from thorough perusal of the Victorian Copyright Register suggests that on several occasions designed products were registered as engravings – see for example the bamboo and rush chair prototypes at A1719, 2746C and 2753C (National Archives of Australia).
[47] Commonwealth of Australia Constitution Act, s. 51(xviii).
[48] Patents Act 1903 (Cth). [49] Copyright Act 1905 (Cth).
[50] Trade Marks Act 1905 (Cth). [51] Designs Act 1906 (Cth).
[52] Presumably this is an error, and in fact the Paris Convention 1883 (which the United Kingdom acceded to in 1884) is intended.
[53] Commonwealth, *Parliamentary Debates*, Senate, 20 June 1906, 392 (Senator John Keating).
[54] Commonwealth, *Parliamentary Debates*, Senate, 20 June 1906, 394 (Senator John Keating).
[55] Ibid.

A second significant change made in the Australian Act was to the definition of 'design'. The 1883 UK Act definition was as follows:

'Design' means any design applicable to any article of manufacture, or to any substance artificial or natural, or partly artificial and partly natural, whether the design is applicable for the pattern, or for the shape or configuration, or for the ornament thereof, or for any two or more of such purposes, and by whatever means it is applicable, whether by printing, painting, embroidering, weaving, sewing, modelling, casting, embossing, engraving, staining, or any other means whatever, manual, mechanical, or chemical, separate or combined, not being a design for a sculpture, or other thing within the protection of the Sculpture Copyright Act of the year 1814 (fifty-fourth George the Third, chapter fifty-six).[56]

The Western Australian, Queensland and Tasmanian Acts had all adopted this definition, but the Federal Act adopted a much shorter one: '"Design" means an industrial design applicable, in any way or by any means, to the purpose of the ornamentation, or pattern, or shape, or configuration, of an article, or to any two or more of those purposes.'[57]

The change to the definition occasioned some debate, mainly driven by Sir Josiah Symon, a lawyer and Senate leader of the Free Traders.[58] Symon's chief objection was not, however, removal of the distinction between sculptures and other articles, but the addition in the Australian Act of the word 'industrial' to 'industrial design', which he considered 'artificial, unnecessary and misleading'.[59] His concerns were echoed by Glynn in the House of Representatives.[60] Those objections were answered by Littleton Groom, pointing out that the word was expressly used in the International Convention, that it was used in the Tasmanian Act and that the definition was 'a decided improvement upon that contained in the English Act'.[61] In fact, the word was only used in the title of the Tasmanian Act and not in the definition of 'design'. The definition was not amended and the term 'industrial design' remained.[62]

[56] Patents, Designs and Trade Marks Act 1883 (UK), s. 60.

[57] Designs Act 1906 (Cth), s. 4.

[58] Symon had made a considerable contribution to the debates over the Copyright Act 1905. See Benedict Atkinson, *The True History of Copyright: The Australian Experience 1905–2005* (Sydney: Sydney University Press, 2007), pp. 18–19, 37–41.

[59] Commonwealth, *Parliamentary Debates*, Senate, 20 June 1906, 402 (Senator Sir Josiah Symon).

[60] Commonwealth, *Parliamentary Debates*, House of Representatives, 1 August 1906, 2163 (Patrick Glynn MP).

[61] Commonwealth, *Parliamentary Debates*, House of Representatives, 1 August 1906, 2165 (Littleton Groom MP).

[62] As Gummow J noted in *Hosokawa Micron International Inc.* v. *Fortune* (1990) 19 IPR 531 at 553, 'the inclusion of the term "industrial" in the Australian definition appears to have been something of a drafting accident to which no great significance should be attached'.

The nature of the right, still referred to as the 'copyright in the design', was defined as meaning 'the exclusive right to apply the design, or to authorize another person to apply the design, to the articles in respect of which it is registered'.[63] This also differed slightly to the UK Act's definition, which referred to 'article of manufacture' and made no reference to authorisation.[64] Infringement of the design copyright was separately defined as applying the design 'or any fraudulent or obvious imitation of it' to any article in respect of which it is registered, or selling or offering for sale such an article, without the licence or authority of the copyright owner.[65] The phrase 'fraudulent or obvious imitation' was taken from the UK Act; although the wording of the rest of the section differed, it essentially achieved the same effect. The author of the design would be the owner of that design and, where the design was made for valuable consideration, the person on whose behalf it was made would be considered the author and therefore the owner.[66]

The Designs Act 1906 came into force on 1 January 1907 – the same day as the Copyright Act 1905, passed a year earlier. Neither statute contained any reference to any potential overlap between them. The Copyright Act 1905 provided for the protection of books, lectures, dramatic works, musical works and artistic works, which were defined to include paintings, drawings, sculptures, engravings, etchings, prints, lithographs, woodcuts, photographs, 'or other work of art produced by any process, mechanical or otherwise, by which impressions or representations of works of art can be taken or multiplied'.[67] The right granted to owners of artistic works extended to reproducing a work, 'or any material part of it, in any manner, form, or size, in any material, or by any process, or for any purpose'.[68] The interaction between copyright in designs and copyright in artistic works was not discussed during debates over the Copyright Bill. While a couple of members expressed concerns that passing the Copyright Act would nullify rights granted under the state acts, their fears were allayed by the assurance that design legislation was forthcoming.[69]

The lack of attention paid to the potential for overlapping protection by designs and copyright legislation may seem odd in retrospect, but it must be remembered that copyright covered a much narrower field at that time. Sherman and Bently suggest that, prior to copyright protection arising automatically, copyright did not offer the same advantages over design

[63] Designs Act 1906 (Cth), s. 12.
[64] Patents, Designs and Trade Marks Act 1883 (UK), s. 60.
[65] Designs Act 1906 (Cth), s. 30. [66] Designs Act 1906 (Cth), s. 14.
[67] Copyright Act 1905 (Cth), s. 4. [68] Ibid., s. 34.
[69] Commonwealth, *Parliamentary Debates*, Senate, 30 August 1905, 1651.

protection. Copyright owners were required to register their works before they could bring an infringement action, except in the case of sculpture. However, sculptures were excluded from design protection under the 1883 Patents, Designs and Trade Marks Act (UK).[70] In the case of drawings, engravings and other two-dimensional works, it was generally thought that reproduction in three dimensions would not amount to infringement. There was thus little scope for overlap.[71] A second explanation can be found in the Gorell Committee's 1909 view that any overlapping should be tolerated to the advantage of copyright and design owners.[72] I have not located any judicial decisions dealing with the overlap during this period, so no further assistance can be found there.

7.2.3 Third Period: 1913–1968: Demarcation

The Copyright Act 1905 did not last long. In 1912, it was repealed and replaced by a statute which implemented the UK's Copyright Act 1911.[73] The UK, or Imperial, Act was annexed in the Schedule to the Copyright Act 1912. This statute specified that copyright subsisted in 'every original literary, dramatic, musical and artistic work' but introduced a different definition of 'artistic works', which was defined to include 'works of painting, drawing, sculpture and artistic craftsmanship', and architectural works of art and engravings and photographs.[74] No criteria or standard of artistic or aesthetic merit was laid down. The statute also introduced a broader approach to the rights created in respect of works, to include the 'right to produce or reproduce the work or any substantial part thereof in any material form whatsoever'.[75] Having extended the rights and the subject-matter, the statute did address the potential overlap between such copyright works and designs. Section 22 provided that the Act did not apply to 'designs capable of being registered under the [Designs Act 1906], except designs which, though capable of being so registered, are not used or intended to be used as models or patterns to be multiplied by any industrial process'.[76]

[70] Patents, Designs and Trade Marks Act 1883 (UK), s. 60.
[71] Sherman and Bently, *Making of Modern IP Law*, p. 164.
[72] This explanation was offered by the High Court in *Burge* v. *Swarbrick* (2007) 232 CLR 336, 347, referring to *Report of the Committee on the Law of Copyright* (1909) Cd. 4976, 10.
[73] An Act relating to Copyright (No. 12 of 1912) (Cth).
[74] Copyright Act 1 & 2 Geo. V (1911) (UK), s. 35.
[75] Copyright Act 1912, Schedule, s. 2.
[76] Ibid, s. 22. The Australian Act instructed that the Designs Act 1906 (Cth) would be read for the Patents and Designs Act 1907 (UK).

The only member who queried the exclusion of registrable designs in the House of Representatives was Sir Robert Best.[77] He argued that the exclusion of designs under the Copyright Act was 'unjust to the enterprising men, who pay highly to secure the designs of great artists, because a design registered under the Designs and Patents Act is protected for five years only'.[78] However, he was assuaged when he was reminded that earlier in the week Parliament had passed legislation allowing registration to be extended for two further periods of five years each, following a similar amendment being made in the UK.[79]

The interpretation of section 22 has given rise to considerable difficulty over the years.[80] Clearly, the intention behind it was to avoid dual protection under both copyright and designs law, forcing artistic works under the former head and industrially produced products under the latter head. However, it did not completely exclude the operation of copyright in relation to designs which can be registered under the Designs Act, but rather 'cut down its ambit'.[81] Thus, a drawing which could also be a registrable design if applied to an article would not be protected by copyright law against being reproduced in three dimensions, and would have to be registered under the Designs Act to gain such protection. However, such a drawing would still be protected against reproduction in two dimensions under the Copyright Act (because in such a case it would not fulfil the criteria of a design under the Designs Act as being applied to an article). Moreover, even where such drawings were also potentially registrable as designs, copyright would continue to treat them as artistic works if there was no intention for such works to be used industrially ('as models or patterns to be multiplied by any industrial process') and they would be protected by the Copyright Act 1912.

With only a few amendments of any significance in the 1930s,[82] the Copyright Act 1912 continued in force for fifty-six years. Despite the

[77] Best had worked in a printing office as a young man before becoming a solicitor and then a politician.

[78] Commonwealth, *Parliamentary Debates*, House of Representatives, 30 October 1912, 4869 (Sir Robert Best MP).

[79] An Act to amend the Designs Act 1906 (No. 14 of 1912) (Cth), s. 3.

[80] See the discussion in *Interlego AG and Another* v. *Croner Trading Pty Ltd* (1992) 39 FCR 348, 355, 366–9.

[81] *Interlego AG and Another* v. *Croner Trading Pty Ltd* (1992) 39 FCR 348, 355 per Gummow J, citing Blanco White, *Patents for Inventions*, 4th edn (London: Stevens, 1974), pp. 331–2.

[82] Copyright Act 1933 (No. 68 of 1933) (Cth); Designs Act 1933 (No. 26 of 1933) (Cth); Designs Act 1934 (No. 42 of 1934) (Cth); Copyright Act 1935 (No. 17 of 1935) (Cth).

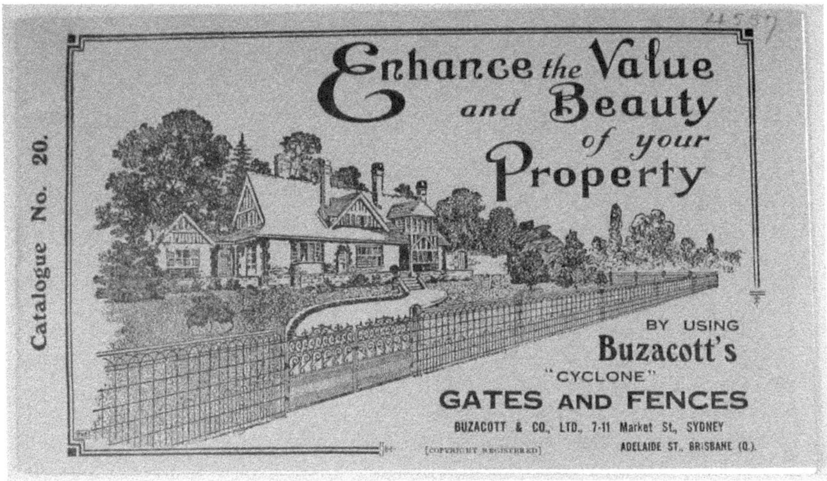

Figure 7.1 Page from a 1915 Buzacott catalogue

steadily rising number of design applications and registrations, only a handful of cases relating to designs came before the courts in the period up to 1968,[83] of which only one involved the operation of section 22 of the Copyright Act. In *Buzacott & Co. Ltd* v. *Dutch*,[84] the plaintiff failed in its action for infringement of copyright in its catalogue containing illustrations of its gates, fences, seats and articles in tube and wire. The NSW Supreme Court found that the illustrations of the articles were engravings under the Copyright Act, but also designs which were capable of registration under the Designs Act 1906 and were intended to be used as models or patterns to be multiplied by an industrial process. Thus, section 22 operated to exclude their protection under copyright law.

Although the judge in this case indicated some unhappiness with the decision he considered he was bound to make,[85] the very small number

[83] *Buzacott & Co. Ltd* v. *Cyclone Proprietary Ltd* (1920) 27 CLR 286; *Buzacott & Co. Ltd* v. *Dutch* (1929) 30 SR (NSW) 22, 46 WN (NSW) 210; *Macrae Knitting Mills Ltd* v. *Lowes Ltd* (1936) 50 CLR 725; *In re Wolanski* (1953) 88 CLR 278; *Inala Industries Pty Ltd* v. *Associated Enterprises Ltd* [1960] Qd R 562; *J. W. Tomlin Pty Ltd* v. *Malleys Ltd* [1960] NSWR 454, 77 WN (NSW) 723, 2 FLR 142; *Malleys Ltd* v. *J. W. Tomlin Pty Ltd* (1961) 180 CLR 120; *D. Sebel & Co. Ltd* v. *National Art Metal Co. Pty Ltd* (1965) 10 FLR 224; *Hella-Australia Pty Ltd* v. *Quinton Hazell (Aust) Pty Ltd* [1968] 1 NSWR 235, 86 WN (Pt 1) (NSW) 243; 10 FLR 86.

[84] *Buzacott & Co. Ltd* v. *Dutch* (1929) 30 SR (NSW) 22, 46 WN (NSW) 210.

[85] Long Innes J stated, 'Although I am clearly of opinion that in its details the defendant's catalogue has been largely copied from those of the plaintiff, as is in fact not denied, I am

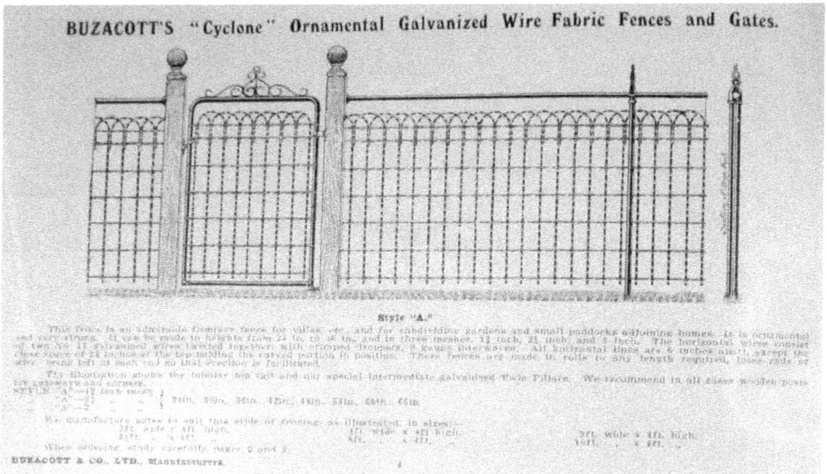

Figure 7.2 Page from a 1915 Buzacott catalogue
Source: Ernest Walter Buzacott and Albert Killear Garven, *Buzacott's Cyclone Gates and Fences*. Copyright Registration 1 Nov. 1915. National Archives of Australia, A1334, 4557

of cases being litigated means no great level of local dissatisfaction with section 22 is perceptible.[86] However, this was not the case in the UK, the jurisdiction to which the Australian courts repeatedly turned for precedent in the small number of decisions coming before them. In *King Features Syndicate* v. *O & M Kleeman*[87] the House of Lords held that the copyright in 'Pop-Eye' cartoons was infringed by the unauthorised manufacture of 'Pop-Eye' dolls and brooches copied from those cartoons, notwithstanding section 22. Although the Pop-Eye merchandise was manufactured industrially, their Lordships found that copyright continued to operate because at the time the cartoons were made the artist had no intention to use them industrially. When the Gregory Committee was appointed ten years later to look into possible reform of copyright law in the UK, it paid particular

unable to give the plaintiff the more extended relief which, but for the provisions of s. 22, I would gladly give him.' *Buzacott & Co. Ltd* v. *Dutch* (1929) 30 SR (NSW) 22, 25.

86 In 1971, the case of *Koloszy* v. *K. Biro & Co. Pty Ltd* [1971] 2 NSWLR 444 also had to decide upon the operation of s. 22, as the works in question were made before the Copyright Act 1968 commenced. Hope J noted the difficulties associated with applying s. 22 in relation to different kinds of works.

87 *King Features Syndicate Inc. and Betts* v. *O & M Kleeman Ltd* [1941] AC 417; (1941) 1B IPR 215; [1941] 2 All ER 403. See Chapter 6, above, for more detail.

attention to this case, stating it demonstrated the inequitable results that could flow from making the protection of copyright turn upon the intention of the artist, as mandated by section 22 of the Imperial Copyright Act. Moreover, the Committee also took the view that the case meant that dual protection would be available under both copyright and designs law, something it considered undesirable.[88]

Five years after the Gregory Committee delivered its report, the UK amended its copyright law.[89] In Australia, this brought to an end the long period of stability which had followed the enactment of the Copyright Act 1912.[90] In 1958 the Attorney-General appointed a Committee, chaired by a former attorney-general and judge, J. A. Spicer, to consider whether any of those amendments should be incorporated into Australian law. The Spicer Committee devoted only nine paragraphs to the question of industrial designs.[91] It took the view that 'extensive inquiry into the revision of the Designs Act'[92] went beyond its terms of reference but did briefly note that a recent New Zealand Committee had recommended that all designs which were original artistic works should be protected as copyright works. The Committee indicated that, had it been authorised to make recommendations regarding reform of design law, it might have taken a similar approach. In the end, however, it simply adopted the discussion of the UK Gregory Committee in relation to the overlap between designs and copyright.

To conclude, during this lengthy period of history, it appears that the approach in Australia was one of demarcation between copyright and designs (notwithstanding the decision in *King Features* v. *Kleeman*). Which regime would apply would depend on the form in which the work was, or was intended, to be exploited. If it was exploited as a design and applied to articles, then it would fall under designs law; if,

[88] Report of the Copyright Committee (1951, Cd. 8662), 82–93. Although note that in his speech Lord Wright stated: 'If the [relevant designs] had been registered and if the [Patents and Designs] Acts had been otherwise complied with, they would have acquired the rights under the Patents and Designs Act, which are much narrower than those given by the Copyright Act . . . Having these rights as designs, they were not to have any further or other rights under the Copyright Act.' *King Features* v. *Kleeman* [1941] AC 417, 439.

[89] Copyright Act 1956, 4 & 5 Eliz. II, c. 74 (UK).

[90] A stability which Ricketson has noted as 'remarkable' in light of the large number of amendments and divisive conflicts generated following the enactment of the Copyright Act 1968: Ricketson, 'Imperial Copyright Act in Australia', 73.

[91] Report of the Committee Appointed by the Attorney-General of the Commonwealth to Consider what Alterations are Desirable to The Copyright Law of the Commonwealth (Australian Government Printer, Canberra, 1959), 82–3.

[92] Ibid., 83.

however, the work was exploited in two dimensions, such as a drawing or painting, it would be protected by copyright.

7.2.4 Fourth Period: 1969–1980: Demarcation

After the Spicer Committee reported, it was to be another seven years before the Australian Government took any legislative action. Eventually it passed the Copyright Act 1968, which made a number of changes to copyright law, including an attempt to re-shape the copyright/designs overlap. The Act continued to provide copyright for a closed list of 'works', being literary, artistic, dramatic and musical works. It remained the case that eligibility for copyright protection turned solely on 'skill, labour and judgment' rather than any artistic merit.[93] It also protected 'subject matter other than works', being films, sound recordings, broadcasts and published editions. As with the Copyright Act 1956 (UK), 'artistic works' were protected against reproduction in 'a material form'.[94] This was limited by section 71, which provided that making an object in three dimensions would not infringe copyright in a work in two dimensions, and vice versa, if the object in question 'would not appear to persons who are not experts in relation to objects of that kind to be a reproduction of the artistic work'.[95] These provisions meant there was potential for designs to be protected under both copyright law and design legislation. The overlap was to be managed in sections 74–77 of the Act which essentially reproduced the scheme of the 1956 UK Act with a few drafting amendments.

The scheme set up by these Acts operated so that the use of an artistic work as an industrial design would not affect any *subsistence* of copyright in that work. It would, however, affect whether certain acts would be found to be *infringements* of that copyright.[96] A new concept, the 'corresponding design', was introduced in an attempt to clarify the distinction between artistic works and designs. This 'corresponding design' was defined as: 'in relation to an artistic work ... a design that, when applied to an article, results in a reproduction of that work'.[97] Two potential situations were addressed: one arising where copyright subsisted in an artistic work, and a 'corresponding design' was registered under the Designs Act 1906; the other arising where copyright subsisted in an artistic work, and a 'corresponding design' was applied industrially to articles which are sold, let for

[93] *Sands and McDougall Pty Ltd* v. *Robinson* (1917) 23 CLR 49.
[94] Copyright Act 1968, s. 31. [95] Copyright Act 1968, s. 71.
[96] J. C. Lahore, 'Industrial Designs and the Copyright Act of 1968 – The Problem of Dual Protection' (1969) 43 *Australian Law Journal* 139, 144.
[97] Copyright Act 1968, s. 74.

hire, offered or exposed for sale or hire, but that corresponding design was *not* registered under the Designs Act in respect of those articles. The Copyright Regulations 1969 provided that a design would be deemed to be 'industrially applied' if it was applied to more than fifty articles.[98]

In both situations, it would not be an infringement of copyright to do anything in relation to an article which would be within the scope of the protection of the Designs Act, whether the design was registered (section 75) or not registered but industrially applied (section 77) either during the fifteen years of actual or putative protection, or thereafter. In relation to protection after the expiration of fifteen years, it would not be an infringement of copyright to do anything within the scope of copyright in the design 'as extended to all associated designs and articles'.[99]

Again, in both situations copyright would remain in the design/artistic work in question, but could only be infringed by doing some other act not covered by the protection granted under the Designs Act. This made more explicit the distinction between works in three dimensions, or as applied to articles, and works in two dimensions. As Attorney-General Bowen explained in his second reading speech: 'Thus, if a cartoon character is used to decorate children's plates, so as to use it after the expiration of 15 years from the time those plates came on the market will not infringe any rights in respect of the artistic copyright in the drawing of the character, but to reproduce it in a magazine would be an infringement of copyright.'[100] Thus, an artistic work, such as a cartoon character, could be registered as a design and exploited industrially during the fifteen years, during which time the owner could use their design registration to control uses that fell within the scope of the registration and the copyright in an artistic work to control other uses; following the expiry of the registration period, copyright would continue to apply to the latter uses.

A further important amendment came in the form of regulations passed the following year. Again echoing the UK scheme to mediate overlaps, the Design Regulations 1969 provided that designs for articles in certain specified classes would be excluded from registration under the Designs Act 1906. These classes were: works of sculpture other than casts or models used or intended to be used as models or patterns to be multiplied by an industrial process; wall plaques; medals; and 'articles that are primarily literary or artistic in character and on which there is printing', such as book jackets, calendars, certificates, dressmaking patterns, maps, plans and postcards.[101] Such articles could not lose copyright protection, even if a

[98] Copyright Regulations 1969, reg. 17. [99] Copyright Act 1968, s. 75.
[100] Commonwealth, *Parliamentary Debates*, House of Representatives, 16 May 1968, 1533 (Attorney-General Nigel Bowen).
[101] Designs Regulations 1969, reg. 2.

corresponding design were to be applied industrially, by virtue of section 74 of the Copyright Act 1968.

Two years after the 1968 Act was passed, a Committee was appointed by the new Attorney-General to give a more thorough examination of the law relating to designs, to recommend whether any changes needed to be made to the law, and also to consider the introduction of a system of 'utility models', or petty patents.[102] This Committee was chaired by Justice Robert Franki and delivered two separate reports in 1973; the first report dealt with designs and the second with patents.

In relation to designs, the Franki Committee considered a number of problems or potential problems with the law as it then stood. Once again, the UK law was taken as the starting point and each section of both statutes was compared, with a discussion of relevant cases. Considerable attention was paid to the copyright/design overlap issues. The Franki Report had noted that since the passing of the Copyright Act 1968, which had adopted the UK position, there had been developments both legislative and judicial in the UK requiring consideration. Indeed, in 1968, the UK had passed an amending Act which altered the position there. The Design Copyright Act 1968 (UK) allowed dual protection lasting fifteen years from the date on which the corresponding design was first published.[103] The Franki Committee made inquiries as to what had motivated such a change, and was informed that it responded to representations made by manufacturers of art metal work and jewellery.[104]

The Franki Committee was not, however, persuaded of the value of such provision and declared it was opposed to dual protection, despite having received a number of submissions ('including some well-documented submissions from the Walt Disney Organisation'[105]) in its favour. It stated firmly: 'It seems to us that a person should be able to make whatever use of an article he pleases if, in accordance with the usual practice in the industrial field, he finds on a proper examination of the records that the article is not covered by any patent or design protection in Australia.'[106] The Report referred to a number of recent UK cases which demonstrated the uncertainty that flowed from dual, or cumulative, protection.[107] It also considered whether it would be desirable from an international point of view to

[102] Designs Law Review Committee, *Report on the Law Relating to Designs* (1973) ('Franki Report').
[103] Design Copyright Act 1968, c. 68 (UK), s. 1. [104] Franki Report, 56.
[105] Franki Report, 52. [106] Franki Report, 53, [255].
[107] The cases referred to were: *IMI Developments Ltd & Anor* v. *R. C. Harrison Ltd* [1970] RPC 299; *Merchant-Adventurers Ltd* v. *M. Grew & Co. Ltd* (1971) 3 WLR 791; *Sifam Electrical Instrument Co. Ltd* v. *Sangamo Weston Ltd* [1971] FSR 337; [1971] 2 All ER 1074; *Antocks Lairn Ltd* v. *I. Bloohn Ltd* [1972] RPC 219; *Temple Instruments Ltd* v. *Hollis Heels Ltd* [1971] FSR 634.

adopt dual protection, noting that some had argued before it that if dual protection were introduced Australian manufacturers would be able to obtain the benefit of copyright protection for works of applied art in other Berne Convention countries, without having to go to the trouble of registering designs. However, the Committee took the view that the breadth of the definition of 'artistic work' in Australia would mean that dual protection would open up copyright protection to a broader range of articles in Australia than would be protected by copyright in overseas countries. It further thought that the imprecise definition of 'works of applied art' would simply lead to greater uncertainty for manufacturers.[108] As a result, the Report recommended retaining sections 74–77 with certain modifications, as well as alterations to a number of other aspects of the Designs Act.

Further developments occurring in the UK in this period also required consideration by the Franki Committee. The first was the case of *Dorling* v. *Honnor Marine Ltd.*[109] In this case, the Court of Appeal had found that where the artistic copyright lay in two-dimensional plans for dinghies, which had been produced industrially in three dimensions, the owner of copyright in the plans retained full copyright because the corresponding design was unregistrable – the plans themselves being unregistrable according to the regulations, and the parts, kits and shape of the completed boat being unregistrable on the basis of functionality.[110] This case, and those which followed it, were said to lead to 'bizarre outcomes'[111] and to be 'illogical'[112] in giving the more expansive protection offered by copyright to things found ineligible for the lesser protection of design rights.

The second development came when the House of Lords was called upon to determine the meaning of the final phrase of the definition of 'design' which excluded from protection features of shape or configuration 'dictated solely by the function which the article to be made in that shape or configuration has to perform'. In *Amp Inc.* v. *Utilux Pty Ltd*, Lord Reid held that: 'If the shape is not there to appeal to the eye but solely to make the article work then this provision excludes it from statutory protection.'[113] The Franki Committee considered that this approach should not be reflected in the Australian legislation, which should be as broad as practicable. While function itself should not be capable of protection through design legislation, it should not be a bar to registration.

[108] Franki Report, 55, [259]–[260].
[109] *Dorling* v. *Honnor Marine Ltd* [1965] 1 Ch 1; [1964] 2 WLR 195; [1964] 1 All ER 241.
[110] *Dorling* v. *Honnor Marine Ltd* [1956] 1 Ch 1, 19 (per Danckwerts LJ).
[111] Whitford Committee (1977, Cmnd. 6732), [97]. [112] Franki Report, 59.
[113] *Amp Inc.* v. *Utilux Pty Ltd* [1972] RPC 103, 110.

In addition, a series of cases confirmed that not only were technical drawings considered artistic works, but that they could be infringed by indirect copying of a three-dimensional work produced from them,[114] thereby expanding the remit of copyright for such works. This undermined the role of the 'non-expert' defence, which provided that the making of an object in three dimensions would not infringe copyright in the artistic work in two dimensions, and vice versa, if it did not appear to a non-expert to be a reproduction.

Notwithstanding these UK developments, there was no case law explicitly concerning the overlap between copyright and designs in Australia during this period. The regime of demarcation continued, but the question of whether functional designs were excluded from design protection did divide opinions in the courts.[115] Because UK developments revealed that such exclusions could re-enliven copyright protection in respect of functional designs, concerns were growing about the potential for over-broad protection for industrial products.

7.2.5 Fifth Period: 1981–1989: Demarcation

Although both Franki Reports were delivered in 1973, the government first took action on the second one, which had found that there was a 'gap' in the law for functional inventions that were not inventive enough for patent protection. In 1979 Parliament passed legislation amending the Patents Act 1952 which created a system of petty patents – patents with the same inventiveness threshold as a standard patent but which were easier and cheaper to obtain and would last only six years.[116]

Two years later, Parliament turned its attention to amendments to the law relating to designs. The Designs Amendment Act 1981 enacted a number of the Committee's recommendations. As a matter of nomenclature, the title of the Designs Act was altered from 'Copyright in Industrial Designs' to simply 'designs'.[117] The Franki Report had observed that the Act did not give merely a right against copying, but rather a monopoly in the design, meaning the use of the word 'copyright' was 'not only inappropriate but . . . likely to be confusing'.[118] The definition of 'design' was also amended and a path between the UK Act

[114] *Solar Thomson Engineering Co. Ltd* v. *Barton* [1977] RPC 537; *L. B. (Plastics) Ltd* v. *Swish Products Ltd* [1979] RPC 551.

[115] See *Mangraviti* v. *Vardi* [1976] 2 NSWLR 225; *Clive Investments Pty Ltd* v. *Paul Segaert Pty Ltd* (1966) 36 *Australian Official Journal of Patents, Trade Marks and Designs* 1577; *Malleys Ltd* v. *J. W. Tomlin Pty Ltd* (1961) 180 CLR 120; *D. Sebel & Co. Ltd* v. *National Art Metal Co. Pty Ltd* (1965) 10 FLR 224.

[116] Patents Amendment Act 1979 (No. 9 of 1979) (Cth).

[117] Designs Amendment Bill Act 1981 (Cth), s. 4.

[118] Franki Report, 30, [133].

and the existing Australian Act was chosen. The UK definition, derived from the 1919 Act as amended in 1949, was as follows:

> In this Act the expression 'design' means features of shape, configuration, pattern or ornament applied to an article by any industrial process or means, being features which in the finished article appeal to and are judged solely by the eye, but does not include a method or principle of construction or features of shape or configuration which are dictated solely by the function which the article to be made in that shape or configuration has to perform.[119]

The definition adopted in the Designs Amendment Act was:

> 'Design' means features of shape, configuration, pattern or ornamentation applicable to an article, being features that, in the finished article, can be judged by the eye, but does not include a method or principle of construction.[120]

The Franki Report had approved of the phrase 'features of shape, configuration, pattern or ornamentation' on the basis that its meaning was reasonably well established by the courts and a new form of words might lead to uncertainty in litigation. It did, however, make what it considered to be some improvements to the drafting.[121] Responding to the developments noted above, in particular the decision in *Amp* v. *Utilux*, the Australian Act also departed from the UK definition in relation to the exclusion of features of shape or configuration 'dictated solely by the function which the article to be made in that shape or configuration has to perform'. Not only was the UK phrase to be omitted from the definition, an additional section was added, stating that: 'An application for registration of a design shall not be refused, and a registered design is not invalid, by reason only that the design consists of, or includes, features of shape or configuration that serve, or serve only, a functional purpose.'[122]

Two other alterations made in 1981 were to abolish the practice of registering designs in classes, as had already occurred in the UK, and to extend the period of protection from a maximum of fifteen years, to a maximum of sixteen years. No specific action was taken in relation to the overlap between copyright and designs at that time, but a new cause for concern was emerging. This was that the expansion of copyright to cover technical drawings, reproduced in both three and two dimensions, would lead to anti-competitive restriction of the spare parts market. Faced with this problem in the UK, the House of Lords created a 'spare parts exception' to copyright law in *British Leyland Motor Corp.*

[119] Registered Designs Act 1949, c. 88 (UK), s. 1.
[120] Designs Amendment Act 1981 (Cth), s. 5. [121] Franki Report, 6–8.
[122] Designs Amendment Act 1981 (Cth), s. 18.

v. *Armstrong Patents Co. Ltd.*[123] The exception was not applied in Australia by Wilcox J, who referred to it in the Federal Court as 'remarkable' and 'a major qualification upon the scheme laid out – wisely or unwisely – under the United Kingdom copyright and designs legislation'.[124] He held that design drawings excluded from the definition of 'design' in the Designs Act 1906, by reason of being 'a method or principle of construction', retained copyright protection.[125]

At the same time, several other cases before the courts demonstrated that the demarcation approach could operate to deny both copyright and design protection in cases where artistic works were registrable as corresponding designs, but had not been registered prior to being industrially applied – results which were perceived to lead to injustice in those particular cases.[126] Nevertheless, the policy of demarcation continued to be considered appropriate, despite the difficulties occasioned by negotiating its boundaries. As Deane J explained in the High Court decision of *Hart* v. *Edwards Hot Water Systems*:

> The present case falls in an area in which one should be conscious of the distinct functions performed by the law of copyright and the law of patents and industrial designs and of the desirability of maintaining at least the semblance of a boundary between their respective fields of operation. The convoluted path by which a three-dimensional object has been held to be an infringement of the copyright in a technical drawing which has been neither factually copied or even seen illustrates the incursions which copyright – with its extended life but more limited protection, its lack of requirement of novelty or true inventiveness and its minimal standards of originality – is capable of making into what would ordinarily be seen as the proper domains of the law of patents and the law of industrial designs.[127]

7.2.6 *Sixth Period: 1990–2003: Partial Cumulation and Demarcation*

In light of the ongoing problems, the Government commissioned a further investigation by the Attorney-General's Department, which published a

[123] *British Leyland Motor Corp.* v. *Armstrong Patents Co. Ltd* [1986] AC 577; (1986) 6 IPR 102.
[124] *Warman International Ltd and Others* v. *Envirotech Australia Pty Ltd and Others* (1986) 11 FCR 478, 499.
[125] Ibid., 496.
[126] *Glamagard Pty Ltd* v. *Enderslea Productions Pty Ltd* (1985) 1 NSWLR 138; (1985) 59 ALR 740; *Hutchence and Others* v. *South Seas Bubble Co. Pty Ltd and Others* (1986) 64 ALR 330; *Flamingo Park Pty Ltd* v. *Dolly Dolly Creation Pty Ltd and Others* (1985) 65 ALR 500.
[127] *S. W. Hart & Co. Pty Ltd* v. *Edwards Hot Water Systems* (1985) 159 CLR 466, 495. See also *Kevlacat Pty Ltd* v. *Trailcraft Marine Pty Ltd* (1987) 79 ALR 534, 550–1.

discussion paper and received submissions in 1987.[128] In 1989 an amending Act was passed, altering a number of aspects of copyright law and commencing on 1 October 1990.[129] In terms of the copyright/design overlap, the Act repealed the much criticised section 71 (the 'non-expert' defence) in its entirety.[130] Still more significantly, it introduced, for the first time, partial cumulation of designs and copyright, by amending sections 74, 75 and 77, in order to ensure that three-dimensional industrial products could not receive copyright protection, but two-dimensional ones could.

It achieved this by amending the definition of 'corresponding design' to add the phrase 'but does not include a design consisting solely of features of two-dimensional pattern or ornament applicable to a surface of an article'.[131] Limiting the exclusion of copyright to three-dimensional works meant that the two-stage process which dealt with the situation during and after registration was no longer necessary. Thus, the sections limiting the operation of copyright where a corresponding design had, and had not, been registered could be simplified.[132] Further language was added to avoid the outcome in *Dorling* v. *Honnor Marine Ltd*,[133] and subsequent cases holding that designs which were unregistrable because they were functional, nor not new and original, or could not be 'judged by the eye', retained copyright protection.[134] Thus, section 77(3) was added in an attempt to make it clear that it was only where the corresponding design was unregistrable through the operation of the Regulations excluding certain designs from registrability that copyright in an artistic work would remain in force.[135]

Copyright protection was not, however, removed for all three-dimensional artistic works that had been industrialised. Section 77 was

[128] Attorney-General's Department's Discussion Paper, *Copyright Protection for Artistic Works Industrially Applied* (Canberra: Australian Government Publishing Service, 1987).

[129] Copyright Amendment Act 1989 (No. 32 of 1989) (Cth).

[130] Copyright Act 1968 (Cth), s. 71, repealed in Copyright Amendment Act 1989 (Cth), Schedule, s. 17. For criticism, see *S. W. Hart & Co. Pty Ltd* v. *Edwards Hot Water Systems* (1985) 159 CLR 466, 475, where Gibbs CJ observed: 'Although the object of the provisions is understandable, the form in which they are expressed, involving the use of a triple negative, is not altogether clear, and their application proves difficult in practice'; see also *Dorling* v. *Honnor Marine Ltd* (1956) 1 Ch 1, 19 and *L. B. (Plastics) Ltd* v. *Swish Products Ltd* [1979] RPC 551, 635–6.

[131] Copyright Act 1968 (Cth), s. 74, amended by Copyright Amendment Act 1989 (Cth), s. 10.

[132] Copyright Act 1968 (Cth), ss. 75, 77, amended by Copyright Amendment Act 1989 (Cth), ss. 10, 11.

[133] *Dorling* v. *Honnor Marine Ltd* [1965] 1 Ch 1.

[134] Copyright Amendment Bill 1988 (Cth), Explanatory Memorandum, cl. 10.

[135] Copyright Act 1968 (Cth), s. 77, amended by Copyright Amendment Act 1989 (Cth), s. 11.

altered to carve out an exception for buildings, models of buildings and works of artistic craftsmanship. Copyright would therefore continue to subsist in such works unless they were registered as designs, whereupon they would lose copyright and rely solely on the protection given by registration. This was not a recommendation of the Franki Committee nor covered in the Attorney-General's discussion paper. According to the Explanatory Memorandum, the reason for introducing this exception was because it was considered that such works are 'more appropriately protected under the [Copyright] Act whether industrially applied or not'.[136]

The 1989 Act had only passed upon the assurance that the Attorney-General's Department would conduct an urgent review of designs law. A Committee was subsequently appointed under Professor James Lahore to carry out an Inquiry into Intellectual Property Protection for Industrial Designs.[137] The Lahore Committee was deeply critical of a number of aspects of the amendments just passed.

First, it considered that the Government's policy decision to deny copyright protection to three-dimensional works could not be successfully implemented unless the definitions of both 'design' and 'corresponding design' were changed.[138] The problem with the definition of 'corresponding design' was that it referred back to the definition of 'design', itself to be found in the Designs Act 1906 rather than the Copyright Act. Designs that did not fall within that definition would likewise also not be 'corresponding designs' and thus would not be affected by the changes in the Copyright Amendment Act designed to deprive them of copyright protection. To take the example given by the Committee, in the case of *Warman* v. *Envirotech* the drawings in question were held not to be designs within the definition of the Designs Act because they constituted a method or principle of construction; therefore they were entitled to copyright protection.[139] This would be unchanged under the amendments, a result the Committee called 'astonishing', given that a principal reason for amending the Act was to deny copyright protection to utilitarian three-dimensional articles.[140] A second problem with the definition of 'corresponding design' was the exclusion of designs consisting solely of features of two-dimensional pattern or ornamentation applicable to the surface of an article. The Committee pointed out it was not clear how this

[136] Copyright Amendment Bill 1988 (Cth), Explanatory Memorandum, cl. 10.

[137] James Lahore, 'Inquiry into Intellectual Property Protection for Industrial Designs' (Presented to Senator the Hon. John Button, Minister for Industry, Technology and Commerce, Canberra, September 1991) ('Lahore Report'), 1.

[138] Ibid., iii. [139] *Warman* v. *Envirotech* (1986) 11 FCR 478. [140] Lahore Report, 15.

definition would apply to woven or embossed designs, or where the pattern lay in the thickness of the material.[141]

Turning to the new definition of 'design', as amended in 1981, the Committee's discussion focused on the explicit exclusion found in the words 'does not include a method or principle of construction'. Recent court decisions interpreting the words had given rise to some dissatisfaction.[142] In *Warman* v. *Envirotech*, an interlocutory hearing, Wilcox J found that design drawings which contained information as to data and tolerances necessary to manufacture the parts in question were excluded from the definition of design because they were 'a method of principle or construction'.[143] Similarly, in *Firmagroup Australia Pty Ltd* v. *Byrne & Davidson Doors (Vic) Pty Ltd*,[144] the High Court upheld lower court decisions which had found there was no infringement of registered designs for handles and locks for shutter (garage) doors because what was copied were general functional features rather than features which 'convey[ed] an idea of unique shape or configuration'.[145] These decisions gave rise to the perception that the Designs Act inadequately protected functional articles, while copyright overprotected them.[146]

The Committee considered that a method or principle of construction was more appropriately protected by patent law than by design law, but it also found that specifically excluding methods or principles of construction from the definition of design had not led to an improvement in designs protection and that, in fact, recent decisions were detrimental to it. It thus recommended changing the definition of design to remove the explicit exclusion and to place more emphasis on the form of an article as being the subject-matter of protection.[147] It considered that the chief problem with giving broad protection to functional designs lay in the definition of infringement and that existing case law gave insufficient guidance on the concept of fraudulent or obvious imitation. The Report recommended abandoning that approach completely, as had already occurred in the UK back in 1949. Instead, it recommended adopting a test of 'substantial reproduction', although it added that since design registration was a monopoly rather than a right to prevent copying, it

141 Ibid., 17. 142 Lahore Report, 31.

143 *Warman* v. *Envirotech* (1986) 11 FCR 478, 496.

144 (1987) 180 CLR 483; 61 ALJR 495; 73 ALR 321. 145 (1987) CLR 483, 488–9.

146 See Janice Luck, 'The Firmagroup Case: Trigger for Designs Law Reform', in Andrew T. Kenyon, Megan Richardson and Sam Ricketson (eds.), *Landmarks in Australian Intellectual Property Law* (Port Melbourne: Cambridge University Press, 2009).

147 Lahore Report, 32, 35.

would be important to ensure that reproduction was not interpreted to require proof of copying.[148]

The Lahore Committee was not alone in considering that the amended provisions of the Copyright Act created as many, if not more, problems than they resolved.[149] And so, shortly after it submitted its report, a reference was made to the Australian Law Reform Commission (ALRC) to review the law of designs.[150] The ALRC carried out the widest-ranging inquiry to date on Australian designs law, consulting with designers, manufacturers, patent attorneys, lawyers and interest groups, as well as the Australian Intellectual Property Office and relevant government departments and agencies. It also conducted a survey of the design industry which involved about 1,000 individual designers and manufacturers around Australia and considered recent developments in the European Community, as well as New Zealand, North America, Asia and Africa.

The ALRC Report stated that 'the law has not kept up with changes in the scope of what designers are doing. Design is an integral part of manufacturing and marketing but designs law tends to treat it as a minor cosmetic aspect of a product. For designers and manufacturers this mismatch and the outdated legal concept of design have been the source of much dissatisfaction over many years.'[151] The Report noted that while modern design encompassed a broad range of activities, concepts and philosophies, the legal concept of design was far narrower and did not extend to non-visual features considered by designers to be important, such as functionality, safety considerations, feel, weight, ergonomics and so on. The ALRC pointed out that some of these aspects would fall to be protected under other areas of intellectual property law, such as trade marks (which now extended to cover shapes, colours, sound and scent), patents, passing off or breach of confidence.[152]

The submissions and the survey revealed to the ALRC that there were a number of perceived problems with the operation of design law in Australia. These included an impression that design law was not regarded highly by those who sought to benefit commercially from their designs, the lack of protection for function, the narrow interpretation of visual

[148] Ibid., 39–41.
[149] See Wayne M. Condon, 'The Copyright Amendment Act 1989 and the Copyright/Design Overlap in Australia' (1990) 12 *European Intellectual Property Review* 84; Ricketson, 'Towards a Rational Basis'.
[150] Australian Law Reform Commission, *Designs Report*, Terms of Reference, No. 74 (1995) ('ALRC Report').
[151] ALRC Report, [2.1]. [152] ALRC Report, [2.20]–[2.27].

appearance, the feeling that registration took too long, was too costly and granted too easily to non-novel designs, that litigation was too costly and victory too uncertain.[153] The ALRC concluded that Australia should continue to provide protection for industrial designs, but that the system was in need of reform. Many of the concerns expressed by stakeholders and others could be addressed within the existing system. However, it also considered that other concerns could not be addressed within the registered design right and that broader review and reform was necessary.

Although many of the submissions to the ALRC identified a gap in protection for functional designs, and called for design protection to be expanded to protect function directly, the ALRC concluded that design legislation should continue to focus narrowly on the visual appearance of a product and that any gap opening up as a result of the failure to protect function was more properly addressed by reforming Australia's petty patent system and not by extending design law.[154] In addition, the ALRC was drawn to arguments in favour of supplementing the current design protection with an unregistered, anti-copying design right. However, as this went beyond its terms of reference, the Commission recommended that a separate review should be commissioned to investigate this.[155]

To sum up, the 1989 amendments introduced a new policy of cumulative protection for two-dimensional artistic works, while retaining demarcation for three-dimensional works. The change in the definition of 'corresponding design' made it clear that when applied to a product also in two dimensions (i.e. as pattern or ornamentation) such works could acquire both design registration and copyright protection. A less strict form of demarcation applied to buildings, models of buildings and works of artistic craftsmanship, in that they could receive either copyright or design protection but not both, while other three-dimensional works were subject to strict demarcation and unable to be protected by copyright if applied industrially. Dissatisfaction continued, however, with the way the boundary was drawn and in particular questions were raised as to whether the language of the legislation adequately implemented its intention.

7.2.7 *Seventh Period: 2004–Present: Partial Cumulation and Demarcation*

The ALRC delivered its report in 1995 but it was not until 2002 that the Government introduced an entirely new design law bill into Parliament – the first in almost one hundred years. In his second reading speech,

153 ALRC Report, [2.42]–[2.48]. 154 ALRC Report, [3.42]–[3.53].
155 ALRC Report, [3.59]–[3.71]. To date, no such review has been commissioned.

Warren Entsch MP explained: 'This Bill is intended to provide a simple to use, cost effective designs system that provides designers with enforceable rights.'[156] The new Act, which received assent on 17 December 2003, implemented many, although not all, of the ALRC's recommendations.

First, the Act introduced a new definition of 'design' as follows: 'design, in relation to a product, means the overall appearance of the product resulting from one or more visual features of the product'.[157] 'Visual features' was in turn defined in section 7 as including 'the shape, configuration, pattern and ornamentation of the product'.[158] The section excluded the feel of a product, the materials used in the product and, in relation to products with one or more indefinite dimensions, the indefinite dimension and more than one repeat of any pattern.[159] The ALRC had recommended changing the word 'article' to the word 'product' as being more 'contemporary' and removing any reference to a design being 'applied to' a product, on the basis that it often required stretching of language to suggest that something like a shape is 'applied to' an article.-[160] The ALRC had further recommended including surface and colour in the list of visual features protected, but these words were not added to the definition.[161] The removal of the phrase 'judged by the eye' followed the ALRC's finding that it was unnecessary, and similarly the ALRC had considered that any reference to consumer or eye appeal, as was found in the UK legislation at that time, was unnecessarily complex.[162]

Finally, the Act attempted once again to ensure that a functional design could fall within the definition of design and would therefore not be excluded from the operation of the copyright exceptions to infringement found in sections 74–77 of the Copyright Act. The 1981 Amendments had proven ineffectual to counter the earlier lines of authority.[163] Section 7 thus provided that a visual feature 'may, but need not, serve a functional purpose'.[164] The exclusion from the definition of design of 'methods and principles of construction' was also removed. The ALRC Report noted that the Federal Court had not been able to identify a clear meaning of the concept dictated solely by function[165] and that the courts had interpreted

[156] Commonwealth, *Parliamentary Debates*, House of Representatives, 11 December 2002, 10080 (Warren Entsch MP).
[157] Designs Act 2003, s. 5. [158] Designs Act 2003, s. 7(1).
[159] Designs Act 2003, s. 7(3). [160] ALRC Report, [4.9], [4.10].
[161] ALRC Report, [4.6], [4.7]. [162] ALRC Report, [4.34]–[4.42].
[163] *Compagnie Industrielle de Precontrainte et d'Equipment des Constructions SA* v. *First Melbourne Securities Pty Ltd and Others* (1999) 44 IPR 512.
[164] Designs Act 2003, s. 7(2).
[165] *Hosokawa Micron International Inc.* v. *Fortune* (1990) 26 FCR 393; (1990) 19 IPR 531.

the exclusion in such a way that design protection was too narrow to cover useful products like locks and pumps.[166]

The second key change made by the 2003 Act was to change the threshold for registration from 'new or original' (which had remained unchanged since 1906) to 'new and distinctive when compared with the prior art base'.[167] This responded to the ALRC's findings that the novelty test was seen as unacceptable by designers and manufacturers, and that the perception was that anything could be registered as long as it was not identical to another registered design. The Act defined a design as being 'new' unless it was 'identical to a design that forms part of the prior art base' and as being 'distinctive' unless it was 'substantially similar in overall impression to a design that forms part of the prior art base'.[168] When assessing substantial similarity, the standard to be applied was to be that of the 'informed user'. The ALRC had drawn this concept from the EC's proposed Council Regulation on designs.[169]

A third change also related to the scope of protection was to alter the definition of infringement. The ALRC's consultations and submissions had revealed high levels of dissatisfaction with the courts' narrow interpretation of design protection, particularly following the High Court decision in *Firmagroup*.[170] The ALRC had proposed that the test for infringement should be one of 'substantial similarity in overall impression' to be assessed by an informed user. It also recommended that the test of 'fraudulent imitation' be removed and a non-exclusive list of factors be provided in the legislation for consideration in cases of infringement.[171] These recommendations were followed in the 2003 Act.[172]

The 2003 Act made a number of other significant changes in relation to the registration process and also reduced the term of protection from a maximum of sixteen years under the 1906 Act to a maximum of ten years – an initial period of five years with a renewal period of five years.[173] The ALRC had in fact recommended reducing protection to fifteen years as this is recommended under the Hague Convention (should Australia decide in future to join), while conceding that

[166] ALRC Report, [4.15]. Relevant cases are: *Firmagroup Australia Pty Ltd* v. *Byrne and Davidson Doors (Vic) Pty Ltd* (1987) 180 CLR 483; (1987) 73 ALR 321; *Warman* v. *Envirotech* (1986) 11 FCR 478; *Malleys Ltd* v. *J. W. Tomlin Pty Ltd* (1961) 180 CLR 120; (1961) 35 ALJR 353; *Stenor Ltd* v. *Whitesides (Clitheroe) Ltd* [1948] AC 107; *Kestos Ltd* v. *Kempat Ltd & Kemp* (1935) 53 RPC 139.

[167] Designs Act 2003, s. 15(1). [168] Designs Act 2003, s. 16.

[169] ALRC Report, [5.18].

[170] *Firmagroup* v. *Byrne and Davidson Doors* (1987) 180 CLR 483.

[171] ALRC Report, [6.6]–[6.13], [6.28]–[6.32]. [172] Designs Act 2003, ss. 19, 71.

[173] Designs Act 2003, s. 46.

'[n]one of the suggested rationales for design protection provide any persuasive argument for any particular period of protection'.[174] The Explanatory Memorandum to the Designs Bill stated it would not be in Australia's interests to provide a period of protection in excess of its international obligations (under TRIPS), as Australia is a net importer of intellectual property.[175]

In relation to ownership, the Act continued to provide, as it had since 1906, that the designer would be the first owner unless the design were created in the course of employment or pursuant to a contract, in which case the employer or other contracting party would be the owner.[176] This echoed the position under the Copyright Act 1968, except in relation to commissioned works, which are owned by the author rather than the commissioner (with some exceptions relating to certain photographs, portraits and engravings).[177]

Another innovation in the 2003 Act was to introduce a spare parts exclusion from design protection.[178] This was not a recommendation of the ALRC, which had examined the issue of spare parts but concluded that the best approach would be to include a procedure for referral of potentially competitive designs to the Trade Practices Commission (now the Australian Competition and Consumer Commission). The Government, however, considered such an exception was necessary to ensure effective competition, particularly in the motor vehicle market.[179]

At the same time as the Designs Bill was introduced, a second bill was introduced to amend sections 74–77 of the Copyright Act. The first amendments made were to the definition of 'corresponding design'. As both the ALRC and the Lahore Report had noted, this definition gave rise to several problems. As noted above, the first problem was that if the work in question did not fall within the definition of 'design' in the Design Act, it could not be a corresponding design and would therefore retain copyright protection, contrary to the intention of the legislation. The second problem arose because section 17A of the Designs Act provided that in the case where copyright subsisted in an artistic work and an application were sought for registration of a corresponding design, that design would not be treated as being other than new or original by reason of any previous use of publication of the artistic work.

[174] ALRC Report, [10.7].
[175] Kathy Bowrey, Michel Handler, Dianne Nicol and Kimberlee Weatherall, *Australian Intellectual Property: Commentary, Law and Practice*, 2nd edn (South Melbourne: Oxford University Press, 2010), p. 356.
[176] Designs Act 2003, s. 13. [177] Copyright Act 1968, s. 35.
[178] Designs Act 2003, s. 72.
[179] Commonwealth, *Parliamentary Debates*, House of Representatives, 11 December 2002, 10080 (Warren Entsch MP).

However, since 'corresponding design' was defined not to include two-dimensional features of pattern or ornament, such aspects would not be rescued by the provision and would be unable to be registered. For example, a published drawing for a fabric design could not be registered prior to manufacturing it because it would no longer be new.[180] A third problem lay in the use of the word 'applicable', which was unclear in relation to designs which are not applied to a surface but form part of an article, such as embroidery, knits, weaves and other textured designs.

The definition was thus altered in the 2003 Act to read:

> Corresponding design, in relation to a design, means visual features of shape or configuration which, when embodied in a product, result in a reproduction of that work, whether or not the visual features constitute a design which is capable of being registered under the *Designs Act 2003*.[181]

Further, 'embodied in' was defined to include 'woven into, impressed on, or worked into' a product.[182] By limiting the definition of 'corresponding design' to 'visual features of shape or configuration', the statute continued the policy of ensuring that two-dimensional features would fall outside the definition and thus outside the exclusion of copyright protection in section 77. They could therefore be protected by both designs law and copyright.

A second change sought to clarify the status of works of artistic craftsmanship. The problem with excluding works of artistic craftsmanship lay in the uncertainty of the category, and the Lahore Committee had noted that the courts in both the UK and Australia had experienced difficulty in determining whether a work was a work of artistic craftsmanship.[183] Under section 10 of the Copyright Act 1968, it was also ambiguous as to whether a work could be simultaneously a work of artistic craftsmanship and another kind of artistic works (such as a painting, sculpture or building). The 2003 Amending Act altered the wording of section 10 to make it clear that this was possible.[184] A related amendment was to add a provision to section 77 that explicitly provided that for the purposes of that section a 'building or model of a building does not include a portable building such as a shed, a pre-constructed swimming pool, a demountable building or similar portable building'.[185] This implemented the conclusion of the ALRC and the Lahore

[180] ALRC Report, [17.31]. [181] Designs (Consequential Amendments) Act 2003, s. 2.
[182] Ibid., s. 3.
[183] Ibid., 18–19. See also *Cuisenaire* v. *Reed* [1963] VR 719; *Federal Commissioner of Taxation* v. *Murray* (1990) 21 FCR 436; (1990) 92 ALR 671; *George Hensher Ltd* v. *Restawile Upholstery (Lancs) Ltd* [1976] AC 64; [1975] RPC 31.
[184] Designs (Consequential Amendments) Act 2003, s. 1. [185] Ibid., s. 13.

Committee that small portable buildings and pools were not suitable for copyright protection.[186] A further amendment to section 77 added a new subsection (1A) which operated to ensure that the manufacture of products reproducing such a specification or representation would not be a copyright infringement.[187]

The problem of 'plan-to-plan' copying was also addressed. This was the issue which arose when engineering drawings were copied (either directly or indirectly), leading to a finding of copyright infringement.[188] Because the immunity in section 77 related only to applying a corresponding design to an article and not to copying in two dimensions as preparatory to making a product, the new section 77A extended the immunity from copyright infringement to cover reproductions of artistic works made in the course of or incidental to making a product where such reproductions were produced by copying the three-dimensional product. However, direct copying of plans remained a copyright infringement.[189]

The amendments made in 2003 therefore did not change the underlying policy of demarcation and partial cumulation, but simply shifted a few of the borders. The dual protection of two-dimensional designs was clarified, works of artistic craftsmanship and architectural works continued to be given the choice of regimes, and other three-dimensional works exploited industrially remained in the design regime. Small portable buildings and pre-fabricated swimming pools were moved from the category of copyright to being required to rely on design protection, as were two-dimensional design drawings.

7.3 Analysis/Assessment

Since the mid-nineteenth century, Australia has moved through different approaches to the design/copyright overlap. For a short period after Federation it had a system of dual or cumulative protection, although this appears to be largely because nobody turned their mind to a potential overlap. For almost eighty years between 1913 and 1990 the system was one of demarcation. After 1990, this developed into a policy that explicitly tolerated dual protection for two-dimensional designs but required three-dimensional designs being exploited industrially to find their

[186] Lahore Report, 17–18. See also *Tefex Pty Ltd* v. *Bowler* (1981) 40 ALR 326.
[187] Ibid., ss. 8, 9.
[188] See *Warman International* v. *Envirotech Australia Pty Ltd* (1986) 11 FCR 478; 67 ALR 253; *Amalgamated Mining Services Pty Ltd* v. *Warman International Ltd and Others* (1992) 111 ALR 269; (1992) 24 IPR 461; *Compagnie Industrielle de Precontrainte et d'Equipment des Constructions SA* v. *First Melbourne Securities Pty Ltd and Others* (1999) 44 IPR 512.
[189] See discussion in David Brennan, 'The Luckless Plan-to-Plan Infringer' (2016) 26 *AIPJ* 131.

protection in design rights. As the ALRC explained, the distinction between two- and three-dimensional works serves a 'rough justice' because designs applied to a surface usually fulfil an aesthetic purpose, while designs applied as shapes usually serve an industrial purpose.[190]

Whether the changes in regime have had any effect on design applications and registrations is difficult to establish. Certainly, there seems to have been a decline in the number of applications around the time that dual protection for two-dimensional designs was introduced, but this is from an unusual high point in 1987 and correlates to a period of recession in the economy. Numbers still remained well above those of earlier decades. A bigger increase in registrations can be seen after the introduction of the new Designs Act 2003, which made only minor changes to the overlap provisions.[191] However, analysis by the Advisory Council on Intellectual Property (ACIP)[192] reveals that this increase is due to a strong rise in use by foreign companies. Use by Australian companies remains largely unchanged, while use by Australian individuals has declined steeply.[193]

A key challenge over the years has been how to formulate the policy of demarcation in sufficiently clear statutory language, and how to deal with works falling on the border between aesthetics and industry. It is probably fair to say that efforts have met with only partial success. In 1995, the ALRC Report had found that there was 'an unacceptable degree of confusion surrounding the designs/copyright overlap'.[194] Since the enactment of the Designs Act 2003, there have been a handful of court decisions interpreting the new provisions. Some of these have clarified the law, while others have revealed ongoing complexity and uncertainty.

In 2007, the High Court gave some useful guidance on the category of 'works of artistic craftsmanship' in the decision of *Burge* v. *Swarbrick*.[195] The central issue in this case was whether a 'Plug' for a racing yacht (that is, 'a hand-crafted full scale model of the hull and deck sections'[196] of the yacht) was a work of artistic craftsmanship, and thus exempt from the limitation on copyright infringement under section 77 of the Copyright

190 ALRC Report, [17.7].
191 See WIPO IP Statistics Data Center, at http://ipstats.wipo.int/ipstatv2/index.htm?tab=industrial, data for Australia, 1980–2014.
192 ACIP was an independent, government-appointed body that has now been abolished.
193 Advisory Council on Intellectual Property, *Review of the Designs System, Final Report* (March 2015), p. 57.
194 ALRC Report, [17.3].
195 (2007) 232 CLR 336. The case arose under the Copyright Act 1968 prior to the amendments of 2003, but there is no reason why the discussion of the meaning of 'works of artistic craftsmanship' would not continue to apply under the new section 77.
196 Ibid., 344.

Act 1968. The Court concluded that while it might be 'impossible, and certainly would be unwise to attempt any exhaustive and fully predictive identification of what can and cannot amount to a work of artistic craftsmanship', the determination turns not on assessing beauty, aesthetic appeal or harmony between visual appeal and utility, but rather on 'assessing the extent to which the particular work's artistic expression, in its form, is unconstrained by functional considerations'.[197] Based on this approach, the Plug was not a work of artistic craftsmanship because matters of visual and aesthetic appeal were subordinated to purely functional aspects, and the work of Mr Swarbrick in designing it was not that of an 'artist-craftsman'.[198] In 2008, the Federal Court confirmed in *Digga Australia* v. *Norm Engineering* that the 2003 amendments to section 77 had the effect that the copyright exception would apply to functional designs created after that date.[199]

Two cases have considered the new definition of 'corresponding design' in section 74 of the Copyright Act, both of them turning on technical discussions of whether certain treatments of fabric can be considered two- or three-dimensional. In *Polo/Lauren Company LP* v. *Ziliani Holdings Pty Ltd*,[200] the court was called upon to decide whether the embroidered polo player logo on Polo Ralph Lauren garments was a 'corresponding design' under the Act. The trial judge considered that it was because the logo was made up of at least 784 stitches, which altered the fabric and meant it was not a 'mere' surface design of pattern or ornamentation.[201] On appeal, however, the Full Court disagreed, appearing to decide (although not altogether clearly) that it would only consider features of shape or configuration to be embodied in three dimensions where the product is made in that shape or configuration in its entirety.

The Court did not, however, explicitly consider how one would decide whether something was three- or two-dimensional, and so questions remain as to where the line will be drawn.[202] Indeed, the issue arose again in the recent case of *Seafolly* v. *Fewstone*.[203] This case involved copying of swimwear and the section 77 defence was raised in relation to an artwork depicting a diamond style smocking pattern placed onto shirred fabric. The judge,

[197] (2007) 232 CLR 336, 364. [198] Ibid., 362, 365.

[199] *Digga Australia* v. *Norm Engineering* (2008) 166 FCR 268; 245 ALR 407; [2008] FCAFC 33.

[200] *Polo/Lauren Co. LP* v. *Ziliani Holdings Pty Ltd* [2008] FCA 49.

[201] *Polo/Lauren Co. LP* v. *Ziliani Holdings Pty Ltd* [2008] FCA 49 at [84].

[202] See discussion in McCutcheon, 'Too Many Stitches in Time?', 45–8, and Janice Luck, 'Section 18 of the Designs Act 2003: The Neglected Copyright/Design Overlap Provision' (2013) 23 *Australian Intellectual Property Journal* 68, 82–4.

[203] *Seafolly Pty Ltd* v. *Fewstone Pty Ltd* (2014) 313 ALR 41; (2014) 106 IPR 85.

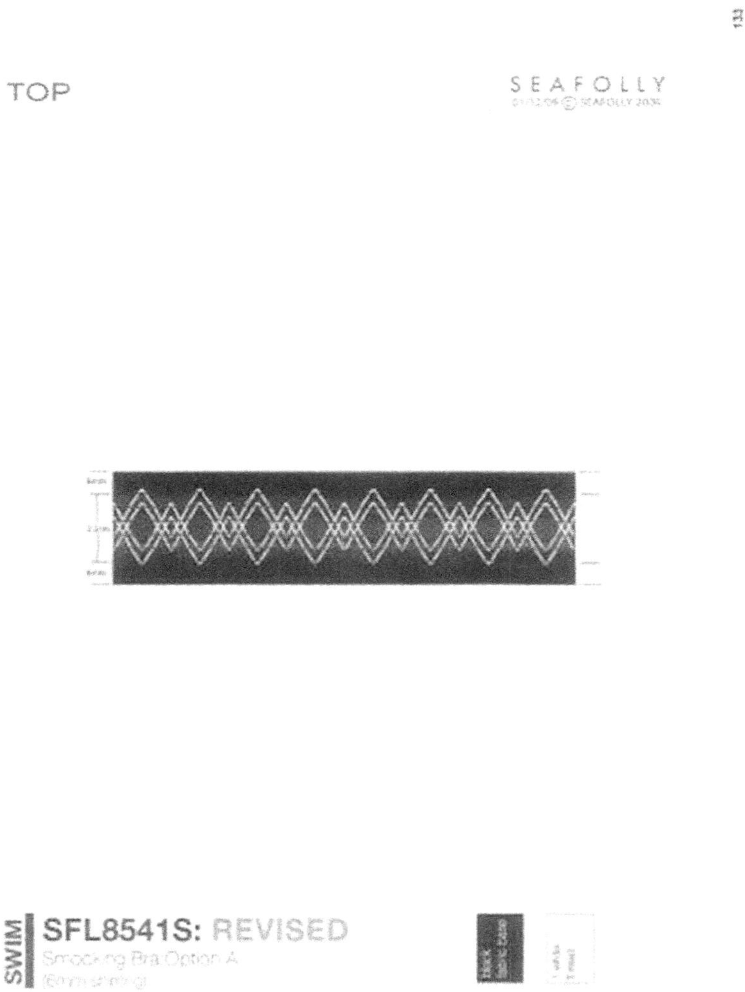

Figure 7.3 The plaintiff's Senorita artwork
Source: © Seafolly Pty Ltd. Image reproduced with permission

Dodds-Streeton J, noted that the Full Court's reasoning in *Polo/Lauren* was 'not consistently explicit, but must be inferred, in some instances, from the materials it cites or extracts'.[204] However, despite conceding that some of

[204] Ibid., 153.

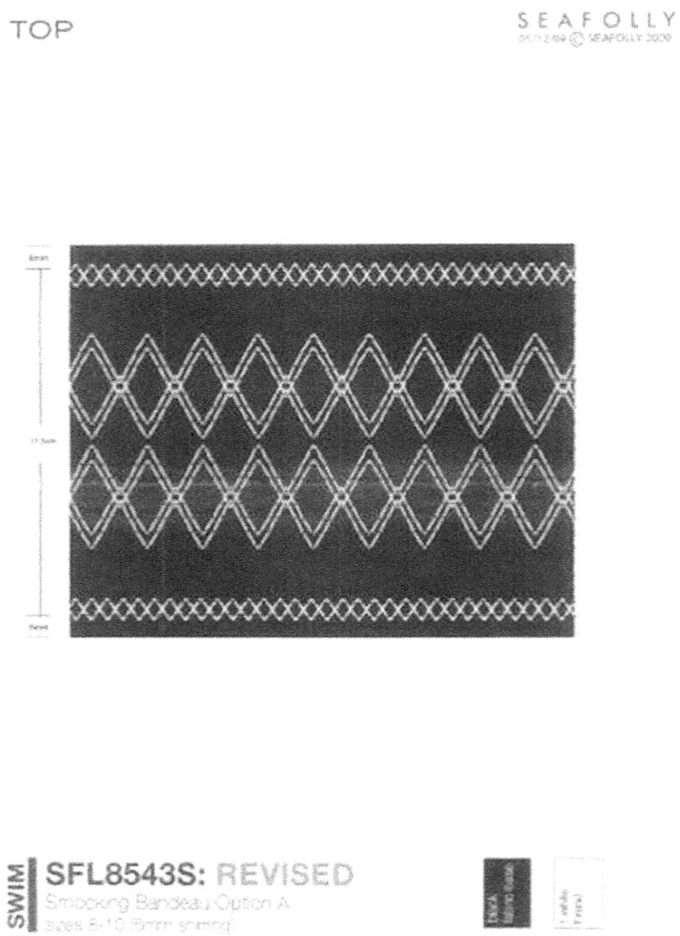

Figure 7.4 The plaintiff's Senorita artwork
Source: © Seafolly Pty Ltd. Image reproduced with permission

its statements could be read in more than one way, Dodds-Streeton J was able to conclude that the Full Court's reasons indicated that it is the features of shape or configuration that must be embodied in a product 'which will occur when the product (in the present case a garment) is

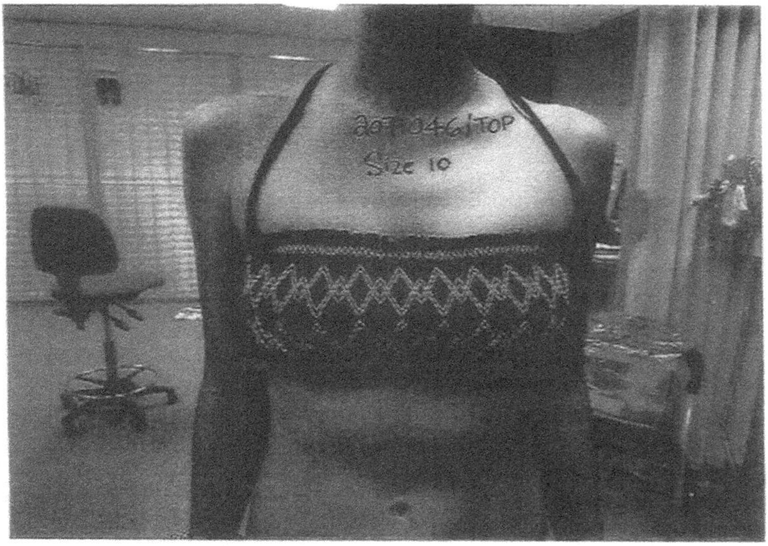

Figure 7.5 The defendant's bandeau-shaped garment
Source: © Fewstone Pty Ltd. Image reproduced in *Seafolly Pty Ltd* v. *Fewstone Pty Ltd* [2014] FCA 321, [13], [14]

made in the shape or configuration of the artwork'.[205] She concluded that in this case the smocking could not be considered three-dimensional because it was only part of a product not itself made in the shape or configuration of the design. She stated that although the fabric was not flat, '[a]ny protrusion of the smocking from the surface is minimal and probably significantly less than that in *Polo/Lauren* itself'.[206]

In 2012, ACIP was asked by the government to review the operation and effectiveness of the Designs Act 2003. ACIP delivered its report in March 2015, having carried out surveys, received submissions and analysed data from IP Australia. It made a number of recommendations for reform of the designs system, ranging from increasing the term of protection to fifteen years, to changing the terminology for registered but uncertified designs to make it clear that such designs do not confer registrable rights and introducing a grace period.[207] It

[205] Ibid., 153. [206] Ibid., 155.
[207] Advisory Council on Intellectual Property, *Review of the Designs System: Final Report* (2015) ('Final Report'). See full list of recommendations at pp. 10–12.

recommended against introducing an unregistered design right, on the basis that there was very little support for it.[208]

In its consideration of the copyright/design overlap provisions, ACIP observed that the rules continued to be 'contentious and unsatisfactory'.[209] Its survey of users of the design system revealed that two thirds of respondents admitted to some level of confusion as to whether their designs were covered by copyright or designs and similar levels of confusion were displayed in relation to whether or not to apply for an innovation patent or a design right.[210] ACIP received submissions for the Arts Law Centre of Australia, the National Association of Visual Artists (NAVA) and the Australian Copyright Council, contending that the provisions operated unfairly in respect of artists as compared to all other kinds of copyright owners and proposed reform that would improve the position of artists in relation to industrially applied artistic works.[211] By contrast, the Law Council of Australia suggested removing entirely the distinction between two-dimensional and three-dimensional embodiments so that the provisions would apply to limit copyright irrespective of whether the artistic work was exploited in two- or three-dimensional form. The Law Council recognised this would reduce the protection of artists but considered removing the uncertainty to be more important. It also argued that the exclusion for works of artistic craftsmanship should apply only where the final products sold were themselves works of artistic craftsmanship, to reduce arguments over prototypes and models for industrial production.[212] Another concern raised in the ACIP review related to the loss of copyright protection for sculptures where 50 or more are made, on the basis it may be in breach of the Berne Convention.[213]

A final problem identified by ACIP and earlier by Janice Luck[214] relates to ongoing inconsistency between section 18 of the Designs Act and section 77 of the Copyright Act. Luck points out that the amendments to the definition of 'corresponding design' in section 74 of the Copyright Act in 1989 and in 2003 were intended to exclude artistic works exploited or registered as two-dimensional designs applied to the surface of articles from the copyright limitations in sections 75 and 77 of the Copyright Act. Section 18 of the Designs Act is intended to allow artistic works to be registered as designs, even though they might otherwise not be considered 'new and distinctive' by reason of having

[208] Ibid., recommendation 22; Advisory Council on Intellectual Property, *Review of the Designs System: Options Paper* (2014) ('Options Paper'), 52–6.
[209] Final Report, p. 33.
[210] Options Paper, pp. 32–3. [211] Final Report, p. 34. [212] Final Report, p. 35.
[213] Options Paper, p. 34.
[214] Luck, 'Section 18 of the Designs Act 2003'.

been used as artistic works (unless that use involved the sale or hire of products to which the design had been applied industrially). However, because section 18 refers to an application for a corresponding design in relation to that artistic work, and because 'corresponding design' is said to have the same meaning as in the Copyright Act,[215] the owner of the registered design can only rely on section 18 where the design consists of visual features of shape and configuration. However, as Luck argues, 'there appears to be no reason why corresponding design for the purposes of designs legislation should not have continued to be defined as a design that reproduces an artistic work regardless of whether the design consists of two-dimensional features of pattern or ornament or three-dimensional figures of shape or configuration'.[216]

In its Options Paper, ACIP had canvassed three alternatives to address the ongoing problems in this field: (1) clarifying areas of uncertainty, in particular the concept of when a design is 'embodied', especially in cases at the boundary of two and three dimensions, and limiting the exclusion for works of artistic craftsmanship to cases where the final marketed product is itself a work of artistic craftsmanship; (2) adopting a limited copyright term for industrially applied artistic works, in a manner similar to an unregistered design right; and (3) allowing full dual protection of designs and copyright works. Its instinct in the Options Paper was to adopt the first option. In relation to the third option, full dual protection, ACIP noted it had received no evidence that copyright protection was needed to provide sufficient incentives for such designs and that it was reluctant to extend copyright to cover mundane items of machinery. Third, it cautioned against using other jurisdictions as an example in favour of dual protection, as such jurisdictions often applied a higher standard of originality to objects of applied art or exclude or give thin protection to functional visual features. Given the ease of acquiring copyright protection for artistic works in Australia, ACIP considered that 'although there are some suggestions in the copyright cases that protection may be limited where the creator's choices are limited, it would be a bold move to assume that these suggestions will be sufficient to ensure that copyright does not entirely take over the field of design and the protection of visual features of products'.[217]

In its Final Report, however, ACIP had changed its position and now considered that a review of the overlap provisions was largely beyond its remit, which was the Designs Act 2003. Its sole recommendation was

[215] Designs Act 2003, s. 5. [216] Luck, 'Section 18 of the Designs Act 2003', 80.
[217] Options Paper, p. 35.

therefore that steps be taken to make section 18 of the Designs Act consistent with the overlap provisions of the Copyright Act.[218] It seems likely, therefore, that Australia will continue to tinker with the provisions regulating the copyright/design interface without any dramatic change of policy in the foreseeable future.

[218] Final Report, p. 35.

8 The Copyright/Design Interface in Italy

*Estelle Derclaye**

8.1 Introduction

As Table 8.1 summarises, the copyright/design interface in Italy has known two main periods, one of full cumulation (1865–1925) and the second of partial cumulation (1925 onwards with a very brief interruption). However, in this second period, partial cumulation was based on different criteria at different times. In the main, separability (*scindibilità*) was used from roughly 1925 until 2001 with high consistency and legal certainty albeit excluding most three-dimensional designs, and from 2001 onwards, the criterion of artistic value took over that of separability, also excluding many designs.[1] Section 8.2 traces the history of the Italian copyright/design interface from the first copyright and design Acts of the Italian state to the adoption of the Design Directive. Section 8.3 analyses the successes and failures of this history and draws conclusions as to which period or system worked best, if any.

8.2 History of the Copyright/Design Interface in Italy

8.2.1 First Period: 1865–1925: Full Cumulation

The first Italian Copyright Act dated from 1865 (Act of 25/6/1865 n. 2237) and the first Design Act from 1868 (30/8/1868 n. 4578).[2] As can be

* I would like to thank Alessandro Cogo, Alberto Musso, Marco Ricolfi and Elisa Vittone for their generous help answering questions and Sabine Jacques, Giorgio Spedicato and Veronica Villa for research assistance. I am also grateful for the support of the German Academic Exchange Service (DAAD), which granted me funding to carry out research for this chapter at the Max-Planck Institute for Intellectual Property and Competition Law.

1 For details especially on the last period, see P. Marzano, 'An ill-designed protection for a well-designed product: Italy and its copyright protection of industrial design' (2014) 240 *Revue Internationale du Droit d'Auteur* 119 at 219–25.

2 There were copyright and design laws before these, but as they pre-dated the modern Italian state, they are not reviewed here. N. Stolfi, *La Proprieta Intelletuale*, 2nd edn (Turin: UTET, 1915), p. 185; G. Valeri, *Corso di Diritto Industriale: Anno Accademico 1928–1929* (Firenze: Poligrafica Universitaria, 1929); M. Fabiani, *Modelli e Design Industriali* (Padova: Cedam, 1975), p. 9.

Table 8.1 *Chronological table of legislation and statistics*

Period	Legislation	Amendments	Interpretation (i.e. by courts)	Further information	Design applications	Design registrations
1. 1865–1925	Copyright Act 1865 Design Act 1868		Full cumulation	Designs were also governed by Industrial Property Acts 1859 and 1864	**** 5,162 (123)	*4,690 (91)
2. 1925–1941	Copyright Act 1925 Design Act 1868 and then 1940		Discrepancy between legislation (full cumulation) and court interpretation (partial cumulation)	Designs were also governed by the Patent Act 1939	14,151 (943)	12,641 (790)
3. 1941–1996	Copyright Act 1941 Design Act 1940	Design Act 1940 lengthens duration of design right to four years. Act of 23/5/1977 lengthens duration of design right to 15 years	Partial cumulation and demarcation for 3D designs		*****151,493 (2,754)	**99,663 (1,812)
4. 1996–1997	Law of 23/12/1996 Copyright Act 1941 Design Act 1940	Abrogated by law of 7/8/1997	1996 Act eliminated higher level of creativity for industrial design =>		See above and below, periods 3 and 5	See above and below, periods 3 and 5

		cumulation? (literature disagreed, norm was unclear) – no reported decision in that period		
5. 1997–2001	Copyright Act 1941 Design Act 1940	Return to previous state of the law, i.e. partial cumulation and demarcation for 3D designs	25,836 (5,167)	17,564 (3,512)
6. 2001–present	Law of 2/2/2001 (Act implementing Design Directive)	Partial cumulation	***28,026 (2,155)	***37,776 (2,905)

Source: Created by the author based on statistical data published by WIPO
Figures in parentheses: average annual numbers
* data incomplete for years before 1874
** data missing for 1942, 1943, 1944, 1958, 1960, 1962, 1966, 1967 and 1965
*** data for applications must be wrong as less high than for registrations; but these are the numbers given by WIPO and no data is missing per year. Another explanation may be that some registrations were delayed and counted from previous years.
**** data incomplete for years before 1883
***** data missing for 1942, 1943, 1944, 1955, 1957, 1958, 1959, 1960, 1962, 1964, 1976 and 1977

expected for copyright laws at the time, the first Italian Copyright Act was rather laconic. It protected all works of the mind and gave their authors a right of reproduction (art. 1).[3] The Act did not spell out a list, even exemplative, of protected works. If a work was jointly created, there was a rebuttable presumption that all co-authors had an equal part and could exercise the right fully (art. 5). The right lasted the life of the author and forty years after his or her death or eighty years from first publication.[4] The rights could be alienated (art. 15) and reproducing the work without the author's consent was infringement (art. 29). The Act did not establish an infringement test nor were there provisions on protection requirements, employee works, commissioned works or limitations to the exclusive rights. However, it was accepted that it was the designer who was the owner *ab initio* of the copyright.[5]

The 1868 Act on industrial designs and models was inspired by the French Act of 18/3/1806.[6] It had just eight articles. Apart from these articles, it referred to the Acts on industrial property rights of 30/10/1859 n. 3731 and 31/1/1864 n. 1637 and the Royal Decree of the same day n. 1674. This meant that designers had to follow the same procedure as that of inventors. In view of the silence of the Act, the literature agreed that ornamental designs and models could be two- or three-dimensional.[7] The 1868 Act referred to the protection requirements for inventions but the literature disagreed on the meaning of this.[8] According to article 3 of the 1859 Patent Act, novelty meant 'never known' or 'when known there was ignorance as to the particular means to actually make the invention'. Some commentators disagreed that novelty equated with originality in the sense of original presentation of existing elements.[9] Otherwise, commentators interpreted the Act as requiring two types of novelty. Intrinsic novelty meant originality or priority of the invention while extrinsic novelty meant that there was no divulgation before the filing of the design or model. Thus it was not an absolute novelty. Even insignificant changes could modify the design's aspect and make it new.[10]

[3] Articles 2 and 3 listed the different modes of reproduction, which included representation, adaptation, etc.

[4] U. Suthersanen, *Design Law in Europe* (London: Sweet & Maxwell, 2000), p. 208.

[5] L. Di Franco, *Trattato della Proprieta Industriale* (Milan: Societa Editrice Libraria, 1933), p. 241.

[6] Fabiani, *Modelli e Design Industriali*, p. 9.

[7] A. Spallino, 'Rassegna di dottrina in tema disegni e modelli industriali 1883–1953' (1954) *Riv. Dir. Industriale* 276 at 277.

[8] Some commentators also thought that a criterion of industriality was necessary. See Di Franco, *Trattato della Proprieta Industriale*, p. 216.

[9] Spallino, 'Rassegna di dottrina in tema disegni e modelli industriali 1883–1953', 278.

[10] Di Franco, *Trattato della Proprieta Industriale*, pp. 228–30.

Likewise, a new application of a known design could be new.[11] Designs contrary to laws, morality and public security could not be protected (art. 6 of the Patent Act 1859).

The patent and design Acts were silent on ownership when the inventor or designer was an employee. It was possible to transfer the design or model in whole or part, according to the general property rules.[12] The transfer was only valid towards third parties if it was registered at the intellectual property office.[13] The designer obtained an exclusive right to reproduce the design in whole or part by any means (art. 2 of the Design Act). The right lasted just two years from the day of publication and it ceased if the designer had not made use of the design within a year of publication (art. 4 of the Design Act). There were no limitations or exceptions to the exclusive right.

Therefore, the Italian system was one of full cumulation.[14] However, as early as 1905, E. Piola Caselli, the father of the separability doctrine (the so-called *scindibilità*), which came to be adopted later by courts and then the Italian legislator (see sections 8.2.2 and 8.2.3), was already advocating the non-cumulation between copyright and design laws.[15] For him, for a work of applied art to remain protected by copyright, it had to keep artistic individuality even if it had practical use. On the other hand, if the aesthetic element was an integral part of the product, the work could only be protected by the Design Act.[16]

The vast majority of commentators thought that the Design Act was very defective owing mainly to the right's short duration.[17] This state of fact was reflected in the very low numbers of designs applied for. In the first ten years of the Act's application (1869–78), only five designs were

[11] Valeri, *Corso di Diritto Industriale: Anno Accademico 1928–1929*, p. 182.

[12] Di Franco, *Trattato della Proprieta Industriale*, p. 257. [13] Ibid.

[14] E. Piola Caselli, *Del Diritto d'Autore Secondo la Legge Italiana Comparata con le Leggi Straniere* (Turin: Marghieri, 1907), p. 297 citing Amar. Greco, Rotondi, Ghiron, Valeri and Messineo also recognise the autonomy of ornamental designs and models and extracted them from the scope of copyright, giving them the same rights as those of inventors of patented inventions. However, some authors negated the autonomy of ornamental designs and models, saying that they were only protected by the Copyright Act: e.g. Di Franco, *Trattato della Proprieta Industriale* and ibid., 'Nozione teorica e disciplina legale dell'arte applicata all'industria' (1940) *D. Aut.* 269. On this, see Spallino, 'Rassegna di dottrina in tema disegni e modelli industriali 1883–1953', at 282–3.

[15] E. Piola Caselli, 'Le opera d'arte applicata e il diritto d'autore', Estratto del Foro Italiano, Anno XXX, Fasc. III, p. 8, Citta di Castello, 1905. See also Piola Caselli, *Del Diritto d'Autore Secondo la Legge Italiana Comparata con le Leggi Straniere*, p. 299.

[16] Piola Caselli, *Del Diritto d'Autore Secondo*, pp. 299–300.

[17] Ibid., p. 293. One commentator even mentions that no other country had such a short term of protection: G. Bertolini, *I Disegni e Modelli di Fabbrica: Tesi per l'Esame di Laurea in Giurisprudenza* (R. Università di Torino, 1914), p. 127. Another defect was the high registration fee. See F. Foà, 'De la protection des arts décoratifs en Italie' (1902) *I diritti d'autore* 125.

deposited.[18] Therefore, the courts did not have much to decide either. Supposedly only one case arose out of the Act.[19] In this case, the Court of Appeal of Milan rejected protection to a sugared almond's design having the shape of a button for lack of novelty (controversially, though, as it was the application of a known design to a new product, which all commentators agreed was sufficient for novelty).[20] Therefore, the gap was filled by the Copyright Act, which protected all works of the mind.[21] Nonetheless, the few decisions dealing with a work of applied art in that period held that they were not protected.[22] In a 1914 decision, the works in question were bronze street lamps. The Court of Appeal of Milan held that for them to be protected by copyright, they had to conserve their artistic individuality, independently from the use they can have in practical life. The court found that even if the lamps had an ornamental and artistic aim, they were not works which could live independently from the industrial product and thus were not artistic works.[23] This 1914 decision thus already embraced the separability doctrine advocated by Piola Caselli.

8.2.2 *Second Period: 1925–1941: Full Cumulation in Theory but Partial Cumulation in Practice – Adoption of the Separability Doctrine*

This period saw two new Acts: the Copyright Act 1925 and the Design Act 1940. As early as 1906, the legislator wanted to reform the Design Act.[24] As a matter of fact, a new Act was adopted in 1934 but never came into force.[25] This Act already stated that the Copyright Act's provisions were not applicable to designs and models, thus incorporating the separability doctrine and codifying the case law and literature.[26] It is only in

[18] Foà, 'De la protection des arts décoratifs en Italie', p. 125. See also Table 8.1.

[19] Foà, 'De la protection des arts décoratifs en Italie', p. 125.

[20] CA Milan, 17/9/1889, *Biancotti* v. *Gabutti, Mon. Trib.*, 1889, p. 891. See also G. Sala, 'La prima sentenza italiana in materia di designi e modeli industriali' (1952) *Riv. Dir. Industriale* 388–90.

[21] The first decision to clearly state that works of applied art were protected by copyright was Cass. Turin (sic), 21/11/1903, *Sirven* v. *Coen and Carli e De Carolis, Il Foro Italiano*, 1905, p. 171.

[22] CA Milan, 17/9/1914, *Il Foro Italiano*, 1914, p. 542 (lamp). See also CA Turin, 20/7/1894, *Il Foro Italiano*, 1894, p. 394 in which the court held that once the author extracts the aesthetic aspect of a work and uses it to decorate an object, copyright protection ceases and only the industrial property protection can apply.

[23] It also did not help that most of the designs were in the public domain.

[24] Bertolini, *I Disegni e Modelli di Fabbrica: Tesi per l'Esame di Laurea in Giurisprudenza*, pp. 128–44.

[25] Royal Decree of 13/9/1934 n. 1612, arts. 66–73.

[26] V. De Sanctis, 'I disegni e modelli ornamentali nella legge di riforma delle privative industriali e dei marchi' (1934) *D. Aut.* 482 at 484.

1940 that the new Design Act, with rules similar to the aborted 1934 Act, came to see the light of day. Since the next Copyright Act dates from 1941, we will examine the Design Act 1940 during the third period.

The Copyright Act of 7/11/1925, n. 1950, made very few substantial changes. Article 1 of the 1925 Copyright Act stated that all works of the mind were protected whatever their merit or destination and its second paragraph specifically included works of applied art. The rest remained almost unchanged, except that the term was increased to fifty years p.m.a. Like the previous Act, there were no provisions on protection requirements, employee works, commissioned works or limitations to the exclusive rights. Thus full cumulation was still applicable as per the legislation and favoured by most commentators.[27] However, as we saw in the previous section, before the new Copyright Act of 1925, Italian courts and commentators had started to drift from the unity of art approach to a partial cumulation system, using the separability test. In fact, both the courts and the literature elaborated several theories to determine under which conditions works of applied art could be protected by copyright, slowly but surely paving the way to a partial cumulation system. There were no less than six different theories,[28] namely means of reproduction (if made industrially or in a high number of copies, the work cannot obtain copyright protection),[29] destination[30] (if the work's essential destination is aesthetic then it can be protected by copyright and vice versa), the accessorial character that the design or model may have in relation to the industrial product, the level of artistic content, the author's intention or aim[31] (art is created without aim whereas a design is a creation with an aim, e.g. a mural as opposed to coins, stamps and labels) and the prevalence of the work's artistic character. The prevailing theory was that of artistic character – one must consider whether the artistic aspect prevails

[27] Valeri, *Corso di Diritto Industriale: Anno Accademico 1928–29*; De Sanctis, 'I disegni e modelli ornamentali nella legge di riforma delle privative industriali e dei marchi'. See also Stolfi cited by E. Piola Caselli, *Trattato del Diritto di Autore e del Contratto di Edizione nel Diritto Interno Italiano Comparato col Diritto Straniero*, 2nd edn (Turin: Marghieri, 1927), p. 106.

[28] Di Franco, *Trattato della Proprieta Industriale*, pp. 218–23 (he lists the different theories). See also L. Biamonti, 'La protezione pratica delle opere dell'arte applicata, Rapporto presentato al congresso di Budapest dell Ass. Litter. et Art. Internazionale del 1930' (1930) *D. Aut.* 563; Fabiani, *Modelli e Design Industriali*, pp. 24–6.

[29] L. Biamonti, 'Sulla natura e sui limiti della tutela giuridica dei lavori d'arte applicata all'industria e dei disegni e modelli ornamentali' (1932) *D. Aut.* 457 highlighted the flaw of the separability doctrine and favoured this theory to complement it.

[30] M. Ghiron, *Corso di Diritto Industriale con Testi di Legislazione e Convenzioni Internationale in Appendice* (Roma: SEFI, 1929), Vol. II, p. 210.

[31] Biamonti, 'La protezione pratica delle opere dell'arte applicata, Rapporto presentato al congresso di Budapest dell Ass. Litter. et Art. Internazionale del 1930', p. 563.

over the industrial one.[32] Only if the utilitarian function can be separated from the artistic one can the design be protected by copyright. This was also known as the separability theory or doctrine. It is not an artistic value criterion. As Marzano puts it, the test was 'a sort of "conceptual reverse engineering" aimed at verifying the persistence in the work, once applied to a useful article, of the characteristics possessed by a corresponding work of "pure", non-applied art'.[33] This theory won in the end. As already mentioned, it had been elaborated by E. Piola Caselli in the first twenty years of the twentieth century, was gradually adopted by courts and culminated in its adoption in the 1941 Copyright Act.[34] This came rather unsurprisingly as Piola Caselli was a judge at the Italian Supreme Court during the period preceding the adoption of the 1941 Copyright Act and then senator and rapporteur of the Copyright Bill. There was therefore a discrepancy between the literature and the case law on the one hand and the Act on the other. Some commentators also lamented that the copyright's term was too long for industrial designs and the Design Act one was too short.[35]

In the 1930s, the judiciary adopted and then devotedly applied the separability doctrine. The first Supreme Court (Court of Cassation) decision which adopted the separability test dated from 1931 and involved a stove. The court rejected the protection of the stove as a work of applied art

[32] Di Franco, *Trattato della Proprieta Industriale*, p. 228; M. Ghiron, *Corso di Diritto Industriale, I marchi, i Segni Distintivi e le Insegne, le Invenzioni, i Modelli ed i Disegni Industriali*, 2nd edn riveduta ed ampliata (Rome: Società editrice del 'Foro Italiano', 1937) XII, 422, p. 387; Biamonti, 'Sulla natura e sui limiti della tutela giuridica dei lavori d'arte applicata all'industria e dei disegni e modelli ornamentali', p. 443 and De Sanctis, 'I disegni e modelli ornamentali nella legge di riforma delle privative industriali e dei marchi', p. 482 (who admits the double protection by copyright and design law, in the case in which the works of applied art can also have the aspect of works of pure art); A. Musatti, 'Opera del ingegno e disegni o modelli di fabbrica' (1915) II *Riv. Dir. Comm.* 1164.

[33] Marzano, 'An ill-designed protection for a well-designed product', p. 121.

[34] For a detailed description of the separability theory, see E. Piola Caselli, *Trattato del Diritto di Autore e del Contratto di Edizione nel Diritto Interno Italiano Comparato col Diritto Straniero*, 2nd edn, p. 109 and 'L'allacciamento della protezione dell'arte industriale con la protezione del diritto d'autore' (1940) 1–2 *D. Aut.* 15. Other proponents of the exclusive application of the Design Act for industrial designs included: M. Ghiron, *Corso di Diritto Industriale con Testi di Legislazione e Convenzioni Internationale* in Appendice, p. 213; ibid., 'Disegni industriali ed opere artistiche alla prossima conferenza di Roma' (1928) *Riv. Pol. Econ.* 1 at 3; Biamonti, 'Sulla natura e sui limiti della tutela giuridica dei lavori d'arte applicata all'industria e dei disegni e modelli ornamentali', 445ff; A. Giannini, 'La protezione delle opere d'arte applicata all'industria' (1939) *Riv. Pol. Econ.* 939 at 950. See F. Morri, 'Le opere dell'industrial design tra diritto d'autore e tutela come modelli industriali: Deve cambiare tutto perché (quasi) nulla cambi?' (2013) *Riv. Dir. Indus.* 177 at 185.

[35] Biamonti, 'La protezione pratica delle opere dell'arte applicata, Rapporto presentato al congresso di Budapest dell Ass. Litter. et Art. Internazionale del 1930'; De Sanctis, 'I disegni e modelli ornamentali nella legge di riforma delle privative industriali e dei marchi'.

in copyright law on the basis of the separability test as well as for absence of originality, which it defined as 'an intellectual creation which reveals the personality of the author'.[36] The Court of Cassation laid down the criterion of separability as follows: 'the industrial product which, because of its nature, cannot be separated from a certain shape matching also with aesthetic lines, can be an artistic entity in as much as the artistic attitudes extrinsic to the making of the object can be dissociated from it and from its industrial destination and assume an autonomous depiction which is added to the object'. A year later the Supreme Court restated its theory but here found that the works were protected. The works were wooden figurines representing ordinary people from the Val Gardena, which were added on top of corks and which had the possibility of moving via a mechanism.[37] The court also confirmed that the fact that the figurines were made industrially did not affect their copyrightability. The Supreme Court then confirmed two decisions which, using the separability doctrine, had held two-dimensional works unprotectable, namely typefaces[38] and the design at the back of playing cards.[39] As regards the latter, the Court of Cassation agreed with the Court of Appeal that any playing cards need to have a design at the back and the author's aim is to make the industrial product more attractive in order for it to be commercially successful. Several decisions from courts of appeal and of first instance also endorsed the doctrine.[40] Of note are two from the Court of Appeal of Milan. One found that an advert was not protectable by copyright for lack of separability and of originality[41] and the other that fashion sketches were protected by copyright as works of pure art.[42]

[36] Cass., 19/12/1931 and 26/1/1932, *Soc. Italiana Triplex* v. *Ditta Galimberti*, *Il Foro Italiano*, 1932, 868; *D. Aut.* 1931, p. 129. One of the judges in this case was Piola Caselli.

[37] Cass., 25/1/1933, *Riffeser* v. *Comploy*, *Riv. Dir. Comm*, pp. 208–12, *aff'ing* CA Brescia, 12/12/1933, *Riv. della Prop. Intell. ed Indus*, 1933, p. 324, also published in *D. Aut.* 1934, p. 46.

[38] Cass., 20/12/1937, *Fonderia tipografica De Luca* v. *Ditta Schriftguss*, *Il Foro Italiano*, 1938, 562.

[39] Cass., 10/6/1938, *Ditta Pignalosa* v. *Ditta Modiano*, *Il Foro Italiano*, 1938, 1642, on appeal from CA Naples, 9/7/1937, *Il Foro Italiano*, 1937, 1404.

[40] See e.g. CA Milan, 31/12/1937, unpublished (bed) cited by L. Pavanello, 'The protection of industrial design under Italian law', in B. Gray and E. Bouzalas (eds.), *Industrial Design Rights: An International Perspective* (The Hague: Kluwer, 2001), p. 160.

[41] CA Milan, 17/7/1933, *Laboratorio Chimico Farmaceutico E. Granelli* v. *Zanoni*, *Riv. Propr. Intell. ed Indus*, 1933, p. 298, also published in *D. Aut.* 1934, p. 39. The advert in question was a panel in wood in the form of a parallelepiped on which were placed on the left a box of San Pellegrino magnesium and on the right a glass with water in it. At the top there was a spoon in wood in which the magnesium was poured into the glass. The spoon was fixed by hooks on the panel. Then there were the words 'Magnesia S. Pellegrino' and 'it is a spoon of health'. For the court, no one with minimal taste and common sense would want to acquire the work for his home, nor appreciate or contemplate it for its artistic value independently from its advertising aim.

[42] CA Milan, 22/10/1935, *Est. Isoldi S.A.R. ed. E. Heimann* v. *Casa Editrice Aracne*, *D. Aut.* 1936, 44.

Thus, by the end of the period, the separability doctrine was well established and accepted in Italian case law and literature.

8.2.3 *Third Period: 1941–1996: Partial Cumulation and Demarcation for 3D Functional Objects*

The new Design Act was adopted on 25 August 1940 and the new Copyright Act on 22 April 1941. During this period, there were two failed attempts at changing design law. First, at the end of the 1970s, a new design Bill added one more year of protection (i.e. five years) but did not change much else.[43] The second attempt (the Minervini Bill of 29 March 1984) aimed at unifying the regulation of industrial design in one single Act, though still rejecting cumulation.[44] Finally, an Act was adopted to lengthen the duration of the design right to fifteen years from filing (Act n. 265 of 23/5/1977).

Apart from its codification of the separability doctrine in its article 2(4) which read '[i]n particular the following shall be protected: works of sculpture, painting, drawing, engraving and similar graphic arts, including scenic art, even when such works are applied to an industrial product if their artistic value is distinct from the industrial character of the product with which they are associated', the Copyright Act 1941 in substance did not change much; it was just more detailed on the rights and added exceptions to the rights.

Article 1 of the Copyright Act 1941 stated: '[i]ntellectual works having a creative character and appertaining to literature, music, the graphic arts, architecture, the theatre and cinematography, whatever their mode or form of expression, shall be protected according to this Law'. The words 'whatever the merit or destination' which appeared in the previous Copyright Act were deleted to avoid protecting trivial works[45] and replaced by 'whatever mode or form of expression'. The Act required two protection requirements, namely creative character and intellectual effort (arts. 1 and 6).[46] The author was the initial owner (art. 6) and there

[43] On this see M. Rotondi, 'Un progetto di legge tipo per brevetti, modelli e marchi e proposta di una legge tipo in materia di diritto di autore' (1977) 1 *D. Aut.* 89.

[44] On this Bill, see G. Floridia, 'La protezione del diritto di autore sulle opere dell'industrial design' (1984) I *Riv. Dir. Ind.* 372; M. Fabiani, 'La protezione dell'arte applicata e dell'industrial design in Italia e negli USA' (1986) *D. Aut.* 414.

[45] M. Fabiani, 'Problemi di protezione del design industriale' (1972) *D. Aut.* 265 at 270; Marzano, 'An ill-designed protection for a well-designed product', p. 145.

[46] For most courts and commentators creative character referred to originality in the sense of the author's personality and not novelty. Contra: M. Franzosi, 'Arte e diritto' (1977) *Riv. Dir. Ind.* 285.

could be joint ownership (art. 10 and arts. 1100–1116 civil code).[47] The Act was silent on employee works, so contract law was applicable. The general rule was that the works made by employees belonged to the employee even if created during the course of employment. But the courts sometimes ruled that economic rights were implicitly transferred to the employer.[48] There were also no rules for commissioned works. In general, the copyright vested in the author unless there was a contract to transfer the right to the commissioner[49] and the transfer was only valid 'to the extent that it [was] necessary to fulfil the purpose of the commissioning agreement'.[50] Transfers needed to be in writing (art. 110) and transfer of future copyright was allowed under certain conditions.[51] Economic rights (reproduction, communication to the public, etc.) were provided for in articles 12–19 and moral rights in articles 20–24. There was infringement even if there were small differences between the work and the infringing copy. What was important was that the essential creative characteristics of the first work were recognisable in the subsequent work and the judge did not have to examine the quality and quantity of all the differences and similarities.[52] A few exceptions and limitations were provided in articles 65–71. The term of protection was fifty years p.m.a. (art. 25).

As in the previous Design Act, article 1 of the new Design Act of 25/8/1940, n. 1411, provided that the Patent Act of 29/6/1939, n. 1127, applied to ornamental designs, except for the provisions expressly stated in the Design Act. Article 5 of the Design Act stated that 'can be registered as ornamental designs and models the new models and designs which can give, to industrial products, a special ornament, either by the shape or the combination of lines, colours or other elements. The provisions of the Copyright Act are not applicable to such designs and models.' The second paragraph of article 5 did not mean that the protection of the Copyright Act and the Design Act could not be cumulated. There could be cumulation if the provisions of the two Acts were fulfilled. In other words, it meant that the provisions of the Copyright Act could not

47 Cass., 29/4–29/7/1957, *Ditta Fontanini* v. *Giardini*, *D. Aut.*, 1958, p. 72 (if a work is created by several persons, all of them must have contributed to the characteristics of the indistinguishability and inseparability which are required by law in order to have copyright protection).
48 Suthersanen, *Design Law in Europe*, p. 214. Contra: Pavanello, 'The protection of industrial design under Italian law', p. 165; the majority opinion was that economic rights belonged to the employer, at least those rights that the parties intended to transfer, citing Trib. Milan, 22/5/1972 (1972) *D. Aut.* 315.
49 Cass., 27/5/1957, *D. Aut.*, 1957, p. 378.
50 Suthersanen, *Design Law in Europe*, p. 214, citing Cass., 7/6/1982, *D. Aut.*, 1983, p. 23.
51 Suthersanen, *Design Law in Europe*, p. 215.
52 Cass. 1st civ., 5/7/1990, n. 2035, *Fiorucci S.p.a.* v. *Manifattura Naj Oleari S.p.a.*, *D. Aut.*, 1991, at p. 69.

apply to registered designs but only the Design Act's provisions could; in other words, copyright protection did not apply to objects actually registered as ornamental designs or models.[53]

Designs had to be new, have industrial application[54] and be lawful.[55] Again, the Act did not define novelty and the literature and courts carried on requiring the twin concepts of intrinsic and extrinsic novelty.[56] Intrinsic novelty now meant more precisely a new creative contribution which gives the object a special 'ornament', i.e. an autonomous aesthetic or decorative value by the shape, a particular combination of lines, colours or other elements.[57] Thus a new form (fulfilling the requirement of extrinsic novelty) could not be protected if anyone could create it without individual creative effort (intrinsic novelty). For the majority of commentators, novelty was relative, unlike in patent law.[58] It was sufficient that the design or model consisted in a different form from that already applied to analogous products, without pretending to be different from all forms

[53] Fabiani commenting on Cass. 1st civ., 5/7/1990, n. 2035, *Fiorucci S.p.a.* v. *Manifattura Naj Oleari S.p.a.*, *D. Aut.*, 1991, p. 70, also citing Greco e Vercellone, 'Le invenzioni e i modelli industriali', in *Trattato Vassali* (Torino, 1968), p. 405; V. De Sanctis, *Il carattere Creativo delle Opera dell'Ingegno* (Milan: Giuffrè, 1977), p. 100.

[54] The requirement of industrial application of the design or model is the one referred to in article 12 of the Patent Act 1939. For Fabiani, 'Problemi di protezione del design industriale', pp. 277–8, industrial application is not a reproducibility of the design or model as pure aesthetic creation but the adaptability of the model to the product object of industrial use, with the aim to confer to it a 'special' ornamental character. For Suthersanen, *Design Law in Europe*, p. 221, industrial applicability means reproduction by mechanical means and also adapting the design to an industrial product for decorative purposes. For G. Guglielmetti, *Le invenzioni e modelli industriali dopo la riforma del 1979* (Turin: Utet, 1982), p. 191, industriality is implied in the destination of the industrial products.

[55] Pavanello, 'The protection of industrial design under Italian law', p. 165; Fabiani, *Modelli e Design Industriali*, p. 61 (only the external aspect of the object is subject to the morality requirement).

[56] For an application, see Trib. Brescia, 25/3/1954, *Santini* v. *Polloni*, *Riv. Prop. Int. ed Indus.*, 1955, 131 (is void for lack of extrinsic novelty the design which is divulged to third parties before application. A typical case of divulgation is the sale of object to an undetermined number of people).

[57] See Fabiani, *Modelli e Design Industriali*, p. 55 and E. Bonasi Benucci, 'Forma del prodotto e sua tutela' (1958) *Riv. Dir. Industriale* 426, at 428. For an application, see Trib. Milan, 6/10/1955, *Ditta Mario Giamperi* v. *Fratelli Mariani S.p.a.*, *Riv. Prop. Int. ed Indus.*, 1955, 257 (simple objective novelty, i.e. a differentiation from what existed before, is not sufficient to have a valid ornamental design or model. One needs the expression of a new ornamental idea, the existence of elements capable to give, to those who cultivate aesthetics in the field of the objects in question, the sensation of a new aesthetic). There were two trends in the courts' interpretation of this criterion, one quite strict and the other more liberal: for decisions, see Guglielmetti, *Le invenzioni e modelli industriali dopo la riforma del 1979*, p. 190 and note 19.

[58] Fabiani, *Modelli e Design Industriali*, pp. 53–6; Suthersanen, *Design Law in Europe*, p. 220. Contra: P. Barbieri, 'Tutela dell'arte applicata all'industria (Brevetti per modello – Concorrenza sleale)' (1955) 2 *D. Aut.* 194 at 203.

considered abstractly.[59] So there was extrinsic novelty when there was a figurative expression which, even if the elements or a combination of these were already known or already applied to other products, met an aesthetic result ulterior and different in the field of the activity considered.[60] There was also no need to show high level of artistry or artistic merit.[61]

According to article 7 of the Design Act, the exclusive right belonged to the author of the new design or its assignees. Unless otherwise provided in a contract, those designs which were made by employees in the course of their employment belonged to the employer (art. 7(2)). The designer had the right to be recognised as the author of the design and have his or her name written in the register of patents. Commissioned designs belonged to the commissionee but the delivery transferred the ownership of the commissioner.[62] Co-authors, i.e. persons who contribute to the creativity, could be co-owners.[63] The rights of the design right holder could be transferred between living persons for free or for a price, or inherited. The transfer of the design right could be limited in time or object and licences were possible.[64] Transfers had to be done in writing, notarised and registered at the intellectual property office.[65] The right holder had the exclusive right to use the design as in the Patent Act.[66] There was infringement if the whole or substantial part of design was used in a commercial context. The test was that of overall impression.[67] Reproduction or importation of the design for personal use was free.[68] The term of protection was four years from filing (art. 9). If a design was not worked within a year of grant, the right was null (art. 13).[69]

59 Fabiani, *Modelli e Design Industriali*, pp. 53–6.

60 Fabiani, 'Problemi di protezione del design industriale', pp. 272–3. For applications, see Cass. Civ., 4/8/1965, n. 1869, *D. Aut.*, 1966, p. 113; Trib. Bologna, 16/5/1974, *Giur. Ann. Dir. Ind.*, n. 613/2; Trib. Milan, 26/9/1974, *Giur. Ann. Dir. Ind.*, 1974, n. 613/2; Trib. Monza, 26/11/1973, *Giur. Ann. Dir. Ind.*, 1973, n. 408/2 (it is sufficient to have novelty in the sector, i.e. that the aesthetic aspect which confers its special ornament to the industrial product was not yet adopted in respect of industrial products entering in this sector); Trib. Florence, 18/8/1978, *Giur. Ann. Dir. Ind.*, 1979, n. 1148/1–2.

61 Suthersanen, *Design Law in Europe*, p. 221.

62 Fabiani, *Modelli e Design Industriali*, pp. 65–6. 63 Ibid., pp. 65–6.

64 Ibid., p. 90; Suthersanen, *Design Law in Europe*, p. 222.

65 Suthersanen, *Design Law in Europe*, p. 222. 66 Ibid., p. 219.

67 Cass. 1st civ., 2/4/1987, *Lecce* v. *S.p.a. Aurora*, *D. Aut.*, 1987, p. 502 (overall impression similar so pen design infringed); Trib. Monza, 21/1/1985, *Foro Padano*, 1985, p. 234, *Frau Poltrone* v. *Zani*, with comment S. Magelli (overall impression similar so furniture design infringed).

68 Fabiani, *Modelli e Design Industriali*, p. 87.

69 Contra: ibid., p. 92 ; Pavanello, 'The protection of industrial design under Italian law', p. 165; Guglielmetti, *Le invenzioni e modelli industriali dopo la riforma del 1979*, pp. 193–4.

In short, nothing much changed compared to the previous Act apart from the provisions about commissioned designs, the infringement test was overall impression, the reproduction or importation for personal use was not an infringement and the term was doubled (four instead of two years).

The transition was therefore a very smooth one compared to the previous period. The vast majority of both courts and literature carried on applying the separability doctrine, clarifying that it was to be understood not in a material, mechanical sense but in a conceptual, ideal sense.[70]

[70] See e.g. Cass. 1st civ., 12/8/1946, *SA Instituto Profilattico e Farmaceutico Candioli & C.* v. *Carlo Frassinelli, Giur. It.*, 1947, I, 76 (typeface); Cass., 20/1/1951, *Giur. Cass. Civ.*, 1951, I, 3; Cass., 22/10/1956, n. 3806, *Franchi* v. *Arti Grafiche Cellerino, Riv. Dir. Comm.*, 1958, pp. 172ff (decorated boxes containing flower seeds; artistic value not separable); Cass., 29/7/1957, *Ditta Fontanini* v. *Giardini, D. Aut.*, 1958, p. 72 (nativity scenes); CA Milan, 16/2/1962, unpublished (bag); Trib. Milan, 3/10/1973, *Foro Italiano*, 1974, item 'Diritto d'autore', n. 13 (ashtray, basket and umbrella stand), both cited by Pavanello, 'The protection of industrial design under Italian law', p. 160; Trib. Milan, 17/6/1974, *Karoflor s.c.r.l.* v. *Rusconi editore S.p.a. and Lanificio Loreto d'Ambrosio S.p.a.*, *Giur. Ann. Dir. Indus.*, 1974, p. 835 (weave pattern for bedspreads and covers not separable); Trib. Milan, 28/4/1975, *Industria Aristica Tito Bianchi s.a.s.* v. *Magazzini Standa S.p.a.*, *Giur. Ann. Dir. Indus.*, 1975, p. 719, *aff'd by* CA Milan, 28/9/1976, *Standa S.p.a.* v. *Industria Aristica Tito Bianchi s.a.s. and Others, Giur. Ann. Dir. Indus.*, 1976, p. 860 (statuettes produced in series and reproducing a work of sculpture separable); Trib. Milan, 30/5/1974, *Giur. Ann. Dir. Ind.*, 1974, p. 562; CA Milan, 19/7/1985, *Fiorucci s.p.a.* v. *Manifattura Naj Oleari S.p.a.*, *Giur. Ann. Dir. Indus.*, 1986, p. 2004 (the design is separable; it can be enjoyed on any support and it is creative so copyright subsists); Cass. Sec. crim., 27/1/1977, n. 3238, *Giur. Ann. Dir. Ind.*, 1978, p. 993 (Rietveld's chair model 'red and blue' inseparable – 'the original design of a dress, a new type of the body of a car, the design of a fabric, shape of a dish, or like in this case, the structure of a piece of furniture, can never be dissociated from the industrial product to which they are applied', Trib. Milan, 12/6/1980, *Mazzucato* v. *Artemide S.p.a.*, *D. Aut.*, 1981, p. 395 ('Nesso' lamp not separable (see Figure 8.1); the court, however, also adds that the lamp had been originally designed to be reproduced in series and its destination was for a competition and seems to deduce its non-copyrightability from these criteria); Cass., 26/6/1980, *Giur. Annotata di Diritto Industriale*, 1980, n. 1258, 61 (Breuer's Wassily chair: see Figure 8.2); Magistrate's Court Alba, 9/1/1992, *Box. S.r.l.* v. *Miroglio Tessile S.p.a.*, *D. Aut.*, 1992, p. 291 (print design (French poems with flowers) separable); Trib. Florence, 28/1/1988, *Giur. Ann. Dir. Ind.*, 1988, n. 2285/1; Cass. 1st civ., 7/12/1994, n. 10516, *Cassina S.p.a* v. *S.r.l. Steel Line, D. Aut.*, 1996, p. 410; Trib. Brescia, 2/12/1995, *D. Aut.*, 1995, 346. V. De Sanctis, Observations under Cass., 10/6/1938, *Ditta Pignalosa* v. *Ditta Modiano, Giur. Comparata di diritto commerciale, marittimo, aeronautico, industriale e d'autore*, 1942, p. 208; Bonasi Benucci, 'Forma del prodotto e sua tutela', p. 426, at 439; Fabiani, 'Problemi di protezione del design industriale', p. 269; Fabiani, *Modelli e Design Industriali*, p. 28; Guglielmetti, *Le invenzioni e modelli industriali dopo la riforma del 1979*, p. 185; and others including Vercellone, Ascarelli, Bergomi, Algardi, Auteri, Benussi and Sena all cited by Morri, 'Le opere dell'industrial design tra diritto d'autore e tutela come modelli industriali: Deve cambiare tutto perché (quasi) nulla cambi?', p. 187 note 27, who notes that the literature is unanimous on this point.

However, this ideal separability was understood in two different ways by courts and commentators.[71] For some commentators, a creation was protectable by copyright if it could be reproduced on media different from the product to which it is originally associated (Auteri[72]), i.e. when one can assume the artistic value even if executed on or with materials other than that of the industrial product (Greco-Vercellone). According to the second interpretation, an object was separable ideally when it could be enjoyed as pure aesthetic fact, e.g. as when one contemplates an exhibition, independently from its use in the practical function to which it is destined (Sena). This interpretation meant a higher artistic level of the object instead or in addition to separability.[73] Whilst the courts embraced the ideal separability concept, it is not always easy to determine which of the two interpretations they adopt as they use ambivalent language.[74] If a court follows the first interpretation, there is never protection by copyright because the object of industrial design is the fusion of the aesthetic with the functional and thus can only be the shape of this object and cannot be thought of in relation to a different object.[75] On the other hand, quasi[76] all two-dimensional designs are protected under this first interpretation. If one follows the second interpretation, industrial design will not normally be protected by copyright but will be only in the rare hypotheses of objects particularly successfully designed.[77]

[71] G. Bergomi, 'Industrial design', in *Contratto e Impresa* (Padova: CEDAM, 1987), pp. 970–1.

[72] For Auteri, 'Industrial design', in *Dizionari di diritto privato a cura d'Irti*, vol. 11, in U. Carnevali, *Diritto Commerciale e Industriale* (Milan (s.d. ma), 1985), p. 588, ideal separability means that it is not necessary that the work can be removed materially from the product but it is sufficient that the creation can be reproduced on different media than the product to which it is originally associated.

[73] See Bergomi, 'Industrial design', at 967 citing V. Mangini and G. Auletta, *Azienda, Opera dell'Ingegno e Invenzioni Industriali, Commentari del cod. Civ. A cura di Scialoja e Branca* (Bologna/Rome: Zanichelli, 1947), pp. 325–6. Di Cataldo, Serra, Sena and Franzosi, for whom the criterion of separability meant artistic value, and Bonasi Benucci, Greco-Vercellone and Guglielmetti, for whom both separability and a value judgment were needed. See also Piola Caselli (above, note 34). For reference to the authors cited above, see Bergomi, pp. 979–81. See Auteri, 'Industrial design', i.e. Greco-Vercellone p. 78, Sena p. 453, Benucci, p. 153. Trib. Roma, 4/9/1963, *Autojournal* v. *Autorama*, *D. Aut.* 1964, p. 49 (car body panel not to be protected by copyright – art. 2(4) and (5) of the Copyright Act 1941 require artistic quality as necessary condition to have protection); Trib. Siena, 30/10/1985, *D. Aut.*, 1988, p. 209 (Le Corbusier's chaise longue copyrightable because of high artistic value but not other furniture designed by the same author), *rev'd by* CA Florence, 4/2/1989, *Zanova S.r.l.* v. *Cassina*, *D. Aut.*, 1989, p. 444. See also CA Florence, 9/1/1978, *Giur. Ann. Dir. Ind.*, 1979, p. 210.

[74] Bergomi, 'Industrial design', p. 971.

[75] Ibid., who prefers the first interpretation because the second makes a value judgment and this is dangerous.

[76] Ibid., p. 973 citing Greco-Vercellone and Trib. Milan, 17/6/1974, *Giur. Ann. Dir. Ind.*, 1974, p. 835.

[77] Bergomi, 'Industrial design', p. 972.

Figure 8.1 The so-called lamp 'Nesso' produced by Artemide and designed by Giancarlo Mattioli

That said, the end result of the application of the doctrine was that a lot of worthy three-dimensional works of applied art, most famously furniture designed by Le Corbusier and other well-known designers,[78] ended

[78] See Cass., 10/10/1975, *Giur. Dir. Int.*, 1978, p. 3, categorically excluding that the structure of a piece of furniture could be protected by copyright; Trib. Monza, 21/1/1985, *Foro Padano*, 1985, I, c. 234, with comment by S. Magelli, 'La tutela brevettuale del design' (armchair 'Cobra' was only susceptible of registered design protection); Trib. Florence, 20/10/1988, *S.p.a. Cassina* v. *S.r.l. Alivar and Matrix S.r.l.*, *D. Aut.*,

Figure 8.2 Marcel Breuer's Wassily chair

up unprotected by copyright law.[79] This meant the courts favoured the first interpretation of the doctrine, i.e. artistic merit or value was not

1989, p. 455 (none of the six chair designs were separable); Magistrate's Court Florence, 26/1/1989, *S.p.a. Cassina* v. *S.r.l. Alivar, D. Aut.*, 1989, p. 82 (Le Corbusier furniture unprotected by copyright as not separable) *aff'd by* CA Florence, 4/2/1989, *Zanova S.r.l.* v. *Cassina, D. Aut.*, 1989, p. 444 and by Cass. 1st civ., 7/12/1994, n. 10516, *Cassina S.p.a* v. *S.r.l. Steel Line, D. Aut.*, 1996, p. 410.

[79] See e.g. Auteri, 'Industrial design', p. 582.

required.[80] On the other hand, paradoxically, two-dimensional works of little value were protected,[81] something the Act had in fact tried to avoid. It was, on the other hand, clear in the case law that the number of copies was an irrelevant criterion,[82] as well as the criterion of aim or destination,[83] even if it was favoured by some commentators.[84] In conclusion, for both the case law and literature, Italy was in a state of partial cumulation.

Then, in the 1990s, the courts embraced an even stricter interpretation of the separability doctrine, based on an article written by another judge of the Court of Cassation, and also expert in copyright law, Paolo Vercellone. Already in 1956, Vercellone advocated 'excluding from copyright protection those three-dimensional works of applied art which, if reproduced on a different substance or embodied in another object, would lose their aesthetic value, since they could be conceived as merely an aesthetic quality of a certain industrial product'.[85] This did not mean that sculptural works were excluded but only useful articles. 'Only sculptures applied to articles could have received copyright protection, not works reflecting designs and modelling activities (for example, the sculpture of the "flying lady" applied to the hood of Rolls Royce automobiles would be copyrightable but not the design – however aesthetically motivated or pleasing – of the car itself).'[86]

This trend started with a 1990 decision of the Court of Cassation, which held that copyright does not apply to those three-dimensional forms which cannot be other than the form of a certain product, e.g. a fork, a television set, a bag, a shoe.[87] The Court added that some

[80] V. De Sanctis, Observations under Cass., 10/6/1938, *Ditta Pignalosa* v. *Ditta Modiano*, *Giur. Comparata di diritto commerciale, marittimo, aeronautico, industriale e d'autore*, 1942, p. 208; Di Franco, 'Nozione teorica e disciplina legale dell'arte applicata all'industria', p. 269. Trib. Florence 20/10/1988, *S.p.a. Cassina* v. *S.r.l. Alivar and Matrix S.r.l.*, *D. Aut.*, 1989, p. 455 (Le Corbusier chairs); Cass. 1st civ., 5/7/1990, n. 2035, *Fiorucci S.p.a.* v. *Manifattura Naj Oleari S.p.a.*, *D. Aut.*, 1991, at 67. Guglielmetti, *Le invenzioni e modelli industriali dopo la riforma del 1979*, p. 185; Auteri, 'Industrial design', pp. 582, 587 also criticising this criterion as arbitrary.

[81] Morri, 'Le opere dell'industrial design tra diritto d'autore e tutela come modelli industriali: Deve cambiare tutto perché (quasi) nulla cambi?', pp. 190–1 and references cited; Marzano, 'An ill-designed protection for a well-designed product', p. 157.

[82] Fabiani, 'Problemi di protezione del design industriale', p. 269. Cass. 1st civ., 5/7/1990, n. 2035, *Fiorucci S.p.a.* v. *Manifattura Naj Oleari S.p.a.*, *D. Aut.*, 1991, p. 63.

[83] Bergomi, 'Industrial design', p. 969 and decisions cited: e.g. CA Milan, 19/7/1985, *Giur. Ann. Dir. Indus.*, 1986, p. 2004, *Fiorucci S.p.a.* v. *Manifattura Naj Oleari S.p.a.* Contra: Trib. Milan, 4/10/1973, *Bruno Danese and Bruno Danese s.n.c.* v. *G.B. Carpano – Antica fabbrica di vermouth S.p.a. and E. Mari*, *Giur. Ann. Dir. Indus.*, 1973, p. 396.

[84] Bonasi Benucci, 'Forma del prodotto e sua tutela', at 430, 446–8.

[85] Marzano, 'An ill-designed protection for a well-designed product', pp. 154–5.

[86] Ibid.

[87] Cass. 1st civ., 5/7/1990, n. 2035, *Fiorucci S.p.a.* v. *Manifattura Naj Oleari S.p.a.*, *D. Aut.*, 1991 (cloth design made of coloured squares), and restated in Cass. 1st civ., 7/12/1994, n. 10516, *Cassina S.p.a* v. *S.r.l. Steel Line*, *D. Aut.*, 1996, p. 410. The court in 1994 seems to go further and rejects the protection of any three-dimensional object. That would go

two-dimensional designs are also excluded because they are not separable, e.g. typographical characters, symbols on a watch or clock and railings, while other two-dimensional designs are separable, such as combinations of lines and colours for scarves, ties and cloth for dresses.[88] It also held that it was clear that the legislator of 1941 rejected all the other criteria except that of separability[89] and that one cannot try to circumvent the separability criterion by trying to classify the work in another category (e.g. work of architecture or an atypical category of work of industrial art) in order to have copyright protection.[90]

Many commentators were still unsatisfied with the new Design Act, for the duration of the right was still too short, the procedure too complex and the fees too high.[91] While many commentators were happy with the separability criterion,[92] and thought cumulation ought to be limited as

too far as it would exclude all sculptures, which have no other function than decorative and are listed as copyright works in the Act. So it probably meant to include only functional objects.

88 Cass. 1st civ., 5/7/1990, n. 2035, *Fiorucci S.p.a.* v. *Manifattura Naj Oleari S.p.a.*, *D. Aut.*, 1991, p. 63 at 67. However, for Morri, 'Le opere dell'industrial design tra diritto d'autore e tutela come modelli industriali: Deve cambiare tutto perché (quasi) nulla cambi?', p. 191, apart from one isolated case, in the few cases decided on two-dimensional works, judges always considered those designs separable, quoting CA Milan, 19/7/1985, in *Giur. Ann. Dir. Ind.*, 1985, n. 2005 (*Naj Oleari*); Cass. 5/7/1990, n. 7077, *Giur. Ann. Dir. Ind.*, 1990, 2474; *D. Aut.*, 1991, 63; *Riv. Dir. Ind.*, 1991, II, 24, with comment Sena, 'Industrial design e diritto d'autore'; in *Giur. it.*, 1991, I, c. 58, with comment M. Ricolfi, 'Il criterio della scindibilità e l'opera "bidimensionale" dell'arte applicata all'industria'; Trib. Como, 12/2/1996 (ord.), 1996, n. 3465 (design of a cloth composed of known elements, i.e. small houses, teddies, flowers and little hearts).

89 Cass., 5/7/1990, n. 2035, *Fiorucci S.p.a.* v. *Manifattura Naj Oleari S.p.a.*, *D. Aut.*, 1991, p. 63 at 66. See also Cass. 1st civ., 7/12/1994, n. 10516, *Cassina S.p.a.* v. *S.r.l. Steel Line*, *D. Aut.*, 1996, p. 410 at 414. However, in its 1994 decision, the court requires not only creativity but also novelty for copyright to subsist.

90 Cass. 1st civ., 7/12/1994, n. 10516, *Cassina S.p.a.* v. *S.r.l. Steel Line*, *D. Aut.*, 1996, p. 410 at 416.

91 E. Valerio, 'Modelli e disegni ornamentali e diritto di autore' (1948) *D. Aut.* 317 at 322–3. Similarly, see also V. De Sanctis, 'Convegno per la tutela delle arti applicate all'industria, Milan 15–16 May 1940, La tutela giuridica dell'arte industriale, Relazioni generale preliminare della S.I.A.E.' (1940) *D. Aut.* 208 at 215; Piola Caselli, 'L'allacciamento della protezione dell'arte industriale con la protezione del diritto d'autore', p. 15, at 23–4; Bonasi Benucci, 'Forma del prodotto e sua tutela', p. 426; Fabiani, *Modelli e Design Industriali*, p. 93 (who would prefer a relatively short period but with possibility to renew); Pavanello, 'The protection of industrial design under Italian law', p. 175; ALAI, Travaux de la réunion d'Amsterdam, 10th report, Report of M. Luzzati, 'L'œuvre d'art appliquée à l'industrie', 1956, p. 138, at 139–40 (term too short).

92 Auletta, Ramella, Biamonti, Ghiron, De Sanctis and anonymous commentators after decisions of Cass., 19/12/1931, *D. Aut.*, 1932, p. 128; CA Milan, 17/7/1933, *Riv. Prop. Intell. e Ind.*, 1933, p. 305; Cass., 20/12/1937, *Riv. Prop. Intell. e Ind.*, 1937, p. 151; CA Brescia, 12/12/1933, *Riv. Prop. Intell. e Ind.*, 1933, p. 88; Cass., 25/1/1933, *Riv. Prop. Intell. e Ind.*, 1933, p. 88, all cited by Spallino, 'Rassegna di dottrina in tema disegni e modelli industriali 1883–1953', p. 276, at 281. See also Fabiani, *Modelli e Design Industriali*, p. 29.

much as possible,[93] some proposed to use other, previous, theories to complement the separability criterion when it does not give satisfactory results, e.g. the function of the product, destination of the form, reproducibility by mechanical means, aesthetic prevalence, autonomous character of the work of art as opposed to the accessorial character that the design or model may have as regards the industrial product, and the absence, in the work of art, of utilitarian aims which would be characteristic of designs and models.[94]

Some other commentators were against the separability doctrine because it is difficult and arbitrary to apply[95] or plainly 'wrong', 'illusory' or 'without sense'.[96]

In conclusion, at the end of this long period, even if the criterion of separability did not find unanimous agreement, it worked rather well even if it excluded most three-dimensional works of applied art. Because of this, if restrictive, effect, the law was very predictable.

[93] Di Franco, 'Nozione teorica e disciplina legale dell'arte applicata all'industria', p. 269, at 276; Barbieri, 'Tutela dell'arte applicata all'industria (Brevetti per modello – Concorrenza sleale)', p. 194 at 202.

[94] Fabiani, 'Problemi di protezione del design industriale', p. 271; P. Greco, *I Diritti sui Beni Immateriali* (Turin: Giappichelli, 1948), p. 171; Auteri, 'Industrial design', p. 583 citing T. Ascarelli, *Teoria della Concorrenza e dei Beni Immateriali* (Milan: Giuffrè, 1960), p. 677; E. Bonasi Benucci, *Tutela della forma nel diritto industriale* (Milan: Giuffrè, 1963), pp. 219ff; Fabiani, *Modelli e Design Industriali*, pp. 18ff. See also Z. Algardi, *Disegno Industriale e Arte Applicata* (Milan: Giuffrè, 1977), cited by Bergomi, 'Industrial design', p. 969. Contra: Vercellone, comment under Cass., 22/10/1956, n. 3806, *Franchi* v. *Arti Grafiche Cellerino*, *Riv. Dir. Comm.*, 1958, pp. 172ff at 174–5.

[95] Barbieri, 'Tutela dell'arte applicata all'industria (Brevetti per modello – Concorrenza sleale)', p. 194 at 198; Bonasi Benucci, 'Forma del prodotto e sua tutela', p. 426 at 441 (if separability is interpreted as artistic value, it leaves the judge arbiter of the merit of the work, who, not knowing how to do so, defers to an expert), also citing E. Valerio and Z. Algardi, *Il Diritto d'Autore* (Milan: Giuffrè, 1943), p. 38; Fabiani, 'Problemi di protezione del design industriale', pp. 270ff; S. Giudici, 'Dell'opera d'arte applicata all'industrial design' (1989) *Riv. Dir. Indus.* 268 at 277–8 (the utilitarian character of the work should not be an obstacle to copyright protection as architectural works and software can be protected, why not industrial design?); Bergomi, 'Industrial design', p. 968, also citing Algardi and De Sanctis.

[96] Morri, 'Le opere dell'industrial design tra diritto d'autore e tutela come modelli industriali: Deve cambiare tutto perché (quasi) nulla cambi?', p. 187 and note 26, citing Auletta-Mangini, *Delle invenzioni industriali. Dei modelli di utilità e dei disegni ornamentali. Della concorrenza, in Commentario al C.C.* a cura di Scialoja and Branca, Libro V, arts. 2584–601 (Bologna/Roma, 1973), 120; V. Di Cataldo, *L'Imitazione Servile* (Milan: Giuffrè, 1979), p. 128; F. Benussi, 'Protezione del disegno industriale – Necessità produttiva e finalità di una normativa', in *Disegno Industriale e Protezione Europea. Atti del Convegno Internazionale di Treviso 12–13 ottobre 1988* (Milan, 1989), 21, 30; W. Duchemin, 'La protection des arts appliqués dans la perspective d'un dépôt communautaire en matière des dessins et modèles industriels' (1978) 97 *Revue Internationale du Droit d'Auteur* 63 at 65.

8.2.4 *Fourth Period: 1996–1997: Back to Full Cumulation but with a Shorter Copyright Term?*

In 1996–7, there was a short period of about eight months during which Italy abolished the separability criterion. On 23/12/1996, Act n. 650 was adopted and its article 1(58) provided that 'copyright on works of industrial design is comprised in the protection of the Act of 22/4/1941, n. 633'. 'The exact limits, the procedure and the requirements for and manner of this protection were left to regulations that should have been issued by the Italian government.'[97] Supposedly, article 1(58) eliminated the separability criterion, thus reverting back to the first period of full cumulation.[98] However, the norm was unclear and the literature disagreed on the meaning of the article. Act n. 650/1996 was abrogated just a few months later by Act n. 266 of 7/8/1997 and, between 1997 and 2001, the country reverted back to the situation in the third period described above in section 8.2.3.

Act n. 266/1997 also enacted in its article 27(2) a rule which said that 'the duration of copyright protection for works of industrial design, under the 25/8/1940 Act n. 1411, cannot be superior to 15 years until the design directive is transposed'. Oddly, the provision did not specify the moment when the fifteen years had to be calculated. The provision was contrary to the EU Term Directive[99] and it was also not clear whether article 27(2) of Act n. 266 abolished article 5(2) of the Design Act 1940 according to which the provisions of the Copyright Act were not applicable to industrial designs and models.[100] Possibly, the provision meant to shorten the copyright term of protection of works of applied art to a maximum of fifteen years to coincide with the term of protection of designs under the new Design Directive but the commentators had different interpretations of the norm.[101]

[97] Pavanello, 'The protection of industrial design under Italian law', p. 154.

[98] Suthersanen, *Design Law in Europe*, p. 209; Pavanello, 'The protection of industrial design under Italian law', p. 153; Morri, 'Le opere dell'industrial design tra diritto d'autore e tutela come modelli industriali: Deve cambiare tutto perché (quasi) nulla cambi?', pp. 193–4. Marzano, 'An ill-designed protection for a well-designed product', p. 199, however, thinks that 'the plausible meaning of this provision was that of eliminating any distinction between the level of creativity requested for the protection of industrial design and that ordinarily required for other works of authorship'.

[99] L. Chimienti, 'Opere del disegno industriale e diritto d'autore, Una discutibile innovazione legislativa' (1997) *D. Aut.* 462.

[100] Ibid.

[101] For a list of commentators and summary of their views, see Morri, 'Le opere dell'industrial design tra diritto d'autore e tutela come modelli industriali: Deve cambiare tutto perché (quasi) nulla cambi?', p. 195.

8.2.5 *Fifth Period: 1997–2001: Back to Partial Cumulation and Demarcation for 3D Functional Objects*

During the fifth period, the 1941 Copyright Act and the 1940 Design Act still applied as well as the 1939 Patent Act. Apart from article 27 of Act n. 266/97 limiting the duration of works of applied art to fifteen years, the fifth period resembled the third in all points. Therefore, separability and demarcation for three-dimensional objects applied.

8.2.6 *Sixth Period: 2001 to Present: 'Artistic Value' Test*

An Act of 2 February 2001 implemented the Design Directive in Italy.[102] For the rest, the copyright remained in the main unchanged in relation to the provisions relevant to works of applied art,[103] and with the Design Directive having left almost no options to Member States, the legal picture is the same as in other Member States.

Article 22 of the Act implementing the Design Directive amended article 2(4) of the 1941 Copyright Act by removing the requirement for separability and adding to the categories of protected works, as a new point 10: 'industrial designs which possess in themselves creative character and artistic value'.[104] Separability is therefore a thing of the past. However, the double criteria of creative character and artistic value have been interpreted in various ways by courts.[105] Some courts have clearly stated these two requirements were different, others merged them into a single criterion and in any case gave either or both very different meanings. Most recently, many courts have interpreted the criterion of artistic value as 'the judgment of history'; in other words, art experts and

[102] Legislative Decree n. 95 of 2 February 2001 implementing Directive 98/71 (GURI N. 79 of 4 April 2001), which entered into force on 19 April 2001.

[103] One exception is that, unless agreed otherwise, the economic rights on works of industrial design created by employees during the course of their employment belong to the employer (art. 12 ter. of the 1941 Copyright Act as amended). Following the adoption of the InfoSoc directive, Act n. 68 of 9 April 2003 also implemented in Italian law more exceptions and re-worded the rights of reproduction, communication to the public and distribution.

[104] Article 2.10's ambiguous wording ('in themselves' and 'artistic value') does not mean that the criterion of separability has been reintroduced. See A. Musso, *Diritto di autore sulle opera dell'ingegno letterarie e artistiche* (Bologna: Zanichelli), p. 80; P. Marchetti and L. Ubertazzi, *Commentario breve alle leggi su proprieta intellettuale e concorrenza*, 4th edn (Padova: CEDAM, 2007), p. 345.

[105] E. Derclaye, 'Are fashion designers better protected in continental Europe than in the United Kingdom? A comparative analysis of the recent case law in France, Italy and the United Kingdom' (2010) 13(3) *Journal of World Intellectual Property* 315 at 323–7 and decisions cited. The article reviews the case law from 2004 to 2009. For details of the litigation post Design Directive, see also Marzano, 'An ill-designed protection for a well-designed product', pp. 219–21.

museums decide which works of applied art are protectable.[106] Much litigation on designs has been fought in this last period with varied results, best illustrated by the continuation, post implementation of the Design Directive, of the Le Corbusier chair saga started in the 1980s and concluded in the mid-1990s.[107] The resulting situation on the copyright/design interface in Italy during that period was therefore one of high legal uncertainty, owing to the different criteria the courts use to determine if a work of applied art can enjoy copyright protection.

However, in 2015, the Supreme Court endorsed the 'judgment of history' criterion and clarified that the two criteria of creative character and artistic value are separate. The first means a 'personal and individual expression'. As to the second, the court first uttered that the criterion cannot be defined exhaustively but a series of objective and subjective parameters can be listed.[108] The subjective parameters, such as the taste, artistic sensibility, aesthetic sense, etc. of the person who considers the work, must be corroborated with objective parameters, the most relevant of which is the recognition, by the relevant cultural institutions, of the value of the design and which transcends functionality and mere elegance. This parameter can be evidenced by the exhibition of the design in museums, prizes, publication in non-commercial specialist reviews, etc. This decision ends the period of uncertainty. That said, the 'judgment of history' criterion is problematic as it decides what is protectable *ex post* and is discriminatory against young, upcoming designers. The court recognised the problem and said that the criterion is not an absolute one and each case has to be decided on a case-by-case basis.

8.3 Analysis

In this final section, we draw conclusions as to the efficiency of the law in the different periods and the reasons for changing it. We also evaluate whether one type of system (full cumulation, partial cumulation or demarcation) is better on the basis of the Italian experience, also drawing from Italian economic and design history.

The Italian history of the copyright/design interface prior to the Design Directive in practice boils down to two periods: one of full cumulation

[106] Marzano, 'An ill-designed protection for a well-designed product', pp. 213 and 227 and references cited.
[107] See above, notes 78 and 80. For details of the Le Corbusier litigation after the implementation of the Design Directive in Italy, see Marzano, 'An ill-designed protection for a well-designed product', pp. 221–5.
[108] Italian Supreme Court, Judgment No. 23292, of 13 November 2015, *Metalco S.p.a., Metalco S.r.l.* v. *City Design S.r.l. and Others* (street shelter lacks artistic value).

and one of partial cumulation with demarcation for 3D functional objects. Over a century and a half, a system of all or nothing shifted between two extremes. The first period spanning sixty years from 1865 to 1925 was definitely a disaster in terms of design protection – since the Act's term of protection was so short, there was an extremely low number of designs registered. What can be said, though, is that in the only reported decision on a registered design, the court held it was unprotected. Copyright therefore filled the gap, but since there was so little litigation, it is hard to say whether full cumulation was a satisfactory system. However, in theory, provided a design was original and new, there could be an overlap and there could have been some regime clashes. While the Patent Act provided for the right to belong to the employer if the employee created the design during the course of his duties, the Copyright Act was silent, so a clash could have occurred if the courts had interpreted the Copyright Act the opposite way. The same could have happened if the courts had interpreted the infringement conditions differently or created different exceptions.

Italian economic and design history for this period and up to the Second World War is a probable additional cause for the small amount of litigation. Italy had a very late industrial revolution. Society was mainly rural and there was very low industrialisation until the 1890s and very little mass production until after the Second World War, so Italian design boomed only thereafter.[109] It must have meant that it was hard to manufacture copies of 3D products at least. In addition, as there was very little export, Italian design must have been barely known abroad, and thus it must have been rare for cheap knock-off copies made abroad to flood the Italian market. Most probably, the combination of a short design protection making knock-off copies less interesting to make as the cost of the original must have gone down anyway after the two or four years of protection had lapsed, and the economic structure in the design industries (a vast majority of small family-owned workshops), must have made it useless to litigate: most designers had no money nor time to sue, while the time that litigation takes would have been working against them.

From 1925 to 2001 (not counting the few months in the mid-1990s where full cumulation arguably resumed during which in any case there was hardly any relevant case law), there were more decisions but the vast majority of the 3D objects were declared unprotected by copyright while the vast majority of 2D designs were declared protectable. On the other hand, design protection was still very short – four years until 1977 – and

[109] P. Sparke, *Design in Italy, 1870 to the Present* (New York: Abbeville Press, 1988), pp. 15–20 at 41.

hardly litigated upon, probably for that very reason. For the period from around 1940 to 1977, one of the factors from the previous period, i.e. in the vast majority, a structure made of very small companies,[110] can also explain the relatively low registered design application and litigation level. In addition, the fact that much design was highly or solely functional[111] may also explain why there was no protection by either copyright or design and thus virtually no litigation on registered design right. Instead, the aura and quality of the design that justified high prices which helped recoup costs, and/or the patronage that designers benefited from,[112] probably meant there was no need for design protection or no need to sue if there was. Also, the mid-1970s were years of profound insecurity in Italy – economically, socially and culturally.[113] Indeed, design applications went down a lot in 1973–5 (there is no data for 1976–7), then go up hugely in 1978–9 (9,464 in 1978 and 8,172 in 1979 from 2,984 in 1975, ca. triple) because by the mid-1970s the economic slump was over but most probably also because of the increase in the duration of registered design protection from four to fifteen years with the 1977 Act. Thereafter and until the 1990s, the economic structure remained rather similar (majority of small firms in the field of design) and high quality design still sold well abroad. From then on, it seems that fluctuations in applications vary with economic slumps.[114] Applications go down a lot in 1981–3, are back up between 1984 and 1986, then down again in 1987–9 and the early 1990s. They shoot off in 1998 until 2002, most likely because of the adoption of the Design Directive (this effect is also seen for many other Member States). Then applications go down dramatically from 2003. (A probable cause is the entry into force of the Community Design System; this effect is also seen in other Member States.) Applications then more or less stabilise between 2008 and 2014.[115] Since 2001, copyright litigation involving designs has carried

[110] P. Sparke, *Design in Italy, 1870 to the Present*, p. 92 and p. 165 respectively. (In 1947, 90 per cent of Italian firms employed only five people and fewer, and in 1971, 81.8 per cent of manufacturing firms had fewer than five workers.)

[111] Ibid., pp. 112–13, 176. For instance, the brothers Castiglioni made lamps whose appearance was dictated solely by their technological and utilitarian constraints, e.g. the Tubino lamp which stood up by twisting its tubular structure (1951). Another example by the brothers is the Luminator consisting of a stand with three feet, a column and a light bulb (1955). Another example is Colombini's plastic dustbin manufactured by Kartell in 1955. See ibid., pp. 121 and 128–9.

[112] Ibid., p. 116. [113] Ibid., p. 195.

[114] Ibid., p. 205. In Italy in 1980–3, there was a slump in domestic demand and exports, with a small recovery in 1983.

[115] For the detailed statistics, see graph in the Annex in the last chapter. Interestingly, the financial crisis does not seem to have had a big effect; a probable reason may be the banks' bail out.

on steadily. Litigation on the registered design also picked up after the implementation of the Design Directive.[116] It could well be because the separability doctrine disappeared leading, among others, to a renewed interest in copyright protection by firms holding rights on iconic designs, as the Le Corbusier recent saga suggests. Of course, empirical analysis must be carried out to verify these suggestions but we have already highlighted a number of important factors which will enable us to start such analysis.

As to why the Italian legislature modified the law on the copyright/design interface in 1941, it was a very particular situation as it was only down to a single man and his special influence as member of the Supreme Court and senator rapporteur of the 1941 Copyright Bill.[117] Of course, Piola Caselli also managed to convince other judges, commentators and members of Parliament and that must have helped. The separability test also had a very long life and the question to be asked at this juncture is whether the separability criterion worked well. It seemed like it did as, in the end, its application by the vast majority of courts was quite consistent and simply boiled down to the exclusion of functional three-dimensional objects and a few functional two-dimensional ones (such as those mentioned as examples by the Court of Cassation in its 1990 decision, e.g. typographical characters, symbols on a watch). Because of its relatively straightforward interpretation, it was rather simple to use, much less arbitrary than some commentators had criticised and certainly better than the current criterion of artistic value, which definitely is arbitrary as it leaves the art experts as judges of the copyrightability of works of applied art. This demarcation for 3D objects helped avoid overlap problems down the line since only one type of protection could apply, that of the Design Act or that of the Copyright Act. In effect, it was impossible to find any decision where an overlap problem arose. This did not mean that overlap problems did not exist in practice but the lack of decisions at least shows that the iceberg was probably very small. The lack of lobbying to change the criterion over such a long period of time shows that the design industry was not so unhappy with the test as to push for reform.[118] On the other hand, the design industry was unhappy with the 1868 and 1940 Design Acts, especially the term of protection, but, despite numerous attempts, did not have enough clout to effect a legal change until the 1977

116 See Derclaye (above, note 105) (at least around twenty reported cases between 2001 and 2009 in the – broadly defined – area of fashion design).

117 Thanks to Prof. Ricolfi for confirming this and adding that Piola Caselli had a lot of personal prestige.

118 M. Ricolfi also shares this view.

Act, which lengthened the duration of the design right, and then until the Design Directive, which gave Italy a 'proper', in the sense of efficient and full-blown, design law. This may mean that design creation (at least for 3D products) was not really affected by the Design Act's poor protection and even possibly in some cases was incentivised by it.[119] A number of factors helped Italian design to thrive including quality, patronage and incessant innovation.[120] Indeed, this constant innovation may well have been caused by the short period of protection especially for designs affected by fashion effects and thus quickly became outdated.

In summary, the separability criterion was a success in terms of its ease of application and relatively strong legal certainty. It seems, therefore, simply on the basis of the Italian experience (for a complete analysis examining all systems, see Chapter 12), that a system based on conceptual separability (understood in the first interpretation explained in section 8.2.3) would work well. However, it would need to be coupled with a reasonably long registered design protection so that 3D designs, and the remainder of uncopyrightable 2D designs, are adequately protected. This is the case now with the Design Directive. As to whether a system of full cumulation would work, it is not possible to say on the basis of the Italian experience as it did not really exist because of the extremely short (two years) period of protection for designs during 1868 and 1925 which led to very low numbers of registered designs and consequently scarce case law. Both the copyright and design laws were also rather sketchy or non-existent on certain points, so it was unclear whether regime clashes could have occurred. Under a full cumulation system, however, legal certainty is also high as it is clear that each design or work of applied art is protected both by the Design and the Copyright Acts if it meets all conditions, provided such conditions are clear. But a full cumulation system can only work if the rules are well aligned so as to avoid regime clashes and overprotection.[121] As the law stands in most EU countries, there is at present a high potentiality of regime clashes, mainly owing to the different tests of infringement and exceptions in copyright and design law. In conclusion, both systems

[119] See e.g. P. Belleflamme, www.ipdigit.eu/2010/09/what-is-the-link-between-competition-and-innovation, pointing out that establishing the link between competition and innovation is complex and depends on many economic relationships that vary across market environments. Many empirical research findings thus have found contradicting results on this issue.

[120] On such innovation, see Sparke, *Design in Italy, 1870 to the Present*, pp. 165, 195, 205.

[121] E. Derclaye and M. Leistner, *Intellectual Property Overlaps: A European Perspective* (Oxford: Hart, 2011), ch. 7, sections 4 and 5.

could therefore work but giving very different results – with full cumulation, double protection creates very strong and long protection for all designs, while under a system of partial cumulation with demarcation for 3D designs, the protection is weaker as it is generally unique (i.e. via design law only) and shorter. The vast majority of 2D designs, on the other hand, are almost always separable, and therefore benefit from both copyright and design protection if they fulfil both laws' protection requirements. Thus full cumulation and the separability doctrine lead to identical results for most 2D designs.

9 'Courts Have Twisted Themselves into Knots' (and the Twisted Knots Remain to Untangle): US Copyright Protection for Applied Art after *Star Athletica*

*Jane C. Ginsburg**

Courts have twisted themselves into knots trying to create a test to effectively ascertain whether the artistic aspects of a useful article can be identified separately from and exist independently of the article's utilitarian function.

Varsity Brands, Inc. v. *Star Athletica, LLC*, 799 F 3d 468, 478 (6th Cir. 2015), *aff'd*, 197 L. Ed. 2d 354 (2017), quoting *Inhale, Inc.* v. *Starbuzz Tobacco, Inc.*, 755 F 3d 1038, 1041 n.2 (9th Cir. 2014), quoting *Masquerade Novelty, Inc.* v. *Unique Indus.*, 912 F 2d 663, 670 (3d Cir. 1990)

9.1 Introduction

United States copyright law explicitly enumerates 'pictorial, graphic or sculptural works' (henceforth 'PGS works') among the subject-matter of copyright.[1] These include 'works of artistic craftsmanship', but copyright covers the design of a useful article 'only if, and only to the extent that, such design incorporates pictorial, graphic, or sculptural features that can be identified separately from, and are capable of existing independently of, the utilitarian aspects of the article'.[2] Inseparable design features, whatever their aesthetic appeal, are not protected under copyright law; any coverage available to the designers must come from other regimes, particularly federal utility or design

* Many thanks to Robert E. Bishop, Columbia Law School class of 2017, and to Nathalie Russell, Columbia Law School class of 2018, for most helpful research assistance, and to Lionel Bently, June Besek, Paul Goldstein, Michael Heller, Rob Kasunic, Philippa Loengard, Paolo Marzano, Bill Patry and Antoon Quaedvlieg for trenchant critiques and valuable suggestions, and to participants in staff seminars at Columbia Law School and at the University of Johannesburg law faculty for probing questions. Portions of this chapter are drawn from an affidavit on US law ('Certificat de coutume') filed (in French) in *Knoll Int'l* v. *M Top Mobilier*, File No. 20150086, Court of Appeals of Paris, GR No. 15/05833 and from an earlier and more extensive (but pre-*Star Athletica*) version published at 40 *Columbia Journal of Law & the Arts* 1 (2016).

[1] 17 USC s. 102(a)(5). [2] 17 USC s. 101.

patent law.[3] The 'separability' test, as we will see, has resisted coherent application, but one thing is clear: in the 1976 Copyright Act, Congress intended to impose a high threshold to copyrightability of useful articles. Copyright, which 'subsists' in a work of authorship upon creation and lasts for seventy years *post mortem auctoris* (or for works made for hire, or anonymous or pseudonymous works, ninety-five years following first publication),[4] was not the appropriate regime for most industrial designs. Whatever 'separability' means, it excludes more designs than would a test that merely inquires whether there exist other designs for the same kind of useful article. The 'separability' threshold therefore will in most cases set a higher bar than the idea/expression 'merger' doctrine. The latter inquires whether the 'idea' is susceptible to multiple forms of expression, or whether instead the plaintiff's work represents the only way, or one of only a few ways, of presenting the idea. By contrast, that the overall shape of a table or chair may be expressed through multiple different designs does not itself suffice to make any one of those designs 'separable' in whole or in part.[5]

This chapter will first review the statutory definitions of a PGS work, and then will address the genesis of the troublesome 'separability' requirement. Next, the chapter will analyse the attempts of administrative and judicial authorities to articulate a predictable test that remains faithful to the text and legislative history of the 1976 Copyright Act, culminating in the US Supreme Court's 2017 decision in *Star Athletica* v. *Varsity Brands*.[6] Finally, this chapter will offer a conclusion and a legislative proposal. I conclude that the statutory requirements of separate identifiability and independent existence apply to 'features' of the design, not to the entire shape of a useful article; attempts to extend separability analysis to the useful article's abstract form as a whole prove unworkable. Accordingly, rather than continuing to struggle with an intractable statutory copyrightability standard, this chapter proposes the enlargement of Title 17's *sui generis* design protection regime to cover original designs of most useful articles.

[3] For a cross-IP discipline view that encompasses design protection, see Peter Lee and Madhavi Sunder, 'The Law of Look and Feel' (2017) 90 S. Cal. L. Rev. 529. For designs that acquire secondary meaning, trade mark law may afford more useful recourse than copyright or design patent law. See, e.g., Dan Hunter and Suzannah Wood, 'The Laws of Design in the Age of Mechanical Reproduction' (2016) 37 *Adelaide Law Review* 403.

[4] At the time of passage of the 1976 Act, the terms were fifty years p.m.a., or seventy-five years after first publication.

[5] See Jane C. Ginsburg and Robert A. Gorman, *Copyright: Concepts and Insights* (New York: Foundation Press, 2012), p. 50.

[6] 197 L. Ed. 2d 354 (2017).

9.2 Statutory Standards

The US Copyright Act protects PGS works, including applied art, but distinguishes the designs of 'useful articles' from non-utilitarian works; the latter include those whose function is 'merely to portray the appearance of the article or to convey information'.[7] While the statute denominates the design of a useful article as PGS work 'only if, and only to the extent that, such design incorporates pictorial, graphic, or sculptural features that can be identified separately from, and are capable of existing independently of, the utilitarian aspects of the article', non-utilitarian works are PGS works in themselves, and there is no need to undertake an inquiry into the 'separability' of aesthetic and useful elements. Such works need not be devoid of purpose, but their potential informational or depictive or even affective utility, such as a religious painting's stimulation of spiritual contemplation,[8] is not the kind of usefulness that the statute reserves to the patent system (or to the public domain).[9] Similarly, a two- or three-dimensional depiction of a useful article, such as a model aeroplane or a drawing of a bottle, is not itself a useful article. The statute, however, makes clear that a protected representation of a useful article gives the author no rights in the article depicted.[10] A blueprint for constructing a car is not a 'useful article' because its functions are to portray the appearance of the car, and to convey information about how to build it. The car, once built, however, is a useful article; any copyright would be limited to elements, such as a hood ornament, that are separable from the car's utilitarian aspects.

Section 113(b) warns that '[t]his title does not afford, to the owner of copyright in a work that portrays a useful article as such, any greater or lesser rights with respect to the making, distribution, or display of the useful article so portrayed than those afforded to such works under the law'.[11] Thus, Claes

[7] 17 USC s. 101, defining 'useful article' as 'an article having an intrinsic utilitarian function that is not merely to portray the appearance of the article or to convey information'.

[8] See, e.g., *Masquerade Novelty* v. *Unique Indus.*, 912 F 2d 663, 671 (3d Cir. 1990):

> When hung on a wall, a painting may evoke a myriad of human emotions, but we would not say that the painting is not copyrightable because its artistic elements could not be separated from the emotional effect its creator hoped it would have on persons viewing it. The utilitarian nature of an animal nose mask or a painting of the crucifixion of Jesus Christ inheres solely in its appearance, regardless of the fact that the nose mask's appearance is intended to evoke mirth and the painting's appearance a feeling of religious reverence.

[9] For detailed discussion of that policy choice, see Viva Moffat, 'The Copyright/Patent Boundary' (2014) 48 *University of Richmond Law Review* 611, 638–9 (the intention to confine functional features of useful articles to the patent realm is implicit in the statute and the legislative history); but see *Star Athletica*, 197 L. Ed. 2d at 371 (rejecting 'argument that the only protectable features are those that play absolutely no role in an article's function').

[10] 17 USC s. 113(b). [11] Ibid.

Oldenburg's monumental sculptures of everyday items such as clothespins, baseball bats and trowels[12] do not give Oldenburg a monopoly in the everyday item. By the same token, the depiction of a useful article such as a chair does not confer on the creator of the two-dimensional drawing or three-dimensional model of the chair the exclusive right to reproduce the chair.[13] In other words, there is no two-step path to chair copyrightability by first drawing a picture of the chair. René Magritte's painting *The Treachery of Images*, captioned 'Ceci n'est pas une pipe' ('This is not a pipe'), helpfully instructs: Magritte has made a picture of a pipe. It is a pictorial work; it is not an actual, functioning pipe (indeed, that is the point of the painting). Under section 113(b), Magritte's copyright does not extend to smoking paraphernalia that looks like his representation of a pipe. Section 113(b) thus reifies Magritte's jest: a picture of a pipe is not an actual pipe; the copyright in a picture of a pipe is not a copyright in an actual pipe.[14]

The statute also specifies, in section 113(a), that the author of a PGS work has the exclusive right to reproduce it 'in or on any kind of article, whether useful or otherwise'.[15] For example, an artist holds the exclusive right to reproduce her drawing onto a t-shirt, a tablecloth, a shower curtain, etc. (thus, Magritte's heirs enjoy the exclusive right in the USA to reproduce the pipe image on a variety of merchandising properties); a sculptor can authorise or prohibit the incorporation of her work into a paperweight or to ornament fireplace andirons.

In the case of three-dimensional works, however, a complication arises, that I have called the 'birth order problem'. The statute's definition of a

[12] See, e.g., http://oldenburgvanbruggen.com/largescaleprojects/lsp.htm (includes photographs of clothespin, baseball bat, trowel and other large-scale depictions of ordinary objects).

[13] See, e.g., *Niemi* v. *American Axle Mfg*, 2006 *WL* 2077590 (ED Mich. 2006) (unauthorised manufacturing of a machine based on copyrighted technical drawing is not infringement).

[14] Cf. *Eliya, Inc.* v. *Kohl's Dept Stores*, 82 USPQ 2d 1088 (SDNY 2006) (holding without reference to s. 113(b), that copyright in a two-dimensional work portraying a three-dimensional useful article – a shoe – does not confer an exclusive right to produce the article portrayed; the court observed that the distinction 'brings to mind Magritte's famous painting of a pipe: [Eliya's two-dimensional rendition of the shoe] n'est pas une chaussure, but is merely a depiction of one').

[15] 17 USC s. 113(a). The examples that follow all illustrate reproduction of the PGS work 'on' a useful article. It is less clear what it means to reproduce the work 'in' a useful article. (Thanks to Paul Goldstein for this observation.) The House Report refers to PGS works 'employed *as the design* of a useful article', H.R. Rep. No. 94–1476, 94th Cong. 2d Sess. at 105 (1976) (emphasis supplied), which suggests that the rights in the pre-existing PGS work extend to authorising or prohibiting the incorporation of the design not only as a discrete decorative element, such as the hood ornament of a car, but also as the entire shape of the useful article, for example a sculpture hollowed out to serve as a vase. As will be discussed further, below, the copyright inheres in the PGS work, not in the useful article 'in or on' which it is reproduced.

PGS work leads to a distinction between incorporating a pre-existing sculptural work 'in or on' a useful article, on the one hand, and altering the form of the work in order to adapt it into a useful article, or designing the work as a useful article from the start, on the other. The copyright in the original standalone sculpture subsists as a PGS work regardless of its reproduction 'in or on' a useful article. But the adapted version becomes a useful article, and, as with the work initially designed to be a useful article, these versions' characterisation as a PGS work in their own right will depend on whether their form, or parts of their form, are 'separable' from the article's function.

For example, imagine a sculpture of a crocodile, with moving jaws. The sculptor's copyright extends to inserting salad tongs into the jaws; in that event, the sculpture is reproduced 'on' a useful article, and its legal status as a PGS work remains unchanged. But if the article consists of salad tongs shaped to resemble a crocodile's toothy maw, then it is a useful article whose status as a PGS work turns on the separability test. In the first crocodile example, the sculpture pre-exists its encounter with a useful article; in the second, the three-dimensional form is contemporaneously a useful article. This birth order distinction may yield arbitrary outcomes, among them the apparent privileging of shapes that are sub-optimally functional (the first set of crocodile salad tongs may not seize salad as well as the second). The Supreme Court has now ruled that 'copyright protection extends to pictorial, graphic and sculptural works regardless of whether they were created as free-standing art or as features of useful articles'[16] – so long as the features can be seen as existing independently of the article's utility. As we shall see, however, as that proviso portends, the Court has not in fact fully eradicated the birth order distinction.

If the article at issue has 'an intrinsic utilitarian function that is not merely to portray the appearance of the article or to convey information', then the statute directs that copyright extends only to those elements (if any) of the object's design that are separable from its function:

> 'Pictorial, graphic, and sculptural works' include ... works of artistic craftsmanship insofar as their form but not their mechanical or utilitarian aspects are concerned; the design of a useful article, as defined in this section, shall be considered a pictorial, graphic, or sculptural work only if, and only to the extent that, such design incorporates pictorial, graphic, or sculptural features that can be identified separately from, and are capable of existing independently of, the utilitarian aspects of the article.[17]

[16] 197 L. Ed. 2d at 367.
[17] 17 USC s. 101 (defining pictorial, graphic and sculptural works).

For our crocodile-shaped salad tongs to be protectable in whole or in part as a PGS work, it would be necessary to determine which if any design features are separable from the function of seizing and serving salad. Perhaps a shaft shaped to resemble the reptile's scaly tail and body would qualify, but the snapping toothsome jaws perform the function of tongs. Do they nonetheless incorporate 'separable' features, so that the entire shape of the tongs would qualify for copyright protection? As the chorus of judicial laments quoted at the outset of this chapter reveals, courts have failed to interpret the meaning of the statutory separability standard in any consistent or coherent manner. Nor, as we shall see, has the Supreme Court succeeded in untangling the 'knots' into which the lower 'courts have twisted themselves'. Before turning to the divergent and often contradictory judicial attempts, we should first detail the genesis of the statutory rule.

9.3 Genesis of the Separability Rule

The 1909 Copyright Act listed 'works of art' within the categories of registrable subject-matter, and further included 'models or designs for works of art'.[18] Copyright Office regulations promulgated in 1910 clarified that the statute did not cover industrial designs. According to the Office:

> *Works of art.*—This term includes all works belonging to the so-called fine arts. (Paintings, drawings, and sculpture). Productions of the industrial arts utilitarian in purpose and character are not subject to copyright registration, even if artistically made or ornamented.[19]

While the regulation might seem to preclude protection for useful articles under copyright law, the Copyright Office nonetheless registered 'clocks, candlesticks, inkstands, door knockers, ashtrays and saltshakers – a far cry from the standard conception of the "fine arts"'.[20]

By the late 1940s, the Copyright Office recognised the need to update its regulations more specifically to address the availability of protection

[18] Act of March 4, 1909, 60th Cong., 2d Sess., 35 Stat. 1075, s. 5(g).

[19] Rules and Regulations for the Registration of Claims to Copyright, Copyright Office Bulletin No. 15, 8 (1910).

[20] Shira Perlmutter, 'Conceptual Separability and Copyright in the Designs of Useful Articles' (1990) 37 *Journal of the Copyright Society of the USA* 339, 342–3. See generally The Meaning of 'Writings' in the Copyright Clause of the Constitution, Study No. 3 in Senate Comm. on the Judiciary, 86th Cong., 1st Session, Copyright Law Revision: Studies Prepared for the Subcomm. on Patents, Trademarks and Copyrights Pursuant to S. Res. 53, Studies 1–4, 63 (Comm. Print 1960) for an in-depth analysis of the evolution of the definition of 'works of art' and the meaning of 'writings' under the statutes and case law of the United States.

for industrial design. Its revised regulations no longer interpolated 'fine' before 'work of art', and explicitly provided protection for useful articles 'includ[ing] works of artistic craftsmanship, insofar as their form but not their mechanical or utilitarian aspect are concerned, such as artistic jewelry, enamels, glassware, and tapestries, as well as all works belonging to the fine arts, such as paintings, drawings and sculpture'.[21] While this regulation did not explicitly impose a separability requirement, the language implied that the 'form' of a work must be distinct from its 'mechanical or utilitarian aspects'.[22]

These regulations figured significantly in the Supreme Court's 1954 decision in *Mazer* v. *Stein*, which concerned statuettes of dancers. The 'statuettes were sold in quantity throughout the country both as lamp bases and as statuettes ... [but] [t]he sales in lamp form accounted for all but an insignificant portion of ... sales'.[23] (See images in Figures 9.1 and 9.2.)[24]

The Court embarked on a review of the relevant statutes, legislative history and Copyright Office practices, noting the evolution of protection from 'works of the fine arts' in 1870 to 'all the writings of an author' in 1909, to limiting protection to the 'form but not ... mechanical or utilitarian aspects' of a work of artistic craftsmanship in 1949.[25] As a first step in its analysis, the Court considered whether the statuettes, as sculptures, were copyrightable. Given the gradual expansion of copyright to cover artistic works in general, the Court declined to find the statuettes too lacking in artistic merit to warrant protection. The Court noted that '[i]individual perception of the beautiful is too varied a power to permit a narrow or rigid concept of art ... Such expression, whether meticulously delineating the model or mental image or conveying the meaning by modernistic form or color, is copyrightable.'[26]

The *Mazer* Court next rejected the proposition that 'congressional enactment of the design patent laws should be interpreted as denying protection to artistic articles embodied or reproduced in manufactured articles'.[27] Emphasising the differences in the nature and scope of copyright law and patent law, the Court ruled that the patent law did not preempt copyright protection for artistic works incorporated in useful articles: 'the patentability of the statuettes, fitted as lamps or unfitted, does not bar copyright as works of art'.[28] The Court noted that the 'dichotomy of

[21] 37 CFR §202.8 (1949). [22] Ibid. [23] *Mazer* v. *Stein*, 347 US 201, 203 (1954).

[24] Photograph of Dancer Statuette, Zvi Rosen, *Mazer and the Balinese Dancer*, www.zvirosen.com/2017/03/23/mazer-and-the-balinese-dancer/ (viewed 24 March 2017) (image located on website identified as Curved Ballet Dancer—Female, H 1723, July 15, 1949, but no additional source information available); image of Lamp Advertisement, http://tushnet.blogspot.com/2012/09/thats-where-light-is.html (image located on website, but no additional source information available).

[25] 347 US 201 at 211–12. [26] Ibid. at 214. [27] Ibid. at 215. [28] Ibid. at 217.

Figure 9.1 Dancer statuette

protection for the aesthetic is not beauty and utility but art for the copyright and the invention of original and ornamental design for design patents'.[29] Hence, a design might be both a work of art for purposes of copyright and, if sufficiently novel, an ornamental design for purposes of

[29] Ibid. at 218.

Figure 9.2 Lamp advertisement

design patents. But, the Court stressed, citing the Copyright Office regulation, 'artistic articles are protected in "form but not their mechanical or utilitarian aspects"'.[30]

Thus, whether the dancer began as a freestanding sculpture subsequently incorporated into a lamp base, or instead was created to serve as a lamp base, the work remained a sculpture, and on that ground was copyrightable as a work of art (assuming sufficient originality).[31] As the

[30] Ibid.

[31] See ibid. at 218–19: 'Nor do we think the subsequent registration of a work of art published as an element in a manufactured article, is a misuse of the copyright. This is

author of a leading study on copyright protection of PGS works observed: '*Mazer* ... established the principle that a work that is otherwise copyrightable does not lose protection when it is incorporated as part of a useful article ... it did not, however, address the more difficult question of how to determine when elements of a useful article may constitute a copyrightable work of art.'[32]

It is that 'more difficult question' that the separability rule, as it emerged from later Copyright Office regulations, was supposed to resolve. Three years after *Mazer*, the Office's first attempt read:

> When the shape of an article is dictated by, or is necessarily responsive to, the requirements of its utilitarian function, its shape, though unique and attractive, cannot qualify it as a work of art. If the sole intrinsic function of an article is its utility, the fact that it is unique and attractively shaped will not qualify it as a work of art. However, where the object is clearly a work of art in itself, the fact it is also a useful article will not preclude its registration.[33]

In 1960, the Copyright Office introduced the separability test, updating the regulation to read:

> If the sole intrinsic function of an article is its utility, the fact that that article is unique and attractively shaped will not qualify it as a work of art. However, if the shape of a utilitarian article incorporates features, such as artistic sculpture, carving, or pictorial representation, which can be identified separately and are capable of existing independently as a work of art such features will be eligible for registration.[34]

The amended regulation failed to produce clarity. It provided no guidance on how to determine the 'sole intrinsic function' of an item, nor did it explain how separability was to be judged. 'Did the artistic features have to be physically separable? In what sense did they have to be "identified" separately? How were these determinations to be made?'[35]

Perhaps as a result of this lack of guidance, few judicial decisions post-*Mazer* contained any meaningful discussion of the separability standard. When courts denied protection, they tended to 'rely on a failure to meet the requirement of original authorship rather than' the separability standard, and when they extended protection, courts tended either simply to state their conclusion that the work was copyrightable, or to 'carve out distinct categories of works as either protectable or not', relying on whether 'the category would traditionally be considered a work of art'.[36]

not different from the registration of a statuette and its later embodiment in an industrial article.'

32 Perlmutter, 'Conceptual Separability', 345. 33 37 CFR §202.100(c) (1957).

34 37 CFR §202.10(c) (1960). 35 Perlmutter, 'Conceptual Separability', 346.

36 Perlmutter, 'Conceptual Separability', 346–7, citing, among other cases, *L. Batlin & Son, Inc.* v. *Snyder*, 536 F 2d 486 (2d Cir. 1976) for failure to meet original authorship,

In a study produced in anticipation of what would become the 1976 Copyright Act, the Copyright Office revisited the problem of applied art, and proposed a new form of protection for useful articles:

> In the years since the *Mazer* decision, full protection under the copyright law has not proved inappropriate for 'works of art' used as a design or decoration of useful articles. We do not believe, however, that it would be appropriate to extend the copyright law to industrial designs as such. In this area there is a delicate balance between the need for protection on the part of those who originate and invest in a design, and the possible effect of protection, if overextended, in restraining competition. The term of copyright . . . is too long for ordinary design protection. And there are other fundamentals of the copyright statute – the provisions on notice, deposit, registration, publication, and liability of innocent distributors of infringing articles, for example – that are not suitable for the entire range of industrial designs.[37]

While recognising that a work of art could serve to decorate a useful article, the Copyright Office disfavoured copyright protection for industrial design in general, largely out of concern for anti-competitive consequences.[38] It preferred a mid-measure between a copyright protection limited to pre-existing works of art incorporated in useful articles (such as the *Mazer* statuette) and full-on copyright protection for the whole domain of industrial design. The Copyright Office therefore recommended protection for the artistic design of a useful article, but for a shorter term, and with more restrictive formalities. But only Congress could establish such a *sui generis* regime for applied art.

The Senate proposed such a system. Title II of the copyright reform bill would have given specific protection to 'ornamental designs of useful articles'.[39] The Title defined a useful article as 'an article which in normal use has an intrinsic utilitarian function that is not merely to portray the appearance of the article or to convey information'.[40] The design was defined to 'consist of those aspects or elements of the article, including its two-dimensional or three-dimensional features of shape and surface, which make up the appearance of the article',[41] and was deemed to be

Tennessee Fabricating Co. v. *Moultrie Mfg Co.*, 421 F 2d 279 (5th Cir. 1970) for finding copyrightability without additional explanation, and a pre-*Mazer* decision involving the same plaintiff and similar statuette-lamp bases, *Rosenthal* v. *Stein*, 205 F 2d 633 (9th Cir. 1953) for relying on categories of works traditionally considered copyrightable works of fine art.

[37] Report of the Register of Copyrights on the General Revision of the US Copyright Law, 87th Cong., 1st Sess. 14–15 (Comm. Print 1961).

[38] Ibid. at 13: 'We do not believe that it would be appropriate to extend the copyright law to industrial designs as such. In this area there is a delicate balance between the need for protection on the part of those who originate and invest in a design, and the possible effect of protection, if overextended, in restraining competition.'

[39] S. Rep. 94–473, Title II. [40] Ibid. at §201(b)(1). [41] Ibid. at §201(b)(2).

ornamental if 'it is intended to make the article attractive or distinct in appearance'.[42] Protection would attach only if the work were original, not commonplace or a minor variation of a pre-existing design, not 'dictated solely by a utilization function of the article that embodies it', and not apparel.[43] Protection would last for an initial term of five years, with the possibility of an additional five years upon application.[44] The Act would create a unique marking symbol – '(D)' – to cover such designs.[45] 'Protection … [would] be lost if application for registration of the design is not made within six months after the date on which the design was first made public.'[46] The Senate proposal, in short, contained what was effectively a *sui generis* regime to cover only the artistic design elements of a useful article.

When the Senate proposal reached the House of Representatives, however, the House Judiciary Committee 'deleted Title II of the bill entirely'.[47] The Judiciary Committee explained that it chose to remove the section 'in part because the new form of design protection provided by Title II could not truly be considered copyright protection and therefore appropriately within the scope of copyright revision'.[48] According to the House Report, the Senate proposal failed to address two key questions: 'first, what agency should administer this new design protection system and, second, should typeface designs be given the protections of the title?'[49] In addition, the Judiciary Committee gave weight to the Justice Department's objection that 'Title II would create a new monopoly which has not been justified by a showing that its benefits will outweigh the disadvantage of removing such designs from free public use'.[50] For the Justice Department, the Senate's amendment would have protected subject-matter that was in fact in the public domain; creation of a new monopoly right in unpatented industrial design therefore required a heavy burden of justification, unmet in this instance.

After eliminating Title II, the House Judiciary Committee chose to 'revise the definition of "pictorial, graphic, and sculptural works" in § 101 to clarify the distinction between works of applied art subject to protection under the bill and industrial designs not subject to copyright protection'.[51] The final bill drafted its definitions of pictorial, graphic and sculptural works as well as of useful articles '[i]n accordance with the Supreme Court's decision in *Mazer*',[52] thus yielding the current § 101 definition with its requirement that the design features of a useful article be separately identifiable and capable of existing independently of the article's utilitarian aspects. The final bill's definition of 'useful article' tracked the 1960 Copyright Office regulation, with one important change: while the

[42] Ibid. at §201(b)(3). [43] Ibid. at §202. [44] Ibid. at §205. [45] Ibid. at §206(a).
[46] Ibid. at §209(a). [47] H.R. Conf. Rep. 94–1733 at 82. [48] H.R. Rep. 94–1476 at 50.
[49] Ibid. [50] Ibid. [51] H.R. Conf. Rep. 94–1733 at 82. [52] H.R. Rep. 94–1476 at 54.

regulation identified an article whose '*sole* intrinsic function . . . is its utility' (emphasis supplied) § 101 defines a 'useful article [as] an article having *an* intrinsic utilitarian function that is not merely to portray the appearance of the article or to convey information . . .' (emphasis supplied). As a result, even a highly decorative item with a single utilitarian function met the definition of a useful article. Broadening the language in this fashion had the effect of narrowing the kinds of works of applied art which would be deemed protectable 'pictorial, graphic or sculptural works', because more works would be required to meet the separability standard.

The House Judiciary Committee explained its reasoning:

> In adopting this amendatory language, the Committee is seeking to draw as clear a line as possible between copyrightable works of applied art and uncopyrighted works of industrial design. A two-dimensional painting, drawing, or graphic work is still capable of being identified as such when it is printed on or applied to utilitarian articles such as textile fabrics, wallpaper, containers, and the like. The same is true when a statue or carving is used to embellish an industrial product or, as in the *Mazer* case, is incorporated into a product without losing its ability to exist independently as a work of art. On the other hand, although the shape of an industrial product may be aesthetically satisfying and valuable, the Committee's intention is not to offer it copyright protection under the bill. Unless the shape of an automobile, airplane, ladies' dress, food processor, television set, or any other industrial product contains some element that, physically or conceptually, can be identified as separable from the utilitarian aspects of that article, the design would not be copyrighted under the bill. The test of separability and independence from 'the utilitarian aspects of the article' does not depend upon the nature of the design – that is, even if the appearance of an article is determined by esthetic (as opposed to functional) considerations, only elements, if any, which can be identified separately from the useful article as such are copyrightable. And, even if the three-dimensional design contains some such element (for example, a carving on the back of a chair or a floral relief design on silver flatware), copyright protection would extend only to that element, and would not cover the over-all configuration of the utilitarian article as such.[53]

Thus, the House Judiciary Committee 'stressed Congress's desire to exclude from protection the general class of industrial products, notwithstanding any "aesthetically satisfying" design'.[54]

[53] Ibid. at 55.

[54] Perlmutter, 'Conceptual Separability', 351.

Star Athletica may make way for broader copyright coverage of applied art; the Court did not allude to this aspect of the legislative history but instead stated 'Congress has provided for limited copyright protection of certain features of industrial design [even when those features may affect the article's utility], and approaching the statute with presumptive hostility toward protection for industrial design would undermine Congress' choice': 197 L. Ed. 2d at 373.

At the same time, however, the House Report appeared to introduce some flexibility into the standard by inserting a term not found in the statute. While the statute covers 'pictorial, graphic, or sculptural features that can be identified separately from, and are capable of existing independently of, the utilitarian aspects of the article', the House Report would extend protection to an 'element that, physically *or conceptually*, can be identified as separable from the utilitarian aspects of that article' (emphasis supplied).[55] A test of physical separability seems fairly easy to apply, *Mazer* offering a paradigmatic example: removing the lampshade, light bulb, dowel and electric cord leaves the freestanding statuette.[56] 'Conceptual' separability, however, has proved far more elusive. Does it mean that one could imagine the design as a separate work of art were it extracted from its utilitarian surroundings, as would be the case for the 'carving on the back of a chair or a floral relief design on silver flatware' cited in the House Report, without needing physically to take an axe to the chair to detach the carving? In the cited examples, the design element appears to be engrafted onto the shape of the useful article without necessarily altering the shape itself. It is not too difficult to 'conceive of' the design being lifted off the useful article, leaving the article otherwise intact. Indeed, this concept of conceptual separability seems the flip side of the artist's § 113(a) right to reproduce a PGS work 'in or on' a useful article. In the latter instance, a pre-existing protectable design is affixed to a pre-existing useful article; in the former, the imagined separation of the design and the useful article yields two standalone items, one of which will be a protectable PGS work. As we will see in the next section, the Copyright Office adhered to this approach to 'conceptual' separability. The Supreme Court, however, while endorsing a 'mirror image' of § 113(a) analysis, and thus finding separability if the extracted design feature yields a standalone PGS work, does not concomitantly require that the object remaining after separation be capable of existing independently as a useful article.[57]

9.4 Administrative Interpretation

The US Copyright Office administers the registration of works of authorship. Registration is not a prerequisite to protection, but no

[55] H.R. Rep. 94–1476 at 55. For a fuller discussion of the legislative history, as well as of the pre-1976 Act treatment of works of applied art, see, e.g., William Patry, *Patry on Copyright* (Eagan: Thomson West, 2016), §§3:125–3:135.

[56] The *Star Athletica* court, however, characterised *Mazer* as an example of conceptual separability, and further declared that it was 'abandon[ing] the distinction between "physical" and "conceptual" separability'. See 197 L. Ed. 2d at 371.

[57] Ibid.

suit may be brought for infringement of a work of US origin unless the work has been registered before the suit is filed.[58] Thus any right holder of a US work of applied art who seeks to enforce her copyright through an infringement action must convince the Copyright Office examiners that the claimed design elements are separable from the utilitarian aspects in order to obtain the necessary certificate of registration.[59] The Compendium of US Copyright Office Practices (Third Edition 2014) states:

924.2(B) Conceptual Separability

The U.S. Copyright Office applies the conceptual separability test only if it determines that the useful article contains pictorial, graphic, or sculptural features that cannot be physically separated from that article.

Conceptual separability means that a feature of the useful article is clearly recognizable as a pictorial, graphic, or sculptural work, notwithstanding the fact that it cannot be physically separated from the article by ordinary means. This artistic feature must be capable of being visualized – either on paper or as a free-standing sculpture – as a work of authorship that is independent from the overall shape of the useful article. In other words, the feature must be imagined separately and independently from the useful article without destroying the basic shape of that article. A pictorial, graphic, or sculptural feature satisfies this requirement only if the artistic feature and the useful article could both exist side by side and be perceived as fully realized, separate works – one an artistic work and the other a useful article. For example, the carving on the back of a chair or an engraving on a vase would be considered conceptually separable, because one could imagine the carving or the engraving as a drawing on a piece of paper that is entirely distinct from the overall shape of the chair and the vase. Even if the carving or the engraving was removed the shape of the chair and the vase would remain unchanged, and both the chair and the vase would still be capable of serving a useful purpose. H.R. REP. NO. 94–1476, at 55 (1976), reprinted in 1976 *USCCAN* at 5668–69.

Under the Copyright Office's approach, in the case of an artistically designed useful article, it is necessary to conceive of two distinct objects, one useful, the other artistic, 'without destroying the basic shape of that article'. This exercise of the imagination lends itself to the kinds of decorative elements envisaged in the House Report: one can imagine a drawing or carving on the back of a chair having an existence independent

[58] 17 USC s. 411(a). Or at least, the plaintiff has filed an application to register. Compare *Cosmetic Ideas* v. *IAC/Interactive Corp.*, 606 F 3d 612 (9th Cir. 2010); *Chicago Bd of Educ.* v. *Substance, Inc.*, 354 F 3d 624 (7th Cir. 2003) ('application approach') with *La Resolana Architects, PA* v. *Clay Realtors Angel Fire*, 416 F 3d 1195, 1202–4 (10th Cir. 2005); *MGB Homes, Inc.* v. *Ameron Homes, Inc.*, 903 F 2d 1486, 1489 (11th Cir. 1990); *Fourth Estate Public Benefit Corp.* v. *Wall-Street.com LLC*, 856 F 3d 1338 (11th Cir. 2017) ('registration approach').

[59] If the Register continues to refuse, the applicant may nonetheless file suit; the Register may choose to become a party to the action, 17 USC s. 411(a).

from the chair, without affecting the functioning of the chair as an item of furniture. In effect, this conceptual effort recalls the author's right to reproduce a pre-existing PGS work 'in or on' a useful article; one can imagine the drawing or carving as a freestanding work subsequently applied to the back of the chair. By contrast, this kind of conceptual exercise does not adapt well to the entire shape of the useful article, because it is difficult to imagine how the entire shape of an object can exist independently of the object itself. The Copyright Office's analysis appears to presume that, in imagining a 'side by side' co-existence of the useful and the decorative elements, the imagined detachment of the decorative aspect will leave the rest of the object intact and functioning. But if the aesthetic element constitutes the entire form of the object, there is no 'rest of' the object to persist independently.[60]

The Compendium continues with examples of 'conceptually separable' elements; none involves the total shape of a useful article. Rather, the Compendium casts doubt on the latter's registrability.

- Artwork printed on a t-shirt, beach towel, or carpet.
- A colorful pattern decorating the surface of a shopping bag.
- A drawing on the surface of wallpaper.
- A floral relief decorating the handle of a spoon.

Merely analogizing the general shape of a useful article to a work of modern sculpture or an abstract sculpture does not satisfy the conceptual separability test, because it does not provide an objective basis for visualizing the artistic features and the useful article as separate and independent works. See *Esquire, Inc.* v. *Ringer*, 591 F 2d 796, 804 (1978) (DC Cir. 1978) [agreeing with the Office's determination that 'the overall design or configuration of a utilitarian object, even if it is determined by aesthetic as well as functional considerations, is not eligible for copyright'].

The Compendium's examples feature artworks effectively 'applied to' useful articles,[61] an approach consistent with what I have called the 'flip side' of the § 113(a) right to reproduce a PGS work 'in or on' a

[60] See, e.g., Humanetics Innovative Solutions Inc., Correspondence ID: 1-JT7IVR, Review Board of the United States Copyright Office (11 September 2014), p. 5, https://ipmall.law.unh.edu/sites/default/files/hosted_resources/CopyrightAppeals/2014/Q1Q10,Q1.52014.pdf (discussed below): ('If one were to conceptually separate the features of [the works identified in the application], there would be no underlying works remaining. The Works, therefore, fail the Copyright Office's test for conceptual separability').

[61] Compare Paolo Marzano, 'An Ill-Designed Protection for a Well-Designed Product: Italy and its Copyright Protection of Industrial Design' (2014) 240 *Revue Internationale du Droit d'Auteur* 119 (suggesting – regarding Italian copyright law, which formerly imposed a separability test – that 'applied art' should not mean industrial design in general, but rather artworks (e.g. drawings, paintings, sculpture) applied to a useful article). Italy, law of 21 April 1941, n. 633, art. 2, since amended by Legislative Decree 2 February 2001, n. 95, implementing EU Directive 98/71/EC.

useful article. Had the 'artwork printed on a t-shirt, beach towel, or carpet' pre-existed the useful article to which the 'artwork' was affixed, the statute establishes that the 'artwork' author's copyright would extend to its being printed on those articles; reproduction of the article bearing the artwork would infringe the author's copyright. If the 'artwork' was created to be 'printed on a t-shirt, beach towel, or carpet' but is nonetheless a separately identifiable PGS work, then it is copyrightable notwithstanding its incorporation in a useful article. The Copyright Office's treatment of conceptual separability thus eliminates differential outcomes based on the birth order of the design relative to the useful article – so long as the design pertains to a discrete aspect of that article.

By contrast, the Copyright Office appears to reject more strenuous efforts of conceptualisation which might imagine the entire shape of a useful article to be 'separable' if the shape in no way affected its function. This approach, however, risks sliding into an idea/expression test, which would deem protectable any design that was not necessary to the functioning of the article. The Compendium rejects that test explicitly with respect to individual features, and necessarily implicitly with respect to the overall design of the article:

> The fact that a useful article could have been designed differently or the fact that an artistic feature is not necessary to or dictated by the utilitarian aspects of that article is irrelevant to this analysis. If the feature is an integral part of the overall shape or contour of the useful article, that feature cannot be considered conceptually separable because removing it would destroy the basic shape of the useful article. See generally H.R. REP. NO. 94–1476, at 55 (1976), reprinted in 1976 *USCCAN* at 5668–69.

The Copyright Office Compendium also details what considerations do not count in assessing the conceptual separability of a design:

> 924.2(C) Factors Not Relevant in Evaluating Separability
>
> In assessing whether certain elements are physically or conceptually separable from the utilitarian functions of a useful article, registration specialists do not consider the following: (i) the aesthetic value of the design; (ii) the fact that the article could have been designed differently; or (iii) the amount of effort or expense that went into the making of the design. H.R. REP. NO. 94–1476, at 55 (1976), reprinted in 1976 *USCCAN* at 5668–69.

Specific applications of the Copyright Office rules can be found in the correspondence of the Review Board of the United States Copyright Office with applicants whose works the Office has declined to register.[62] A pattern emerges from these letters. First, the Review Board ascertains if the design

[62] The University of New Hampshire maintains a database of Decision of the Appeals Board – US Copyright Office 1995–2014, http://ipmall.info/hosted_resources/copyright

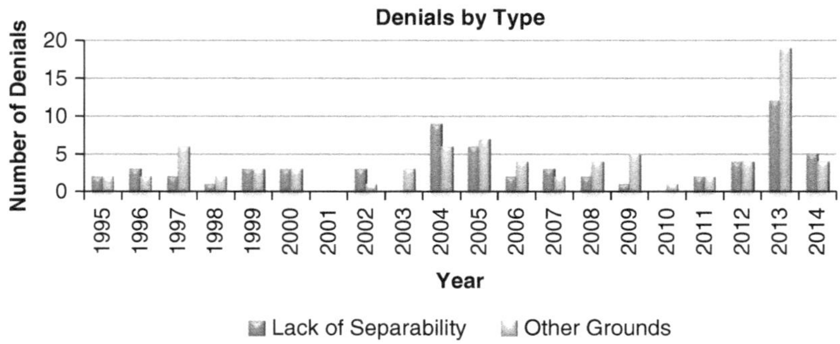

Figure 9.3 Denials of registration by the Review Board of the United States Copyright Office, by type

of the useful article presents separable elements. Secondly, the Review Board examines those elements for minimal originality. Between 1995 and 2014 the Review Board resolved 396 appeals, of which 146 concerned useful articles. Three appeals resulted in registration of the design.[63]

The chart[64] in Figure 9.3 illustrates the grounds for denying the remaining 143 appeals. Of these, sixty-three were denied registration because the Board found the design features physically or conceptually inseparable from their utilitarian function. Another eighty were rejected on other grounds: seventy-nine because the design features, even if separable, lacked minimal originality, and one for a lack of fixation and authorship.

Where the registrant has sought to claim the entire form of the article as a PGS work, the Review Board has declined to find separability. For example, where the applicant sought to register the overall shape of 'crash dummy' human forms designed for testing the impact of automobile crashes on the human body (pictured in Figures 9.4–9.6),[65] the Review Board ruled:

> [Y]ou argue that the Works' overall visual aesthetic appearances are conceptually separable from the utilitarian functions of a crash test dummy. We find your

appeals.asp. The statements in the text are based on a search of that database for rejections of form VA (visual art) applications from 1995 to 2014.

[63] In two of those cases, the Board reversed its prior decision and granted copyright on grounds of originality. The other accepted appeal – after a previous finding of a lack of separability – was registered under the Rule of Doubt due to an inability of the Board to determine if the work was a *model* of a useful article or a useful article itself.

[64] Thanks to Robert E. Bishop, Columbia Law School class of 2017, for preparing the chart.

[65] Humanetics Innovative Solutions Inc., Correspondence ID: 1-JT7IVR, Review Board of the United States Copyright Office (11 September 2014), p. 2, https://ipmall.law.unh.edu/sites/default/files/hosted_resources/CopyrightAppeals/2014/Q1Q10,Q1.52014.pdf (images located in appeal, but no additional source information available).

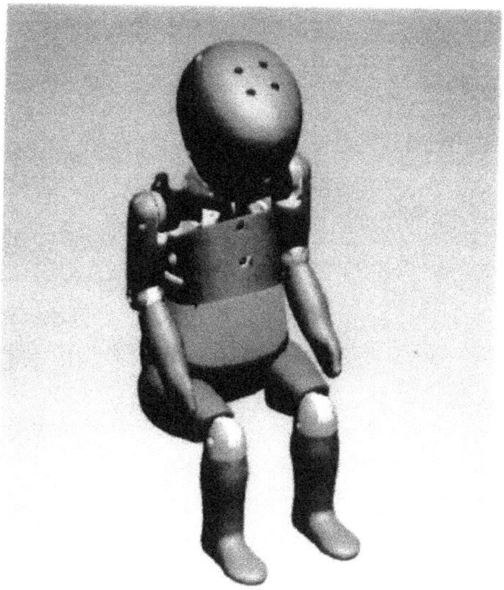

Figure 9.4 Crash dummy

arguments to be unpersuasive. Specifically, we find it impossible to imagine a way to conceptually separate the aesthetic design elements from the Works without destroying their shape and configuration as human-based testing devices. In order for Q1, Q1O, and Q1.5 to be useful as crash test dummies, designed to measure the forces imposed on the human body during an impact, the Works necessarily need to be designed in the basic image of a human. It is well settled that copyright protection is not available based on the 'overall shape or configuration' of a utilitarian article 'no matter how aesthetically pleasing that shape or configuration might be.' To argue that the Works' aesthetic appearances are separable from the useful articles underneath is to claim that the Works' overall shapes and forms are distinguishable from their intended function. We do not agree.

... The sculptural aspects of the Works cannot be envisioned separately without completely destroying their images or configurations. If one were to conceptually separate the features of Q1, Q1O, and Q1.5, there would be no underlying works remaining. The Works, therefore, fail the Copyright Office's test for conceptual separability.[66]

By excluding the 'overall shape or configuration' of a useful article, the Copyright Office's application of the separability test effectively assesses only those elements that one may imagine physically detaching from the article. As we shall see, the Supreme Court, while disagreeing in some respects with the Copyright Office approach, now also appears to limit

[66] Ibid. at p. 5 (citation omitted).

Figure 9.5 Crash dummy

copyright protection to design features that do not constitute the shape of the useful article as a whole.

9.5 Judicial Interpretation

The case law preceding *Star Athletica* offered a plethora of tests of conceptual separability,[67] some of which could have extended

[67] Compare *Brandir Int'l, Inc.* v. *Cascade Pacific Lumber Co.*, 834 F 2d 1142, 1145 (2d Cir. 1987) ('if design elements reflect a merger of aesthetic and functional considerations, the artistic aspects of a work cannot be said to be conceptually separable from the utilitarian elements. Conversely, where design elements can be identified as reflecting the designer's artistic

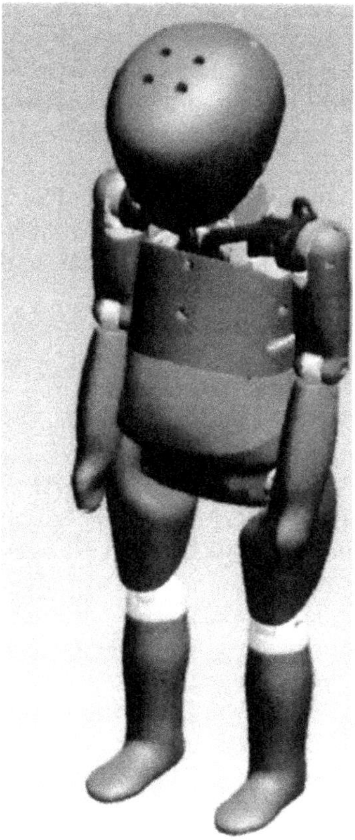

Figure 9.6 Crash dummy

judgment exercised independently of functional influences, conceptual separability exists'), with *Varsity Brands* v. *Star Athletica*, 799 F 3d 468, 488 (6th Cir. 2015) ('What are the utilitarian aspects of the useful article? ... Can the viewer of the design identify pictorial, graphic, or sculptural features separately from the utilitarian aspects of the useful article? ... Can the pictorial, graphic, or sculptural features of the design of the useful article exist independently of the utilitarian aspects of the useful article?'), with *Pivot Point Int'l* v. *Charlene Prods, Inc.*, 372 F 3d 913 (7th Cir. 2004) (independence of design decisions from utilitarian functions), with *Leicester* v. *Warner Bros*, 232 F 3d 1212, 1219 (9th Cir. 2000) (conceptual separability requires that the claimed design feature 'can stand on its own as a work of art traditionally conceived, and ... the useful article in which it is embodied would be equally useful without it'), with *Progressive Lighting, Inc.* v. *Lowe's Home Centers, Inc.*, 549 *Federal Appendix* 913, 920 (11th Cir. 2013) (conceptual separability concerns 'ornamental, superfluous designs contained within useful objects'; '[c]onceptual separability does not apply to functional components of useful articles, no matter how artistically designed ... unless they are physically separable from the useful article').

copyright protection to the entirety of a useful article's form. One widely adopted approach considered the extent to which an article's function affected the designer's aesthetic choices, an approach that endeavoured to locate copyrightability on a sliding scale from form-follows-function (inseparable) to functionally gratuitous (separable).[68] Another inquired whether the claimed design features enjoyed market value independently of the article's utilitarian aspects.[69] The Supreme Court has now rejected both of those tests, and proclaimed a single standard, but as we shall see, its application, particularly to three-dimensional forms, proves elusive.

9.5.1 *Threshold Question: What Is a 'Useful Article'?*

The separability test applies only to 'features' of articles 'having an intrinsic utilitarian function' (other than to portray or convey information). The statute distinguishes between PGS features comprised within the '*design of* a useful article' (emphasis supplied) and PGS works *applied to* a useful article.[70] Courts have unduly complicated their inquiries by searching for separability when they should first have inquired whether the disputed design was in fact a useful article.[71] Indeed, *Star Athletica* was such a case.[72]

There, the Sixth Circuit ruled that team insignia applied to cheerleader uniforms (pictured in Figure 9.7)[73] were separable and protectable from the overall design of the uniforms. While the court found separability because 'the arrangement of stripes, chevrons, color blocks, and zigzags are "wholly unnecessary to the performance of" the garment's ability to cover the body, permit free movement, and wick moisture',[74] it should

[68] See, e.g., *Universal Furniture*, 618 F 3d 417 (4th Cir. 2010); *Jovani Fashion, Ltd* v. *Fiesta Fashions*, 500 *Federal Appendix* 42 (2d Cir. 2012) (prom dresses); *Brandir Int'l, Inc.* v. *Cascade Pacific Lumber Co.*, 834 F 2d 1142, 1145 (2d Cir. 1987); and *Pivot Point Int'l* v. *Charlene Prods, Inc.*, 372 F 3d 913 (7th Cir. 2004).

[69] See, e.g., *Kieselstein-Cord* v. *Accessories by Pearl, Inc.*, 632 F 2d 989, 991 (2d Cir. 1980); Melville B. Nimmer and David Nimmer, *Nimmer on Copyright* (New York: M. Bender, 2016), 2A-75, §2A.08[B][4] ('conceptual separability exists where there is substantial likelihood that even if the article had no utilitarian use it would still be marketable to some significant segment of the community simply because of its aesthetic qualities'); *Galiano* v. *Harrah's Operating Co., Inc.*, 416 F 3d 411, 419 (5th Cir. 2005). For an extensive review of the case law, see an earlier version of this chapter published at 40 Colum. J. L. & the Arts 1 (2016).

[70] Accord, W. Patry, *Patry on Copyright*, §3:143.50 (distinguishing between the design 'of' a useful article, and a design applied 'to' a useful article).

[71] See, e.g., *Home Legend* v. *Mannington Mills*, 784 F 3d 1404 (11th Cir. 2015) (depictions of wood grain drawn on paper laminated to floor boards).

[72] See 197 L. Ed. 2d at 375–6 (Ginsburg, J concurring in the judgment).

[73] 799 F 3d at 473 (image located in opinion, but no additional source information available).

[74] Ibid. at 491.

Figure 9.7 Varsity team insignia applied to cheerleader uniforms

instead have treated those elements as fabric design, a category long recognised as a pictorial or graphic work.[75] Copyright does not protect the garments into which the design-bearing fabric is cut, but neither does

[75] See, e.g., *LA Printex Industries* v. *Aeropostale, Inc.*, 676 F 3d 841 (9th Cir. 2012); *Knitwaves, Inc.* v. *Lollytogs Ltd (Inc.)*, 71 F 3d 996 (2d Cir. 1995); *Eve of Milady* v. *Impression Bridal, Inc.*, 957 F Supp. 48 (SDNY 1997). By contrast, in *Jovani Fashion, Ltd* v. *Fiesta Fashions*, 500 *Federal Appendix* 42 (2d Cir. 2012), the Second Circuit affirmed the

the fashioning of the fabric into an article of clothing cancel out the copyright of the design imprinted thereon.

Rather than addressing the cheerleading garments as a whole (and detailing ten different tests of conceptual separability), the court should have recognised that the design elements at issue – the fabric designs representing team insignia – were not useful articles in the first place. The facts the court discussed might have alerted it to the difference between the design elements (insignia) and the useful article (the garment). Indeed, the court distinguished between the 'graphic design' and the uniform:

> The five Varsity designs are examples of how a cheerleading uniform still looks like a cheerleading uniform no matter how different the arrangement of the stripes, chevrons, colorblocks, and zigzags appear on the surface of the uniform. All of Varsity's graphic designs are interchangeable. Varsity's customers choose among the designs in the catalog, including the five designs at issue, select one of the designs, and then customize the color scheme. The interchangeability of Varsity's designs is evidence that customers can identify differences between the graphic features of each design, and thus a graphic design and a blank cheerleading uniform can appear 'side by side'—one as a graphic design, and one as a cheerleading uniform.[76]

In highlighting the graphic designs' 'interchangeability', the Sixth Circuit effectively applied the statutory standards of separate identifiability and independent existence of the designs relative to the uniforms. But the court would have made shorter work of its analysis had it drawn a different conclusion from its characterisation of 'the stripes, chevrons, colorblocks, and zigzags' as the 'graphic design', and from the customers' selection among the graphic designs: these elements are PGS works 'reproduced on' the uniform (the useful article); the graphic designs' status as PGS works did not require assessing the characteristics of the uniforms.[77]

District Court's dismissal of a complaint alleging that defendant competitor infringed the design of plaintiff's prom dress. According to the District Court, plaintiff 'conceded that the individual elements of the dress (such as the pattern of sequins) were not copyrightable in isolation. Jovani acknowledged that there is no discernible pattern of sequins ... Jovani has conceded that it is not claiming a copyright in the fabric designs of its dress.' *Jovani Fashion, Ltd* v. *Cinderella Divine, Inc.*, 808 F Supp. 2d 542 (SDNY 2011). The sequin pattern's lack of originality indicates that, unlike *Varsity Brands*, which involved 'multiple graphic designs that appear on the cheerleading uniforms and warm-ups they sell', 799 F 3d at 470, *Jovani* could not have been reconceptualised as a fabric design case.

76 799 F 3d at 491. Toward the end of its opinion, the Sixth Circuit finally recognised 'we believe that the graphic features of Varsity's cheerleading-uniform designs are more like fabric design than dress design', ibid. at 493.

77 The court acknowledged that, 'If the design is not the design of a useful article, then there is no need to inquire into whether there are "pictorial, graphic, or sculptural features that can be identified separately from, and are capable of existing independently of, the utilitarian aspects of the [useful] article." 17 USC § 101.' But it then stated that the design at issue was the design of the uniform rather than 'the graphic features of each design [uniform]', ibid. at 487. See also *Patry on Copyright*, §3:143.50 (*Varsity Brands* exemplifies designs applied to a useful article).

The Supreme Court, however, asserting that the parties had not raised the issue of whether the designs were 'useful articles',[78] proceeded directly to separability, thus depriving lower courts of guidance on a potentially dispositive definitional issue. Nonetheless, the Court's subsequent statement that a 'separable' feature 'cannot itself be a useful article'[79] will likely require lower courts to grapple with the meaning of that term.

9.5.2 Separability: The 'Mirror Image' Approach

Eschewing distinctions between 'physical' and 'conceptual' separability,[80] *Star Athletica* turned to the statutory text, which defines a useful article's 'pictorial, graphic, or sculptural features' as PGS works if [1] they 'can be *identified separately* from, and [2] are capable of *existing independently* of, the utilitarian aspects of the article'.[81] The Court stated:

> The first requirement—separate identification—is not onerous. The decisionmaker need only be able to look at the useful article and spot some two- or three-dimensional element that appears to have pictorial, graphic, or sculptural qualities.
>
> The independent-existence requirement is ordinarily more difficult to satisfy. The decisionmaker must determine that the separately identified feature has the capacity to exist apart from the utilitarian aspects of the article. In other words, the feature must be able to exist as its own pictorial, graphic, or sculptural work as defined in §101 once it is imagined apart from the useful article. If the feature is not capable of existing as a pictorial, graphic, or sculptural work once separated from the useful article, then it was not a pictorial, graphic, or sculptural feature of that article, but rather one of its utilitarian aspects.
>
> Of course, to qualify as a pictorial, graphic, or sculptural work on its own, the feature cannot itself be a useful article or '[a]n article that is normally a part of a useful article' (which is itself considered a useful article).[82]

As construed by the Supreme Court, the statutory text best fits the kind of pictorial, graphic or sculptural design elements exemplified by the *Mazer* statuette lamp base: these clearly can be 'identified separately from' and can be imagined as 'existing independently of' the useful article's functional elements; indeed, the lamp bases were also sold as freestanding statuettes. As we have seen in the Copyright Office's approach, interpreting the statutory phrase '*capable* of existing independently' to extend to the imaginary removal of the feature as a predicate to its existing independently from the article meets the dual statutory requirements of separate identifiability and independent existence. As we observed,[83] this conceptual effort in effect imagines the design feature as a pre-existing PGS work reproduced on or in

[78] 197 L. Ed. 2d at 366. [79] Ibid. at 367. [80] Ibid. at 371.
[81] 17 USC s. 101 (emphasis supplied). [82] 197 L. Ed. 2d at 367 (citations omitted).
[83] Above, text after note 61.

the useful article. Interpreting separability as the mirror image of § 113(a) is consonant with the statutory text: if notwithstanding its application to or incorporation in a useful article, the design element could have been a freestanding PGS work, then it is both separately identifiable, and *capable* of separate existence.

The Supreme Court adopted a similar analysis:

> The Copyright Act provides 'the owner of [a] copyright' with the 'exclusive righ[t] ... to reproduce the copyrighted work in copies.' §106(1). The statute clarifies that this right 'includes the right to reproduce the [copyrighted] work in or on any kind of article, whether useful or otherwise.' §113(a). Section 101 is, in essence, the mirror image of §113(a). Whereas §113(a) protects a work of authorship first fixed in some tangible medium other than a useful article and subsequently applied to a useful article, §101 protects art first fixed in the medium of a useful article. The two provisions make clear that copyright protection extends to pictorial, graphic, and sculptural works regardless of whether they were created as freestanding art or as features of useful articles. The ultimate separability question, then, is whether the feature for which copyright protection is claimed would have been eligible for copyright protection as a pictorial, graphic, or sculptural work had it originally been fixed in some tangible medium other than a useful article before being applied to a useful article.[84]

It is not clear how far the Court's application of the reverse §113(a) approach goes. In the case before it:

> Applying this test to the surface decorations on the cheerleading uniforms is straightforward. First, one can identify the decorations as features having pictorial, graphic, or sculptural qualities. Second, if the arrangement of colors, shapes, stripes, and chevrons on the surface of the cheerleading uniforms were separated from the uniform and applied in another medium—for example, on a painter's canvas—they would qualify as 'two-dimensional ... works of ... art,' §101. And imaginatively removing the surface decorations from the uniforms and applying them in another medium would not replicate the uniform itself. Indeed, respondents have applied the designs in this case to other media of expression—different types of clothing—without replicating the uniform. The decorations are therefore separable from the uniforms and eligible for copyright protection.[85]

By contrast, had the separated features 'replicated the uniform', then it appears the features would not have been separable because 'the [extracted] feature cannot itself be a useful article'. 'Replication' does not mean 'representation'. The Court analogised to a design that covers the full surface of a guitar: if the designs are lifted off, their contours will depict the shape of the guitar, but they will not *be* a guitar.[86] By the same token, the Varsity stripes were 'surface decorations': they followed the cut of the uniforms, but did not

[84] 197 L. Ed. 2d at 367–8. [85] Ibid. [86] Ibid.

shape them (as evidenced by the interchangeability of the team-designating designs on the same basic – unadorned – uniform).

The announced rule that 'to qualify as a pictorial, graphic, or sculptural work on its own, the feature cannot itself be a useful article' appears to preclude PGS status for the full shape of most useful articles. Indeed, 'features' suggests aspects or components of the design, not the entirety of the form of the useful article. Furthermore, the Court appears to exclude from PGS status even some portion of the shape of the article less than its entirety because 'the feature cannot itself be ... "[a]n article that is normally a part of a useful article" (which is itself considered a useful article)'.

Are there nonetheless circumstances in which the 'mirror image' approach to separability would embrace the full form of a three-dimensional useful article (or some substantial portion of it)? For example, were the complete abstraction of the article's form from its function possible, and the shape could stand on its own as a work of art, perhaps the overall shape might be a 'feature'.[87] In fact, the Court's separability standard may not require that the form be completely unnecessary to the article's function: the Court rejected a proposed requirement 'that the statute protects only "solely artistic" features that have no effect whatsoever on a useful article's utilitarian function'.[88] Thus, it appears that the useful article's separable form may even 'make [the article] more useful'.[89] Thus, to return to the crocodile salad tongs posited earlier, the Court might consider both the pre-existing sculpture outfitted with tongs, and the tongs designed in the shape of a crocodile, to be protectable PGS works. Similarly, the Court disapproved the Copyright Office requirement that the conceptual separation of the PGS features from the useful article must result in two intact objects, the extracted PGS work on the one hand, and the remaining utilitarian article on the other:

> The focus of the separability inquiry is on the extracted feature and not on any aspects of the useful article that remain after the imaginary extraction. The statute does not require the decisionmaker to imagine a fully functioning useful article without the artistic feature. Instead, it requires that the separated feature qualify as a nonuseful pictorial, graphic, or sculptural work on its own.[90]

It is correct that the statutory text requires only that the PGS feature be capable of existing independently without the useful article; the Copyright

[87] See Paul Goldstein, *Goldstein on Copyright*, 3rd edn (New York: Wolters Kluwer, 2016), 2:79, §2.5.3 (applying a 'stand alone' test to construe 'conceptual separability' generally, and citing example of a slipper in the shape of a bear paw).

[88] 197 L. Ed. 2d at 371. [89] Ibid. [90] Ibid. at 370–1.

Office interpolated the reverse proposition that the useful article should be capable of existing independently without the design element. If the conceptual extraction of the PGS features does not require that the remainder still be capable of serving as the useful article that it was pre-extraction, then the Court would appear to be opening the way to widening the universe of protectable shapes of useful articles.

That said, the Court did pose some limit to the extraction approach:

> Of course, because the removed feature may not be a useful article—as it would then not qualify as a pictorial, graphic, or sculptural work—there necessarily would be some aspects of the original useful article 'left behind' if the feature were conceptually removed.[91]

If 'some aspects of the original useful article' must be 'left behind', then perhaps the extraction approach necessarily stops short of extending to the useful article's entire form.

The Court also declined to find in Congress' frequent failure to enact a *sui generis* industrial design right a congressional 'intent to entirely exclude industrial design from copyright'.[92] Rather, 'Congress has provided for limited copyright protection for certain features of industrial design'[93] that the separability test should accommodate. On the other hand, the Court stressed that 'our test does not render the shape, cut, and physical dimensions of the cheerleading uniforms eligible for copyright protection'.[94] The Court's enumeration of what its separability test does not protect suggests a narrow scope of copyright coverage. If the listed features are not copyrightable per se, then the Court has implicitly rejected an approach to separability that inquires whether other designs could achieve the utilitarian aspects of the article. After all, many different shapes, cuts or physical dimensions could permit a cheerleading uniform to attain its characteristic objectives to 'cover the body, permit free movement, and wick away moisture'.[95] But, unlike the stripes, chevrons and colour blocks at issue in *Star Athletica*, whose reproduction would not 'replicate' the uniforms, 'shape, cut, and physical dimensions' do constitute the article itself. That the article may be one example of many different variations of uniforms does not matter; 'shape, cut, and physical dimensions' define the particular resulting uniform, and that is all that is needed to produce a copyright-excluded 'useful article'.

Applying the non-replication rule to three-dimensional design 'features' of useful articles should similarly result in a very limited

[91] Ibid. at 371. [92] Ibid. at 372. [93] Ibid. at 373. [94] Ibid.
[95] *Varsity Brands*, 799 F 3d at 491.

universe of copyright-protectable forms constituting the object as a whole. The claimed shape, after all, will 'replicate' the object (or a part of it), and the object will have 'an intrinsic utilitarian function'. Consider an amoeba-shaped table top. A table is a useful article, and its top 'is normally part of' it; accordingly, is its shape not separable? That table tops can come in many shapes would not matter. Which shapes are 'normally part of a useful article'? The answer may turn on whether the particular shape has 'an intrinsic utilitarian function that is not merely to portray the appearance of the article or to convey information'. If the shape has no utilitarian function (as might be the case for carvings that shape the edges of the table[96]), then separating the shape would not 'replicate' a 'useful article'. But if the shape does have an intrinsic utilitarian function, then its extraction would 'replicate' a 'useful article'. An amoeba shape for a table top might at first blush seem arbitrary and devoid of utility. But amoeba-shaped conference tables in fact exist and serve the utilitarian purpose of dividing the larger group sitting around the whole table into smaller discussion groups.[97] As a result, the three-dimensional form of the table top, even if it might be perceived as a sculptural work, would not pass the second step of the *Star Athletica* Court's analysis.

The Supreme Court's new test will in application probably yield the same representational art-favouring results as those obtained under most prior interpretations of the statutory standard: Courts more easily perceive figurative designs as 'separable' than abstract forms. A federal district court found the bear paw shape of a slipper separable (see Figure 9.8).[98]

Similarly, the sheep-shaped seat of a stool (image in Figure 9.9[99]) may readily be identified separately and conceived as existing independently of the rest of the stool.[100]

[96] See, e.g., *Universal Furniture* v. *Collezione Europa*, above, note 68.

[97] See, e.g., www.miencompany.com/shop/by-category/tables-desks/classroom-tables-and-desks/item/F2-Amoeba-Table.

[98] *Animal Fair, Inc.* v. *AMFESCO Indus.*, 620 F Supp. 175, 188 (D. Minn. 1985), *aff'd without opinion*, 794 F 2d 678 (8th Cir. 1986) (finding the bear-depictive sculptural features of the slippers separable from and 'wholly unrelated' to the footwear function). Figure 9.8 image source: www.myboothang.com/bear-paw-slippers/. The depicted slippers may not have been the ones at issue in *Animal Fair*: that company ceased operations in 2015; see www.theridgefieldpress.com/44570/animal-fair-to-close-its-doors-after-15-years-in-business/ (1 April 2015).

[99] County Engraving Online (2015), www.countyengraving.co.uk/childrens-wooden-step-or-stool-sheep-design-personalised-109-p.asp.

[100] The *Star Athletica* ruling brings the sheep stool even more comfortably within the zone of separability because the court has clarified that the extraction of the PGS feature need not leave a 'fully functioning' useful article behind, 197 L. Ed. 2d at 371. A stool without a seat is not fully functional, but that no longer appears to be an impediment to the 'separability' of the design of the seat.

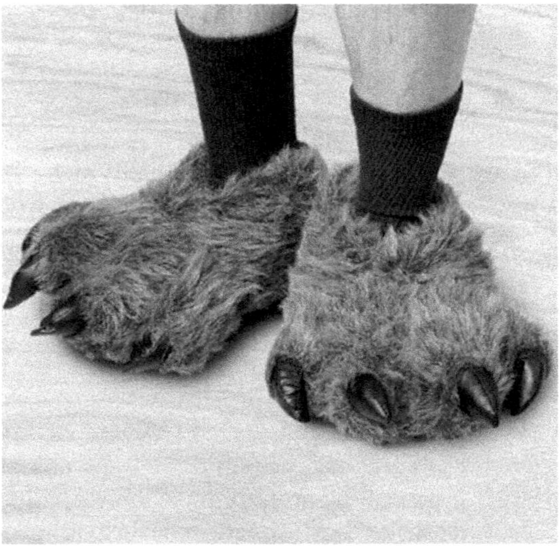

Figure 9.8 Bear paw slippers

Figure 9.9 County Engraving, 'Children's wooden step or stool sheep design personalised'

In *Mazer* v. *Stein*, while the placement of the bulb and shade atop the dancer (see image in Figure 9.2) may have facilitated ruling the ballerina sculpture protectable despite its incorporation in the lamp, one might predict that even were the lighting elements fully integrated into the sculpture – for example, were the illumination to emanate from the ballerina's tutu – a court would still find the sculpture separable from the useful article of the lamp. By contrast, the abstract form of the lighting fixture in *Esquire* v. *Ringer* did not elicit a perception of the object as a distinct sculpture.[101] Moreover, the simpler or sleeker the shape, the less likely courts may be to identify separate PGS features, much less perceive them as capable of existing independently of the article's utilitarian aspects. Similarly, the more the form follows the article's function, the less will be 'left behind' after the extraction exercise, but the Court has told us that 'there necessarily would be some aspects of the original useful article "left behind" if the feature were conceptually removed'.[102]

Ultimately, the Court's reverse-§113(a) analysis fails to supply the sword that cuts through the tangle of 'separability' case law. Even if the overall form of a useful article (or of parts of it) can be 'identified' as a sculptural work, its ability to exist independently of the utilitarian aspects of the article will now be assessed under the non-replication rule: if the shape of the object is a useful article, then it is not separable, even if other articles of similar utility might be differently shaped (just as cheerleader uniforms may come in many shapes, cuts or proportions).

How do we know if the shape is a useful article? The statutory definition of a useful article tells us that the object has 'an intrinsic utilitarian function that is not merely to portray the appearance of the article or to convey information'. So long as the form is not gratuitous relative to the function, just about any three-dimensional shape of a useful article (or of a part of it) will enable 'an intrinsic utilitarian function'. Courts' perception of representational shapes (such as the *Mazer* ballet dancer) as separable suggests a tendency to overlook the role the shape may play in the attainment of the article's functional objectives. For example, much of the form of the fish pitcher depicted in Figure 9.10[103] bears a relationship to its function; the open mouth serves as the spout and the curved tail furnishes the handle. Nonetheless, *Star Athletica*'s refusal to require that the claimed PGS elements be '"solely artistic" features that have no effect whatsoever on

[101] 591 F 2d 796 (4th Cir. 1978). [102] 197 L. Ed. 2d at 371.
[103] Image source: www.etsy.com/listing/84000688/glug-jug-pitcher-ceramic-golden-fish.

Figure 9.10 Fish pitcher

a useful article's utilitarian function'[104] accommodates the copyright protection at least of representational shapes, despite the apparent tension of the rejection of a 'solely artistic' standard with the definition of a useful article as having '*an* intrinsic utilitarian function' (emphasis supplied).

9.5.3 *Birth Order Redux: Indirect Copyright Protection for Some Industrial Design?*

The above analysis leads to a paradox: although the *Star Athletica* Court sought a test under which

> copyright protection extends to pictorial, graphic, and sculptural works regardless of whether they were created as freestanding art or as features of useful articles. The ultimate separability question, then, is whether the feature for which copyright protection is claimed would have been eligible for copyright protection as a pictorial, graphic, or sculptural work had it originally been fixed in some tangible medium other than a useful article before being applied to a useful article[105]

birth order continues to matter because under *Star Athletica* the claimed PGS 'feature' may not 'replicate' the useful article whose form it constitutes. By contrast, had the design shaped a standalone sculpture, it would be a PGS

[104] 197 L. Ed. 2d at 371. [105] 197 L. Ed. 2d at 367.

Figure 9.11 Chair inside a trunk (*Heptagon Creations, Ltd* v. *Core Group Marketing LLC*)

work, and its subsequent incorporation in a useful article would not deprive the underlying sculpture of copyright protection. This outcome suggests that producers of artistically designed useful articles should first create non-useful sculptures, register them as such, and then convert them to useful articles. That the conversion may introduce changes needed to adapt the sculpture into a useful article does not matter because the protected work remains the sculpture, not its utilitarian adaptation.

The divergent outcomes seem a product of pure formalism. (Which may be one reason for the Court's attempt to abolish the 'birth order' distinction.) Consider the application of the two-step 'first-a-sculpture, then-a-useful-article' approach[106] to the item in Figure 9.11.[107]

[106] Cf. *Universal Furniture* v. *Collezione Europa*, above, note 68, at 434 (reflecting judicial approval of this process in reverse: the designer first designed the useful parts of the furniture, and then in a separate step designed the artistic flourishes).

[107] Complaint, *Heptagon Creations, Ltd* v. *Core Group Marketing LLC*, 2011 *WL* 6600267 (SDNY 2011) (no. 11-cv-01794-LTS), p. 47 (image located in complaint, but no additional source information available).

In the actual litigation,[108] the court ruled that the plaintiff had failed to plead with particularity which elements of the item were conceptually separable and why. After *Star Athletica*, a court might identify the design of the hollowed tree trunk base and arms separately from the seat, but the base and arms' capacity for existence independently of the chair function could founder on the rule that the design may not replicate a part of a useful article. The base and arms of a chair are indeed a part of the chair: albeit fanciful, they still fulfil the 'intrinsic utilitarian function' of providing arm rests and a base for the seat. On the other hand, if the shape of the useful article, or part of it, also represents a figurative form – the ballet dancer lamp base (part of the useful article), or the ballet dancer-shaped lamp with the illuminated tutu (the entire useful article) – then a court might perceive the representational features (even if they constitute the whole of the design) as existing separately from their utilitarian aspects. Applied to the chair base and arms, if a court perceived them as the representation of a tree trunk, it might envision their independent existence notwithstanding their functional role. The reverse-§113(a) analysis could in theory apply equally well to abstract shapes – imagine the chair base and arms no longer depicted a tree trunk, but instead formed an atypical polygon. But the less representational the form, the less likely it may be to pass the first step of the *Star Athletica* test, which requires the court initially to identify separate PGS elements. By the same token, while *Star Athletica* now tells us that the useful article's form need not be fully independent of its function, the more they are intertwined, the less courts may be likely to identify the formal elements 'separately from the utilitarian aspects of the article'.

By contrast, if the designer had first created the hollowed tree trunk-like external shell as a sculptural form in its own right, then there would be no doubt that the copyright in the underlying sculpture would remain unaffected by the subsequent addition of the seating element. As a result, the sculptor would have a copyright infringement claim against an unlicensed furniture designer who adopted the shell for seating. Moreover, the sculptor's protection would extend to the reproduction of the sculpture with any kind of seating, or, for that matter, as any other kind of useful article, such as the table that might result from turning the shell upside down (see Figures 9.12 and Figure 9.13).

Admittedly, the two-step approach does not yield copyright protection for the useful article, only for the underlying sculpture on which the useful article is based. In practice, however, this distinction may be without a meaningful difference, because the designer of the useful article could

[108] *Heptagon Creations, Ltd* v. *Core Group Marketing LLC*, 2011 *WL* 6600267 (SDNY 2011).

Figure 9.12 Chair removed from the trunk (*Heptagon Creations, Ltd* v. *Core Group Marketing LLC*)

Figure 9.13 Chair reincluded in the trunk (*Heptagon Creations, Ltd* v. *Core Group Marketing LLC*)

obtain an exclusive licence from the sculptor, thus giving her enforceable rights against competing designers of useful articles.

As a result, even indirect protection for artistically designed useful articles significantly broadens the *de facto* application of copyright to works of applied art. Direct protection via a reverse-§113(a) approach seems more troublesome still. The wider that approach sweeps, the greater the risk that the distinction Congress sought to make between PGS works (protectable) and aesthetically designed useful articles (generally not copyrightable as a whole, albeit potentially copyrightable as to parts) returns to the knot-twisted muddle from which we started. If the reverse-§113(a) approach works well in the context of distinct component part 'features' of a useful article, it may ultimately be unconvincing as applied to the entire form of the article because it tends toward over-inclusiveness. If, to paraphrase Gertrude Stein, 'a chair is a chair is a chair', so that the shapes of most useful articles should resist recharacterisation as non-useful PGS works, the universe of forms that effective advocates might conceptually convert to 'sculptures' could nonetheless prove ever-expanding. Consider the item in Figure 9.14:[109] it does not require great labour of the imagination to conceive of the 'Tube chair' as a sculpture.

Or the Sori Yanagi 'Butterfly stool' (1954) (Figure 9.15),[110] as its name suggests, could be conceptualised as an abstract representation of a butterfly.

Or either of the items in Figures 9.16 and 9.17, displayed in the Helsinki Design Museum.[111]

Or, the Le Corbusier 'LC2' armchair (1928) (Figure 9.18)[112] looks more like a chair and less like an abstract form than the earlier examples, but could nonetheless be imagined as a sculpture of an indented cube.

Other examples likely abound, some more, some less obviously at first blush a piece of furniture or other useful article, but all of them arguably capable of being imagined as non-useful works of art. Sadly, then, for the attempt to forge a path to copyright coverage of innovative and attractive furniture and other useful article designs, the reverse-§113(a) interpretation of the statutory definition of a PGS work toward which *Star Athletica* points presents two daunting risks: either a run down the slippery slope, or, to halt that slide, judicial resort to a gut sense of

[109] Joe Colombo, 'Tube chair' (1969–70). Photo: www.metmuseum.org/toah/works-of-art/1987.98.1a-d/.
[110] Image source: www.vitra.com/en-us/product/butterfly-stool.
[111] See www.designmuseum.fi/en/. Image credits: Jane C. Ginsburg.
[112] Image source: www.cassina.com/en/collection/sofas-and-armchairs/lc2-maison-la-roche.

Figure 9.14 Joe Colombo, 'Tube chair'

Figure 9.15 Sori Yanagi, 'Butterfly stool'

Figure 9.16 Ball-chair, by designer Eero Aarnio, 1966, producer Asko Oy

whether or not the disputed object is 'art'. *Star Athletica* offers two limiting principles (though the majority opinion also contains language inconsistent with those guidelines): first, the claimed PGS work cannot be the entire form or a functional part of the useful article. Secondly, the requirement that the alleged PGS features be perceived as separate PGS works will tend to confine the reconception of the useful article as a standalone three-dimensional PGS work to representational forms. Without those limiting principles, the §113(a) mirror-image approach in practice is likely often to present intractable problems of line-drawing, and for that reason may well prove unworkable.

Figure 9.17 Flying carpet sofa, by designer Ilkka Suppanen, 1998

Figure 9.18 Le Corbusier 'LC2' armchair

9.6 Congress Should Untie the Knot

Attempts to apply the statutory tests of separate identification and capacity for independent existence to the overall designs of useful articles have yielded a plethora of interpretations, but predictable and even-handed treatment of applied art continues to elude courts and creators. It may well be time for Congress to revisit the question. Happily, the solution need not demand extensive Congressional intervention, because a statutory framework already exists in Chapter 13 of the Copyright Act, added in 1998, establishing 'Protection of original designs'.[113] Chapter 13 largely tracks the abandoned Title II of the 1976 Copyright Act,[114] covering original designs of useful articles for a ten-year term following registration, if registration occurs within two years of the date on which the design is first made public.[115] The statute excludes coverage for unoriginal or commonplace designs, as well as for those 'dictated solely by a utilitarian function of the article that embodies it',[116] thus welcoming designs that accommodate the article's function, so long as utilitarian considerations do not exclusively influence design choices. This 'not dictated by' standard encompasses a broader range of full article designs than would *Star Athletica's* interpretation of the statutory separability test for PGS works. The scope of protection prohibits the making or distribution of copies that are 'substantially similar in appearance', but, unlike copyright in a PGS work, does not confer a derivative works right.[117]

[113] Vessel Hull Design Protection Act, title V of the Digital Millennium Copyright Act, Pub. L. No. 105–304, 112 Stat. 2860, 2905 (1998) (codified as amended at 17 USC §§1301–1332).

[114] See above, text at notes 39–50.

[115] 17 USC ss. 1301, 1305, 1310. There is also a notice requirement; see ibid. ss. 1306, 1307.

[116] Ibid. §1302. Designs not subject to protection:

> Protection under this chapter shall not be available for a design that is —
> (1) not original;
> (2) staple or commonplace, such as a standard geometric figure, a familiar symbol, an emblem, or a motif, or another shape, pattern, or configuration which has become standard, common, prevalent, or ordinary;
> (3) different from a design excluded by paragraph (2) only in insignificant details or in elements which are variants commonly used in the relevant trades;
> (4) dictated solely by a utilitarian function of the article that embodies it; or
> (5) embodied in a useful article that was made public by the designer or owner in the United States or a foreign country more than 2 years before the date of the application for registration under this chapter.

[117] Ibid. §1308. Exclusive rights:

> The owner of a design protected under this chapter has the exclusive right to —
> (1) make, have made, or import, for sale or for use in trade, any useful article embodying that design; and
> (2) sell or distribute for sale or for use in trade any useful article embodying that design.

Chapter 13 thus would offer a ready-made design protection regime, were it not for its definition of a useful article, which currently is limited to vessel hulls.[118] But the origins of this legislation in special pleading from the Florida and California boat-building industries[119] need not preclude its revision into a genuine design protection statute. Indeed, bills (so far unenacted) to extend intellectual property protection to fashion design have taken Chapter 13 as their starting points.[120] To bring the design of a broader range of useful articles within statutory coverage, a few modest amendments to Chapter 13 would suffice.

First, the initial declaration that '[t]he designer or other owner of an original design of a useful article which makes the article attractive or distinctive in appearance to the purchasing or using public may secure the protection provided by this chapter upon complying with and subject to this chapter'[121] could remain, albeit preferably without the requirement that the design be 'attractive to the purchasing or using public'. The introduction of a merit standard is troublesome, given copyright law's traditional rejection of inquiries into artistic worthiness.[122] Admittedly, Chapter 13 establishes a

Ibid. §1309(e):

(e) Infringing Article Defined. – As used in this section, an 'infringing article' is any article the design of which has been copied from a design protected under this chapter, without the consent of the owner of the protected design. An infringing article is not an illustration or picture of a protected design in an advertisement, book, periodical, newspaper, photograph, broadcast, motion picture, or similar medium. A design shall not be deemed to have been copied from a protected design if it is original and not substantially similar in appearance to a protected design.

118 Ibid. §1301(b)(2).

119 See, e.g., US Copyright Office. Compendium of US Copyright Office Practices, s. 1302 (3d ed. 2014) ('Vessel design protection is not a form of copyright protection. Congress enacted the VHDPA to provide a new, separate form of special protection for vessel designs in response to the needs of the boat industry, not as an amendment to the copyright law'). Susanna Monseau, 'The Challenge of Protecting Industrial Design in a Global Economy' (2012) 20 *Texas Intellectual Property Law Journal* 495, 535 ('[The VHDPA] came about because the Supreme Court struck down a Florida statute protecting boat hulls on the basis of federal preemption, and once boat designers were prevented from using state unfair competition laws to protect their designs they lobbied Congress for federal protection of boat hull designs').

120 See, e.g., s. 3523 – Innovative Design Protection Act of 2012, 112th Congress, 2d sess. (2012), available at: www.congress.gov/bill/112th-congress/senate-bill/3523?q=S.3523; S. Rep. 112–259, available at: www.congress.gov/congressional-report/112th-congress/senate-report/259/1?q=S.3523. See generally Scott Hemphill and Jeannie Suk, 'The Law, Culture, and Economics of Fashion' (2009) 61 *Stanford Law Review* 1147. See also Susan Scafidi, 'IDPPPA: Introducing the Innovative Design Protection and Piracy Prevention Act, a.k.a. Fashion Copyright' (2010) Counterfeit Chic, www.counterfeitchic.com/2010/08.

121 Ibid. §1301(a)(1).

122 See, e.g., *Bleistein* v. *Donaldson Lithographing Co.*, 188 US 239 (1903); see generally Robert A. Gorman, 'Copyright Courts and Aesthetic Judgments: Abuse or Necessity?' (2002) 25 *Columbia-VLA Journal of Law & the Arts* 1.

sui generis design protection regime that borrows from other intellectual property regimes as well as from copyright. For example, distinctiveness is a characteristic of trade marks,[123] and a requirement that the design stand out from its predecessors is not an unreasonable means of limiting the universe of protectable designs. On the other hand, Chapter 13 already captures that restriction in its list of excluded designs, which denies coverage not only to unoriginal or banal designs, but also to a design 'different from a design excluded [as banal or commonplace] . . . only in insignificant details or in elements which are variants commonly used in the relevant trades'. In any event, the Copyright Office does not appear to view attractiveness or distinctiveness as conditions of protection; neither registration Form D-VH[124] nor the Compendium of Copyright Office Practices[125] allude to, much less implement, any requirement that the applicant demonstrate that the design is attractive or distinctive to the purchasing public.

Secondly, and similarly, the amendment would largely retain the first part of the current definition, which specifies that 'a design is "original" if it is the result of the designer's creative endeavor that provides a distinguishable variation over prior work pertaining to similar articles which is more than merely trivial and has not been copied from another source'.[126] To make clear that originality is not limited to providing a distinguishable variation on prior designs, but can also refer to creative designs not based on prior designs, it might be desirable to revise the phrase to read 'a design is "original" if it is the result of the designer's creative endeavor, *including one* that provides a distinguishable variation . . .' (emphasis supplied).

Finally, the definition of a 'useful article' could reprise the definition in § 101 of the Copyright Act.[127] Several limiting factors, some of them already in the statute, could assuage fears that such a broad definition would result in overprotection of utilitarian design. For one thing, not every design of a useful article will qualify. Threshold criteria in Chapter 13 set the level of creativity and exclude designs dictated by functional objectives. Legitimate concerns may nonetheless arise regarding subject-matter that would cross the statutory threshold but whose protection would entail unacceptably anti-competitive consequences. Spare parts for automobiles and other devices may well fall into this category. To confront the problem of potential overprotection, Congress would need

[123] Lanham Act s. 45 (definition of a trade mark).
[124] Form D-VH, The Copyright Office, available at www.copyright.gov/forms/formdvhi.pdf.
[125] See Copyright Office Compendium, above, ss. 1300–1305. [126] Ibid. §1301(b)(1).
[127] 'A "useful article" is an article having an intrinsic utilitarian function that is not merely to portray the appearance of the article or to convey information. An article that is normally a part of a useful article is considered a "useful article".'

to choose between two approaches. It could expand the universe of protectable designs piecemeal from vessel hulls to specifically identified kinds of useful articles, for example furniture, or apparel, or handbags, leaving all other kinds of designs uncovered. Or it could adopt an encompassing definition of protectable subject-matter while excluding specified categories, such as spare parts in general, or the designs of motor vehicles in particular.

Congress would also need to determine whether a claimant may cumulate forms of intellectual property protection. Currently, Chapter 13 requires a claimant to elect between vessel hull protection and design patent.[128] By contrast, Chapter 13 allows for the co-existence of copyright and design protection; the latter for the shape of the vessel hull as a whole, the former for particular design components.[129] Amending Chapter 13 to cover a broader range of useful articles need not alter that result, so long as it remained clear that copyright protection was limited to 'features', i.e. separable parts of the design of the useful article, rather than its entirety. Copyright should not provide a back-up extension of protection for the entire design of a useful article after the ten-year design protection term expires.

9.7 Conclusion

The 1976 Copyright Act and its legislative history adopt a restrictive standard that embraces individual design features while largely excluding the overall form of useful articles. Yet, under §113(a), if the design

[128] See 17 USC §1329. Relation to design patent law:

The issuance of a design patent under title 35, United States Code, for an original design for an article of manufacture shall terminate any protection of the original design under this chapter.

The H.R. 2696 Vessel Hull Design Protection Act was initially proposed as a form of design patent protection. 'The legislation creates a new design patent for vessel hulls. Confusion between copyright patent and trademark protection for hull models over the years has apparently produced a proliferation of unattributed and bad copies of expensive designs, and this legislation articulates clearer standards for the grant of a design patent.' *Vessel Hull Design Protection Act*, 144 Cong. Rec. H. 1243, 1247.

[129] See Compendium s. 1302 ('Vessel designs – the overall shape and form of a water craft's deck or hull – are useful articles and, as such, cannot be protected by copyright law . . . Purely ornamental two- and three-dimensional decorations on or in the surfaces of the deck or hull might be copyrightable, but the deck and hull themselves are not'). See also Hearings Before the Subcommittee on Courts and Intellectual Property on H.R. 2652, H.R. 2696 and H.R. 3163, 144 Cong. Rec. H. 521–57, Prepared Statement of Marybeth Peters, Register of Copyrights for the United States ('We do not believe that the existence or enforcement of protection under the Copyright Act should bear upon the existence or enforcement of protection under design legislation. The standards for obtaining the two forms of protection differ, as do the scope and duration of the protection').

previously existed as a freestanding original work of art, its application to or incorporation in the overall form of a useful article would not deprive the pre-existing PGS work of copyright protection. The resulting useful article will enjoy indirect copyright protection in whole or in part by virtue of the copyright in the underlying PGS work. The Supreme Court in *Star Athletica* now instructs courts to interpret the statutory separability test to mirror the §113(a) exclusive right of the author of a PGS work to reproduce that work in or on a useful article. This approach offers an effective way to discern separability of particular design elements, but proves more problematic in the case of the form of the article as a whole. While limiting the reverse-§113(a) analysis to discrete design 'features' better hews to the statute, it nonetheless leaves us with the paradox of the disparate treatment of pre-existing artworks applied to useful articles relative to artistic designs created as useful articles.

Because the statutory separate identifiability plus independent existence standard best accommodates individual design features that are representational or superfluous to the article's function, it arguably privileges design frivolity over sobriety, excrescence over simplicity, often disfavouring the cleaner elegance that may appeal to exponents of the modernist, 'form follows function' aesthetic (and to at least some judges and law professors). Accordingly, one may be sympathetic to endeavours to interpret the statute to encompass a wider range of overall forms of useful articles.[130] From the designer's perspective, more capacious standards would be desirable, especially in the absence of a design protection regime such as exists in the European Union.[131] But that is the point: in the absence of the kind of specially tailored coverage this chapter has proposed, Congress has determined that copyright, by and large, is not the appropriate vehicle. Thus, the 'separability' line Congress has drawn, albeit often difficult to discern coherently even (or especially) after *Star Athletica*, places most overall designs of useful articles in the public domain.

[130] In addition to the reverse-§113(a) approach, several such endeavours are detailed in *Varsity Brands, Inc.* v. *Star Athletica, LLC*, 799 F 3d 468, 484–5 (6th Cir. 2015), cert. granted 194 *Lawyers' Edition* 2d 829 (2016). See also Goldstein, 'Goldstein on Copyright', §2.5.3(c) ('it seems appropriate to place designs that are not essential to the utility of the useful article on the copyrightable side of the line'). The 'not essential to' standard resembles the rejected 'not dictated by' standard; both are variants on the idea/expression merger test.

[131] Directive 98/71/EC of the European Parliament and of the Council of 13 October 1998 on the Legal Protection of Designs, OJ 1998 L 289/28; see also Graeme Dinwoodie, 'Federalized Functionalism: The Future of Design Protection in the European Union' (1996) 24 *AIPLA Quarterly Journal* 611 (discussing the considerations underlying the Design Protection Directive in the European Union).

10 US Design Patent Law: A Historical Look at the Design Patent/Copyright Interface

*Jason J. Du Mont and Mark D. Janis**

Table 10.1 *Chronological table of legislation and statistics*

	Legislation		Applications[1]		Grants[1]	
	Main	Amend	Total	Avg/Y	Total	Avg/Y
1 – Isolation	1842		‡	‡	1,365	76
	1861		‡	‡	2,444	272
2 – Demarcation	1870[2]	1874,[3] 1887, 1902, 1939	238,680‡	2,911‡	161,758	1,973
3 – Shift to Partial Cumulation	1952	1982, 1994, 1999/2012	838,372	13,100	580,169	9,065

* The authors would like to thank Mayank Garg and Scott Skiles for their excellent research assistance on this project. We also benefited greatly from feedback on prior versions from Estelle Derclaye and Lionel Bently. Our thanks also go to Lynne Chave for editing our footnotes.

1 This table was added to conform with the other chapters in the book, and requires a few caveats. First, we make no causal claims about the impact of demarcated or cumulative rights and the quantity of design patent applications or grants. Secondly, due to limitations in the United States Patent & Trademark Office's ('USPTO') dataset and the lack of any clear effective date for many of the early patent statutes, the total number of applications and grants under each period are tied to the calendar year that the legislation was passed. For example, Period 2 – which begins with the passage of the 1870 Act on 8 July 1870 and ends with the passage of the 1952 Act on 19 July 1952 – combines all of the applications and grants from the calendar years of 1870 through to the end of 1951. As a result, the cumulative output from each period should only be used as a rough approximation. Thirdly, data on design patent applications is unavailable from the USPTO prior to 1880. Double dagger symbols (‡) are included next to all impacted periods. Fourthly, at the time of this writing, the output from the third period was capped at 2015. Finally, the dataset for this table can be found on the USPTO's website. Pat. Tech. Monitoring Team, 'US Patent Activity: Calendar Years 1790 to the Present', USPTO (last visited 15 July 2016), www.uspto.gov/web/offices/ac/ido/oeip/taf/h_counts.htm [https://perma.cc/Q4BS-XGNG].

2 Insofar as design patent law is concerned, the 1870 Act effectively merged and consolidated its two predecessors, the 1861 and 1842 Acts. It incorporated some elements of the 1842 Act (those not inconsistent with the 1861 Act) and omitted others (those intended to be repealed by the 1861 Act). We address some of these developments below in 10.3.1.1 and 10.3.1.2. For a more complete account of these nineteenth-century legislative developments, see Jason J. Du Mont, 'A Nonobvious Design: Reexamining the Origins of the Design Patent Standard' (2009) 45 *Gonzaga Law Review* 531, 546–8, 560–5, 573–82.

3 While the Revised Statutes of 1874 were principally intended to consolidate and simplify all US laws found in the Statutes at Large – by, among other things, removing repealed

10.1 Introduction

This chapter addresses the interface between the US design patent and copyright regimes. Comparatively little has been written about this subject.[4] A number of scholars, ourselves included, have instead directed attention to other interfaces of significance in design law: that between the utility patent and design patent systems,[5] and between the trademark and design patent systems.[6] And, of course, many scholars have analysed

laws and pooling those that remained in their original or amended states – they introduced some changes into the law, including into the design patent provisions. As a result, we have listed the Revised Statutes as an amendment to the 1870 Act, although they were intended to be treated as a restatement of it. See Du Mont, 'A Nonobvious Design', 560–1, 573–8.

[4] But cf. Ralph S. Brown, 'Copyright-like Protection for Designs' (1989) 19 *University of Baltimore Review* 308; Jerome Reichman, 'Design Protection After the Copyright Act of 1976: A Comparative View of the Emerging Interim Models' (1983) 31 *Journal of the Copyright Society* 267; Jerome Reichman, 'Design Protection and the New Technologies: The United States Experience in a Transnational Perspective' (1989) 19 *University of Baltimore Review* 6; Ryan Vacca, 'Design Patents: An Alternative When the Low Standards of Copyright are Too High?' (2007) 31 *Southern Illinois University Law Journal* 325. Older scholarship touching on the issue includes Gregory R. Mues, 'Dual Copyright and Design Patent Protection: Works of Art and Ornamental Designs' (1975) 49 *St John's Law Review* 543; Richard W. Pogue, 'Borderland: Where Copyright & Design Patent Meet' (1953) 52 *Michigan Law Review* 33; Note, 'Protecting the Artistic Aspects of Articles of Utility: Copyright or Design Patent?' (1953) 66 *Harvard Law Review* 877.

[5] See, e.g., Christopher V. Carani, 'Design Patent Functionality: A Sensible Solution' (2014) 7 *Landslide* 19; Jason J. Du Mont and Mark D. Janis, 'Functionality in Design Protection Systems' (2012) 19 *Journal of Intellectual Property Law* 261; Jason J. Du Mont and Mark D. Janis, 'Functionality in US Design Patent & Community Design Law', in Henning Hartwig (ed.), *Research Handbook on Design Law* (Cheltenham: Edward Elgar Publishing, forthcoming 2017), available at: https://papers.ssrn.com/sol3/papers.cfm?abstract_id=2773070; Christopher J. Gaspar, 'The Federal Circuit Locks Down the Ornamentality Requirement: Best Lock v. Ilco Unican' (1997) 23 *Iowa Journal of Corporation Law* 179; Fredrick L. Medlin, 'Functionality of Individual Features in Design Patents: A New Role After Egyptian Goddess' (2008) 77 *Patent, Trademark & Copyright Journal* 139; Perry J. Saidman, 'Functionality & Design Patent Validity & Infringement' (2009) 91 *Journal of the Patent & Trademark Office Society* 313; Perry J. Saidman and John M. Hintz, 'The Doctrine of Functionality in Design Patent Cases' (1989) 19 *University of Baltimore Law Review* 352.

[6] See, e.g., Margreth Barrett, 'Consolidating the Diffuse Paths to Trade Dress Functionality: Encountering TrafFix on the Way to Sears' (2004) 61 *Washington & Lee Law Review* 79; Graeme B. Dinwoodie, 'The Death of Ontology: A Teleological Approach to Trademark Law' (1999) 84 *Iowa Law Review* 611, 626; Anthony E. Dowell, 'Trade Dress Protection of Product Designs: Stifling the Progress of Science & the Useful Arts for an Unlimited Time' (1994) 70 *Notre Dame Law Review* 137; Jay Dratler, Jr, 'Trade Dress Protection for Product Configurations: Is There a Conflict with Patent Policy?' (1996) 24 *AIPLA Quarterly Journal* 427; Paul Heald, 'Sunbeam Products, Inc. v. The West Bend Co.: Exposing the Malign Application of the Federal Dilution Statute to Product Configurations' (1998) 5 *Journal of Intellectual Property Law* 415; Deborah J. Krieger, 'The Broad Sweep of Aesthetic Functionality: A Threat to Trademark Protection of Aesthetic Product Features' (1982) 51 *Fordham Law Review* 345, 354–9; Russell L. Law and Philip D. Junkins, 'Registrability of Packages & Configuration of Goods on the Supplemental Register: Design Patent vs. Trade-Mark Registration' (1954) 36 *Journal of the Patent & Trademark Office Society* 900; Mark P. McKenna, '(*Dys*)Functionality' (2011) 48 *Houston Law Review* 823, 843–8; Perry J. Saidman, 'Kan TrafFix Kops Katch the Karavan Kopy Kats? or Beyond Functionality:

intellectual property overlaps and the cumulation of rights at a more general level.[7]

Under modern US law, concurrent copyright and design patent protection for a given design is permissible; no election between regimes is required.[8] The goal of this chapter is to explain how US law arrived at this point, specifically by asking how design patent law has demarcated its protectable subject-matter over the course of its lengthy history, and by looking outwards from the perspective of design patent law to observe how US copyright law has evolved over that same time period.[9]

Although disputes about design patent/copyright cumulation have arisen only infrequently in recent reported decisions, the issue presents a number of difficult conceptual puzzles that still warrant attention. Consider, for example, a photograph. A photograph qualifies as a potentially copyrightable pictorial work of authorship under the express language of the 1976 Copyright Act.[10] The same photograph 'standing alone' would be ineligible for design patent protection according to the Patent and Trademark Office (PTO), because the design patent regime presumes that the design will be associated with an article of manufacture, rather than being mere 'abstract design'.[11] But the matter is hardly that simple. It would be entirely reasonable to characterise a photograph as surface ornamentation embedded in an article of manufacture (the article being the tangible print of the photograph on paper backing, or the electronic screen on which the

Design Patents are the Key to Unlocking the Trade Dress/Patent Conundrum' (2000) 82 *Journal of the Patent & Trademark Office Society* 839.

7 See, e.g., Laura A. Heyman, 'Overlapping Intellectual Property Doctrines: Election of Rights Versus Selection of Remedies' (2013) 17 *Stanford Technology Law Review* 239; Mark P. McKenna and Katherine J. Strandburg, 'Progress & Competition in Design' (2013) 17 *Stanford Technology Law Review* 1; Peter Lee and Madhavi Sunder, 'Design Patents: Law Without Design' (2013) 17 *Stanford Technology Law Review* 277; Jerome Reichman, 'Charting the Collapse of the Patent-Copyright Dichotomy: Premises for a Restructured International Intellectual Property System' (1995) *Cardozo Arts & Entertainment Law Journal* 475; Jerome Reichman, 'Legal Hybrids Between the Patent & Copyright Paradigms' (1994) 94 *Columbia Law Review* 2432.

8 See below, 10.4.

9 Another chapter in this volume addresses the design patent/copyright interface using copyright law as the frame of reference: see Chapter 9.

10 17 USC § 102(a)(5) (listing 'pictorial, graphic, and sculptural' works as a category of copyrightable subject-matter); 17 USC § 101 (defining 'pictorial, graphic, and sculptural' works as including photographs).

11 US Patent and Trademark Office, Manual of Patent Examining Procedure § 1504.01 (9th ed. Rev. 07.2015, Oct. 2015) (hereinafter 'MPEP').

photograph is displayed). A claim to surface ornamentation associated with an article of manufacture is unquestionably within the scope of design patent-eligible subject-matter. The PTO's practice of declaring photographs as falling outside of the design patent system may be a sound administrative decision, and may reflect a commonly held impulse about where in the intellectual property landscape photographs should reside, but it is not conceptually coherent.[12] Indeed, that sort of incoherence may become increasingly important as the design patent system encounters a rising wave of designs for computer-generated icons and other types of virtual designs.[13]

In 10.2, below, we consider the approaches of the earliest US design patent acts, which became effective in 1842 and 1861, respectively. We characterise this era as one in which the design patent and copyright regimes were quite isolated from one another. We show that while the design patent provisions reached many classes of subject-matter that are associated primarily with copyright today (for example statues, busts, labels and commercial prints), copyright at the time had a relatively limited reach, such that cumulation issues were rare.

In 10.3, we bring the analysis forward from 1870 to the early twentieth century, a time period characterised primarily by the expansion of copyright into the realm of commercial works, and the contraction of design patent law as a consequence of the adoption of an express ornamentality requirement. Here we show the emergence of copyright practices that seemed to suggest a strict separation between the design patent and copyright regimes, and a requirement to elect between design patent and copyright protection.

Finally, in 10.4, we conclude briefly with an overview of the pertinent case law of the modern era. Our focal point here is the *Yardley* decision,[14] in which the Court of Customs and Patent Appeals rejected the election requirement.

[12] In other work, we have argued that some of the cases are better understood within the context of patent law's disclosure doctrines. See Jason J. Du Mont and Mark D. Janis, 'Disclosing Designs' (2017) 69 *Vanderbilt Law Review* 1631.

[13] See Jason J. Du Mont and Mark D. Janis, 'Virtual Designs' (2014) 17 *Stanford Technology Law Review* 107, 135 (documenting the influx of design patents granted for virtual designs).

[14] 493 F 2d 1389 (CCPA 1974).

10.2 Isolationism: The 1842 and 1861 Design Patent Legislation (1842–1870)

In hindsight, the collision between design patent law and copyright law appears foreordained.[15] The initial proposal for a design patent regime was styled as a 'copyright' law[16] and drew heavily from a patchwork of British copyright and design laws.[17] Although this proposal did not pass, another proposal, derived from suggestions found in Patent Commissioner Henry Ellsworth's annual report,[18] became law the following year.[19] Recast as a design 'patent' law, the 1842 Act afforded design patent holders the exclusive right to make, use and sell their novel designs for a term of seven years. The Act required that design patent applications be subjected to pre-grant examination, and that they be governed by other utility patent rules.[20] But the Act also retained some of the copyright character of the original proposal – notably, in its provision defining categories of design-patent-eligible subject-matter.

Specifically, the subject-matter provision encompassed:

> [(1)] any new and original design for a manufacture, whether of metal or other material or materials, or
> [(2)] any new and original design for the printing of woolen, silk, cotton, or other fabrics, or
> [(3)] any new and original design for a bust, statue, or bas relief or composition in alto or basso relievo, or
> [(4)] any new and original impression or ornament, or to be placed on any article of manufacture, the same being formed in marble or other material, or
> [(5)] any new and useful pattern, or print, or picture, to be either worked into or worked on, or printed or painted or cast or otherwise fixed on, any article of manufacture, or
> [(6)] any new and original shape or configuration of any article of manufacture . . .[21]

This is an odd patchwork of subject-matter categories that might seem to the modern reader to spill out across the boundaries of many different intellectual

[15] For a history of the first design patent act, see Jason J. Du Mont and Mark D. Janis, 'The Origins of American Design Patent Protection' (2013) 88 *Indiana Law Journal* 837.

[16] Senator John Ruggles' 'copy-right' Bill also had many of the core hallmarks of modern patent regimes, such as pre-grant examination. A Bill for Promoting the Progress of Useful Arts, by Securing the Right of Invention and Copy-right to Proprietors of New Designs for Manufactures, for Limited Times, S. 269, 26th Cong., §4 (1841) (hereinafter '1841 Design Bill').

[17] For context on the British design and copyright legislation, see Chapter 6.

[18] Report from the Commissioner of Patents: Showing the Operation of the Patent Office During the year 1841, S. Rep. No. 169, 2 (1842) (hereinafter 'Ellsworth's Report for 1841').

[19] Act of 29 Aug. 1842, ch. 263, §3, 5 Stat. 543, 543–4 (1842). [20] Ibid.

[21] Act of 29 Aug. 1842 (above, note 19); see also William Edgar Simonds, *The Law of Design Patents* (New York: Baker, Voorhis & Co., 1874), p. 177 (disaggregating the 1842 Act into ten subject-matter classes).

property regimes. It covered the products of many disparate industries; it extended to both two- and three-dimensional designs; and it reached designs commonly associated with the useful arts, as well as those typically thought to fall within the fine arts. Viewed as a matter of the design enterprise, there was little that unified this collection of subject-matter. But seen as a product of the Whig protectionist agenda, the provision is at least coherent: it reflected Congress' concern about providing American manufacturers with every intellectual property right that their British competitors enjoyed under British law – whether they stemmed from British copyright or design laws.[22]

Congress' kitchen-sink approach to drafting the 1842 Act set the stage for questions concerning the interface between design patent law and other intellectual property regimes. It lifted the first three categories from Commissioner Ellsworth's annual report,[23] each reflecting a different subset of British design or copyright protection that was lacking in the US at the time.[24] One protected designs for manufactures made of metal or other materials, which iron manufacturers and others could use to protect the shapes of their stoves or the ornamentation applied to them. Another protected designs for surface ornamentation applied to textiles, whose manufacturers had long applied weaving and printing techniques to produce unique designs for rugs, clothing and other materials. And, lastly, one protected designs for sculptures, like busts or statues, which had long been unprotected by US copyright law.[25] Thus, Ellsworth's proposal contained separate categories of two- and three-dimensional designs from the useful arts, and another category of three-dimensional designs from the fine arts.[26]

To these three categories, Congress added three additional categories drawn from some of the same British sources.[27] Not surprisingly, the result

[22] See Du Mont and Janis, 'Origins', 871–3.

[23] See Ellsworth's Report for 1841 (above, note 18), at 2.

[24] The first class in the 1842 Act was intended to generically reflect the subject-matter found in the British Design Registration Act 1839, the second class incorporated the British Textile Act 1839 (and the omitted fabrics it haphazardly lumped into the Design Registration Act 1839), and finally the third class transplanted the British Sculptures Act 1814. See An Act to Secure to Proprietors of Designs for Articles of Manufacture the Copyright of such Designs for a Limited Time, 2 & 3 Vict., c. 17, s. 1 (1839) (Eng.) (hereinafter 'British Design Registration Act 1839'); An Act for extending the Copyright of Designs for Calico Printing to Designs for printing other woven Fabrics, 2 & 3 Vict., c. 13, s. 1 (1839) (Eng.) (hereinafter 'British Textile Act 1839'); An Act to Amend and Render Effectual an Act of His present Majesty, for Encouraging the Art of Making New Models and Casts of Busts, and other Things therein mentioned, and for giving further Encouragement to such Arts, 1814, 54 Geo. 3, c. 56, s. 1 (Eng.) (hereinafter 'British Sculptures Act 1814').

[25] See Ellsworth's Report for 1841 (above, note 18), at 2.

[26] See ibid. (describing his proposal as providing 'the exclusive benefit of new and original designs for articles of manufacture, both in the fine and useful arts . . .').

[27] Whether Congress derived this language directly from the British Design Registration Act 1839, or indirectly from it via the 1841 US Bill, is not entirely clear. Consider the language reproduced below from the 1841 US Bill and the 1839 British legislation. We have indicated how the language compares to categories four, five and six from the 1842 Act:

was a provision that seemed to be comprehensive on first blush, but also appeared to be littered with internal inconsistencies upon closer inspection. For example, it was not clear how category two in the statute (covering prints for fabric) related to category five (covering patterns, prints or pictures on any article of manufacture). In addition, category one, covering designs for 'manufactures', could be read to encompass all of the remaining categories.[28]

These overlap problems – so typical of intellectual property provisions that attempt to draw lines on the basis of subject-matter – easily could have been avoided.[29] Whereas the British legislation needed to use the multi-category structure because the legislation afforded different rights to different categories of subject-matter,[30] the American design patent

1841 Design Bill:
[Category 5] First. For the pattern or print to be either worked, ~~stamped~~, printed, or painted, into or on any article of manufactured linen, cotton, calico, muslin, or other textile fabric;
[Category 4] Second. ~~For the modelling, or the casting, or the embossment, or the chasing, or engraving, or for~~ any other kind of impression or ornament, on any article of manufacture ~~not being textile fabric;~~
[Category 6] Third. For the shape or configuration of any article of manufacture not included or embraced in the class first mentioned.

British Design Registration Act 1839:
[Category 5] First. For the Pattern or Print, to be either worked into or worked on, or printed on or painted on, any Article of Manufacture, ~~being Tissue or textile Fabric, except Lace, and also except Linens, Cottons, Calicoes, Muslins, and any other Article within the Meaning of the Acts mentioned in the Schedule hereto annexed:~~
[Category 4] Second~~. For the Modelling, or the Casting, or the Embossment, or the Chasing, or the Engraving, or for~~ any other Kind of Impression or Ornament, on Article of Manufacture, ~~not being a Tissue or textile Fabric:~~
[Category 6] Third. For the Shape or Configuration of any Article of Manufacture, ~~except Lace, and also except Linens, Cottons, Calicoes, Muslins, and any other Article within the Meaning of the Acts mentioned in the Schedule hereto annexed:~~

Congress likely omitted the language protecting engravings from the second class of the 1841 Design Bill and the British Design Registration Act of 1839 because engravings were already protected in US copyright law at the time. See Act of 3 Feb. 1831, ch. 16, § 1, 4 Stat. 436, 436 (1831) (hereinafter 'Act of 3 Feb. 1831'). Unaccounted for in the text, Congress added a reference to impressions made of marble to the fourth class of the 1842 Act, and it added pictures to the patterns and prints found in class five.

28 See discussion below, notes 43–44 (tracing the statutory origins of this term).

29 For a more in-depth explanation of product-specific and open-ended class structures in the corresponding British legislation, see Brad Sherman and Lionel Bently, *The Making of Modern Intellectual Property Law* (Cambridge: Cambridge University Press, 1999), pp. 74–5.

30 For example, under the British regimes at the time, statues or busts falling under the British Sculptures Act 1814 would have been protected for a term of fourteen years, textiles under the British Textile Act 1839 would have been protected for three months, while those registered under the British Design Registration Act 1839 would have been protectable for twelve months, and the remaining articles of manufacture falling under the British Design Registration Act 1839 would have received a twelve-month term, unless they were for an impression or ornament made of metal, whereby they would have been eligible for a three-year term of protection. Compare British Sculptures Act 1814 (above, note 24), at s. 1, and British Textile Act 1839 (above, note 24), at s. 1, with British Design Registration Act 1839 (above, note 24), at s. 1.

legislation provided the same package of rights to all categories of design. Congress could have dispensed with the category structure altogether, substituting generic umbrella language,[31] or, alternatively, compressing the multiple categories into a single, internally consistent list (as the utility patent subject-matter provision does). The problematic multi-category structure of the design patent subject-matter provision, and the sheer miscellany of subject-matter covered under it, created confusion about the purpose and function of the design patent system.

Yet the overlap with copyrightable subject-matter, which seems profound when viewed from a modern perspective, was actually minimal in early practice.[32] When the design patent act was passed in 1842, copyright law only extended protection to books, maps, charts, musical compositions and a limited set of prints and engravings.[33] Equally important, copyright had yet to develop a unifying conception of the act of authorship, and so there was no clear conceptual path for expanding copyright protection from its existing realm to other endeavours – such as those in the visual arts – that might have been considered authorial acts (i.e. beyond bald natural law or Lockean labour-centric assertions).[34]

In time, the oddities of the design patent subject-matter categories, and the newly extended reach of copyright, combined to give rise to questions about the design patent/copyright interface. Below, we survey two areas of subject-matter in which the interface was important: designs for busts or statues, and designs for prints or pictures.

10.2.1 Statues and Busts

To modern observers, the 1842 Act's class protecting designs for 'bust[s], statue[s], or bas relief[s] or composition[s] in alto or basso relievo' is probably the most ill-fitting. Indeed, it protected a range of sculptural works that are today more commonly associated with copyright law, such as the bust and statue shown in Figures 10.1 and 10.2 respectively.[35]

While this subject-matter class encompassed designs for some traditional works of fine art, whose value was derived from their aesthetic

[31] Congress eventually did so, in legislation enacted in 1902. See discussion below, at 10.3.2.

[32] See also Chapter 6 (finding commentary in the UK similarly quiet about design/copyright overlaps until the early twentieth century).

[33] Act of 3 Feb. 1831 (above, note 27), at 436.

[34] See Oren Bracha, 'Owning Ideas: A History of Anglo-American Intellectual Property', S.J.D. Dissertation, Harvard Law School (2005), p. 376.

[35] The drawings from both design patents were lightly edited for publication by removing scanning artefacts.

Figure 10.1 Philip Garbeille, bust of Zachary Taylor
Source: US Patent No. D172 (issued 28 Mar. 1848)

Figure 10.2 Clark Mills, equestrian statue
Source: US Patent No. D704 (issued 15 May 1855)

appeal only, the remaining classes covered designs for the useful arts – that is, objects having some utility beyond aesthetics.

Congress might have included statues and busts because it intended to use the design patent regime as the exclusive vehicle for protecting any three-dimensional work whose commercial value stemmed from its appearance. After all, no other intellectual property regime was specifically calibrated to protect this category of subject-matter at the time.[36] In retrospect, copyright might have been the most logical place, but it did not protect works of art (beyond a narrow band of etchings, engravings and prints).[37] Indeed, copyright was still focused on protecting works that were reproduced in two dimensions.[38]

Another theory is that Congress simply viewed the design patent act as a gap-filling measure for copyright law. Indeed, Congress had already failed to pass copyright protection for busts and casts after being petitioned in 1838,[39] and perhaps some members viewed the new design regime as a logical alternative, without considering deeply how that subject-matter category would fit alongside the others in the design patent provisions. Because the differences between patent and copyright had not yet fully crystallised, it may have seemed to be of little consequence whether the subject-matter ended up in one type of regime or the other.

Yet another explanation for the decision to include statues and busts in the design patent subject-matter provisions relates to the methods by which these works were created and reproduced. Writing in hindsight over thirty years after the 1842 Act's passage, William Simonds – patent practitioner and eventual Patent Commissioner – hinted at this account in his 1874 design patent treatise:

> Statues and other productions of the sculptor's art, intended solely to gratify a taste for the ideal and the beautiful, cannot, perhaps, be classed logically in every respect with the other things named, whose chief purpose is a useful one . . . but they can be logically classed together in that it requires the same faculty, power or talent to

[36] See George Ticknor Curtis, *Treatise on the Law of Copyright* (Boston: Little & Brown, 1847), p. 115.

[37] See Act of 29 Apr. 1802, ch. 36, § 2, 2 Stat. 171 (extending copyright protection to 'who [ever] shall invent and design, engrave, etch or work, or from his own works and inventions, shall cause to be designed and engraved, etched or worked, any historical or other print or prints'); Act of 3 Feb. 1831, ch. 16, § 1, 4 Stat. 436 (removing the 'historical' limitation from this class and protecting 'who shall invent, design, etch, engrave, work, or cause to be engraved, etched, or worked from his own design, any print or engraving').

[38] Even musical compositions – which were added to the copyright statute in 1831 – still had to be fixed, printed and published before obtaining protection. See Robert Brauneis, 'Musical Work Copyright for the Era of Digital Sound Technology' (2014) 17 *Tulane Journal of Technology and Intellectual Property* 1, 12.

[39] See S. Doc. No. 25-475, at 1 (2d Sess. 1838).

produce the one as the other. It requires the exercise of the same power or faculty, in kind, to produce a beautiful vase as to model a beautiful statue.[40]

While Simonds's assertions might be plausible,[41] the 'faculties' shared by these groups were likely more pragmatic, and oriented around the trades or skills used to produce these works at scale. Indeed, the cast-iron manufacturers – who, not coincidentally, were also the group that lobbied for design protection in the first place – relied on similar moulding and casting techniques to mass produce three-dimensional works of art, and would have benefited from having these works protected.[42] When Commissioner Ellsworth first suggested that statues and busts be included as eligible subject-matter,[43] he also might have been trying to subtly reinforce ties to mass production by referring to the output from all of the categories as 'articles of manufacture'.[44] In fact, many of the design patents granted for statues and busts during this era – like the one depicted above for a bust of General (and eventually President) Zachary Taylor – included specifications that expressed the sculptors' intention to mould and reproduce the work.[45] Although these reproductions did not function as perfect substitutes, they helped satisfy the working class's

[40] Simonds, *Law of Design Patents*, pp. 183–4.

[41] Simonds's argument also fails to explain why the design patent act was deemed more appropriate than copyright law for statues and busts. In fact, there is no evidence from lawmakers that copyright protection was perceived as inappropriate at the time of the design patent act's passage, nor that design patent protection was somehow preferable. A preference for design patent would also have been curious given the fact that copyright seemed to be expanding. See above, note 37 (documenting the expansion of the prints under the 1802 and 1831 statutes).

[42] See Petition of a Number of Manufacturers & Mechanics of the US, Praying the Adoption of Measures to Secure to Them Their Rights in Patterns & Designs, S. Doc. 26-154 (2d Sess. 1841) (hereinafter 'Manufacturers' Petition').

[43] Commissioner Ellsworth described the proposed regime as protecting 'new and original designs for articles of manufacture, both in the fine and useful arts . . .' Ellsworth's Report for 1841 (above, note 18), at 2.

[44] While the British Design Registration Act 1839 was the first to use the term 'article of manufacture' when referring to its protected subject-matter, statues and busts were not explicitly included within its categories (or excluded, for that matter). See British Design Registration Act of 1839 (above, note 24). British manufacturers did not need to rely on their design regime for the protection of statues and busts because these works already enjoyed copyright protection under separate legislation, whose term of protection also lasted longer. Compare Registration Act 1839 (above, note 24) (lasting fourteen years), with British Sculptures Act 1814 (above, note 24) (lasting one to three years depending on its material and classification). Senator John Ruggles' initial Bill also used the term 'article of manufacture' as an open-ended category, but the proposal lacked specific reference to statues and busts – which were unique to Ellsworth's proposal. See 1841 Design Bill (above, note 13); Ellsworth's Report for 1841 (above, note 18), at 2.

[45] US Patent No. D172 (issued 28 Mar. 1848) ('I provide a pattern for a bust of Gen. Z. Taylor by modeling or otherwise, and from this prepare moulds in the usual way for casting duplicates of my pattern').

demand for small-scale reproductions, like miniature statuettes, figurines, souvenirs and trinkets.

Whatever the reason for their inclusion,[46] statues and busts were not commonly patented under the first two design patent acts.[47] As shown in

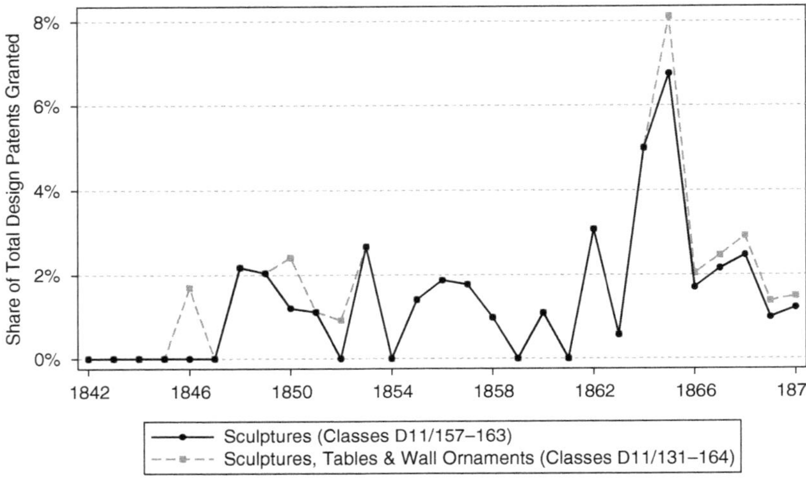

Figure 10.3 Annual share of total design patents granted for sculptures[48]

Figure 10.3 by the solid line, sculptures never rose above 6.76 per cent of the annual design patents granted. But that number does not tell the full story.

[46] Additional explanations might include: (1) the wish to create a public central repository for innovative statues and busts at the Patent Office, which did not exist in copyright law until 1870; (2) belief in the importance of pre-grant examination, which was renewed in utility patent law by the 1836 Patent Act and first design Bill's drafter, Senator John Ruggles; and (3) the view that three-dimensional works were not 'writings' under the US Constitution and were therefore inappropriate for copyright protection. See, e.g., Du Mont, 'A Nonobvious Design', 544 (addressing the Patent Office's potential role as repository); Du Mont and Janis, 'Origins', 862 (discussing the role of examination); Ralph D. Clifford and Richard J. Peltz-Steele, 'The Constitutionality of Design Patents' (2015) 14 *Chicago-Kent Journal of Intellectual Property* 553, 575 (asserting, to the contrary, that sculptures 'have long been considered "writings" under the Constitution' but basing this assertion on dicta in a Supreme Court case decided in 1954).

[47] Except for the table at the beginning of the chapter, all of the empirical analysis in this chapter was generated using a dataset that we began building in March of 2013 through a series of Freedom of Information Act requests with the USPTO. See Jason J. Du Mont and Mark D. Janis, *American Design Patent Law: A Legal History* (Cambridge: Cambridge University Press, forthcoming).

[48] Under the US Patent Classification System ('USPC'), sculptures are aggregated with tables and wall ornaments. To help parse the data, we offer two different points of comparison in Figure 10.3. The first is more narrowly tailored to sculptures, counting only design patents whose primary classification falls between D11/157 to 163 of the

Indeed, the ebbs and flows that can be seen in Figure 10.3, in large part, reflect the small quantity of design patents granted during this initial era (e.g. in 1865 there were only 15 design patents granted for sculptures of the 222 total). Even if one takes a broad view of sculptural works that includes all table and wall ornaments – which are depicted in Figure 10.3 by the dotted line – the maximum share of total design patents granted to these works never rose above 8.11 per cent during this period.[49]

10.2.2 *Useful Patterns, Prints or Pictures for Articles of Manufacture*

The second category of subject-matter that eventually sparked questions about its interaction with copyright law extended protection to 'any new and useful pattern, or print, or picture, to be either worked into or worked on, or printed or painted or cast or otherwise fixed on, any article of manufacture' (category five, above).[50] Much of the confusion about the scope of this category stemmed from its relationship to another category in the 1842 Act (category two, above), which protected designs for prints applied to 'woolen, silk, cotton, or other fabrics'. From the statute's language, the former category's open-ended application to any 'article of manufacture' appears to subsume the later category's product-specific application to fabrics (i.e. woollens, silks and cottons are all articles of manufacture). And its legislative history appears to support this construction.[51] Yet when coupled with a few terms bearing no legislative

USPC (so-called simulative designs for two- or three-dimensional ornamental art forms). This approach yielded the fewest false positives, as we confirmed by manually reviewing all of the design patents granted for this time period that fell within the mainline class D11/131. Nonetheless, this approach tends to under-report the quantity of designs that might qualify as sculptures. This is caused by three things. First, some design patents are simply misclassified. For example, after running some text-based searches using the patents' titles, we uncovered a handful of design patents that should have been classified in classes D11/157 to 163. See, e.g., US Patent No. D16 (issued 31 Jan. 1844) (labelling the patent's figures as fine arts and sculptures, titling the patent as a 'Design for a Bust of (Robert) Burns', and yet classifying the patent under D5/39, which covers designs for simulative sheet material). Secondly, to avoid double counting, we ignored cross-classifications, which would not capture design patents whose principal classifications fall outside classes D11/157 to 163. This is relatively rare within these classes, during this era, but nonetheless unaccounted for above. And, finally, this approach omits design patents classified in the more general (mainline) class D11/131, rather than in the more specific subclasses D11/157–163.

The second point of comparison takes a much broader view of sculptures by including all design patents granted under D11/131 (i.e. all sculptures, tables and wall ornaments). While this approach over-reports the number of sculptures, it was included to show that sculptures made up the bulk of these types of works – as shown by the proximity of the two lines in Figure 10.3.

[49] See ibid. [50] See Act of 29 Aug. 1842 (above, note 19).

[51] See discussion above, note 44 (tracing the use of the phrase 'article of manufacture' in the 1842 Act and its antecedents).

antecedent, the Act's structure leads to questions about the scope of the category protecting design for patterns, prints and pictures.

As a testament to the 1842 Act's confusing framework, when it was amended in 1861 to provide applicants with different term and pricing options – replacing the Act's fixed seven-year term and pricing structure with a three-and-a-half-, seven- or fourteen-year term, and the ability to extend the term under certain circumstances – the product-specific category was entirely omitted by Congress (i.e. removing a 'new and original design for the printing of woolen, silk, cotton, or other fabrics').[52] When in conference, '[t]he Senate was unwilling to agree to so much of the section as related to designs for patterns, regarding it as too complicated'.[53] The omission does not appear to have had any effect on the operation of the design patent system. According to the Patent Office's records surrounding the 1861 Act's passage, the quantity and share of design patents granted for sheet material[54] remained substantial, comprising a whopping 44 per cent of the design patents granted in 1861.[55] Presumably, the Patent Office must have assumed that the omitted category was subservient to the open-ended category that was retained.[56]

Although the exact relationship between the categories might not have mattered any longer, there were still questions about scope of the open-ended category. On the one hand, it was intended to protect designs for

[52] Du Mont, 'A Nonobvious Design', nn. 89–103 (and accompanying text); see Act of 2 Mar. 1861, ch. 88, § 11, 12 Stat. 246, 248 (1861).

[53] See *Congressional Globe*, 26th Congress, 2d Sess. 1248 (1861).

[54] Three important caveats should be noted. First, to avoid double counting, we have ignored design patents with cross-reference classifications to sheet material, and used the primary parent classes only. Within the USPC, sheet material is classified as under D5. Secondly, this data includes some false positives, since class D5 also includes both textile and paper yard goods, and the USPC does not distinguish between the materials. However, it appears that the vast majority of the relevant design patents were for fabrics, since the assignees of record largely track with large carpet manufacturers from this period. Finally, this data omits design patents granted for prints, patterns and pictures that are classified by product application, rather than raw material (i.e. sheet material). For example, there are many patents granted for carpets and rugs that are classified as furnishings and not sheet material. Whether the under-counting from failure to account for product applications or the over-counting from paper goods dominates is not clear.

[55] The concentration of patents classified as sheet material undergo several ebbs and flows under the 1861 Act. However, they remain the most highly concentrated design patent class over this time period: from 1861 to 1870, comprising 44.37%, 46.67%, 54.55%, 38.57%, 25.68%, 21.43%, 15.08%, 30.11%, 20.67% and 20.84% of the total patents granted, respectively. See discussion above, note 48 (providing caveats for interpreting this data).

[56] See *Ex parte Bartholomew*, 1869 *Decisions of the Commissioner of Patents* 103, 103 (noting that '[t]he definition of the subject-matter, or, in other words, of a "design," is the same in both acts'); Hector T. Fenton, *The Law of Patents for Designs* (Philadelphia: William J. Campbell, 1889), p. 3 (noting 'that the later [(i.e. the remaining class)] is inclusive of the former [(i.e. the omitted class)]'); Simonds, *Law of Design Patents*, p. 179 (describing the omission of this class as '. . . more apparent than real' because of the retention of the broader class for new and useful patterns).

mass-produced two-dimensional surface ornamentation applied to a broader range of products than just fabrics – like wall-papers and tissues – but its outer bounds remained fuzzy. Indeed, applicants commonly relied on this class to justify the protection of several different commercially oriented works that were not protected within the federal intellectual property system. For example, design patents like the ones in Figures 10.4 and 10.5 were often used to protect labels and other commercial prints that were not yet protectable through copyright law, which was limited to a narrow band of engravings and prints (and eventually photographs in 1865).[57]

The Patent Office also routinely granted design patents – like those in Figures 10.6 and 10.7 – to commercial prints that incorporated trademarks (titled as 'Design(s) for Trade-Marks').[58] Since there was no federal trademark system at the time, it is not surprising that manufacturers exploited this category's broad language to obtain protection, whatever the resulting scope of protection might have been. But the Patent Office's endorsement of this practice was extraordinary, and not particularly consistent.

For example, the 1865 Patent Office's rules under Commissioner Holloway provided a roadmap that outlined how to obtain design patents for the graphic elements of trademarks:

> § 76. Names, titles, bill-heads, and other matters intended for use as circulars or trade-marks, if printed in the ordinary movable types, are not held to be patentable as designs.
>
> § 77. When any such matter is the special work of an artist for a specified purpose, as when engraved, it may be patented as a design. Hence when a patent is desired for a design to be used as a trade-mark, it is recommended that the same be engraved.[59]

Presumably, it was the emphasis on artistry that pushed these works into the realm of design patent law. Although trademarks were not protectable per se, design patents could be used to protect their artistic elements, as well as those found in other commercial prints and labels. But the Patent Office's emphasis on mere material changes – especially engravings, which were already protected by copyright law – illustrates the flimsy nature of these subject-matter boundaries, and raises questions about the scope of protection that these design patents provided.

[57] See Act of 3 Feb. 1831 (above, note 27), at 436 (protecting those 'who shall invent, design, etch, engrave, work, or cause to be engraved, etched, or worked from his own design, any print or engraving'); Act of 3 Mar. 1865, ch. 126, § 1, 13 Stat. 540 (1865) (extending protection to 'photographs and the negatives thereof').

[58] See also *American Artisan & Patent Record*, 10 May 1865, 15 (containing an advertisement for a firm specialising in design patent-related matters that described '[l]abels and trade-marks for medicines, perfumery in bottles, boxes, or other objects ...' as suitable subject-matter for design patents).

[59] Rules & Directions for Proceedings in the Patent Office 23 (1 Jan. 1865).

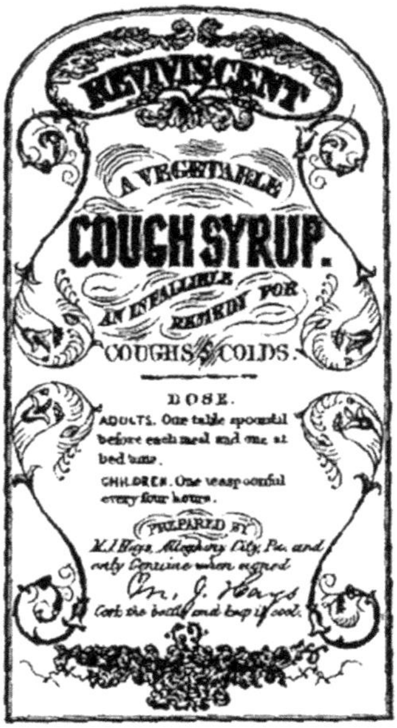

Figure 10.4 Margaret J. Hays, design for a label
Source: US Patent No. D2,914 (issued 4 Feb. 1868)

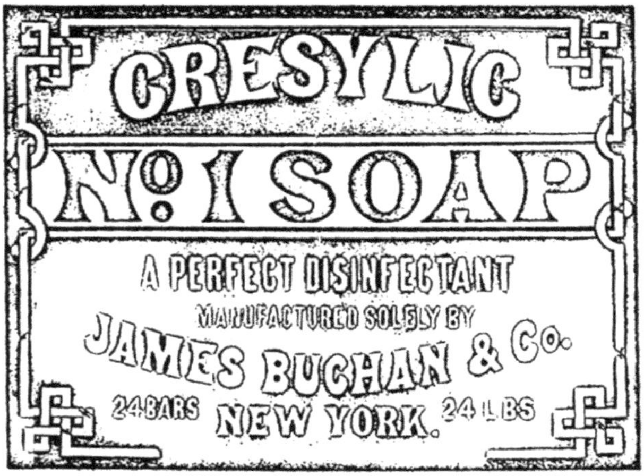

Figure 10.5 John Fahnestock, design for a label
Source: US Patent No. D2,715 (issued 6 Aug. 1867)

Figure 10.6 John W. Carroll, design for a trademark
Source: US Patent No. D2,487 (issued 9 Oct. 1866)

Figure 10.7 John and Lysander Hamlin, design for a trademark
Source: US Patent No. D3,435 (issued 20 Mar. 1869) (lightly edited to remove scanning artifacts)

Around the same time as Commissioner Holloway's rule changes, the Patent Office also began granting more patents for designs titled as trademarks.

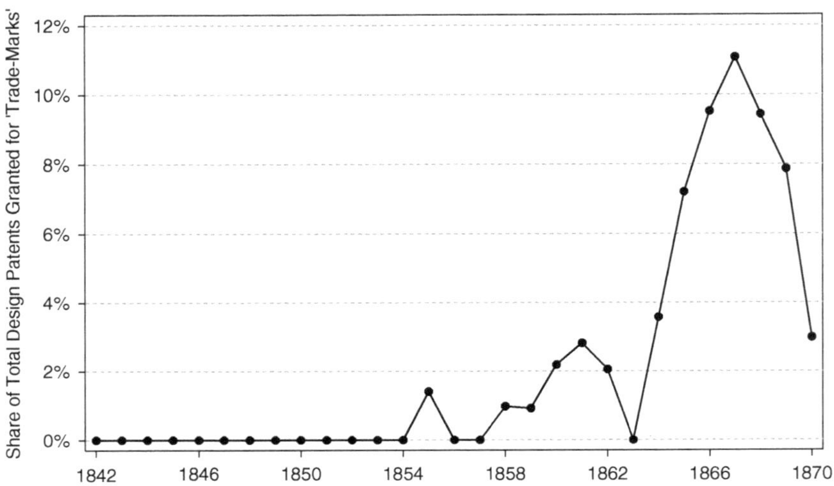

Figure 10.8 Annual share of total design patents granted for 'trade-marks'[60]

To place Figure 10.8 in context, from 1842 until the 1870 Act's passage, the Patent Office granted at least 202 such design patents.[61] They reached their peak total in 1868, when the Patent Office granted 42 of them, and their peak share of total patents in 1867, when they comprised 11.08 per cent of all design patents granted.

Despite the popularity of these design patents, subsequent administrations struggled to refine design patent law's relationship with trademark law, oscillating between extremes. In 1867, Commissioner Theaker expunged Sections 76 and 77 of the 1865 rules (above) and substituted a provision stating that '[t]rade-marks merely are not patentable. There must be some new design, such as is contemplated by . . . [the design patent act].'[62] Yet only two years later, a new administration under Commissioner Fisher construed

[60] These quantities are likely under-representative because our identification strategy depended on use of the term 'trademark' (or a derivative) in the title of the design patent. For obvious reasons, this was necessary because there is no class in the USPC for trademarks.

[61] The first was granted in 1855, and the last was granted in 1870. As detailed in the following section, the Patent Office halted this practice after federal trademark protection was incorporated into the 1870 Act – granting only two more design patents for trademarks under the new regime before bringing it to a halt. See discussion below, at 10.3.1.

[62] Rules & Directions for Proceedings in the Patent Office 21 (1 Aug. 1867).

the class protecting patterns, prints or pictures for articles of manufacture as referring to 'ornament combined with utility, as in the case of trade-marks'.[63] Consequently, more than any other class, it was the protection of patterns, prints and pictures that helped set the stage for more difficult questions involving the cumulation of intellectual property rights.

10.3 A New Grey: Design Patents in an Era of Copyright Expansionism (1870–1952)

While the initial design patent acts covered a broad array of subject-matter, the regime remained relatively isolated from other areas of intellectual property.[64] From 1842 to 1870, there was no federal trademark or unfair competition protection for designs. Similarly, copyright law failed to protect most commercial prints and three-dimensional works of art. Although there is evidence that manufacturers used the design patent regime to plug some of these gaps, each body of law largely remained sealed away from the next, providing little opportunity for interface questions.

In 1870, this model was fundamentally altered when Congress enacted the first comprehensive intellectual property act in US history.[65] The Act not only brought copyright and patent laws under the same roof, but it also included the US's first federal trademark regime.[66] Within this new ecosystem, design patent law struggled to find its identity. Indeed, much of the debate during this era was sparked by the expansion of copyright law into spaces once thought unique to design patent law, such as three-dimensional works and commercial prints. In this section, we cover how the Patent Office, courts and Congress responded to these difficult questions under the 1870 and 1902 Acts.

[63] *Ex parte Bartholomew*, 1869 *Decisions of the Commissioner of Patents* 103, 104. Fisher's emphasis on utility was presumably tied to the class's text, which protected 'any new and *useful* pattern, or print, or picture ... [for an] article of manufacture'. See Act of 2 Mar. 1861 (above, note 52) (emphasis added).

[64] Commissioner Samuel Fisher regarded the subject-matter of utility patent, design patent and copyright law as wholly distinct from each other. See *Ex parte Sellers*, 1870 *Decisions of the Commissioner of Patents* 58, 58 (comparing utility patents to design patents and noting that they were intended 'for a new class of patents, granted to a different class of persons and for a different class of subjects, for different periods of time, and upon the payment of different fees ... [, and that t]hese subjects of invention or contrivance are in truth as distinct from each other as either is from copyright'). Nonetheless, most administrations struggled to define the relationship between design and utility patents.

[65] For a complete account of the 1870 Act's legislative history, see Du Mont, 'A Nonobvious Design', 561–7, 573–8 (and accompanying notes).

[66] Act of 8 Jul. 1870, ch. 230, 16 Stat. 198 (1870).

10.3.1 Repositioning Design Patents within the New Ecosystem

The design patent portions of the 1870 Act underwent several changes.[67] Beyond the removal of its US citizenship requirement, however, these changes were largely cosmetic.[68] In addition to breaking up the design patent statute into six smaller subcomponents, the 1870 Act also included some alterations to its class structure: (1) removing any reference to marble in the class protecting impressions or ornaments, and combining this class with the one protecting patterns, prints or pictures; (2) combining the broad catch-all class protecting any design for a manufacture, with the class protecting busts and statues; and (3) adding back the class protecting specific fabrics, which was errantly omitted from the 1861 Act.[69]

It appears that Congress did not intend for these changes to alter the scope of design patent-eligible subject-matter. To be certain, one might assume, for example, that Congress' omission of marble and its decision to combine statues and busts within the generic class for manufactures reflected Congress' intent to remove the fine arts altogether from design patent protection. But this was not the case. In fact, because of the unique circumstances that gave rise to the 1870 Act, we know these changes were merely cosmetic. Unlike most patent bills from this era, the 1870 Act's text did not originate from the Committee on Patents. Rather, the Committee started with a draft from another commission that Congress appointed to consolidate and simplify all federal laws in the wake of the Civil War.[70] It then excised the copyright and patent provisions, and subsequently amended them to effectuate the changes it wished to incorporate into the laws at the time, like the creation of a federal trademark

[67] Compare Act of 8 Jul. 1870 (above, note 66), at §§ 71–76, with Act of 2 Mar. 1861 (above, note 52), at § 11, and Act of 29 Aug. 1842 (above, note 19), at § 3.

[68] See, e.g., Act of 8 Jul. 1870 (above, note 66), at § 71. However, the Act did introduce some confusion about the designs available for extension. See ibid. at § 74; Simonds, *Law of Design Patents*, pp. 207–13.

[69] Compare Act of 8 Jul. 1870 (above, note 66), at § 71 (' ... any person who, by his own industry, genius, efforts, and expense, has invented or produced any new and original design for a *manufacture, bust, statue, alto-relievo, or bas-relief*; any new and original design for the printing of *wool[l]en, silk, cotton, or other fabrics*; any new and original impression, ornament, pattern, print or picture, to be printed, painted, cast or otherwise placed on or worked into any article of manufacture; or any new, useful, and original shape or configuration of any article of manufacture ...') (emphasis added), with Act of 2 Mar. 1861 (above, note 52), at § 11.

[70] For background on this commission and the Patent Committee's subsequent incorporation of their work into the 1870 Act, see Du Mont, 'A Nonobvious Design', 573–8 (and accompanying notes) and P. J. Federico, 'Commentary on the New Patent Act' (1993) 75 *Journal of the Copyright Society* 161, 165 (originally printed in 1954).

regime.[71] Most important, for our purposes, the commission that supplied the Patent Committee with its draft of the copyright and patent provisions was not supposed to substantively alter the laws (i.e. from those not already overruled or amended).[72] So, the initial draft that it provided to the Patent Committee should reflect the law as it was at the time when the commission consolidated the Statutes at Large. This is critical because a careful comparison of the commission's draft and the resulting 1870 Act reveals that their respective class structures were identical[73] – meaning that alterations should be understood as artefacts of the consolidation process, not as substantive amendments.[74] As a result, we can safely infer that the changes to the subject-matter provisions in the 1870 Act were not intended to change the scope of eligible subject-matter of design patents.[75]

However, simply by including the design patent provisions as part of the comprehensive legislative scheme of the 1870 Act, Congress may have changed the way in which the design patent regime was perceived.[76] Instead of being tucked away in the Statutes at Large alongside amendments to the utility patent laws, design patents now had a permanent

[71] This is also apparent from the 1870 Act's title, which added the term 'amend' to the commission's draft. Compare A Bill to Revise, Consolidate, and Amend the Statutes Relating to Patents & Copyrights, H.R. 1714, 41st Cong. § 72 (as reported by H. Comm. on Patents, 7 Apr. 1870) (hereinafter '1870 Bill') (describing the Bill as revising, consolidating and *amending* the copyright and patent laws), with The Statutes Relating to Patents & Copyrights as Revised, Simplified, Arranged, & Consolidated by the Commission Appointed for that Purpose (on file at The National Archives, Records of the US House of Representatives, Record Group 233) (hereinafter '1869 Draft of Revised Statutes') (describing the draft as revising, simplifying, arranging and consolidating the copyright and patent laws, but not *amending* them).

[72] Frustrated by what it perceived as overreach, the committee overseeing the revision subsequently appointed a third party to take the commission's output and to remove and notate any changes it had made. See Ralph H. Dawn and Ernest R. Fiedler, 'The Federal Statutes: Their History & Use' (1938) 22 *Minnesota Law Review* 1008, 1013.

[73] Indeed, the Committee on Patents only altered one word found in the commission's recitation of classes, which we address in 10.3.2 below. See 1870 Bill (above, note 71), at § 72 (adding the word 'useful' to the class protecting shapes or configurations or articles of manufacture).

[74] Based on the commission's citation to the 1842 Act in the margins of this section of its draft, the inclusion of the class for fabrics – which was omitted in the 1861 Act – likely made it back into the 1870 Act because it was found in the 1842 Act, and had never been expressly overruled by the 1861 Act. See 1869 Draft of Revised Statutes (above, note 71), at § 69.

[75] See also Simonds, *Law of Design Patents*, p. 180 (describing the 1870 Act's subject-matter provision as adopting a 'more concise phraseology').

[76] See *Sellers*, 1870 *Decisions of the Commissioner of Patents* at 58 (noting just prior to the 1870 Act's passage that 'I regard the … [design patent Act] as distinct from the remainder of the law as if it formed the subject of a separate statute, and the codified of the patent laws evidently so regarded it, for they collected all the matter relating to design patents in a separate chapter').

home.[77] Up until this point, it had been difficult to discern whether utility and design patent law were connected deeply in practice, despite the existence of an incorporation clause in the statute. But the structure of the new Act seemed to reinforce the expectation that the utility patent provisions usually would be applied along common lines, forcing the Patent Office to explain anew the relationship between the regimes as applications under the 1870 Act began to arrive.

Simultaneously, copyright law entered a new era of growth. Under the new Act, protection was extended to certain types of two- and three-dimensional works in the fine arts, covering 'painting[s], drawing[s], chromo[s], statue[s], statuar[ies], and ... models or designs intended to be perfected as works of the fine arts'.[78] In addition, the protection of commercial prints expanded during this period. Collectively, these events created new pressures on the design patent system. We address both below.

10.3.1.1 Commercial Prints

Immediately following the passage of the 1870 Act, the Patent Office was forced to reassess its past practice of allowing design patents to be granted for various types of commercial prints, such as labels and advertisements (especially those containing trademarks). Before addressing the design patent regime's interaction with copyright, however, this issue arose in the context of its new federal trademark regime.[79] Under the Act, manufacturers could register their marks for use with a class of goods for twenty-five dollars, and obtain thirty years of protection.[80] Nonetheless, many price-sensitive manufacturers continued to apply for design patents in an effort to game the system and avoid paying the higher costs associated with trademark registration.[81] Frequently, this was accomplished by staging the design patent application as directed to a print or picture

[77] See, e.g., Act of 2 Mar. 1861 (above, note 52), at § 11 (one of seventeen total provisions); Act of 29 Aug. 1842 (above, note 19), at § 3 (one of five total provisions).

[78] Act of 8 Jul. 1870 (above, note 66), at § 86.

[79] The Patent Office had actually began accepting the deposit of trademarks from the citizens of a select few countries prior to the 1870 Act's passage under various treaty obligations. See, e.g., Rules & Directions for Proceedings in the Patent Office 18 (1 Nov. 1869) (discussing the deposit system for trademarks within the design patent section). Indeed, these obligations played a big role in the Committee's decision to incorporate federal trademark protection into the 1870 Act. See 'The Federal Trademark Statutes' (1879) 19 *The Albany Law Journal: A Weekly Record of the Law & The Lawyers* 5, 6.

[80] Act of 8 Jul. 1870 (above, note 66), at §§ 77–78.

[81] See *Ex parte Whyte*, 1871 *Decisions of the Commissioner of Patents* 304, 306 ('It is more likely that applicant chose the present form of application, thinking that by securing the exclusive use of the design he could apply it at pleasure to all classes of goods; and that, being protected in that exclusive use, he would thus, in the lapse of time, become possessed of a veritable trade-mark for as many different classes of goods as he might himself have manufactured or might have procured to be manufactured by others, while

applied to a fabric, and then subsequently using that fabric design as a product label for numerous types of goods – rewarding the manufacturer with an exclusive right to the design while allowing them to avoid paying for protection on a per-class basis, which was required for trademark registration.[82]

Regardless of the applicant's justification, the Patent Office came down harshly on this practice. Just a few months after the 1870 Act's passage, Commissioner Fisher – who was instrumental in the Act's drafting, and had previously allowed for this use – discontinued the Patent Office's practice of allowing design patents to be granted for designs that applicants intended to use as trademarks. According to Fisher, the trademark 'provision, by prescribing the statutory mode of obtaining protection for a trade-mark, excludes all other modes not expressly provided for, and operates as a construction of . . . [the design patent provision], in excluding trade-marks from the list of subjects intended to be protected as designs'.[83] If the design looked like it was intended for use as a trademark, then it was barred from design patent protection.[84] It did not matter whether it contained artistic elements. For Fisher, because the subject-matter was clearly demarcated between the two regimes, there was no need to address the potential for cumulative protection; the mere possibility of trademark protection foreclosed the design from patent protection.[85]

As a cost-saving measure, these manufacturers also attempted to exploit the copyright system by registering these labels as prints. At the time, copyright registration only cost fifty cents and lasted for twenty-eight years (and could be extended for another fourteen years),[86] whereas even the cheapest design patent application cost the applicant ten dollars

under the trade-mark sections of the law a single fee would have secured registration for the design as a trade-mark in its application to a single class of goods only').

[82] In the first case dealing with this interface, Commissioner Fisher seemed puzzled why the applicant might prefer design patent protection. See *Ex parte King*, 1870 *Decisions of the Commissioner of Patents* 109, 109 (noting a few months after the Act's passage, that since trademark 'protection is more ample, and covers more than double the time for less money, it is difficult to see why [the] applicant, or any one else, should now seek a design patent for a trade-mark'). Within a year, however, the Patent Office seemed more attuned with the economic incentives for obtaining design patent protection. See *Whyte*, 1871 *Decisions of the Commissioner of Patents* at 306.

[83] *King*, 1870 *Decisions of the Commissioner of Patents* at 109.

[84] See, e.g., *Whyte*, 1871 *Decisions of the Commissioner of Patents* at 305–6 (requiring the design to be intrinsically incorporated into the final article of manufacture and further filtering the issue through its disclosure analysis).

[85] *King*, 1870 *Decisions of the Commissioner of Patents* at 109. ('In accordance with this opinion, the present application, and all others which are intended to cover trade-marks, or "designs for trade-marks," must be presented under the [trademark] provisions . . . of the act of July 8, 1870, and not otherwise').

[86] See Act of 8 Jul. 1870 (above, note 66), at §§ 87, 88, 92.

for only three-and-a-half years of protection.[87] While this practice occurred prior to the 1870 Act's passage, it drew more attention now that registration was removed from the district courts and consolidated within the Library of Congress. By 1872, Ainsworth Spofford, the Librarian of Congress, began calling for the removal of prints from the copyright system altogether.[88] According to Spofford, if they merited any protection at all, 'they should be protected by registry at the Patent Office, either as trade-marks or as designs for labels'.[89] Eventually in 1874 – after being registered in the thousands, according to one account[90] – Congress amended the copyright laws so that only prints associated with the fine arts could be registered with the Library of Congress.[91] Instead of denying the remaining 'prints or labels' protection or forcing them back into the design patent system, however, Congress allowed them to remain within copyright, with the caveat they be registered at the Patent Office for a higher price (six dollars).[92]

Now tasked with its administration, the new copyright registry brought the interface between copyright and design patent law into new light.[93] Under the express terms of the 1874 Act, the Patent Office was supposed to register 'prints or labels designed to be for any articles of manufacture' that were not trademarks.[94] While this language was squarely intended to demarcate the new regime from trademarks and copyrights granted to prints from the fine arts (i.e. at the Library of Congress), scant attention was paid to its relationship with design patents. After all, under the 1870 Act, design patents still protected designs for patterns, prints or pictures

[87] Rules of Practice in the USPTO 25 (1 Aug. 1871) (requiring $10 for a 3½-year term, $15 for a 7-year term and $30 for a 14-year term).

[88] Report of the Librarian of Congress, S. Mis. Doc. No. 13, 42d Cong., 3d Sess., 2 (1872).

[89] Ibid. at 2–3.

[90] Report of the Librarian of Congress, S. Mis. Doc. No. 3, 43d Cong., 2d Sess., 2 (1874).

[91] Act of 18 June 1874, ch. 310, § 3, 18 Stat. 78.

[92] Initially, there was a tremendous amount of confusion concerning whether the print/label registry was still within the purview of copyright law – thus requiring these works to meet its other requirements, like originality or notice – or whether it was some form of *sui generis* protection, close in kind to trademark law. See, e.g., *Rosenbach* v. *Dreyfuss*, 2 F 217, 223 (SDNY 1880). However, in 1891, the Supreme Court solidified the view that the print/label registry fell within the copyright regime (albeit with registration at the Patent Office), and therefore must meet its requirements for protection. See *Higgins* v. *Keuffel*, 140 US 428, 433 (1891).

[93] For a more complete account of the print/label regime than we can offer here, see Zvi S. Rosen, 'Reimagining Bleistein: Copyright for Advertisements in Historical Perspective' (2012) 59 *Journal of the Copyright Society* 347. See also P. J. Federico, 'Copyrights in the Patent Office' (1939) 21 *Journal of the Patent and Trademark Office Society* 911; Herbert Howell, 'The Print & Label Law' (1922) 70 *University of Pennsylvania Law Review* 95; Walter J. Derenberg, 'Commercial Prints & Labels: A Hybrid in Copyright Law' (1940) 49 *Yale Law Journal* 1212.

[94] Act of 18 June 1874 (above, note 91), at § 3.

applied to any article of manufacture.[95] The Patent Office's rules also failed to add much clarity, defining prints and labels as follows:

By the word 'print,' as used in said act, is meant any device, picture, word, or words, figure or figures (not a trade-mark) impressed or stamped directly upon the articles of manufacture, to denote the name of the manufacturer, or place of manufacture, style of goods, or other matter.

By the word 'label,' as therein used, is meant a slip or piece of paper, or other material, to be attached in any manner to manufactured articles, or to bottles, boxes, and packages contained in them, and bearing an inscription, (not a trade-mark,) as, for example, the name of the manufacturer or the place of manufacture, the quality of goods, directions for use &c.[96]

Most importantly, the Office failed to indicate whether prints or labels containing designs with similar descriptive information could still be protected through the design patent system, as they had prior to the 1874 Act's passage.

Despite the apparent overlap, there were comparatively few Patent Office or court decisions dealing with the interface between design patents and the copyrights in the print or label registry.[97] Most case law within this space wrestled with the more nebulous distinction between the print and label registry and trademark or copyright protection (for fine art pictorial works).[98] For designs that straddled the divide between design

[95] Act of 8 July 1870 (above, note 66), at § 71 (protecting 'any new and original impression, ornament, pattern, print, or picture, to be printed, painted, cast, or otherwise placed on or worked into any article of manufacture'); Rev. Stat. § 4929 (1874) (same except for a typo, mistakenly changing 'pattern' to 'patent').

[96] Initially the prints and labels were viewed as separate and distinct categories. See Rules of Practice in the US Patent Office (1 Nov. 1876) (Appendix) (reproduced above in text). By 1881, however, Commissioner Marble found the distinction artificial and construed the terms synonymously, as a printed label. *Ex parte Schumacher & Ettlinger*, 1881 *Decisions of the Commissioner of Patents* 18, 19; Rules of Practice in the US Patent Office (1 Nov. 1876) (Appendix) (reproduced in Orlando Bump, *The Law of Patents, Trade-Marks, Labels & Copy-Rights*, 2nd edn (New York: Baker, Voorhis & Co., 1884), pp. 579–80) ('The words "prints" and "labels" as used in this act, so far as it relates to registration in the Patent Office, are construed as synonymous, and are defined as any device, picture, word, or words, figure or figures, (not as a trade-mark) impressed or stamped directly upon the articles of manufacture, or upon a slip or piece of paper or other material, to be attached in any manner to manufactured articles, or to bottles, boxes, and packages containing them, to indicate the contents of the package, the name of the manufacturer or the place of manufacture, the quality of goods, directions for use, etc.'). Following the Supreme Court's decision in *Higgins*, discussed below, the Patent Office would both redefine and separate prints and labels again. See discussion below, notes 109–12 and accompanying text.

[97] See also *US ex rel. Schumacher* v. *Marble*, 3 Mackey 32, 50 (D.C. 1883) (demanding that registration be treated like a ministerial task, which would not involve substantive examination).

[98] See, e.g., *Ex parte Godillot*, 1874 *Decisions of the Commissioner of Patents* 120; *Ex parte Schumacher & Ettlinger*, 1876 *Decisions of the Commissioner of Patents* 75; *Ex parte Simpson*

patent and copyright, the incentives largely pointed towards copyright (as a pictorial work, if possible, or within the print/label registry). It was cheaper to acquire, it was not subject to the same stringent patentability requirements, it lasted longer, and it often provided a more generous set of remedies against infringers.[99] As a result of this incentive structure, a large number of these disputes likely played out at the Library of Congress, an institution that lacked an open and transparent registration process at the time.

Nonetheless, the issue did arise at the Patent Office when applicants attempted to shoehorn their designs into the print and label registry. For example, in *Ex parte Parker*, the Office was forced to assess which regime was appropriate for a print applied to a matchbook consisting primarily of an image of a boy with the words 'Scratch my back' below (an obvious homage for how to light the match).[100] Assistant Commissioner Doolittle began his assessment by noting that trademarks and prints/labels must be 'affixed, in some way, to goods, as merchandise, and not as constituting the merchandise itself'.[101] Presumably treating the merchandise as a matchbook and not the matches, Doolittle reasoned that the print in this case was 'the article itself—a fanciful pattern wrought into or upon the article—forming part of the article, and giving to it a certain value by way of a new appearance, like a new pattern worked upon a slipper'.[102] Now squarely out of the realm of trademarks or prints/labels, next, the Assistant Commissioner summarily rejected the possibility of copyright protection as a pictorial work because the matchbook was not a work of fine art. Left with only the possibility of design patent protection, Doolittle turned back to the physical nature of the relationship between the image and the underlying matchbook and concluded that the print was more appropriate for the design patent regime because its design was 'incorporated into the structure of the article, to be a permanent part thereof'.[103] Recognising the argument's circularity, Doolittle acknowledged:

(1876) 10 *USPTO Office Gazette* 333; see also 'New Law Concerning Copyrights for Labels' (11 July 1874) 31 *Scientific American* 17 (noting that the Patent Office's duty to avoid granting labels for 'trademarks, will doubtless serve to introduce office red tape-ism, vexation and delay into the business of obtaining copyrights, from which it has heretofore been free').

99 See Rev. Stat. (above, note 95), at §§ 4953, 4954, 4958, 4964, 4965.

100 The applicant had applied for registration under the print/label regime. *Ex parte Parker*, 1878 *Decisions of the Commissioner of Patents* 14 (1877).

101 Ibid. at 15. 102 Ibid.

103 Ibid. at 15–16. In reaching this conclusion, Commissioner Doolittle relied on a prior decision that distinguished whether a print was more appropriate for a trademark or design patent by its level of permanence or incorporation into the underlying article of manufacture. See *Ex parte Whyte*, 1871 *Decisions of the Commissioner of Patents* 304. By comparison to design patents, trademarks were perceived as more artificial or tacked

The subjects to be protected under the design, copyright, label, and trade-mark acts are often so nearly the same in character that it is difficult always to say to which class they belong, specially in the absence of definitions in the statutes, but these provisions differ in some respects so widely that the executive departments must give them some positive interpretation to insure an orderly administration of public business.

While Doolittle's analysis in *Ex parte Parker* emphasised that the key to policing the interface between design patents and copyrights for prints/labels was to focus on the permanence of its design features and their relationship to consumer demand, it left open questions about the fundamental nature of the print/label regime. At bottom, what made the image appropriate for the print/label regime in the first place? While it might have lacked any reference to the manufacturer or its place of business, the words 'scratch my back' could at some level be interpreted as a direction for using the matchbook, which presumably was intended to spark the matches it held. Relatedly, how did Doolittle's classification of the article as a matchbook anchor his analysis of the design's permanency? By defining the article by its trade dress (i.e. matchbook v. matches), it is hard to imagine a print that is not stuck to the back of its packaging as ever qualifying for anything but a design patent.

In any event, the resulting lack of any first order principles governing the intended subject-matter for the print and label regime took on new significance in 1891 when the Supreme Court, in *Higgins* v. *Keuffel*, found the protection of labels unconstitutional.[104] Because of the close relationship between labels and trademarks, the Court followed its prior decision declaring the federal trademark regime unconstitutional,[105] and held that the protection of labels went beyond Congress' power under Article 1, Section 8, Clause 8 of the US Constitution (the so-called 'IP clause').[106] Arguably conflating copyright protection under the print/label registry with its protection as a fine art (at the Library of Congress), the Court reasoned that '[t]o be entitled to a copyright the article must have by itself some value as a composition, at least to the extent of having some purpose

onto the underlying article. Ibid. Although Doolittle does not address it in *Ex parte Parker* – which uses the same logic to distinguish prints/labels from design patents – Doolittle presumes the same reasoning applies, but this time treating prints/labels as the subject-matter with the more transitory relationship with the underlying article of manufacture. 1878 *Decisions of the Commissioner of Patents* 15–16.

104 140 US 428, 431 (1891).

105 Compare *Higgins*, 140 US at 431, with *Trade-Mark Cases*, 100 US 82, 94 (1879).

106 *Higgins*, 140 US at 431 ('It cannot, therefore, be held by any reasonable argument that the protection of mere labels is within the purpose of the [IP] clause . . .'). The Court did not address whether the regime might have been constitutional under the commerce clause. See also Act of 3 Mar. 1881, ch. 138, § 1, 21 Stat. 502 (justifying the new trademark regime on commerce clause grounds).

other than as a mere advertisement or designation of the subject to which it is attached'.[107] In addition, the Court offered an alternative holding: even if the protection of labels was constitutional, the plaintiff failed to comply copyright law's general notice requirement, and was therefore not entitled to recovery.[108]

Instead of treating *Higgins* as upending the entire print/label registry, the Patent Office continued to register prints in its aftermath, evidently on the grounds that *Higgins* was limited to its alternative holding, and that there was a meaningful difference between prints and labels. Picking up on *Higgins*' reasoning, in 1892 Commissioner Simonds also reopened registration for labels, this time requiring the same level of 'artistic excellence' as pictorial works registered at the Library of Congress.[109] After granting only six label registrations in 1892,[110] Simonds updated the Patent Office rules in 1893, enshrining the new quasi-originality standard,[111] and also redefining the regime's subject-matter:

> A label is a device or representation borne by an article of manufacture or vendible commodity.
>
> A print is a device or representation not borne by an article of manufacture or vendible commodity, but in some fashion pertaining thereto—such, for instance, as a *pictorial advertisement* thereof.[112]

By removing all references to any descriptive content – such as business names, locations or directions for use – the Commissioner was clearly

[107] *Higgins*, 140 US at 431 (relying, in part, on reasoning from *Scoville* v. *Toland*, 21 F Cas 863 (C.C.D.Oh. 1848) (No. 12,553), a copyright case decided before the print/label registry was created – by Justice McLean, while riding circuit – where the court found a label for a medicine uncopyrightable).

[108] 140 US at 434.

[109] See *Ex parte Palmer* (1892) 58 *Office Gazette of the US Patent Office* 383, 384 (noting, in light of *Higgins*, that 'to be entitled to registry under the copyright law in the Patent Office needs to possess just as much artistic excellence, and no more, as would entitle it to copyright in the office of the Librarian of Congress . . .').

[110] Annual Report of the Commissioner of Patents for the Year 1892, S. Doc. No. 53, 52 Cong., 2d Sess., x (1893). But it would not grant another label registration until 1896 (granting one). Annual Report of the Commissioner of Patents for the Year 1896, S. Doc. No. 183, 54 Cong., 2d Sess., iv (1897). In 1897, it granted fourteen label registrations, and then within a couple of years registrations picked up at a much higher rate than even before *Higgins*. See Annual Report of the Commissioner of Patents for the Year 1897, S. Doc. No. 185, 55 Cong., 2d Sess., iv (1898).

[111] 'Construction of Statutes Relating to the Registration of "Prints" and "Labels"' (1893) 62 *Office Gazette of the US Patent Office* 909 (notice dated 9 Feb. 1893) (updating the prints/labels rules to, among other things, require that '[b]oth labels and prints, in order to be entitled to registry, must be intellectual productions in the degree required by the copyright law'); *Ex parte H.J. Heinz Co.*, 1893 *Decisions of the Commissioner of Patents* 21, 24–5.

[112] 'Construction of Statutes Relating to the Registration of "Prints" and "Labels"', 909.

trying to further distance the regime from *Higgins*, but he might have pushed things too far.

Simonds' decision to redefine prints as pictorial advertisements is fascinating. At the time, courts were struggling to apply the fine arts distinction to pictorial works,[113] and this was an obvious manoeuvre to capture that subject-matter.[114] To the extent that the Library of Congress was actually registering these works for their artistic qualities, this reorientation would have created a new overlap between the two copyright regimes. As for Simonds' new definition of labels, this also placed it more squarely at odds with some of the design patents being granted for prints applied to articles of manufacture. While the number of grants certainly dropped after the print/label regime was opened in 1874, the Patent Office still occasionally granted design patents for labels whose visual elements were inventive enough to warrant protection (both with and without descriptive text).[115] Consequently, by emphasising the need for artistic excellence and redefining labels without reference to their descriptive material, Simonds appears to have created greater redundancy between the two regimes.

10.3.1.2 Works of Fine Art

The line between a copyrightable three-dimensional work of fine art and a patentable design for an article of manufacture was often just as difficult to draw. Not long after the 1870 Act's passage, in *Gorham* v. *White*,[116] the Supreme Court provided some helpful markers when describing the design patent regime's normative foundation:

> The acts of Congress which authorize the grant of patents for designs were plainly intended to give encouragement to the *decorative arts*. They contemplate not so much utility as appearance, and that, not an abstract impression, or picture, but an aspect given to those objects mentioned in the acts ... The law manifestly contemplates that giving certain new and original *appearances to a manufactured article* may enhance its salable value, may enlarge the demand for it, and may be a meritorious service to the public.[117]

[113] See, e.g., *Ehret* v. *Pierce*, 10 F 553 (CCEDNY 1880) (denying copyrightability); *Yuengling, Jr* v. *Schile*, 12 F 97 (CCSDNY 1882) (confirming copyrightability); *J. L. Mott Iron Works* v. *Clow*, 82 F 316 (7th Cir. 1897) (denying copyrightability).

[114] Presumably, Simonds' interpretation would have captured prints for 'mere advertisements', a distinction that some courts used during this period to deny copyright protection to prints under the main statute when they lacked sufficiently distinct artistic elements. See, e.g., *J. L. Mott Iron Works*, 82 F at 318.

[115] Compare, e.g., US Patent No. D16,779 (issued 6 July 1886) (with text), with US Patent No. D30,711 (issued 9 May 1899) (without text).

[116] The Court did not apply the 1870 Act, however, as the design patent was granted under the 1861 Act. *Gorham* v. *White*, 81 US 511 (1872).

[117] Ibid. at 524–5.

By focusing on the decorative arts, the Court seemed to ignore the three-dimensional fine arts (such as statues and busts) that had been protected from the regime's inception.[118] Nonetheless, the decorative arts were always more central to the regime's purpose. And this was especially true when *Gorham* was decided, because the 1870 Act had opened these works of fine art up to copyright protection.

Although the 1870 Act did not simultaneously remove this subject-matter from the design patent regime, sculptures never made up more than 1.2 per cent of the total design patents granted after the Act's passage.[119] In most years they amounted to no more than 1 per cent. One notable exception was the work of the venerated sculptor John Rogers. His iconic figurines of scenes from contemporary life in the US around the time of the Civil War were not only immensely popular with the public, but they also show up prominently within the patent record.[120] The sculptor's personal letters from the 1860s, written when Rogers was launching his career, reveal an understanding of the importance of intellectual property protection. Regarding one sculpture, he told his aunt: 'I wish to get a patent right . . . so as to prevent its being copied & to enable me to sell the right in other places.'[121] The sculpture was called the *Slave Auction*, depicting the tragic scene of a family of slaves being divided at auction. It was so unpopular amongst Southerners that even some stores in the North refused to carry it.[122] But it won Rogers notoriety, which propelled the sales of subsequent works like the one in Figure 10.9.[123] Despite the availability of copyright protection for these new statuettes created after the 1870 Act, he still continued to obtain design patents.

118 See generally Steven B. Shubert, 'The Decorative Arts: A Problem in Classification' (1993) 12 *Art Documentation* 77 (outlining some of the problems with the distinction between the decorative and fine arts).

119 This high mark occurred in 1875, when eleven design patents were granted for sculptures.

120 See generally David H. Wallace, 'The Art of John Rogers: "So Real and So True"' (1972) 4 *American Art Journal* 59, 62.

121 Letter from John Rogers to Mary Jane Derby Peabody (19 Jan. 1860), in NY Historical Society, *Selected Letters*, John Rogers: American Stories (last visited 15 July 2016), www.johnrogers-history.org/learn-more/selected-letters/01-19-1860.html [https://perma.cc/E38D-6BHE] (hereinafter 'Rogers Letter').

122 See Rogers Letter (above, note 121); Wallace, 'The Art of John Rogers', 61 (describing the *Slave Auction* as a 'distinct failure').

123 The statuette depicted – called *Coming to the Parson* – was Rogers' most popular, selling about 8,000 copies. Michael Clapper, 'Imaging the Ordinary John Rogers's Anticlassical Sculptures as Purposely Popular Art' (2009) 43 *Winterthur Portfolio* 1, 1. The image in Figure 10.9 was not taken directly from its design patent, since the PTO's scanned version is difficult to decipher. See US Patent No. D4,287 (issued 9 Aug. 1870).

Figure 10.9 John Rogers, figurine of a couple asking to be wed
Source: Vrest Orton, *The Famous Rogers Groups: A Complete Check-list and Collectors' Manual* (Vermont: Weston, 1960)

As the most widely recognised source of high-quality mass-produced sculptures during this time,[124] Rogers might have viewed design patent protection as a more reliable form of protection than copyright.[125]

[124] Clapper, 'Imaging the Ordinary', 16 (noting that '[h]is process combined mass-reproduced affordability with a believable appearance of artistic authenticity, which helped make it possible for his clients to display the groups in their homes as genuine art').

[125] With few exceptions, most of the design patents granted during this era were for small figurines that also appear – from their images and descriptions – to be cast and produced at scale.

Indeed, Rogers had reason to be concerned about whether small mass-produced sculptural works were going to be accommodated by copyright law's narrow definition of the fine arts (or, more narrowly, whether a copyrighted fine art sculpture would be considered infringed by serial reproductive techniques, more characteristically applied in the decorative arts).[126] Copyright law was in flux during this time, and contemporary observers questioned how to categorise Rogers' work. For example, in 1864, the celebrated art critic James Jackson Jarves seemed puzzled when he reviewed Rogers' wartime works, stating: 'Although diminutive, they possess real elements of greatness. In their execution there is no littleness, artifice or affection ... *His is not high art, but it is genuine art* of a high naturalistic order, based on true feeling and a right appreciation of humanity.'[127] Consequently, while copyright protection lasted longer and might have been easier to obtain, design patent protection was clearly the safer bet.

In any event, the Library of Congress' (and, eventually, the Copyright Office's) rules distinguished between copyrightable works of fine art and design patent subject-matter. Perhaps picking up on the language in *Gorham*, the 1892 rules defined the fine arts for copyright purposes as including 'only painting and sculpture', and specified that 'articles of *merely ornamental* and *decorative art* should be sent to the Patent Office, as subjects for Design Patents'.[128] The 1899 rules took a different approach, simply listing objects that were not copyrightable.[129] The list explicitly excluded articles of manufacture, decorative articles, mechanical devices, advertisements, engravings of manufactured articles, prints for articles of manufacture, patterns, and perhaps most notably 'articles subject to patents for designs'.[130] However futile these exclusions might have been in practice, this era ended with both offices clinging to the idea that they could keep the subject-matter from design patents and copyrights separate.

10.3.2 Copyright Expansionism and the Election Era

At the beginning of the twentieth century, design patent law underwent a face lift, shedding its complex list of subject-matter categories in favour of one category covering 'any new, original, and ornamental design for an

126 Irrespective of his work's artistic merit, Rogers had become well known for perfecting his modelling and casting techniques. See Wallace, 'The Art of John Rogers', 62; Clapper, 'Imaging the Ordinary', 8.

127 Wallace, 'The Art of John Rogers', 62 (quoting James Jackson Jarves) (emphasis added).

128 Directions for Securing Copyrights, Library of Congress, § 11 (1895) (emphasis added).

129 Directions for Securing Copyrights, Library of Congress, Bull. No. 2, 16–17 (Mar. 1899).

130 Ibid.

article of manufacture'.[131] The statute's overhaul in 1902 was intended to address the regime's interface with utility patent law by removing the term 'useful'[132] from the category protecting shapes or configurations, and adding the requirement that they be 'ornamental'.[133] Commissioner Paine, whose petition propelled Congress into action, believed this change would help realign the regime:

> It is thought that if the present bill shall become a law the subject of design patents will occupy its proper philosophical position in the field of intellectual production, having upon the one side of it the statute providing protection to mechanical constructions possessing utility of mechanical function, and upon the other side the copyright law, whereby objects of art are protected, reserving to itself the position of protecting objects of new and artistic quality pertaining, however, to commerce, but *not justifying their existence upon functional utility*.[134]

Paine also thought it prudent to dismantle the statute's product-specific class structure because it was under-inclusive, and the statute's special remedies provision passed in 1887 had already adopted the open-ended phrase 'design for an article of manufacture'.[135] The 1902 Act was not intended to shrink the scope of subject-matter protected under the design patent statute,[136] but it may have had that effect for some types of subject-matter. For example, because statues and busts were no longer explicitly designated as a class of eligible subject-matter (even though they remained under the umbrella of the 'design for an article of manufacture'), the Patent Office may have considered itself to have more discretion to extend design patent protection only to those statues and busts that were created for large-scale reproduction.[137]

While design patent law was repositioning itself – and, if anything, contracting in light of the types of designs that could meet the new ornamentality requirement – copyright law was clearly headed in the opposite

[131] Act of 19 May 1902, ch. 783, 32 Stat. 193 (emphasis added).

[132] See generally Du Mont, 'A Nonobvious Design', 553–9, 565–8, 569, 571–2, 583, 586, 588–9 (cataloguing many of the disparate uses of this term by courts and the Patent Office, and tracing the 1902 Act's legislative history); Du Mont and Janis, 'Functionality in Design Protection Systems', 264–5 (providing background on the 1902 Act and its subsequent applications).

[133] Initially, the Commissioner had recommended adding the term 'artistic' but the Senate's Committee on Patents recommended changing it to 'ornamental'. S. Rep. No. 1139 at 2, 57 Cong., 1st Sess. (15 Apr. 1902).

[134] S. Rep. No. 1139 at 3 (emphasis added).

[135] S. Rep. No. 1139 at 1; see Act of 4 Feb. 1887, ch. 105, § 1, 24 Stat. 387.

[136] S. Rep. No. 1139 at 2; *Ex parte Fulda*, 1913 *Decisions of the Commissioner of Patents* 206, 207; see also *In re Schnell*, 46 F 2d 203, 205–6 (CCPA 1931) (citing *Fulda* for the same proposition).

[137] See discussion above (notes 119–27) and accompanying text (discussing John Rogers and the protection of sculptural works from 1870 to 1902).

direction. The Supreme Court's 1903 decision, in *Bleistein* v. *Donaldson Lithographing Co.*, helped lead the way.[138] In that case, the Court reversed an appeals court decision declaring a series of chromolithographs for circus advertisements uncopyrightable.[139] Today, the case is often cited as adopting a content-neutral market definition of originality that effectively lowered the bar for protection.[140] But what Holmes left unstated might have had a bigger impact on the scope of copyright's subject-matter. Instead of addressing what made the circus advertisement a work of fine art under the statute, Holmes gave the limitation short shrift by rolling it into his originality analysis – emphasising that the prints' popularity and quality did not make them any less of a work of fine art.[141] When coupled with the originality standard's changes, the Court's new analytical framework substantially eroded the barriers between works protectable via copyright registration at the Copyright Office and those protectable via print/label registration or design patents.[142]

In 1909, Congress overhauled the Copyright Act.[143] In addition to extending the renewal term for another fourteen years – bringing the total term, after renewal, up to fifty-six years – Congress also expanded the reach of copyrightable subject-matter, adding a new catch-all provision that protected 'all of the writings of an author' and expanding some of the specific classes included in the Act.[144] Most relevant here, Congress also slightly expanded the reach of the class protecting three-dimensional works: whittling away the 'fine arts' limitation by changing this class' language from protecting 'works of the *fine* arts' to 'works of art'.[145] During the Act's legislative development, the Librarian of Congress, Herbert Putnam, told Congress:

[138] See 188 US 239, 250–1 (1903). [139] Ibid. at 252.

[140] See, e.g., Bracha, 'Owning Ideas', 396.

[141] Holmes questioned whether the fine arts limitation even applied to chromos, like the circus posters in the case, but then conceded that, even if the work was classified as a print that was subject to the limitation, it did not change the case's outcome. See *Bleistein*, 188 US at 250.

[142] Oddly enough, Holmes still appeared to have some grasp of the fine arts limitation. Even if just paying it mention, he recognised that the '"antithesis to illustrations or works connected with the fine arts" is ... "prints or labels designed to be used for any other articles of manufacture"'. Ibid. at 251. However, this distinction was not very helpful. By this time, the Patent Office and many courts had already accepted advertisements, like the circus poster, as 'prints' within the print and label registry – a point left unaddressed in Holmes' opinion. In effect, Holmes opened the main copyright regime up to advertisements, without closing the gate to protection in the print/label registry.

[143] Act of 4 Mar. 1909, ch. 320, 35 Stat. 1075. [144] Ibid. at §§ 4, 5.

[145] Compare Act of 4 Mar. 1909 (above, note 143), at § 5(g) ('Works of art; models or design for works of art'), with Rev. Stat. (above, note 95), at § 4952 ('painting, drawing, chromo, statue, statuary, and of models or designs intended to be perfected as works of the fine arts').

The term 'works of art' is deliberately intended as a broader specification than 'works of the fine arts' in the present statute with the idea that there is subject-matter (for instance, of applied design, not yet within the province of design patents), which may properly be entitled to protection under the copyright law.[146]

However, Putnam's pronouncements did not necessarily align with his practices as Librarian of Congress. On the one hand, his testimony seemed to indicate that the new language was intended to expand copyright's reach beyond the fine arts. If, for example, the applied arts fit within copyright law's 'works of art' under the 1909 Act, then the copyright regime certainly would have reached into the realm of design patents (notwithstanding Putnam's claim to the contrary). If anything, the 1902 Act's amendment to the design patent statute – requiring that designs be ornamental – would have pushed the design patent regime in this direction already. On the other hand, under Putnam's leadership, the Copyright Office's rules promulgated immediately after the 1909 Act gave the impression that it was business as usual.[147] In defining 'works of art' under the Act, the Copyright Office's rules stated:

This term includes all works belonging to the so-called fine arts. (Paintings, drawings, and sculpture.)

Productions of the industrial arts utilitarian in purpose and character are not subject to copyright registration, even if artistically made ornamented.[148]

Similar to its rules under the 1870 Act, the Copyright Office eventually updated the second provision to include a notice that the industrial arts 'depend[ed] upon action under the patent law ...'[149] Consequently, while the two regimes' statutes appeared to be headed for collision, each respective office initially tried to maintain the façade of independence.

[146] Arguments Before the Comm. on Patents of the Senate & House of Reps. Conjointly on the Bills S. 6330 & H.R. 195853, To Amend & Consolidate the Acts Respecting Copyright, 59th Cong., 1st Sess., 11 (6–9 June 1906) (statement of Herbert Putnam, Library of Congress); see also *Mazer* v. *Stein*, 347 US 201, 213–14 n. 28 (indicating that these are the only statements explaining the change to this class).

[147] Arthur Weil, *American Copyright Law* (Chicago: Callaghan & Co., 1917), p. 83 (challenging the Copyright Office's practice and advocating a more expansive approach).

[148] Rules & Regulations For the Registration of Claims To Copyright, Library of Congress, Bull. No. 15, § 12 (1910) (approved by the Register of Copyrights, Thorvald Solberg, and Herbert Putnam, the Librarian of Congress). They also included analogous lists of uncopyrightable works, like before.

[149] It is also noteworthy that, added to the same provision, the Copyright Office indicated that artistic drawings of industrial objects could be copyrighted. Rules & Regulations For the Registration of Claims To Copyright, Library of Congress, Bull. No. 15, § 12 (1917) ('... but registration in the Copyright Office has been made to protect artistic drawings notwithstanding they may afterwards be utilized for articles of manufacture'); see also 17 USC § 113(b).

A year after the 1909 Act was passed, matters finally came to a head in *Louis De Jonge & Co.* v. *Breuker & Kessler Co.*[150] In that case, Louis De Jonge & Co. owned the copyright for a small painting of holly, mistletoe and spruce – that was registered as a work of fine art, under the prior act – but was applying the images from the painting to holiday wrapping paper.[151] In fact, the artist and company had never intended to reproduce the image as a work of art, but had always intended it for this type of mass production.[152] In defence, the Breuker & Kessler Co. argued that the painting's application to wrapping paper meant that it was not the proper subject of copyright, but should have been registered as a print/label or a design patent. But like the courts in a line of commercial print cases that was slowly building prior to the 1909 Act's passage – culminating in *Bleistein*, and its progeny – the *Louis De Jonge* court did not find Louis De Jonge & Co.'s use in a commercial medium fatal. From its perspective, the painting was 'artistic in thought and execution', and so 'when the painting left the artist's hand, it was of such a character as made it eligible either for copyright or for patenting, at the option of the author or owner'.[153] In other words, the painting's intended mode of reproduction did not negate the fact that it had been created initially as a work of art, and neither should its scope of rights be limited to that particular application.[154]

While the court's analysis and holding did not deviate from the reasoning of the commercial print cases, it was the court's statements in dicta that made the decision so important.[155] Instead of pretending the image had to be copyrighted as a painting, or that it had to be patented as a design for wrapping paper, Judge McPherson acknowledged that it could qualify for both.

> But it could *not* enter both. The method of procedure, the term of protection, and the penalties for infringement, are so different that the author or owner of a painting that is eligible for both classes must decide to which region of intellectual effort the work is to be assigned, and he must abide by the decision. Ordinarily, of course, there is no difficulty. Not many paintings are suitable for use as designs, and only a few designs possess the qualities demanded by the fine arts. But it is easily conceivable that here and there a painting may be eligible for either class, and the water color in question is, I think, an excellent example. Such a work may be used in both the fine and the useful arts; but it can have protection in only one of these classes. *The author or owner is driven to his election, and must stand by his choice.*[156]

[150] 182 F 150 (CCED Pa. 1910). [151] Ibid. at 151. [152] Ibid. [153] Ibid.
[154] Ibid. at 154–5.
[155] Ultimately, the plaintiff failed to comply with the copyright act's notice/marking requirements, making the copyrightability question moot. Ibid. at 154. On appeal, the Third Circuit affirmed on the same grounds, and did not address the issue of election. *Louis De Jonge & Co.* v. *Breuker & Kessler Co.*, 191 F 35 (3d Cir. 1911).
[156] *Louis De Jonge & Co.*, 182 F at 152 (emphasis added).

Whether driven by growing anti-monopoly sentiment in the US during this period, or some other force, McPherson did not articulate why the author or owner had to elect between the two intellectual property regimes. Indeed, McPherson's statements indicate that he understood some of the differences in the acquisition and enforcement of rights under both regimes, yet he was unwilling to allow for cumulative protection.[157]

Just a few years later, in *Ex parte Fulda*, Commissioner Moore endorsed *Louis De Jonge & Co.*'s election requirement in dicta, and the Patent Office began paying closer attention to circumstances where applicants tried to obtain cumulative protection.[158] However, given the administrative costs and technological challenges associated with design examination during this period, it is unlikely that the Patent Office had the capacity to adequately police this requirement. The obvious exception was when applicants attempted to convert one application into another, within the Patent Office. For example, in *In re Blood*, the Court of Appeals for the District of Columbia endorsed the Patent Office's election practice, where a design patent applicant had applied to protect a design for a hosiery ticket and had previously registered the design as a print/label,[159] which was still handled by the Patent Office at the time.[160] Citing *Louis De Jonge & Co.*, the court affirmed the Patent Office's rejection and voiced concerns that any other approach 'would result for all practical purposes in an extension of the design monopoly'.[161]

10.4 Cumulative Protection in the Modern Era (1952–Present)

In the modern era, the design patent system has been under pressure to absorb newly emergent utility patent jurisprudence,[162] and (like most intellectual property regimes) also has struggled to accommodate new areas of creative endeavour. These and other influences have triggered oscillations between more restrictive and more expansive design patent protection over the course of the twentieth century and into the twenty-first.[163]

[157] See generally Weil, *American Copyright Law*, pp. 84–5 (arguing, in his popular copyright treatise from this era, that works like those in *Louis De Jonge & Co.* should be both copyrightable and patentable).

[158] *Fulda*, 1913 *Decisions of the Commissioner of Patents* at 210.

[159] *In re Blood*, 23 F 2d 772, 772 (CCPA 1927).

[160] Act of 31 July 1939, ch. 396, 53 Stat. 1142 (transferring the registration of prints and labels back to the Library of Congress).

[161] *Blood*, 23 F 2d at 772. [162] Du Mont and Janis, 'Origins', 874.

[163] Du Mont, 'A Nonobvious Design', 598–609.

By contrast, copyright protection has steadily expanded. It embraced the notion that copyrightable expression could reside in commercial products, extended the reach of copyright owners over derivative rights, and developed broader notions of authorship. Consistent with this pattern, in *Mazer* v. *Stein*, the Supreme Court ruled that a copyright on a statuette was valid and infringed when the statuette was reproduced or incorporated in other commercial articles, like a table lamp.[164] *Mazer* relied on the principle that copyright could inhere in the segregable artistic elements of industrial objects.[165] Moreover, it dispensed with the argument that the possibility of design patent protection forecloses copyright protection as a matter of law.[166] But the Court declined to rule on whether a designer could hold design patent rights and copyrights cumulatively, merely noting that 'other courts have passed upon the issue'.[167]

In 1974, in *In re Yardley*, the Court of Customs and Patents Appeals picked up where *Mazer* had left off.[168] The case involved a design patent application for a watch face design depicting a cartoon figure of Spiro Agnew.[169] In the course of responding to an obviousness rejection, the applicant submitted photographs of a watch bearing the design in which a copyright notice was visible on the watch face (reproduced in Figure 10.10).[170] By contrast, in the drawings submitted with the original application, the applicant had depicted the watch face without the copyright notice, and also without other surface indicia (reproduced in Figure 10.11). In light of the copyright notice, the examiner added a new ground of rejection: 'estoppel', based on the fact that the applicant evidently held copyright registrations directed to the design.[171] The Board upheld the rejection,[172] and the applicant appealed to the Court of Customs and Patent Appeals.

164 347 US 201, 218 (1953); see also *In re Deister Concentrator Co.*, 289 F 2d 496, 500 n. 2 (CCPA 1961) (identifying *Mazer*, despite the long history of issues described throughout this chapter, as the inflection point for the overlap between design patents and copyright).

165 For more on *Mazer* or its adaptation and incorporation into the 1976 Copyright Act, see Chapter 9.

166 *Mazer*, 347 US at 217 (holding that 'the patentability of the statuettes, fitted as lamps or unfitted, does not bar copyright as works of art', and observing that 'neither the Copyright Statute nor any other says that because a thing is patentable it may not be copyrighted').

167 Ibid. The copyright holder had not obtained design patent protection, so the cumulation issue was not directly before the Court.

168 *In re Yardley*, 493 F 2d 1389 (CCPA 1974).

169 Ibid. at 1391.

170 Ibid. at 1391–2. The court's opinion contains a low-quality reproduction of the photograph as it appeared in a newspaper article. Ibid. at 1391. We have improved the image quality for publication purposes, but we have not made any changes that would materially affect the issues being discussed.

171 Ibid. at 1391.

172 Ibid. at 1392.

Figure 10.10 The Novelty Watch Company, photograph from office action that includes a copyright notice

Figure 10.11 The Novelty Watch Company, original drawing from patent application that lacks a copyright notice

The court reversed, reasoning that nothing in either the copyright or patent statute required a designer to elect between copyright and design patent protection for designs that could qualify under both regimes.[173] Likewise, no election requirement could be derived from

[173] Ibid. at 1394.

the Supreme Court's *Sears, Roebuck & Co.* v. *Stiffel Co.* decision. *Sears* had involved an issue of federal supremacy – namely, whether state unfair competition law could be used to restrict the copying of a lamp pole shape that was previously protected by federal intellectual property rights (specifically, utility and design patents, which were ultimately held invalid).[174] *Yardley* dealt with no such supremacy issue. It involved the intersection between two *federal* intellectual property regimes, and it presented the real prospect of concurrent protection, since Yardley's copyright registrations remained extant (unlike the utility and design patents in *Sears*). The CCPA declined to extend the reasoning of *Sears*, commenting that 'the Supreme Court [in *Sears*] was not thinking of the present fact situation where similar subject matter is protected by a federal copyright'.[175] Indeed, rather than ruling that the constitution, as interpreted in *Sears*, mandated election between design patent and copyright protection, the CCPA asserted in *Yardley* that the constitutional aspiration of promoting progress in the field of design actually would be facilitated by allowing concurrent protection.[176]

From the viewpoint of those who argue that the Constitution demands an unqualified 'right to copy' the subject-matter of expired patents or copyrights, *Yardley* has few redeeming qualities. Under *Yardley*, a designer might concurrently hold a design patent and a copyright directed to the same design, and after the design patent expires (fifteen years after issuance under current law), the copyright term might have several decades left to run. This is just the type of scenario that raises the hackles of those who defend the right to copy, even if it is less extreme than concurrent design patent and trade dress protection, where trade dress protection might endure indefinitely after the design patent expires.

But for those who remain unconvinced the right to copy is quite so robust, *Yardley* presents a close case that raises a number of difficult questions, most of which remain unanswered. For example, how common is it for a designer to hold (and assert) concurrent design patent rights and copyrights in the same subject-matter?[177] Relatedly, how often do courts actually find concurrent design patents and copyrights in the same design valid and infringed? Beyond a very narrow band of designs, this group remains sceptical that design

[174] 376 US 225, 231–2 (1964). [175] *Yardley*, 493 F 2d at 1395. [176] Ibid. at 1396.
[177] It would be difficult to assess the prevalence of concurrent protection because registration is not required for copyright protection.

patent/copyright stacking is much more than a theoretical threat to the public domain.[178]

In any event, it would take some time after *Yardley*, but the Patent and Trademark Office lifted the election requirement and updated its rules to allow applicants to include notices of copyright registration in the drawings of their design patents.[179] The Copyright Office also eventually followed suit. It began by clearing away exclusions for particular classes of subject-matter (such as textiles) that were previously deemed uncopyrightable because they were considered the exclusive domain of design patent law.[180] Finally, in the mid-1990s, the Copyright Office removed its election requirement.[181]

Since these changes, copyright law and design patent law have also continued to evolve and respond to new subject-matter,[182] but these regimes' solutions have not changed much. Copyright law's (rightfully) harsh separability requirement ensures that most forms of industrial design result in a very narrow set of rights, if any.[183] This helps channel industrial design towards the design patent regime (or into the public domain). On the other hand, design patent law has a comparatively permeable functionality doctrine, channelling only extreme cases into the utility patent regime (or into the public domain). However, design patent law lacks a corresponding channelling doctrine with copyright law, which might push subject-matter from design patents to copyrights.[184] Within this narrow band of works, while there is some opportunity for overlapping protection, in most cases the resulting scope of protection is so different between the two regimes that it can only be described in terms of partial cumulation.[185]

[178] Copyright law's separability requirement and design patent law's many substantive and procedural hurdles – as well as other pragmatic considerations related to these articles' brief commercial lifespans – would seem to limit any such concern to a fairly narrow subset of designs.

[179] MPEP § 1512 (5th ed. Rev. 4, Oct. 1986).

[180] See 37 CFR § 202.10 (1959) (noting that 'the fact that it [(i.e. the work)] appears on a textile material or textile product' does not affect its registrability but still clinging to an election requirement); see also *Peter Pan Fabrics, Inc.* v. *Acadia Co.*, 173 F Supp. 292, 299 (SDNY 1959).

[181] 60 Federal Regulation 15605, 15605–6 (24 Mar. 1995). The Vessel Hull regime, however, requires election. 17 USC § 1329.

[182] See, e.g., Du Mont and Janis, 'Virtual Designs'.

[183] For a complete account of the separability requirement, see Chapter 9.

[184] But see *Ex parte Cady*, 1916 *Decisions of the Commissioner of Patents* 57, 62 (denying design patent protection to a disembodied picture of Peter Rabbit).

[185] If we ignore circumstances where design patents are granted for *elements* of an object – which are more likely to qualify for both design patent and copyright protection, like a statuette of a Balinese dancer attached to a lamp – then two-dimensional designs probably present the greatest opportunity for cumulative rights. As detailed above, commercial prints – like a design for a business card or a sign – might be one such example.

10.5 Conclusion

The history of the American design patent/copyright interface reflects a theme that will be familiar to intellectual property scholars: the interface developed over time through piecemeal litigation and shifting political influence as the respective regimes evolved, not instantaneously through a comprehensive (or coherent) *a priori* legislative exercise.

Initially, both the design patent and copyright regimes defined their respective boundaries by provisions that listed categories of eligible subject-matter. As long as the categories did not overlap, there could be little occasion for boundary disputes, at least in theory. However, in the late nineteenth century, the categories of copyrightable subject-matter expanded rapidly, encompassing subject-matter such as three-dimensional works of art and commercially oriented two-dimensional images or prints – once seemingly the exclusive domain of design patent law. This triggered a series of reflexive manoeuvres by various patent commissioners attempting to regularise the design patent/copyright interface, which proved largely unsatisfactory.

Subsequently, the copyright law developed the concept of the protectable 'work', and the design patent statute dispensed with the subject-matter categories altogether in favour of the rubric of the 'design for an article of manufacture'. This created a significantly greater potential for conflict, because it was not self-evident from the face of either statute where the outermost boundaries of protectable subject-matter lay for either regime. At first, early in the twentieth century, some courts and administrative decision-makers reacted by requiring applicants to elect between design patent and copyright protection. Later in the twentieth century, divergence between the regimes became manifest: the respective protectability requirements differed, as did the scope of protection afforded under the regimes. Eventually, the election requirement was rejected.

Today, the design patent system is in its ascendancy. As the strategic significance of design patent protection grows, we may see yet another reassessment of the design patent/copyright interface.

11 The Copyright/Design Interface in Japan

*Masahiro Motoyama**

11.1 Japanese Design Protection System and Its Development

11.1.1 Establishment of Design Law

The Japanese design protection system began with the Design Bylaws (Imperial Ordinance No. 85 of 20 December 1888), which was enacted in 1888 under the influence of the UK design protection system (Patents, Designs and Trade Marks Act 1883).[1] The Design Bylaws, along with the Trademark Bylaws and the Patent Bylaws, were drafted by Korekiyo Takahashi, who was later to become the first Commissioner of the Japan Patent Office (JPO).[2] After Takahashi returned to Japan from an inspection tour to Europe and the United States to investigate the industrial property systems from 1885 to 1886, he remarked on the need for creating a design protection system in Japan, stating that 'since Japanese people's skills and fortes are centred on design, a legal protection system relating to it is indispensable without doubt'.[3] As implied by Takahashi's words, establishment of Japan's first design protection system was not only intended for meeting the mere formalistic demand to develop modern law at an early stage, but is considered to have stemmed from the practical demand to protect designs as intellectual property, in order to ensure the export competitiveness[4] and trading values of Japanese designs.

* In this chapter, quotations from Japanese literature are translated into English for convenience.

[1] Tadashi Takada, *Ishō* (Designs) (Tokyo: Yuhikaku, 1969), p. 12; Tsunehisa Katō, *Bubun ishō ron: ishō hō no mokuteki to sono gendaiteki tenkai* (Partial design theory: purpose of the Design Act and its modern development) (Tokyo: Shougaku Sha, 2002), p. 73.

[2] Korekiyo Takahashi, *Takahashi Korekiyo jiden (jō)* (Takahashi Korekiyo autobiography, vol. I) (Tokyo: Chuoukouron Shinsha, 1976), p. 260.

[3] Yoshinori Amagai, *Ōyō bijutsu shisō dōnyū no rekishi: Wīn haku sandō yori ishō jōrei seitei made* (History of the introduction of the idea of applied art: From participation in World Exposition 1873 Vienna to enactment of the Design Bylaws) (Kyoto: Shibunkaku, 2010), p. 343.

[4] Japan Patent Office, *Kōgyō shoyūken seido hyakunenshi: jōkan* (One-hundred-year history of the industrial property right system: vol. I) (Tokyo: Hatsumei Kyoukai, 1985), p. 78.

Table 11.1 *Chronological table of legislation and statistics*

Period	System/legislation	Amendments	Interface/interpretation	Total design applications	Annual average	Total design registrations	Annual average
1889–1899	Design Bylaws of 1888		Copyright Act still not legislated	3,256	296	833	76
1900–1909	Design Act of 1899 Copyright Act of 1899		Demarcation	12,073	1,207	4,746	475
1910–1921	Design Act of 1909 Copyright Act of 1899		Demarcation	34,664	2,889	14,927	1,244
1922–1960	Design Act of 1921 Copyright Act of 1899		Demarcation Japanese government delegates asserted demarcation at the 1928 Rome Conference for the Revision of the Berne Convention	341,939	8,768	178,257	4,571
1961–1970	Design Act of 1959 Copyright Act of 1899		Demarcation	365,463	36,546	160,694	16,069
1971–2015	Design Act of 1959 Copyright Act of 1970		Basic demarcation as the legislative intent (Copyright Act) Partial or total cumulation as judicial precedents (Copyright Act)	1,974,967	43,888	1,442,767	32,061

Source: Created by the author based on statistical data published by the Japan Patent Office

The current design protection system is the system under the Design Act (Act No. 125 of 13 April 1959) legislated in 1959. Protection of registered design is the only way to protect design rights in Japan. There is no protection system for unregistered designs such as the one in the EU today. While the outline of the current Design Act will be reviewed later in relation to individual issues, the major characteristics of the development of the design protection in Japan, from the system under the first Design Bylaws to that under the current Act, can be summarised as follows. First, the concept of a protectable design has become narrower in terms of its relationship with the product to which it is designated. Specifically, the notion of design was reduced from the concept that can be grasped independently from the concrete product to the concept that can be grasped only as inseparable from the product (addition of the requirement of a product to the notion of 'design': reviewed later in 11.1.2). Secondly, the entity entitled to protection is basically the design creator, who is a natural person. At the same time, however, since the time of establishment of the design system, there has also been a system whereby a company's employer acquires an exclusive design right for a design created by an employee of the company (the system of employee designs: reviewed later in 11.1.3.2). Thirdly, as major requirements for registration of a design, a design needed to be mass-producible and not identical or similar to a publicly known design (novelty), since the time of establishment of the design system. Later, under the current Act, creative difference from an existing publicly known general motif (creative difficulty) was additionally stipulated as a requirement (reviewed later in 11.1.4.1). Fourthly, with regard to the scope of a design right, it has not changed since the time of establishment of the design system that the exclusive effect of a design right extends to exploitation of a design identical to the registered design, as a business, for a specific product that was designated at the time of filing the application for design registration. In contrast, exploitation of a design similar to the registered design had been prohibited merely by penal provisions under the design system during some time in the past, but under the current Act, a design right's exclusive effect itself extends to exploitation of a similar design (reviewed later in 11.1.4.2). Indeed, interpretation of the concept of 'similarity' that determines the scope of a design right has been subject to heated discussions that also involved the essence of the Japanese design protection system (reviewed later in 11.1.4.3). Fifthly, and finally, with regard to the issue of adjustment with subject-matter protected by copyright (applied art), Japan never had a system to recognise cumulation for applied art in general under the Copyright Act and the Design Act. Accordingly, the Design Act has consistently protected applied art under a fundamentally demarcated relationship with the Copyright Act since the establishment of its system (reviewed later in 11.1.5). Nevertheless, there have been some developments in courts' interpretations of the Copyright Act to recognise the possibility of partial cumulation (reviewed later in 11.2).

Since the Design Bylaws of 1888 to the current Design Act of 1959, the subject-matter protected under the design right has been statutorily expressed by the term 'ishō'. While 'ishō' is a Japanese translation of the term 'design', at the time of enactment of the Design Bylaws of 1888, the subject-matter 'ishō' meant nothing but 'applied art'. In other words, the statement of the legislative reason of the Design Bylaws sets forth that 'establishment of design protection law will contribute to the development of *applied art* and the emergence of a wave of new works, leading to development of industry . . .' in explaining the purpose of introducing the system.[5] Also, the part explaining the provisions of the bylaws states that the purpose of protecting 'ishō' is 'to develop new, excellent ideas relating to *applied art* by rewarding the efforts of persons who created works by using their time, funds and intelligence'.[6]

Indeed, Article 1 of the Design Bylaws defines the subject-matter as 'novel *ishō* pertaining to the shape, patterns or colours to be applied to industrial products'. The statement of the legislative reason also indicated that '*ishō ("design" in English)* is a contrivance that should be applied to industrial products'. Here, the general term 'applied art' was not used in the actual statute as a legal term, but the bylaws used the wording 'ishō' instead of 'applied art' to refer to design, which is the subject-matter, merely due to the idea that 'since there is no other appropriate Japanese word for it, it will be translated as "ishō"'.[7] The underlying cause of the decision to use the term 'ishō' in Japan's first design protection system to refer to the subject-matter – 'a contrivance that should be applied to industrial products' – instead of the literal expression 'applied art', is considered to be that the concept of 'art' was undifferentiated whereas the concept of 'ishō' was idiomatic at the time.[8]

The Japanese design protection system which started out from the Design Bylaws of 1888 subsequently underwent four sweeping amendments leading to the current Act. They were the Design Act of 1899 (Act No. 37 of 2 March 1899), the Design Act of 1909 (Act No. 24 of 5 April

[5] Ministry of Agriculture and Commerce, 'Ishō jōrei wo sadamu' (Establishment of the Design Bylaws), *Kōbun ruiju dai 12 hen mingyōmon fu 3* (Collection of official documents, part 12, private business, industry sector, 3) (1888).

[6] Ibid.

[7] Design Division, Japan Patent Office, *Ishō seido 120 nen no ayumi* (120-year progress of the design system) (Tokyo: Japan Patent Office, 2009), p. 11.

[8] Ibid., p. 79.

1909), the Design Act of 1921 (Act No. 98 of 30 April 1921), and the current Design Act of 1959 (Act No. 125 of 13 April 1959). At the time when the Design Bylaws of 1888 were established, Japan still did not have copyright law in the modern sense that covers the contents of the Berne Convention for the Protection of Literary and Artistic Works. It was in 1899 when a Copyright Act covering artistic works as its subject-matter was enacted. In other words, more than a decade before Japan established a modern copyright law protecting also artistic works, the Japanese design protection system had already made a start as a protection system covering overall applied art, ahead of the Copyright Act.

In fact, some of the typical design registrations under the old system were tasteful or decorative applied art that were not directly related to functional designs of products. For example, among the total of 725 designs registered under the Design Bylaws of 1888 during the period from 1889 to 1898, a particularly large number of designs were registered for the fields of textiles (148 designs) and paper products (109 designs).[9] The typical registered designs were textile patterns relating to plants, flowers, ancient paintings, everyday life scenes, birds, written characters, animals, landscapes, bugs and fish or wallpaper patterns relating to flowers, birds, people, animals and fish.[10] Meanwhile, typical designs registered under the Design Act of 1899 included designs of shawls imitating shapes in nature, such as butterflies, bats and birds, designs of gas lamps with three-dimensional decorations depicting plant branches and leaves entwined around them, designs of table clocks with three-dimensional patterns of various animals, and designs of ornamental clocks with three-dimensional decorations of a herd of monkeys on rocks.[11]

Nevertheless, the role expected of these initial design laws as a system mainly for protecting tasteful/decorative applied art itself gradually changed in the course of developments, leading to the enactment of the current Act, especially through the change in the notion of 'ishō = design' as the subject-matter, which will be reviewed below.

11.1.2 Design as the subject-matter

Article 2(1) of the current Act, the Design Act of 1959, defines the concept of 'design' as the shape, patterns or colours, or any combination thereof, of an article, which creates an aesthetic impression through the eye. According to this definition, a design, which is the subject-matter of the Design Act, is roughly comprised of the following three requirements:

[9] Japan Patent Office, *Kōgyō shoyūken seido hyakunenshi*, p. 113. [10] Ibid., pp. 127–9.
[11] Ibid., pp. 236–9.

a design must be an appearance inseparable from a product (hereinafter referred to as the 'First Requirement'); the appearance of a design must consist of a 'shape, patterns or colors, or any combination thereof' (hereinafter referred to as the 'Second Requirement'); and a design must create a visually recognisable aesthetic impression (hereinafter referred to as the 'Third Requirement').

11.1.2.1 Definitional Inseparability from the Product

To be protected subject-matter, a design must consist of the appearance of a product (First Requirement). Here, a product means a tangible object which is a movable.[12] In other words, a 'design' is a notion that contains a product which is a tangible movable as an element, and not a notion that is understood abstractly separate from an actual product. Accordingly, the design differs if its designated product differs.[13] For example, a design of an automobile will be understood to differ from a design of a toy car that has the same appearance. This is because an automobile as transportation machinery and a toy car as an entertainment item are different products. This approach is substantially different from the idea of copyright, which regards the aesthetic expression of applied art itself as the subject-matter independently of the product to which it is applied.

Such a notion of 'design', which is as a definition inseparable from the product designated, had not been adopted legislatively from its start. The Design Bylaws of 1888, the Design Act of 1899 and the Design Act of 1909 had all defined a 'design' as an appearance (shape, pattern or colour) that can be applied to a product. Under these laws, a 'design' had been understood as a notion that is separate and independent from a product to which it was applied. However, this notion of 'design' was substantially modified under the Design Act of 1921. The Act redefined a 'design' as an appearance devised in relation to a product. In other words, it was clarified that a design could never exist separately and independently from a product. Since then, until the current Act, a design has been a notion inseparable from a product. Indeed, in the JPO's examination practice under the Act of 1921, an explanation was given that a pattern of a clothing fabric and the same pattern of a wallpaper were different designs since the products to which they are exploited were different.[14]

The following two circumstances can be pointed to as reasons for the notion of design being substantially modified from a notion unrestricted

[12] Design Division, Japan Patent Office, *Ishō shinsa kijun* (Design examination standards) (July 2011), p. 8.

[13] Takada, *Ishō*, p. 34. [14] Ibid.

by the requirement of a product to a notion inseparable from a product. One is the influence of modern design thinking. Specifically, it is thinking that an appearance of a product does not exist abstractly, independently of the product, but is rather defined based on the functions specific to the product.[15] The other is negative concern against the excessively broad scope of design right. Upon Diet deliberations on the Design Act of 1921, a government delegate who submitted the Bill stated that, if a design right could exist abstractly beyond the tangible limitation of the product to which it is designated, 'the scope of right would be far too broad', and it would also deviate from the purpose of devising a design.[16]

11.1.2.2 Consequence of the Requirement of a Product and Its Partial Modification

Yet, some problems could occur as the consequence of interpreting that a design, which is the subject-matter, is inseparable from the product.

First, there had been a problem of whether the appearance of a part of a product can constitute a design. A product is a tangible movable, and it needs to be independently tradable by itself. In such case as a headlight of an automobile, where a part of a product (complex product) can be independently tradable by itself as a component, the appearance of that component can constitute a design. There was a court decision concerning a dispute over whether the part of a turntable for a record player other than the motor (unfinished product) satisfied the requirement of a product, where the court found that the turntable can be regarded as a product.[17] However, if a part of a product is not tradable by itself, such as in the case of the handle part of a refrigerator, the appearance of that part cannot constitute a design of a component even if it satisfies the other requirements for protection, and cannot be fully protected from imitation by others. Nonetheless, as is typically also the case with the appearance of the image display part of a digital camera, if a part whose impression is made characteristic among the overall design cannot be the subject-matter of the Design Act, it will not be appropriate for the protection system to promote the actual design development. Consequently, in order to overcome this problem, it was provided upon the Design Act's amendment in 1998 that a 'part of a product' is included in the concept of

[15] Ryoji Saito, in Shigeaki Mitsuda and Kazuko Matsuo (eds.), *Chūkai Ishō Hō* (Commentary on Design Act) (Tokyo: Seirinshoin, 2010), p. 112.

[16] The 44th Imperial Diet, House of Representatives, Minutes of the first committee meeting on a Bill for amendment of the Patent Act and four other agenda items (24 February 1921), 3.

[17] *Turntable*, Judgment of the Tokyo High Court of 26 July 1978, Mutai Saishū (Intellectual Property Law Reports), vol. 10, no. 2, 369.

a 'product' constituting a design. It meant the introduction of the system of so-called 'partial designs'. As a result, the appearance of a part of a product that is not independently tradable by itself could also become the subject-matter as a design.

Secondly, there is a problem of restriction on elements that constitute the appearance of a design. According to the provisions of the Design Act, the elements of the appearance of a design are a shape, patterns or colours, or any combination thereof. However, when a design is interpreted to be inseparable from a tangible 'product', there can be no design that solely consists of patterns and colours without a shape. Consequentially, if the inseparability between a design and a 'shape' are interpreted strictly, there will be cases where the appearances of today's products cannot be protected sufficiently, such as the graphical user interface (GUI). Therefore, in order to address this problem, GUI on a screen that is necessary for achieving the purpose or functions of the product was added to the subject-matter upon the Design Act's amendment of 2006.

11.1.2.3 Appearance that Can Constitute a Design

The appearance of a design that can be the subject-matter must consist of a shape, patterns or colours, or any combination thereof (Second Requirement). These three kinds of constituent elements have not changed since the Design Bylaws of 1888.

First, with regard to the first element of a shape, as long as a product is to be a constituent element of a design, a shape will be an indispensable element of a design since there is no product without a tangible shape, as discussed in 11.1.2.2. However, a shape that can constitute a design is only the regular shape of the product itself, and an irregular shape that is secondarily created from the product is not construed to be a design. For example, the shape of a flower made by tying knots in a handkerchief upon sales and display of handkerchiefs is not regarded as a design.[18] This is because the shape of the flower is not the shape of the handkerchief itself.

Next, with regard to the second element of patterns, there is a question of whether or not written characters can constitute a pattern. Since there is no statutory definition of a pattern, the determination on whether or not written characters can constitute a pattern is left to interpretation. Court decisions have determined this point based on whether or not the written characters are readable. Specifically, in a case concerning a dispute over whether or not the stylised characters 'CUP NOODLE' indicated on a

[18] Japan Patent Office, *Ishō shinsa kijun*, p. 10.

packaging container constitute a design (pattern), the Tokyo High Court stated that there is room to find written characters to constitute a design as a pattern if they are deemed to have lost their original function as a means of linguistic communication as a result of having been made into a pattern. However, the court stated that the written characters in question have not lost their original function as characters since it is sufficiently possible to understand the linguistic meaning of the characters, and held that the characters do not constitute a pattern.[19] The Tokyo High Court subsequently made a similar determination in a case concerning a dispute over whether the stylised characters 'Coca-Cola' and 'COKE' indicated on a packaging can constitute a design (pattern), and ruled that the written characters do not constitute a pattern on the basis that the characters are readable as a language.[20]

Lastly, with regard to questions relating to the third element of colours, there is an argument over whether or not the gloss or visual material feel of a product can be included in the element of colours. As an example of legislation concerning this point other than the Design Act, the Unfair Competition Prevention Act that regulates unauthorised imitation of the configuration of another person's goods expressly provides that the 'configuration of goods' means the shape of goods and the pattern, colour, gloss and texture combined with such shape.[21] In that definition, gloss and texture are categorised under law as elements that differ from colour. In light of this, gloss and texture will not be included in the elements of shape, patterns and colours that are restrictively listed under the Design Act as elements of an appearance. Also, there are no court decisions that treated gloss or texture as an element of an appearance constituting a design.

11.1.2.4 Meaning of the Requirement of Aesthetic Impression through the Eye

To be protected subject-matter, a design must create a visually recognisable aesthetic impression (Third Requirement).

This requirement of aesthetic impression through the eye (visibility) was stipulated under law for the first time upon establishment of the current system under the 1959 Design Act. Nevertheless, even under

19 *CUP NOODLE*, Judgment of the Tokyo High Court of 25 March 1980, Mutai Saishū, vol. 12, no. 1, 108. This determination was also upheld by the Supreme Court in the final appellate instance of the same case (Judgment of the Supreme Court of 16 October 1980, Hanrei Jihō, vol. 986, 49).

20 *Packaging Can*, Judgment of the Tokyo High Court of 7 March 1990, Mutai Saishū, vol. 22, no. 1, 142.

21 Article 2(4) of the Unfair Competition Prevention Act.

the previous system, it had been construed through literature that an aesthetic impression is required for a design.[22] The underlying intention was to distinguish between the subject-matter of the Design Act and that of the Utility Model Act which also protects the appearance (shape) of a product. The subject-matters of the two Acts were interpreted to be fundamentally different, with one representing the utility/functional aspect (Utility Model Act) and the other representing the tasteful/decorative aspect (Design Act) of the shape of a product, and the element that decided the tasteful/decorative aspect indispensable for the subject-matter of the Design Act was the aesthetic impression of the appearance.[23] Under the previous system, the aesthetic impression required for a design was construed to be a tasteful/decorative aesthetic impression.

Meanwhile, with regard to the understanding of the requirement of aesthetic impression stipulated under the current Act, there can be various theories as to whether it should be construed either as decorative aesthetics or as functional aesthetics.[24] It is difficult to understand the legislators' intention with regard to this point from legislative documents.[25] Certainly, one factor behind the practice adopted since the Design Act of 1921 to deem a design to be inseparable from the product was the influence of modern design thinking that considers a design to be inseparable from functions of the product. Then, to construe the aesthetic impression of a design to mean functional aesthetics seems compatible. However, it is difficult to consider that tasteful/decorative designs that had been typical designs registered under the previous system were excluded from the subject-matter solely based on the requirement of 'aesthetic impression' under the Design Act. It is interpreted that the requirement of aesthetic impression under the current Act can be satisfied either by decorative aesthetics or functional aesthetics, and therefore this requirement practically has a weak function to limit the subject-matter.[26]

Nonetheless, the aesthetic impression to be created by a design must at least be visually recognisable. This raises a question of whether or not an

[22] Ichiro Kiyose, *Kōgyō shoyūken gairon* (Overview of industrial property rights) (Tokyo: Ganshoudou, 1911) (Tokyo: Gakujyutsusensho, 2002 reprinted edition), p. 214; Takatsugu Yoshihara, *Jitsuyō Shin'an Hō Ishō Hō shōron* (Detailed discussions on the Utility Model Act and the Design Act) (Tokyo: Yuhikaku, 1928), pp. 303–4 and 306; Kojiro Murayama, *Tokkyo shin'an ishō shōhyō yonpō yōron* (Essence of the four laws on patents, utility models, designs and trademarks) (Tokyo: Ganshoudou, 1928), pp. 237 and 316.

[23] Kiyose, *Kōgyō shoyūken gairon*, p. 214; Yoshihara, *Jitsuyō Shin'an Hō Ishō Hō shōron*, p. 306; Murayama, *Tokkyo shin'an ishō shōhyō yonpō yōron*, p. 315.

[24] Takada, *Ishō*, pp. 83–5.

[25] Takashi Morimoto, in Mitsuda and Matsuo (eds.), *Chūkai Ishō Hō*, p. 148.

[26] Takada, *Ishō*, p. 85; Takashi Morimoto, in Mitsuda and Matsuo (eds.), *Chūkai Ishō Hō*, p. 149.

excessively small design and a design that cannot be seen from outside satisfy the requirement of visual recognisability. With regard to this point, in a case concerning a dispute over whether an extremely small connector terminal (approx. 1.2 mm wide and 1.3 mm long) constitutes a design, the Intellectual Property High Court (established in April 2005 as a special division of the Tokyo High Court) determined that the small product in question in this case satisfies the requirement of visibility if, when actually trading the product, it is a normal practice to observe the shape of the product by magnifying the shape through use of a magnifying glass.[27] This means that visibility does not require recognition by the naked eye. Also, in a case concerning a dispute over whether or not a design right on a speed reducer used for a motor is infringed by a motor with a speed reducer (finished product) which incorporates said speed reducer as its part, the Tokyo High Court held that a hidden shape of a product which does not show in the external appearance and cannot be recognised through the eye in the distribution process cannot be taken into consideration in determining infringement of said design.[28] In both cases, the courts indicated an approach to determine the visual recognisability by taking into consideration the actual conditions of trading or distribution process in the market.

11.1.3 Entities Entitled to Protection: Vesting of Right

11.1.3.1 Design Creator

The entity entitled to protection under the Design Act, that is, the person who is entitled to obtain a design registration, is, basically, the creator of the design. The right to obtain a design registration is initially vested in the design creator at the same time as the creation of the design. Of course, a design creator is able to cause another person to succeed to this right, but a design application filed by a person who does not have the right is refused in examination,[29] and even if a registration is granted for such an application, it becomes subject to a ground for invalidation.[30]

Here, the design creator refers to the person who was actually involved in the very act of creating the design. Therefore, a person who merely ordered, assisted or provided advice on the act of creation or a person who merely provided funds or facilities cannot be a design creator. Also, since an act of creation is a factual act, neither an agent nor a juridical person may be a creator of a design. There is also a court case in which the design

[27] *Connector Terminal*, Judgment of the Intellectual Property High Court of 31 March 2006, Hanrei Jihō, no. 1929, 84.

[28] *Speed Reducer*, Judgment of the Tokyo High Court of 30 June 2003.

[29] Article 17(iv) of the Act of 1959. [30] Article 48(1)(iii) of said Act.

creator who is entitled to obtain a design registration was interpreted as a person who directly reflected his or her own intention in the act of creation and participated in making a concrete form.[31]

11.1.3.2 System of Employee Designs

Although the right to file a design application is initially vested in the design creator alone, in principle, a design creator often belongs to a company and, as an employee of such organisation, creates designs by receiving funds, facilities, materials, etc. from the employer. For such a case, there is a system for providing a design-creating incentive to the employer, such as a company. It is the system of employee designs.[32]

A design is categorised as an employee design if the design was created as the present or past duty of an employee of a company, within the scope of business of the employer. When a design is an employee design, first of all, even if the employee himself or herself obtains a design right through registration, the employer will have a non-exclusive licence on the design right under the law. As a result, the employer will be able to exploit (manufacture, use, assign, lease, etc.) the design free of charge without obtaining the authorisation of the employee, who is the holder of design right. Furthermore, in the case of an employee design, there leaves the way for the employer to obtain an exclusive, monopoly right on the design. In other words, the employer may conclude an agreement with the creator, before the completion of the design, that the creator will assign the right to obtain a design registration or the design right after design registration to the employer, or grant an exclusive licence to the employer. In addition, the employer may conclude an agreement with the creator in advance that the right to obtain a design registration will be initially vested in the employer. In other words, it is possible to have the right to obtain a design registration vested in the employer instead of the creator from the time the right emerges (the time the design is created). This system, which was introduced upon the law amendment in July 2015, ensures higher legal stability to the employer than the above case (of assigning the right to obtain a design registration to the employer after the right emerges), as a means whereby the employer owns an exclusive right on an employee design, thus avoiding the risk of double assignment.

[31] *Clamp*, Judgment of the Osaka High Court of 27 May 1994, Chiteki Saishū (Intellectual Property Law Reports), vol. 26, no. 2, 447.
[32] Article 15(3) of the Act of 1959.

11.1.4 Requirements for Protection (Requirements for Registration) and the Scope of the Effect of the Right (Requirements for Infringement)

The Japanese Design Act adopts an examination and registration system for protection of designs. The examination conducted has been not only a formality, but also a substantive examination already since the Design Bylaws of 1888. An examination is conducted on whether a design satisfies the statutory requirements for registration in regard to similarity with existing designs, etc., and a design right, which is an exclusive, monopoly right, is granted only for a design that satisfies the requirements. The scope of the exclusive, monopoly effect of the design right is also stipulated under law.

In this manner, the Japanese Design Act substantively provides for the protection requirements and the scope of protection of a design by explicit provisions. However, some debate could arise surrounding their interpretation, that is, in the understanding of what substantially the Design Act protects and how, depending on differences in standpoint when interpreting the intention and purpose of the Design Act.

11.1.4.1 Requirements for Registration

The first requirement for registration is mass-producibility.[33] When a design (as a notion inseparable from a product) is not mass-producible, it is usually difficult to say that production of the design is conducted as an industrial activity. Since the purpose of the Design Act is the 'development of industry' (Article 1 of the current Act), the object of monopoly by a design right must be limited to designs that can be industrially mass-produced, also in light of such purpose of the Act. At the same time, in relation with the Copyright Act, this requirement also serves as a standard for distinguishing between applied art which is the subject-matter of the Copyright Act and a design which is the subject-matter of the Design Act. Specifically, a work of artistic craftsmanship, which is a one-of-a-kind product, is excluded from the subject-matter of the Design Act due to lack of mass-producibility, but it is expressly included in artistic works as applied art that is protected under the Copyright Act.[34] Due to this mass-producibility requirement, the aesthetic appearance of real property, such as a garden or building, is not protected under the Design Act. Meanwhile, the Copyright Act sets forth architectural works as a different category from artistic works in its provisions illustrating examples of protected works.[35]

[33] Article 3(1) of the Design Act of 1959. [34] Article 2(2) of the Copyright Act of 1970.
[35] Article 10(1)(v) of the Copyright Act of 1970.

The second requirement for registration is novelty.[36] A design that lacks this novelty requirement is a design that was publicly known, that was described in a distributed publication or that was made available to the public through the Internet prior to the filing of the application for design registration, and a design similar to such design. The geographical area for determining novelty is not only Japan, but also foreign countries. For example, a design that is identical or similar to a design that is not publicly known in Japan but is publicly known in a foreign country is regarded as lacking the requirement for registration. While novelty is an objective requirement unrelated to the subjective fact of whether or not the creator had accessibility to the prior design, it is not always determined in an absolute manner. For instance, as is often the case in a design development workplace, if a design is known among a large number of people who are mutually under a duty of confidentiality, the design is not construed as a design 'that was publicly known'.[37] In addition, an exceptional grace period is set for lack of novelty. When a third party has disclosed a design against the will of the person having the right to obtain a design registration or when the person having such right has disclosed a design on a trial basis by the person's own will, the novelty requirement is satisfied as long as the application for design registration is filed within six months from such disclosure.[38]

The third requirement for registration is creative difficulty. A design must not be one that can be easily created by a person with average knowledge of designs in the industry of said design based on existing publicly known appearances or motifs at the time of the filing of the application.[39] Under this requirement, even where a design satisfies the abovementioned novelty requirement and is objectively found to be a new creation, if it could be easily created by a person having average knowledge of the design, grant of a monopoly right on said design will be refused. The geographical area for determining creative difficulty was expanded upon the law amendment of 1998, from Japan to also include foreign countries, similar to the case of the novelty requirement. On the other hand, existing publicly known appearances or motifs with which the filed design should be compared are not subject to restriction based on products, which differs from the case of the novelty requirement. In other words, the creative difficulty requirement questions whether the conception of the design has distinctiveness when compared with appearances or

[36] Article 3(1) of the Design Act of 1959.

[37] Takashi Morimoto, in Mitsuda and Matsuo (eds.), *Chūkai Ishō Hō*, p. 151; Naoko Matsumoto, in Shigeki Chaen (ed.), *Ishō Hō* (Design Act) (Tokyo: Yuhikaku, 2012), p. 64.

[38] Article 4 of the Design Act of 1959. [39] Article 3(2) of the Design Act of 1959.

motifs of existing designs regardless of identity or similarity of the products.[40] According to the current Design Examination Standards, for example, making the shape of a paperweight resemble a green pepper, which is a natural object, and making the shape of a toy motorbike resemble a real publicly known motorbike, can be seen as lacking this requirement.[41]

Lastly, there are cases where an application is refused even if the design satisfies all of the abovementioned requirements for registration. One is the case of unregistrable designs. A design cannot be registered in the following three cases: when the design is liable to injure public order or morality; when the design is liable to create confusion with an indication of source of another person's business; and when the shape of the design is indispensable for securing functions of the product.[42] The other is the case where two or more applications filed for identical or similar designs compete with each other. For example, even when two or more applications are filed for identical designs on different filing dates, and the filed designs all satisfy the novelty and other requirements for registration, only the application that was filed first is protected by registration, and the other applications are refused.[43]

11.1.4.2 Scope and Limits of the Effect of a Design Right

The effect of exclusive monopoly of a design right extends to an act of exploiting a design that is identical or similar to the registered design on a repeated and ongoing basis, that is, as a business.[44] An act of exploiting a design has no broad sense but is explicitly and restrictively defined as an act of manufacturing, using, assigning, leasing, offering for assignment or lease (including displaying for the purpose of assignment or lease), or importing or exporting of a product of the design.[45] Design right infringement through unauthorised exploitation becomes subject to civil liability such as an injunction[46] or compensation for damage,[47] as well as to criminal punishments (imprisonment with work and fines) under the penal provisions of the Design Act.[48] Infringement of a right includes not only unauthorised imitation, but also exploiting registered design irrespective of the accessibility. Japanese design right is an absolute

[40] *Flexible Hose*, Judgment of the Supreme Court of 19 March 1974, Saikō Saibnasho Minji Hanreishū (Supreme Court Reports), vol. 28, no. 2, 308.
[41] Japan Patent Office, *Ishō shinsa kijun*, pp. 42–51.
[42] Article 5 of the Design Act of 1959. [43] Article 9 of the Design Act of 1959.
[44] Article 23 of the Design Act of 1959. [45] Article 2(3) of the Design Act of 1959.
[46] Article 37(1) of the Design Act of 1959. [47] Article 709 of the Civil Code.
[48] Article 69 of the Design Act of 1959.

monopoly right differing from an anti-copying right like copyright[49] or Community unregistered design right in the European Union.

The scope of protection of a registered design extends to not only designs that are identical, but also to those that are similar to the registered design. As mentioned earlier, the notion of design is inseparable from its designated product, so whether or not a design is identical or similar to the registered design must be considered in relation to both the product of the design and its appearance. In other words, a design identical to a registered design means a design for an identical product and which has an identical appearance (such as shape, patterns or colours) as the registered design. In contrast, a design similar to a registered design means a design for an identical product and which has a similar appearance, a design for a similar product and which has an identical appearance, or a design for a similar product and which has a similar appearance. Incidentally, in determination of similarity between designs, the determining entity is not the creator of the design or an expert, but consumers in the actual market of the design.[50] For instance, consumers who are to determine similarity are, in the case of a design of a face puff, females who have an interest in face washing if only a little,[51] while in the case of a design of a pile for building, they are builders who purchase piles for building and brokers of such transactions,[52] and in the case of a design of a shopping basket used in stores such as supermarkets, they are purchasing agents of the supermarket, etc.[53]

However, an infringing relation is not restricted to one between mutually identical or similar designs. That is to say, exploiting a design which contains others' registered design as a whole is prohibited, even though both designs are mutually different because of the difference of each product.[54] For example, exploiting a bicycle design including another's registered design for a bicycle handle infringes the design of the handle, despite lacking similarity between each product.

Also in the way of the infringement test, we can find, by contrast to copyright law, a specific feature for design law. The infringement test of design right is done considering not only the commonality but also the

[49] *One Rainy Night in Tokyo*, Judgment of the Supreme Court of 7 September 1978, Saikō Saibnasho Minji Hanreishū, vol. 32, no. 6, 1145.
[50] Article 24(2) of the Design Act of 1959.
[51] *Face Puff*, Judgment of the Osaka District Court of 15 December 2005, Hanrei Jihō, no. 1936, 155.
[52] *Foundation Pile*, Judgment of the Intellectual Property High Court of 27 January 2009.
[53] *Shopping Basket*, Judgment of the Osaka High Court of 30 August 2006, Hanrei Jihō, no. 1965, 147.
[54] Article 26 of the Design Act of 1959.

difference in appearance between both designs.[55] As is usual in the case law, when dispute arises over infringement between the registered design and another design, after grasping the most characteristic part of the appearance of the registered design, which can draw consumers' attention, and clarifying commonality as well as difference in the appearance of both designs, whether infringement is affirmed or not will be decided by comparing the total impression of them from the consumers' perspective.[56] When commonality surpasses difference, infringement should be affirmed; when difference surpasses commonality, it will be denied.[57] This assessment of infringement is essentially different from that of copyright infringement as anti-copying right.

The duration of the design right as outlined above is up to twenty years from the date of the registration establishing the design right.[58] The duration depends on the payment of the registration fee every year. Therefore, in practice, a design right is a right that can be renewed annually for up to twenty years. There are also exceptional cases where the effect of right is restricted even within the valid duration of the design right. For example, the effect of a design right does not extend to an act of exploiting a design for experimental or research purposes.[59] Meanwhile, since the effect of a design right extends only to an act of exploiting the design right on a repeated and ongoing basis as a business, an act of exploiting the design only within a family or within a personal scope falls beyond the effect of the design right in the first place.

11.1.4.3 Debate over Similarity of Designs: Discussions on the Essential Nature of the Design Act

A design 'similar' to a publicly known design is refused registration, and the effect of a design right extends to 'similar' designs. Therefore, in determining the scope of protection of a design right, the meaning of the concept of 'similarity' is decisively important. Interpretation of the concept of 'similarity', which relates to both requirements for registration and requirements for infringement, has been discussed as an issue that also relates to understanding the essence of the Japanese Design Act. The discussions centred on confrontation between two opinions: one understanding the intention and purpose of design protection to be protecting the *creative character* inherent

55 Shigeki Chaen, in Shigeki Chaen (ed.), *Ishō Hō* (Design Act) (Tokyo: Yuhikaku, 2012), p. 109.

56 Article 24(2) of the Design Act of 1959.

57 Kazuo Komatsu, 'Saikin no ishō shingai soshō ni okeu ishō no ruihi ni tsuite' (On similarity between designs in recent lawsuits for design right infringement), in Ryuichi Shitara et al. (eds.), *Gendai chiteki zaisan hō, jitsumu to kadai* (Modern intellectual property law, practice and issues) (Tokyo: Hatsumeisuishin Kyoukai, 2015), p. 853.

58 Article 21 of the Design Act of 1959.

59 Article 36 of the Design Act of 1959.

in the design, and recognising 'similarity' based on commonality in the *creativity* that is objectively identified from a *design creator* perspective (so-called 'creation theory');[60] and one understanding the intention and purpose of design protection to be maintaining the *distribution/market order* for design, and recognising 'similarity' based on the possibility of causing misunderstanding or confusion in the market from the perspective of *the market*, such as purchasers of articles (so-called 'confusion theory').[61]

Historically, the theoretical origin of the confusion theory dates back earlier. Literature in 1911 had already set forth that similarity of designs, which determines registrability on one hand and determines infringement on the other, means causing misunderstanding of the designs among general consumers.[62] In contrast, the Tokyo High Court adopted the creation theory[63] and clearly denied the confusion theory[64] successively in the *Flexible Hose* case and the *Hat* case in the 1970s which related to interpretation of the requirement for registration. However, in the final appellate instance of both of these cases, the Supreme Court conversely gave a clear holding that the entity that is to determine similarity between designs is general consumers, and successively denied the Tokyo High Court's determination that was based on the creation theory.[65] Subsequently, upon the 2006 amendment of the Design Act, a rule was stipulated determining similarity as a requirement for infringement from the consumers' perspective.[66] As a result, there is no longer room to apply interpretation based on the creation theory, which regards creators to be the determining entity, in limiting the scope of the effect of a design right.

After the abovementioned Supreme Court decisions that denied the creation theory, there have been some court decisions that expressly endorsed the confusion theory.[67] There were also cases where the court relied on the confusion theory in determining not only similarity between

[60] Riichi Ushiki, *Ishō Hō no kenkyū* (Study on the Design Act), 4th revised edn (Tokyo: Hatsumei Kyoukai, 1994), p. 123.
[61] Takada, *Ishō*, p. 149; Mitsue Toyosaki, *Kōgyō shoyūken hō* (new enlarged edition) (Tokyo: Yuhikaku, 1980), p. 326; Minoru Takeda, 'Ishō no ruihi ni tsuite' (About similarity between designs) (1990) 87, no. 2, *Hatsumei* (The Invention), 48; Toshisuke Kiyonaga, 'Ishō no ruihi' (Similarity between designs) (1985) 9 *Saiban jitsumu taikei* (Judicial practice overview), 409.
[62] Kiyose, *Kōgyō shoyūken gairon*, p. 221.
[63] *Flexible Hose*, Judgment of the Tokyo High Court of 29 January 1970, Mutai Reishū, vol. 2, no. 1, 16.
[64] *Hat*, Judgment of the Tokyo High Court of 31 May 1973, Mutai Reishū, vol. 5, no. 1, 184.
[65] *Flexible Hose*, Judgment of the Supreme Court of 19 March 1974, Saikō Saibnasho Minji Hanreishū, vol. 28, no. 2, 308; *Hat*, Judgment of the Supreme Court of 28 February 1975, Hanrei Taimuzu, no. 320, 160.
[66] Article 24(2).
[67] For example, *Fence*, Judgment of the Kanazawa Branch of the Nagoya High Court of 10 July 1991, Hanrei Jihō, no. 1408, 113; *Clothes Storage Case*, Judgment of the Tokyo High

the appearances of designs, but also similarity between the products for which the appearances are designated. In a case in which infringement of a design right relating to a face puff was disputed,[68] the Osaka District Court held that whether or not the products are similar should also be determined based on whether or not there is likelihood of confusion of the products among general consumers, clearly taking the standpoint of the confusion theory. Specifically, the court found similarity between a registered design of a face puff and a design of a face-washing tool on the basis that, for females, who are the main consumers of a face puff, a face puff not only has its original use/function to apply foundation, etc. to the facial skin, but also a use/function as a face-washing tool, and the court affirmed infringement of the design right. Also, in the recent 'K-SWISS' case, the Intellectual Property High Court found that five zonal forms applied to the lateral sides of athletic shoes as a well-known logo mark constituted a *design*, and suggested that protection under the Design Act could extend to the design's ability, which can be formed on the actual distribution market, to identify the source of the article to which it is applied, independent of the creative elements of the design.[69]

By taking the standpoint of the confusion theory, when determining infringement, for example, the presence of commonality in creative elements between designs does not necessarily lead to a conclusion of finding infringement. Even if a creative element of a registered design is found in part of the design of the defendant, provided that from the consumers' perspective in actual market the overall impression of the two designs (considering also differences between them) differs and there is no likelihood of confusion of the products, the two designs will be found not to be similar, and a conclusion of non-infringement will be derived. Hence, the confusion theory may be evaluated as compatible with the above-mentioned infringement test, particularly for design right, which has been practised through court decisions.

11.1.5 Relationship between the Copyright Act and Applied Art

As mentioned earlier, the first modern Copyright Act was enacted in Japan in 1899, which was about ten years after the enactment of the Design Bylaws of 1888. This previous Copyright Act (Act No. 39 of 4

Court of 13 April 1995, Hanrei Jihō, no. 1536, 103; *Time Card*, Judgment of the Tokyo High Court of 26 September 1995, Chiteki Saishū, vol. 27, no. 3, 682.

68 *Face Puff*, Judgment of the Osaka District Court of 15 December 2005, Hanrei Jihō, no. 1936, 155.

69 *K-SWISS*, Judgment of the Intellectual Property High Court of 28 May 2008.

March 1899) had no specific provisions on protection of applied art. The intention of its legislators did not include application of copyright to the domain of useful applied art either. Dr Rentaro Mizuno, who drafted the Bill, clearly stated in his comprehensive book on the Copyright Act that a tasteful design, that is, applied art, which is the subject-matter of the Design Act, is not included in the subject-matter of the Copyright Act.[70] Mizuno also asserted that protection of applied art was not included in the intention of the legislators of the previous Japanese Copyright Act even when the 1908 Berlin amendment of the Berne Convention inserted a provision to protect applied art, which is not obligatory for the countries of the Union, in Article 2(4).[71]

Such demarcating concept of the previous Copyright Act to leave protection of applied art totally to the Design Act coincides with the legislative intent of the Design Act at the time, which was structured as a system for protecting decorative/tasteful applied art that is identified separately from concrete products. A similar idea can be observed in the argument made by the Japanese delegate at the International Conference for the Amendment of the Berne Copyright Convention held in Rome in 1928. When a proposal was made at the amendment conference in Rome to insert a provision to protect applied art, the Japanese delegate stated that the proposal could in no way be accepted since making applied art the subject-matter of the Copyright Act would cause confusion to the existing protection order formed by the Design Act, and led to the proposal being rejected.[72] In other words, even under the Design Act of 1921, which had shifted to the notion of design being inseparable from products and which had gradually begun to include not only decorative designs but also functional designs in its subject-matter, there was no change in the demarcation between copyright and applied art among legislators and government officials.

However, there was some literature that supported protection of applied art under the previous Copyright Act. Specifically, it was an idea of not imposing any special restriction on the possibility of copyright protection for applied art,[73] but interpreting the aesthetic creativity

[70] Rentaro Mizuno, *Chosakuken Hō* (Copyright Act) (Tokyo: Reibunsha, 1905) (1974 reprinted edition), p. 66.

[71] Rentaro Mizuno, 'Chosakuken hogo bankoku kaigi no seika to naikoku hō' (Outcome of the international conference on copyright protection and national law) (1909) 27, no. 10 *Hōgaku Kyōkai zasshi* (Journal of the Jurisprudence Association), 1528.

[72] Ministry of Education, *Bungaku Teki Oyobi Bijutsu Teki Chosakubutsu Hogo Jōyaku Rōma kaigi hōkokusho* (Report on the Rome conference on the Convention for the Protection of Literary and Artistic Works) (1928), p. 104.

[73] Kiyose, *Kōgyō shoyūken gairon*, p. 217; *Shiro Mitsuishi, Ishō Hō shōsetsu* (Detailed explanation on the Design Act) (Tokyo: Teikokuchihougyouseigakkai, 1969), pp. 77ff.

required for copyright protection to be relatively higher in level than that required for design right protection, and recognising partially cumulative copyright protection for applied art (design) that has a high level of aesthetic creativity.[74]

In contrast to the previous Copyright Act, the current Copyright Act (Act No. 48 of 6 May 1970) introduced express provisions on protection of works of artistic craftsmanship from among applied art.[75] A work of artistic craftsmanship means the design of a one-of-a-kind useful handicraft product, such as an artistic pot or wall hanging.[76] Hence, the Act expressly recognised copyright protection only for such applied art that had not been protected under the Design Act of 1959 due to lack of the mass-producibility requirement (reviewed earlier in 11.1.4.1).

Due to this measure, at least works of artistic craftsmanship are protected by copyright, similar to other categories of works, such as literary works, paintings, musical works and images. This protection includes moral rights.

The requirement for copyright protection (copyrightability) is that the expression must be creative.[77] Creativity is generally interpreted to require no special level. It is rather difficult to positively define creativity. In other words, creativity can be interpreted negatively, such as not being an imitation, not being commonplace, and not being an inevitable expression. When a work of artistic craftsmanship fulfils this condition of creativity, its designer (author) obtains a property right that prohibits unauthorised exploitation (reproduction, exhibition, Internet transmission, rental of reproductions, etc.) of the design itself separately from its tangible product;[78] and moral rights that prohibit making the work first available to the public, changing the name of the author and destroying the integrity of the work without authorisation,[79] and that prohibit exploitation that would harm the honour or reputation of the designer.[80] The term of protection is fifty years after the death of the designer (author). However, although the 'author' will nonetheless be protected, if the requirements for a work made for hire in the course of his or her duties[81] are met, not the actual designer, but the employer, such as the corporation to which the

[74] Murayama, *Tokkyo shin'an ishō shōhyō yonpō yōron*, p. 325; Sen'ichi Shinmura, *Chosakuken Hō gairon* (Overview of the Copyright Act) (Tokyo: Ganshoudou Shoten, 1933), p. 43.
[75] Article 2(2) of the Copyright Act of 1970.
[76] Moriyuki Kato, *Chosakuken Hō chikujō kōgi* (Article-by-article lecture on the Copyright Act), 6th newly revised edn (Tokyo: CRIC, 2013), p. 68.
[77] Article 2(1)(i) of the Copyright Act of 1970.
[78] Articles 21–28 of the Copyright Act of 1970.
[79] Articles 18–20 of the Copyright Act of 1970.
[80] Article 113(6) of the Copyright Act of 1970.
[81] Article 15 of the Copyright Act of 1970.

designer belongs, will initially acquire all property rights and moral rights as the 'author'. In the case of a work made for hire, the term of protection of a work of artistic craftsmanship will be fifty years after the work is made public. Of course, such copyright protection is not without restriction. There are provisions restricting the effect of copyright, such as allowing reproduction for private use, and allowing certain acts of exhibition by the owner of the original of the work of artistic craftsmanship.

As mentioned above, the current Japanese Copyright Act provides a statutory protection system for applied art through Article 2(2), which is a provision on protection of works of artistic craftsmanship. Meanwhile, protectability of applied art other than works of artistic craftsmanship has been one of the important interpretation issues of the Japanese Copyright Act since the legislation of the current Act until today. That is the interpretation issue concerning the interface with the Design Act, which will be discussed in the following.

11.2 Interface between the Design Act and Copyright Act with regard to Design Protection

11.2.1 Status of Interface and Its Evaluation (Advantages/Disadvantages)

11.2.1.1 Conflict between the Legislative Intent and the Interpretations by the Courts

Fundamental Demarcation and Exceptional Cumulation as the Legislative Intent

Under the current Copyright Act, the only provision concerning protection of applied art is Article 2(2), which clarifies the protection of works of artistic craftsmanship. It was the first statutory provision enacted in 1970 that made it clear that the Japanese Copyright Act can protect applied art.

The basic concept adopted in the process of legislative deliberation of this provision is found to have the following two characteristics.[82] First is the idea to avoid the standpoint taken under the previous Act to keep silent about the relationship between applied art and copyright, in accordance with the Brussels amendment of the Berne Convention in 1948 which explicitly added works of applied art to subject-matter. Second is the idea to limit the copyrightable applied art strictly and to concurrently provide for measures to adjust copyright protection and design right

[82] Ministry of Education, *Chosakuken Seido Shingikai tōshin setsumeisho* (Explanation on the report of the Copyright System Council) (1966), p. 9; Ministry of Education, *Chosakuken Seido Shingikai shingi kiroku (1)* (Records of deliberations at the Copyright System Council (1)) (1966), pp. 196–7.

protection, in order to avoid allowing copyright protection from causing confusion to the existing protection order of the Design Act in establishing a protection system for applied art. Cases that were assumed to be confusing the existing market order of the Design Act included, for example, a case where applied art, which can be freely exploited under the order of the Design Act, becomes subject to the exclusive effect of copyright.[83]

Based on this fundamental concept, two kinds of system were proposed. The first system proposed was as follows. First, with regard to the appearance of a product itself, copyright protection would be allowed only for a work of artistic craftsmanship that cannot be the subject-matter of the Design Act due to being a one-of-a-kind product and lacking mass-producibility as one of its protection requirements. Next, with regard to drawing plans and patterns that serve as the basis for manufacture of mass-produced products, protection of such drawing plans and patterns would be allowed, and a measure to make adjustment with the Design Act would be implemented whereby a choice would be made between copyright protection and design right protection before and after the industrial exploitation.[84] The influence of UK law could be observed in this adjustment measure.[85]

However, the scheme actually adopted in Article 2(2) of the current Act was not this first system, but the second system which was prepared in case it would turn out to be difficult to institutionalise the measure for adjustment with the Design Act that was planned by the first system. This is an idea to clearly stipulate copyright protection under law only for works of artistic craftsmanship that do not require a measure for adjustment with the Design Act due to lack of protection requirement thereof and hence have no likelihood of causing cumulative protection. At the same time, it basically shelved copyright protection for drawing plans and patterns of mass-produced articles that require adjustment measures, making it a future legislative issue, and exceptionally allowed copyright protection for graphic works, such as posters, postcards and calendars, that were considered to have no room to cause confusion to the protection order of the Design Act.[86] In actuality, at the 63rd session of the Diet in 1970 where legislation of the current Copyright Act was deliberated, the issue of protection of applied art was positioned as an unsolved legislative issue to be addressed in the future in the supplementary resolution

[83] Ministry of Education, *Chosakuken Seido Shingikai shingi kiroku* (1), p. 197.
[84] Ministry of Education, *Chosakuken Seido Shingikai tōshin setsumeisho*, pp. 9–10.
[85] Ministry of Education, *Chosakuken Seido Shingikai shingi kiroku* (1), p. 198.
[86] Ministry of Education, *Chosakuken Seido Shingikai tōshin setsumeisho*, pp. 10–11.

adopted by both the House of Representatives and the House of Councillors.[87]

In short, Article 2(2) of the current Copyright Act is a system that was devised in case an adjustment measure of selecting either the copyright or the design right system before and after industrial exploitation (the first system proposed) cannot be realised. Namely, its main or fundamental purpose is to prevent confusion in the order of the market with regard to protection of applied art that has been formed on the basis of the design law system in the past. That is an idea to basically abandon copyright protection for applied art of mass-produced articles from the start of their creation process. Therefore, although cumulative protection is exceptionally allowed only for applied art of graphic works, such as posters and postcards, the basic intention of this provision can be construed to be an even stricter and more cautious demarcation than the first system which was basically to allow copyright protection for unrestricted applied art before industrial exploitation.[88]

Such a demarcating idea can be regarded as rational to a certain extent, in light of the history of design protection in Japan. In Japan, only the design law system that started in 1888 had assumed the role of protecting applied art ahead of the enactment of the current Copyright Act, and it played such a role alone (without copyright protection) for more than eighty years. In addition, such a design protection system differed from that of the Copyright Act, especially in terms of substantial features: the notion of the subject-matter (design), which was restrictedly defined as inseparable from its designated product; the scope of protection, which was determined not solely by the creative elements of design from a creator perspective, but by considering the distinctiveness or confusion between designs from the perspective of consumers; and the infringement test, which featured consideration of not only the commonality but also the differences between designs and comparing overall impressions of both designs. As long as the purpose of laws is inevitably to preserve and protect social order, it is considered to have been a natural demand for the current Copyright Act to preserve the existing protection order for applied art that has been formed by the Design Act.

[87] Minutes of the Committee on Education of the House of Representatives at the 63rd Diet session, no. 12, 1; Minutes of the Committee on Education of the House of Representatives at the 63rd Diet session, no. 13, 25.

[88] Masahiro Motoyama, 'Ōyō bijutsu mondai no honshitsu to sono tenkai' (Essence of the issue of applied art and its development), in Ryu Takabayashi et al. (eds.), *Chiteki zaisan hō no rironteki tankyū* (Theoretical inquiry of intellectual property law) (Tokyo: Nihonhyouron Sha, 2012), p. 304.

Development of Partial Cumulation for Applied Art by the Courts

However, unlike such fundamental demarcation of the current Copyright Act, many conventional court decisions have constantly developed interpretations that approve partial cumulation for applied art protection.

Major court decisions that have indicated interpretations concerning the possibility of protecting applied art and were rendered during the period from 1971 when the current Act came into effect until 2014 include the following nineteen decisions, in chronological order:

(i) the 'Hakata Doll' provisional disposition case (the court *upheld* copyright protection of the appearance of a Japanese ornamental doll);

(ii) the 'Buddhist Altar Carvings' case (the court *upheld* copyright protection of the design for decorating a Buddhist altar);

(iii) the 'T-shirt Pattern Original Drawing' case (the court *upheld* copyright protection of a poster-like design on the chest part of a T-shirt);

(iv) the 'Commercial Advertisement' case (the court *upheld* copyright protection for a poster for commercial advertisement);

(v) the '*Saga-nishiki* Double Woven *Obi*' case (the court *denied* copyright protection for the pattern of *obi* (sash) for kimono);

(vi) the 'NY Chair' case (the court *denied* copyright protection for the design of a chair that has become a permanent collection of the Museum of Modern Art, New York);

(vii) the 'Wood-grain Decorative Paper' case (the court *denied* copyright protection for adhesive paper for decorating the surface of furniture);

(viii) the 'Decorative Window Lattice' case (the court *denied* copyright protection for the master drawing for an exterior material for a building);

(ix) the 'Decorative Street Lamp' case (the court *denied* copyright protection for the design of street lamps for a shopping street);

(x) the 'Furby' case (the court *denied* copyright protection for the appearance of an electronic toy pet);

(xi) the 'Writing Paper Picture' case (the court *upheld* copyright protection for the picture of insects, etc. that was drawn as an illustration on a writing paper);

(xii) the '*Shokugan* (chocolate toy) Figures' case (the court partially *upheld* copyright protection for three-dimensional representations of animals and monsters that appear in illustrated reference books of animals or ancient literature);

(xiii) the 'Shiro Sendai' case (the court *denied* copyright protection for a portrait drawing drawn on mug cups, etc.);

(xiv) the 'Petite Holder' case (the court *denied* copyright protection for a stuffed dog with the function of a holder for small items);

(xv) the 'Tripp-Trapp I' case (the court *denied* copyright protection for the children's chair 'Tripp-Trapp');

(xvi) the 'Pot Handle Design' case (the court *denied* copyright protection for the cylindrical design of cooking pot handles);

(xvii) the 'Customized Dolls' Body Parts' case (the court *denied* copyright protection for nude body parts that can be clothed or coloured according to preference);

(xviii) the 'Chateau Katsunuma' case (the court *denied* copyright protection for the design of a signboard showing the direction to a winery); and

(xix) the 'Tripp-Trapp II' case (the court *denied* copyright protection for the children's chair 'Tripp-Trapp') (see Figure 11.2 below).[89]

These court decisions can be statistically summarised as follows. Of the nineteen court decisions, six decisions upheld copyright protection for applied art of mass-producible products, while the remaining thirteen decisions denied cumulative copyright protection. In other words, over two-thirds of the court decisions rendered a conclusion denying copyright protection. When focusing on the instance level of the court, five out of the six decisions that upheld copyright protection were rendered by district courts of first instance (one case was a provisional disposition case), and the remaining one was rendered by an appellate court, while six

[89] (i) Decision of the Sasebo Branch of the Nagasaki District Court of 7 February 1973, Mutai Reishū, vol. 5, no. 1, 18; (ii) Judgment of the Himeji Branch of the Kobe District Court of 9 July 1979, Mutai Reishū, vol. 11, no. 2, 371; (iii) Judgment of the Tokyo District Court of 20 April 1981, Mutai Reishū, vol. 13, no. 1, 432; (iv) Judgment of the Osaka District Court of 29 March 1985, Mutai Reishū, vol. 17, no. 1, 132; (v) Judgment of the Kyoto District Court of 15 June 1989, Hanrei Jihō, no. 1327, 124; (vi) Judgment of the Osaka High Court of 14 February 1990; (vii) Judgment of the Tokyo High Court of 17 December 1991, Chiteki Saishū, vol. 23, no. 3, 808; (viii) Judgment of the Tokyo High Court of 30 September 1992; (ix) Judgment of the Osaka High Court of 23 January 2001; (x) Judgment of the Sendai High Court of 9 July 2002, Hanrei Jihō, no. 1813, 150; (xi) Judgment of the Tokyo District Court of 11 July 2003; (xii) Judgment of the Osaka High Court of 28 July 2005, Hanrei Jihō, no. 1928, 116; (xiii) Judgment of the Sendai District Court of 2 October 2007; (xiv) Judgment of the Tokyo District Court of 4 July 2008; (xv) Judgment of the Tokyo District Court of 18 November 2010; (xvi) Judgment of the Intellectual Property High Court of 22 March 2012; (xvii) Judgment of the Tokyo District Court of 29 November 2012; (xviii) Judgment of the Intellectual Property High Court of 17 December 2013; and (xix) Judgment of the Tokyo District Court of 17 April 2014.

out of the thirteen decisions that denied copyright protection were rendered by courts of first instance, and the remaining seven decisions were rendered by appellate courts.

In this manner, these nineteen court decisions statistically show a slight inclination toward denying cumulative protection in their conclusions. However, in all of these court decisions, except for case (iv) where the court upheld copyright protection for a poster for advertisement without referring to generalities, the courts upheld a theoretical possibility for copyright protection of mass-producible applied art other than works of artistic craftsmanship, suggesting the possible interpretation of partial cumulation. In other words, with regard to applied art other than one-of-a-kind works of artistic craftsmanship, the courts did not deny their copyright protection (cases (iii), (v), (vi), (vii), (xi), (xvii), (xviii) and (xix)), or clearly uphold their copyright protection (cases (i), (ii), (viii), (ix), (x), (xii), (xiii), (xiv), (xv) and (xvi)). As the specific standards for determining the protectability, except for case (i) where the court upheld protection of applied art without setting any special requirements, the courts indicated such standards as whether or not the applied art in question has independent aesthetic appreciability or aesthetic effect (cases (v), (vi) and (xvi)), whether or not its aesthetic expression is under any restriction (cases (iii) and (viii)) and whether or not it has a high level of artistic quality, aesthetic creativity or aesthetics (cases (ii), (vii), (ix), (x), (xi), (xii), (xiii), (xiv), (xv), (xvii), (xviii) and (xix)), and considered these standards in a combined manner in some cases.

In other words, in case (i), the court indicated full cumulation, and in the other cases, it indicated partial cumulation that allows design right protection and copyright protection in a phased manner mainly according to the level of aesthetic creativity of the object. In any case, the idea of fundamental demarcation, which was the legislative intent, cannot be found in conventional court decisions on applied art.

Incidentally, under Japanese copyright law, protectability of applied art is treated as a separate interpretation issue from protectability of typefaces as forms of practical fonts. With regard to the possibility of copyright protection of typefaces, the Supreme Court indicated a goal for interpretation in the 'Gona Font' case.[90] The interpretation was to deny monopolistic copyright protection, in principle, considering the characteristics of letters as communication means. The Supreme Court set an extremely high level of creativity standard for font expressions that can be the subject-matter of copyright, in order to contribute to the development of the culture of publication of printed matter and to prevent the

[90] Judgment of the Supreme Court of 7 September 2000, Saikō Saibansho Minji Hanreishū, vol. 54, no. 7, 2481.

recognition of copyright from causing confusion upon the use of written characters. However, this extremely high level of creativity standard stems not from interpretation of the provision providing for applied art (Article 2(2)), but from interpretation of the provision defining a work (Article 2(1)(i)) taking into account the purpose of the Copyright Act. Since a typeface as a means of linguistic communication is generally not categorised as a 'pattern' which is a constituent element of a 'design' (the aforementioned 'CUP NOODLE' case and 'Packaging Can' case), and lacks the requirement of a product in the case of a digital font, it cannot constitute a 'design' which is the subject-matter of the Design Act. Therefore, unlike in the case of the appearances of products, copyright protection of typefaces does not present the problem of interface with the Design Act. The Supreme Court appropriately limited the protectability of typefaces based on problem awareness specific to typefaces, which is the risk of adverse effects being caused by granting copyright to written characters.

11.2.1.2 Analysis and Evaluation of Court Decisions

Conclusions Derived from Court Decisions

As discussed above, with regard to the Japanese system of copyright protection for applied art (Article 2(2) of the current Act), the legislative intent was to fundamentally demarcate the protection between the Copyright Act and the Design Act, whereas courts have basically indicated the possibility of interpretation as partial cumulation between the Copyright Act and the Design Act.

However, when the conclusions derived by the respective court decisions are analysed, it is questionable whether the court has practically realised cumulative protection as an interface with the Design Act.

First, in the earlier-mentioned nineteen court decisions, the court upheld cumulative protection by copyright for applied art as a conclusion only in a relatively small number of cases. They are the six cases of (i), (ii), (iii), (iv), (xi) and (xii). In other words, in the remaining over two-thirds of the decisions, the courts denied protection of applied art as a conclusion, despite presenting an interpretation recognising partial cumulation for applied art.

Moreover, in the six (relatively small number of) cases in which protection was upheld, there remains a question as to whether these were cases in which it was absolutely necessary to bring up interpretation of partial cumulation against the legislative intent as demarcation.[91] Specifically, the poster-like design on the chest part of a T-shirt (case (iii)), the poster

[91] Motoyama, 'Ōyō bijutsu mondai no honshitsu to sono tenkai', pp. 317–22.

for commercial advertisement (case (iv)) and the picture on a writing paper (case (xi)) for which copyright protection was upheld all correspond to so-called graphic works, for which the current Act since its original enactment had recognised cumulative protection exceptionally and restrictively not inconsistent with its legislative intent as demarcation. Therefore, they could be positioned as the subject-matter of the current Copyright Act irrespective of the copyrightability for applied art in general. On the other hand, in examining the copyrightability of three-dimensional representations of animals and monsters that have already appeared in existing literature (case (xii)), it would have been sufficient to determine whether or not they could be evaluated as derivative works of the pre-existing two-dimensional expressions of monsters, etc., as there is no doubt that a three-dimensional expression based on a pictorial expression of a cartoon character can be categorised as a derivative work.[92] As mentioned above (in 11.1.4.1) regarding the protection requirement for design, a design based on an existing and publicly known motif of expression lacks creative difficulty; hence where applied arts are made from figures of ancient literature, as in the '*Shokugan* Figures' case (case (xii)), there is no room for design registration and therefore no room to bring up the issue of interface. Furthermore, the 'Hakata Doll' provisional disposition case (case (i)) and the 'Buddhist Altar Carvings' case (case (ii)) are both cases of so-called slavish imitation of appearances created by other people. Today, cases on imitation of appearances that are similar to these court decisions, including the legislative durational limitation of the protection (three years from the date the goods were first sold), can be dealt with under the regulation of Article 2(1)(iii) of the Unfair Competition Prevention Act which prohibits slavish imitation of the configuration (appearance) of products. The issue of protectability of the doll and carvings which was questioned in these two cases can be absorbed into the issue of application of the Unfair Competition Prevention Act, without having to bring up interpretation of the Copyright Act with regard to general applied art.

In sum, even if there are six court decisions upholding copyright protection for mass-producible applied art in their conclusion, it is difficult to find in them the significance of precedents that practically recognised cumulative copyright protection for general applied art.

On the other hand, almost all of the relatively large number of cases in which copyright protection was denied were related to applied art, for which

[92] Fumio Sakka, *Shōkai Chosakuken Hō* (Detailed explanation on the Copyright Act), 4th edn (Tokyo: Gyousei, 2010), p. 150; Nobuhiro Nakayama, *Chosakuken Hō* (Copyright Act), 2nd edn (Tokyo: Yuhikaku, 2014), p. 155.

legislators of the Copyright Act abandoned the conclusion to extend copyright protection. In other words, except in case (xviii), the applied art in cases where protection was denied was all that of mass-produced products, namely a pattern of *obi* for kimono (case (v)), the design of a chair (cases (vi), (xv) and (xix)), a pattern of decorative paper for a building material (case (vii)), the drawing for a material for a building (case (viii)), the design of a street lamp (case (ix)), the appearance of a toy or a stuffed animal (cases (x), (xiv) and (xvii)), and a drawing on or the shape of tableware or a cooking utensil (cases (xiii) and (xvi)). None of these works of applied art correspond to works of artistic craftsmanship or graphic works, such as posters, for which protection is intended by the current Copyright Act; instead, they are categorised as drawing plans and patterns of mass-produced products for which protection has been abandoned due to the protection with the Design Act.

After all, the conventional court decisions have indicated a possible interpretation recognising partial cumulation for mass-producible applied art, unlike the legislators' intention, but it is hard to say that the decisions have practically succeeded in modifying the demarcating interface, which was intended by the legislators.

Theories Adopted by Court Decisions

In addition, theoretical defects can also be observed in the interpretation adopted by court decisions to derive partial cumulation.

As summarised above, many of the court decisions that derived partial cumulation used the level of aesthetic creativity as the standard for distinguishing between the subject-matter of copyright and that of design right (cases (ii), (vii), (ix), (x), (xi), (xii), (xiii), (xiv), (xv), (xvii), (xviii) and (xix)). They adopted an idea to recognise partial cumulation by copyright for applied art that has a relatively high level of aesthetic creativity, and to recognise only protection by design right for applied art that does not reach that level. Since the general interpretation of the Japanese Copyright Act is to require no specific level of creativity as a requirement for protection of works, this idea, which uses the level of aesthetic creativity as a standard, is a unique approach that differs from the general theory. However, the idea is extremely similar[93] to the so-called 'two-level theory' (Stufentheorie) that was applied in Germany until recent years.[94]

[93] Masahiro Motoyama, 'Ōyō bijutsu no hogo wo meguru chosakuken no genkai zuke to ishōken no hogo taishō' (Limitation of copyright over protection of applied art and the subject-matter of design right), in *Ishō Hō oyobi shūhen hō no gendaiteki kadai* (Modern issues of the Design Act and related Acts) (Tokyo: Hatsumei Kyoukai, 2005), p. 482.

[94] *Geburtstagszug*, Federal Court of Justice (2014) *Gewerblicher Rechtsschutz und Urheberrecht* 175.

The German 'two-level theory' is an idea to limit the applied art that can be the subject-matter of copyright based on a high level of creativity, on the basis of protectability of applied art under the previous German Design Act (Gesetz betreffend das Urhebererrecht an Mustern und Modellen vom 11 Januar, 1876).[95] Under the theory, what lies between design right and copyright is understood to be not an essential difference, but a difference in grade (Grad), and the subject-matter of the two rights are distinguished in a continuous and graded manner based on the level of aesthetic creativity or the level of originality (Gestaltungshöhe).[96] However, there is no room for applicability of 'two-level theory' to the relationship between the Japanese Design Act and Copyright Act. As discussed earlier in relation to interpretation of the concept of 'similarity' that decides the scope of protection of a design right, the essence of the Japanese Design Act is not protection of creative elements that may be continuous with the Copyright Act but protection of distinctiveness or prevention of confusion in the market of designs that are not continuous with the Copyright Act (protection of distinctive elements). Rather, under the concept of the confusion theory of the Design Act, there was even a possibility that creative elements themselves would not be protected. In other words, the courts' idea, that is *similar* to the '*two-level theory*', which tries to recognise partial cumulation for applied art by using a high level of aesthetic creativity as the standard, is theoretically *incompatible* with the nature of the Japanese Design Act which is not in a graded relationship with the Copyright Act.[97] This is also clear from the fact that the German Supreme Court, when it abandoned its 'two-level theory' for copyrightability of applied art after more than 100 years in 2013, mentioned as the theoretical ground for it that the current German Design Act has changed the nature of the previous Design Act and the Design Act lost its graded relationship with the Copyright Act.[98]

In conclusion, the conventional copyright court decisions have indicated an interpretation to recognise partial cumulation as an interface, but their theoretical foundation was not necessarily free from criticism.

[95] Wilhelm Nordemann, 'Zur Abgrenzung des Geschmacksmusterschutzes vom Urheberschutz' (1967) *Archiv für Urheber- und Medienrecht*, 906 and 908.

[96] H. P. Knöbl, *Die 'kleine Münze' im System des Immaterialgüter- und Wettbewerbsrechts* (2002), p. 90.

[97] Motoyama, 'Ōyō bijutsu no hogo wo meguru chosakuken no genkai zuke to ishōken no hogo taishō', p. 485; Masahiro Motoyama, 'Chiteki zaisanken no hirogari to kōsaku—Dezain hogo' (Spread and intersection of intellectual property protection: Design protection) (2006) *Chizai nenpō 2006* (I.P. annual report 2006), 230.

[98] *Geburtstagszug*, Federal Court of Justice (2014) *Gewerblicher Rechtsschutz und Urheberrecht* 175, para. 34.

11.2.1.3 Development of Interpretation in Recent Judgments by the Intellectual Property High Court

In contrast, the judgments successively rendered by the Intellectual Property High Court in August 2014 and April 2015 are considered to have been intended to overcome such theoretical drawbacks of the conventional court decisions.

First, the 'Fashion Show' case of 28 August 2014[99] was a case concerning a dispute over copyrightability of expressions of coordination of clothes and accessories at a fashion show (see Figure 11.1). This court decision is notable in that it cited the Supreme Court judgment on the 'Gona Font' case concerning typeface protection as a precedent for copyrightability of applied art for the first time. As mentioned earlier, the Supreme Court judgment on the 'Gona Font' case was theoretically unrelated to interpretation of applied art with regard to the interface with the Design Act. However, the Intellectual Property High Court cited the judgment as a precedent. The underlying intention was considered to be to free the discussion on interpretation on copyright protection of applied art from the issue of relationship with the Design Act, and to restructure it as discussion on interpretation of the Copyright Act alone.

Figure 11.1 Fashion show
Source: Judgment of the Intellectual Property High Court of 28 August 2014

[99] *Hanrei Jihō*, no. 2238, 91.

The theoretical drawbacks of conventional court decisions stemmed from the fact that the standard of an extremely high level of aesthetic creativity similar to that of the 'two-level theory' which was adopted in these decisions had no theoretical foundation in the systematic relationship between the Japanese Design Act and Copyright Act. Indeed, as indicated by this Intellectual Property High Court judgment, if the relationship between copyrightability of applied art and the Design Act were cut off, discussion on interpretation of applied art would gain a free hand with setting of the protection standards, without confronting the theoretical issue originating from the systematic relationship with the Design Act. However, such an idea has not been sufficiently successful as a response to the issue of protection of applied art in Japan. This is because, as long as the Design Act exists as a system for protecting appearances of products, in the process of thinking about the appropriateness of copyrightability for applied art, which means also appearances of products, the question of how to address the need to preserve the protection order that has already been constructed on the basis of the Design Act inevitably arises. In short, making the issue of copyrightability of applied art free from the context of the relationship between the Copyright Act and the Design Act may provide more interpretative flexibility for the Copyright Act, but it will merely be an unrealistic approach to forming an actual protection order for design in the market.

Next, the 'Tripp-Trapp II' case of 14 April 2015 was a case concerning a dispute over copyright protection for a children's chair (see Figure 11.2), and it was a judgment of the appellate court for the same case (xix) in which the protection was denied. This court decision is notable in that, as a general interpretation on copyrightability of applied art, it abandoned the standard of a higher level of aesthetic creativity similar to that of the 'two-level theory' which was typically adopted in conventional court decisions, and recognised cumulation without any mechanisms to regulate the interface for applied art based on the normal creativity standard just the same as other categories of works. As a result, unlike in the original instance, copyrightability for the Tripp-Trapp chair was upheld, although its similarity with the defendant's chair was denied as a result of determining a narrow scope of protection, and, as a conclusion, the claim for injunction of sales of the defendant's chair was dismissed.

The text of the judgment does not sufficiently mention the reason for which the standard of high level of aesthetic creativity for applied art should be abandoned. Even so, the idea of abandoning the standard itself should be affirmatively evaluated as an approach to overcome the theoretical defect in the conventional interpretation similar to German 'two-level theory'. However, on the other hand, the interpretation of full

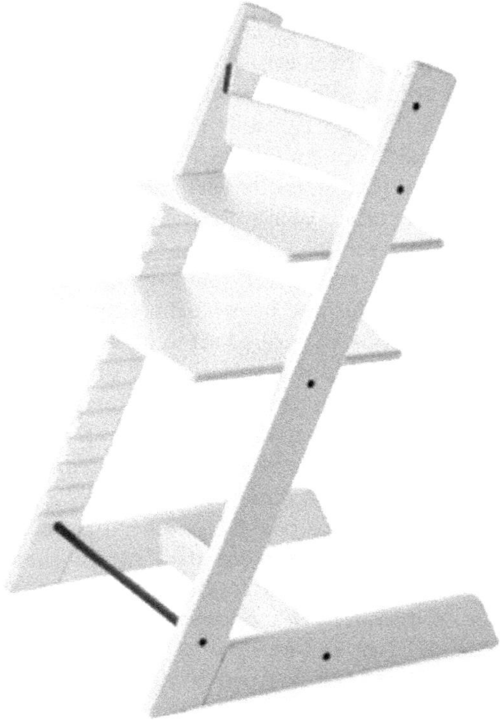

Figure 11.2 Tripp-Trapp chair
Source: Judgment of the Intellectual Property High Court of 14 April 2015

cumulation indicated by the court is not exactly sufficient for preserving the design protection order formed up to the present by the Design Act.

According to the decision, theoretically, the creative elements of the Tripp-Trapp chair, even if they were partial, would be subject to anti-copying with a clear scope of protection under copyright even after the design right is extinguished. This will undoubtedly give rise to a new design protection order that was not experienced under the conventional design protection order that was shaped by the Design Act. Specifically, the partial creative appearances of the Tripp-Trapp chair, even if once registered, which could have been freely exploited as public domain after twenty years from registration, will become subject to a long-term exclusive right as well as moral rights protection under the Copyright Act. In addition, under the design protection order where creative elements themselves were not always made subject to exclusive right according to the confusion theory of the Design Act, the partial creative forms of the Tripp-Trapp become subject to an anti-copying right in themselves. Such an outcome will open the path to copyright protection of general applied art without providing any answer to the task of making adjustment with the order under the Design Act, which had been left as a future task by the supplementary resolution upon legislation of the current Copyright Act.

In any case, the fact that attempts to correct defects in the conventional interpretation similar to the 'two-level theory' began to be observed in interpretation by the courts themselves deserves high evaluation, but in order to develop the theory of correction into a stable and convincing interpretation, there is a need for further accumulation of lower court decisions and unification of the interpretation by the Supreme Court.

11.2.2 What Would Be the Appropriate Interface Rules?

11.2.2.1 Interpretation Approach

The desirable interface between the Design Act and Copyright Act over protection of applied art should rely on the historical background of the two Acts in respect to formation of the design protection order, if the discussion is to only focus on the domestic relationship between the two Acts as national laws.

In this regard, the system for protecting the aesthetic appearances of products in Japan has been dominantly built by the Design Act for over eighty years, ahead of the Copyright Act. Under such circumstances, the practices of distribution and bringing in the market of aesthetic appearances of products must have been reasonably formed according to the original rules of the Design Act. Assuming this as a premise, it is essential to avoid a situation where confusion will be caused to the existing design trading order as a result of the Copyright Act – with, for example, clearly different protection requirements (distinctiveness in the case of a design ↔ creativity in the case of a work), list of rights (limited right of exploitation in a design ↔ property right including the right of adaptation and extensive moral rights in a work), scope of protection (limitation with product and prevention of confusion considering also differences of designs ↔ prohibition of imitation of creative elements itself) and term of protection (twenty years after design registration ↔ fifty years after the death of the author) – starting to protect applied art more widely than before. If the legal system is a means for forming social order, causing social confusion by allowing legal protection will run contrary to the purpose of law.

In other words, if the history of protection of aesthetic appearances of products is to be considered as a background, applied art that can be the subject-matter of the Copyright Act in Japan should inevitably be limited to (i) applied art that fundamentally cannot be the subject-matter of the Design Act in light of the objective mode of the creation or (ii) applied art that can be the subject-matter of the Design Act but whose cumulative protection does not cause confusion to the existing order of design trading in the actual market. The former applied art (i) may include one-of-a-kind works of artistic craftsmanship that are not mass-producible, the appearances of products that cannot be 'designs' under the Design Act due to lacking a repeatable and fixed shape (such as coordination of clothes and accessories at a fashion show), and such existing pictorial expressions created independent of specific products, that are applicable to some products, but are not as design registrable because of lacking protection requirements (novelty and creative difficulty) (for example, the design of the chest part of a T-shirt). All of these are works of applied art that cannot pass through the filter of the design protection system. Therefore, as in the case of typefaces, there is less probability to form the legal order for such applied art under the Design Act. On the other hand, the latter applied art (ii) may include graphic works, such as posters and postcards, which were due to be protected under the legislative intent of the current Copyright Act. Meanwhile, it is difficult to find a practical foundation for expanding copyright protection beyond this domain as rigid precedent, and no such national consensus can be easily found that could alter the legislators' intention as fundamental demarcation. Copyright protection should be denied for applied art for which a design registration has already or formerly been granted or applied art which is categorised as an appearance designated just for a specific product even without a design registration.

11.2.2.2 Legislative Approach

However, the above interpretation only focuses on Japan's domestic system.

In light of the reciprocity rule under Article 2(7) of the Berne Convention as revised in Paris, there is a theoretical possibility that applied art which only receives protection under the Design Act in Japan as the country of origin can receive only design protection in another country of the Union, even when general interpretation in that country recognises copyrightability for that applied art.[100] For example, if the shape of a chair like the Tripp-Trapp is not to receive protection under

[100] Annete Kur, in A. Kur and H. Eichmann (eds.), *Designrecht: Praxishandbuch*, 2nd edn (2016), pp. 468ff, para. 61.

the Copyright Act in Japan (aforementioned cases (xv) and (xix)), it is possible that in Germany, where similar types of chairs created by nationals of other countries of the Union can receive copyright protection (BGH GRUR 2009, 856 Rdnr.22-Tripp-Trapp-Stuhl), the shape of such chair created in Japan cannot obtain copyright and can only be protected under the German Design Act.

If there is a policy or political determination that such a situation is not necessarily favourable from the viewpoint of Japan's strategy to export applied art, the system will need to be altered. In short, from the economic policy perspective of securing export competitiveness, the possibility of copyright protection for applied art in Japan should be expanded in order to secure the possibility of copyright protection for Japanese applied art overseas. This idea is no longer related to the problem awareness of whether or not the existing design protection order within Japan should be preserved. The basis of the idea is the strategy and policy for exporting Japanese designs to overseas. The viewpoint is completely different from the idea of supporting the system for protection of applied art under the current Copyright Act.

Therefore, such alteration of the system will be beyond the limits of interpretation of the current legislation. Of course, the possibility cannot be denied that such institutional amendment will temporarily cause a certain level of confusion to the design protection order that has been formed by the Design Act. In order to ease such concerns, a transitional measure could be taken, for instance, to exclude the copyright effect of designs whose duration has expired in the interim.

Nonetheless, such expansion of the domain of copyright protection is not expected to weaken the significance of the existence of the Design Act. That is because the Japanese Design Act actually functions as a system to protect the distinctiveness of designs and prevent confusion between designs, unlike the concept of the Copyright Act to protect creative elements themselves. The Design Act and Copyright Act protect different legal interests (the Design Act protects market interests by preventing confusion between designs, while the Copyright Act protects the economic interests and moral interests of the creative elements of designs themselves). The situations where design right and copyright each actually function also differ (design right functions when preventing confusion between products, while copyright functions when preventing imitation of expressions). Therefore, even if cumulation is introduced, copyright will not always take over on behalf of design right; in other words, copyright infringement may not always be affirmed more easily than design right infringement with regard to all sorts of applied art (designs). Rather, under the standpoint of the confusion theory, even a design which lacks any creative elements in the sense of copyrightability (and this seems not to be seldom especially in the case of functional designs) will enjoy design right protection, as long as there is distinctiveness against other designs from the viewpoint of market consumers, and against its non-authorised exploitations design right infringement will be affirmed. Design right in itself can be expected to work individually, not as a measure to protect human creative activity but for maintaining the distribution/trading order for design.

The Design Act and Copyright Act are mutually independent legal systems. Hence, cumulative protection of applied art by the Copyright Act does not in any way undermine the significance of the Design Act as a legislative existence.

12 A Model Copyright/Design Interface: Not an Impossible and Undesirable Task?

*Estelle Derclaye**

12.1 Introduction and Preliminary Thoughts

This final chapter draws from all the chapters in an attempt to determine the most adequate rules to regulate the interface between copyright and design protection. The main standard to determine such rules is a balanced protection, namely avoiding both under- and over-protection. To achieve such balanced protection, criteria to regulate the interface used in the countries reviewed are evaluated, and simplicity and efficiency of the system for both designers and users are also important criteria which guide the chapter. The chapter starts with a historical account of the efforts made both at international and EU level to regulate the interface (12.2). It then compares the experiences of the countries reviewed in this volume over the years to discover similarities, differences and trends (12.3). The chapter carries on by assessing the adequacy of the possible models and criteria to organise the interface (12.4). It then compares the experiences of the countries reviewed in this volume over the years to discover similarities, differences and trends (12.3 and Annex at 12.7). The chapter carries on by assessing the adequacy of the possible models and criteria to organise the interface (12.4) and finishes by proposing a model copyright/design interface (12.5–12.6).

The first thing to discuss before embarking on this chapter is if it makes sense or is desirable to find a model for the copyright/design interface. Two arguments can be made against finding such a model. The first argument is whether harmonisation is always by definition a good thing.[1] This first

* I would like to thank Yves Gaubiac, Jean-Michel Bruguière and Pascale Tréfigny for sending me materials and Lionel Bently and Marco Ricolfi for generously and tirelessly answering countless questions about the Italian and UK systems. I am also grateful to Isabella Alexander, Lionel Bently, Jason Du Mont, Jane Ginsburg, Masahiro Motoyama, Maria-Daphne Papadopoulou, Antoon Quaedvlieg and Irini Stamatoudi for their comments on a previous version of this chapter, and Lynne Chave for the data compilation and graphs as well as insights from her practitioner's perspective. All potential errors remain my own. Unless otherwise stated, all footnotes in quotes are omitted.

[1] A. Kingsbury, 'International harmonisation of designs law: The case for diversity' (2010) EIPR 382, at 392 and references cited at note 63; see the many contributions and especially A. Ohly, 'Concluding remarks, postmodernism and beyond', in A. Ohly and J. Pila (eds.), *The Europeanisation of Intellectual Property Law* (Oxford: Oxford University Press, 2013), p. 260.

argument is further divided in two. First, harmonisation is contestable because there is not always one good way of doing something but several equally good ways; and, secondly, it prevents the possibility of testing different laws – several countries toying with different laws can act as laboratories, showing which laws work and which do not. In response to this second argument, one can say that this has already been done for the copyright/design interface for over a century. So many different models have been used or, if not, discussed extensively that the interface has reached a level of maturity so that we know with a high degree of certainty which experiments work and which do not. As to the first argument, if several equally good models can work, there is no reason not to leave a choice to countries if such choice does not lead to negative effects including at international level, i.e. for the relations between countries' industries and communities, creators and users.

The second argument is well known: it is that a single *level* of IP protection is not always suited for all of the world's countries.[2] This is not specific to design protection. Countries are at different stages of development, are IP importers or exporters and may need more or less IP protection. Provided all countries are at more or less the same level of development, and are net exporters of IP, and the vast majority of those reviewed in this book are, they can adopt the same IP laws. Provided every country eventually aspires to an elevated level of development, once they reach it, such a model can be adopted. In the meantime, articles 25 and 26 of the TRIPs Agreement (TRIPs) allows them to choose a minimal level of protection.

12.2 Historical Lessons from International Efforts

As the national chapters of this book show, there were and still are wide divergences between countries in the way they deal with the interface, not only between the countries but also during different periods in each individual country. This was, and still is, at the origin of the difficulty in attempting to reach a solution to the interface in international conventions.

12.2.1 International Efforts

12.2.1.1 *Sui Generis* Design Right

International efforts on a *sui generis* right for designs were launched by the Association Litteraire et Artistique Internationale (ALAI) in 1956.[3] In 1958,

[2] Kingsbury, 'International harmonisation of designs law', 385: 'The concept that there exists a single solution to designs protection that would be optimal across all jurisdictions is itself highly challengeable. What constitutes an appropriate designs regime will vary considerably across jurisdictions, depending on factors including level of development, indigenous design requirements, competition and tax regimes, and trade policy.' And ibid., 395.

[3] The 1956 ALAI congress took a unanimous resolution stating that there should be a study at international level on the topic between the international organisations. See 7th edn

the three unions (Berne, Paris and Geneva) agreed to form a group of experts tasked to find a solution for the protection of designs at international level. In 1959, experts from twenty-one countries agreed that a *sui generis* right was necessary but did not agree on how the interface with copyright law would work, thus leaving countries to choose between cumulation and demarcation.[4] They also thought that cumulation would not pose many problems.[5] The group discussed subject-matter, protection requirements and formalities, but reached no agreement on those.[6] They only agreed on minimal aspects, mainly duration (minimum ten years) and prohibition of exact reproduction.[7]

Meanwhile, the question of a *sui generis* right for designs was debated at the 1960 congress of the Association Internationale pour la Protection de la Propriété Intellectuelle (AIPPI) and again in 1964 with a text unanimously adopted at the AIPPI Tokyo congress in 1966. This text in short states that: the object of protection of a design right is appearance and it can be two-dimensional (2D) and three-dimensional (3D); cumulation is possible but not mandatory; and if a design or model shows no creative effort or if it is exclusively dictated by a technical necessity, registration can be refused. The designs and models must be deposited to be protected and there can be secrecy for one year. Protection is for a minimim of ten years and is against exact reproduction and imitation.[8] The experts again did not think cumulation would create many difficulties.[9] Incidentally, the text closely resembles that of TRIPs adopted thirty years later, showing no further progress to reach

séance de travail, 'La protection des œuvres des arts appliqués et des dessins et modèles', in ALAI (ed.), *Travaux de la Réunion d'Amsterdam* (1956), p. 63 at 67.

4 M.-A. Pérot-Morel, *Les Principes de Protection des Dessins et Modèles dans les Pays du Marché Commun* (La Haye: Mouton, 1968), pp. 299–300; W. Duchemin, 'La protection des arts appliqués dans la perspective d'un dépôt communautaire en matière de dessins et modèles industriels' (1978) 97 *RIDA* 4 at 67; S. Ladas, *Patents, Trademarks and Related Rights, National and International Protection* (Cambridge, MA : Harvard University Press, 1975), pp. 836–7, also stating that UNESCO was involved, citing UNESCO Report (1959) XII, no. 1 *Copyright Bulletin*.

5 Ladas, *Patents, Trademarks and Related Rights*, pp. 836–7.

6 Ladas, *Patents, Trademarks and Related Rights*, p. 837.

7 Pérot-Morel, *Les Principes de Protection des Dessins et Modèles dans les Pays du Marché Commun*, p. 301; Duchemin, 'La protection des arts appliqués dans la perspective d'un dépôt communautaire en matière de dessins et modèles industriels', 71.

8 See Pérot-Morel, *Les Principes de Protection des Dessins et Modèles dans les Pays du Marché Commun*, pp. 302–6; Ladas, *Patents, Trademarks and Related Rights*, pp. 868–9; J. Reichman, 'Design protection in domestic and foreign copyright law: From the Berne Revision of 1948 to the Copyright Act of 1976' (1983) *Duke Law Journal* 1143 at 1166. Duchemin, 'La protection des arts appliqués dans la perspective d'un dépôt communautaire en matière de dessins et modèles industriels', 67–9, also mentions the parallel work (draft model law) of the Milan Institute of Comparative Law which met on this issue in 1964, 1965 and 1968.

9 S. Ricketson and J. Ginsburg, *International Copyright and Neighbouring Rights* (Oxford: Oxford University Press, 2006), p. 469.

agreement on more details at international level. While it does not appear in the text, the experts generally preferred relative to absolute novelty.[10] BIRPI and WIPO also came up with a model design law in 1970.[11] Lastly, the latest AIPPI resolution on the interface advocates cumulation, and a very broad one at that, but without many more details (in short the scope of copyright for industrial products should not be different from that for other copyright works, and designs solely dictated by technical function can be excluded).[12]

However, even if there is a WIPO model law, it is optional and the design protection as enshrined at international level in TRIPs is extremely flexible and thus could lead countries to adopt the 'right type' of *sui generis* design protection which, if coupled with the 'wrong type' of copyright protection,[13] will not produce the desired effects.

12.2.1.2 Copyright Protection of Designs

Copyright protection of designs has encountered even slower and more meagre progress and this since the nineteenth century and both at international and regional level.

Since the beginning, the issue was a thorny one as there were great differences in how to approach the protection of works of applied art between Berne members, mainly between France on one hand and Italy, the UK and Japan on the other. The question was not raised until the revision of the Berne Convention in 1908, and only one article applying national treatment to works of art was adopted. However, this led to a serious imbalance since nationals of countries applying unity of art or full cumulation would not be protected in countries with a demarcation system and vice versa. Therefore, some countries gave reservations on this article so they could escape this imbalance.[14] During the Rome revision in 1928, countries could not find a compromise and thus nothing changed.[15] A solution by way of articles 2(7) and 7(4) was found in Brussels in 1948 albeit with difficulty[16] and

10 Pérot-Morel, *Les Principes de Protection des Dessins et Modèles dans les Pays du Marché Commun*, p. 302. Ladas, *Patents, Trademarks and Related Rights*, p. 832 also reporting that the patent approach for designs was criticised for its stringent criteria including absolute novelty.

11 BIRPI and WIPO, *Model Law for Developing Countries on Industrial Designs*, Geneva, 1970. See Ladas, *Patents, Trademarks and Related Rights*, p. 871; Reichman, 'Design protection in domestic and foreign copyright law', 1143 at 1165; Ricketson and Ginsburg, *International Copyright and Neighbouring Rights*, p. 469.

12 See Resolution on question 231, Seoul Congress, 2012, available at http://aippi.org/wp-content/uploads/committees/231/RS231English.pdf.

13 Or vice versa: the 'wrong type' of design protection with the 'right type' of copyright protection. For more on this, see below, sections 12.3–12.5.

14 Ricketson and Ginsburg, *International Copyright and Neighbouring Rights*, pp. 456–7.

15 Ibid., pp. 458–60.

16 M. Oppenheimer, 12th report, 'Dessins et modèles d'art appliqué', ALAI (ed.), *Travaux de la réunion d'Amsterdam*, 1956, p. 149 at 151.

remained unchanged until the last revision in 1971.[17] Because no solution was found to entirely resolve the problem, countries' choice was limited to embarking on bilateral negotiations.[18]

ALAI did work in parallel. ALAI was always in favour of copyright protection for works of applied art[19] even in the presence of a *sui generis* design right.[20] Over the course of twenty-seven years, from 1956 to 1983, ALAI accumulated the declarations and resolutions, in the main repeating its attachment to a copyright protection of works of applied art, even if a *sui generis* design right is adopted.[21] However, while ALAI was in favour of cumulation, it did not specify its form (partial or full).

12.2.2 *EU Efforts*

EU design law is the most harmonised regional design regime in the world. It is an amazing feat since it saw the light of day from a wild patchwork of design laws and some countries had no design law at all

[17] Ricketson and Ginsburg, *International Copyright and Neighbouring Rights*, p. 461; Ladas, *Patents, Trademarks and Related Rights*, pp. 833–4.

Article 2(7) reads: 'Subject to the provisions of Article 7(4) of this Convention, it shall be a matter for legislation in the countries of the Union to determine the extent of the application of their laws to works of applied art and industrial designs and models, as well as the conditions under which such works, designs and models shall be protected. Works protected in the country of origin solely as designs and models shall be entitled in another country of the Union only to such special protection as is granted in that country to designs and models; however, if no such special protection is granted in that country, such works shall be protected as artistic works.'

Article 7(4) reads: 'It shall be a matter for legislation in the countries of the Union to determine the term of protection of photographic works and that of works of applied art in so far as they are protected as artistic works; however, this term shall last at least until the end of a period of twenty-five years from the making of such a work.'

[18] J. L. Duchemin, 11th report, 'La protection internationale des œuvres des arts appliqués', ALAI (ed.), *Travaux de la réunion d'Amsterdam*, 1956, p. 141 at 146; M. Poirier, 9th report, General report established for the special commission, 'The protection of works of the applied arts and of designs and models', ALAI (ed.), *Travaux de la réunion d'Amsterdam*, 1956, p. 130 at 135.

[19] Duchemin, 'La protection internationale des œuvres des arts appliqués', 143; M. Poirier, 'The protection of works of the applied arts and of designs and models', 135.

[20] M. F. Hepp, 'La protection légale des produits des arts appliqués dans le domaine international', ALAI (ed.), *Travaux de la réunion de 1958*, p. 211 at 216.

[21] Ibid., referring to the 1957 ALAI declaration to keep copyright even if a special protection of designs is adopted at international level; at the Munich congress of 1963, ALAI adopted a resolution on the interface and constituted a study commission on works of applied art but then not much followed. See Pérot-Morel, *Les Principes de Protection des Dessins et Modèles dans les Pays du Marché Commun*, p. 307; in 1965 ALAI was in favour of cumulation: see Duchemin, 'La protection des arts appliqués dans la perspective d'un dépôt communautaire en matière de dessins et modèles industriels', 67–9; H. Cohen Jehoram, 'Protection of industrial design, between copyright and design laws: A comparative study', ALAI (ed.), *Travaux de la Réunion de la Mer Egée*, 1983, p. 77 at 125 referring to the 1983 resolution declaring the same.

(Greece).[22] While EU design law is highly harmonised and has had tremendous success, it nevertheless left the copyright/design interface untouched.

The work at EU level started as early as 1960 with a committee formed of staff in charge of IP services in the different Member States of the then European Community and a report on the work of this committee written by Professor Roscioni. However, there was no follow-up, probably because the issue was not yet ripe.[23] Then the Max Planck Institute for Intellectual Property Law drafted a model design law[24] which was presented at a symposium in 1990. Another model law was also drafted by an international group of experts in connection with a seminar about design law held in 1988 in Treviso and was close to the Max Planck draft.[25] The European Commission's proposal for a legal protection of design was similar to the Max Planck draft in most part[26] and the said draft is also quite close to the text of the Directive and Regulation.[27] However, again the Max Planck draft left the copyright/design interface untouched. The drafters thought that the Member States' copyright laws on the topic were too hard to reconcile,[28] with which I can certainly agree. But they also

[22] Greece enacted special legislation on the protection of industrial designs and models in 1996. For more details, see Chapter 3. Writing a decade before the adoption of the Design Directive and Design Regulation, H. Cohen Jehoram insightfully described the situation concerning design laws in the then EC as follows: 'In no other field of intellectual property do national legal systems vary so widely as in design protection.' See H. Cohen Jehoram, 'Cumulative design protection: A system for the EC?' (1989) *EIPR* 83. Firth and Griffiths also describe the widely different design laws before the Design Directive in relation to protection requirements, term and procedure: H. Griffiths, 'Overview of developments in Europe on industrial design protection' (1993) 4 *Fordham Intell. Prop. Media & Ent. L.J.* 359 at 359–63; A. Firth, 'Aspects of design protection in Europe' (1993) *EIPR* 42 at 42–3.

[23] Pérot-Morel, *Les Principes de Protection des Dessins et Modèles dans les Pays du Marché Commun*, p. 24; Duchemin, 'La protection des arts appliqués dans la perspective d'un dépôt communautaire en matière de dessins et modèles industriels', 67.

[24] See Max Planck Institute for Foreign and International Patent, Copyright and Competition Law, 'Towards a European design law', 1991. The draft law was drafted by Kur, Levin, Beier and Haertel.

[25] 'Towards a European design law', 14.

[26] See European Commission, *Green Paper on the Legal Protection of Industrial Design*, Brussels, June 1991, III/F/5131/91-EN, pp. 11 and 144.

[27] The system is described in 'Towards a European design law', 5 and 6. In short, it adopts a design approach because the patent approach is suitable for big business but not SMEs and this is the category that needs an efficient protection of design the most. It is a two-tier system, i.e. a short (two-year) unregistered right along with a registered right. The right had a grace period, duration for an initial five years renewable up to twenty-five years, and had a criterion of relative novelty and distinctiveness. Years before, many experts also were in favour of relative novelty and a grace period: see e.g. Cohen Jehoram, 'Protection of industrial design, between copyright and design laws: A comparative study', 106 and 114, reporting interventions by Pérot-Morel and Mout-Bouwman.

[28] 'Towards a European design law', 46–7. G. Dinwoodie, 'Federalized Functionalism: The Future of Design Protection in the European Union' (1996) 24 *AIPLA Quarterly Journal* 647, 711–716.

thought that their proposed design system, which included an unregistered design right, would reduce the problem of the interface to nought.[29] Hence it did not have to be resolved. Cumulation would exist in theory but not in practice. The Commission also wanted to leave copyright untouched[30] and thought the need for copyright would diminish because of the Community registered and unregistered design rights.[31] So both the Max Planck drafters and the Commission were rather naïve because it is clear – and this will be discussed in detail below – that if the copyright's level of originality is low, even if the design law is attractive, many designers will not use it since there is no need to register or, if designers register, their two rights will cumulate and they will obtain double protection, because of an unresolved interface.

In conclusion, all twenty-eight Member States now have almost identical substantive national registered design laws and, in addition, every designer can benefit from the Community unregistered design right (UCD) and Community registered design right (RCD). It is undoubtedly a major advancement compared to the period before 1998 and, indirectly, a major achievement in relation to the interface, as a well-functioning and balanced design system is crucial to a well-functioning interface, as we shall see in section 12.3. However, like at international level, the copyright/design interface was left unregulated at EU level (in article 17 Design Directive and article 96(2) Design Regulation[32]), leading most Member States to keep their systems of full cumulation, partial cumulation or demarcation. Only one thing is clear: that following the CJEU decision in *Flos*, the term of copyright protection for works of applied art may not be shorter than the full term, i.e. seventy years p.m.a.,[33] and this despite the relatively clear or at least very broad language of article 17 Design Directive. What is less clear following the same decision is

[29] Ibid., 5: 'the problem of the relation between design law and copyright law that has led to enormous difficulties in all countries, is to be mitigated by offering an efficient design protection so that the need for an additional protection will be confined to exceptional cases'; and at 55: draft provisions 'will render it unnecessary for designers to have much resort to copyright law'.

[30] *Green Paper on the Legal Protection of Industrial Design*, p. 142. [31] Ibid., p. 151.

[32] Article 17 reads: 'A design protected by a design right registered in or in respect of a Member State in accordance with this Directive shall also be eligible for protection under the law of copyright of that State as from the date on which the design was created or fixed in any form. The extent to which, and the conditions under which, such a protection is conferred, including the level of originality required, shall be determined by each Member State.' Article 96(2) reads: '2. A design protected by a Community design shall also be eligible for protection under the law of copyright of Member States as from the date on which the design was created or fixed in any form. The extent to which, and the conditions under which, such a protection is conferred, including the level of originality required, shall be determined by each Member State.'

[33] Case C-168/09, *Flos SpA* v. *Semeraro Casa & Famiglia SpA* [2011] ECDR 161, para. 39.

whether the level of originality for all designs (registered and unregistered) is harmonised.[34]

12.3 Comparing National Experiences: Similarities, Differences and Trends

The foremost and strongest commonality in the countries' experiences is that a badly designed design law is not going to help the interface. This is because if the system is one of full or partial cumulation with a high level of originality in the copyright Act and a patent approach in the design Act, i.e. a strict registered design system, inevitably, designers use the more protective unfair competition law (if it exists) and/or copyright law, convincing courts to lower the originality level to compensate the inadequate registered design protection. The pendulum then switches from under-protection to over-protection.[35] This happened in France, the Benelux, the Nordic countries and the USA at various moments of their history. An adequate level of design protection is fixed now in the EU at least[36] so that such issue is resolved at EU level.

Two other very strong commonalities emerge from the statistics on the number of design applications and, to a lesser extent, design registrations.[37] Granted, it is hard to measure the effects of a piece of legislation.[38] In the case of designs, there are many other factors which can affect design applications such as industrial ones (sectoral composition, shorter product lifecycles, industry structure, awareness and knowledge of design rights), legal ones (legal traditions, legal strength of unregistered rights, wide or narrow range of IPR options, enforcement regimes, diffuse qualification, existence and efficacy of competing private databases, rise of open source collaborations) and administrative ones (simplicity and ease of application procedure and registration cost).[39] And there may be others such as the abolition of copyright formalities making copyright more attractive than

[34] Ibid., para. 34. Arguably only unregistered designs must abide by the level imposed by *Infopaq* and its progeny. L. Bently, 'The return of industrial copyright?' (2012) *EIPR* 654 at 660ff. See Chapter 3 (Greece) in this book where it is argued that the issue of originality has been fully harmonised on the basis of the CJEU's case law.

[35] J. Reichman, 'Design protection and the legislative agenda' (1992) 55(2) *Law and Contemporary Problems* 281 at 287.

[36] It may be argued that a similar situation now exists in Australia as it has adopted a design law very similar to that of the EU except for the relatively short duration (ten years).

[37] See the graphs and the consolidated country tables in the annex at the end of this chapter.

[38] J. Schovsbo and S. Teilmann-Lock, 'We wanted more Arne Jacobsen chairs but all we got was boxes – Experiences from the protection of designs in Scandinavia from 1970 till the directive' (2016) *IIC* 418 at 426.

[39] BOP Consulting 2011, 'Design economics chapter four: Design rights, an international comparison', UK Intellectual Property Office, p. 14.

registered design right. Last but not least, the national and global economic history is also a strong determining factor.[40] It is thus very difficult to analyse the statistics in a meaningful way, especially to determine the effect of a change in legislation or judicial trend, without embarking in proper statistical, empirical economic research. This is something which I will not do in this chapter but leave for future research.

That said, there are some cases where one can venture rather confidently to say that it is hard to see what factors other than the legislation could have influenced the statistics. This is the case for design applications. The first striking feature is the huge decrease in national applications in the EU Member States reviewed in this book[41] and the commensurate enormous rise in EUIPO (former OHIM) applications from 2003 onwards, which corresponds with the introduction of the RCD. The Benelux is the most striking illustration in this respect: applications go from 3,649 in 2003 to a drastic and steady decrease down to 72 applications in 2014. This general trend may be explained by the relatively cheap fees, and easy and quick procedure, including the possibility of online filing at the EUIPO, considering the right is applicable in all the EU Member States.

When one compares the applications by residents and non-residents for the periods prior to and post design regulation, one sees that residents tend to carry on filing for national design rights in their country rather than RCDs while the non-residents tend to prefer filing RCDs. This may be explained by the fact that most non-residents are probably companies looking to protect specific export markets, whereas national applications are preferred by nationally based non-exporting businesses.[42] That said, some of these foreign companies may also prefer to file national designs rather than RCDs or in addition to RCDs to prevent a 'central attack'. In any case, these statistics show the great success of the RCD.

The second striking feature is that whereas at first sight, generally, legislative changes do not seem to have affected design applications, there are some cases where it is hard to see what factors other than the legislation could have had an influence. As J. Schovsbo and S. Teilmann-Lock note about Denmark:

[40] Strangely the BOP Consulting 2011 report does not mention this factor.

[41] At least those reviewed in this book but the statistics show a very similar trend exists in the other EU Member States.

[42] For similar findings, see Europe Economics, 'Economic review of industrial design in Europe', Final Report, MARKT/2013/064/D2/ST/OP, January 2015, p. 44 and 'Legal review on industrial design protection in Europe under the contract with the Directorate General Internal Market, Industry, Entrepreneurship and SMEs', Final Report, MARKT 2014/083/D, 15 April 2016, pp. 29–30.

Clearly the shortage of litigation suggests that right holders did not consider registrations to be important enough to warrant the costs of litigation. Yet, the fact that parties did engage in registration and chose to incur the costs thereof indicate some level of impact of the system. Hence, registration practices may be a useful measure of the effects of the Act. At any rate user behaviour as evidenced by registration and litigation activity are markers of whether the Act did in fact produce the effects *intended* by the legislator.[43]

The statistics show a similar effect as that described by J. Schovsbo and S. Teilmann-Lock in other countries. Italy had a very low level of applications until 1940 when the right's duration was doubled to four years, with an increase then, and again a big surge in 1977 when the term was increased to fifteen years. Equally, there was very little litigation on registered designs until the implementation of the Design Directive in Italy. In Sweden, the design Act seems to have had a huge impact as applications shot from ca. 500 to ca. 3,500 in the space of one year (1971), stayed around that level until the introduction of the RCD and then decreased dramatically from 2003 onwards down to 437 in 2014. It makes sense as Sweden had a stricter level of originality for a much longer period than Denmark and there is a slight decrease in applications in the 1990s onwards when Sweden started to lower its copyright's originality level. Another interesting example is Japan. For most of its history (1899 until today), the Japanese interface was the strictest of all countries reviewed in this book, with a high hurdle design law (visibility requirement, absolute novelty, principle of speciality and confusion as infringement test) as well as virtually no copyright protection for mass-reproducible 3D designs. Despite a slight decrease in applications since the 1990s, it seems that the Japanese legislation does not deter applications, which remain very high in Japan especially in comparison with other big economies such as the UK, France and Germany. A probable explanation is that designers have no choice but to register whether the design system is generous or strict because they cannot fall back on copyright or unfair competition law.

Nevertheless, it seems, unsurprisingly, as it is the case for each country examined, that the key driver for the level of design applications is not so much the law but the economic history[44] of each country as well as global

[43] Schovsbo and Teilmann-Lock, 'We wanted more Arne Jacobsen chairs but all we got was boxes' (2016) *IIC* 418 at 426.

[44] This includes the decline in manufacturing as is apparent in France, Germany and the UK after the Second World War, with a much bigger decline in the UK compared to France and Germany. See BOP Consulting 2011, 'Design economics chapter four: Design rights, an international comparison', 15–17. Other reasons why the UK could have fewer applications compared to France and Germany are: a weaker awareness of

economic history, especially world wars and world recessions.[45] The most striking examples are Australia and Japan, which have known sustained economic booms; the continuous general upward trend of design applications for these countries seems to reflect this economic success. This is also shown, generally, in the amount of domestic applications over time compared to foreign ones. Also, generally, smaller markets receive fewer applications, so the Nordic countries, the Benelux and Greece have constantly lower numbers of applications than Germany, France, the UK and Japan.[46] Italy is an outlier here as numbers never reach 10,000 and are more often, on average, between 4,000 and 6,000. The USA is an outlier too, as numbers only pick up and continuous grow at the end of the 1970s (before that the number of applications was between 5,000 and 10,000 maximum). Several factors, unrelated to change in the statutory law as such, explain this surge in design patent applications: (1) more favourable case law; (2) faster turn-around times at the USPTO; (3) the USPTO grants the vast majority of design applications; and (4) increase in the application and thus registrations for design patents on computer icons.[47]

When one compares the number of applications with the number of registrations per country, the number of registrations is quite close to the number of applications even if obviously it is lower. This is because the procedural aspects in most countries are straightforward and examination formal, i.e. not substantive. Two interesting examples are the USA and Japan. In these two countries, the contrast between applications and registrations is far starker, owing to the substantive examination of design applications. At all times except between the 1970s and now, there is a huge difference between the number of applications and the

design law among designers; less favourable procedural aspects such as no simplified procedure for short-term designs; no online filing; higher registration fees; higher enforcement costs and the courts' less IP-friendly attitude; and one substantive law aspect, namely that unlike other countries, there is a national unregistered design right. See ibid., 17–34. The UK introduced online filing on 30 September 2015.

45 For a consideration of this in Italy, see Chapter 8.

46 Yearly design application figures look roughly like this. In the Benelux, the peak was around 3,500. The Nordic countries have between 1,000 and 4,000 on average depending on country. Greece peaks at 2,000. By contrast, France, Germany and the UK postwar applications are generally around the 10,000 mark on average; Australia's application numbers have always been growing, from zero to ca. 7,000 at present; Japan peaks at ca. 60,000 and has on average around 30,000 applications.

47 M. Leaffer, presentation at ALAI Congress, Rome, 15–16 September 2016. See also J. Reichman, 'Design protection after the copyright act of 1976: A comparative view of the emerging interim models' (1983) 31 *Journal of the Copyright Society* 267 at 364 stating: 'Since 1974 however the US has had a better functioning design patent law in the sense that it now better covers 3D objects not covered by copyright law via a less stringent non-obviousness condition.' See also Reichman, 'Design protection and the legislative agenda', 285, mentioning more favourable case law since the 1980s.

number of registrations: only about a third of designs get registered in Japan and about half in the USA. However, it does not seem to have deterred applications in Japan, the probable explanation being that designers have no choice, having no recourse to copyright or unfair competition. In the USA, examination became far less stringent at the start of the 1970s and the statistics show a corresponding increase in applications and registrations, which is explained partly because of that, as stated in the previous paragraph. And the test for works of applied art to acquire copyright protection was also a little less stringent than in Japan, probably explaining at least partly the lower level of design applications. Thus a strict procedural system, i.e. one with substantive examination such as the Japanese one (and the US one before the 1970s), shows that it lowers drastically the number of registrations compared to other countries which have a formal check, where the number of applications is close to the number of registrations (Germany, Greece, France, the Benelux, Italy).[48] This shows that the law has a strong effect in lowering the number of registrations. The experience of the USA also seems to show that if the substantive examination is replaced by a more lax examination, applications increase.

Leaving the statistical analysis and coming back to the legal analysis alone, differences but also common trends exist in the mechanisms used to regulate the interface. The countries can be classed in two broad categories, depending on the period: the full cumulation system on the one hand and the partial cumulation and demarcation systems on the other hand. The partial cumulation and demarcation systems use first a mechanism or test to pass at the level of protection requirements in order to limit the number of designs which can obtain copyright protection. In the main, two tests emerge as 'winners' over time: a higher level of originality via a criterion of artistic value or merit (be it judged by experts (Denmark, Italy, Germany and the UK at times), the (educated) public (UK and Germany at times) or the courts themselves (Japan, Australia)); and the separability test (Italy and USA). Other tests were proposed by the literature and sometimes adopted by the legislature or courts but were abandoned for their inadequacy (such as intention in the UK, Australia and the Netherlands) or simply pre-empted by authority (other tests

[48] The Nordic countries also had a substantive examination until the implementation of the Design Directive but only Sweden shows a similar pattern as the USA and Japan. Australia and the UK had substantive examination at times (Australia 1906–2003) and formal examination at other times (Australia 2003–present), and show a similar trend in the difference between the number of applications and the number of registrations, albeit less pronounced than that of the USA and Japan.

proposed in Italy and France were ‘crushed’ by the overwhelming influence of respectively E. Piola Caselli and E. Pouillet[49]).

The full and partial cumulation systems also vary in their regulation of the conflicts or clashes caused by the overlap. They range from no mechanism to some to many. In France, the interface is not regulated at all at legislative level but courts often align the copyright framework with the design framework in some troublesome areas, namely ownership and exploitation contracts. In Japan, Norway and Sweden, courts sometimes use a narrower scope of protection if the design is functional. In the Benelux, there is alignment for ownership and duration at legislative level; in Japan the ownership rules are aligned. In the UK and Australia, over the years, the legislatures adopted a detailed regulation of the interface in relation to ownership, rights, defences and duration.

Yet another interesting emerging aspect is that some countries’ legislatures always wanted demarcation or partial cumulation and never full cumulation, namely the UK, Australia and Japan. These countries grappled with how to do it, so did not think it was impossible – unlike France, which adopted unity of art by giving up trying to find an interface after deciding that all criteria were flawed.

These evaluations lead us to two main interim conclusions. First, even if it is not the only factor, legislation does often have an important effect on the success of the design regime and of its interface with copyright. Secondly, there have been and still are very big differences between countries in the way they regulate the interface. As we shall see, such entrenched national positions owed to legal cultures are probably the biggest hurdle to overcome before a single copyright/design interface model can be adopted at regional let alone international level.

12.4 Possible Models and Criteria

As we have seen in section 12.3, a deeper statistical analysis needs to be done to have a conclusive account of the relative impact of the several factors influencing the level of design applications, which is beyond the scope of this book. What can be done at this stage is compare the success and failure of the different models (section 12.4.1) and of the different

[49] Y. Gaubiac and A.-E. Khan confirmed to me that Pouillet had a lot of prestige and influence and thus also a lot of followers. Gaubiac adds that it is really the arguments in favour of the thesis which were decisive and shared by many protagonists. Reichman, ‘Design protection in domestic and foreign copyright law’, 1154–5, 1159, also mentions ‘Pouillet and his followers’. Note that according to Z. Algardi, *Disegno Industriale e Arte Applicata* (Milan: Giuffrè, 1977), pp. 65–6, Pouillet was anticipated by Huard, so Pouillet was not the first to propose the theory of unity of art.

criteria used to regulate the interface (section 12.4.2) by reviewing the legal history and by examining arguments developed by the literature and the courts.

12.4.1 The Models: Copyright or Sui Generis *Design Right(s), Artistic Property or Industrial Property, or Both?*

For a long time, there were heated discussions about whether designs should be classified as part of intellectual or instead industrial property law.[50] Design law as a branch of industrial property originates from the French 1806 Act, which was copied by other countries afterwards.[51] Before that time, copyright protected designs and models, as for instance in the UK. So the classification of designs as industrial property can be said to be a historical accident.[52] The French courts then on the basis of this law made a differentiation between artistic and industrial designs.[53] They also required novelty and more generally the patent approach rather than the copyright approach, and then most European countries followed this example.[54] That being said, because of the hybrid nature of 3D design which combines function and aesthetics, the grant of such industrial property protection may have happened anyway later in another country. So maybe it is only a historical accident that it happened in France at that very specific point in time.

This division is now enshrined in international instruments and it is clearly difficult to go backwards now even if the Paris Convention and TRIPs still give a choice between the two types of property rights.[55] More convincingly, it seems fairer to have both systems so that designers can choose which one suits their needs best. This is because the field of design varies enormously, from 2D to 3D, and from fashion design (which is quickly outdated) to other more lasting designs such as the Tripp-Trapp or Le Corbusier chairs.[56] A deposit system is necessary to provide

[50] Ladas, *Patents, Trademarks and Related Rights*, para. 483, p. 828. [51] Ibid., p. 829.
[52] Ibid., p. 829. [53] Ibid., p. 830. [54] Ibid., p. 830.
[55] Confirming this for the Paris Convention, see S. Ricketson, *The Paris Convention for the Protection of Industrial Property: A Commentary* (Oxford: Oxford University Press, 2015), p. 487, n. 11.20.
[56] Cohen Jehoram, 'Protection of industrial design, between copyright and design laws: A comparative study', 107, reporting intervention by Duchemin (everyday thousands of designs are created but the vast majority will never be exploited; one should not simply put the two systems, i.e. industrial property and copyright, as antagonistic to protect designs, as there are many shades (i.e. potential systems between copyright and industrial property) in between, so to speak, which correspond better to the reality); Cohen Jehoram, 'Protection of industrial design, between copyright and design laws: A comparative study', 121, reporting intervention by Levin. (For M. Levin, formal requirements (i.e. registration, cost, etc.) for designs do not fit the designers' needs as they are

industry and third parties with certainty but the system must take into account the interest of small creators too[57] and thus provide an unregistered right. As we have seen in section 12.2.2, this is what drew the Max Planck Institute to propose not only a choice between copyright and a registered design right but also an unregistered design right. Submissions to the European Commission before it issued its Green Paper on the legal protection of industrial design also stated that the mode of protection, i.e. registered or not, depends a lot on 'the nature of the design, type of product it is applied to and the market in which the product manifests itself'.[58] Hence, the toy, textile and fashion industries prefer unregistered design rights, whereas the manufacturing industries prefer the registered design right.[59]

The vast majority of commentators echo this and advocate choice and potential cumulation between copyright and design right.[60] Most commentators also prefer a design approach rather than a patent approach for the design right, be it registered or not.[61] They also believe that the

mostly unaware of the law, e.g. that the design loses novelty if it is made public. So she stresses that works of applied art must be protected by copyright law.) See also, in a similar vein, the Johnston Committee's views, as referred to in Chapter 6, above (UK), which also thought that cumulation is an adequate system as registration does not serve the interests of all design industries.

57 Duchemin, 'La protection des arts appliqués dans la perspective d'un dépôt communautaire en matière de dessins et modèles industriels', 75.

58 U. Suthersanen, *Design Law in Europe* (London: Sweet & Maxwell, 2000), p. 14.

59 Ibid.

60 For Duchemin, 'La protection des arts appliqués dans la perspective d'un dépôt communautaire en matière de dessins et modèles industriels', 35, the number of design registrations is low and depends on the country and sector. The number of registrations has little relation to the mass of creations generally. Also the costs often outweigh advantages to register, especially for short-lived designs and for individual designers of SMEs. So he thinks that copyright is necessary for the small creator so he or she can fall back on it. P. Combeau, then co-president of the International Commission within AIPPI studying the protection of designs (stating a report will soon be presented in Paris), H. Papakonstantinou, A. Argyriadis (adding that it is better without a too-long term for design protection so as not to stifle follow-on competition) and J. Liedes all thought a cumulative system is better. See respectively at pp. 108, 112 and 114 in Cohen Jehoram, 'Protection of industrial design, between copyright and design laws: A comparative study'. Very few commentators advocated protecting designs only by copyright. In 1989, Cohen Jehoram, 'Cumulative design protection: A system for the EC?', 87, proposed a single copyright uniform law to deal with the interface issue so there would no longer be any interface but reckons it may be too much for some countries to abolish their registered design laws entirely. Six years earlier, he advocated cumulation and suggested that the European Community should opt for it, especially as most Member States had a cumulative system. See Cohen Jehoram, 'Cumulative design protection: A system for the EC?', 87. Also, nowadays very few countries protect designs only by copyright; in other words, most countries have a design act.

61 See e.g. Ladas, *Patents, Trademarks and Related Rights*, p. 832; A. Muhlstein and M. Wilkinson, 'Whither industrial design' (1999–2000) 14 *Intellectual Property Journal* 1, criticising the patent approach taken by the US design patent, preferring the UCD and

copyright protection for designs must be limited so as not to be over-protective, as the experience of some countries has shown.[62] It is only French commentators and courts, albeit a decreasing majority of them since the Design Directive, who believe that full cumulation is the only way to go.[63] The reason is historical. As A.-E. Kahn's chapter recounts, during the entire nineteenth century, France battled for years with five different criteria, trying to find the right one to distinguish between artistic and industrial designs. But it failed and France adopted the unity of art in 1902.[64] French commentators supporting the unity of art theory thus think it either impossible or subjective and therefore arbitrary to make this distinction.[65] Some also think the unity of art solution is simple.[66] Indeed it avoids the complexity of fixing the boundary between artistic and industrial designs.[67] However, the simplicity of a solution is not a sufficient argument as simplicity does not by definition entail

adding that Canada could adopt something similar; also Reichman, 'Design protection in domestic and foreign copyright law', 1223–4, also criticising the US design patent system. See also AIPPI in section 12.2.1.1 above.

62 Reichman, 'Design protection in domestic and foreign copyright law', 1223ff. For instance, prior to the Benelux design law, Belgium protected designs by copyright without requiring any level of originality.

63 See Duchemin, 'La protection des arts appliqués dans la perspective d'un dépôt communautaire en matière de dessins et modèles industriels', 65. Reichman, 'Design protection in domestic and foreign copyright law', 1159–60, notes, however, that 'the "unity of art" theory continues to elicit scepticism even in France ... Arguably, France and Belgium, which had sought to rescue artistic designs from the exigencies of patent law, were now converting copyright law into a de facto industrial property law without the characteristic safeguards of the industrial property paradigm.' More recently see F. Greffe, *Propr. industr.* 2013, chron. 4. A. Lucas, H.-J. Lucas and A. Lucas-Schloetter, *Traité de la Propriété Littéraire et Artistique*, 4th edn (Paris: Lexis-Nexis, 2012), n. 94, p. 109, however, recognise that full cumulation undermines the coherence of authors' rights and industrial property. However, P. Y. Gautier, *Propriété Littéraire et Artistique*, 7th edn (Paris: PUF, 2010), n. 100, p. 120, criticises the theory and P. Kamina, 'Fasc. 1155: Règles Spécifiques a Certaines Oeuvres – Arts appliqués', JurisClasseur Propriété Littéraire et Artistique, 2016, J. Passa, *Droit de la propriété industrielle*, 2nd edn (Paris: LGDJ, 2009), pp. 6ff, and A.-E. Kahn, 'Un an de droit de la mode', *Communication Commerce électronique* no. 9, Septembre 2016, chron. 10, are not for total cumulation but full or partial cumulation.

64 Reichman, 'Design protection in domestic and foreign copyright law' reports at 1159 that 'the soundest writers caution that it was a victory by default rather than by persuasion'.

65 Duchemin, 'La protection des arts appliqués dans la perspective d'un dépôt communautaire en matière de dessins et modèles industriels', 45, 63, 73; Cohen Jehoram, 'Protection of industrial design, between copyright and design laws: A comparative study', reporting intervention by A. Francon, 115; Ricketson and Ginsburg, *International Copyright and Neighbouring Rights*, pp. 454–5; Pérot-Morel, *Les Principes de Protection des Dessins et Modèles dans les Pays du Marché Commun*, p. 315.

66 Duchemin, 'La protection des arts appliqués dans la perspective d'un dépôt communautaire en matière de dessins et modèles industriels', 46–8.

67 Ricketson and Ginsburg, *International Copyright and Neighbouring Rights*, p. 455; Lucas, Lucas and Lucas-Schloetter, *Traité de la Propriété Littéraire et Artistique*, n. 94. Except that it is not that simple to exclude functional designs according to the application of the idea/expression dichotomy, which some of these commentators do not acknowledge.

adequacy. Often a complex situation, such as that concerning designs, needs a sophisticated answer. Also I do not think that it is impossible to find a workable criterion, as will be shown in the following sections. I would therefore reject it in view of the obvious overprotection and subsequent stifling of competition it leads to and on the basis of some countries' actual experience proving this.

Advocates of demarcation are rare and are not surprisingly coming from countries which have had the system, such as Italy and Japan. However, it has become quite clear that forcing registration with no choice for either a limited copyright or unregistered design right protection is unfair to many designers, namely those whose designs are short-lived and do not justify the expense, thus those mainly created by individuals and SMEs.

In conclusion, it seems clear, and the experience of the European Union has now proved it,[68] that a cumulative system of some sort rather than either copyright only or registered design right only is the best way to accommodate all the different design sectors. What the EU system has not done but the experience of many EU Member States prior to the EU design system has shown is that since the interface is concerned with two branches of the IP system – copyright and design laws – one cannot envisage regulating the interface by tweaking, fixing or tinkering with only one of the two systems: the two have to be dealt with in a holistic way.[69]

The next problem is therefore to determine how the two, or possibly three, rights interact with each other; in other words, how to regulate the copyright/design interface.

12.4.2 The Criteria to Fix the Boundary of the Interface

Over the years, countries have toyed with a variety of criteria to fix the boundary between artistic and industrial designs, i.e. the subject-matter

[68] In 2016, the European Commission commissioned a report on the status of design law in the EU. The purpose of the study was to find out in the main if the harmonised and unitary design system in the EU works well or whether further harmonisation or changes are required. See 'Legal review on industrial design protection in Europe'. The report found that both the level of harmonisation and the functioning of internal market in relation to goods embodying designs have been achieved but also that there are areas where the smooth functioning of the internal market has not been achieved. See ibid., 2016, 11. For instance, registration and administration costs are usually cheap; there is less delay than with multi-jurisdictional applications; and the filing/grant success rate has been overwhelming. Ibid., 13. However, some notions such as those of design, individual character, industrial sector, functionality, disclosure and the scope of protection need further clarification at legislative level. That said, harmonisation should carry on via the EUIPO and CJEU and national courts should carry on aligning their case law with that of EUIPO and CJEU. Ibid., 12–14.

[69] As explained in Chapter 4 (Scandinavia).

of protection. Some criteria have proved inadequate (12.4.2.1), whereas some, if not perfect, have proved more suitable (12.4.2.2). In addition, countries have also used different legal mechanisms to regulate the interactions between the different rights (these will be examined in detail in section 12.5). When I refer to one of the legal systems reviewed in this book, I automatically refer, without adding a footnote, to the contributors' chapters for more detail. Also, as a reminder, the criterion to fix the borderline applies in addition to the normal copyright protection requirements, i.e. that only original expressions are protectable.

First of all, it seems clear that fixing the border is really only necessary, in the main, for 3D designs. Designers of 2D designs have been allowed to cumulate copyright and design rights in most countries most of the time (e.g. even in partial cumulation and demarcation countries such as the UK, Australia and Italy in most cases, although not always in Japan). The monopoly is much less powerful on a 2D design since it does not concern a functional object but its 'decoration'. The only problem is to demarcate the border between 2D and 3D designs, but this is not insurmountable. In the UK, the case law developed well and the tests are now well established. The distinction is more precisely between non-functional surface decoration and functional surface decoration. Surface decoration is excluded from UK unregistered design right (UKUDR) and covers not only 2D designs but also 3D designs which are decorating the object.[70] Some 2D designs can be excluded because they are mass-produced. This was the case in the UK with, for example, carpets and wallpaper as per the Copyright (Industrial Process and Excluded Articles) (No. 2) Order 1989, at 2(b), which provided that an article is meant to be made by an industrial process (and therefore its duration reduced to twenty-five years from first marketing[71]) if 'it consists of goods manufactured in lengths of pieces, not being hand-made goods'.

[70] *Mark Wilkinson* v. *Woodcraft Designs* [1998] FSR 63, 72–3 ('The expression "surface decoration" in section 213(3) and in section 51 is apt to include both decoration lying on the surface of the article (for example, a painted finish) and decorative features of the surface itself (for example, beading or engraving)'). *Jo-Y-Jo Ltd* v. *Matalan Retail Ltd* [2000] ECDR 178 (embroidery was surface decoration since it was comprised of stitches added to the garment after it was made). *A. Fulton Co. Ltd* v. *Grant Barnett & Co. Ltd* [2001] RPC 257 (the seams at the edges and corners of an umbrella case were not surface decoration). *Dyson Ltd* v. *Qualtex (UK) Ltd* [2006] RPC 31, paras. 80, 81 and 83 (there was no reason why the decoration should not come into existence with the surface. Surface decoration can be in 3D. Surface features which had significant function should not be regarded as 'surface decoration'). In Australia, there remains uncertainty whether embroidered designs are 2D or 3D. The last case on this issue held they were 2D as they were not part of the shape of garment, but the previous case did not give such a clear-cut answer. See Australian chapter.

[71] Section 52 UK Copyright Act prior to 2016. Mass-produced 2D designs of primarily artistic character such as book jackets and postcards were, however, excluded from s. 52's application.

12.4.2.1 Inadequate or Unworkable Criteria

1. A first criterion is that of **destination**. It was proposed by some commentators in Italy before the adoption of the separability doctrine and was the prevailing theory in France before the adoption of the unity of art theory. According to this criterion, if the designed object's (essential) destination is aesthetic then it is protected by copyright, but if it is industrial or functional then it is protected by design right. There is an evident problem with the criterion; it occurs when the object has no predominant destination or utilitarian purpose but is both aesthetic and functional.[72] Another objection is, why should copyright protection be refused to a beautiful object simply because it is utilitarian?[73] Therefore, commentators are generally against the criterion of destination and currently none of the legal systems reviewed in this book are using it.[74]
2. The designer's **intention** has been used in the UK and Australia's copyright legislation respectively in 1911 and 1912, and was most famously applied in the *King Features* v. *Kleeman* decision.[75] In the USA, the designer's intention may in some cases determine the outcome of the separability test. It was also proposed by some Italian commentators before the adoption of the separability test. In the UK, the Gregory Committee was against this criterion because making the protection of copyright turn upon the intention of the artist can lead to inequitable results. It can be used strategically in order to gain the protection that the designer wants rather than the one suited to the object. Indeed, the author can also always claim *a posteriori* that he or she wanted to do something aesthetic. Taking the user's perspective, he or she can almost never be certain of the author's intention, making the criterion almost always work in favour of the author. Therefore, the user will always have to err on the side of caution and refrain from using the work, even if the author's intention was not to create a work of art. The criterion was more generally criticised and abandoned in Australia but is still found in the UK for sculptures,[76] although not works of artistic craftsmanship, the latter constituting the vast majority of 3D designs.

[72] Ricketson and Ginsburg, *International Copyright and Neighbouring Rights*, p. 455.
[73] Cohen Jehoram, 'Protection of industrial design, between copyright and design laws: A comparative study', 108.
[74] Perot-Morel, *Les Principes de Protection des Dessins et Modèles dans les Pays du Marché Commun*, 319; Duchemin, 'La protection des arts appliqués dans la perspective d'un dépôt communautaire en matière de dessins et modèles industriels', 93.
[75] *King Features Syndicate Inc. and Betts* v. *O & M Kleeman Ltd* [1941] AC 417, HL.
[76] See *Lucasfilm* v. *Ainsworth* [2008] EWHC 1878 (Ch), *aff'd* by [2011] UKSC 39. However, it is not the artist but the judge who decides according to a list of criteria.

3. The criterion of the **status of the author** was used in France before the adoption of the unity of art theory. If the author was a manufacturer or a craftsman, design law applied, but if he was an artist, copyright law applied. It is also used for works of artistic craftsmanship in the Australian *Burge* v. *Swarbrick* case, even if arguably not in isolation.[77] However, like the criterion of destination, the criterion does not work if the manufacturer or craftsman is also an artist or when the artist transfers his or her rights to a company.[78]
4. The French also experimented with the criterion of the **method of reproduction**. The Italian literature also proposed it. Japan arguably still uses it. According to this criterion, handcrafted items were copyrightable while works reproduced by mechanical means were not.[79] The criterion was famously rejected in the UK in *George Hensher* v. *Restawile*,[80] even if the House of Lords agreed it could be an indicator to determine craftsmanship. The criterion has been criticised as inequitable and arbitrary.[81] Indeed, even if it can arguably be less frequent, a work can be very artistic even if it is not handmade.
5. Another criterion the French experimented with was that of the **secondary or accessory character of the aesthetic features** in the work embodying the design.[82] The Italian literature also suggested it. However, it is impossible to use when form follows function as the aesthetic features of the work do not have a secondary or accessory character.
6. Last but not least, the criterion of **artistic merit or value** has been used a lot over the years and is still used by countries such as the UK, Germany, Italy and Japan. The French also used this criterion as a last resort after having tried all the others.[83] Because of its subjectivity, France rejected it to adopt the unity of art theory. Indeed, a criterion based on artistic value leaves the decision to the whim of judges (or the experts or the public) and thus is highly subjective, inevitably leading to inconsistent decisions. It is therefore uncertain and bad for creators

[77] (2007) 232 CLR 336.
[78] Y. Gaubiac, 'La théorie de l'unité de l'art' (1982) 111 *RIDA* 2 at 46–7.
[79] Ibid., 44–5.
[80] *George Hensher Ltd* v. *Restawile Upholstery (Lancs) Ltd* [1975] RPC 31 (HL).
[81] Duchemin, 'La protection des arts appliqués dans la perspective d'un dépôt communautaire en matière de dessins et modèles industriels', 63.
[82] Gaubiac, 'La théorie de l'unité de l'art', 46–7.
[83] Ibid., 48–9; M.-A. Pérot-Morel, 'Specific protection of designs and its relation to protection by copyright in French law', in H. Cohen Jehoram (ed.), *Specific Design Protection and Copyright in Benelux and Dutch Law* (Leiden: Sijthoff, 1976), p. 49; G. Finniss, 'The theory of "unity of art" and the protection of designs and models in French law' (1964) 46 *Journal of the Patent Office Society* 615 at 621.

and users alike.[84] This is perhaps most famously illustrated by the still ongoing 'saga' relating to works of artistic craftsmanship in the UK, where there is no agreed criterion at Supreme Court level but a plurality of different ones (although it seems lower courts are now settling for the criterion of artistic merit judged by a substantial part of the public[85]). Italy had its 'Le Corbusier saga' which ended with the Supreme Court holding in 2015 that artistic merit was to be judged by experts (museums and the like).[86] Nevertheless, whether it is the judge, the experts or the public deciding whether a work is artistic or not, it is clear that the criterion is subjective and unfair to the designer. Some young designers may see their designs unfairly refused protection because they are ahead of their time (just think of Van Gogh in the field of painting).[87] The criterion of artistic merit or value can therefore definitely not be adopted. In fact, it goes totally against the copyright's principle of originality which categorically rejects such a criterion. Why then should it be reintroduced for works of applied art? When a high threshold of originality is set for works of applied art, it distorts copyright law in the sense that the criterion of originality is harder to achieve and thus it does not reward many authors, whereas it is the aim of copyright law to foster creativity. The argument according to which such criterion also has the perverse effect that more mundane works such a as directories, simple drawings, etc. are protected but not highly creative 3D works is, however, not valid. It is fine to exclude highly creative works of applied art from copyright law if artists can fall back on (an) adequately crafted design right(s).[88]

[84] Duchemin, 'La protection des arts appliqués dans la perspective d'un dépôt communautaire en matière de dessins et modèles industriels', 46; Reichman, 'Design protection after the copyright act of 1976', 368.

[85] *Guild* v. *Eskandar* [2001] FSR 38.

[86] See Italian chapter. Marzano criticises the Italian criterion for its possible corruptibility (having connections helps artists place their work in a museum) and that not all museums are equally relevant, e.g. national gallery as opposed to municipal museum of the designer's summer residence.

[87] See also Oliver Wendel Holmes' famous rejection of a merit criterion in copyright law in general in *Bleistein* v. *Donaldson Lithographing*, 188 US 239, 251–2 (1903):

> It would be a dangerous undertaking for persons trained only to the law to constitute themselves final judges of the worth of pictorial illustrations, outside of the narrowest and most obvious limits. At the one extreme some works of genius would be sure to miss appreciation. Their very novelty would make them repulsive until the public had learned the new language in which their author spoke. It may be more than doubted, for instance, whether the etchings of Goya or the paintings of Manet would have been sure of protection when seen for the first time. At the other end, copyright would be denied to pictures which appealed to a public less educated than the judge.

Many thanks to Jane Ginsburg for pointing this out to me.

[88] Reichman, 'Design protection after the copyright act of 1976', 369–70.

Clearly, the first five criteria have been rightfully rejected. The criterion of artistic merit or value does not stack up either even if it has been used for years and is still used nowadays in some countries. Surely a more objective criterion can be found.

12.4.2.2 Possible Workable Criteria

A first objective criterion is that of **the number of copies** made. This is the system that the UK had prior to 1968 and which excluded from copyright protection works embodying designs made in more than fifty copies,[89] and that Australia still uses.[90] This system was praised as workable by a French expert even if she doubted it was the best criterion.[91] More enthusiastic was H. Cohen Jehoram who thought it was 'a nicely clear cut and arbitrary system' which provided maximum certainty.[92] An Italian commentator also found the UK criterion adequate because once the work has been reproduced so many times it loses its aesthetic value.[93] However, it is doubtful whether this is a valid reason for the adequacy of the criterion. Rather, it is to do with the fact that, since the object is functional, the protection should be less strong to prevent undue monopolisation. It is true that the criterion of the number of copies is arbitrary but, on the other hand, contrary to all the others reviewed above, it is not subjective and it is extremely predictable for both the designer and the public. Presumably it is sufficient for the artist to stamp the numbers of copies at the back of the article, e.g. '1 of 40', '10 of 100' or '5 of 2,000', or simply the public can assume that if an object is available in supermarkets or similar stores it is produced in more than the amount of copies set out by the legislature. For 2D works such as wallpaper and carpets, like in the UK order of 1989, the criterion would be lengths or pieces, not the number of copies.[94]

The main trouble with this criterion is that it is against the Berne Convention if works of applied art are classified as artistic works.[95] And in

[89] See UK chapter, s. 22 of the Copyright Act 1911 and Design Rules of 26 June 1912.

[90] See Copyright Regulations 1969, reg. 17. However, it is treated as a non-exhaustive deeming provision, such that a court might decide that, in a particular case, fewer than fifty copies would satisfy the criterion if they are made 'industrially'. See *Press-Form Pty Ltd* v. *Henderson's Ltd* (1993) 26 IPR 113; *Gold Peg International Pty Ltd* v. *Kovan Engineering (Aust) Pty Ltd* [2005] FCA 1521.

[91] Perot-Morel, *Les Principes de Protection des Dessins et Modèles dans les Pays du Marché Commun*, 314–15, 318, still thinking that the best way to deal with the issue of designs is a system close to the unity of art.

[92] Cohen Jehoram, 'Protection of industrial design, between copyright and design laws: A comparative study', 97.

[93] E. Bonasi Benucci (1958) *Riv. Dir. Industriale* 426 at 430 and 446–50.

[94] See note 95.

[95] This does not mean that it is per se impossible to adopt this criterion but, of course, it is extremely difficult to change the convention so, realistically, one has to work with it.

a system of partial cumulation as advocated here, works of applied art have to be protectable by copyright and thus classed as artistic works. It is possible, though, to tweak this criterion to reduce the copyright term to twenty-five years so that it is compliant with article 7(4) of the said convention. This is what the UK did with section 52 of the 1988 Copyright Act, which, after almost thirty years of existence, was repealed in 2016.[96] The number of copies can be set at fifty or whatever number one wants to choose. It could also be a different number depending on the sector. An additional criterion can be added to it to make it less harsh, namely excluding some works even if they are reproduced in more than fifty copies, as the UK did in its Copyright (Industrial Process and Excluded Articles) (No. 2) Order 1989:[97]

> a) sculptures, other than casts or models used or intended to be used as models or patterns to be multiplied by an industrial process, b) wall plaques, medals and medallions and c) printed matter primarily of literary or artistic character including book jackets, calendars, certificates, coupons, dress-making patterns, greeting cards, labels, leaflets, maps, plans, playing cards, postcards, stamps, trade advertisements, trade forms and cards, transfers and similar articles.

However, if such exclusion is added, we go back to the distinction problem: what is a sculpture and what is printed matter primarily of literary or artistic character, as the order phrases the latter as a non-exhaustive list. Indeed, as reported in the UK chapter, the courts and literature sometimes struggled to make this distinction.

A system similar to the old section 52 of the UK Copyright Act overprotects if a number of copies below the number that triggers the section's effect overcompensates the designer because he or she can sue on both copyright and registered right. This is a risk when one uses such a criterion unless the law stipulates, like in the UK per section 236 of the Copyright Act, that infringement of one right gives way to the other if both rights are infringed. The UK did not have a provision similar to section 236 for the infringement of registered design right and copyright but section 52 was combined with the criterion of artistic merit for works of artistic craftsmanship (in which the vast majority of 3D designs fall), which reduces the number of cumulation cases. However, we saw that this criterion was not adequate.

A second possibly workable criterion is **separability**. Despite its troubled application in the USA, which has not ended with the

96 See also the similar provisions in Australia: Designs Regulations 1969, reg. 2. The UK had a similar, but more complex, section prior to s. 52 of the 1988 Copyright Act, namely s. 10 of the 1956 Copyright Act. See UK chapter for more details.

97 SI 1989/1070. See the similar system of the 1956 Copyright Act.

Supreme Court decision in *Varsity Brands*,[98] the criterion was more successfully applied in Italy, even if more harshly (i.e. excluding the vast majority of 3D designs). Some commentators also find it more suited than all the others, among others not surprisingly many Italian commentators.[99] For Pérot-Morel, even if the separability criterion is difficult to apply, it can give a more adequate protection to such designs than copyright protection. This leads her to conclude that separability could be kept in principle as it can conciliate the points of view of partisans and adversaries of the unity of art theory.[100] Reichman praises separability for its degree of precision and finds it 'more successful than others in drawing the distinction without offending the principle that forbids discrimination on the basis of merit'.[101] It is objective,[102] if it is not travestied into a subjective criterion such as that of artistic value or merit[103] (as some courts have done in Italy) or that of the creator's intention, as some courts have done in the USA. Defenders of the separability criterion also prefer it to the artistic value criterion as it does less violence to copyright law principles.[104]

Separability (at least 'Italian style') has the additional advantage that it clearly separates copyright and design protection. There is very rarely cumulation for 3D designs, so very rarely overprotection. There is also rarely underprotection: even if the author does not have copyright protection and does not register his or her design, at least in the EU and the UK, the author can potentially benefit from the unregistered design right(s) if the work meets those regimes' protection requirements.

The current US Copyright Office regulations seem to match closely the Italian regime which existed until 2001, in short excluding all entire

[98] *Varsity Brands, Inc.* v. *Star Athletica, LLC*, 799 F 3d 468, 478 (6th Cir. 2015), *aff'd* 2017 US Lexis 2026. For a discussion of this decision, see Chapter 9.

[99] See e.g. T. Ascarelli, *Teoria della concorrenza e dei beni immateriali* (Milano: Giuffrè, 1960), p. 677; G. Floridia, 'La protezione del diritto d'autore sulle opere dell'industrial design' (1984) *Rivista di Dirirtto Industriale*, 372ff; D. Sarti, *La tutela dell'estetica del prodotto industriale* (Milan: Giuffrè, 1990), p. 26; P. Vercellone, comment under Cass., 22/10/1956, n. 3806 (1958) *Rivista di Diritto Commerciale*, 172ff, *Franchi* v. *Arti Grafiche Cellerino*, pp. 174–5.

[100] Pérot-Morel, *Les Principes de Protection des Dessins et Modèles dans les Pays du Marché Commun*, 318–19.

[101] Reichman, 'Design protection in domestic and foreign copyright law', 1181. Reichman wrote in the 1980s when the US case law was not as chaotic as it is now. He also wrote about the separability doctrine in general and not only how it is applied in the US courts.

[102] Reichman, 'Design protection after the copyright act of 1976', 376. It is arguable that the very purpose of the separability theory is to avoid making value judgements.

[103] Reichman, 'Design protection in domestic and foreign copyright law', 1121.

[104] Reichman, 'Design protection after the copyright act of 1976', 369. However, it is contentious that this is the case especially if the separability test in fact favours certain kinds of designs over others, namely ornate as opposed to simple. On this, see below.

shapes of useful articles and considering aesthetic value as an irrelevant factor. However, unlike Italian courts, the US judiciary has struggled to interpret the separability requirement. In her chapter, Jane Ginsburg explains that the Supreme Court's recent approach to separability could still pose an intractable line-drawing exercise in some cases, and thus may well prove unworkable anyway. As a result of this almost impossible line-drawing exercise, the test may also not avoid being discriminatory. 'Form follows function' objects would be excluded from copyright protection even if they are very aesthetically pleasing, and equally or less aesthetically pleasing designs may fall on the (copy) right side of the line, or, pushing aesthetics aside as this is not an adequate criterion anyway, if we use the originality criterion, designs could fall on either side of the line.

P. Goldstein believes that, alternatively, normal copyright criteria, namely the idea/expression dichotomy (excluding elements dictated by function), merger doctrine and originality, can do the trick.[105] However, then a lot of designs would fall within copyright's scope (even form-follows-function designs[106]) and be protected for the full term. In effect, this boils down to the unity of art principle.

Drawing from the lessons of this vast and lengthy experience, is it possible to draft the contours of a model copyright/design interface?

12.5 A Model Copyright/Design Interface

A model copyright/design interface is one which is as clear and simple for everyone involved so that it entails strong legal certainty and is as balanced as possible in the sense that there is as little over- and under-protection as possible. To have a working copyright/design interface, as we stated in section 12.3, countries' experiences show that **we first need an adequate *sui generis* design right**. This means a design law which does not follow a patent approach (i.e. high fees, absolute novelty, speciality principle, too short a duration), otherwise there is underprotection and designers revert to unfair competition or to copyright and courts tend

[105] P. Goldstein, *Goldstein on Copyright*, 3rd edn (New York: Aspen, 2014), 2015 Supplement, §2.5.3.c. If these criteria work, it is not necessary to use separability; separability need only be used in the 'hard' cases. A. Quaedvlieg also suggested this to me in view of the relatively adequate way the system functions in the Benelux.

[106] This is because lamps, chairs, etc. can come in (quasi?) infinite types of shapes and still perform their function (allowing lighting, sitting), so almost no shape is dictated by function except the shape of entirely new products perhaps. Even so, it will be rare. Consider, for instance, the shape of the very first vacuum cleaner ever invented; its shape might at first be thought to be dictated by function but we now know there are also an almost limitless number of shapes for vacuum cleaners.

to push the criterion of originality down in order to protect designs, and then there is overprotection.[107]

We have ascertained that the EU design system in terms of its substance is a (near) adequate model[108] and we can therefore adopt its provisions for the model. We have two possibilities: this unregistered right is copyright or it is a new unregistered design right which can be added to copyright. If it is copyright and protection is based on a criterion such as separability or the number of copies, it can be rather harsh to small creators who may be deprived of any protection and sometimes as soon as the object is marketed. This is because they cannot rely on an automatic unregistered design right unfettered by these criteria and often will not have thought to register at all or to register within the grace period if there is one (like in the EU). So it seems that taking all designers into account, big and small, IP-savvy and not, a three-rights system would be best.[109] However, this is without taking into account a rule, as the one I propose below, shortening the term of copyright to twenty-five years if the number of copies set out in the legislation is reached. In that situation, and if the requirements for copyright protection are easy to meet, which is the case

[107] This is well illustrated by the Dutch story and the UK legislative changes in 1968 where cumulation made design registrations fall dramatically. See also Reichman, 'Design protection in domestic and foreign copyright law', 1223ff; ibid., 'Design protection after the copyright act of 1976: A comparative view of the emerging interim models' (1983) 31 *Journal of the Copyright Society* 267 at 354 and also stating at 364 that since 1974 the USA has had a better functioning design patent law in the sense that it now better covers 3D objects not covered by copyright law because the Patent Office interprets the non-obviousness condition less stringently; Reichman, 'Design protection after the copyright act of 1976', 369, 371; Reichman, 'Design protection and the legislative agenda', 281–5. See also Schovsbo and Teilmann-Lock, 'We wanted more Arne Jacobsen chairs but all we got was boxes' and J. Ginsburg's chapter in which she proposes the adoption of a *sui generis* design right based on the current Vessel Hull design act.

[108] The authors of the report written for the European Commission in 2016 ('Legal review on industrial design protection in Europe') suggested some improvements (in the main clarification of some notions). See above, note 68. Some doubt remains as to whether the scope of protection of the design right is strong enough at least in the UK after the UK Supreme court decision in *PMS* v. *Magmatic* [2016] UKSC 12. The strength of such scope would thus depend on how the Court of Justice of the European Union would interpret it when a case is referred to it on this issue.

[109] In the same vein, see A. Ohly, 'Where is the birthday train heading? The copyright design interface in German law', in G. Karnell et al., *Liber Amicorum Jan Rosen* (Visby: Eddy, 2016), p. 603: 'A model of graded protection – three years protection against imitation for unregistered designs, up to twenty-five years absolute protection with registration, full copyright term for highly creative designs – is by no means outdated. On the contrary it takes account of the need to allow future designers the freedom they need.' The Commission in its *Green Paper on the Legal Protection of Industrial Design* hinted at this (p. 143): 'a fair overall protection of industrial design may require the possibility of invoking, at least in certain cases, copyright protection'.

in most countries, this makes an unregistered design right redundant. The proposal thus is to have only registered design right and copyright.

In the correct EU system, whether **cumulation between an EU and a national right is necessary, whether it is the unregistered or registered design right**, is however **controversial**. The Commission had taken the view that the national and Community registered rights should not be cumulative.[110] And in fact, this is the case for plant variety rights (PVR).[111] A system like the PVR could very well work for designs too. So if a designer opts for a national registered design, he or she cannot then obtain a Community registered design, but if he or she changes his or her mind, he or she can convert the national right into a Community one and vice versa.

In order to avoid underprotection, demarcation is out. To avoid overprotection, **a model copyright/design interface means partial cumulation** rather than a total or full cumulation. Having chosen this approach, **another important aspect of a good interface is to have a simple, precise, objective and non-discriminatory criterion or criteria** so that all designers, especially the non-IP savvy ones, as well as third parties, can know their rights with relative ease.[112] In that respect, then, as developed in section 12.4, a criterion based on the number of copies is superior to any other, including one based on separability.

The system would work as follows. It is based on the UK rules regulating the interface between the registered design right and copyright as it is a good starting point to find a model copyright/design interface, but the proposed rules are also more refined compared to the UK rules. To start with, the criterion of the number of copies used in the now repealed section 52 of the current UK Copyright Act could be adopted.[113] If the designer makes more than the amount of copies set by the legislature, copyright and registered design right would co-exist for the minimum of twenty-five years from the making of the work set by article 7(4) of the Berne Convention (or less if we were not constrained by the Convention[114]). This number of copies can be lower or higher than fifty (the old section 52 stated fifty) and could vary depending on the design sector. If the designer makes fewer copies than the

[110] *Green Paper on the Legal Protection of Industrial Design*, p. 138. It had left the cumulation of the UK unregistered right (UKUDR) with the UCD intact as UKUDR replaces copyright in some cases. Ibid., p. 139.

[111] Council Regulation (EC) No. 2100/94 of 27 July 1994 on Community plant variety rights, OJ 1994 L 227/1.

[112] Cohen Jehoram, 'Protection of industrial design, between copyright and design laws: A comparative study', 107, reporting intervention by Duchemin.

[113] G. Ghidini, 'Cumulation of copyright with registration protection of products of industrial design: An alternative proposal', Working Paper, 11 March 2016 (available on www.ssrn.com), shares this opinion and proposes a system to regulate the interface based on the old s. 52 of the UK Copyright Act.

[114] See below for the ideal term of protection.

amount set by the legislature, there will be works which can be registered as designs as well, namely sculptures and works of applied art, and both copyright and registered design right could also co-exist if the designer chooses to register. Arguably, this will be less frequent since probably the designer would not go through that expense if he or she is not going to make that many copies.

UK law is also good as it aligns the provisions on ownership in copyright and design right regimes.[115] Thus, first, one would make the provisions on commissioned and employee designs coincide in the two rights. Secondly, the UK also has the same primary and secondary infringement provisions for copyright and UKUDR; again, this could be extended to the registered design right. Thirdly, a system based on section 236 of the UK Copyright Act would also be good. Section 236 ensures that where a design is infringed and attracts both UKUDR and copyright, a claimant can only sue on the basis of copyright. This avoids overprotection[116] for what is in essence the same act of infringement. The rule laid out in section 236 could be made applicable to the registered design right. But in this case since the claimant has registered his or her design, it should be the registered design right that prevails at the level of infringement. Granting a narrower scope of copyright protection if the design is rather functional (along the lines of Swedish and Norwegian case law[117]) could also be a nifty mechanism to avoid overprotection. Arguably, the idea/expression dichotomy already plays that role. Finally, all exceptions and excluded subject-matter should be aligned. This means that copyright law should include a repair exception or alternatively exclude must-fit and must-match features from its scope. This system would leave purely functional designs out of copyright protection and out of registered design right protection if the designer chooses not to register. This is not leaving a gap since it is filled by patent law. Last but not least, one would leave the rights of attribution and integrity untouched or one could make the right of attribution inapplicable as the UK Copyright Act did when section 52 was applicable. The contractual protection of authors which exists in many civil law countries may also have to be watered down or made inapplicable.

[115] See ss. 11, 51, 53, 215, 224, 226, 227, 236, 244A and 244B of the UK Copyright Act and s. 2 UK Registered Designs Act, some of which were amended by the Intellectual Property Act 2014. The exceptions are aligned between all design rights but not with copyright. The Benelux law also aligns ownership provisions.

[116] There is a real risk of overprotection here as the infringement tests for copyright and unregistered design are different, leading to one right not being infringed while the other could very well be, thereby 'filling the protection gap'. The same applies for copyright and registered design infringements.

[117] Although, at EU level, this is now probably conflicting with the *Painer* decision (Case C-145/10, *Eva-Maria Painer* v. *Standard Verlags GmbH* [2011] ECDR 297), this is not reversible provided counter-legislation is passed.

As the UK example shows, it is not distorting copyright law to 'twist' its rules to accommodate designs. In fact, the Berne Convention allows it and there are other works which have a special regime in copyright law such as computer programs and databases. Borderline cases require adjusting the rules. This does not mean that the copyright framework is weakened or no longer coherent.

A good working copyright/design interface also needs **an adequate duration** for both copyright and design rights. If the copyright term is too long, in a similar way as the level of originality being too low, it will undermine the design rights, and even if it does not have that effect because the interface criterion works well, the term makes copyright law arguably overprotective. As the Italian experience shows, if the registered design right term is too short (e.g. a term of two years or less, and arguably four is too short too), the right will very rarely be used.

How long should the registered design right last for? For many commentators, fifteen is an adequate number of years for a design right.[118] Before the implementation of the Design Directive, this was the term in Germany, in Italy as of 1977, in the UK from 1907 to 1988, and in the Benelux and Nordic countries.[119] Some also suggested a term no longer than the patent term.[120] That makes sense as many 3D designs are functional, and in that respect thus closer to inventions than works. The term could also vary depending on the sector, e.g. a shorter term for the fashion sector and a longer term for the manufacturing sector.[121] This is somewhat the case in the EU with the Community unregistered design right but also via the possibility to renew the national or Community registered right every five years, up to a maximum of twenty-five years. So, in a system which gives the choice between unregistered and registered design rights, one can vary the term of the registered and unregistered design rights to match the different sectors' interests, and allow one to be transformed into the other after a grace period, as is the case in the EU. In my proposal, the grace period would function between copyright and the registered design. In sum, a term of between fifteen and twenty-five years

[118] Duchemin, 'La protection des arts appliqués dans la perspective d'un dépôt communautaire en matière de dessins et modèles industriels', 85; W. Cornish, 'Cumulative protection for industrial designs' (1973) 8 *University of British Columbia Law Review* 219 at 242, 243, 245 citing in agreement the Johnston Committee report of 1962, also citing that a Canadian Commission recommended five or seven years.

[119] During her presentation at the ALAI annual conference in Rome on 15–16 September 2016, D. Lipszic mentioned that a significant number of Latin American countries such as Argentina, Brazil, Paraguay and Uruguay also have a fifteen-year term of protection.

[120] Cornish, 'Cumulative protection for industrial designs', 242.

[121] Pérot-Morel, *Les Principes de Protection des Dessins et Modèles dans les Pays du Marché Commun*, p. 322.

for the registered design right would be adequate and arguably the EU system of renewals provides flexibility to the different designing sectors.

Virtually every expert agrees that the Berne standard copyright term of life of the author plus fifty years is too long for works of applied art. If one wants to protect works of applied art as artistic works and wants to respect international law, then the minimum copyright term must be twenty-five years from the making of the work as per article 7(4) of the Berne Convention.[122] But it could be lower than twenty-five, say fifteen, if the Berne Convention did not have to be respected or did not apply, i.e. if a country decided not to classify works of applied art as artistic works. So if it was felt that twenty-five years was too long for industrial designs/works of applied art, an alternative would be to exclude them from copyright protection and have an unregistered design right lasting less than twenty-five years and a registered design right modelled on what we already have in the EU, five years renewable to a maximum of twenty-five years, or, if this was felt to be too long, a maximum of fifteen years. I am not ruling out this system but simply then copyright would be replaced by an unregistered design right, and the same rules I propose above in this section to regulate the interface between copyright and RDR would apply between the UDR and the RDR. I have a preference for the copyright/RDR interface over the UDR/RDR interface as we already have a well-settled body of copyright case law to rely on and, as we have seen with the database *sui generis* right, new rights create uncertainties. One possibility is to say that the copyright rules will apply to the newly created UDR, but in my view, it is still a riskier option.

In a partial cumulation scenario, twenty-five years is certainly enough since the right is cumulated at least potentially with the registered design right. If it is not cumulated, whether the duration is adequate is debatable as any term is. It will be too much for some designs and too little for others. At the end of the day, as with any IP right, duration is by definition arbitrary. For some, it would be a good idea to match the copyright and design right term to twenty-five years[123]. (it was almost the case for artistic works made in more than fifty copies, or in lengths or pieces in UK law prior to the repeal of section 52 in 2016). This is certainly a good idea which works at international level if one wants to keep protecting works of applied art by copyright, but it is problematic in the EU owing to the

122 In 1992, the Australian Law Reform Commission had recommended this term for any protection an article would receive. See S. Ricketson, 'Towards a rational basis for the protection of industrial design in Australia' (1994) 5 *Australian IP Journal* 193 at 207.

123 Duchemin, 'La protection des arts appliqués dans la perspective d'un dépôt communautaire en matière de dessins et modèles industriels', 91.

Term Directive and the *Flos* decision. A modification of either the case law or the directive would be in order to allow such alignment.

To sum up, a model copyright/design interface would have two rights: copyright and registered design right (or alternatively unregistered design right and registered design right) either only at national level or leaving a choice of the regional and national level, but once that choice is made it would not be cumulative, yet it would be reversible (like the PVR). The system would be a partial cumulation system, based on the number of copies (or lengths or pieces for 2D designs), with provisions in all the rights aligned as far as possible. The duration would be no longer than twenty-five years for both copyright and the registered right and the length of the registered right may be set differently depending on the sectors. A grace period like the one provided in the EU legislative framework between the UCD and the RCD could work but instead between copyright and the registered design. This model respects both Berne and TRIPs but runs counter to EU statutory law and CJEU case law. This is not problematic since this case law can be overridden by a legislative initiative. Of course, whether the EU legislature's agenda will include this issue in the near or distant future is guesswork.

12.6 Conclusion

The copyright/design interface has been on the agenda of international organisations and bodies for over a century. Despite years of discussion and negotiations, almost no progress has been made even at regional level, as exemplified by the EU treatment of the interface. Countries have rarely changed their positions (e.g. Japan) or if they have, like France or Greece, it is because they have had to as required by EU law. Countries' positions nowadays still seem entrenched. This has led S. Ricketson and J. Ginsburg to write that the current Berne text on the issue is probably the most that can still be achieved at the moment and that the current situation under which each member remains free to choose which protection to give to works of applied art under *sui generis* design laws is unlikely to change in the near future.[124] Therefore, trying to find a workable interface may well be an impossible and thus useless task. That may be so at international level, but it does not prevent individual countries having a go. At EU level it may well be that the interface will get harmonised 'by the back door', i.e. by CJEU case law 'generously' interpreting the current legislative framework rather than or before the EU legislature acts on it, as it has already done with *Flos*

[124] Ricketson and Ginsburg, *International Copyright and Neighbouring Rights*, pp. 465, 469.

and *Infopaq* and the subsequent case law on originality.[125] What is clear is that a holistic approach looking both at copyright and design law together rather than in isolation is needed to solve the problem.[126] And this is not what the CJEU has done so far; on the contrary, its decisions have arguably started to undermine the EU design system. But it is never too late to correct course. My modest hope is that this book sheds some light on how to deal efficiently with the copyright/design interface so that no legislature or court repeats the mistakes of the past. My less modest hope is that this book has shown that solving the interface is not as difficult and therefore as utopian as it seems at first sight.

[125] See Joined Cases C-403/08 and C-429/08, *Football Association Premier League* v. *QC Leisure* and *Karen Murphy* v. *Media Protection Services* [2011] ECR I-9083; Case C-393/09, *Bezpečnostní softwarová asociace–Svaz softwarové ochrany* v. *Ministerstvo kultury* [2011] ECDR 70; *Painer*, above, note 117; Case C-604/10, *Football Dataco* v. *Yahoo UK!* [2012] 2 CMLR 24; Case C-406/10, *SAS Institute Inc.* v. *World Programming Ltd* [2012] 3 CMLR 4. On the CJEU case law on originality, see e.g. E. Rosati, 'Originality in a work, or a work of originality: The effects of the *Infopaq* decision' (2011) EIPR 476; I. Stamatoudi, 'Originality under EU copyright law', in P. Torremans (ed.), *Copyright Law: A Handbook of Contemporary Research*, 2nd edn (Cheltenham: Edward Elgar Publishing, 2017), p. 57.

[126] See the Nordic countries chapter, speaking of the EU.

12.7 Annex: Graphs

Design Application and Registration Figures by Country

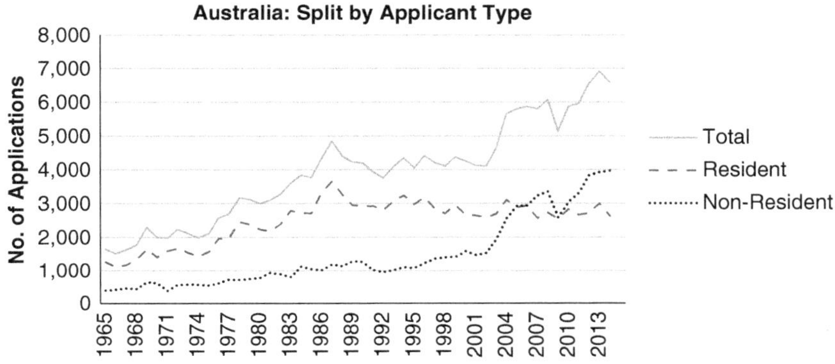

Figure 12.1 Total number of design applications, Australia, split by applicant type

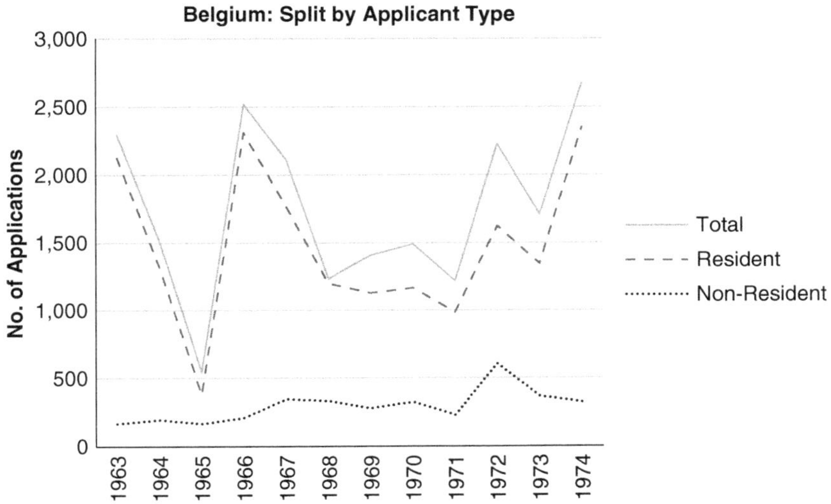

Figure 12.2 Total number of design applications, Belgium, split by applicant type

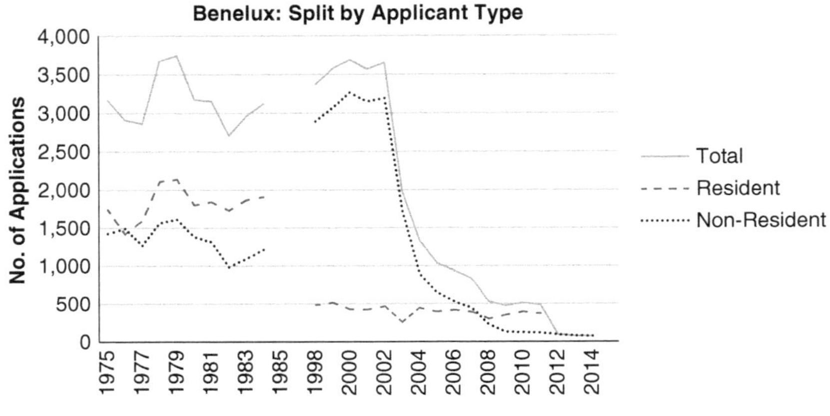

Figure 12.3 Total number of design applications, Benelux, split by applicant type

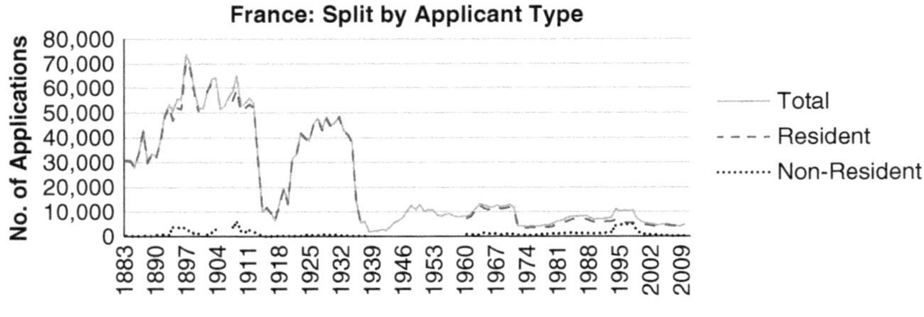

Figure 12.4 Total number of design applications, France, split by applicant type

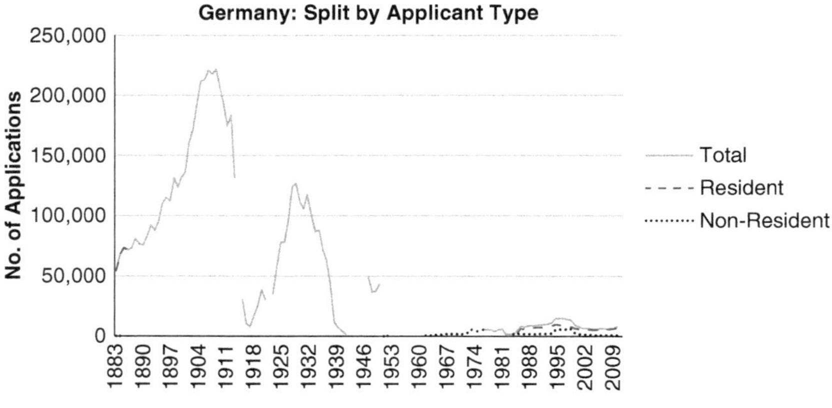

Figure 12.5 Total number of design applications, Germany, split by applicant type

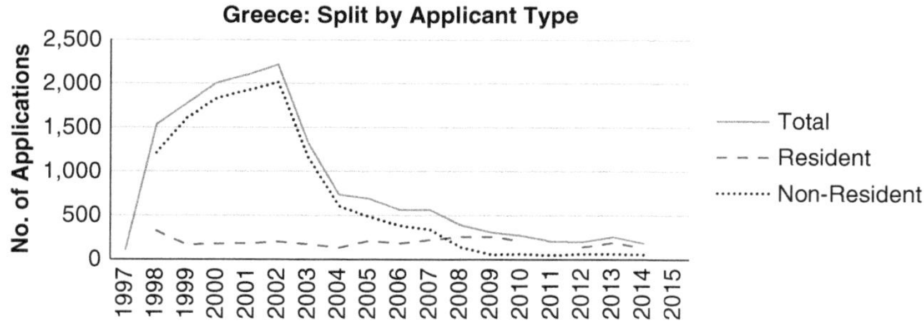

Figure 12.6 Total number of design applications, Greece, split by applicant type

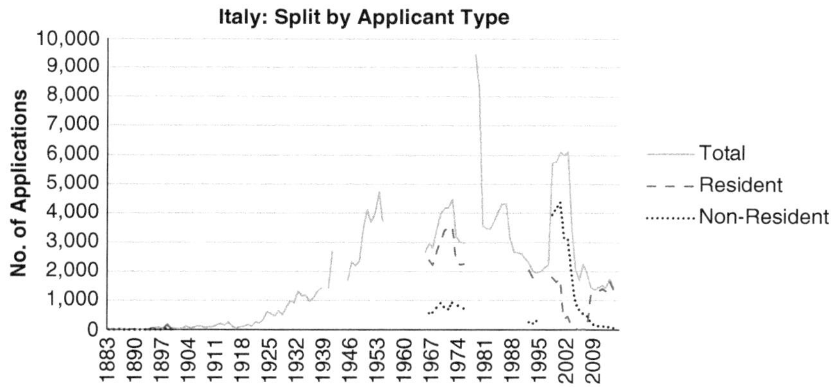

Figure 12.7 Total number of design applications, Italy, split by applicant type

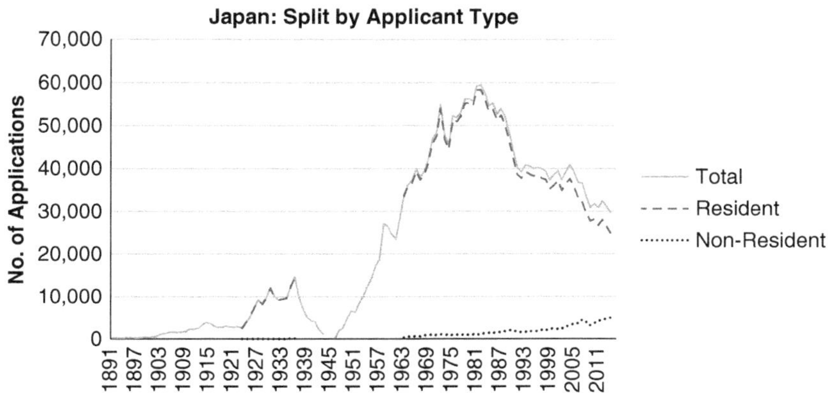

Figure 12.8 Total number of design applications, Japan, split by applicant type

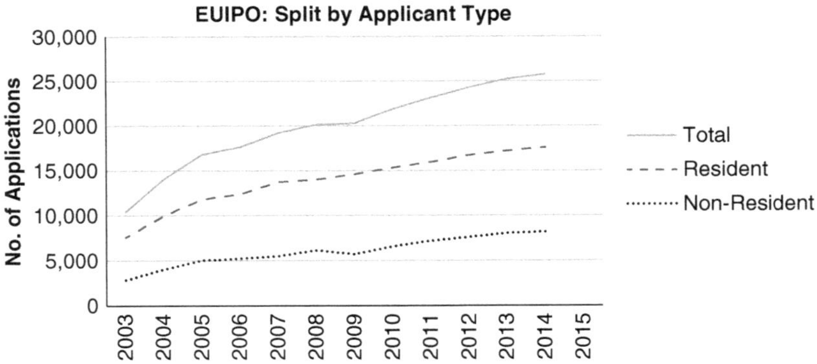

Figure 12.9 Total number of design applications, EUIPO, split by applicant type

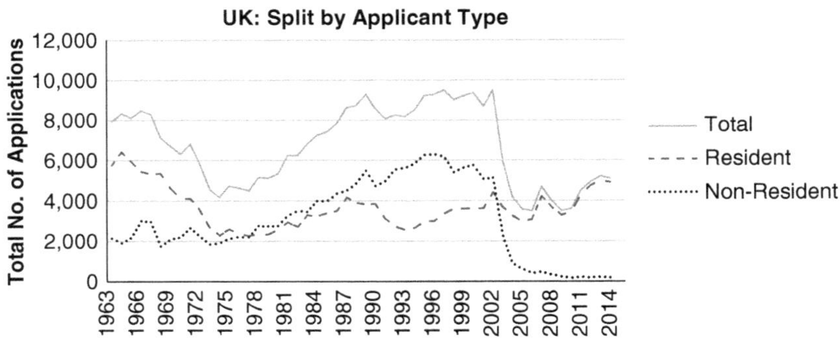

Figure 12.10 Total number of design applications, UK, split by applicant type

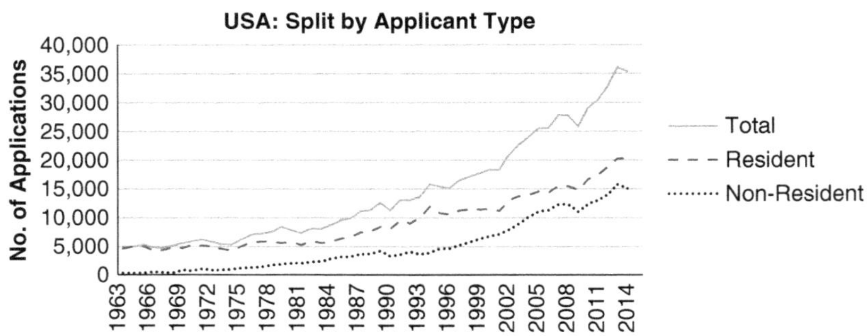

Figure 12.11 Total number of design applications, USA, split by applicant type

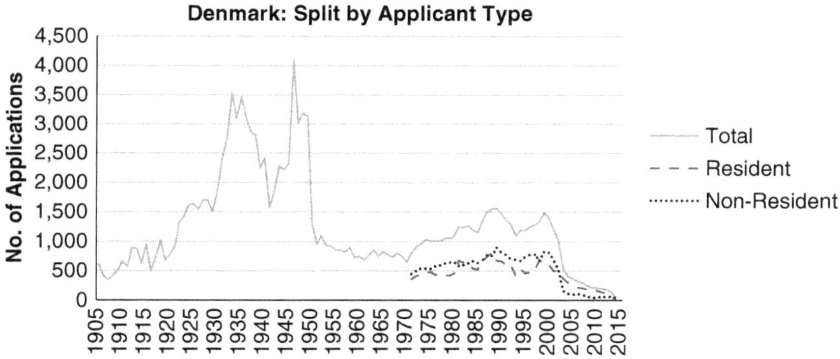

Figure 12.12 Total number of design applications, Denmark, split by applicant type

Figure 12.13 Total number of design applications, Finland, split by applicant type

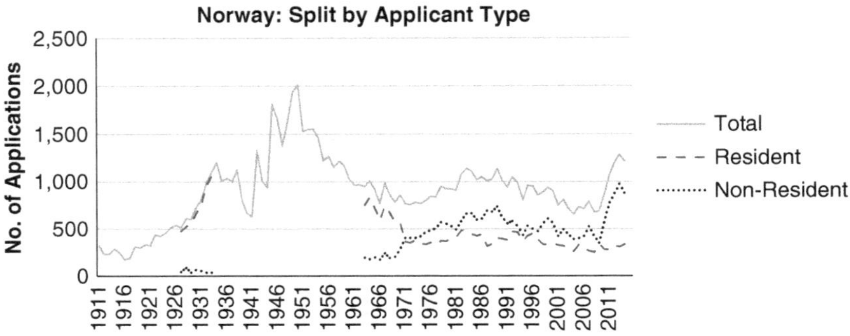

Figure 12.14 Total number of design applications, Norway, split by applicant type

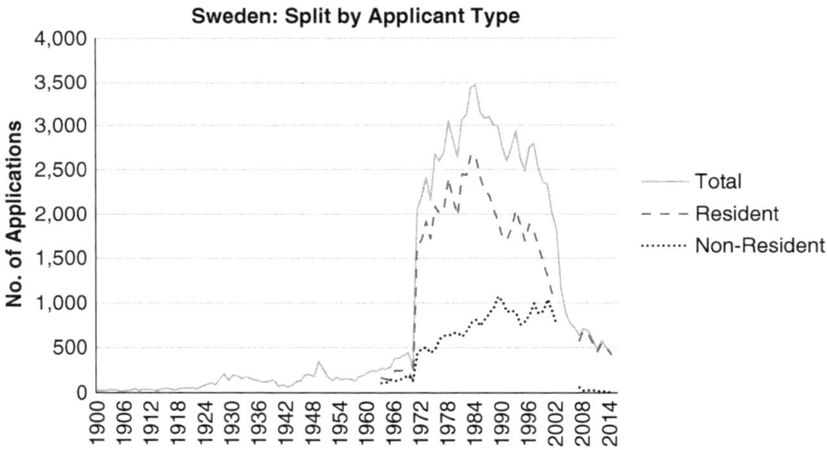

Figure 12.15 Total number of design applications, Sweden, split by applicant type

Index

Cambridge Intellectual Property and Information Law

Titles in the series (formerly known as *Cambridge Studies in Intellectual Property Rights*)

Brad Sherman and Lionel Bently *The Making of Modern Intellectual Property Law*
Irini A. Stamatoudi *Copyright and Multimedia Products: A Comparative Analysis*
Pascal Kamina *Film Copyright in the European Union*
Huw Beverly-Smith *The Commercial Appropriation of Personality*
Mark J. Davison *The Legal Protection of Databases*
Robert Burrell and Allison Coleman *Copyright Exceptions: The Digital Impact*
Huw Beverly-Smith, Ansgar Ohly and Agnès Lucas-Schloetter *Privacy, Property and Personality: Civil Law Perspectives on Commercial Appropriation*
Catherine Seville *The Internationalisation of Copyright Law: Books, Buccaneers and the Black Flag in the Nineteenth Century*
Philip Leith *Software and Patents in Europe*
Geertrui Van Overwalle *Gene Patents and Clearing Models*
Lionel Bently, Jennifer Davis and Jane C. Ginsburg *Trade Marks and Brands: An Interdisciplinary Critique*
Jonathan Curci *The Protection of Biodiversity and Traditional Knowledge in International Law of Intellectual Property*
Lionel Bently, Jennifer Davis and Jane C. Ginsburg *Copyright and Piracy: An Interdisciplinary Critique*
Megan Richardson and Julian Thomas *Framing Intellectual Property: Legal Constructions of Creativity and Appropriation 1840–1940*
Dev Gangjee *Relocating the Law of Geographical Indications*
Andrew Kenyon, Megan Richardson and Ng-Loy Wee-Loon *The Law of Reputation and Brands in the Asia Pacific Region*
Annabelle Lever *New Frontiers in the Philosophy of Intellectual Property*
Sigrid Sterckx and Julian Cockbain *Exclusions from Patentability: How the European Patent Office is Eroding Boundaries*
Sebastian Haunss *Conflicts in the Knowledge Society: The Contentious Politics of Intellectual Property*
Helena R. Howe and Jonathan Griffiths *Concepts of Property in Intellectual Property Law*
Rochelle Cooper Dreyfuss and Jane C. Ginsburg *Intellectual Property at the Edge: The Contested Contours of IP*
Normann Witzleb, David Lindsay, Moira Paterson and Sharon Rodrick *Emerging Challenges in Privacy Law: Comparative Perspectives*
Paul Bernal *Internet Privacy Rights: Rights to Protect Autonomy*
Peter Drahos *Intellectual Property, Indigenous People and their Knowledge*
Susy Frankel and Daniel Gervais *The Evolution and Equilibrium of Copyright in the Digital Age*
Edited by Kathy Bowrey and Michael Handler *Law and Creativity in the Age of the Entertainment Franchise*

Sean Bottomley *The British Patent System and the Industrial Revolution 1700–1852: From Privileges to Property*

Susy Frankel *Test Tubes for Global Intellectual Property Issues: Small Market Economies*

Jan Oster *Media Freedom as a Fundamental Right*

Sara Bannerman *International Copyright and Access to Knowledge*

Andrew T. Kenyon *Comparative Defamation and Privacy Law*

Pascal Kamina *Film Copyright in the European Union, Second Edition*

Tim W. Dornis *Trademark and Unfair Competition Conflicts*

Ge Chen *Copyright and International Negotiations: An Engine of Free Expression in China?*

David Tan *The Commercial Appropriation of Fame: A Cultural Critique of the Right of Publicity and Passing Off*

Jay Sanderson *Plants, People and Practices: The Nature and History of the UPOV Convention*

Daniel Benoliel *Patent Intensity and Economic Growth*

Jeffrey A. Maine and Xuan-Thao Nguyen *The Intellectual Property Holding Company: Tax Use and Abuse from Victoria's Secret to Apple*

Megan Richardson *The Right to Privacy: Origins and Influence of a Nineteenth Century Idea*

Martin Husovec *Injunctions Against Intermediaries in the European Union: Accountable But Not Liable?*

Edited by Estelle Derclaye *The Copyright/Design Interface: Past, Present and Future*

For EU product safety concerns, contact us at Calle de José Abascal, 56–1°, 28003 Madrid, Spain or eugpsr@cambridge.org.

www.ingramcontent.com/pod-product-compliance
Ingram Content Group UK Ltd.
Pitfield, Milton Keynes, MK11 3LW, UK
UKHW020837290926
15470UKWH00004B/1410
* 9 7 8 1 1 0 7 1 9 8 6 7 8 *